MATHS QUEST 8 for the Australian Curriculum

MATHS QUEST 8 for the Australian Curriculum

CATHERINE SMITH | ELENA IAMPOLSKI
LYN ELMS | LEE ROLAND | ROBERT ROWLAND

CONTRIBUTING AUTHORS

ANITA CANN | DOUGLAS SCOTT | IRENE KIROFF | KELLY WAI TSE CHOY | KELLY SHARP
PAUL TARQUINIO | ROBERT CAHN | JO BRADLEY | PAUL NUGENT | SONJA STAMBULIC

SUPPORT MATERIAL

KYLIE BOUCHER

First published 2011 by
John Wiley & Sons Australia, Ltd
42 McDougall Street, Milton, Qld 4064

Typeset in 10/12pt Times LT

National Library of Australia
Cataloguing-in-Publication data

Author:	Smith, Catherine.
Title:	Maths quest 8 for the Australian Curriculum / Catherine Smith … [et al.].
ISBN:	9781742162843 (student ed. : pbk) 9781742462363 (student ed. : eBook) 978 1 118 39564 6 (flexisaver) 9781742162867 (teacher ed. : pbk) 9781742462387 (teacher ed. : eBook)
Notes:	Includes index.
Target audience:	For secondary school age
Subjects:	Mathematics — Textbooks.
Other authors/ contributors:	Smith, Catherine.
Dewey number:	510

Illustrated by Aptara and the Wiley Art Studio

Typeset in India by Aptara

Printed in Singapore by
Craft Print International Ltd

10 9 8 7 6 5 4 3

Contents

Introduction *ix*
About eBookPLUS *xi*
Acknowledgements *xii*

CHAPTER 1

Numeracy 1

1A **Set 1A 2**
Calculator allowed 2
1B **Set 1B 7**
Calculator allowed 7
1C **Set 1C 12**
Calculator allowed 12
1D **Set 1D 17**
Non-calculator 17
1E **Set 1E 22**
Calculator allowed 22
1F **Set 1F 26**
Non-calculator 26

CHAPTER 2 NUMBER AND ALGEBRA
NUMBER AND PLACE VALUE

Integers 31

Are you ready? 32
2A **Adding and subtracting integers 33**
Exercise 2A 34
2B **Multiplying integers 37**
Exercise 2B 39
2C **Dividing integers 40**
Exercise 2C 41
2D **Combined operations on integers 42**
Exercise 2D 43
Summary 45
Chapter review 46
eBookPLUS activities 48

CHAPTER 3 NUMBER AND ALGEBRA
NUMBER AND PLACE VALUE

Index laws 49

Are you ready? 50
3A **Review of index form 51**
Exercise 3A 52
3B **First Index Law 53**
Exercise 3B 55
3C **Second Index Law 56**
Exercise 3C 58
3D **Third Index Law 59**
Exercise 3D 61
3E **Fourth Index Law 62**
Exercise 3E 63
Summary 65
Chapter review 66
eBookPLUS activities 69

ICT ACTIVITY PROJECTS*PLUS*

Attack of the killer balloons 70

CHAPTER 4 NUMBER AND ALGEBRA
REAL NUMBERS

Real numbers 73

Are you ready? 74
4A **Addition and subtraction of fractions 75**
Exercise 4A 79
4B **Multiplication and division of fractions 81**
Exercise 4B 83
4C **Terminating and recurring decimals 85**
Exercise 4C 87
4D **Addition and subtraction of decimals 88**
Exercise 4D 90
4E **Multiplication and division of decimals 91**
Exercise 4E 94
4F **Percentages, fractions and decimals 95**
Exercise 4F 97
4G **Estimation 98**
Exercise 4G 102
Summary 105
Chapter review 107
eBookPLUS activities 110

CHAPTER 5 NUMBER AND ALGEBRA
REAL NUMBERS

Ratios and rates 111

Are you ready? 112
5A **Introduction to ratios 113**
Exercise 5A 114
5B **Simplifying ratios 116**
Exercise 5B 118
5C **Proportion 120**
Exercise 5C 122
5D **Comparing ratios 124**
Exercise 5D 125

5E Dividing in a given ratio 126
Exercise 5E 128
5F Rates 129
Exercise 5F 130
Summary 133
Chapter review 134
eBookPLUS activities 136

CHAPTER 6 NUMBER AND ALGEBRA
MONEY AND FINANCIAL MATHEMATICS
Application of percentages 137
Are you ready? 138
6A Common percentages and shortcuts 139
Exercise 6A 141
6B Discount 143
Exercise 6B 145
6C Profit and loss 148
Exercise 6C 150
Summary 153
Chapter review 154
eBookPLUS activities 156

CHAPTER 7 MEASUREMENT AND GEOMETRY
GEOMETRIC REASONING
Congruence and transformations 157
Are you ready? 158
7A Congruent figures 160
Exercise 7A 161
7B Triangle constructions 163
Exercise 7B 165
7C Congruent triangles 166
Exercise 7C 169
7D Quadrilaterals 171
Exercise 7D 173
Summary 176
Chapter review 178
eBookPLUS activities 180

CHAPTER 8 NUMBER AND ALGEBRA
PATTERNS AND ALGEBRA
Algebra 181
Are you ready? 182
8A Using variables 183
Exercise 8A 184
8B Substitution 187
Exercise 8B 188
8C Working with brackets 189
Exercise 8C 190
8D Substituting positive and negative numbers 191
Exercise 8D 193
8E Number laws and variables 193
Exercise 8E 197
8F Simplifying expressions 199
Exercise 8F 200
8G Multiplying and dividing expressions with variables 201
Exercise 8G 204
8H Expanding brackets 205
Exercise 8H 207
8I Factorising 208
Exercise 8I 210
Summary 211
Chapter review 213
eBookPLUS activities 216

CHAPTER 9
Problem solving I 217
9A Introduction to problem solving — create a table 218
Exercise 9A 220
9B Draw a diagram 222
Exercise 9B 223
9C Look for a pattern 224
Exercise 9C 225
9D Work backwards from the answer 226
Exercise 9D 226
9E Elimination 227
Exercise 9E 228
9F Simplify the problem 229
Exercise 9F 231
9G Guess and check 232
Exercise 9G 233
9H Mixed problems I 233
Exercise 9H 235
9I Mixed problems II 236
Exercise 9I 236
9J Mixed problems III 237
Exercise 9J 237

CHAPTER 10 MEASUREMENT AND GEOMETRY
UNITS OF MEASUREMENT
Measurement 239
Are you ready? 240
10A Perimeter 241
Exercise 10A 244
10B Circumference 246
Exercise 10B 248

10C Area of rectangles, triangles, parallelograms, rhombuses and kites 251
Exercise 10C 255
10D Area of a circle 258
Exercise 10D 259
10E Area of trapeziums 262
Exercise 10E 263
10F Volume of prisms and other solids 265
Exercise 10F 268
10G Time 270
Exercise 10G 273
10H 24-hour clock and time zones 275
Exercise 10H 278
Summary 282
Chapter review 285
eBookPLUS activities 290

CHAPTER 11 NUMBER AND ALGEBRA
LINEAR AND NON-LINEAR RELATIONSHIPS

Linear equations 291
Are you ready? 292
11A Identifying patterns 294
Exercise 11A 297
11B Backtracking and inverse operations 298
Exercise 11B 300
11C Keeping equations balanced 301
Exercise 11C 302
11D Using algebra to solve problems 303
Exercise 11D 307
11E Equations with the unknown on both sides 309
Exercise 11E 312
Summary 314
Chapter review 315
eBookPLUS activities 318

CHAPTER 12 STATISTICS AND PROBABILITY
DATA REPRESENTATION AND INTERPRETATION

Representing and interpreting data 319
Are you ready? 320
12A Samples and populations 321
Exercise 12A 325
12B Organising and displaying data 328
Exercise 12B 333
12C Measures of centre 337
Exercise 12C 341
12D Measures of spread 343
Exercise 12D 347
12E Analysing data 349
Exercise 12E 353
Summary 356
Chapter review 358
eBookPLUS activities 361

ICT ACTIVITY PROJECTS*PLUS*
How to burglar-proof your bedroom 362

CHAPTER 13 STATISTICS AND PROBABILITY
CHANCE

Probability 365
Are you ready? 366
13A Probability scale 367
Exercise 13A 369
13B Experimental probability 370
Exercise 13B 373
13C Sample spaces and theoretical probability 376
Exercise 13C 380
13D Complementary events 383
Exercise 13D 385
13E Venn diagrams 386
Exercise 13E 390
13F Tree diagrams and two-way tables 392
Exercise 13F 397
Summary 400
Chapter review 401
eBookPLUS activities 404

CHAPTER 14 NUMBER AND ALGEBRA
LINEAR AND NON-LINEAR RELATIONSHIPS

Coordinates and linear graphs 405
Are you ready? 406
14A The Cartesian plane 407
Exercise 14A 408
14B Linear patterns 410
Exercise 14B 411
14C Plotting linear graphs 412
Exercise 14C 414
14D Extension: The y-intercept and gradient 417
Exercise 14D 421
14E Extension: Sketching linear graphs 425
Exercise 14E 427
Summary 428
Chapter review 430
eBookPLUS activities 433

CHAPTER 15

Problem solving II 435

Exercise 15A 436
Exercise 15B 437
Exercise 15C 438
Exercise 15D 439
Exercise 15E 440
Exercise 15F 441
Exercise 15G 442
Exercise 15H 444
Exercise 15I 446
Exercise 15J 447

Answers 449
Glossary 491
Index 493

Introduction

Australian Mathematics education is entering a historic phase. A new curriculum offers new opportunities to engage future generations of students in the exciting and challenging world of Mathematics.

The Australian Mathematics Curriculum provides students with essential mathematical skills and knowledge through the content strands of *Number and algebra, Measurement and geometry* and *Statistics and probability*. The Curriculum focuses on students becoming proficient in mathematical understanding, fluency, reasoning and problem solving.

Maths Quest 8 for the Australian Curriculum is specifically written and designed to meet the requirements and aspirations of the Australian Mathematics Curriculum.

This resource contains:
- a student textbook with accompanying eBookPLUS
- a teacher edition with accompanying eGuidePLUS.

Student textbook

Full colour is used throughout to produce clearer graphs and headings, to provide bright, stimulating photos, and to make navigation through the text easier.

Are you ready? sections at the start of each chapter provide introductory questions to establish students' current levels of understanding. Each question is supported by a SkillSHEET that explains the concept involved and provides extra practice if needed.

The first chapter, *Numeracy*, consists of six sets of 30 questions. Three sets are calculator-allowed questions and three sets are non-calculator questions. These questions are designed to promote the use of mathematics in real life.

Clear, concise *theory sections* contain *worked examples* and *highlighted important text* and *remember boxes*.

Icons appear for the eBookPLUS to indicate that interactivities and eLessons are available online to help with the teaching and learning of particular concepts.

Worked examples in a Think/Write format provide clear explanation of key steps and suggest presentation of solutions.

Exercises contain many carefully graded skills and application problems, including multiple-choice questions. Cross-references to relevant worked examples appear with the first 'matching' question throughout the exercises.

Each chapter concludes with a *summary* and *chapter review* exercise containing examination-style questions (multiple-choice, short-answer and extended-response), which help consolidate students' learning of new concepts.

A *glossary* is provided to enhance students' mathematical literacy.

There are two problem-solving chapters designed to encourage students to apply their mathematical skills in non-routine situations.

Student website — eBookPLUS

The accompanying eBookPLUS contains the entire student textbook in HTML plus additional exercises. Students may use the eBookPLUS on laptops, school or home computers, and cut and paste material for revision, assignments or the creation of notes for exams.

WorkSHEET icons link to editable Word documents, and may be completed on-screen, or printed and completed by hand.

SkillSHEET icons link to printable pages designed to help students revise required concepts, and contain additional examples and problems.

Interactivity icons link to dynamic animations, which help students to understand difficult concepts.

eLesson icons link to videos or animations designed to elucidate concepts in ways that are more than what the teacher can achieve in the classroom.

Hungry brain activities provide engaging, whole-class activities to introduce each chapter.

Test yourself tests are also available. Answers are provided for students to receive instant feedback.

Word searches and *crosswords* are available for each chapter.

Two *ProjectsPLUS* activities provide students with the opportunity to work collaboratively and creatively, online, on a mathematics project.

Teacher website — eGuidePLUS

The accompanying eGuidePLUS contains everything in the eBookPLUS and more. Two tests per chapter, fully worked solutions to *WorkSHEET*s, the work program and other curriculum advice in editable Word format are provided. Maths Quest is a rich collection of teaching and learning resources within one package.

Maths Quest 8 for the Australian Curriculum provides ample material, such as exercises, problem-solving questions, projects, worksheets and technology files, from which teachers can assess their students.

Next generation teaching and learning

About eBookPLUS

This book features eBookPLUS: an electronic version of the entire textbook and supporting multimedia resources. It is available for you online at the JacarandaPLUS website (**www.jacplus.com.au**).

Using the JacarandaPLUS website

To access your eBookPLUS resources, simply log on to **www.jacplus.com.au**. There are three easy steps for using the JacarandaPLUS system.

Step 1. Create a user account

The first time you use the JacarandaPLUS system, you will need to create a user account. Go to the JacarandaPLUS home page (**www.jacplus.com.au**) and follow the instructions on screen. An activation email will be sent to your nominated email address. Click on the link in this email and your activation will be complete. You can now use your nominated email address and password to log in to the JacarandaPLUS system.

Step 2. Enter your registration code

Once you have activated your account and logged in, enter your unique registration code for this book, which is printed on the inside front cover of your textbook. The title of your textbook will appear in your bookshelf. Click on the link to open your eBookPLUS.

Step 3. View or download eBookPLUS resources

Your eBook and supporting resources are provided in a chapter-by-chapter format. Simply select the desired chapter from the drop-down list. The student eBook tab contains the entire chapter's content in easy-to-use HTML. The student resources tab contains supporting multimedia resources for each chapter.

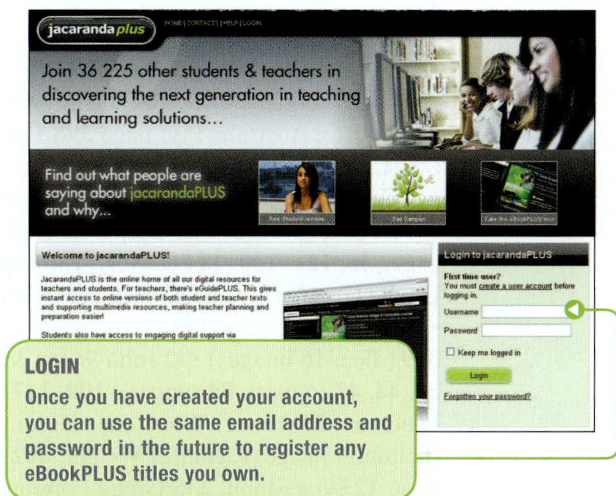

Using eBookPLUS references

eBook*plus*

eBookPLUS logos are used throughout the printed books to inform you that a multimedia resource is available for the content you are studying.

Searchlight IDs (e.g. int-0001) give you instant access to multimedia resources. Once you are logged in, simply enter the searchlight ID for that resource and it will open immediately.

Minimum requirements

- Internet Explorer 7, Mozilla Firefox 1.5 or Safari 1.3
- Adobe Flash Player 9
- Javascript must be enabled (most browsers are enabled by default).

Troubleshooting

- Go to the JacarandaPLUS help page at **www.jacplus.com.au**
- Contact John Wiley & Sons Australia, Ltd.
  Email: support@jacplus.com.au
  Phone: 1800 JAC PLUS (1800 522 7587)

Acknowledgements

The authors and publisher would like to thank the following copyright holders, organisations and individuals for their assistance and for permission to reproduce copyright material in this book.

Images

• © iStockphoto: pages **3** (lower)/DNY59, **7** (upper)/ranplett, **13** (lower)/Valentin Casarsa, **18** (2 images)/organicpixel, **108**/manley099, **323**/Winston Davidian, **353**/pixduluxe • © Ateco Automotive Australia Pty: page **398** • AAP Image/Gary Dowse: page **36** (lower) • © Banana Stock: pages **329**, **334** (lower), **441** (upper) • Catherine Smith: pages **157**, **181**, **435** • © Comstock: page **403** (upper) • © Corbis Corporation: pages **115** (upper), **154**, **369** • © Digital Stock/Corbis Corporation: pages **29**, **185**, **342**, **367**, **385**, **431** • © Digital Vision: pages **46**, **121**, **130**, **184** (lower), **186** (upper), **378**, **441** (lower) • © Fairfax Photo Library/Estelle Grunberg: page **236** (lower) • © Image Disk Photography: pages **142** (lower), **358** • © Image 100: page **349** • Creative Cohesions — Jennifer Wright: pages **131**, **137**, **264**, **287**, **399** (dice, 16 images) • © John Wiley & Sons Australia: page **319**; pages **3** (upper), **36** (upper), **37**, **44**, **47** (upper), **84** (upper), **109**, **147** (phone)/Taken by Kari-Ann Tapp; **47** (lower)/Jo Patterson; **23** (lower), **146**/Renee Bryon; **190**/Malcolm Cross; **359**/Shukla Chakraborty; **375** (bottom 6 images)/Jennifer Wright; **402** (left)/Werner Langer • © Newspix: pages **104**/Julie Best, **125**/Joe Mann, **235**/Gregg Porteous, **237** (lower)/Ross Marsden, 321/Phil Hillyard, **326**/Gary Graham • © Photodisc, Inc.: pages **9** (upper, middle), **84** (lower), **90**, **114**, **115** (lower), **119**, **142** (upper), **144**, **147** (bike), **151** (upper, lower), **186** (lower), **188**, **241**, **250** (left, right), **257** (upper, middle, lower), **269** (upper, lower), **270** (upper, lower), **272**, **280** (upper, lower), **286**, **336**, **337**, **341**, **354**, **355** (upper, lower) **368**, **371**, **375** (upper, middle), **377**, **380**, **381**, **391** (upper, lower), **397**, **405**, **425**, **445** • Photolibrary: pages **15**/Jan Baldwin, **245**/Claver Carroll • © PhotoAlto/Frederic Cirou: page **9** (lower) • Used under license from Shutterstock.com: pages **1**/© Alexey Karyagin, **2**/© Lori Martin, **7** (bottom)/© Alexey Demidov, **8**/© Wallenrock, **10** (lower)/© Paul Prescott, **10** (upper)/© Vaide Seskauskiene, **12**/© Vadim Kozlovsky, **13** (top)/© Tomasz Trojanowski, **14**/© DPiX Center, **16**/© Alvinku, **19**/© Brian Erickson, **21** (upper)/© Ilin Sergey, **21** (lower)/© Smart-foto, **22**/© Ragnarock, **23** (upper)/© Giovanni Benintende, **28**/© Mike Flippo, **31**/© palmenpep, **49**/© Tomasz Nieweglowski, **66**/© Yuri Arcurs, **67** (upper)/© Carlos E. Santa Maria, **67** (lower)/© Dan Ionut Popescu, **73**/© Chris Curtis, **81**/© vgstudio, **88**/© Petrenko Andriy, **90–1**/© Zhiltsov Alexandr, **95**/© Tupungato, **98**/ © Paul Matthew Photography, **103**/© Dmitriy Shironosov, **124**/© Elnur, **132**/© Gusev Mikhail Evgenievich, **143**/© magicinfoto, **147** (iPod)/© Morgan Lane Photography, **147** (surfboard)/© Evgenia Bolyukh, **150**/© Margo Harrison, **215**/© fonats, **217**/© Feverpitch, **227**/© M. Wolf, **228**/© Elnur, **233**/© Stephen Coburn, **236** (upper)/© Taras Vyshnya, **237** (upper)/© Tim Evans, **238** (upper)/© riekephotos, **238** (lower)/© Elena Elisseeva, **239**/© BEST PICTURES, **273**/© Vladimir Wrangel, **281**/© Olinchuk, **288**/© Filipp Obada, **289**/© Greg da Silva, **291**/© Alistair Scott, **328**/© Evgeny Kovalev spb, **334** (upper)/© MadTatyana, **360**/© Max Blain, **362** (left)/© Monkey Business Images, **362** (right)/© Sue Smith, **362–3**/© iDesign, **365**/© erperlstrom, **402** (right)/© Hugo Maes, **403** (lower)/© mmm, **438**/© Paul Cowan, **443**/© Kurhan, **447**/© Erik Lam, **448**/© ilker canikligil • © Stockbyte: page **417** • Approval granted Tattersalls Sweeps Pty Ltd: page **128** • © Tetra Images: page **127** • © Viewfinder Australia Photo Library: pages **111**, **390** • © Alex Wild 2004: page **184** (upper)

Other contributors

The contributions of the following authors are also acknowledged: Brett Barber, Roger Blackman, Stephen Broderick, Robert Cahn, Steve Craven, Caroline Denney, Andrea Dineen, John Dowsey, Rodney Ebbage, Chris Evangelou, Dennis Fitzgerald, Ray Hawkins, Stephen Heames, Linda Johnson, Robert Johnson, Carolyn Mews, Mario Panaccio, Poppy Pantelidis, David Phillips, Tony Priddle, Colin Shnier, David Tynan, Jill Vincent, Don Wagstaff, Jenny Watson.

Every effort has been made to trace the ownership of copyright material. Information that will enable the publisher to rectify any error or omission in subsequent editions will be welcome. In such cases, please contact the Permissions Section of John Wiley & Sons Australia, Ltd.

Numeracy

1A Set 1A
1B Set 1B
1C Set 1C
1D Set 1D
1E Set 1E
1F Set 1F

WHAT DO YOU KNOW?

1. List what you know about numeracy. Create a concept map to show your list.
2. Share what you know with a partner and then with a small group.
3. As a class, create a large concept map that shows your class's knowledge of numeracy.

OPENING QUESTION

If it takes 4 possums 4 minutes to eat 4 plants, how long will it take 40 possums to eat 40 plants?

In this chapter there are six sets of questions. These questions provide the opportunity for students to use their numeracy skills in everyday situations.

1A Set 1A

eBook*plus*

Weblinks
Problems and puzzles 1
Problems and puzzles 2

Calculator allowed

1 The original Ferris Wheel opened to the public in Chicago in 1893. The distance around the outside of the ferris wheel is approximately three times the diameter. This ferris wheel has a diameter of 76.2 m. If you were to string lights to the outside edge of the ferris wheel, what would be the approximate length of lights needed to the nearest metre?

A 119 m B 120 m
C 200 m D 229 m

2 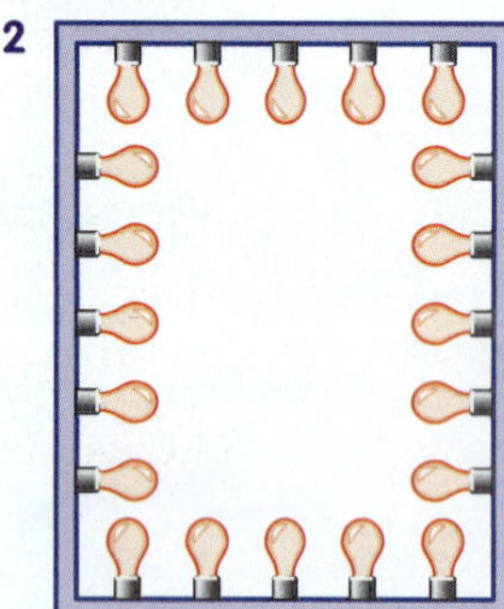 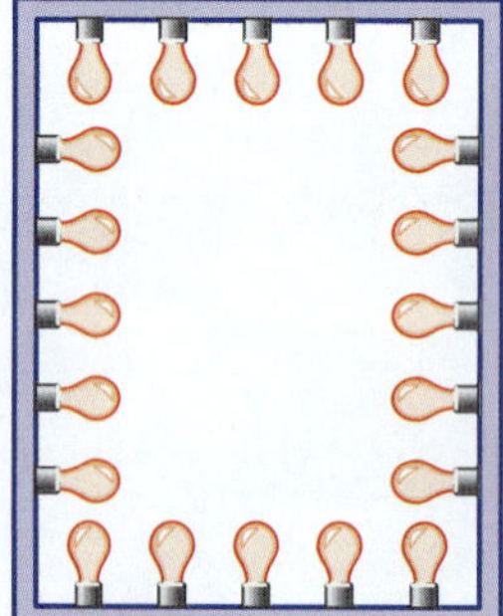

You want to string lights around two windows that measure 90 cm by 120 cm. What is the minimum length of lights needed?

A 2.5 m B 3.5 m
C 6.5 m D 8.5 m

3 The quilt design is a square with four identical parallelograms.
What is the unshaded area of the quilt design?

A 65 cm^2
B 129 cm^2
C 149 cm^2
D 159 cm^2

5 cm
2 cm
13 cm

4 During the January holidays, Anna works in a café in Queenscliff. She saves 75% of her earnings. If Anna earns \$750, what is the best estimate of the amount of money that she saves?

A \$550 B \$300
C \$150 D \$100

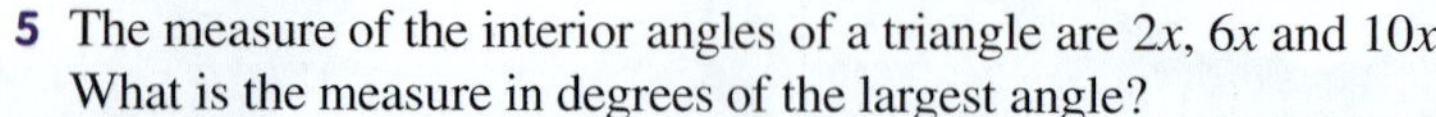

5 The measure of the interior angles of a triangle are $2x$, $6x$ and $10x$. What is the measure in degrees of the largest angle?

A 20 B 100
C 200 D 250

6 A regular octagon has an area of 100 cm^2. A square surrounds the octagon and has a perimeter of 60 cm. What is the area of one of the triangles if they are all the same size?

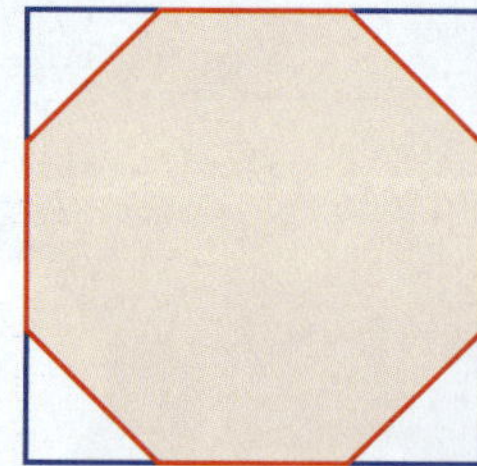

7 You have a rectangular storage box that is 55 cm high. You cut off a 5-cm strip around the top of the box. What will be the new volume of the box in cubic centimetres?

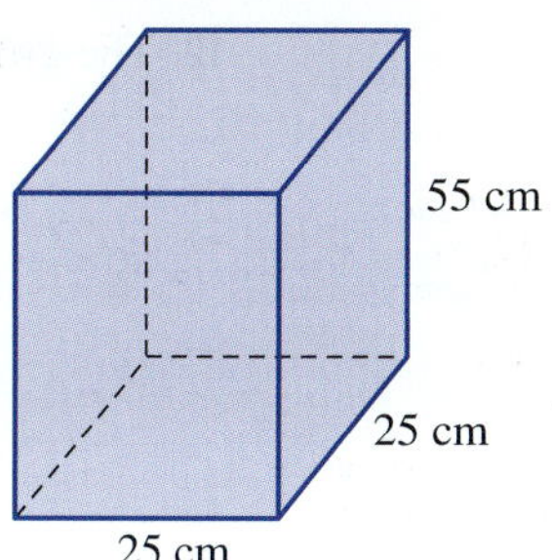

A $31\,250 \text{ cm}^3$
B $27\,500 \text{ cm}^3$
C $22\,000 \text{ cm}^3$
D $20\,000 \text{ cm}^3$

8 Triangle ABC is equilateral. What is the measure of angle x?

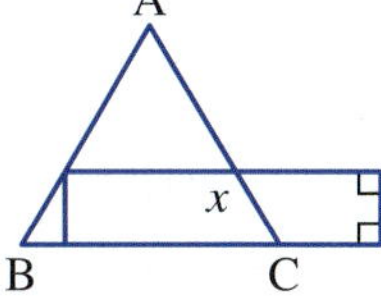

9 A shop reduces the price of sports shoes by 40%. The new price is \$72. What was the original price of the sports shoes?

A \$120
B \$115.20
C \$100.80
D \$100

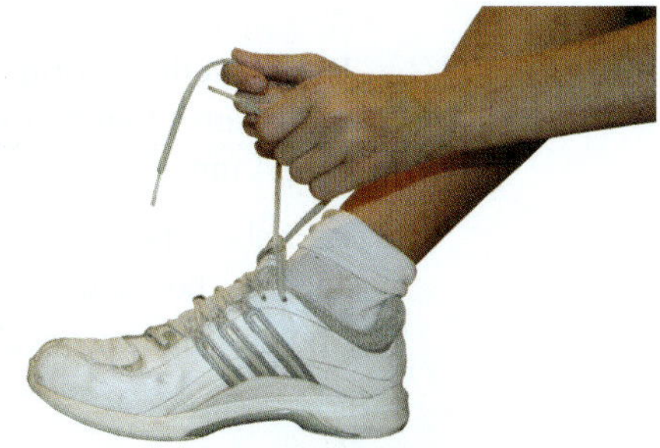
SALE 40% OFF

10 High-speed label applicators can put labels onto envelopes at a rate of 200 per second. Which of the following represents the number in a day?

A 1.728×10^5
B 1.728×10^6
C 1.728×10^7
D 1.728×10^8

11 Alex and his six friends played a game at Timezapp in which the person with the lowest final score wins. The table shows the final scores for each person except Alice.

Player	Score
Alex	151
Ben	153
Julie	149
Lee	139
Alice	
Aysha	135
Keta	143

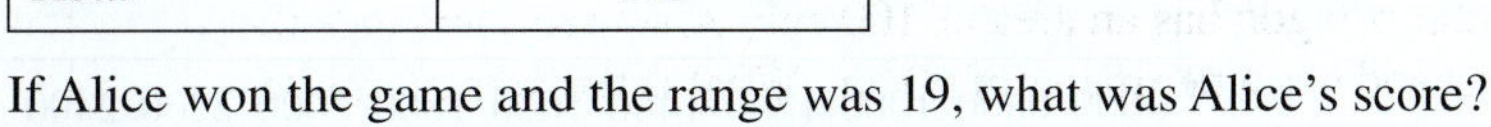

If Alice won the game and the range was 19, what was Alice's score?

A 132 B 134
C 170 D 172

12 The growth rate of hair is shown below.

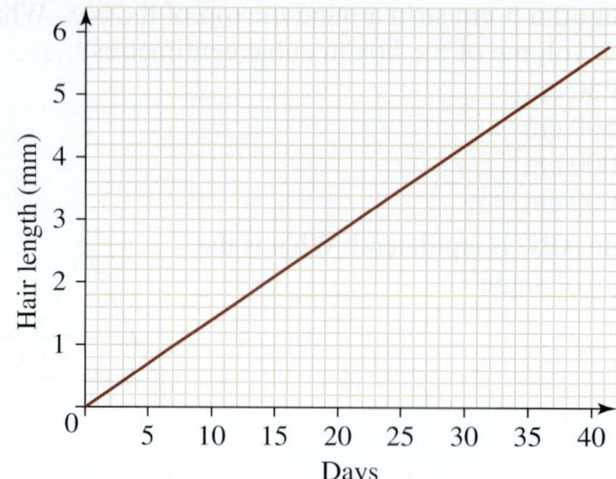

Based on the information in the graph, which figure best represents the number of millimetres that hair grows in 30 days?

A 2.4 mm **B** 3.6 mm **C** 4.2 mm **D** 5.7 mm

13 A Frisbee fits inside a cube. The top of the cube has a perimeter of 72 cm. If the Frisbee occupies 250 cm^3, how much space is left in the box?

14 You are hanging towels on a clothes line. You use two pegs per towel.

However, as you continue you realise that you will run out of pegs. Instead, you attach the end of the new towel to the old towel. In this way the towels share a peg.
If t represents the number of towels and P represents the number of pegs, which of these equations represents the number of pegs needed?

A $P = 2 \times t + 1$ **B** $P = 2 \times t + 2$ **C** $P = 3 \times t$ **D** $P = t + 1$

15 A cyclist is competing in an 80-km race. The record time for the race is 2 hours and 40 minutes. What will his speed, s (in km/h), need to be to beat this record?

A $s < 30$ **B** $s > 30$ **C** $s < 33$ **D** $s > 20$

16 The depth of the water inside Blue Lagoon Bay has been recorded over a time period as shown on the graph below.

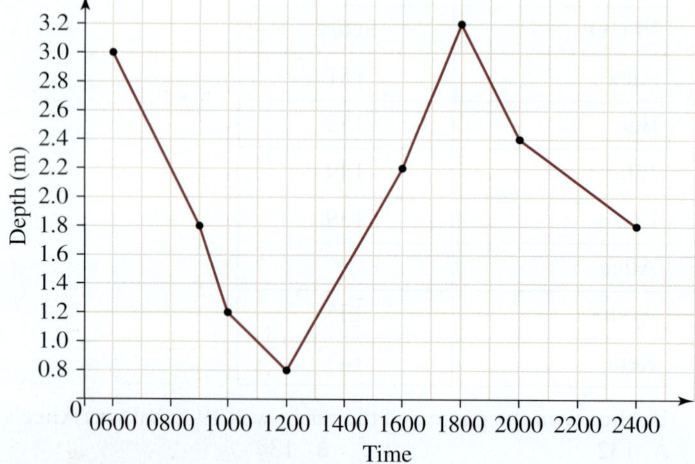

What is the depth at 10 pm?

17 Sing and Nam each buy a health bar at lunchtime from the vending machine. There are four different types: ANZAC, chocolate chip, triple fruit and yogurt to choose from. What is the probability that they choose exactly the same type of bar?

18 A triangle with two identical sides and an angle of 119° is:

A scalene and acute
B isosceles and acute
C isosceles and obtuse
D isosceles and right-angled.

19 Alex wants to find the perimeter of the isosceles trapezium shown below.

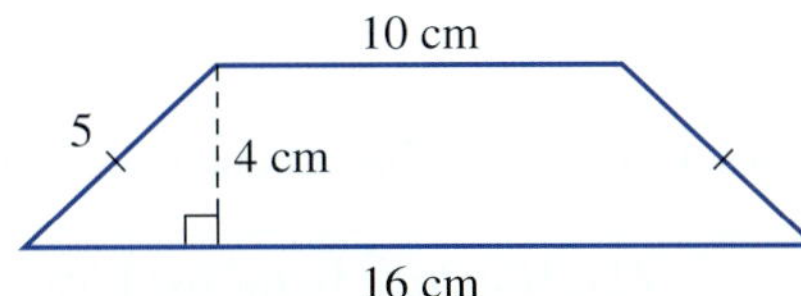

Which equation could Alex use to find the perimeter of the trapezoid?

A $P = 10 + 16 + 4 + 5$
B $P = 10 + 16 + (2 \times 5)$
C $P = 10 + 16 + 4 + 5$
D $P = (10 + 16) \times 4 + 2$

20 Which point on the number line could represent the value of $\sqrt{10}$?

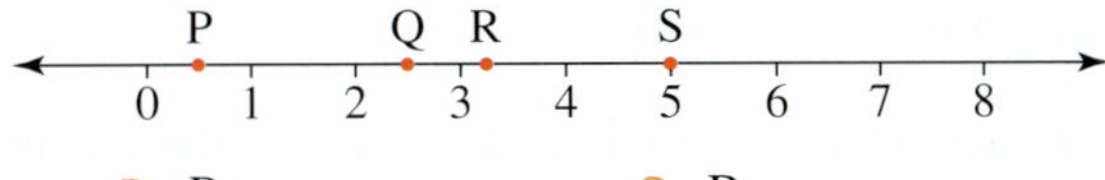

A S
B P
C R
D Q

21 Lightning quickly heats the air, causing it to expand. This produces the sound of thunder. Sound travels approximately 1 km in 3 seconds. How far away is a thunderstorm when you notice a 2-second delay between the lightning and the sound of thunder?

A 1 km away
B $\frac{1}{3}$ km away
C $\frac{1}{2}$ km away
D $\frac{2}{3}$ km away

22 The bar graph shows 120 students in Year 8 and their different swimming levels. What percentage of students, to the nearest whole number, have reached the bronze level?

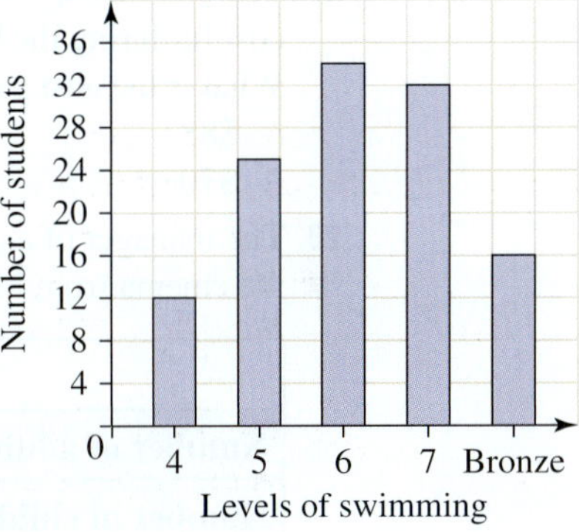

A 13%
B 15%
C 17%
D 19%

23 A reservoir has a total capacity of 1 068 000 megalitres. Suppose the water is to be drained by a pump at a constant daily rate. If $\frac{9}{10}$ of the volume of the reservoir remains after the first day's pumping, how many megalitres (to the nearest megalitre) have been lost over 3 days? (Round to the nearest megalitre)

A 772 740
B 320 400
C 289 428
D 1068

24 The current storage level of Melbourne's water supply is shown below.

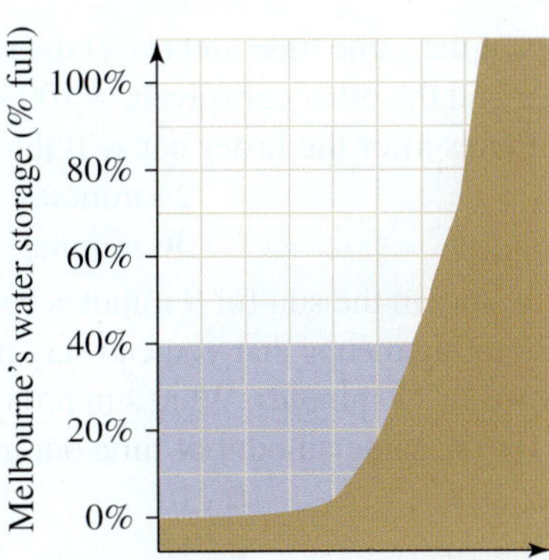

If the total capacity is 1 670 500 megalitres, how much water is available (to the nearest ten thousand megalitres)?

A 700 000 B 670 000
C 669 000 D 660 000

25 One student in the Japanese class is to make name tags, 50 mm × 50 mm square, from stiff card. The sheet of card measures 25 cm by 30 cm.
What is the maximum number of name tags that can be made from one sheet?

A 10 B 20
C 30 D 40

26 The table shows the cost of hiring a band called *The Hotshots*.

***The Hotshots* band for hire**	
Monday to Friday	$55 per hour
Saturday	$110 per hour
Acoustic Rental	$60 per booking
Deposit 20% of total cost	

A booking is made for Saturday for 4 hours, along with acoustic rental.
Which of the following represents the deposit?

A $(110 \times 4 + 60) \times \frac{20}{100}$ B $(110 \times 4 + 60) \times \frac{100}{20}$

C $(110 + 60) \times 4 \times \frac{20}{100}$ D $(110 + 60) \times 4 \times \frac{100}{20}$

27 The *Queenscliff Marine Centre* hires a boat for 12 biologists to go diving for six days. The cost for hiring the boat for six days is usually $880. The Marine centre obtains a 10% discount.
What is the cost per person with the discount?

A $88 B $74
C $70 D $66

28 The manager of a cinema complex records the number of people attending the 2 pm session at the cinema from Monday to Friday.

	Monday	Tuesday	Wednesday	Thursday	Friday
Number of adults	120	170	147	160	183
Number of children	37	42	52	62	85

What is the mean number of adults attending the 2 pm session for that week?

A 120 B 150
C 156 D 160

29 Two cars begin at the same time and travel the same distance of 160 km. One car travels at 80 km per hour and the other car travels at 100 km per hour.
How many minutes after the faster car will the slower car complete the journey?

A 20 minutes B 24 minutes
C 30 minutes D 36 minutes

30 You can usually stay in the sun for 9 minutes before burning. Using a sun protecting lotion with an SPF 20 rating means that you can stay in the sun for 9 × 20 minutes before burning. Your friend burns in 15 minutes. What sun protection factor would she need to use so that you can both stay for the same amount of time out in the sun? (Of course remember to wear a hat!)

A 8 B 10
C 12 D 15

1B Set 1B

Non-calculator

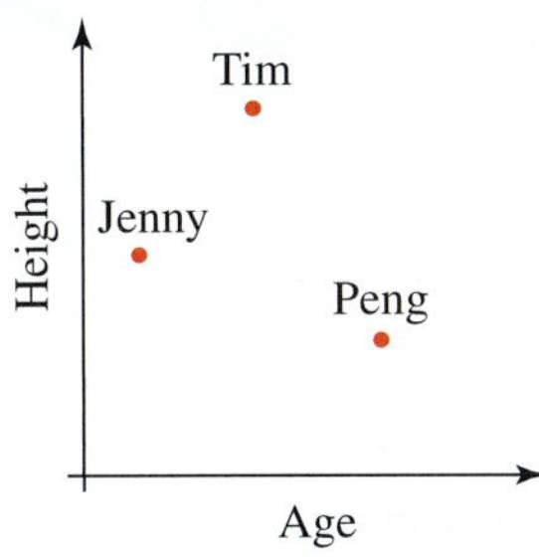

1 The width of the rectangular computer screen is 8 cm, and its area is 80 cm^2. The perimeter of the screen is:

A 32 cm **B** 36 cm
C 38 cm **D** 40 cm

2 The sum of $3x$ dollars and $3x$ cents, in cents, is:

A $3x + 3$ **B** $3x$
C $303x$ **D** $3x + 3x$

3 The graph below shows the ages and heights of three Year 8 students.

Tim
Jenny
Peng
Height
Age

Which one of the following statements is true?

A Tim is the eldest and the tallest.
B Jenny is older than Peng and younger than Tim.
C Peng and Tim are the same age.
D Peng is the shortest.

4 Two angles of a triangle are 63° and 57°. Which of the following could not be the measure of an exterior angle of the triangle?

A 110° **B** 117° **C** 120° **D** 123°

5 Susan claims that the weight of her cat is at most 8 kg. What inequality represents her claim?

A $w < 8$ **B** $w > 8$
C $w \leq 8$ **D** $w \geq 8$

6 The diagram below shows two parallel streets, Yarra Street and Myers Street, intersected by Moolap St. The obtuse angle that Myers Street forms with Moolap Street is four times the measure of the acute angle that Yarra Street makes with Moolap Street. What is the measure of the acute angle at Yarra Street and Moolap Street?

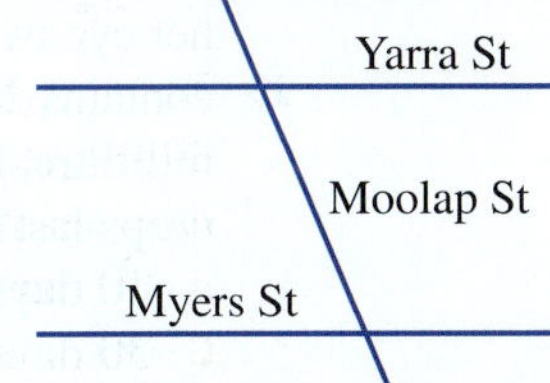

A 30° **B** 36°
C 108° **D** 144°

7

Input	1	2	3	4	?
Output	2	5	8	11	59

Ann and Jack are playing a game where Ann gives an Input number for Jack to put in to the same expression to give an Output number.

What is the Input number that Ann gave Jack for an Output number of 59?

A 18 **B** 20

C 22 **D** 24

8 Five students competed in a 200-m race. Their finishing times were 47.5 s, 46.8 s, 47.3 s, 48.0 s and 48.2 s.

What is their average time for running a 200-m race, correct to 2 decimal places?

9 A triangle has been drawn on 1-cm grid paper. Which statement is incorrect?

A The triangle is isosceles.

B The triangle is right-angled.

C The perimeter is 24 cm.

D The area is 16 cm^2.

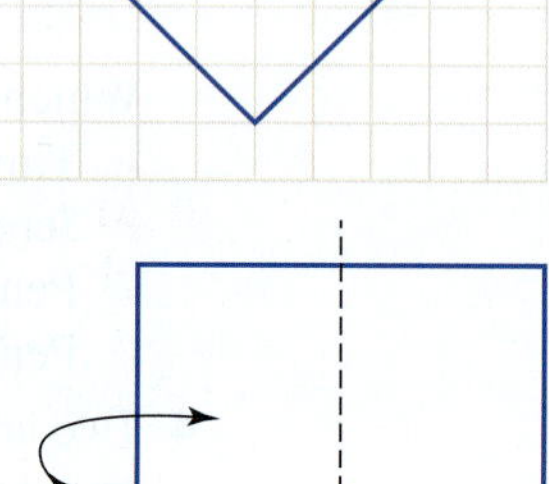

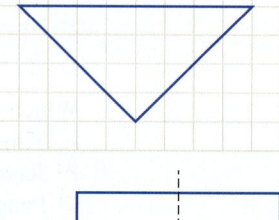

10 Fold a paper square in half vertically and then cut it along the fold line. What is the ratio of the perimeter of one of the resulting two smaller rectangles to the large square?

A $\frac{1}{2}$ **B** $\frac{2}{3}$

C $\frac{3}{4}$ **D** $\frac{5}{6}$

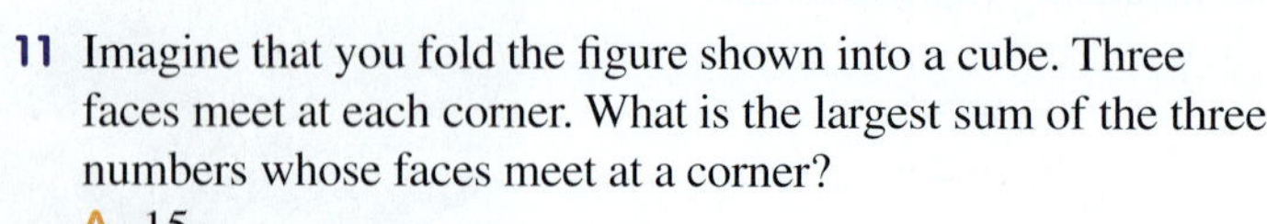

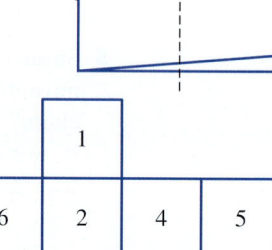

11 Imagine that you fold the figure shown into a cube. Three faces meet at each corner. What is the largest sum of the three numbers whose faces meet at a corner?

A 15

B 14

C 13

D 12

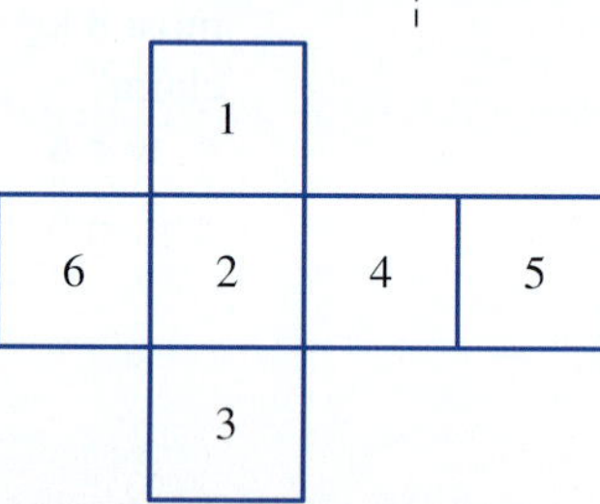

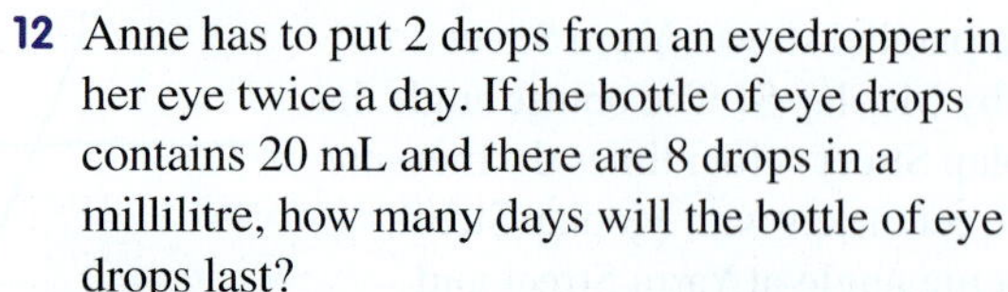

12 Anne has to put 2 drops from an eyedropper in her eye twice a day. If the bottle of eye drops contains 20 mL and there are 8 drops in a millilitre, how many days will the bottle of eye drops last?

A 10 days **B** 20 days

C 30 days **D** 40 days

13 Two hundred Year 8 students are doing a science experiment in which 25 mL of an alkaline solution will be used by each student. How much solution is needed in total?

A 50 litres **B** 5 litres

C 0.5 litres **D** 0.05 litres

14 You have made 15 muffins for your class. You realise that this is only $\frac{3}{5}$ of the total that you need? How many more do you need to make?

A 3
B 5
C 9
D 10

15 A market gardener noted that 6 boxes of cherry tomatoes and 2 kg weighed the same amount as 5 boxes of cherry tomatoes and 4 kg. If x represents the weight of a box of cherry tomatoes in kg, which equation best represents the information?

A $8x = 9x$
B $12x = 20x$
C $6x + 2 = 5x + 4$
D $6x - 2 = 5x + 4$

16 Mulching the garden in the summertime is a great way of saving water.
A bale of pea straw costs $5.00 and the delivery charge is $15.00.
Olivia spent $90 in total. How many bales of pea straw did she buy for the garden?

A 18 B 15
C 12 D 9

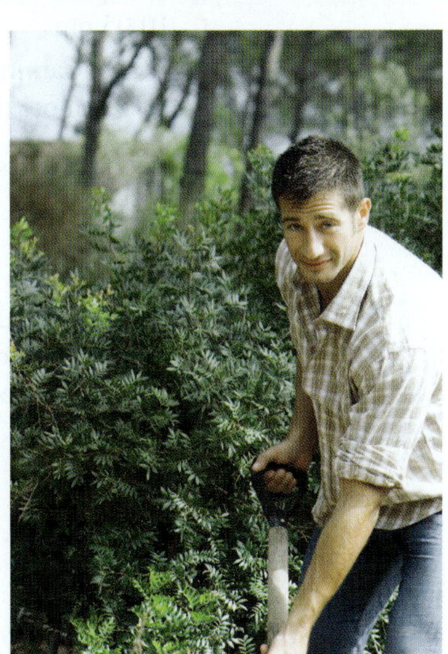

17 In Yen's class, the ratio of the number of students who walked to school on Tuesday to the number of students who took some form of transport was 12 : 18.
Which fraction is an equivalent form of this ratio?

A $\frac{2}{8}$ B $\frac{4}{9}$
C $\frac{2}{3}$ D $\frac{3}{4}$

18 The Cheetahs and the Leopards are two school netball teams. The table shows the scores of their games.

	Game 1	Game 2	Game 3	Game 4	Game 5
Cheetahs	45	40	35	49	64
Leopards	28	50	27	52	63

Based on the scores in the table, which statement is true?

A The Cheetahs won 20% of the games.
B The Cheetahs won 30% of the games.
C The Leopards won 40% of the games.
D The Leopards won 60% of the games.

19 The following is a diagram of a proposed floor plan for an office space. The proposed plan has four areas. Three of the areas are rectangular and the fourth is a square.
What is the length of y?

A 3 m **B** 5 m
C 15 m **D** 25 m

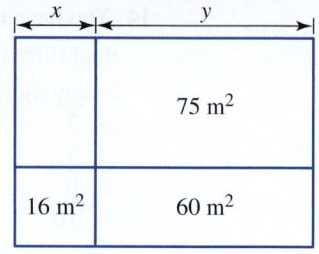

x y
75 m^2
16 m^2 60 m^2

20 Adults, on average, have 5.5 litres of blood in their bodies.
How many millilitres of blood are in the kidneys?

A 25 **B** 500
C 1000 **D** 1375

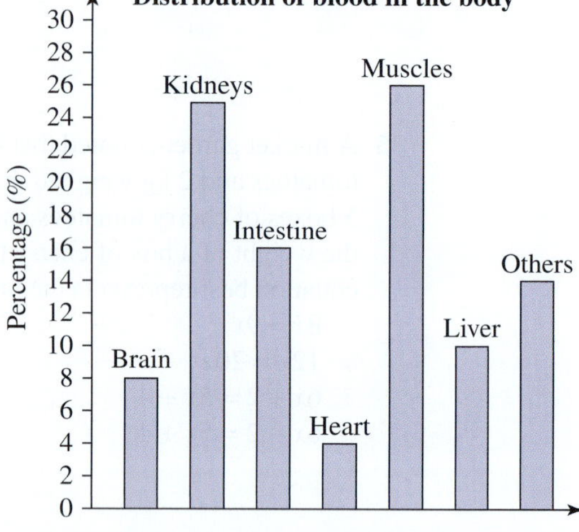

21 Anne and her friends decided to watch a DVD. They started it at 8.30 pm and it ran for 105 minutes. At what time did the DVD end?

A 9.30 pm **B** 9.35 pm
C 10.05 pm **D** 10.15 pm

22 A 900-car parking lot is divided into 3 sections. There are 330 spots in Section 1. Section 2 holds 160 more than will fit into Section 3. How many spots are in Section 3?

23 A chef assembles a cake in $\frac{2}{3}$ of an hour. If he works for $7\frac{1}{2}$ hours, how many cakes will he fully assemble?

A $10\frac{3}{4}$ **B** 11 **C** $11\frac{1}{4}$ **D** 12

24 A roll of material contains 6 metres of cloth. Four lengths, each of x centimetres, are cut from the cloth. What length of material (in centimetres) remains?

A $6 - 4x$
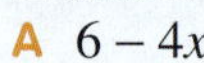
B $4x - 6$
C $600 - 4x$
D $100(6 - 4x)$

25 Two roads cross. What is the size of angle A?
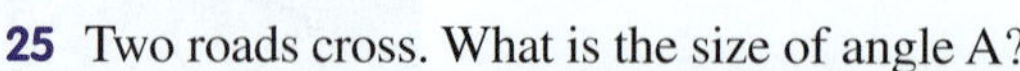

26 A survey is taken of a Year 8 group to determine the length of time students spend on homework each night.

Time spent in minutes	Number of pupils
0	6
15	10
30	14
40	2
50	4
60	8
70	10
80	5
90	1

What percentage of the group spend 60 minutes or more on homework each night?

27 In the following diagram of yellow and blue buckets, each bucket of the same colour contains the same number of pegs.

Total number of pegs in 4 yellow buckets = 28 pegs

Total number of pegs in 1 yellow bucket and 2 blue buckets = 43 pegs

How many pegs are in each of the given coloured buckets?

28 Which of these is the lightest?

A 25 000 grams
B 2.50 kilograms
C 25 000 000 milligrams
D 2.5 tonnes

29 A piece of wire is cut into the exact number of pieces needed to create the edges of a cube.
If the volume of the cube is 125 cm^3, what was the length of wire to begin with?

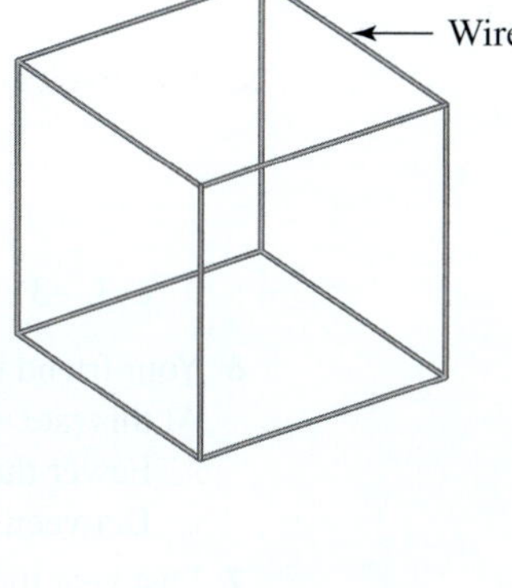

A 5 cm
B 30 cm
C 50 cm
D 60 cm

30 Given the balance, what is the value for x?

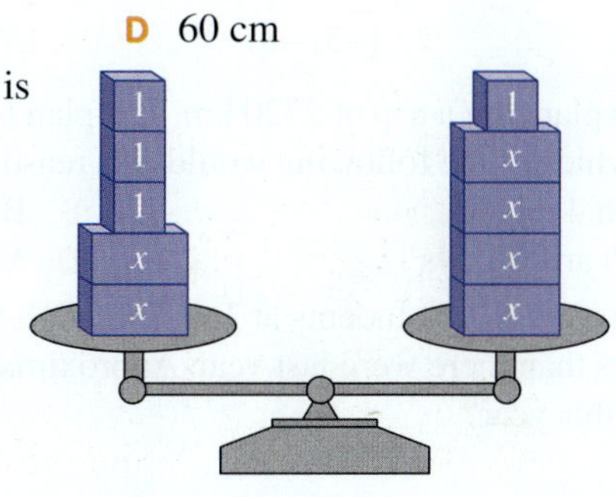

A $\frac{1}{2}$

B 1

C 2

D 4

1C Set 1C

Calculator allowed

1 Each year, the area of tree logging in the Otway Ranges is approximately equivalent to clearing 200 football ovals. The area of a football oval is given by Area = $3.142 \times A \times B$ (see the diagram). If the width of the football oval is 110 m and the length is 160 m, approximately how many square metres of trees are felled each year in the Otways?

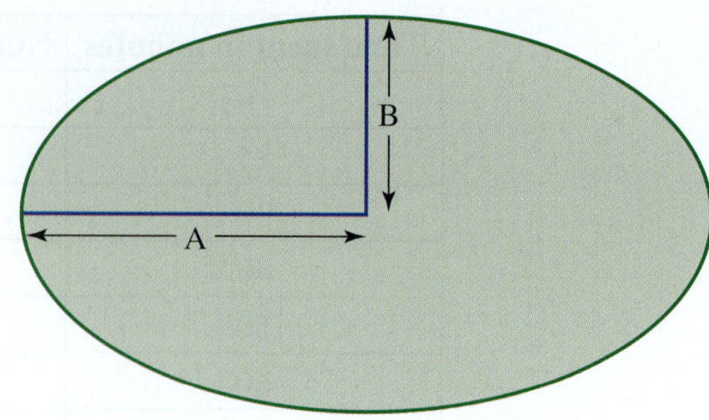

A 1.9×10^4 **B** 2.76×10^4 **C** 1.9×10^6 **D** 2.76×10^6

2 A designer wants to enlarge a cylinder to 150% of its original size.
If the diameter is 37 mm, what was the radius of the copy of the cylinder?

A 27.75 mm **B** 46.25 mm
C 55.5 mm **D** 92.5 mm

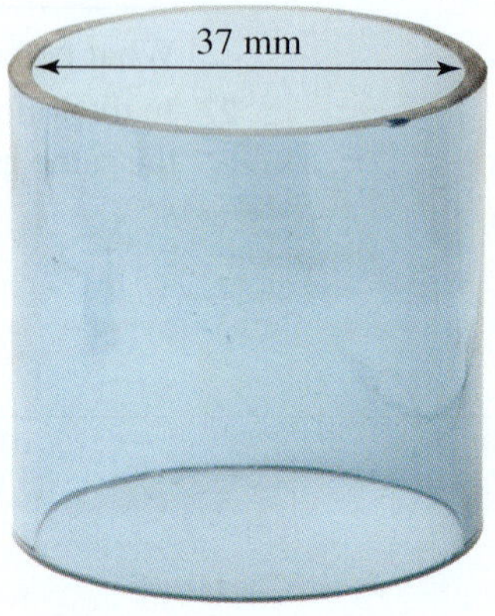

3 A teenager is to receive 750 mL of saline solution. The drip rate is adjusted to 60 mL per hour. When will it be necessary to change the saline solution if the drip rate begins at 10.30 am?

4 The area of a square is 73 square metres. Which is the closest to the length of each side?

A 8.4 m **B** 8.5 m **C** 8.6 m **D** 8.7 m

5 A kite is drawn as shown below with the coordinates of D being omitted. What are the coordinates of D?

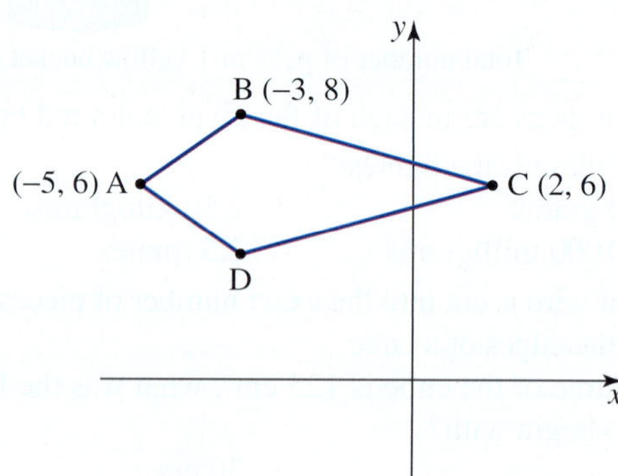

A (–3, –3) **B** (–3, –8) **C** (–3, 4) **D** (–3, 6)

6 Your friend is planning a trip of 2320 km. The plan is to drive between 400 and 480 km each day. At this rate, which of the following would be a reasonable number of days to complete the trip?

A Fewer than 4 days **B** Between 4 and 6 days
C Between 6 and 8 days **D** More than 8 days

7 Last year there were 225 students at Top End High School. This year there are 20 per cent fewer students than there were last year. Approximately how many students are at Top End High School this year?

A 205 **B** 245 **C** 270 **D** 180

8 This column graph shows four test results for Bill, Wanda and Neale.
Which of the following options represents the test results?

A Bill has a higher average than Neale but a lower average than Wanda.
B Bill has a lower average than Wanda but a higher average than Neale.
C Wanda has a higher average than Bill but a lower average than Neale.
D Wanda has a higher average than Neale and Bill.

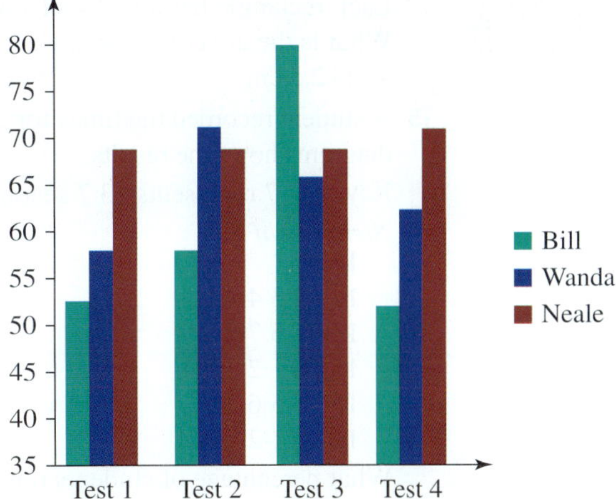

9 A prepared workout on a treadmill consists of intervals of walking at various rates and angles of incline. A 3% incline means 3 units of vertical rise for every 100 units of horizontal run.
My treadmill, when set at a 3% incline, has a horizontal run of 1.6 m. What will be the vertical rise?

A 4.8 m
B 48 cm
C 48 mm
D 4.8 mm

10 You are about to play your final game in a computer tournament. Your previous scores have been 134, 99, 109, 117 and 101. To win the tournament your average must be at least 114. What is the minimum score you must achieve in this game to win?

11 Suppose your heart rate is 72 beats per minute. How many days will it take your heart to beat 1 000 000 times? Round your answer to the nearest number of days.

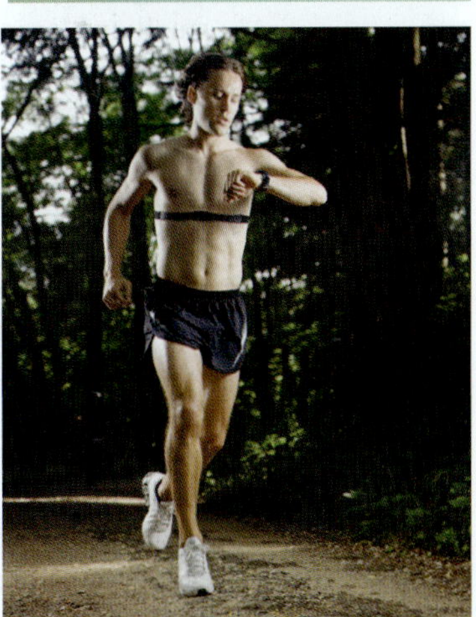

12 A gardener wants to put 12 cm of mulch on his garden, whose dimensions are 20 m by 13 m.
How many trailer loads will he require if his trailer holds 1.5 m^3.

A 20 B 21 C 46 D 47

13 A machine packs grain at a rate of $1\frac{1}{5}$ tonnes of grain per hour. How long will the machine take to pack 18 000 kg of grain?

A 15 hours
B 21 hours 6 minutes
C 21 hours 24 minutes
D 216 hours

14 In the diagram below, the shape is made from four identical rectangles.

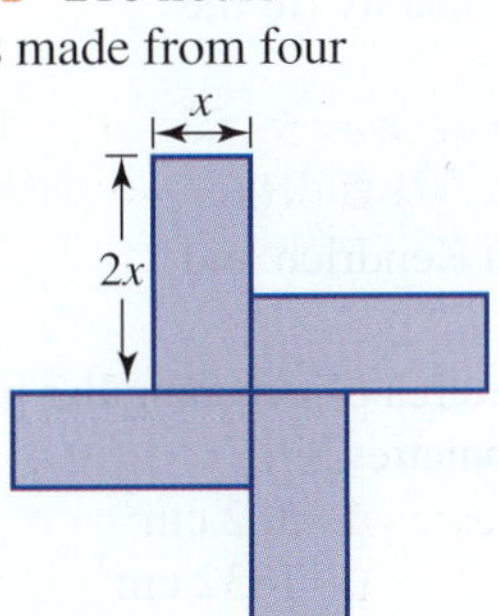

Each rectangle has a width of x and a length of $2x$. If the perimeter of the shape is 48 cm, What is the area of the shape?

A 112.5 cm^2 **B** 72 cm^2 **C** 60 cm^2 **D** 180 cm^2

15 A student recorded the times for 25 people running a 200-metre race. The stem-and-leaf diagram shows the results.

Key: 13 | 7 represents 13.7 seconds

Stem	*Leaf*
13	7
14	2 3 4 4
14	5 5 7 7 8 9
15	0 1 2 2 3 4
15	5 5 6 7 9
16	0 1 2

What percentage of students ran no more than 14.8 seconds?

A 36% **B** 40% **C** 45% **D** 48%

16 A student recorded the times for 25 people running a 200-metre race. The stem-and-leaf diagram shows the results.

Key: 13 | 7 represents 13.7 seconds

Stem	*Leaf*
13	7
14	2 3 4 4
14	5 5 7 7 8 9
15	0 1 2 2 3 4
15	5 5 6 7 9
16	0 1 2

What percentage of students ran more than 14.8 but less than 15.5?

A 28% **B** 32%
C 36% **D** 40%

17 Tsing works in a bakery. One of her chores is to take cardboard sheets and to fold them into small and large trays. It takes 2 minutes to fold a small tray and 3 minutes to fold a large tray. Can she complete 80 small and 45 large trays in the allocated time of 3.5 hours?

A Yes, Tsing will finish in 2.6 hours.
B No, Tsing will take 4 hours and 25 minutes.
C Yes, Tsing will finish exactly on 3.5 hours.
D No, Tsing will take 4 hours and 55 minutes.

18 The maximum quantity of air that can fill your lungs is called Force Vital Capacity (L). This can be modelled by the formula $L = 4.43 \times H - 0.026 \times A - 2.89$ where H = your height (metres) and A = your age (years).
If you are 165 cm tall and 15 years old, what is your capacity (to the nearest litre)?

A 4 **B** 5
C 70 **D** 106

(Formula based on Kendrich and Smith 1992)

19 What is the surface area of a rectangular prism that has a length of 11 cm, a width of 6 cm and a height of 50 millimetres?

A 170 cm^2 **B** 302 cm^2
C 330 cm^2 **D** 1832 cm^2

20 You have a piece of string 3.7 metres long. You cut it into 6 pieces of equal length to tie to 6 balloons, and there is 22 cm of string left. How long were each of the 6 pieces?

21 My teacher and I boarded a tram together. At the second stop, three people got on. At the third stop, three people got on and one got off. At the fourth stop, three got off. At the fifth stop, six people got off. At the sixth stop, one-half of the passengers got off and I was the only passenger left on the tram. How many passengers were on the tram when my teacher and I got on?

22 Examine the expression $3k^2 + 6k - 5 + 6k^2 + 2$.
When it is simplified, which of the following is the equivalent expression?
A $3k^2 + 12k - 3$
B $9k^2 + 6k - 3$
C $9k^2 + 6k + 7$
D $15k^2 + 6k - 3$

23 Jane and Lance each have a rectangular piece of paper of the same dimensions. The length is labelled x cm and the width is 12 cm.
Jane and Lance each cut their paper in half in two different ways as illustrated below.
Jane's cutting.

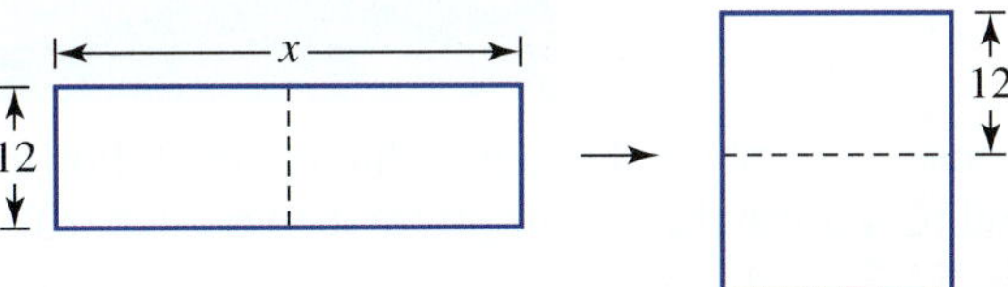

Lance's cutting

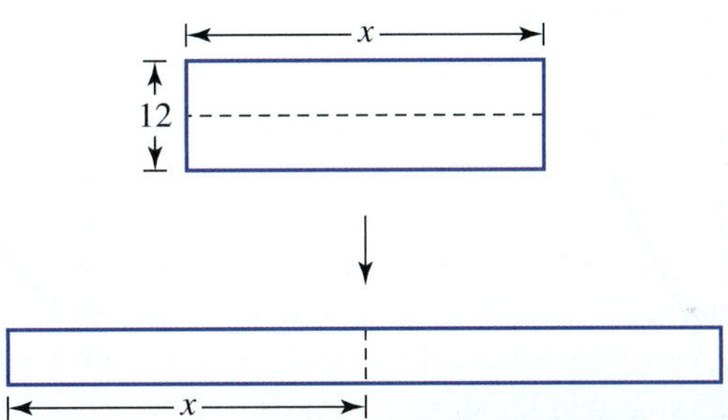

Which of the following represents the sum of the perimeters of the two new designs?
A $P = 5x + 48$
B $P = 5(x + 12)$
C $P = 6x + 60$
D $P = 6(x + 12)$

24 To make a Chinese dish called 'Dragon's beard noodles' a process for making it by hand is as follows.
Take a 100-cm strand of dough and fold it in half. Stretch the dough back to its original length so that the two thinner strands are formed. Repeat this process over and over increasing the number of noodles as they get progressively thinner.
After the 6th fold how many noodles strands will you have?
A 12
B 32
C 64
D 128

25 The steps on the foreshore have a horizontal width of 24 cm and a height of 18 cm, as shown below.

For someone climbing the steps, which of the following graphs models the height above the ground (h) against the distance from the first step (d)?

A

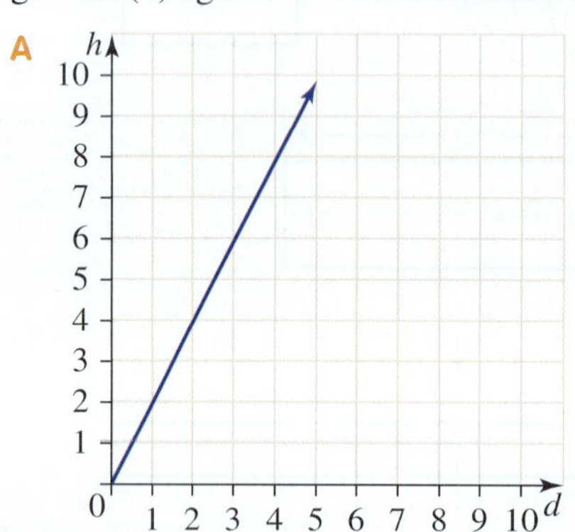

B

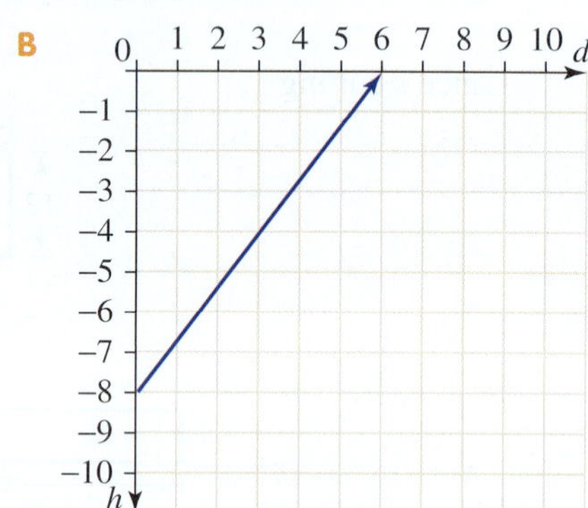

C

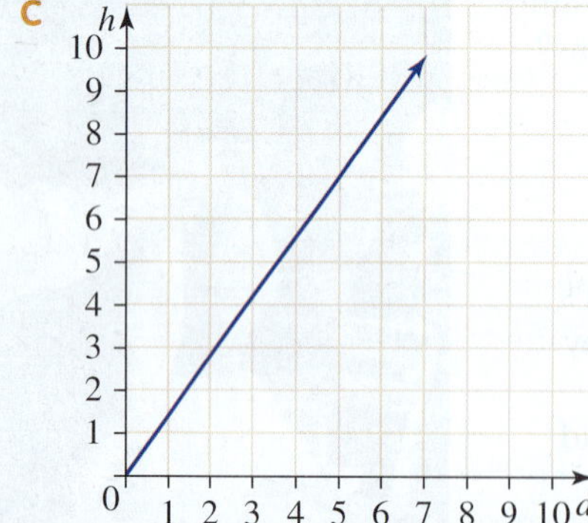

D

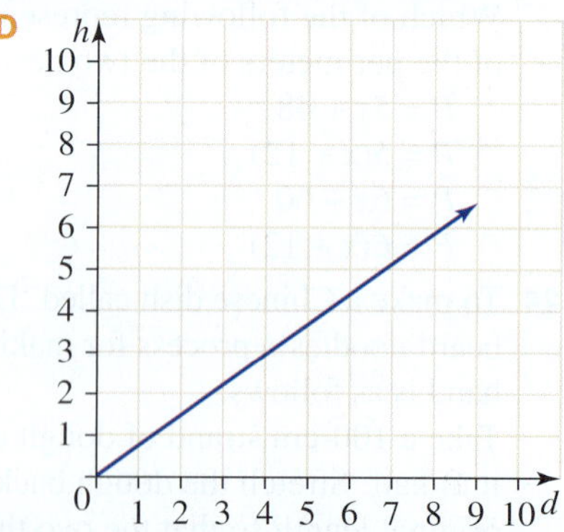

26 A recipe for pizza dough requires a 20 cm × 40 cm rectangular pan. However, you have only a square pan, with dimensions of 25 cm × 25 cm.
Approximately what will be the difference in the size of your pizza by using the square pan?

A Smaller by 22% **B** Larger by 22% **C** Smaller by 28% **D** Larger by 28%

27 Alice ripped a piece of paper into three parts, and tore each of those parts into three more parts. If she repeated this action 3 times, how many pieces of paper would she have?

A 15 **B** 81 **C** 243 **D** 729

28 Ning was throwing darts at a target as shown at right. When his dart landed on or inside the circle (bullseye) of the target board, he earned 7 points. However, when his dart landed outside the circle he earned 2 points. After 50 throws his friend reported his score to be 140 points. Ning wanted to know how many bullseyes he had hit, but his friend did not know. How many bullseyes did Ning hit? (Assume he hits inside the circle.)

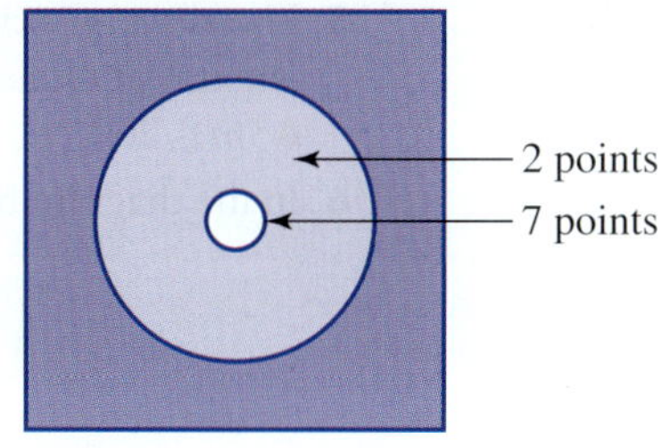

Let x = number of hits on the bull's eye.

Which of the following equations could be used to solve for x?

A $7x + 50 - x = 140$ **B** $7x + 2(50 - x) = 140$

C $7x + 2x = 140$ **D** $2x + 2(50 - 7x) = 140$

29 John bushwalked 36 km through the Flinders Ranges in 3 days. On the first day he hiked 50% of the total distance. On the second day he hiked 25% of the distance that remained. How many kilometres did he hike on the third day?

A $11\frac{1}{2}$ **B** $13\frac{1}{2}$ **C** $22\frac{1}{2}$ **D** 27

30 Two pencil boxes as shown have the following information.

The volume of one pencil box is 24 cm^2 more than the volume of the other pencil box. One box has two of its sides measuring 3 cm and 4 cm, while the other box has sides that measure 1.5 cm and 6 cm. The third sides of the boxes are the same length. What is that length?

A 2 cm **B** 4 cm

C 6 cm **D** 8 cm

1D Set 1D

Non-calculator

1 A 130 cm long strand of wire is cut into three pieces.
The longest piece is three times as long as the second shortest piece.
The second longest piece is three times as long as the shortest piece.
How long is the shortest piece?

A 18 cm **B** 10 cm

C 17.5 cm **D** 15 cm

2 One litre of paint covers an area of 20 square metres.
How much paint will cover one square metre?

A 0.005 litre **B** 0.002 litre

C 0.05 litre **D** 0.02 litre

3 A pancake recipe requires $4\frac{1}{2}$ cups of milk. If you wish to make one-fifth of the recipe, how many cups of milk will you need?

A 0.2 **B** 0.5

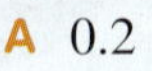

C 0.8 **D** 0.9

$2x + 3$ $6x - 9$ $4x + 12$

4 Each card pictured at right is labelled with a value. What is the mean value of these cards?

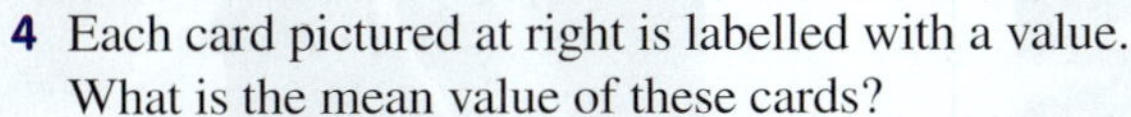

A $12x + 6$ **B** $12x + 24$

C $4x + 6$ **D** $4x + 2$

5 In order to purchase a new iPod you must save at least \$260. What inequality represents the amount of money, m, that you must save?

A $m \leq 260$ **B** $m < 260$ **C** $m \geq 260$ **D** $m > 260$

6 In the diagram below, $\angle A$ and $\angle B$ are complementary.

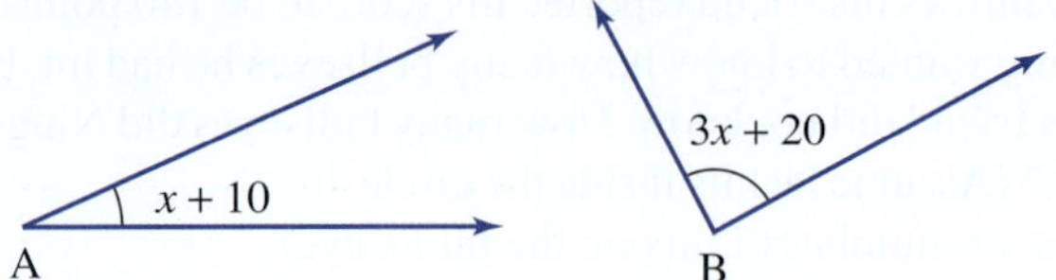

What is the measure of $\angle B$?

A 65° **B** 45° **C** 30° **D** 15°

7 A swimming pool is being filled with water. The pool already contained 5000 litres of water. The table shows the number of litres of water in the pool after t hours.

Litres of water in pool (L)	Number of hours (t)
5000	0
7500	1
10 000	2
12 500	3
15 000	4

Which rule can be used to determine the number of litres, L, of water in the pool after t hours?

A $L = 2500t$ **B** $L = 5000t$ **C** $L = 5000t + 2500$ **D** $L = 5000 + 2500t$

8 Anne wants to solve the equation shown.

$$2x - 3 = 13.$$

Which steps could she use to find the solution?

A Add 3 to both sides, then divide both sides by 2.
B Subtract 3 from both sides, then divide both sides by 2.
C Divide both sides by 2, then add 3 to both sides.
D Multiply both sides by 2, then subtract 3 from both sides.

9 The photograph of a dragonfly is shown with its dimensions.

You decide to enlarge the photograph, and the new length is 12 cm. What is the new width?

A 14 cm B 15 cm C 16 cm D 17 cm

10 Madeline noticed that in one minute she blinked 50 times. At this rate, approximately how many days will it take her to blink 1 000 000 times?

A 8 B 10 C 12 D 14

11 A parcel of land is to be subdivided as shown below. The shaded area is to be sold.

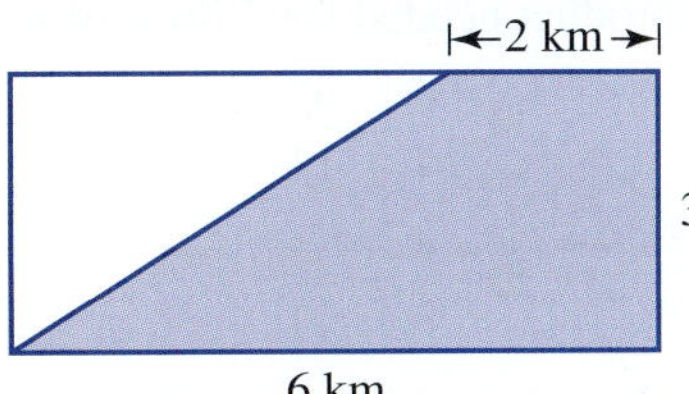

What percentage of the total area does this represent?

A $33\frac{1}{3}$ B 50 C $66\frac{2}{3}$ D 75

12 When the diagram shown is folded to make a cube, what symbol is on the face opposite the face marked Δ?

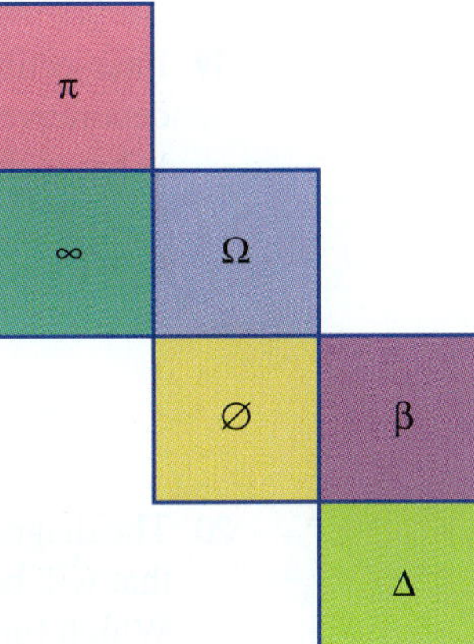

A β

B Ω

C ∅

D ∞

13 You have an envelope that has a perimeter of 35 cm. If the ratio of the length to the width is 4 : 3, what are the dimensions of the envelope?

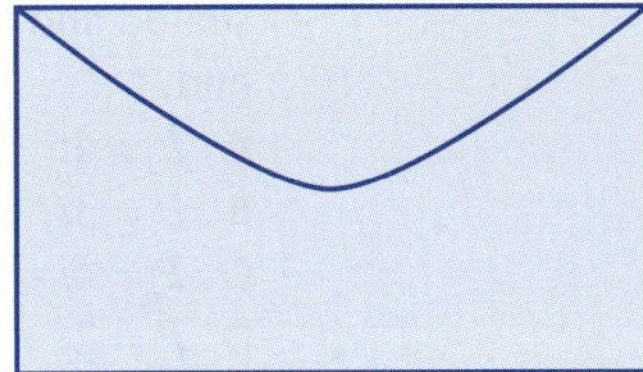

A $L = 20$ cm, $W = 15$ cm B $L = 10$ cm, $W = 7.5$ cm

C $L = 15$ cm, $W = 20$ cm D $L = 7.5$ cm, $W = 10$ cm

14 A triangle ABC was drawn on coordinate axes as shown. What would be the coordinates of the triangle reflected in the y-axis?

A (1, 3) (1, 1) (−1, −3) B (3, −1) (1, 1) (−1, −2)

C (−3, 1) (−1, −1) (1, 3) D (3, 1) (1, 1) (1, −3)

15 Evaluate the following expression.

$$2\frac{2}{5} - 1\frac{2}{3}$$

16 An electronic device counted 4500 vehicles passing through an intersection during an 8-hour period. If the number of vehicles passing through the intersection per hour remains the same, what proportion can be used to find x, the number of vehicles that would be counted during a 10-hour period?

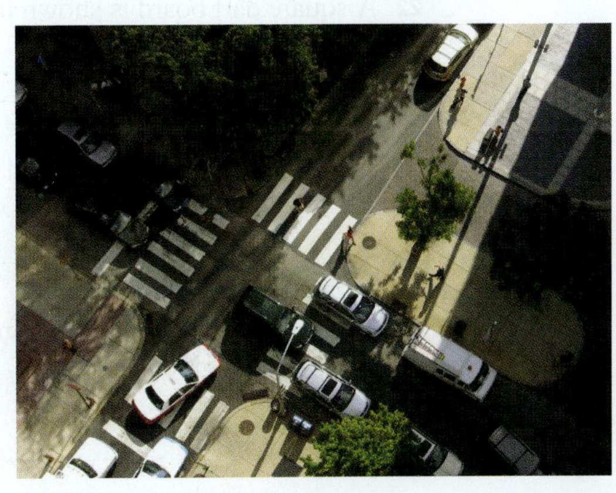

A $\frac{4500}{8} = \frac{x}{10}$

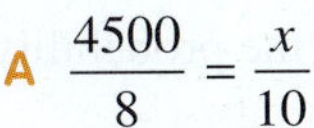

B $\frac{8}{4500} = \frac{x}{10}$

C $\frac{8}{x} = \frac{10}{4500}$

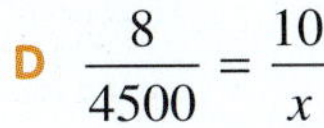

D $\frac{8}{4500} = \frac{10}{x}$

17 John has five fewer marbles than Liam, and Tang has three times as many as John. If Liam has n marbles, which of the following represents the number of marbles that Tang has?

A $3n - 5$ **B** $3n$
C $5 - 3n$ **D** $3(n - 5)$

18 The directions for using a concentrated cleaning product say to add 3 capfuls of the product to every 4 litres of water. Which of the following equations can be used to calculate c, the number of capfuls of the product needed for 7 litres of water?

A $\frac{3}{4} = \frac{c}{7}$ **B** $\frac{3}{4} = \frac{c}{11}$

C $\frac{4}{3} = \frac{c}{7}$ **D** $\frac{4}{3} = \frac{c}{11}$

19 Intersecting paths have been constructed to surround a decorative garden bed.
What is the angle measurement for x?

A 128° **B** 102°
C 87° **D** 61°

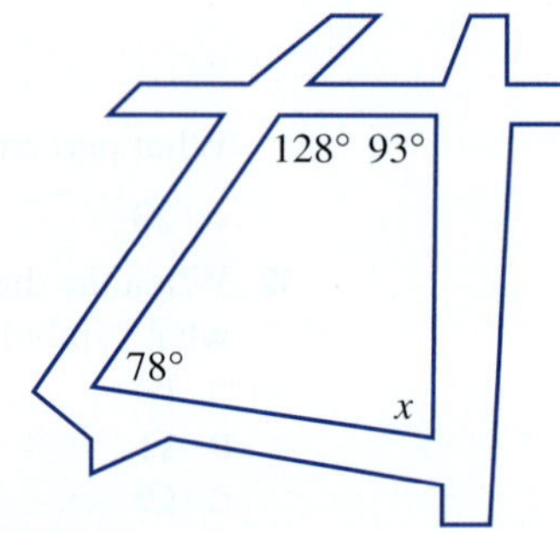

20 The diagrams show the seating arrangements that will be used if tables are placed end to end. Which formula represents the relationship between the number of people (P) that can be seated and the number of tables (t) placed end to end.

A $P = 4t$
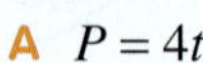
B $P = 3t$
C $P = 4t - 2$
D $P = 2t + 2$

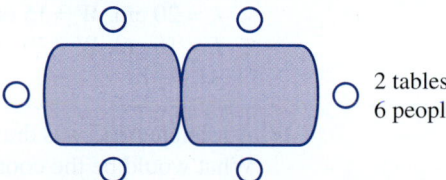

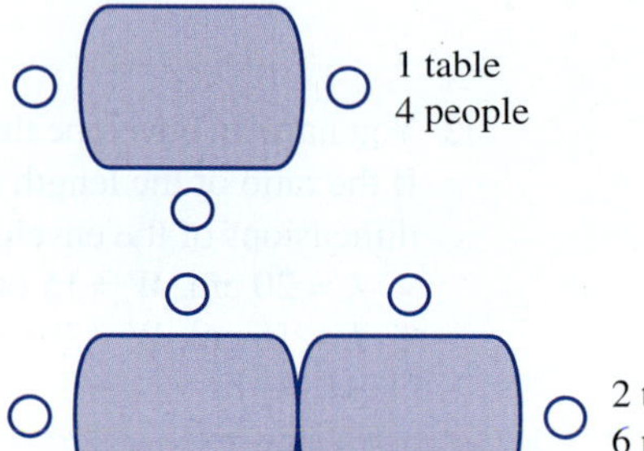

21 The diagram shows a rhombus. The midpoints of two of its sides are joined with a straight line.
What is the measure of angle x?

A 76° **B** 104°
C 142° **D** 152°

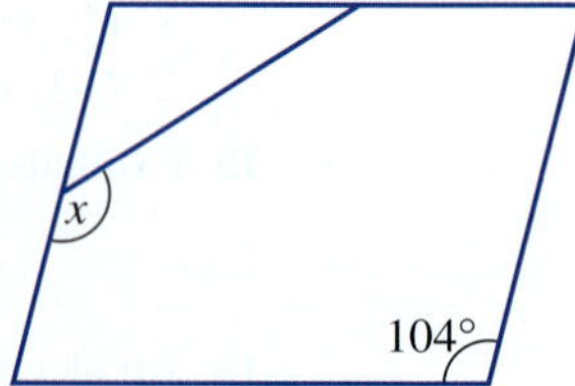

22 A square dart board is shown below.

Suppose a dart, thrown randomly, hits the board. Determine the probability of the dart's landing on a green segment.

A $\frac{7}{12}$ **B** $\frac{1}{8}$ **C** $\frac{7}{24}$ **D** $\frac{1}{14}$

23 In how many different ways could these bollards be arranged in a line?

24 What is the solution for the following expression?

$$5 + \frac{70}{10} \times (1 + 2)^2 - 1$$

A 95 **B** 71
C 67 **D** 46

25 A helicopter has a rotor that moves at a rate of 720 revolutions per minute. Through how many degrees does the rotor turn per second?

A 0.03 **B** 12
C 4320 **D** 259 200

26 You counted a total of 40 goldfish in a pond in the Botanical Gardens. The gardener told you that the ratio of female fish to male fish was 3 : 5. What was the total of the number of male goldfish?

A 24 **B** 25
C 26 **D** 30

27

Polygons	
Number of sides (n)	**Sum of interior angle measures (S)**
3	180°
4	360°
5	540°
6	720°
7	900°

Based on the table, which statement is true?

A The sum of the interior angle measures decreases by $\frac{1}{2}$ for each side increase of 1.
B The sum of the interior angle measures increases by 180° for each side increase of 1.
C The sum of the interior angle measures doubles for each side increase of 1.
D The sum of the interior angle measures is a whole number multiple of 360°.

28 The sum of x and y is:

A 196°
B 180°
C 135°
D 113°

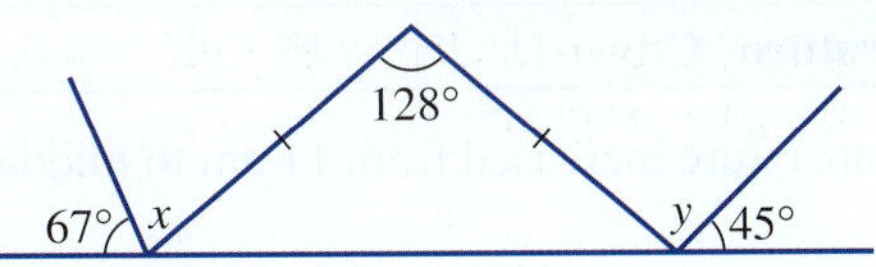

29 A box is displayed on the top of a shop counter as shown in the photograph. Its dimensions are length = $1\frac{1}{4}$ m, width = $1\frac{2}{5}$ m, height = 0.8 m.
What is the volume of the box?

A 1.2 m^3 B 1.25 m^3
C 1.4 m^3 D 1.65 m^3

30 If two sides of a triangle are 12 cm and 20 cm, the third side must be:

A between and including 8 cm and 32 cm.
B between but not including 8 cm and 32 cm.
C greater than 8 cm.
D less than 32 cm.

1E Set 1E

Calculator allowed

1 The students in a class measure their heights in cm.
The following stem-and-leaf plot shows their heights.
Key: 13 | 5 means 135 cm.

Stem	*Leaf*
13	5 8
14	0 4 9
15	3 5 5
16	3

What is the mean height?

A 148 cm B 149 cm C 155 cm D 163 cm

2 You have a rectangular box with a lid. The top of the lid has an area of 392 square centimetres. The ratio of the width to the length of the lid is 1:8. What are the dimensions of the lid?

A 4 cm by 98 cm B 7 cm by 56 cm
C 8 cm by 49 cm D 8 cm by 64 cm

3 The following is a design of a quilt square (ACEF) whose sides are 5 cm long.
B and D are the mid-points of sides AC and CE respectively.
What is the area of the triangle BDF?

A 6.25 B 9.375
C 12.5 D 15.625

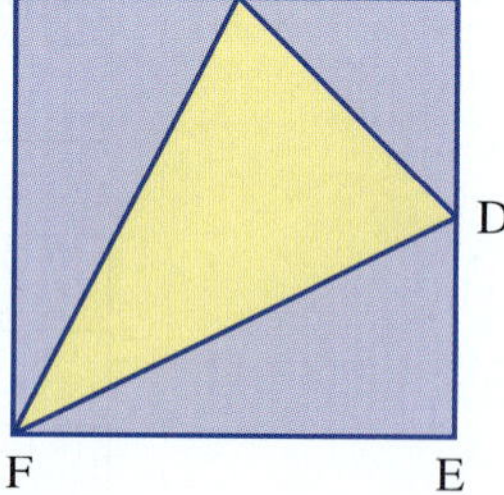

4 A photograph is placed on a card measuring 8.5 cm by 10 cm. A 1.5-cm edging is left all around. What area (in square cm) does the photograph cover?

A 59.5 cm^2 B 49 cm^2 C 46.75 cm^2 D 38.5 cm^2

5 A student recorded the temperature outside her classroom every hour for one school day. She drew up the following table.

Time	9 am	10 am	11 am	12 pm	1 pm	2 pm	3 pm
Temperature °C	11	13		34	36	33	29

If the temperature increased from 11 am to midday by $41\frac{2}{3}\%$, what was the temperature at 11 am?

A 22° B 23° C 24° D 25°

6 The school bus took $1\frac{1}{4}$ hours to travel 80 km. How far did it travel in $2\frac{1}{2}$ hours?

7 Consider the pattern below.

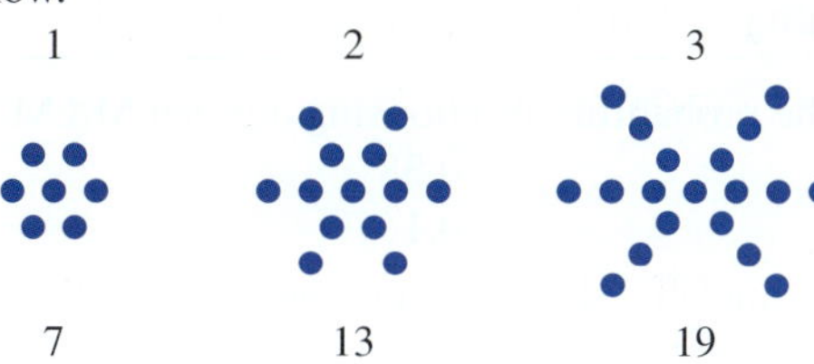

Which one of the following equations could model the design, where C represents the total number of dots (the numbers shown below) and n represents the series number (the numbers shown above).

A $C = 7n - 1$ **B** $C = 6n$ **C** $C = 6n + 1$ **D** $C = 6n - 1$

8 A bag of fertiliser is made by mixing nitrates, potash and phosphates in the ratio of 3 : 2 : 5. How much fertiliser will be produced if 15 kg of nitrates are used?

A 22 kg **B** 25 kg **C** 45 kg **D** 50 kg

9 Fuel for a two-stroke engine is made by mixing petrol and oil in the ratio 30 : 1. If you have 250 mL of oil, how much petrol needs to be added to make a two-stroke mixture?

A 0.12 litre **B** 1.2 litres **C** 7.5 litres **D** 8.3 litres

10 The Venn diagram shows how many of the 200 Year 8 students have an iPod only, a mobile phone only, or both an iPod and a mobile phone.
Use the information in the diagram to find the probability that a student chosen at random has neither an iPod nor a mobile phone.

A $\frac{1}{30}$ **B** $\frac{3}{20}$ **C** $\frac{6}{10}$ **D** $\frac{1}{30}$

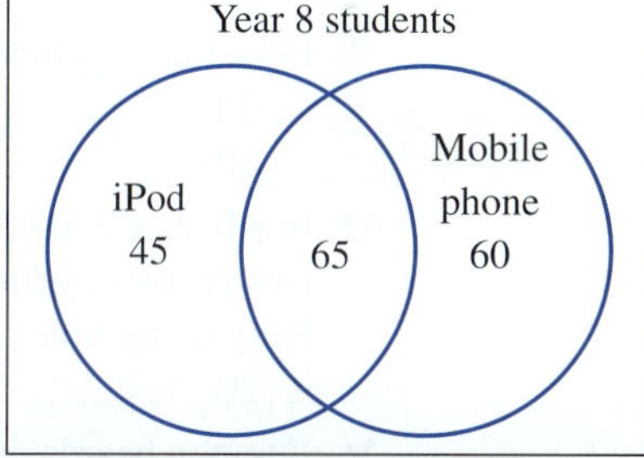

11 The Orion nebula is approximately 1.5×10^3 light-years away from Earth. It is visible with the naked eye. One light-year is approximately 9.5×10^{12} km. What is the approximate distance in kilometer between Earth and the Orion nebula?

A 1.425×10^{15} **B** 1.425×10^{16}
C 1.1×10^{11} **D** 6.33×10^9

12 An express train leaves from Geelong at 8.55 am and arrives in Altona station at 9.37 am. If the train travelled 52 km, what was the train's average speed in km/h?

A 98 km/h **B** 84 km/h
C 74 km/h **D** 71 km/h

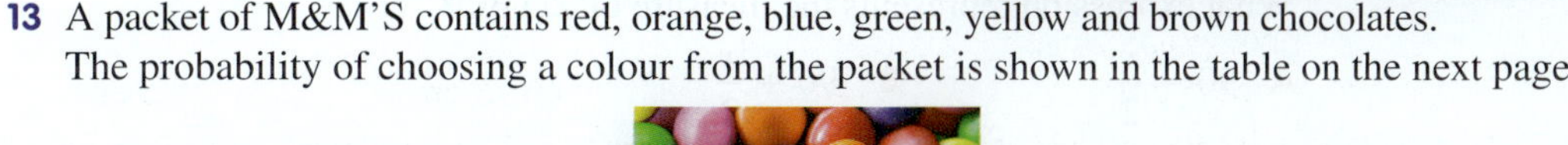

13 A packet of M&M'S contains red, orange, blue, green, yellow and brown chocolates. The probability of choosing a colour from the packet is shown in the table on the next page.

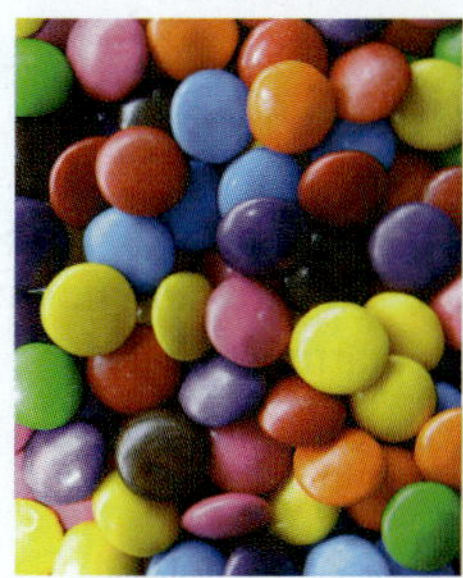

Colour	Red	Orange	Blue	Green	Yellow	Brown
Probability	0.3	0.13	0.12		0.25	0.09

What is the probability of choosing a green M&M?

A 0.9 B 0.38

C 0.11 D 0.1

14 The following table shows the number of M&M'S of different colours in a particular bag.

Colour	Number	Expression
Red		x
Orange		$x - 2$
Blue		$x - 1$
Green		$x + 1$
Yellow		$x - 3$
Brown		$x + 2$
Total	33	

How many yellow M&M'S are in the bag?

A 30 B 20

C 10 D 3

15 In a bag of 200 jelly beans, the following distribution of colours was found.
Brown 13%, yellow 14%, red 13%, blue 24%, orange 20%, green 16%
How many blue jelly beans are in the bag?

A 20 B 24 C 48 D 40

16 'Dragon beards' is a special Chinese dish. The noodles are hand-pulled until they are extraordinarily fine. It has been calculated that a piece of paste prepared with 1.5 kilograms of wheat flour can make 144 000 hair-thin noodles, each 20 centimetres long.
If you joined all the strands together, what would be their total length?

A 28.8 km B 288 km C 28 800 km D 288 000 km

17 The angles below are supplementary. The measure of ∠DEF is $\frac{x}{2}$.

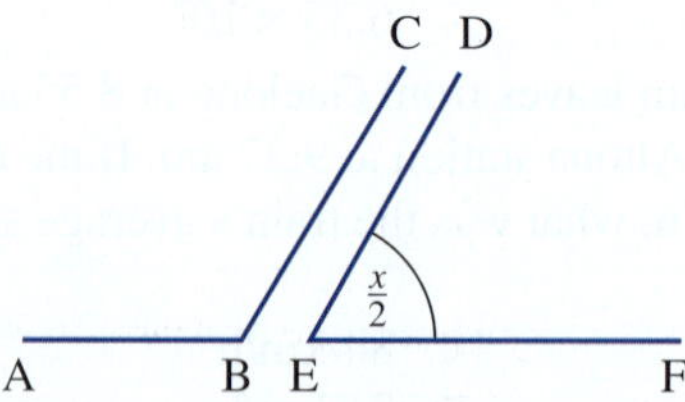

What expression represents the measure of ∠ABC?

A $90 - \frac{x}{2}$ B $90 + \frac{x}{2}$

C $180 - \frac{x}{2}$ D $180 + \frac{x}{2}$

18 A driver drives 8 km south, then 6 km east followed by 2 km south. He then travels 3 km west. Next, in order to avoid a traffic jam, he turns and travels 6 km north. How many kilometres is the driver south of his starting point?

19 If the ratios of the sides of a quadrilateral are given in order as 3 : 3 : 4 : 4, what type of quadrilateral must it be?

A Rectangle B Square C Kite D Parallelogram

20 The angles of a triangle are in the ratio 3 : 5 : 7. Which diagram has angles in this ratio?

A

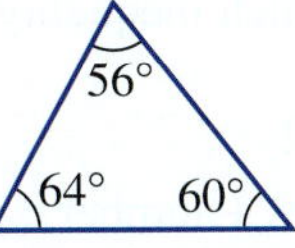

B

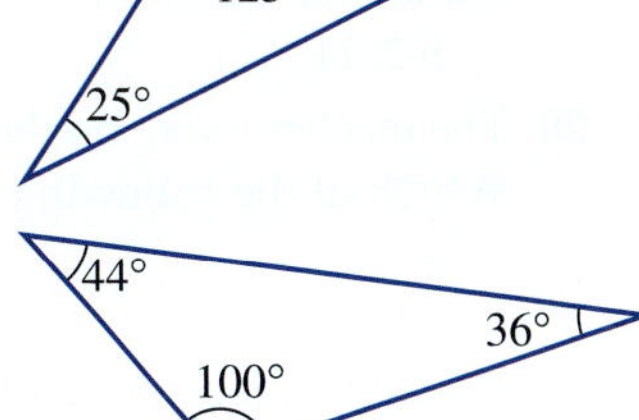

C

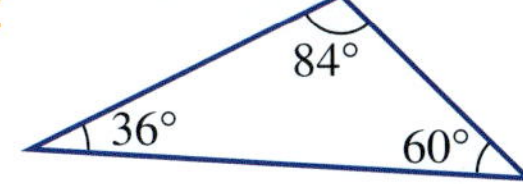

D

21 A trapezium was created on a Cartesian plane using the coordinates A(2, 0), B(–2, 0), C(–3, 4) and D(x, 4).
What is the value for x if the area of the trapezium is 24 units?

22 Ann is drawing a right-angled isosceles triangle on a coordinate grid. She has plotted two of the corners of the triangle at (–2, 3) and (1, 2).
Which of the coordinates below would make the third corner a right-angled isosceles triangle?

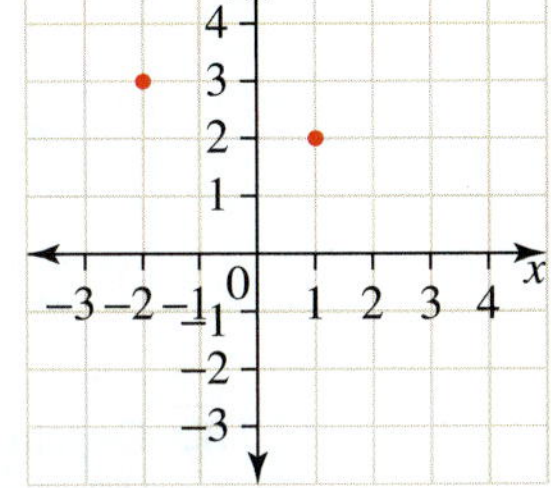

A (–1, 4)
B (4, 3)
C (0, –1)
D (3, 5)

23 Ann recorded the highest temperature each day over a 7-day period in February.
Which statement describes the data?

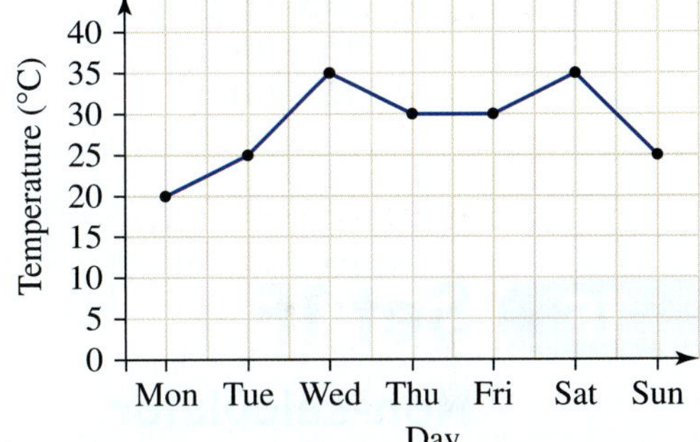

A Median > mean
B Mean = mode
C Median = mean
D Median < mean

24 Ethan wants to solve for x in this equation.

$$1\tfrac{2}{5} - x \times \tfrac{2}{3} = 1\tfrac{2}{3}$$

Which step should he perform first?

A Divide both sides by $\frac{2}{3}$.
B Multiply both sides by $\frac{2}{3}$.
C Subtract $1\frac{2}{5}$ from both sides.
D Add $1\frac{2}{5}$ to both sides.

25 Al-Samaw'al was simplifying the expression $6x - 3(x - 5)$.
Which is the equivalent expression?

A $3x - 5$
B $3x + 5$
C $3x - 15$
D $3x + 15$

26 In the parallelogram ABCD below, AC and DB intersect at E.
AE = $3x - 3$ and EC = $x + 13$.

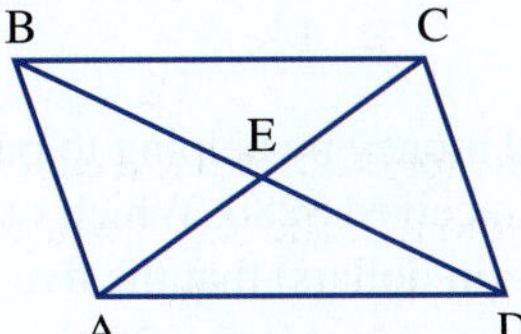

What is the value of x?

A 8
B 16
C 20
D 40

27 There are 520 students and 25 teachers taking buses to the Deakin Great Hall for a speech night. Each bus can take a maximum of 48 passengers. Which inequality represents the least number of buses (b) for the trip?

A $b \geq 11$ **B** $b \leq 11$ **C** $b \geq 12$ **D** $b \leq 12$

28 The teacher wrote on the board: 'Eight less than three times a number n is greater than 15'. Which of the following numbers could be a solution for n?

A $7\frac{1}{5}$ **B** $7\frac{1}{3}$ **C** $7\frac{2}{3}$ **D** $8\frac{1}{3}$

29 Which graph could represent the solution set for $x < \sqrt{3}$?

A

−4 −3 −2 −1 0 1 2 3 4

B

−4 −3 −2 −1 0 1 2 3 4

C

−4 −3 −2 −1 0 1 2 3 4

D

−4 −3 −2 −1 0 1 2 3 4

30 Descartes has drawn a cube on a Cartesian plane. What are the coordinates of B?

A (20, −10)
B (−15, −10)
C (15, −10)
D (15, −15)

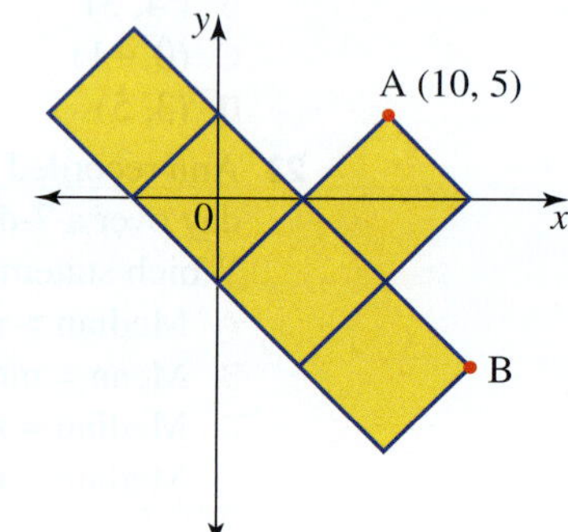

Set 1F

Non-calculator

1 A room has four identical walls that are being painted. For decorative purposes, each of the four walls is being painted in a variety of colours. One of the colours is blue, and the four walls will each have different areas that are painted this colour. The fraction of each wall that is painted blue is shown on the diagram.

What fraction of all 4 walls will be painted with this colour?

Room

$\frac{1}{6}$ $\frac{3}{7}$ $\frac{1}{3}$ $\frac{1}{2}$

A  $\frac{5}{7}$ **B** $\frac{6}{7}$

C $\frac{5}{14}$ **D** $1\frac{5}{7}$

2 Five friends earned money by helping to build a wall in a garden. After they divided the money equally, they each received \$280. Which of the following equations could be used to determine x, the total amount (in dollars) that the five friends earned?

A $5x = 280$ **B** $x - 5 = 280$

C $x + 5 = 280$ **D** $\frac{x}{5} = 280$

3 There are 150 Scouts at a camp. For 40% of them, this is their first camp. One-fifth of the remainder have been to one other camp. The others have been to three camps. Which of the following represents the percentages of students on camp for the first, second and third times?

A

B

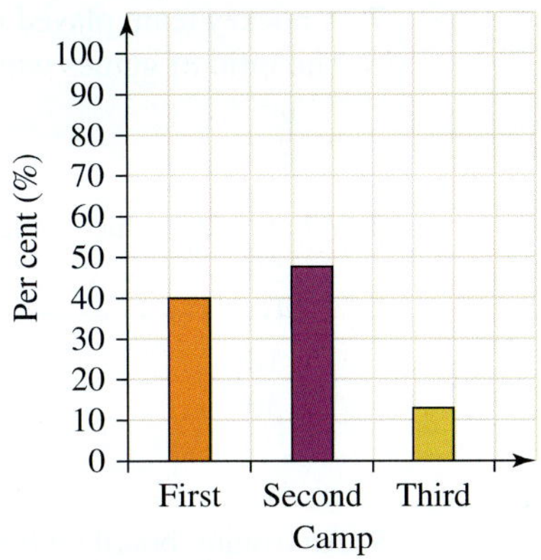

C

D

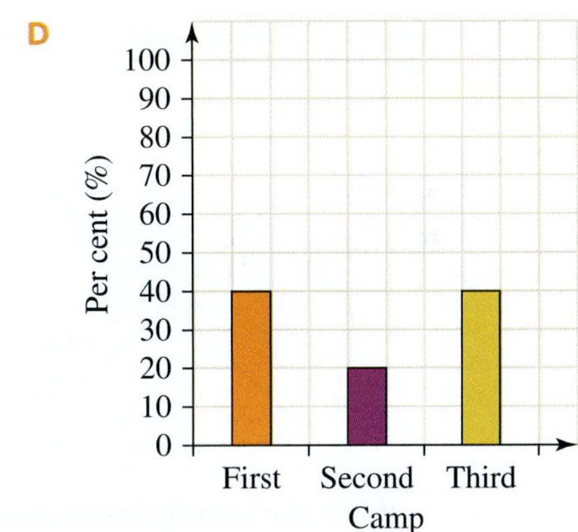

4 Ash spins the arrow twice on the spinner. Which tree diagram shows all the possible outcomes?

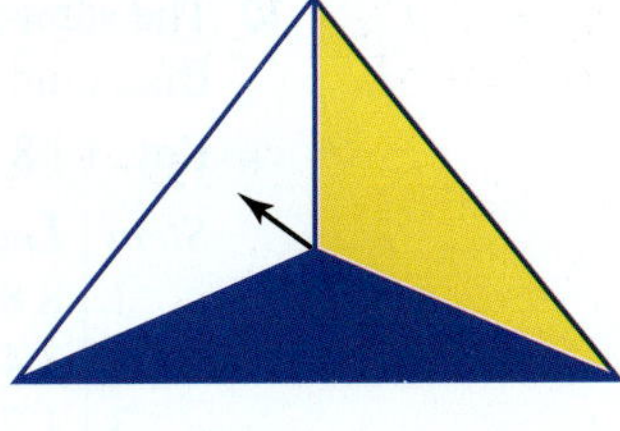

A

W W B B Y Y

B

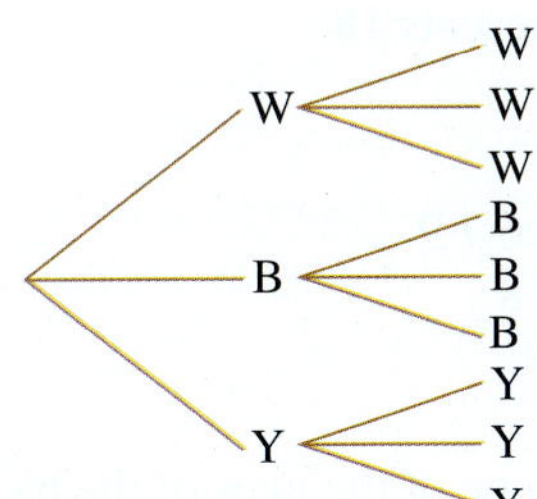

C

W: W B Y
B: W B Y
Y: W B Y

D

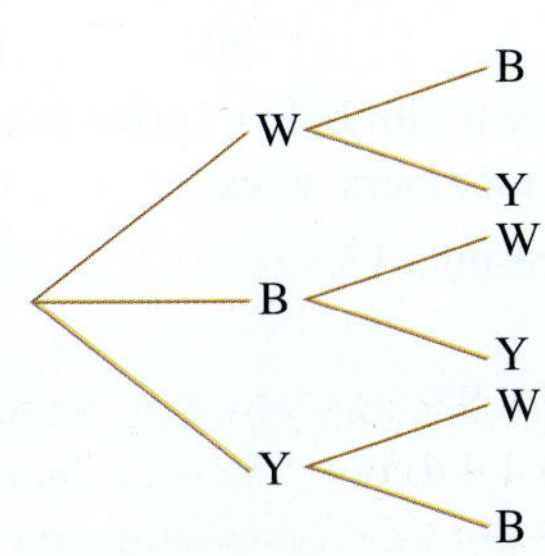

5 The human heart beats an average of 37 800 000 times in one year. Which of the following is an equivalent value?

A 3.78×10^{-7} **B** 3.78×10^{-6} **C** 3.78×10^{6} **D** 3.78×10^{7}

6 Which unit of measurement would be most appropriate for measuring the area of a page of newspaper?

A mm^2 **B** cm^2 **C** m^2 **D** km^2

7 A hockey team played n games, losing five of them and winning the rest. The ratio of games won to games lost is:

A $\frac{n}{5}$ **B** $\frac{n-5}{5}$ **C** $\frac{5}{n}$ **D** $\frac{5}{n-5}$

8 What is the value of the angle x?

A 85°
B 70°
C 110°
D 130°

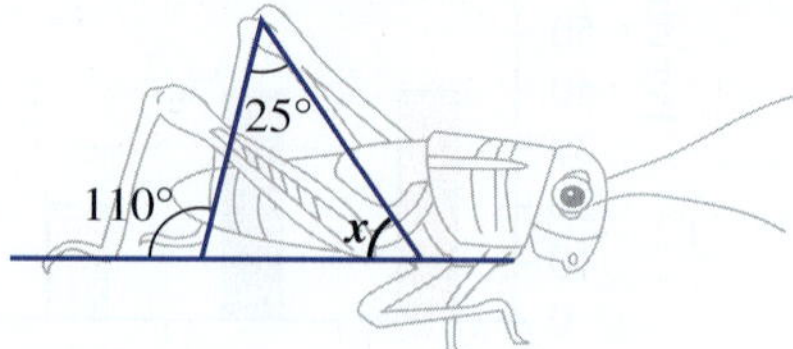

9 An ironing board with the measurements shown is advertised online.

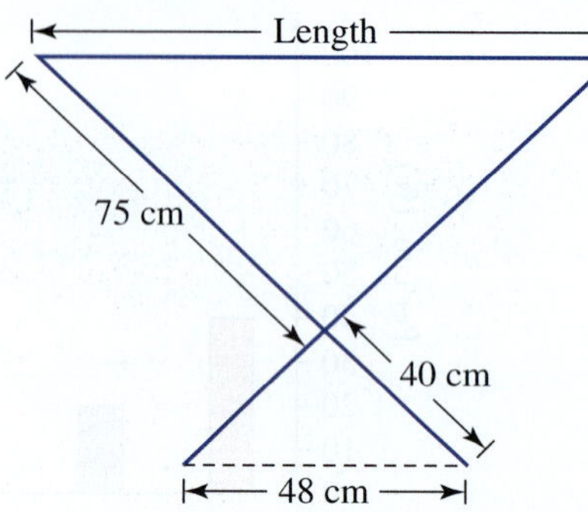

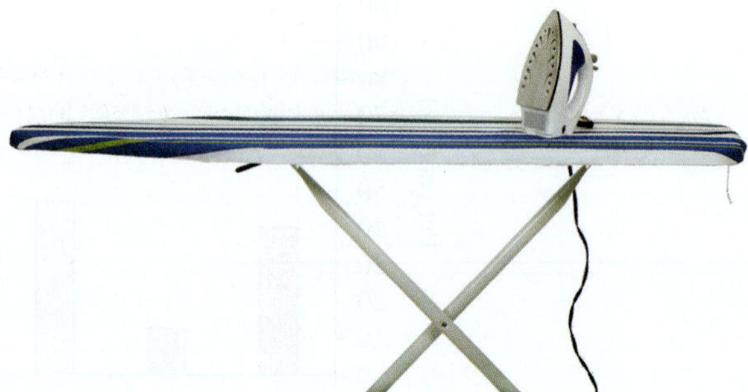

When the ironing board is set up, two similar triangles are formed. How long is the top?

A 90 cm **B** 62.5 cm **C** 51.2 cm **D** 48 cm

10 The stem-and-leaf plot below shows the age of each member of a bicycle club.

Bike club members' ages

Key: 1 | 8 represents 18

Stem	*Leaf*
1	8 8 9
2	3 4 6 6 6 7 9
3	1 2 5 7 8
4	0 2 5
5	2 7

What is the range of the ages of the bicycle club members?

A 57 **B** 39
C 36 **D** 30

11 The stem-and-leaf plot below shows the age of each member of a running club.

Running club members' ages

Key: 1 | 3 represents 13

Stem	*Leaf*
1	3 5 6 7 8 8 9
2	0 1 2 3 4 4 4 5
3	0 2 3 4 5

What is the median age of the club members?

A 22 **B** 22.5
C 24 **D** 24.5

12 The *Chef and Cook* television show produces two square-based cakes. The small cake has a side length of 8 cm while the large cake has a side length of 16 cm. Which of the following statements is true?

A The area of the base of the large cake is 2 times the area of the small cake.
B The area of the base of the large cake is 4 times the area of the small cake.
C The area of the base of the large cake is 8 times the area of the small cake.
D The area of the base of the large cake is 16 times the area of the small cake.

13 Calculate the value of the following.
$25 \times (2768 + 2768 + 2768 + 2768)$

14 The stage in the hall at League School has the shape of a quadrilateral, as shown. Which of these are the most likely values of x and y?

	x	y
A	30	160
B	45	145
C	63	117
D	72	118

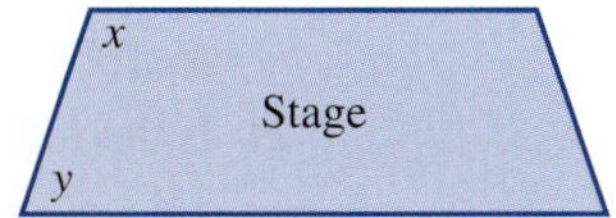

15 The numbers of passengers on a train over a 20-day period were recorded as follows:
59, 65, 73, 83, 90, 83, 71, 92, 60, 58, 96, 66, 75, 76, 85, 77, 86, 79, 87, 79
The data are displayed below on a stem-and-leaf plot.

Key: 5 | 9 represents 59

Stem	*Leaf*
5	8 9
6	0 5 ?
7	1 3 5 6 7 9 9
8	3 3 5 6 7
9	0 2 6

What is the missing number?

16 The table shows the results of a survey, which asked drivers how many accidents they had over the previous 5 years. What is the median number of accidents per year?

Number of accidents	0	1	2	3	4	5	6
Number of drivers	16	14	21	4	3	1	1

A 0.5 **B** 1
C 1.5 **D** 2

17 Alex wants to know the answer to the following expression.
$(5 \times 10^4) + (2 \times 10^2) + (4 \times 10) = \square$
Which of the following is correct?

A 502 400 **B** 52 400
C 50 240 **D** 5240

18 What is the missing number in the following equation?

$$\frac{4}{3} \div \frac{?}{3} = \frac{1}{8}$$

19 My mother is 4 times as old as I am. My sister is 75% of my age and 10% of my grandfather's age. My father is 50, which is 2 years older than my mother. How old are my sister and grandfather?

20 In the quilt design below, what is the measure of x?

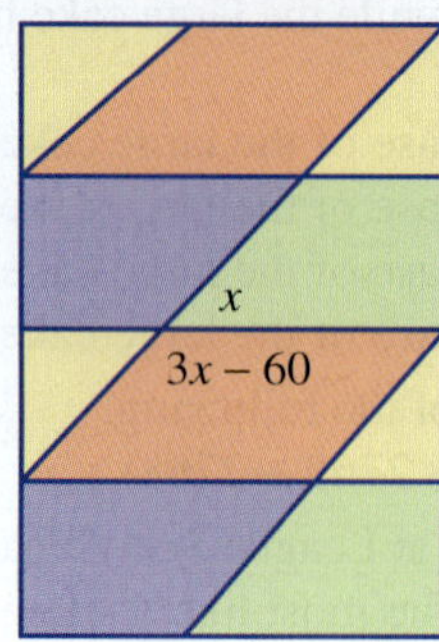

A $10°$ B $30°$ C $40°$ D $60°$

21 Is the following equation true or false?

$12 + (5 \times 9) - (108 \div 2) = 3$

22 The solid brick shown is made of small cubic bricks of sides 1 unit. When the large brick is disassembled into its component small bricks, the total surface area of all the small bricks is how much greater than the surface area of the large brick?

A 32 B 40 C 56 D 96

23 Jane ate 0.2 parts of pizza and her friend ate 0.02 parts of the same pizza. Find the ratio between the parts they ate.

A 10 : 1 B 5 : 2 C 1 : 1 D 1 : 10

24 A marble is selected at random. What is the probability that the marble will not be blue?

A $\frac{5}{6}$ B $\frac{1}{6}$ C $\frac{3}{14}$ D $\frac{3}{7}$

25 Write 70 as a percentage of 200.

26 If $4x + 3 = 22$, what is the value of $4x - 3$?

A -3 B 0 C 16 D 19

27 If this pattern continues, how many cubes will it take to make 10 layers?

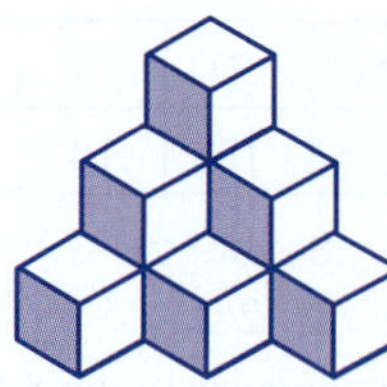

28 The first number in a pattern is 48. To go from one number to the next the rule is to divide by 4. What is the fourth number in the pattern?

A $\frac{4}{3}$ B $\frac{3}{4}$ C $\frac{1}{3}$ D $\frac{1}{4}$

29 Which of the following is equivalent to the expression $2^6 \times 2^4$?

A 2^{24} B 2^{10} C 4^{24} D 4^{10}

30 Andrew wants to find the value for the expression $\frac{6x + 5}{8x + 5}$ when $x = -10$. What is the value?

A $\frac{2}{3}$ B $\frac{-2}{3}$ C $\frac{11}{15}$ D $\frac{-11}{15}$

Integers

2A Adding and subtracting integers
2B Multiplying integers
2C Dividing integers
2D Combined operations on integers

WHAT DO YOU KNOW?

1. List what you know about positive and negative integers. Create a concept map to show your list.
2. Share what you know with a partner and then with a small group.
3. As a class, create a large concept map that shows your class's knowledge of positive and negative integers.

eBook*plus*

Digital doc
Hungry brain activity
Chapter 2
doc-6386

OPENING QUESTION

A dolphin can leap up to 5 metres above the surface of the water. If a particular dolphin was swimming at a depth of –2.7 metres, how many metres would the dolphin need to travel vertically to reach the maximum distance above the surface?

Are you ready?

Try the questions below. If you have difficulty with any of them, extra help can be obtained by completing the matching SkillSHEET located on your eBookPLUS.

eBook*plus*
Digital doc
SkillSHEET 2.1
doc-6387

Integers on the number line

1 Label this number line with 10 equal intervals from 0 to 10.

Mark each of the following with a dot on the number line.

a 7   b 4   c 0

2 Use the number line drawn for question 1 to find the numbers that are:

a 3 units away from 5
b 2 units away from 2
c 4 units away from 6.

eBook*plus*
Digital doc
SkillSHEET 2.2
doc-6388

Adding and subtracting integers

3. Evaluate each of the following.

a $4196 + 673$ b $903 - 268$ c $65 + 518 + 2361$

eBook*plus*
Digital doc
SkillSHEET 2.3
doc-6389

Arranging numbers in order

4 Arrange the numbers 25, 39, 12, 56, 17, 30, 45, 29 in:

a ascending order   b descending order.

eBook*plus*
Digital doc
SkillSHEET 2.4
doc-6390

Multiplying integers

5 Calculate 739×56 using:

a short multiplication   b long multiplication.

6 Calculate 483×72 using:

a short multiplication   b long multiplication.

eBook*plus*
Digital doc
SkillSHEET 2.5
doc-6391

Dividing integers

7 Calculate each of the following.

a $27 \div 9$ b $132 \div 11$ c $21 \div 7$

eBook*plus*
Digital doc
SkillSHEET 2.6
doc-6392

Order of operations and directed numbers

8 Calculate each of the following, using the correct order of operations.

a $23 - 4 \times 3$ b $2^3 + \sqrt{16} \times 5$ c $\sqrt{3^2 + 4^2}$

d $18 \div 2 \times 3$ e $\sqrt{3 \times 12} + 3^2$ f $(8 - 3)^2 + 8^2 - 3^2$

2A Adding and subtracting integers

Integers

- Integers are positive whole numbers, negative whole numbers and zero.
- The group of integers is often referred to as the set Z.
- $Z = \{\ldots -4, -3, -2, -1, 0, 1, 2, 3, 4, \ldots\}$

eBook*plus*

eLesson
Directed numbers
eles-0040

Addition of integers

- A number line can be used to add integers.
- To add a positive integer, move to the right.
- To add a negative integer, move to the left.

WORKED EXAMPLE 1

Calculate the value of each of the following.

a $-3 + +2$
b $-3 + -2$

THINK

THINK		WRITE
a 1	Start at −3 and move 2 units to the right, as this is the addition of a positive integer.	**a** $-3 + +2$
2	Write the answer.	$3 + +2 = -1$
b 1	Start at −3 and move 2 units to the left, as this is the addition of a negative integer.	**b** $-3 + -2$
2	Write the answer.	$-3 + -2 = -5$

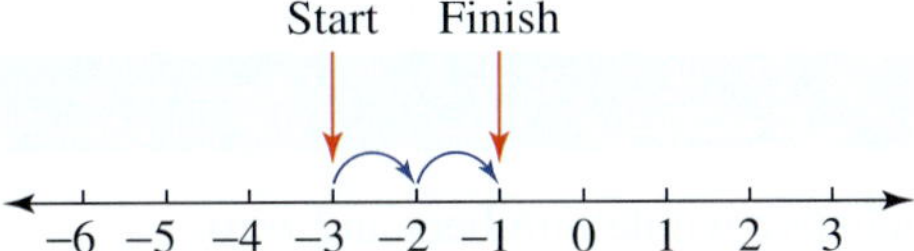

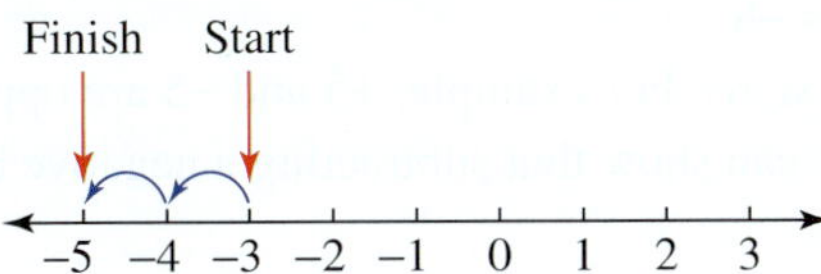

Subtraction of integers

- Subtracting an integer gives the same result as adding its opposite.
  For example, $-3 - 5 = -3 - +5 = -3 + -5 = -8$.
  Note that +5 and −5 are opposites.
- By developing and extending a pattern, we can show that subtracting a negative has the same effect as adding a positive. Look at the pattern shown at right.
  It can be seen from the table that subtracting a negative is the same as adding its inverse. For example, $8 - -4 = 8 + +4 = 12$.

8 − 3 =	5
8 − 2 =	6
8 − 1 =	7
8 − 0 =	8
8 − −1 =	9
8 − −2 =	10
8 − −3 =	11

- In mathematics, a number without a positive or negative sign is considered to be positive. So 8 + +4 can be written as 8 + 4 and −5 − +1 can be written as −5 − 1.

WORKED EXAMPLE 2

Calculate the value of each of the following.

a −7 − +1 **b** −2 − −3

THINK	WRITE
a 1 Subtracting an integer gives the same result as adding its opposite.	**a** −7 − +1
2 Using a number line, start at −7 and move 1 unit to the left.	= −7 + −1
3 Write the answer.	= −8
b 1 Subtracting an integer gives the same result as adding its opposite.	**b** −2 − −3
2 Using a number line, start at −2 and move 3 units to the right.	= −2 + +3
3 Write the answer.	= +1

REMEMBER

1. Integers are positive whole numbers, negative whole numbers and zero.
2. A number line can be used to add integers.
   (a) To add a positive integer, move to the right.
   (b) To add a negative integer, move to the left.
3. Subtracting an integer gives the same result as adding its opposite.
   For example, −3 − 5 = −3 − +5 = −3 + −5 = −8.
4. Opposite numbers are those with opposite signs. For example, +5 and −5 are opposites.
5. By developing and extending a pattern, we can show that subtracting a negative has the same effect as adding a positive.
6. In mathematics, a number without a positive or negative sign is considered to be positive.

EXERCISE 2A Adding and subtracting integers

FLUENCY

1 Which of the following numbers are integers?

3, $\frac{1}{2}$, −4, 201, 20.1, −4.5, −62, $-3\frac{2}{5}$

2 Copy and complete the following addition and subtraction number patterns by placing the correct integers in the boxes.

a 6, 4, 2, □, □, □ **b** −5, −10, −15, □, □, □
c □, □, □, −1, −3, −5 **d** □, □, □, −2, 0, 2

INDIVIDUAL PATHWAYS

eBook*plus*

Activity 2-A-1
The Game of Pirates — standard
doc-6394

Activity 2-A-2
The Game of Pirates — variation 1
doc-6395

Activity 2-A-3
The Game of Pirates — variation 2
doc-6396

eBook*plus*

Interactivity
Directed number target
int-0074

3 **WE1** Calculate the value of each of the following.

a −3 + 2 **b** −7 + −3 **c** 6 + −7
d −8 + −5 **e** 13 + +6 **f** 12 + −5
g −25 + +10 **h** 16 + −16

4 **WE2** Calculate the value of each of the following.

a 7 − +2 **b** −18 − +6 **c** 3 − +8
d 11 − +6 **e** 17 − −9 **f** −28 − −12
g 14 − −8 **h** −17 − −28

5 Calculate the value of each of the following.

a −3 + −5 **b** 6 − −5 **c** −17 + +3
d −14 − −13 **e** 28 − −23 **f** −48 + −3
g −57 − −18 **h** −32 − −40

6 Simplify the following.

a −4 + −3 **b** −6 − +3 **c** 5 + −2
d 17 − +5 **e** −13 − −3 **f** 10 − −3
g −26 + −14 **h** 25 + −7 **i** 32 − +5
j −16 − +18 **k** −26 − −15 **l** 124 − −26
m −3 + −4 − −6 **n** 27 + −5 − −3 **o** −10 + +3 − +6
p 23 + −15 − −14 **q** 15 − −4 + −10 **r** −37 − −5 − −10

UNDERSTANDING

7 Copy and complete the following tables. For the subtraction table, subtract the number on the side from the number at the top.

a

+	−8	+25	−18	32
−6	−8 + −6 = −14			
−13				
−16				
−19				

b

−	+15	−17	−27	57
+7	+15 − +7 = 8			
−6				
−9				
+12				

c

+	−11		13	
	−16			
+17		36		
		18	12	
−28				−35

d

−	+9			42
	−17			
−14			−1	
		23		
+23		−2		

8 Design your own addition and subtraction of integers tables like those in question **7**. Fill in all answers in your tables.

9 In a kitchen, some food is stored at −18 °C in a freezer and some at 4 °C in the fridge. A roast is cooking in the oven at a temperature of 180 °C.

Before answering each of the following questions, draw a number line to show the positions of the temperatures.

- **a** What is the difference in temperature between the food stored in the freezer and the food stored in the fridge?
  (*Hint:* Difference = largest value − smallest value)
- **b** What is the difference in temperature between the food stored in the fridge and the roast cooking in the oven?
- **c** What is the difference in temperature between the food stored in the freezer and the roast cooking in the oven?

10 Calculate the difference between the two extreme temperatures recorded at Mawson Station in Antarctica in recent times.

11 Locate the button on your calculator that allows you to enter negative numbers. Use it to answer the following.

- **a** $-458 + 157$
- **b** $-5487 - 476$
- **c** $-248 - -658 - -120$
- **d** $-42 + 57 - -68 + -11$

12 Write out these equations, filling in the missing numbers.

- **a** $-7 + \square = 6$
- **b** $8 - \square = 12$
- **c** $-15 - \square = -26$
- **d** $42 - \square + -17 = 35$
- **e** $-7 - \square - -31 = -28$
- **f** $\square - 13 + 21 = 79$

13 The following is a homework sheet done by a student in Year 8. Correct her work for her and give her a mark out of six. Make sure you include the correct answer if her answer is wrong.

a $-3 + -7 = -10$
b $-4 - -10 = -6$
c $-7 - 8 = 15$
d $9 - -8 + -7 = 10$
e $42 + 7 - -11 = 60$
f $-17 + 4 - 8 = 23$

REASONING

14 Evaluate and compare the following pairs of expressions.
a $-4 + 1$ and $+1 - 4$
b $-7 + 5$ and $+5 - 7$
c $-8 + 3$ and $+3 - 8$

15 What did you notice about the answers in question **14**? Use a number line to help you explain why this is the case.

16 Evaluate and compare the following pairs of expressions.
a $-2 + -5$ and $-(2 + 5)$
b $-3 + -8$ and $-(3 + 8)$
c $-7 + -6$ and $-(7 + 6)$

17 What did you notice about the answers in question **16**? Explain why this is the case.

REFLECTION
What strategy will you use to remember how to add and subtract integers?

2B Multiplying integers

- Patterns in the answers in multiplication tables can be used to determine the product when two directed numbers are multiplied. Consider the following patterns.

$3 \times 3 = 9$	$-3 \times 3 = -9$
$3 \times 2 = 6$	$-3 \times 2 = -6$
$3 \times 1 = 3$	$-3 \times 1 = -3$
$3 \times 0 = 0$	$-3 \times 0 = 0$
$3 \times -1 = -3$	$-3 \times -1 = 3$
$3 \times -2 = -6$	$-3 \times -2 = 6$
$3 \times -3 = -9$	$-3 \times -3 = 9$
Answers go down by 3.	Answers go up by 3.

- When multiplying two directed numbers:
  - if their signs are the same, the answer is positive
  - if their signs are different, the answer is negative.

$+ \times + = +$	$+ \times - = -$
$- \times - = +$	$- \times + = -$

WORKED EXAMPLE 3

Evaluate each of the following.

a $-3 \times +7$

b -8×-7

THINK	WRITE
a The two numbers have different signs, so the answer is negative ($7 \times 3 = 21$).	a $-3 \times +7$ $= -21$
b The two numbers have the same signs, so the answer is positive ($8 \times 7 = 56$).	b -8×-7 $= 56$ (or $+56$)

Powers and square roots of directed numbers

- Calculating powers of negative numbers uses the same process as calculating powers of positive numbers.
- There are two possible answers when you take the square root of a number. For example:

$$4^2 = 4 \times 4 = 16 \qquad (-4)^2 = (-4) \times (-4) = 16$$

Therefore when asked to take the square root of 16, the answer could be $\pm\sqrt{16}$.
$\pm\sqrt{16} = -4$ or $+4$, which can also be written as ± 4 (positive or negative 4).

WORKED EXAMPLE 4

Evaluate each of the following.

a $(-5)^3$

b **The square root of 64**

THINK	WRITE
a 1 Write the question in expanded form.	a $(-5)^3 = (-5) \times (-5) \times (-5)$
2 Evaluate by working from left to right beginning with $-5 \times -5 = +25$.	$= +25 \times (-5)$ $= -125$
b Look for the numbers that, when squared, result in 64 ($8 \times 8 = 64$ and $-8 \times -8 = 64$).	b $\pm\sqrt{64} = +8$ or -8 $= \pm 8$

REMEMBER

1. When multiplying two directed numbers:
   (a) if their signs are the same, the answer is positive
   (b) if their signs are different, the answer is negative.
2. Calculating powers of negative numbers uses the same process as calculating powers of positive numbers.
3. There are two possible answers when you take the square root of a number: a positive answer and a negative answer.

EXERCISE 2B

Multiplying integers

INDIVIDUAL PATHWAYS

eBook*plus*

Activity 2-B-1
Integer multiplication
doc-6397

Activity 2-B-2
More integer multiplication
doc-6398

Activity 2-B-3
Advanced integer multiplication
doc-6399

FLUENCY

1 Copy and complete the following tables.

$4 \times 4 =$ ____	$-5 \times 4 =$ ____	$-6 \times -4 =$ ____
$4 \times 3 =$ ____	$-5 \times 3 =$ ____	$-6 \times -3 =$ ____
$4 \times 2 =$ ____	$-5 \times 2 =$ ____	$-6 \times -2 =$ ____
$4 \times 1 =$ ____	$-5 \times 1 =$ ____	$-6 \times -1 =$ ____
$4 \times 0 =$ ____	$-5 \times 0 =$ ____	$-6 \times 0 =$ ____
$4 \times -1 =$ ____	$-5 \times -1 =$ ____	$-6 \times 1 =$ ____
$4 \times -2 =$ ____	$-5 \times -2 =$ ____	$-6 \times 2 =$ ____
$4 \times -3 =$ ____	$-5 \times -3 =$ ____	$-6 \times 3 =$ ____
$4 \times -4 =$ ____	$-5 \times -4 =$ ____	$-6 \times 4 =$ ____

2 WE3 Evaluate each of the following.

a -2×5 **b** 3×-8 **c** -6×-7
d 2×-13 **e** -8×-6 **f** -7×6
g -10×75 **h** -115×-10 **i** -7×9
j $+9 \times -8$ **k** -11×-5 **l** 150×-2

3 Use an appropriate method to evaluate the following.

a $-2 \times 5 \times -8 \times -10$ **b** $8 \times -1 \times 7 \times -2 \times 1$
c $8 \times -4 \times -1 \times -1 \times 6$ **d** $-3 \times -7 \times -2 \times -1 \times -1 \times -1$
e $-5 \times -8 \times -2 \times -2$

4 Complete the following equations.

a $7 \times$ ____ $= -63$ **b** $-3 \times$ ____ $= 21$ **c** $16 \times$ ____ $= -32$
d ____ $\times -3 = 36$ **e** ____ $\times 7 = -42$ **f** ____ $\times -9 = -72$
g ____ $\times -4 = 80$ **h** $-10 \times$ ____ $= 60$ **i** $-11 \times$ ____ $= 121$

5 WE4a Evaluate each of the following.

a $(-2)^3$ **b** $(-3)^2$ **c** $(-2)^4$ **d** $(-3)^4$
e $(-2)^5$ **f** $(-4)^2$ **g** $(-5)^3$ **h** $(-4)^4$
i $(-5)^4$ **j** $(-6)^3$

6 Use your answers to question **5** to help complete the following statements.

a If a negative number is raised to an even power the answer is (positive/negative).
b If a negative number is raised to an odd power the answer is (positive/negative).

7 WE4b Evaluate the square root of the following numbers.

a 25 **b** 81 **c** 49 **d** 121 **e** 100

8 If $a = -2$, $b = -6$, $c = 4$ and $d = -3$, calculate the values of the following expressions.

a $a \times b \times c$ **b** $a \times -b \times -d$ **c** $b \times -c \times -d$
d $c \times -a \times -a$ **e** $d \times -(-c)$ **f** $a \times d \times b \times c^2$

UNDERSTANDING

9 For each of the following, write three possible sets of integers that can be placed in the boxes to make the equation a true statement.

a $\square \times \square \times \square = -12$
b $\square \times \square \times \square = 36$
c $\square \times \square \times \square \times \square = -36$

10 For each of the following, determine whether the result is a positive or negative value. You do not have to work out the value.

a $-25 \times 54 \times -47$ **b** $-56 \times -120 \times -145$ **c** $-a \times -b \times -c \times -d \times -e$

11 What happens when a number is multiplied by -1? Use some examples to illustrate your answer.

eBook*plus*

Digital doc
WorkSHEET 2.1
doc-6400

12 The notation $-(-3)$ is a short way of writing -1×-3. Write the expression represented by each of the following and then use an appropriate method to determine the answer.

a $-(-2)$
b $-(+3)$
c $-(-5)$
d $-(-(+5))$
e $-(-(-7))$
f $-(-(+4))$

REFLECTION
Can we find square roots, cube roots, fourth roots and so on for negative numbers?

2C Dividing integers

- Division is the inverse operation of multiplication. We can use the multiplication facts for directed numbers to discover the division facts for directed numbers.

Multiplication fact	Division fact	Pattern
$2 \times 3 = 6$	$6 \div 3 = 2$ or $\frac{6}{3} = 2$ and $6 \div 2 = 3$ or $\frac{6}{2} = 3$	$\frac{\text{positive}}{\text{positive}} = \text{positive}$
$-2 \times -3 = 6$	$6 \div -3 = -2$ or $\frac{6}{-3} = -2$ and $6 \div -2 = -3$ or $\frac{6}{-2} = -3$	$\frac{\text{positive}}{\text{negative}} = \text{negative}$
$-2 \times 3 = -6$	$-6 \div 3 = -2$ or $\frac{-6}{3} = -2$ and $-6 \div -2 = 3$ or $\frac{-6}{-3} = 3$	$\frac{\text{negative}}{\text{positive}} = \text{negative}$ and $\frac{\text{negative}}{\text{negative}} = \text{positive}$

- When dividing two directed numbers:
  - if their signs are the same, the answer is positive
  - if their signs are different, the answer is negative.
- Remember that division statements can be written as fractions and then simplified. For example,

$$\begin{aligned}-12 \div -4 &= \frac{-12}{-4} \\ &= \frac{12 \times -1}{4 \times -1} \\ &= 3\end{aligned}$$

$\frac{+}{+} = +$	$\frac{+}{-} = -$
$\frac{-}{-} = +$	$\frac{-}{+} = -$

WORKED EXAMPLE 5

Evaluate each of the following.

a $-56 \div 8$ **b** $\frac{-36}{-9}$

THINK

a The two numbers have different signs, so the answer is negative ($56 \div 8 = 7$).

b Cancel the common factors (-1). The two numbers have the same signs, so the answer is positive.

WRITE

a $-56 \div 8$
$= -7$

b $\frac{-36}{-9} = \frac{-1 \times 36}{-1 \times 9}$
$= \frac{36}{9}$
$= 4$

WORKED EXAMPLE 6

Evaluate the following.

a $234 \div -6$ **b** $-182 \div -14$

THINK	WRITE
a 1 Complete the division as if both numbers were positive numbers.	**a** $6\overline{)23^{5}4}$ = 39
2 Determine the sign of the answer. A positive number divided by a negative number is a negative number.	$234 \div -6 = -39$
b 1 Complete the division as if both numbers were positive numbers.	**b** $14\overline{)182}$ = 13; 14, 42, 42, 0
2 Determine the sign of the answer. A negative number divided by a negative number is a positive number.	$-182 \div -14 = 13$

REMEMBER

When dividing two directed numbers:

- if their signs are the same, the answer is positive
- if their signs are different, the answer is negative.

EXERCISE 2C Dividing integers

INDIVIDUAL PATHWAYS

eBook*plus*

Activity 2-C-1 Integer division doc-6401

Activity 2-C-2 More integer division doc-6402

Activity 2-C-3 Advanced integer division doc-6403

FLUENCY

1 WE5a Evaluate each of the following.

a $-63 \div 9$ **b** $8 \div -2$ **c** $-8 \div 2$

d $-6 \div -1$ **e** $88 \div -11$ **f** $0 \div -5$

g $48 \div -3$ **h** $-129 \div 3$ **i** $-56 \div -7$

j $+184 \div -4$ **k** $-55 \div -11$ **l** $304 \div -8$

2 WE5b Evaluate each of the following.

a $\frac{-121}{-11}$ **b** $\frac{-12}{3}$ **c** $\frac{-36}{-12}$

d $\frac{21}{-7}$ **e** $\frac{-100}{-50}$ **f** $-3 \times \frac{2}{-3}$

3 WE6 Evaluate the following.

a $960 \div -8$ **b** $-243 \div 9$ **c** $-266 \div -7$

d $-132 \div -4$ **e** $-282 \div 6$ **f** $1440 \div -9$

g $324 \div -12$ **h** $-3060 \div 17$ **i** $-6000 \div -24$

j $-2294 \div -37$ **k** $4860 \div 15$ **l** $-5876 \div -26$

UNDERSTANDING

4 Write three different division statements, each of which has an answer of −8.

5 Copy and complete the following by placing the correct integer in the box.

a $-27 \div \square = -9$ **b** $-68 \div \square = 34$
c $72 \div \square = -8$ **d** $-18 \div \square = -6$
e $\square \div 7 = -5$ **f** $\square \div -4 = -6$
g $-132 \div \square = 11$ **h** $-270 \div \square = 27$

6 Calculate the value of each of the following by working from left to right.

a $-30 \div 6 \div -5$ **b** $-120 \div 4 \div -5$
c $-800 \div -4 \div -5 \div 2$

7 If $a = -12$, $b = 3$, $c = -4$ and $d = -6$, calculate the value of each of the following expressions.

a $a \div c$ **b** $a \div b$
c $a \div d$ **d** $b \div c$
e $b \div d$ **f** $a \div b \div d$

8 If $a = -24$, $b = 2$, $c = -4$ and $d = -12$, calculate the value of each of the following expressions.

a $a \div b \times c$ **b** $d \times c \div b \div c$
c $b \div c \div d \times a$ **d** $c \times a \div d \div b$
e $a \times b \div d \div d$ **f** $a \div d \times c \div b$

9 Copy and complete the following tables:

a

×			−6	+8
			18	
−10		−40		
	10		30	
−7				−56

b

×			−9	
+6	30			−42
		36		
	−55		99	
		−6	−18	

10 Copy and complete the following tables. Divide the number on the top by the number on the side.

a

÷	4	−10	12	−8
−2				
7				
−3				
−10				

b

÷				−4
		−2		
−8	−4	3		
6			−6	
				1

REFLECTION

Can you list 4 areas in real life where directed numbers are used?

2D Combined operations on integers

- The mathematical rules about order of operations apply when we work with directed numbers.
- BIDMAS helps us to remember the correct order in which we should perform the various operations. This means that we do brackets first; then powers or indices; then × and ÷ (working from left to right); and finally + and – (working from left to right).

WORKED EXAMPLE 7

Calculate the value of each of the following.

a $54 \div -6 + 8 \times -9 \div -4$

b $-8 \div 2 + (-2)^3$

THINK		WRITE
a	1 Write the question.	a $54 \div -6 + 8 \times -9 \div -4$
	2 There are no brackets or powers, so, working from left to right, complete all multiplication and division, then the addition.	$= -9 + 18$
	3 Write the answer.	$= 9$
b	1 Write the question.	b $-8 \div 2 + (-2)^3$
	2 Simplify the cubed term.	$= -8 \div 2 + -8$
	3 Complete the division.	$= -4 + -8$
	4 Write the answer.	$= -12$

REMEMBER

1. The mathematical rules about order of operations apply when we work with directed numbers.
2. BIDMAS helps us to remember the correct order in which we should perform the various operations. This means that we do brackets first; then powers or indices; then × and ÷ (working from left to right); and finally + and – (working from left to right).

EXERCISE 2D Combined operations on integers

INDIVIDUAL PATHWAYS

eBook*plus*

Activity 2-D-1 Match-'em Game A doc-6404

Activity 2-D-2 Match-'em Game B doc-6405

Activity 2-D-3 Match-'em Game C doc-6406

FLUENCY

1 WE7a Calculate the values of the following expressions.

a $-4 - 6 - 2$
b $-4 \times 2 + 1$
c $8 \div (2 - 4) + 1$
d $7 - (3 - 1) + 4$
e $6 \times (4 + 1)$
f $-3 - 40 \div 8 + 2$
g $-4 + 5 - 6 - 7$
h $-5 \times 12 + 2$
i $12 \div (2 - 4) - 6$
j $13 - (4 - 6) + 2$
k $7 \times (6 + 2)$
l $-6 - 36 \div 9 + 3$

2 WE7b Evaluate each of the following.

a $-7 + 6 \times -2$
b $-9 - 15 + 3$
c $(-63 \div -7) \times -3 + -2$
d $(-3)^3 - 3 \times -5$
e $-5 \times -7 - [5 + (-8)^2]$
f $[(-48 \div 8)^2 \times 36] \div -4$

3 Calculate the values of the following expressions.

a $-3 + 15 - 26 - 27$
b $-8 \times 11 + 12$
c $52 \div (-9 - 4) - 8$
d $23 - (16 - 4) + 7 - 3$
e $15 \times (-6 + 2)$
f $-6 - 64 \div -16 + 8$
g $-3 \times -4 \times -1 \times 5$
h $-6 \times (-13 + 5) + -4 + 2$

UNDERSTANDING

4 A class of year 8 students were given the following question to evaluate.

$$4 + 8 \div -(2)^2 - 7 \times 2$$

a A number of different answers were obtained, including −8, −12 and −17. Which one of these is the correct answer?

b Using only brackets, change the question in two ways so that the other two answers would be correct.

5 In a particular adventure video game, a player loses and gains points based on who or what they come in contact with during the game. See the list below right for the number of 'hit' points associated with each contact. Calculate the number of points a player has at the end of each round of the game below.

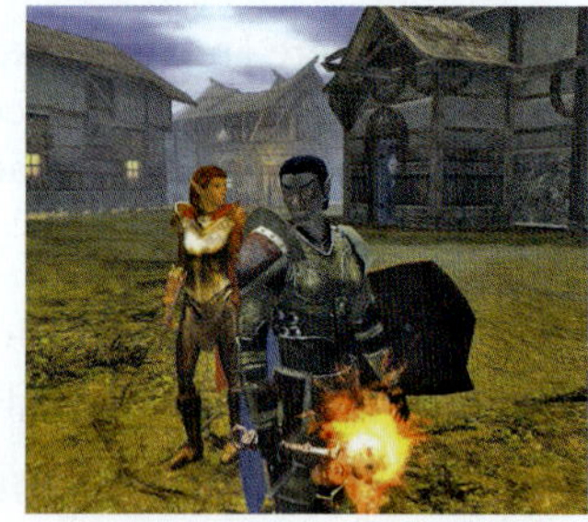

Round number	Points at the start of the round	Contacts during the round	Points at the end of the round
1	100	20 gnomes, 10 goblins and 3 healing potions	
2		3 gnomes, 5 goblins, 6 orcs and 5 healing potions	
3		3 orcs, 6 trolls and a cleric	
4		5 trolls, 1 balrog and a cleric	

Character	'Hit' points
Balrog	−100
Troll	−10
Orc	−5
Goblin	−2
Gnome	−1
Healing potion	+20
Cleric	+50

eBook*plus*

Digital doc
WorkSHEET 2.2
doc-6407

REFLECTION

What effects do directed numbers have on order of operations?

Summary

Adding and subtracting integers

- Integers are positive whole numbers, negative whole numbers and zero.
- A number line can be used to add integers.
  - To add a positive integer, move to the right.
  - To add a negative integer, move to the left.
- Subtracting an integer gives the same result as adding its opposite.
  For example, $-3 - 5 = -3 - +5 = -3 + -5 = -8$.
- Opposite numbers are those with opposite signs. For example, +5 and −5 are opposites.
- By developing and extending a pattern, we can show that subtracting a negative has the same effect as adding a positive.
- In mathematics, a number without a positive or negative sign is considered to be positive.

Multiplying integers

- When multiplying two directed numbers:
  - if their signs are the same, the answer is positive
  - if their signs are different, the answer is negative.
- Calculating powers of negative numbers uses the same process as calculating powers of positive numbers.
- There are two possible answers when you take the square root of a number: a positive answer and a negative answer.

Dividing integers

- When dividing two directed numbers:
  - if their signs are the same, the answer is positive
  - if their signs are different, the answer is negative.

Combined operations on integers

- The mathematical rules about order of operations apply when we work with directed numbers.
- BIDMAS helps us to remember the correct order in which we should perform the various operations. This means that we do brackets first; then powers or indices; then × and ÷ (working from left to right); and finally + and − (working from left to right).

MAPPING YOUR UNDERSTANDING

Using terms from the summary, and other terms if you wish, construct a concept map that illustrates your understanding of the key concepts covered in this chapter. Compare your concept map with the one that you created in *What do you know?* on page 31.

Have you completed the two *Homework sheets*, the *Rich task* and two *Code puzzles* in your *Maths Quest 8 Homework Book*?

Chapter review

FLUENCY

1 True or false? The number –2.5 is called an integer.

2 True or false? $-6 < -2$

3 List the integers between –11 and –7.

4 Arrange these numbers in ascending order: 7, 0, –3, 10, –15.

5 Calculate the value of each of the following.
- a $-6 + -8$
- b $16 - -5$
- c $-3 - +7 + -2$
- d $-1 - -5 - +4$

6 Write out the following equations and fill in the missing numbers.
- a $7 - \square = -14$
- b $-19 + \square = 2$
- c $\square - 13 - -12 = 10$
- d $-28 - \square = -17$

7 MC Which of the following statements is true?
- A Multiplying an even number of negative numbers together gives a negative answer.
- B The square root of 16 is +4.
- C Dividing a negative number by another negative number gives a positive answer.
- D Adding two negative numbers together gives a positive answer.

8 Evaluate each of the following.
- a -12×-5
- b $-(-10) \times 3 \times -2$
- c $-24 \div -3$
- d $-48 \div -4 \div -3$
- e $6 \times -3 \div -2$
- f $-36 \div 3 \div -4 \times -9$
- g $-8 \times -3 - (4 - -1) + -63 \div 7$
- h $-9 + -9 \div -9 \times -9 - -9$

PROBLEM SOLVING

1 Give an example of two numbers that fit each of the descriptions that follow. If no numbers fit the description, explain why.
- a Both the sum and the product of two numbers are negative.
- b The sum of two numbers is positive and the quotient is negative.
- c The sum of two numbers is 0 and the product is positive.

2 On a test, each correct answer scores 5 points, each incorrect answer scores –2 points and each question left unanswered scores 0 points.
- a Suppose a student answers 16 questions correctly and 3 questions incorrectly, and does not answer 1 question. Write an expression for the student's score and find the score.
- b Suppose you answered all 20 questions on the test. What is the greatest number of questions you can answer incorrectly and still get a positive score? Explain your reasoning.

3 Write each of the following problems as equations using directed numbers and then find the answer.
- a You have \$25 and you spend \$8 on lollies. You then spend another \$6 on lunch. A friend gives you \$5 to buy lunch, which comes to only \$3.50. You then find another \$10 in your pocket and buy an ice cream for \$3. How much money do you have left in total before you return your friend's change from lunch?
- b Two friends are on holiday; one decides to go skydiving and the other decides to go scuba diving. If the skydiving plane climbs to 4405 m above sea level, and scuba diver goes to the ocean floor, which is 26 m below the surface, what is the vertical distance between the two friends?

4 Insert the integers from –6 to +2 into the circles on the figure below so that each line of three circles has each of the following totals.
- a –6
- b –3
- c –9

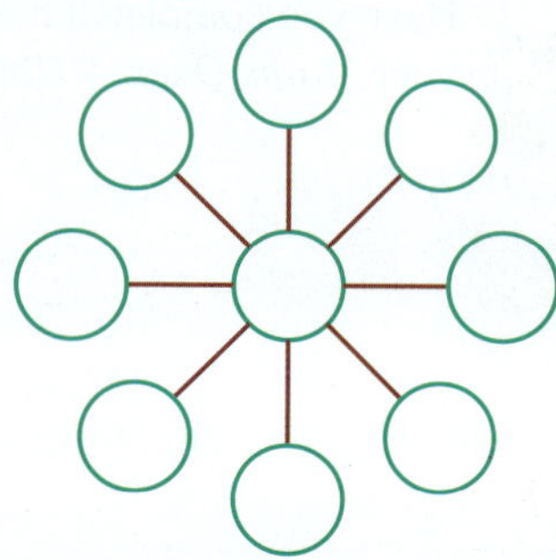

5 For each of the following:

i represent the situation with a multiplication of directed numbers

ii solve the problem.

a You receive several letters in the mail: two cheques worth \$100 each, three bills worth \$75 each and a voucher for \$20. How much money do you end up with?

b You earn \$150 each time you work at the local races. If you work at three race meetings in one month, how much do you earn that month?

c For your birthday, you get three cards with \$40 in each of them. As a present, your brother tears up the IOUs you gave him when he did your chores. There were four IOUs worth \$10 each. In total, how much more money do you have after your birthday?

In science, directed numbers are often used to describe a direction or an increase or decrease in a measurement.

6 Directed numbers can describe the distance of an object from a reference point (known as the *displacement*, *d*, of the object). For example, if we are 200 km east of a town, and east is defined as a negative direction, we are –200 km from the town.

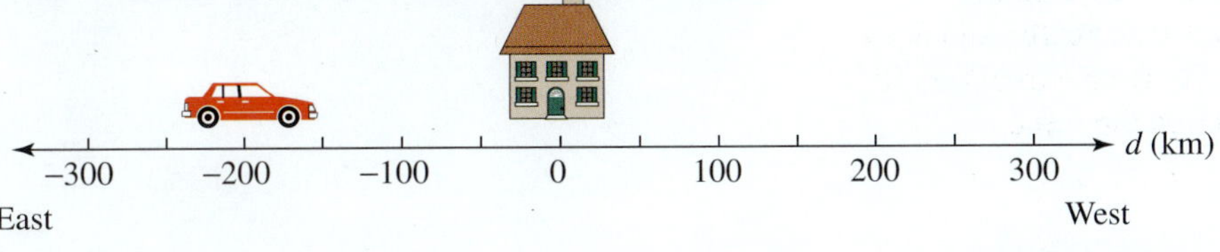

a If a car travels 150 km in a westerly direction from –200 km, describe the displacement of the car from the town.

b If a car travels from 300 km west of the town, describe the displacement of the car after it has travelled 450 km in a westerly direction.

7 Directed numbers can describe the direction that an object is travelling. For example, in question **6**, travelling towards the west is travelling in a positive direction; towards the east is a negative direction. A car travelling east at 100 km/h goes at –100 km/h. Scientists use the term *velocity*, *v*, to mean a speed in a particular direction.

a If a car travels past the town at –100 km/h, where will it be in 2 hours time?

b If a car goes past the town travelling at –100 km/h, where was the car an hour ago?

eBook*plus*

Interactivities

Test yourself Chapter 2 int-2722

Word search Chapter 2 int-2724

Crossword Chapter 2 int-2723

eBookplus ACTIVITIES

Chapter opener

Digital doc *(page 31)*
- Hungry brain activity Chapter 2 (doc-6386)

Are you ready?

Digital docs *(page 32)*
- SkillSHEET 2.1 (doc-6387) Integers on the number line
- SkillSHEET 2.2 (doc-6388) Adding and subtracting integers
- SkillSHEET 2.3 (doc-6389) Arranging numbers in order
- SkillSHEET 2.4 (doc-6390) Multiplying integers
- SkillSHEET 2.5 (doc-6391) Dividing integers
- SkillSHEET 2.6 (doc-6392) Order of operations and directed numbers

2A Adding and subtracting integers

Digital docs *(page 35)*
- Activity 2-A-1 (doc-6394) The Game of Pirates — standard
- Activity 2-A-2 (doc-6395) The Game of Pirates — variation 1
- Activity 2-A-3 (doc-6396) The Game of Pirates — variation 2

eLesson *(page 33)*
- Directed numbers (eles-0040)

Interactivity *(page 35)*
- Directed number target (int-0074)

2B Multiplying integers

Digital docs *(page 39)*
- Activity 2-B-1 (doc-6397) Integer multiplication
- Activity 2-B-2 (doc-6398) More integer multiplication
- Activity 2-B-3 (doc-6399) Advanced integer multiplication
- WorkSHEET 2.1 (doc-6400) *(page 40)*

2C Dividing integers

Digital docs *(page 41)*
- Activity 2-C-1 (doc-6401) Integer division
- Activity 2-C-2 (doc-6402) More integer division
- Activity 2-C-3 (doc-6403) Advanced integer division

2D Combined operations on integers

Digital docs *(page 43)*
- Activity 2-D-1 (doc-6404) Match-'em Game A
- Activity 2-D-2 (doc-6405) Match-'em Game B
- Activity 2-D-3 (doc-6406) Match-'em Game C
- WorkSHEET 2.2 (doc-6407) *(page 44)*

Chapter review

Interactivities *(page 47)*
- Test yourself Chapter 2 (int-2722) Take the end-of-chapter test to test your progress.
- Word search Chapter 2 (int-2724)
- Crossword Chapter 2 (int-2723)

To access eBookPLUS activities, log on to

www.jacplus.com.au

Index laws

3A Review of index form
3B First Index Law (multiplying numbers in index form with the same base)
3C Second Index Law (dividing numbers in index form with the same base)
3D Third Index Law (the power of zero)
3E Fourth Index Law (raising a power to another power)

WHAT DO YOU KNOW?

1 List what you know about index laws. Create a concept map to show your list.
2 Share what you know with a partner and then with a small group.
3 As a class, create a large concept map that shows your class's knowledge of index laws.

eBook*plus*

Digital doc
Hungry brain activity
Chapter 3
doc-6833

OPENING QUESTION

At 9 am there were 2 bacteria in a Petri dish. If the number of bacteria doubles every minute, how many bacteria were in the Petri dish by 10 am?

Are you ready?

Try the questions below. If you have difficulty with any of them, extra help can be obtained by completing the matching SkillSHEET located on your eBookPLUS.

eBook*plus*

Digital doc
SkillSHEET 3.1
doc-6834

Factor trees

1 Use factor trees to write each of the following numbers as the product of its prime factors.

a 32 **b** 81 **c** 1000

eBook*plus*

Digital doc
SkillSHEET 3.2
doc-6835

Squaring numbers

2 Evaluate each of the following squares.

a 6^2 **b** 11^2 **c** 50^2

eBook*plus*

Digital doc
SkillSHEET 3.3
doc-6836

Equivalent fractions

3 Simplify the following.

a $\frac{7}{21}$ **b** $\frac{12}{30}$ **c** $\frac{15}{20}$

eBook*plus*

Digital doc
SkillSHEET 3.4
doc-6837

Simplifying algebraic expressions

4 Simplify each of the following.

a $a \times b \times 6 \times c$ **b** $2 \times z \times 3 \times w$ **c** $4 \times l \times l \times 5$

Digital doc
SkillSHEET 3.5
doc-6838

Simplifying algebraic fractions

5 Simplify each of the following.

a $\frac{a \times b}{b}$ **b** $\frac{2m^2}{6}$ **c** $\frac{14kn}{7n}$

3A Review of index form

- If a number or a variable is multiplied by itself several times, it can be written using short-cut notation referred to as **index form**.
- When written in index form, the number or the variable that is being multiplied is written once only. To indicate how many times it is being multiplied by itself, a small number is written above and to the right of it. For example, if number 2 is multiplied by itself 4 times, it can be written as $2 \times 2 \times 2 \times 2$ (factor form), or as 2^4 (index form).
- When written in index form, the number or variable that is being multiplied is called the *base*, while the number showing how many times it is being multiplied is called the *power*, or *index*. For example, in the number 2^4, 2 is the base and 4 is the power or index.
- When the base is multiplied by itself the number of times indicated by the power, the answer is called a *basic numeral*. For example,

$$\underbrace{2^4}_{\text{Index form}} = \underbrace{2 \times 2 \times 2 \times 2}_{\text{Factor form}} = \underbrace{16}_{\text{Basic numeral}}$$

WORKED EXAMPLE 1

State the base and power for the number 5^{14}.

THINK	WRITE
1 Write the number.	5^{14}
2 The base is the number below the power.	The base is 5.
3 The power or index is the small number just above and to the right of the base.	The power is 14.

WORKED EXAMPLE 2

Write 12^4 in factor form.

THINK	WRITE
1 Write the number.	12^4
2 The base is 12, so this is what will be multiplied.	
3 The power is 4, so this is how many times 12 should be written and multiplied.	$= 12 \times 12 \times 12 \times 12$

WORKED EXAMPLE 3

Write $2 \times 5 \times 2 \times 2 \times 5 \times 2 \times 5$ in index form.

THINK	WRITE
1 Write the problem.	$2 \times 5 \times 2 \times 2 \times 5 \times 2 \times 5$
2 Write the factors in numerical order.	$= 2 \times 2 \times 2 \times 2 \times 5 \times 5 \times 5$
3 The number 2 has been written 4 times and multiplied. The number 5 has been written 3 times and multiplied.	$= 2^4 \times 5^3$

WORKED EXAMPLE 4

Write $7 \times 5^3 \times 6^5$ in factor form.

THINK	WRITE
1 Write the problem.	$7 \times 5^3 \times 6^5$
2 List the factors: 7 is written once, 5 is written 3 times and multiplied, and 6 is written 5 times and multiplied.	$= 7 \times 5 \times 5 \times 5 \times 6 \times 6 \times 6 \times 6 \times 6$

REMEMBER

1. A number written in index form has:
   (a) a base, which is the large number below
   (b) a power or index, which is the small number written just above and to the right of the base.

   base $\rightarrow 2^5 \leftarrow$ index

2. The base tells us what will be multiplied.
3. The power tells us how many times the base will be written and multiplied.
4. Factor form is when all the multiplications are shown.
5. After multiplying out to remove the index, the answer is called a basic numeral.

$$\underbrace{2^5}_{\text{index form}} = \underbrace{2 \times 2 \times 2 \times 2 \times 2}_{\text{factor form}} = \underbrace{32}_{\text{basic numeral}}$$

EXERCISE 3A Review of index form

INDIVIDUAL PATHWAYS

eBook*plus*

Activity 3-A-1
Review of index form
doc-2143

Activity 3-A-2
More index form
doc-2144

Activity 3-A-3
Advanced index form
doc-2145

FLUENCY

1 WE1 State the base and power for each of the following.

a 8^4 **b** 7^{10} **c** 20^{11} **d** 19^0 **e** 78^{12}
f 3^{100} **g** m^5 **h** c^{24} **i** n^{36} **j** d^{42}

2 Write the following in index form.

a $2 \times 2 \times 2 \times 2 \times 2 \times 2$ **b** $4 \times 4 \times 4 \times 4$
c $x \times x \times x \times x \times x$ **d** $9 \times 9 \times 9$
e $11 \times l \times l \times l \times l \times l \times l$ **f** $44 \times m \times m \times m \times m \times m$

3 WE2 Write the following in factor form.

a 4^2 **b** 5^4 **c** 7^5 **d** 6^3 **e** 3^6
f n^7 **g** a^4 **h** k^{10}

4 Write each of the following as a basic numeral.

a 3^5 **b** 4^4 **c** 2^8 **d** 11^3 **e** 7^4
f 6^3 **g** 1^{10} **h** 5^4

5 a MC What does 6^3 mean?

A 6×3 **B** $6 \times 6 \times 6$ **C** $3 \times 3 \times 3 \times 3 \times 3 \times 3$
D $6 + 6 + 6$ **E** 3×6

b What does 3^5 mean?

A 3×5 **B** 5×5 **C** $3 + 3 + 3 + 3 + 3$
D $3 \times 3 \times 3 \times 3 \times 3$ **E** 5×3

6 WE3 Write each of the following in index form.

a $6 \times 2 \times 2 \times 4 \times 4 \times 4 \times 4$

b $7 \times 7 \times 7 \times 7 \times 3 \times 3 \times 3 \times 3$

c $19 \times 19 \times 19 \times 19 \times 19 \times 2 \times 2 \times 2$

d $13 \times 13 \times 4 \times 4 \times 4 \times 4$

e $66 \times p \times p \times m \times m \times m \times m \times m \times s \times s$

f $21 \times n \times n \times 3 \times i \times i \times i \times 6 \times r \times r \times r$

g $16 \times k \times e \times e \times e \times 12 \times p \times p$

h $11 \times j \times j \times j \times j \times j \times 9 \times p \times p \times l$

7 WE4 Write each of the following in factor form.

a $15f^3j^4$

b $7k^6s^2$

c $4b^3c^5$

d $19a^4n^3m$

e $8r^2l^4t^2$

REFLECTION

How will you remember the meaning of the base and that of the index?

UNDERSTANDING

8 Write each of the following numbers as a product of its prime factors, using indices.

a 64

b 40

c 36

d 400

e 225

f 2000

9 Some basic numerals (see below) are written as the product of their prime factors. Identify each of these basic numerals.

a $2^3 \times 3 \times 5$

b $2^2 \times 5^2$

c $2^3 \times 3^3$

d $2^2 \times 7 \times 11$

e $3^2 \times 5^2 \times 7$

f $2^6 \times 5^4 \times 19$

10 a Write each of the following numbers in index form with base 10.

i 10 ii 100 iii 1000 iv 1 000 000

b Use your knowledge of place value to rewrite each of the following basic numerals in expanded form using powers of 10. The first number has been done for you.

	Basic numeral	Expanded form
i	230	$2 \times 10^2 + 3 \times 10^1$
ii	500	
iii	470	
iv	2360	
v	1980	
vi	5430	

c Write each of the following as a basic numeral.

i $7 \times 10^4 + 5 \times 10^3$

ii $3 \times 10^4 + 6 \times 10^2$

iii $5 \times 10^6 + 2 \times 10^5 + 4 \times 10^2 + 8 \times 10^1$

3B First Index Law (multiplying numbers in index form with the same base)

- The numbers in index form with the same base can be multiplied together by being written in factor form first. For example, $5^3 \times 5^2 = (5 \times 5 \times 5) \times (5 \times 5) = 5^5$.
- The simpler and faster way to multiply numbers in index form with the same base is to use the first index law. The First Index Law states: $a^m \times a^n = a^{m+n}$. This means that when numbers in index form with the same base are multiplied by each other, the powers (indices) are added together. For example, $5^3 \times 5^2 = 5^{3+2} = 5^5$ (as above).
- If the variables in index form that are being multiplied have coefficients, the coefficients are multiplied together and the variables in index form by each other. For example, $2a^4 \times 3a^5 = (2 \times 3) \times (a^4 \times a^5) = 6a^9$.

WORKED EXAMPLE 5

Simplify $2^3 \times 2^6$ after first writing in factor form, leaving the answer in index form.

THINK	WRITE
1 Write the problem.	$2^3 \times 2^6$
2 Write in factor form.	$= (2 \times 2 \times 2) \times (2 \times 2 \times 2 \times 2 \times 2 \times 2)$
3 Simplify by writing in index form.	$= 2^9$

WORKED EXAMPLE 6

Simplify $7^4 \times 7 \times 7^3$, giving your answer in index form.

THINK	WRITE
1 Write the problem.	$7^4 \times 7 \times 7^3$
2 Show that the 7 in the middle has an index of 1.	$= 7^4 \times 7^1 \times 7^3$
3 Check to see if the bases are the same. They are all 7.	
4 Simplify by using the First Index Law (add indices).	$= 7^{4+1+3}$ $= 7^8$

WORKED EXAMPLE 7

Simplify $5e^{10} \times 2e^3$.

THINK	WRITE
1 Write the problem.	$5e^{10} \times 2e^3$
2 The order is not important when multiplying, so place the numbers first.	$= 5 \times 2 \times e^{10} \times e^3$
3 Multiply the numbers.	$= 10 \times e^{10} \times e^3$
4 Check to see if the bases are the same. They are both e.	
5 Simplify by using the First Index Law (add indices).	$= 10e^{10+3}$ $= 10e^{13}$

Multiplying expressions containing numbers in index form with different bases

- When there is more than one variable involved in the multiplication question, the First Index Law is applied to each variable separately.

WORKED EXAMPLE 8

Simplify $7m^3 \times 3n^5 \times 2m^8 \times n^4$.

THINK	WRITE
1 Write the problem.	$7m^3 \times 3n^5 \times 2m^8 \times n^4$

2 The order is not important when multiplying, so place numbers first and group the same variables together.	$= 7 \times 3 \times 2 \times m^3 \times m^8 \times n^5 \times n^4$
3 Simplify by multiplying the numbers and using the First Index Law for bases that are the same (add indices).	$= 42 \times m^{3+8} \times n^{5+4}$ $= 42m^{11}n^9$

REMEMBER

1. The First Index Law states: $a^m \times a^n = a^{m+n}$. This means that when numbers or variables in index form with the same base are multiplied by each other, the powers (indices) are added together.
2. If the expression contains coefficients, the coefficients are multiplied together and the numbers and variables in index form by each other.
3. When there is more than one variable involved in the multiplication question, the First Index Law is applied to each variable separately.

EXERCISE 3B

First Index Law (multiplying numbers in index form with the same base)

INDIVIDUAL PATHWAYS

eBookplus

Activity 3-B-1 First Index Law doc-6839

Activity 3-B-2 More of the First Index Law doc-6840

Activity 3-B-3 Advanced use of the First Index Law doc-6841

eBookplus

Digital doc Spreadsheet **Multiplying with indices** doc-2160

FLUENCY

1 WE5 Simplify the following after first writing in factor form.

a $2^2 \times 2^4 = (2 \times 2) \times (\square \times \square \times \square \times \square)$
$= 2^{\square}$

b $5^3 \times 5^5 = (5 \times 5 \times 5) \times (\square \times \square \times \square \times \square \times \square)$
$= 5^{\square}$

c $f^6 \times f \times f^2 = (\square \times \square \times \square \times \square \times \square \times \square) \times \square \times (\square \times \square)$
$= f^{\square}$

2 Simplify each of the following.

a $3^7 \times 3^2$ b $6^{14} \times 6^3$ c $10^6 \times 10^4$
d $11^3 \times 11^3$ e $7^8 \times 7$ f $2^{11} \times 2^3$
g $5^2 \times 5^2$ h $8^9 \times 8^2$ i $13^7 \times 13^8$
j $q^{23} \times q^{24}$ k $x^7 \times x^7$ l $e \times e^3$

3 WE6 Simplify each of the following, giving your answer in index form.

a $3^4 \times 3^6 \times 3^2$ b $2^{10} \times 2^3 \times 2^5$ c $5^4 \times 5^4 \times 5^9$
d $6^8 \times 6 \times 6^2$ e $10 \times 10 \times 10^4$ f $17^2 \times 17^4 \times 17^6$
g $p^7 \times p^8 \times p^7$ h $e^{11} \times e^{10} \times e^2$ i $g^{15} \times g \times g^{12}$
j $e^{20} \times e^{12} \times e^6$ k $3 \times b^2 \times b^{10} \times b$ l $5 \times d^4 \times d^5 \times d^7$

4 a MC What does $6 \times e^3 \times b^2 \times b^4 \times e$ equal?

A $6e^4b^6$ B $6e^3b^6$ C $6eb^9$
D $6eb^{10}$ E $6e^3b^8$

b What does $3 \times f^2 \times f^{10} \times 2 \times e^3 \times e^8$ equal?

A $32f^{12}e^{11}$ B $6f^{12}e^{11}$ C $6fe^{23}$
D $6f^{20}e^{24}$ E $3f^{12}e^{24}$

5 WE7 Simplify each of the following.

a $4p^7 \times 5p^4$ b $2x^2 \times 3x^6$ c $8y^6 \times 7y^4$
d $3p \times 7p^7$ e $12t^3 \times t^2 \times 7t$ f $6q^2 \times q^5 \times 5q^8$

6 WE8 Simplify each of the following.

a $2a^2 \times 3a^4 \times e^3 \times e^4$ **b** $4p^3 \times 2h^7 \times h^5 \times p^3$ **c** $2m^3 \times 5m^2 \times 8m^4$

d $2gh \times 3g^2h^5$ **e** $5p^4q^2 \times 6p^2q^7$ **f** $8u^3w \times 3uw^2 \times 2u^5w^4$

g $9y^8d \times y^5d^3 \times 3y^4d^7$ **h** $7b^3c^2 \times 2b^6c^4 \times 3b^5c^3$ **i** $4r^2s^2 \times 3r^6s^{12} \times 2r^8s^4$

j $10h^{10}v^2 \times 2h^8v^6 \times 3h^{20}v^{12}$

UNDERSTANDING

7 Simplify each of the following.

a $3^x \times 3^4$ **b** $3^y \times 3^{y+2}$ **c** $3^{2y+1} \times 3^{4y-6}$ **d** $3^{\frac{1}{2}} \times 3^{\frac{2}{3}} \times 3^{\frac{3}{4}}$

8 **a** Express the following basic numerals in index form: 9, 27 and 81.

b Use your answers to part **a** to help you simplify each of the following expressions. (Give each answer in index form.)

i $3^4 \times 81 \times 9$

ii $27 \times 3^n \times 3^{n-1}$

REFLECTION

The First Index law can only be applied if the bases are the same. Why is that so?

3C Second Index Law (dividing numbers in index form with the same base)

- The numbers in index form with the same base can be divided by first being written in factor form. For example,

$$2^6 \div 2^4 = \frac{2^6}{2^4} = \frac{2\times2\times2\times2\times2\times2}{2\times2\times2\times2}$$

$$= \frac{\cancel{2}\times\cancel{2}\times\cancel{2}\times\cancel{2}\times2\times2}{\cancel{2}\times\cancel{2}\times\cancel{2}\times\cancel{2}} = 2\times2$$

$$= 2^2.$$

- The simpler and faster way to divide the numbers in index form is to apply the Second Index Law. The Second Index Law states: $a^m \div a^n = a^{m-n}$. This means that when the numbers in index form with the same base are divided, the powers are subtracted. For example, $2^6 \div 2^4 = 2^{6-4} = 2^2$ (as above).

WORKED EXAMPLE 9

Simplify $\frac{5^{10}}{5^3}$ after first writing in factor form, leaving your answer in index form.

THINK	WRITE
1 Write the problem.	$\frac{5^{10}}{5^3}$
2 Write in factor form.	$= \frac{5\times5\times5\times5\times5\times5\times5\times5\times5\times5}{5\times5\times5}$
3 Cancel 5s.	$= 5\times5\times5\times5\times5\times5\times5$
4 Write in index form.	$= 5^7$

WORKED EXAMPLE 10

Simplify $d^{12} \div d^4$ using an index law.

THINK	WRITE
1 Write the problem and express it as a fraction.	$d^{12} \div d^4$
2 Check to see if the bases are the same. They are both d.	$= \dfrac{d^{12}}{d^4}$
3 Simplify by using the Second Index Law (subtract indices).	$= d^{12-4}$ $= d^8$

Dividing with coefficients

- When the coefficients are present, we divide them as we would divide any other numbers and then apply the Second Index Law to the variables.
- In examples where the cofficients do not divide evenly, we simplify the fraction that is formed by them.
- When there is more than one variable involved in the division question, the Second Index Law is applied to each variable separately.

WORKED EXAMPLE 11

Simplify $36d^7 \div 12d^3$ giving your answer in index form.

THINK	WRITE
1 Write the problem and express it as a fraction.	$36d^7 \div 12d^3 = \dfrac{36d^7}{12d^3}$
2 Divide the numbers (or coefficients) and apply the Second Index Law to the variables.	$= \dfrac{3d^7}{d^3}$
3 Simplify by using the Second Index Law (subtract indices).	$= 3d^{7-3}$ $= 3d^4$

WORKED EXAMPLE 12

Simplify $\dfrac{7t^3 \times 4t^8}{12t^4}$.

THINK	WRITE
1 Write the problem.	$\dfrac{7t^3 \times 4t^8}{12t^4}$
2 Multiply the numbers in the numerator and apply the First Index Law (add indices) in the numerator.	$= \dfrac{28t^{11}}{12t^4}$
3 Simplify the fraction formed and apply the Second Index Law for the variable (subtract indices).	$= \dfrac{7t^7}{3}$

REMEMBER

1. The Second Index Law states: $a^m \div a^n = a^{m-n}$. This means that when the numbers or variables in index form with the same base are divided, the powers are subtracted.
2. When the coefficients are present, we divide them as we would divide any other numbers and then apply the Second Index Law to the variables.
3. If the coefficients do not divide exactly, we simplify the fraction that is formed by them.
4. When there is more than one variable involved in the division question, the Second Index Law is applied to each variable separately.

EXERCISE 3C

Second Index Law (dividing numbers in index form with the same base)

INDIVIDUAL PATHWAYS

eBook*plus*

Activity 3-C-1 Second Index Law doc-6842

Activity 3-C-2 More of the Second Index Law doc-6843

Activity 3-C-3 Advanced use of the Second Index Law doc-6844

eBook*plus*

Digital doc Spreadsheet **Dividing with indices** doc-2161

FLUENCY

1 WE9 Simplify each of the following after first writing in factor form, leaving your answer in index form.

a $\frac{2^5}{2^2}$ b $\frac{7^7}{7^3}$ c $\frac{10^8}{10^5}$

2 WE10 Simplify each of the following using the index law, leaving your answer in index form.

a $3^3 \div 3^2$ b $11^9 \div 11^2$ c $5^8 \div 5^4$

d $12^6 \div 12$ e $3^{45} \div 3^{42}$ f $13^{75} \div 13^{74}$

g $6^{23} \div 6^{19}$ h $\frac{10^{13}}{10^9}$ i $\frac{15^{456}}{15^{423}}$

j $\frac{h^{78}}{h}$ k $\frac{b^{77}}{b^7}$ l $\frac{f^{1000}}{f^{100}}$

3 WE11 Simplify each of the following, giving your answer in index form.

a $3x^5 \div x^3$ b $6y^7 \div y^5$ c $8w^{12} \div w^5$

d $12q^{34} \div 4q^{30}$ e $16f^{12} \div 2f^3$ f $100h^{100} \div 10h^{10}$

g $80j^{15} \div 20j^5$ h $\frac{45p^{14}}{9p^4}$ i $\frac{48g^8}{6g^5}$

j $\frac{12b^7}{8b}$ k $\frac{81m^6}{18m^2}$ l $\frac{100n^{95}}{40n^5}$

4 a MC What does $21r^{20} \div 14r^{10}$ equal?

A $7r^{10}$ B $\frac{3r^2}{2}$ C $7r^2$ D $\frac{3r^{10}}{2}$ E $\frac{2}{3}r^{10}$

b What does $\frac{2m^{33}}{16m^{11}}$ equal?

A $\frac{m^{22}}{8}$ B $\frac{8}{m^{22}}$ C $8m^{22}$ D $\frac{m^3}{8}$ E None of the above

5 Simplify each of the following.

a $\frac{15p^{12}}{5p^8}$ b $\frac{18r^6}{3r^2}$ c $\frac{45a^5}{5a^2}$

d $\frac{60b^7}{20b}$ e $\frac{100r^{10}}{5r^6}$ f $\frac{9q^2}{q}$

6 WE12 Simplify each of the following.

a $\dfrac{8p^6 \times 3p^4}{16p^5}$ **b** $\dfrac{12b^5 \times 4b^2}{18b^2}$ **c** $\dfrac{25m^{12} \times 4n^7}{15m^2 \times 8n}$

d $\dfrac{27x^9y^3}{12xy^2}$ **e** $\dfrac{16h^7k^4}{12h^6k}$ **f** $\dfrac{12j^8 \times 6f^5}{8j^3 \times 3f^2}$

g $\dfrac{8p^3 \times 7r^2 \times 2s}{6p \times 14r}$ **h** $\dfrac{27a^9 \times 18b^5 \times 4c^2}{18a^4 \times 12b^2 \times 2c}$ **i** $\dfrac{81f^{15} \times 25g^{12} \times 16h^{34}}{27f^9 \times 15g^{10} \times 12h^{30}}$

UNDERSTANDING

7 Simplify each of the following.

a $2^{10} \div 2^p$

b $2^{7e} \div 2^{3e-4}$

c $\dfrac{5^{4x} \times 5^{3y}}{5^{2y} \times 5^x}$

d $\dfrac{3^{2-3m} \times 3^{7m}}{3^{5m} \times 3}$

8 Consider the fraction $\dfrac{8 \times 16 \times 4}{2 \times 32}$.

a Rewrite the fraction, expressing each basic numeral as power of 2.

b Simplify by giving your answer

i in index form **ii** as a basic numeral.

c Now check your answer by cancelling and evaluating the fraction in the ordinary way.

eBook*plus*

Digital doc
WorkSHEET 3.1
doc-6851

9 Consider the fraction $\dfrac{6 \times 27 \times 36}{12 \times 81}$.

a Rewrite the fraction, expressing each basic numeral as the product of its prime factors.

b Simplify, giving the answer

i in index form **ii** as a basic numeral.

REFLECTION

How will you remember that when numbers in index form are divided, powers are subtracted, but coefficients are divided?

3D Third Index Law (the power of zero)

- Consider the following two different methods of simplifying $2^3 \div 2^3$.

Method 1

$$2^3 \div 2^3 = \frac{2 \times 2 \times 2}{2 \times 2 \times 2} = \frac{8}{8} = 1$$

Method 2

$$2^3 \div 2^3 = \frac{2^3}{2^3} = 2^{3-3} \text{(using the Second Index Law)} = 2^0$$

Since the two results should be the same, 2^0 must equal 1.

- Any base that has an index power of 0 is equal to 1.
- The Third Index Law states: $a^0 = 1$. This means that any base that is raised to the power of zero is equal to 1.
- If it is in brackets, any numeric or algebraic expression that is raised to the power of zero is equal to 1. For example $(2 \times 3)^0 = 1$, $(2abc^2)^0 = 1$.

WORKED EXAMPLE 13

Find the value of 15^0.

THINK	WRITE
1 Write the problem.	15^0
2 Any base with an index of zero is equal to one.	$= 1$

WORKED EXAMPLE 14

Find the value of $(25 \times 36)^0$.

THINK	WRITE
1 Write the problem.	$(25 \times 36)^0$
2 Everything within the brackets has an index of zero, so the answer is 1.	$= 1$

WORKED EXAMPLE 15

Find the value of $19e^5a^0$.

THINK	WRITE
1 Write the problem.	$19e^5a^0$
2 Only *a* has a power of zero, so replace it with a 1 and simplify.	$= 19e^5 \times 1$ $= 19e^5$

WORKED EXAMPLE 16

Simplify $\dfrac{6m^3 \times 11m^{14}}{3m^{10} \times 2m^7}$.

THINK	WRITE
1 Write the problem.	$\dfrac{6m^3 \times 11m^{14}}{3m^{10} \times 2m^7}$
2 Multiply the numbers and apply the First Index Law in both the numerator and denominator.	$= \dfrac{66m^{17}}{6m^{17}}$
3 Divide the numbers and simplify using the Second Index Law.	$= 11m^{17-17}$ $= 11m^0$
4 Simplify using the Third Index Law.	$= 11 \times 1$ $= 11$

REMEMBER

Any base that has an index (power) of zero is equal to 1.
Third Index Law: $a^0 = 1$

EXERCISE
3D Third Index Law (the power of zero)

INDIVIDUAL PATHWAYS

eBook*plus*

Activity 3-D-1
The power of zero
doc-6845

Activity 3-D-2
More of the power of zero
doc-6846

Activity 3-D-3
Advanced use of the power of zero
doc-6847

FLUENCY

1 WE13 Find the value for each of the following.
a 16^0 b 44^0 c f^0 d h^0

2 WE14 Find the value of each of the following.
a $(23 \times 8)^0$ b $7^0 \times 6^0$ c $(35z^4)^0$ d $(12w^7)^0$

3 Find the value of each of the following.
a 4×3^0 b $9^0 + 11$ c $c^0 + 10$ d $3p^0 + 19$

4 WE15 Find the value of each of the following.
a $12m^3k^0$ b $7c^0 + 14m^0$ c $32g^0 + 40h^0$ d $\frac{8k^0}{7j^0}$
e $\frac{16t^0}{8y^0}$ f $\frac{6b^2 \times 5c^0}{3s^0}$ g $\frac{4d^0 \times 9p^2}{12q^0}$ h $\frac{3p \times 4d^0}{2z^0 \times 6p}$

5 Find each of the following.
a $e^{10} \div e^{10}$ b $a^{12} \div a^{12}$ c $(4b^3)^0 \div (4b^3)^0$ d $84f^{11} \div 12f^{11}$
e $30z^9 \div 10z^9$ f $99t^{13} \div 33t^{13}$

6 Simplify each of the following.
a $\frac{21p^4}{21p^4}$ b $\frac{40f^{33}}{10f^{33}}$ c $\frac{54p^6q^8}{27p^6q^8}$ d $\frac{16p^{11}q^{10}}{8p^2q^{10}}$
e $\frac{24e^{10}a^9}{16e^6a^9}$ f $\frac{x^4y^2z^{11}}{x^4yz^{11}}$ g $\frac{7m^6r^4i^7}{21m^3r^4i^7}$ h $\frac{3c^5d^3l^9}{12c^2d^3l^9}$

7 a MC You are told that there is an error in the statement $3p^7q^3r^5s^6 = 3p^7s^6$. To make the statement correct, what should the left-hand side be?
A $(3p^7q^3r^5s^6)^0$ B $(3p^7)^0q^3r^5s^6$ C $3p^7(q^3r^5s^6)^0$ D $3p^7(q^3r^5)^0s^6$

b You are told that there is an error in the statement $\frac{8f^6g^7h^3}{6f^4g^2h} = \frac{8f^2}{g^2}$. To make the statement correct, what should the left-hand side be?
A $\frac{8f^6(g^7h^3)^0}{(6)^0f^4g^2(h)^0}$ B $\frac{8(f^6g^7h^3)^0}{(6f^4g^2h)^0}$ C $\frac{8(f^6g^7)^0h^3}{(6f^4)^0g^2h}$ D $\frac{8f^6g^7h^3}{(6f^4g^2h)^0}$ E None of the above

c What does $\frac{6k^7m^2n^8}{4k^7(m^6n)^0}$ equal?
A $\frac{3}{2}$ B $\frac{3n^8}{2}$ C $\frac{3m^2}{2}$ D $\frac{3m^2n^8}{2}$ E None of the above

8 WE16 Simplify each of the following.
a $\frac{2a^3 \times 6a^2}{12a^5}$ b $\frac{3c^6 \times 6c^3}{9c^9}$ c $\frac{5b^7 \times 10b^5}{25b^{12}}$ d $\frac{8f^3 \times 3f^7}{4f^5 \times 3f^5}$
e $\frac{9k^{12} \times 4k^{10}}{18k^4 \times k^{18}}$ f $\frac{2h^4 \times 5k^2}{20h^2 \times k^2}$ g $\frac{p^3 \times q^4}{5p^3}$ h $\frac{m^7 \times n^3}{5m^3 \times m^4}$
i $\frac{8u^9 \times v^2}{2u^5 \times 4u^4}$ j $\frac{9x^6 \times 2y^{12}}{3y^{10} \times 3y^2}$

REFLECTION
Explain how the Second and the Third Index Law are connected?

3E Fourth Index Law (raising a power to another power)

- The Fourth Index Law states that when raising a power to another power, the indices are multiplied; that is, $(a^m)^n = a^{m \times n}$. For example, $(5^3)^2 = 5^{3 \times 2} = 5^6$.
- Every number and variable inside the brackets should have its index multiplied by the power outside the brackets. That is,

$$(a \times b)^m = a^m \times b^m$$

$$\left(\frac{a}{b}\right)^m = \frac{a^m}{b^m}$$

(These are sometimes called the Fifth and Sixth Index Law.)

- Any number or variable that does not appear to have an index really has an index of one; that is, $2 = 2^1$, $a = a^1$.
- Every number or variable inside the brackets must be raised to the power outside the brackets. For example, $(3 \times 2)^4 = 3^4 \times 2^4$ and $(2a^4)^3 = 2^3 \times a^{4 \times 3} = 8a^{12}$.

WORKED EXAMPLE 17

Simplify the following, leaving answers in index form.

a $(7^4)^8$ **b** $\left(\frac{3^2}{5^3}\right)^3$

THINK	WRITE
a 1 Write the problem.	**a** $(7^4)^8$
2 Simplify using the Fourth Index Law (multiply the indices).	$= 7^{4 \times 8}$ $= 7^{32}$
b 1 Write the problem.	**b** $\left(\frac{3^2}{5^3}\right)^3$
2 Multiply the indices.	$= \frac{3^{2\times3}}{5^{3\times3}}$
3 Simplify.	$= \frac{3^6}{5^9}$

WORKED EXAMPLE 18

Simplify $(2b^5)^2 \times (5b^8)^3$.

THINK	WRITE
1 Write the problem.	$(2b^5)^2 \times (5b^8)^3$
2 Simplify using the Fourth Index Law.	$= 2^{1 \times 2}b^{5 \times 2} \times 5^{1 \times 3}b^{8 \times 3}$ $= 2^2b^{10} \times 5^3b^{24}$
3 Calculate the coefficient.	$= 4b^{10} \times 125b^{24}$ $= 500b^{10} \times b^{24}$
4 Simplify using the First Index Law.	$= 500b^{34}$

WORKED EXAMPLE 19

Simplify $\left(\dfrac{2a^5}{d^2}\right)^3$.

THINK	WRITE
1 Write the problem.	$\left(\dfrac{2a^5}{d^2}\right)^3$
2 Simplify using the Fourth Index Law for each term inside the grouping symbols.	$=\dfrac{2^{1\times3}a^{5\times3}}{d^{2\times3}}$ $=\dfrac{2^3a^{15}}{d^6}$
3 Calculate the coefficient.	$=\dfrac{8a^{15}}{d^6}$

REMEMBER

1. The Fourth Index Law states that when a power is raised to another power, the indices are multiplied. That is, $(a^m)^n = a^{m\times n}$.
2. Every variable and every number inside the brackets should have its index multiplied by the power outside the brackets. That is,

$$(a\times b)^m = a^m \times b^m$$

$$\left(\frac{a}{b}\right)^m = \frac{a^m}{b^m}$$

3. Any number or variable that does not appear to have an index really has an index of one; that is, $2 = 2^1$, $a = a^1$.

EXERCISE 3E

Fourth Index Law (raising a power to another power)

INDIVIDUAL PATHWAYS

eBook*plus*

Activity 3-E-1
Mammal dot to dot A
doc-6848

Activity 3-E-2
Mammal dot to dot B
doc-6849

Activity 3-E-3
Mammal dot to dot C
doc-6850

FLUENCY

1 WE17 Simplify each of the following leaving your answers in index form.

a $(3^2)^3$ b $(6^8)^{10}$ c $(11^{25})^4$
d $(5^{12})^{12}$ e $(3^2\times10^3)^4$ f $(13\times17^3)^5$
g $\left(\dfrac{3^3}{2^2}\right)^{10}$ h $(3w^9q^2)^4$ i $\left(\dfrac{7e^5}{r^2q^4}\right)^2$

2 WE18 Simplify each of the following.

a $(p^4)^2\times(q^3)^2$ b $(r^5)^3\times(w^3)^3$ c $(b^5)^2\times(n^3)^6$
d $(j^6)^3\times(g^4)^3$ e $(q^2)^2\times(r^4)^5$ f $(h^3)^8\times(j^2)^8$
g $(f^4)^4\times(a^7)^3$ h $(t^5)^2\times(u^4)^2$ i $(i^3)^5\times(j^2)^6$

3 Simplify each of the following.

a $(2^3)^4\times(2^4)^2$ b $(t^7)^3\times(t^3)^4$ c $(a^4)^0\times(a^3)^7$
d $(b^6)^2\times(b^4)^3$ e $(e^7)^8\times(e^5)^2$ f $(g^7)^3\times(g^9)^2$
g $(3a^2)^4\times(2a^6)^2$ h $(2d^7)^3\times(3d^2)^3$ i $(10r^{12})^4\times(2r^3)^2$

eBook*plus*

Digital doc
Spreadsheet
Raising a power to another power
doc-2162

4 a MC What does $(p^7)^2 \div p^2$ equal?

A p^7 B p^{12} C p^{16} D $p^{4.5}$ E p^{11}

b What does $\dfrac{(w^5)^2 \times (p^7)^3}{(w^2)^2 \times (p^3)^5}$ equal?

A w^2p^6 B $(wp)^6$ C $w^{14}p^{36}$ D w^2p^2 E w^6p^{19}

c What does $(r^6)^3 \div (r^4)^2$ equal?

A r^3 B r^4 C r^8 D r^{10} E r^{12}

eBook*plus*

Interactivity
Indices
int-2360

5 Simplify each of the following.

a $(a^3)^4 \div (a^2)^3$ b $(m^8)^2 \div (m^3)^4$ c $(n^5)^3 \div (n^6)^2$
d $(b^4)^5 \div (b^6)^2$ e $(f^7)^3 \div (f^2)^2$ f $(g^8)^2 \div (g^5)^2$
g $(p^9)^3 \div (p^6)^3$ h $(y^4)^4 \div (y^7)^2$ i $\dfrac{(c^6)^5}{(c^5)^2}$
j $\dfrac{(f^5)^3}{(f^2)^4}$ k $\dfrac{(k^3)^{10}}{(k^2)^8}$ l $\dfrac{(p^{12})^3}{(p^{10})^2}$

6 WE19 Simplify each of the following.

a $\left(\dfrac{3b^4}{d^3}\right)^2$ b $\left(\dfrac{5h^{10}}{2j^2}\right)^2$ c $\left(\dfrac{2k^5}{3t^8}\right)^3$
d $\left(\dfrac{7p^9}{8q^{22}}\right)^2$ e $\left(\dfrac{5y^7}{3z^{13}}\right)^3$ f $\left(\dfrac{4a^3}{7c^5}\right)^4$

UNDERSTANDING

7 Simplify each of the following using the index laws.

a $g^3 \times 2g^5$ b $2p^6 \times 4p^2$ c $(w^3)^6$
d $12x^6 \div 2x$ e $(2d^3)^2$ f $5a^6 \times 3a^2 \times a^2$
g $15s^8 \div 5s^2$ h $4bc^6 \times 3b^3 \times 5c^2$ i $\dfrac{14x^8}{7x^4}$
j $(f^4g^3)^2$ k $\dfrac{16u^6v^5}{6u^3v}$ l $x^2y^4 \times xy^3$
m $5a^6b^2 \times a^2 \times 3ab^3$ n $x^2y^4 \div xy^3$ o $(4p^2q^5)^3$

8 Simplify each of the following, giving your answer in index form.

a $(w^3)^4 \div w^2$ b $\dfrac{4x^5 \times 3x}{2x^4}$ c $(2a^3)^2 \times 3a^5$
d $12x^6 \times 2x \div 3x^5$ e $2d^3 + d^2 + 5d^3$ f $\dfrac{(2k^3)^2}{4k^4}$
g $\dfrac{4p^5}{p^4 \times 6p}$ h $15s^8t^3 \div 5s^2t^2 \times 2st^4$ i $12b^4c^6 \div 3b^3 \div 4c^2$
j $(f^4g^3)^2 - fg^3 \times f^7g^3$ k $\dfrac{(3p^3)^2 \times 4p^7}{2(p^4)^3}$ l $2(x^2y)^4 \times 8xy^3$
m $5a^6b^2 + a^2 \times 3a^4b^2$ n $24x^2y^4 \div 12xy^3 - xy$
o $\dfrac{4p^2q^7 \times (3p^3q)^2}{6(pq)^3 \times p^5q^4}$

eBook*plus*

Digital doc
WorkSHEET 3.2
doc-6852
Weblink
Multiplying numbers in index form

REFLECTION
How will you remember to raise all coefficients to the power outside the brackets?

Summary

Review of index form

- A number written in index form has:
  - a base, which is the large number below
  - a power or index, which is the small number written just above and to the right of the base.

$$\text{base} \rightarrow 2^5 \leftarrow \text{index}$$

- The base tells us what will be multiplied.
- The power tells us how many times the base will be written and multiplied.
- Factor form is when all the multiplications are shown.
- After multiplying out to remove the index, the answer is called a basic numeral.

$$\underbrace{2^5}_{\text{index form}} = \underbrace{2 \times 2 \times 2 \times 2 \times 2}_{\text{factor form}} = \underbrace{32}_{\text{basic numeral}}$$

First Index Law (multiplying numbers in index form with the same base)

- The First Index Law states: $a^m \times a^n = a^{m+n}$. This means that when numbers or variables in index form with the same base are multiplied by each other, the powers (indices) are added together.
- If the expression contains coefficients, the coefficients are multiplied together and the numbers and variables in index form by each other.
- When there is more than one variable involved in the multiplication question, the First Index Law is applied to each variable separately.

Second Index Law (dividing numbers in index form with the same base)

- The Second Index Law states: $a^m \div a^n = b^{m-n}$. This means that when the numbers or variables in index form with the same base are divided, the powers are subtracted.
- When the coefficients are present, we divide them as we would divide any other numbers and then apply the Second Index Law to the variables.
- If the coefficients do not divide exactly, we simplify the fraction that is formed by them.
- When there is more than one variable involved in the division question, the Second Index Law is applied to each variable separately.

Third Index Law (the power of zero)

- Any base that has an index (power) of zero is equal to 1. Third Index Law $a^0 = 1$

Fourth Index Law (raising a power to another power)

- The Fourth Index Law states that when a power is raised to another power, the indices are multiplied. That is, $(a^m)^n = a^{m \times n}$.
- Every variable and every number inside the brackets should have its index multiplied by the power outside the brackets. That is,

$$(a \times b)^m = a^m \times b^m$$

$$\left(\frac{a}{b}\right)^m = \frac{a^m}{b^m}$$

- Any term that does not appear to have an index really has an index of one; that is, $2 = 2^1$, $a = a^1$.

MAPPING YOUR UNDERSTANDING

Using terms from the summary, and other terms if you wish, construct a concept map that illustrates your understanding of the key concepts covered in this chapter. Compare this concept map with the one that you created in *What do you know?* on page 49.

Have you completed the two *Homework sheets*, the *Rich task* and the two *Code puzzles* in your *Maths Quest 8 Homework Book*?

Chapter review

FLUENCY

1 State the base for each of the following.
a 5^{10} **b** 9^4 **c** x^8 **d** w^7

2 State the power or index for each of the following.
a 11^6 **b** 23^5 **c** C^{17} **d** L^{100}

3 Write the following in index form.
a $7 \times 7 \times 7 \times 7$ **b** $3 \times 3 \times 3 \times 3 \times 3 \times 3 \times 3$
c $m \times m \times m \times m \times m$
d $k \times k \times k \times n \times n \times n \times n \times n$

4 Write each of the following as a basic numeral.
a 6^2 **b** 8^2 **c** 3^4 **d** 2^7 **e** 5^3

5 Evaluate each of the following.
a $7^2 - 4^2$ **b** $9^2 + 3^3 - 5^2$

6 Simplify each of the following.
a $3^5 \times 3^6$ **b** $10^{11} \times 10^4$ **c** $7^3 \times 7^6$
d $j^4 \times j^6 \times j^9$ **e** $t^4 \times t^5 \times t$ **f** $2z^5 \times 6z \times z$
g $5w^3 \times 7w^{12} \times w^{14}$ **h** $2e^2p^3 \times 6e^3p^5$

7 Simplify each of the following.
a $6^5 \div 6^2$ **b** $12^{10} \div 12$ **c** $5^{24} \div 5^{14}$
d $2^6 \div 2^2$ **e** $\dfrac{3^{20}}{3^{11}}$ **f** $\dfrac{m^{99}}{m^{66}}$
g $\dfrac{p^{15}}{p}$ **h** $\dfrac{h^7 \times h^{11}}{h^5}$ **i** $\dfrac{L^6 \times L^2 \times L^4}{L^8}$
j $\dfrac{y^5 \times y^7 \times y^2}{y^8}$ **k** $\dfrac{a^7 \times a \times a^5}{a^3 \times a^6}$
l $\dfrac{c^4 \times c^2 \times c \times c^7}{c^3 \times c^8 \times c^4}$

8 Simplify the following.
a 4^0 **b** 9^0 **c** 1966^0
d m^0 **e** n^0 **f** zb^0
g $7w^0$ **h** $8q^0 - 2q^0$ **i** $4s^0 + 60t^0$
j v^0w^5 **k** $(x^3y^6)^0$ **l** klm^0
m $d^2e^6f^0$ **n** $r^4s^0u^9$

9 Raise each of the following to the given power.
a $(2^4)^3$ **b** $(6^9)^2$ **c** $(7^4)^{10}$
d $(n^{21})^6$ **e** $(r^{16}i^{12})^2$ **f** $(b^2d^8)^{20}$
g $(2pm^3)^3$ **h** $(9wz^4)^2$

10 MC What does $\left(\dfrac{4b^4}{d^2}\right)^3$ equal?
A $\dfrac{4b^3}{d^3}$ **B** $\dfrac{12b^{12}}{d^6}$ **C** $\dfrac{64b^{12}}{d^6}$
D $\dfrac{64b^7}{d^5}$ **E** $\dfrac{12b}{d^5}$

PROBLEM SOLVING

1 a Evaluate each of the following.
i $(-1)^1$ **ii** $(-1)^2$ **iii** $(-1)^3$
iv $(-1)^4$ **v** $(-1)^5$ **vi** $(-1)^6$

b Use your answers to part **a** to complete the following sentence:
'If negative one is raised to the even power, the result is ….; if it is raised to the odd power, the result is …. .'

c Consider the expression $(-1)^k + (-1)^l$. Find all possible values of the above expression. Specify the values of k and l for which each result occurs.

2 At 9 am there were 10 bacteria in a Petri dish.
a If the number of bacteria doubles every minute, find out how many bacteria were in a Petri dish after:
i 1 minute **ii** 2 minutes
iii 3 minutes **iv** 10 minutes.
b Develop the rule that connects the number of bacteria, N, and the time, t (in minutes) after 9 am.
c Use your answer to part **b** to find the number of bacteria in a dish at 10 am. Give your answer in index form (do not evaluate).

3 Lena receives an email containing a chain letter. She is asked to forward this letter to 5 friends (or else she will have a lot of bad luck!). Lena promptly sends 5 letters as required. (Let's call it the *first round* of letters.) Each of Lena's 5 friends also sends 5 letters. (Call this the *second round* of letters.)
a How many letters were sent in the second round? Give your answer as
i a basic numeral **ii** in index form.

b How many letters were sent in the third round? Give your answer as

i a basic numeral **ii** in index form.

c Assuming the chain is not broken, and each recipient sent out 5 letters, what was the total number of letters sent in the first four rounds? Give your answer as

i a basic numeral **ii** in index form.

4 Nathan is considering participating in the Premier's Reading Challenge. He decided to test himself first by trying to read a 400-page book in 6 days. Nathan read 7 pages on Day 1. After performing some basic arithmetic computations he realised that he needed to increase that amount to be able to finish the book on time. Nathan decided to double the amount of read pages every day.

a How many pages did Nathan read on

i Day 2 **ii** Day 3?

b Develop the formula connecting the number of pages P read per day and the number of days d.

c Use your answer to part **b** to find the number of pages Nathan will read on Day 6.

d If Nathan continues according to plan, will he finish the book in 6 days? Justify your answer with mathematical calculations.

5 Alex bought a second-hand car for \$25 000. Each year the car depreciates by 20% (that is, each year it loses 20% of its value).

a Find the value of the car at the end of the first year.

b Find the value of the car at the end of the second year.

c The value, V, of the car can be found using the formula $V = 25\,000 \times 0.8^t$, where t is the number of years after purchase. Explain the meaning of the numbers 25 000 and 0.8.

d Use the formula to find the value of the car after 5 years.

e Alex decided that he will sell his car when its value falls below \$5000. How soon will he be able to do that?

6 The number, E, of employees in a large firm grows according to the rule $E = 60 \times 1.15^t$, where t is the number of years from the year 2000.

a How many people did the firm employ in the year 2000?

b How many employees were there in

i 2001

ii 2002?

c How many years will it take for the number of employees to exceed 200?

7 When money is invested in a bank, it earns interest. Interest is calculated as a percentage of the money invested. The term *compound interest* means that the interest earned in one year is added to the account at the end of that year, and that next year the interest is calculated on the larger amount. Compound interest can be found using the formula

$A = P\left(1 + \frac{r}{100}\right)^t$, where P is the principal (the invested amount), r is the yearly interest rate and t is the number of years the money has been invested. A is the total amount of money (principal plus interest) accumulated after t years.

a Find the total amount of money accumulated if \$2000 was invested at 4.5% p.a. for 6 years. (*Note:* p.a. stands for 'per annum', which means 'per year'.)

b Find the total amount of money accumulated if \$10 000 was invested at 7% p.a. for 3 years.

c For part **b**, calculate the total amount of interest earned on the investment over the 3 year period.

8 Four rabbits were accidentally introduced to a small island. The population of rabbits doubled every 4 weeks.

a How many rabbits were on an island

i 8 weeks later

ii 24 weeks later

iii 1 year later?

b After one year, to cope with the rabbit problem, some foxes were brought to the island. As a result, the population of rabbits started declining by 10% each week. After the foxes had been brought in, how many rabbits were left after
i 1 week **ii** 2 weeks **iii** 10 weeks?

9 There were 50 bacteria of Type X and 30 bacteria of Type Y in a Petri dish. The number of bacteria of Type X doubles every 4 hours; the number of bacteria of Type Y quadruples every 6 hours.

Find the total number of bacteria in the dish after
a 12 hours **b** 1 day **c** 2 days **d** 1 week.

10 A basic numeral can be expressed in a standard form (also called a scientific notation) by writing it as a number between 1 and 10 multiplied by power of 10. For example, number 4000 in standard form is written as 4.0×10^3. For each of the following situations express the basic numeral in standard form.

a A company declares an annual profit of 3 billion dollars.

b The diameter of Earth is (approximately) 40 000 km.

c The half-life of a certain radioactive element is 5 000 000 years.

d Light travels at a speed of 300 000 km/s.

11 **a** Express the basic numerals 4, 8 and 16 as powers of 2.

b Use your answers from part **a** to simplify the following:

i $\dfrac{4^x \times 8^y}{16}$

ii $\dfrac{8^{2m} \times 16^m}{4^{3m} \times 2^{4m}}$.

12 If $a^2 = 7$, find the value of:
a $a^4 + 1$ **b** $2a^6$ **c** $3a^6 - 4a^4$.

13 A rubber ball is dropped from a balcony which is 10 m above the ground. The ball bounces to $\frac{3}{4}$ of its previous height after each bounce.

a Find the height of the ball above the ground after
i 1 bounce
ii 3 bounces
iii 5 bounces.

b When will the height of the ball above the ground be less than 1 m?

eBook*plus*

Interactivities

Test yourself
Chapter 3
int-2750

Word search
Chapter 3
int-2619

Crossword
Chapter 3
int-2620

eBookplus ACTIVITIES

Chapter opener

Digital doc *(page 49)*

- Hungry brain activity Chapter 3 (doc-6833)

Are you ready?

Digital docs *(page 50)*

- SkillSHEET 3.1 (doc-6834) Factor trees
- SkillSHEET 3.2 (doc-6835) Squaring numbers
- SkillSHEET 3.3 (doc-6836) Equivalent fractions
- SkillSHEET 3.4 (doc-6837) Simplifying algebraic expressions
- SkillSHEET 3.5 (doc-6838) Simplifying algebraic fractions

3A Review of index form

Digital docs *(page 52)*

- Activity 3-A-1 (doc-2143) Review of index form
- Activity 3-A-2 (doc-2144) More index form
- Activity 3-A-3 (doc-2145) Advanced index form

3B First Index Law

Digital docs *(page 55)*

- Activity 3-B-1 (doc-6839) First Index Law
- Activity 3-B-2 (doc-6840) More of the First Index Law
- Activity 3-B-3 (doc-6841) Advanced use of the First Index Law
- Spreadsheet (doc-2160) Multiplying with indices

3C Second Index Law

Digital docs *(page 58)*

- Activity 3-C-1 (doc-6842) Second Index Law
- Activity 3-C-2 (doc-6843) More of the Second Index Law
- Activity 3-C-3 (doc-6844) Advanced use of the Second Index Law
- Spreadsheet (doc-2161) Dividing with indices
- WorkSHEET 3.1 (doc-6851) *(page 59)*

3D Third Index Law

Digital docs *(page 61)*

- Activity 3-D-1 (doc-6845) The power of zero
- Activity 3-D-2 (doc-6846) More of the power of zero
- Activity 3-D-3 (doc-6847) Advanced use of the power of zero

3E Fourth Index Law

Digital docs *(page 63)*

- Activity 3-E-1 (doc-6848) Mammal dot to dot A
- Activity 3-E-2 (doc-6849) Mammal dot to dot B
- Activity 3-E-3 (doc-6850) Mammal dot to dot C
- WorkSHEET 3.2 (doc-6852) *(page 64)*
- Spreadsheet (doc-2162) Raising a power to another power *(page 64)*

Weblink *(page 64)*

- Multiplying numbers in index form

Interactivity *(page 64)*

- Indices (int-2360)

Chapter review

Interactivities *(page 68)*

- Test yourself Chapter 3 (int-2750) Take the end-of-chapter test to test your progress.
- Word search Chapter 3 (int-2619)
- Crossword Chapter 3 (int-2620)

To access eBookPLUS activities, log on to

www.jacplus.com.au

ICT ACTIVITY

projectsplus

Attack of the killer balloons

SEARCHLIGHT ID: PRO-0095

Scenario

Ms Lovely is a Math teacher at Scholar High School and during last week she had her 30th birthday. Mr Handsome, her adoring husband, secretly placed a balloon and flowers in her classroom before the beginning of her first class. Unfortunately, he had unknowingly purchased a killer balloon from Mr Loon, of Angry Balloons! During Ms Lovely's class, the balloon developed a strange looking face and burst open.

To everyone's amazement, there were now five balloons, all with strange faces! During the following period when Ms Lovely was taking a new class, the five balloons also burst, and during the day continued to multiply in this way. Eventually it became apparent that the balloons were hostile, and were going to attack.

Terrified, Ms Lovely and the threatened children escaped, but the killer balloons had taken control of her classroom and were threatening to spread. The students and staff were evacuated from the school, and the Australian Centre for the Study of Extraordinary and Unexplained Phenomena (ACSEUP) was called to investigate. The ACSEUP re-created the events to produce a simulation video so they could study the balloons, and work out how to defeat them. They realised that if they could work out the mathematical pattern of the increasing numbers of balloons perhaps they could find a plan for defeating them. However, after extensive analysis, they were stumped. The ACSEUP researchers had heard that your school had some clever maths students, and have asked your mathematics class to help Ms Lovely's students solve the mystery of the killer balloons.

Task

Watch the case study video that ACSEUP has provided for your class, and simultaneously track the growth of the killer balloons on a chart. Use the data that you have collected to create a graph showing the growth rate of the killer balloons. From these, create a mathematical equation that simulates the attack.

When you have finished this research and understand the problem, you will answer some other questions that ACSEUP has asked about similar balloon scenarios. These will include how to go about defeating the killer balloons. Using your solutions to these questions, combined with your charts, graphs and equations, you will present a comprehensive report about the attack of the killer balloons to ACSEUP.

Summary of tasks

- Record and graph the growth of the balloons.
- Create a mathematical formula that simulates the growth of the balloons.
- Answer questions about other balloon growth scenarios.
- Record and graph the popping of the balloons.
- Create a mathematical formula that simulates the destruction of the balloons.
- Answer questions about other balloon destruction scenarios.
- Prepare a report on the attack of the killer balloons for ACSEUP.

Process

- Open the ProjectsPLUS application for this chapter in your eBookPLUS. Watch the Attack of the Killer Balloons case study, navigate to your Media Centre, and print Template 1 provided in the Template section. Watch the case study video again and fill in the required data in Template 1. Your Media Centre includes the re-enactment of the killer balloon take-over.
- Next, press the 'Start Project' button and then set up your project group. You will need to create a group of two or three of your classmates before you begin this project. Save your group settings and the project will be launched.
- Navigate to the Media Centre, then to the Documents section and answer the questions in the six ACSEUP worksheets.
- Navigate to the Media Centre, then to the Template section and print Presentation guidelines.
- Use the Presentation guidelines to choose a topic for your presentation, then read about the guidelines for the project.
- Navigate to the Media Centre to access Geogebra and the corresponding user manual.
- If possible, use a SMARTBoard or overhead projector and computer to display your Geogebra graph and tables during the presentation.

SUGGESTED SOFTWARE
- ProjectsPLUS
- Microsoft Word
- Geogebra

Your ProjectsPLUS application is available in this chapter's Student Resources tab inside your eBookPLUS. Visit www.jacplus.com.au to locate your digital resources.

Interactivity

KILLER BALLOONS

SEARCHLIGHT ID: int-2447

If a quantity doubles or triples over a consistent time period, it is said to be increasing exponentially. Use this interactivity to change the exponential rate of growth and then predict the number of balloons that will appear. Watch the graph of the number of balloons against time plotted on the wall.

MEDIA CENTRE

Your Media Centre contains:
- a Document section with ACSEUP worksheets
- a Template section with presentation guidelines
- Geogebra software and its user manual
- an assessment rubric.

Real numbers

4A Addition and subtraction of fractions
4B Multiplication and division of fractions
4C Terminating and recurring decimals
4D Addition and subtraction of decimals
4E Multiplication and division of decimals
4F Percentages, fractions and decimals
4G Estimation

WHAT DO YOU KNOW?

1 List what you know about problems involving fractions, decimals and percentages. Create a concept map to show your list.
2 Share what you know with a partner and then with a small group.
3 As a class, create a large concept map that shows your class's knowledge of problems involving fractions, decimals and percentages.

eBook*plus*

Digital doc
Hungry brain activity
Chapter 4
doc-6853

OPENING QUESTION

In 1926, the cactus moth was introduced to control the prickly pear cactus (itself introduced in the 1830s). The moth lays egg sticks (a row of connected eggs) containing about 70 eggs that are 2.4 cm long. What is the length of a single egg?

Are you ready?

Try the questions below. If you have difficulty with any of them, extra help can be obtained by completing the matching SkillSHEET located on your eBookPLUS.

eBook*plus*

Digital doc
SkillSHEET 4.1
doc-6854

Order of operations I

1 Evaluate each of the following.

a $4 + \frac{1}{2}$ of 12
b $5 \times (13 - 7)$

eBook*plus*

Digital doc
SkillSHEET 4.2
doc-6855

Factors

2 Find all the factors of:

a 20
b 48.

eBook*plus*

Digital doc
SkillSHEET 4.3
doc-6856

Multiples

3 List the first 5 multiples of:

a 6
b 8.

eBook*plus*

Digital doc
SkillSHEET 4.4
doc-6857

Adding and subtracting fractions I

4 Calculate each of the following, writing your answer as a mixed number if appropriate.

a $\frac{3}{7} + \frac{6}{7}$
b $\frac{3}{8} - \frac{1}{4}$

eBook*plus*

Digital doc
SkillSHEET 4.5
doc-6858

Multiplying and dividing fractions

5 Calculate each of the following.

a $\frac{2}{9} \times \frac{7}{6}$
b $\frac{5}{8} \div \frac{3}{4}$

eBook*plus*

Digital doc
SkillSHEET 4.6
doc-6859

Adding and subtracting decimals

6 Calculate each of the following.

a $7.6 + 15.1$
b $126.35 - 83.49$

eBook*plus*

Digital doc
SkillSHEET 4.7
doc-6860

Multiplying and dividing decimals

7 Calculate each of the following.

a 3.7×1.2
b $182.72 \div 5$

eBook*plus*

Digital doc
SkillSHEET 4.8
doc-6861

Rounding to the first (leading) digit

8 Round each number.

a 87 to the nearest ten
b 539 to the nearest 100

eBook*plus*

Digital doc
SkillSHEET 4.9
doc-6862

Operations with fractions

9 Calculate each of the following.

a $\frac{1}{3} + \frac{1}{2}$
b $\frac{3}{5} - \frac{2}{7}$
c $2\frac{3}{4} + 1\frac{2}{3}$
d $\frac{5}{6} \times \frac{3}{7}$
e $\frac{3}{8} \div \frac{1}{4}$
f $3\frac{2}{5} \div 2\frac{1}{2}$

eBook*plus*

Digital doc
SkillSHEET 4.10
doc-6863

Operations with decimals

10 Calculate each of the following.

a $0.5 + 0.26$
b $2.73 - 1.49$
c 0.3×0.2
d $(0.4)^2$
e $4.8 \div 0.5$
f $0.032 \div 0.04$

4A Addition and subtraction of fractions

Introduction to real numbers

- Number systems have become more sophisticated as societies have developed.
- Different types of numbers can be classified into specific groups.
- The **real number** system contains the set of **rational** and **irrational** numbers. It can be denoted by the symbol R.
- The set of real numbers contains a number of groups or subsets that can be classified as shown in the chart below.

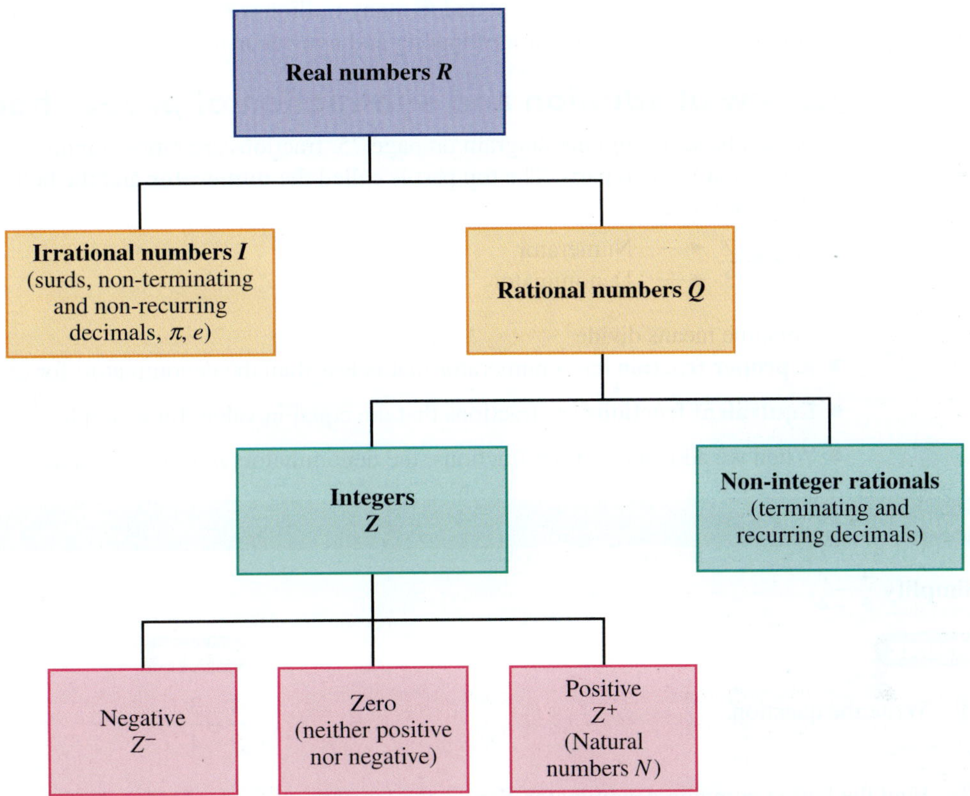

Rational numbers

- A rational number is any number that can be expressed as a ratio of two whole numbers in the form $\frac{a}{b}$, where a and b are whole numbers and $b \neq 0$.
- The set of rational numbers is given the symbol Q. Examples include $\frac{1}{4}, -3, \frac{4}{7}, 100, -63, 1.5, -0.8$ and $1.\overline{45}$.
- Rational numbers include all integers (symbol Z), as integers can be expressed in the form $\frac{a}{b}$. For example, $100 = \frac{100}{1}, -3 = \frac{-3}{1}$.
- Rational numbers include all fractions, both those that can be expressed as terminating decimals and those that can be expressed as recurring decimals. For example, $\frac{2}{5} = 0.4$ is a terminating decimal and $\frac{1}{3} = 0.33\ldots.. = 0.\dot{3}$ is a recurring decimal. These are rational numbers as they can be expressed in the form $\frac{a}{b}$, where a and b are whole numbers and $b \neq 0$.

Irrational numbers

- Numbers that cannot be expressed in the form $\frac{a}{b}$, where a and b are whole numbers and $b \neq 0$, are called irrational numbers. Examples of these numbers are $\sqrt{5}, \sqrt{7}$ and $2\sqrt{11}$. These numbers can be expressed as decimals, but their decimal values do not terminate or repeat in any pattern.
- A special irrational number is π (pi). This is the distance around the circumference of a circle with a diameter of 1. It can be approximated as a decimal that is non-terminating and non-recurring.

  In decimal form, $\pi = 3.141\,592\ldots$

  The value of π has been calculated to many millions of decimal places with the aid of a computer, but it is still non-terminating and non-recurring.

Review of addition and subtraction of proper fractions

- As can be seen from the diagram on page 75, fractions are rational numbers.
- A fraction has two parts. The top part is called the **numerator** and the bottom part is called the **denominator**.

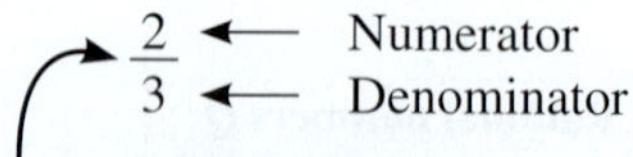

This line means divide

- A **proper fraction** has a numerator that is less than the denominator; for example, $\frac{3}{5}$.
- **Equivalent fractions** are fractions that are equal in value; for example, $\frac{1}{2} = \frac{2}{4}$.
- When we add and subtract fractions, the denominators *must* be the same.

WORKED EXAMPLE 1

Simplify $\frac{4}{5} - \frac{3}{4}$.

THINK	WRITE
1 Write the question.	$\frac{4}{5} - \frac{3}{4}$
2 Find the lowest common denominator, that is, the lowest multiple common to both.	$= \frac{4 \times 4}{5 \times 4} - \frac{3 \times 5}{4 \times 5}$
3 Write both fractions with the same denominator, that is, the lowest common denominator.	$= \frac{16}{20} - \frac{15}{20}$
4 Subtract the fractions.	$= \frac{1}{20}$
5 Write the answer.	

Addition and subtraction of mixed numbers

- An **improper fraction** has a numerator greater than the denominator; for example, $\frac{7}{3}$.
- A **mixed number** contains a whole number part and a proper fraction part; for example, $7\frac{5}{8}$.
- When we are adding and subtracting mixed numbers, we must first change them to improper fractions, and then solve them as shown in Worked example 1. However, it is often better to add or subtract the whole number parts first and then the fraction parts.

WORKED EXAMPLE 2

Calculate $2\frac{2}{3} + 3\frac{1}{2}$.

THINK	WRITE
1 Write the question.	$2\frac{2}{3} + 3\frac{1}{2}$
2 Change each mixed number to an improper fraction.	$= \frac{8}{3} + \frac{7}{2}$
3 Write both fractions with the same denominator using equivalent fractions.	$= \frac{8 \times 2}{3 \times 2} + \frac{7 \times 3}{2 \times 3}$ $= \frac{16}{6} + \frac{21}{6}$
4 Add the fractions.	$= \frac{37}{6}$
5 Write the answer as a mixed number if appropriate.	$= 6\frac{1}{6}$

- A rough estimate can be found by adding or subtracting the whole number parts. For example, $2 + 3 = 5$, so $2\frac{2}{3} + 3\frac{1}{2} > 5$.
- If the first fraction part is smaller than the second fraction part when subtracting fractions, use equal addition. In this method, a fraction is added to both terms that will make the second fraction a whole number.

WORKED EXAMPLE 3

Calculate $4\frac{1}{5} - 1\frac{1}{2}$.

THINK	WRITE
1 Write the question.	$4\frac{1}{5} - 1\frac{1}{2}$
2 Change each mixed number to an improper fraction.	$= \frac{21}{5} - \frac{3}{2}$
3 Write both fractions with the same denominator using equivalent fractions.	$= \frac{21 \times 2}{5 \times 2} - \frac{3 \times 5}{2 \times 5}$ $= \frac{42}{10} - \frac{15}{10}$
4 Subtract the second fraction from the first.	$= \frac{27}{10}$
5 Write the answer as a mixed number if appropriate.	$= 2\frac{7}{10}$

Negative fractions

- Positive and negative numbers have both size and direction, so they are often called **directed numbers**.
- Directed numbers include zero, integers and fractions.

WORKED EXAMPLE 4

Graph each of the following sets of directed numbers on a number line.

a $x > -2\frac{1}{2}$

b $x \leq 1\frac{3}{4}$

c $-2\frac{1}{3} < x \leq 3.4$

THINK

a $>$ means greater than, so x takes on all values to the right of $-2\frac{1}{2}$. Use an *open* or *unshaded* circle to indicate that the number itself is not included.

b $\leq$ means less than or equal to, so x takes on all values to the left of and including $1\frac{3}{4}$. Show all points fitting the description. Use a *closed* or *shaded* circle to show that the number itself is included.

c $-2\frac{1}{3} < x \leq 3.4$ means all numbers lying between the given boundaries, including 3.4 itself. Use an open dot to show that $-2\frac{1}{3}$ is not included and a closed dot to show that 3.4 is included. Use estimation to locate the boundary points.

WRITE

a

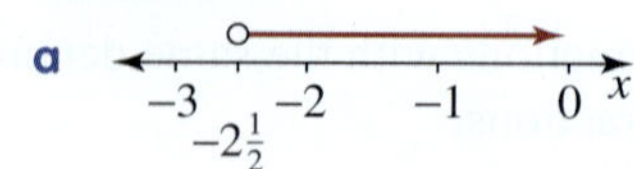

b

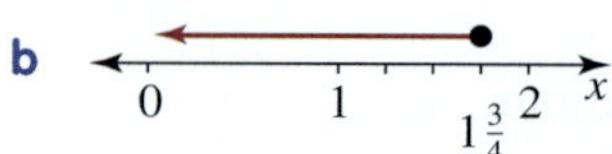

c

−3 −2 −1 0 1 2 3 4 x

$-2\frac{1}{3}$ 3.4

Addition and subtraction of positive and negative fractions

- The rules for adding and subtracting integers apply to the addition and subtraction of positive and negative fractions.
  1. When adding same signs, add and keep the sign.
  2. When adding different signs, find the difference between the 'sign-less' numbers (that is ignoring the sign) then use the sign of the number furthest from zero.
  3. When subtracting, add the opposite.
- The rules for addition and subtraction of fractions apply:
  Write all fractions with the same denominator, then add or subtract the numerators:
  $\frac{2}{3} + \frac{1}{2} = \frac{4}{6} + \frac{3}{6} = \frac{7}{6} = 1\frac{1}{6}$.

WORKED EXAMPLE 5

Calculate $-\frac{1}{3} + \frac{1}{2}$**.**

THINK / **WRITE**

1. Write the expression. — $-\frac{1}{3} + \frac{1}{2}$
2. Write both fractions with the same denominator. — $= -\frac{2}{6} + \frac{3}{6}$
3. Add the numerators.
   Note: They are different signs, so find the difference and use the sign of the number furthest from zero. — $= \frac{1}{6}$
4. Write the answer.

WORKED EXAMPLE 6

Calculate $-\frac{3}{4}-\frac{1}{6}$.

THINK	WRITE
1 Write the expression.	$-\frac{3}{4}-\frac{1}{6}$
2 To subtract, add the opposite.	$=-\frac{3}{4}+-\frac{1}{6}$
3 Write both fractions with the same denominator.	$=-\frac{9}{12}+-\frac{2}{12}$
4 Add the numerators. *Note:* They are the same sign, so add and keep the sign.	$=-\frac{11}{12}$
5 Write the answer.	

REMEMBER

1. The real number system contains the set of rational and irrational numbers. It can be denoted by the symbol R. Fractions are rational numbers.
2. To add or subtract fractions with the same denominator, add or subtract the numerators.
3. To add or subtract fractions with different denominators, make the denominators the same by using equivalent fractions and then add or subtract.
4. To add or subtract mixed numbers, change the mixed numbers to improper fractions and then add or subtract.
5. *Addition.* Write all fractions with the same denominator, then add numerators. If the sign is the same, add and keep the sign. If the sign is different, then find the difference between the signless numbers and use the sign furthest from zero.
   Opposites add to zero.
6. *Subtraction.* Write all fractions with the same denominator, then subtract numerators by adding the opposite.

EXERCISE 4A Addition and subtraction of fractions

FLUENCY

1 WE1 Simplify the following.

a $\frac{2}{5}+\frac{1}{4}$ **b** $\frac{3}{4}+\frac{5}{8}$ **c** $\frac{6}{10}-\frac{2}{5}$ **d** $\frac{8}{25}+\frac{34}{50}-\frac{7}{25}$

e $\frac{3}{4}+\frac{5}{6}$ **f** $\frac{9}{10}-\frac{2}{7}$ **g** $\frac{8}{12}+\frac{5}{7}-\frac{1}{2}$ **h** $\frac{21}{30}+\frac{5}{6}+\frac{9}{10}$

2 Simplify the following fractions, working from left to right.

a $\frac{3}{17}+\frac{6}{17}$ **b** $\frac{21}{27}-\frac{16}{27}$ **c** $\frac{6}{17}+\frac{2}{17}+\frac{4}{17}$ **d** $\frac{3}{15}+\frac{11}{15}-\frac{2}{15}$

INDIVIDUAL PATHWAYS

eBook*plus*

Activity 4-A-1
Addition and subtraction of fractions
doc-6864

Activity 4-A-2
More addition and subtraction of fractions
doc-6865

Activity 4-A-3
Advanced addition and subtraction of fractions
doc-6866

3 Simplify the following fractions, writing the answer as a mixed number if appropriate.

a $\frac{3}{5}+\frac{4}{5}$ **b** $\frac{7}{8}+\frac{3}{8}$ **c** $\frac{7}{8}+\frac{3}{8}+\frac{6}{8}$ **d** $\frac{41}{50}-\frac{24}{50}+\frac{6}{50}$

4 **WE2** Calculate the following and check answers with the aid of a calculator.

a $2\frac{3}{5}-4\frac{1}{5}$ **b** $6\frac{7}{9}-3\frac{5}{9}$ **c** $8\frac{4}{5}-4\frac{1}{5}$

d $8\frac{5}{6}-4\frac{1}{6}$ **e** $6\frac{7}{8}-4\frac{3}{8}$ **f** $1\frac{4}{9}+5\frac{5}{9}$

g $6\frac{1}{4}+3\frac{2}{8}$ **h** $12\frac{2}{5}+8\frac{7}{9}$ **i** $4\frac{3}{4}-5\frac{1}{6}+3\frac{2}{12}$

j $1\frac{2}{5}+3\frac{1}{3}-2\frac{4}{15}$

5 **WE3** Calculate the following and check answers with the aid of a calculator.

a $5\frac{3}{5}-2\frac{3}{10}$ **b** $6\frac{1}{2}-3\frac{5}{6}$

c $10\frac{1}{4}-5\frac{2}{5}$ **d** $4\frac{1}{8}-2\frac{3}{5}$

6 **WE4** Graph each of the following sets of directed numbers on a number line.

a $x>-3\frac{1}{2}$ **b** $x<-2\frac{1}{3}$ **c** $x\geq-4.5$

d $x\leq 6.25$ **e** $-2<x<1$ **f** $-1\frac{2}{3}<x\leq\frac{1}{2}$

g $-6\frac{3}{4}\leq x<-4\frac{1}{2}$ **h** $x\geq 2.75$ **i** $x<-1\frac{4}{5}$

j $2\frac{3}{5}\leq x\leq 3.8$

7 Describe the directed numbers graphed on each number line. Use number sentences such as: $x>-2\frac{1}{2}$, $x\leq 4.8$ and so on.

a -2 $-1\frac{1}{2}$ -1 0

b 5 6 $6\frac{3}{4}$ 7

c -8 $-7\frac{1}{2}$ -7 $-6\frac{1}{3}$ -6

d -1 0 $\frac{2}{3}$ 1

e -5 -4 -3

f 10 11 12

g -9 -8

h -3 -2 -1 0 1

8 Arrange the following in ascending order.

a $6, -3, 0, 5.8, -4\frac{1}{2}$ **b** $3\frac{2}{3}, -1, -4.2, 1\frac{1}{2}, -\frac{3}{4}$

c $0, -\frac{2}{3}, \frac{1}{4}, -6.8, -8.6$

9 **WE5** Calculate.

a $-\frac{3}{5}+\frac{1}{5}$ **b** $-\frac{3}{8}+-\frac{5}{8}$ **c** $\frac{1}{4}+-\frac{1}{2}$

d $-\frac{1}{6}+-\frac{2}{3}$ **e** $\frac{1}{2}+-\frac{3}{8}$ **f** $-\frac{1}{2}+-\frac{1}{3}$

g $-\frac{3}{5}+\frac{1}{2}$ **h** $\frac{3}{4}+-\frac{1}{3}$ **i** $-2\frac{1}{2}+-1\frac{3}{4}$

j $1\frac{2}{3}+-2\frac{3}{5}$ **k** $-2\frac{1}{2}-3\frac{1}{3}$ **l** $3\frac{1}{4}+1\frac{3}{5}$

eBook*plus*

Interactivity
Adding and subtracting fractions
int-2357

10 WE6 Calculate.

a $\frac{1}{2}-\frac{3}{4}$ b $-\frac{1}{2}-\frac{1}{3}$ c $-\frac{1}{3}-\frac{2}{5}$
d $-\frac{3}{4}--\frac{2}{5}$ e $2\frac{1}{2}-3\frac{1}{4}$ f $-3\frac{3}{5}--1\frac{1}{3}$

UNDERSTANDING

11 If Mary eats $\frac{5}{8}$ of a block of chocolate for afternoon tea and $\frac{3}{8}$ after dinner, how much of the block has she eaten altogether?

12 Seven bottles of soft drink were put out onto the table at a birthday party. How much soft drink was left over after $5\frac{2}{9}$ bottles were consumed?

REASONING

13 Frank has a part-time job at the local newsagency. If he spends $\frac{1}{3}$ of his pay on comic books, and $\frac{2}{5}$ on lollies, what fraction of his pay does he have left over?

14 In my class, $\frac{1}{3}$ of the students ride their bikes to school, $\frac{1}{4}$ catch the bus and the rest get a lift. What fraction of my class get a lift to school?

15 A Year 8 class organised a cake stall to raise some money. If they had 10 whole cakes to start with, sold $2\frac{3}{4}$ cakes at recess and then $5\frac{7}{8}$ at lunch time, how much cake was left over?

REFLECTION
Why do we normally leave the answer as a mixed number instead of an improper fraction?

4B Multiplication and division of fractions

Multiplication of fractions

- Change mixed numbers to improper fractions before multiplying.
- Multiply the numerators and multiply the denominators.

WORKED EXAMPLE 7

Simplify $2\frac{1}{4}\times 1\frac{5}{7}$.

THINK	WRITE
1 Write the question.	$2\frac{1}{4}\times 1\frac{5}{7}$
2 Change the mixed numbers to improper fractions and cancel if possible.	$=\frac{9}{\cancel{4}^{1}}\times\frac{\cancel{12}^{3}}{7}$
3 Multiply the numerators and then multiply the denominators.	$=\frac{27}{7}$
4 Change to a mixed number and simplify if appropriate.	$=3\frac{6}{7}$

- To divide by a fraction, multiply by the reciprocal.

WORKED EXAMPLE 8

Find $2\frac{1}{4} \div \frac{3}{8}$.

THINK	WRITE
1 Write the question.	$2\frac{1}{4} \div \frac{3}{8}$
2 Change mixed numbers to improper fractions.	$= \frac{9}{4} \div \frac{3}{8}$
3 Change ÷ to × and tip the second fraction, (× and tip), and cancel if appropriate.	$= \frac{\not{9}^{3}}{\not{4}^{1}} \times \frac{\not{8}^{2}}{\not{3}^{1}}$
4 Multiply the numerators and then multiply the denominators.	$= \frac{3}{1} \times \frac{2}{1}$
5 Simplify if appropriate.	$= 6$

Multiplication and division of positive and negative fractions

- To multiply fractions, express any mixed numbers as improper fractions. Multiply the numerators and denominators, applying the rules for multiplying positive and negative numbers.

WORKED EXAMPLE 9

Simplify $\frac{2}{5} \times -\frac{5}{8}$.

THINK	WRITE
1 Write the expression and cancel the common factors in numerators and denominators.	$\frac{\not{2}^{1}}{\not{5}^{1}} \times \frac{-\not{5}^{1}}{\not{8}^{4}}$
2 Multiply the numerators and then multiply the denominators. *Note:* positive × negative = negative	$= \frac{1}{1} \times -\frac{1}{4}$
3 Write the answer.	$= -\frac{1}{4}$

- When dividing by a fraction, express any mixed numbers as improper fractions and multiply by the reciprocal.

WORKED EXAMPLE 10

Evaluate $-\frac{3}{4} \div -1\frac{1}{2}$.

THINK	WRITE
1 Write the expression using a division sign.	$-\frac{3}{4} \div -1\frac{1}{2}$
2 Change the divisor to an improper fraction.	$= -\frac{3}{4} \div -\frac{3}{2}$

3 Change ÷ to ×, tip the divisor (multiply and tip) and cancel common factors in numerators and denominators. $= -\frac{\cancel{3}^1}{\cancel{4}^2} \times -\frac{\cancel{2}^1}{\cancel{3}^1}$

4 Multiply the numerators and then multiply the denominators. *Note:* negative × negative = positive $= -\frac{1}{2} \times -\frac{1}{1}$

5 Write the answer. $= \frac{1}{2}$

REMEMBER

1. *Multiplication*. Cancel common factors in numerators and denominators then multiply numerators and multiply denominators. If the signs are the same, the result is positive. If the signs are different, the result is negative.
2. *Division*. Change ÷ to × and invert the divisor, then follow the rules for multiplication. If mixed numbers are involved in multiplication and division of fractions, change them to improper fractions.

EXERCISE 4B Multiplication and division of fractions

INDIVIDUAL PATHWAYS

eBook plus

Activity 4-B-1 Multiplication and division of fractions doc-6867

Activity 4-B-2 More multiplication and division of fractions doc-6868

Activity 4-B-3 Advanced multiplication and division of fractions doc-6869

FLUENCY

1 Simplify the following.

a $\frac{3}{4} \times \frac{1}{2}$ b $\frac{1}{8} \times \frac{1}{7}$ c $\frac{2}{5} \times \frac{3}{5}$

d $\frac{5}{7} \times \frac{1}{3}$ e $\frac{1}{2} \times \frac{5}{6}$ f $\frac{3}{7} \times \frac{7}{9}$

g $\frac{11}{20} \times \frac{2}{3}$ h $\frac{1}{3} \times \frac{3}{5}$ i $\frac{5}{8} \times \frac{11}{20}$

j $\frac{2}{3} \times \frac{9}{10}$ k $\frac{6}{7} \times \frac{14}{15}$ l $\frac{5}{6} \times \frac{3}{10}$

2 WE7 Simplify the following and check your answers with the aid of a calculator.

a $3\frac{1}{2} \times 1\frac{3}{5}$ b $1\frac{2}{10} \times 1\frac{1}{5}$ c $2\frac{2}{3} \times 1\frac{1}{2}$

d $3\frac{2}{4} \times 2\frac{1}{2}$ e $8\frac{9}{10} \times \frac{7}{10}$ f $5\frac{3}{4} \times 2\frac{2}{5}$

g $6 \times 2\frac{1}{6}$ h $1\frac{3}{5} \times \frac{5}{8}$ i $4\frac{3}{4} \times 2\frac{1}{2}$

3 Simplify the following.

a $\frac{1}{3} \div \frac{1}{2}$ b $\frac{7}{8} \div \frac{3}{2}$ c $\frac{4}{14} \div \frac{1}{3}$

d $\frac{2}{5} \div \frac{1}{4}$ e $\frac{3}{4} \div \frac{7}{8}$ f $\frac{5}{6} \div \frac{8}{9}$

g $\frac{12}{15} \div \frac{4}{3}$ h $\frac{1}{5} \div \frac{10}{12}$ i $\frac{3}{4} \div \frac{3}{8}$

eBook plus

Interactivity **Dividing fractions** int-2358

4 WE8 Find the following.

a $1\frac{6}{10} \div 1\frac{3}{5}$ b $3\frac{5}{7} \div 2\frac{1}{6}$ c $1\frac{1}{6} \div \frac{2}{1}$

d $1\frac{5}{7} \div \frac{1}{3}$
e $1\frac{1}{3} \div \frac{5}{6}$
f $\frac{7}{9} \div 1\frac{7}{18}$
g $3\frac{1}{2} \div 1\frac{3}{5}$
h $10\frac{4}{5} \div 2\frac{1}{2}$
i $7\frac{8}{9} \div 7\frac{1}{2}$

5 WE9 Simplify.

a $-\frac{1}{2} \times \frac{1}{3}$
b $-\frac{3}{4} \times -\frac{1}{5}$
c $-\frac{2}{3} \times 7$
d $\frac{1}{3} \times -\frac{3}{4}$
e $-\frac{3}{4} \times \frac{5}{6}$
f $-\frac{5}{6} \times \frac{3}{10}$
g $-\frac{8}{9} \times 1\frac{3}{4}$
h $-3\frac{1}{7} \times -\frac{7}{8}$
i $-2\frac{1}{2} \times \frac{4}{5}$

eBook*plus*

Digital doc
Spreadsheet
Four operations with fractions
doc-2130

6 WE10 Evaluate the following.

a $-\frac{1}{5} \div \frac{1}{2}$
b $\frac{2}{3} \div -\frac{3}{4}$
c $-\frac{7}{4} \div -\frac{2}{1}$
d $\frac{3}{2} \div -4$
e $-\frac{1}{8} \div \frac{3}{4}$
f $-1\frac{4}{5} \div 6$
g $-2\frac{1}{4} \div -\frac{1}{2}$
h $2\frac{2}{3} \div -1\frac{1}{9}$
i $-\frac{3}{5} \div 2\frac{5}{8}$

UNDERSTANDING

7 Find $\frac{3}{4}$ of 16. ('of' has the same meaning as multiplying.)

8 An assortment of 75 lollies is to be divided evenly among 5 children.

a What fraction of the total number of lollies will each child receive?
b How many lollies will each child receive?

9 Evaluate the following.

a $-\frac{2}{3} + \frac{1}{6} \times -\frac{2}{5}$
b $1\frac{1}{2} \times -\frac{5}{6} \div \frac{4}{7}$
c $-\frac{7}{8} \div -1\frac{3}{4} - \frac{1}{2}$
d $\left(\frac{2}{5} - \frac{6}{7}\right) \times -3\frac{1}{3}$
e $\left(-1\frac{1}{2} - 3\frac{4}{5}\right) \div \frac{3}{5}$
f $\frac{9}{10} \times -\frac{5}{3} \div \left(1\frac{2}{7} - 2\frac{1}{2}\right)$

REASONING

10 Sam has been collecting caps from all around the world. If he has a total of 160 caps and $\frac{1}{5}$ of them are from the USA, how many non-American caps does he have?

11 In the staff room there is $\frac{7}{8}$ of a cake left over from a meeting. If 14 members of staff would all like a piece, what fraction will they each receive?

12 Year 8's cake stall raised $120. If they plan to give $\frac{1}{4}$ to a children's charity, and $\frac{2}{3}$ to a charity for the prevention of cruelty to animals, how much will each group receive and how much is left over?

eBook*plus*

Digital doc
WorkSHEET 4.1
doc-6870

REFLECTION
Do the rules of operation order apply to positive and negative fractions?

4C Terminating and recurring decimals

Fractions to decimals

- Numbers that can be written as fractions are called rational numbers.
- To write a fraction as a decimal, divide the numerator by the denominator.
- Fractions expressed as decimals will be **terminating decimals**, which have a fixed number of decimal places; or **recurring decimals**, which have an infinite number of decimal places.
- Recurring decimals that have one recurring digit are written with a dot above the recurring digit. Recurring decimals with more than one digit are written with a line above the recurring digits:
  $0.3\,3\,3\,3\,3\,3\ldots\ldots = 0.\dot{3}$
  $0.484848\ldots\ldots = 0.\overline{48}$
- If the only factors of the denominator are powers of 2 or 5, you will be able to find an exact decimal equivalent.
- Unless you are told otherwise, round to 2 decimal places.
- Negative fractions are converted using the same method (remember that a negative fraction will result in a negative decimal).
- A calculator can also be used to convert fractions to decimals.

WORKED EXAMPLE 11

Convert the following fractions to decimals. State if the decimal is a recurring decimal or a terminating decimal.

a $\frac{1}{5}$ **b** $4\frac{5}{12}$ **c** $-\frac{5}{8}$ **d** $\frac{2}{3}$

THINK	WRITE
a 1 Write the question.	**a** $\frac{1}{5}$
2 Rewrite the question using division.	$= 1 \div 5$
3 Divide, adding zeros as required.	$5\overline{)1.0}$ = 0.2
4 Write the answer.	$\frac{1}{5} = 0.2$ This is a terminating decimal.
b 1 Write the question.	**b** $4\frac{5}{12}$
2 Convert mixed numbers to improper fractions.	$= \frac{53}{12}$
3 Rewrite the question using division.	$= 53 \div 12$
4 Since 12 is not a power of 2 or 5, it will be a recurring decimal.	
5 Divide, adding zeros so until a pattern occurs.	$12\overline{)53.{}^{5}0{}^{2}0{}^{8}0{}^{8}0{}^{8}0}$ = 4. 4 1 6 6 6
6 Write the answer with a dot above the recurring number.	$4\frac{5}{12} = 4.41\dot{6}$ This is a recurring decimal.
c 1 The size of the decimal will be the same as for $\frac{5}{8}$.	**c** $\frac{5}{8}$
2 Rewrite the question using division.	$= 5 \div 8$
3 $8 = 2^3$, so an exact answer will be found. Divide, adding zeros as required.	$8\overline{)5.{}^{5}0{}^{2}0{}^{4}0}$ = 0. 6 2 5

THINK	WRITE
4 Write the answer, remembering that the original fraction was negative.	$-\frac{5}{8} = -0.625$ This is a terminating decimal.
d 1 Rewrite the question using division.	**d** $\frac{2}{3} = 2 \div 3$
2 Since 3 is not a power of 2 or 5, it will be a recurring decimal.	$3\overline{)2.000}$ = .666
3 Write the answer, remembering to place a dot above the recurring number.	$\frac{2}{3} = 0.\dot{6}$ This is a recurring decimal.

- When changing a decimal to a fraction, rewrite the decimal as a fraction with the same number of zeros in the denominator as there are decimal places in the question. Simplify the fraction by cancelling.
- If the decimal has a whole part, it is easier to write it in expanded form; for example, $2.365 = 2 + 0.365$
- Negative decimals are converted using the same method (remember that a negative decimal will result in a negative fraction).

WORKED EXAMPLE 12

Convert the following decimals to fractions in simplest form.
a 0.25 b 1.342 c −0.8

THINK	WRITE
a 1 Write the question.	**a** 0.25
2 Rewrite as a fraction with the same number of zeros in the denominator as there are decimal places in the question. Simplify the fraction by cancelling.	$= \frac{\cancel{25}^{1}}{\cancel{100}^{4}}$
3 Write the answer.	$= \frac{1}{4}$
b 1 Write the question.	**b** 1.342
2 Rewrite the decimal in expanded form.	$= 1 + 0.342$
3 Write as a mixed number with the same number of zeros in the denominator as there are decimal places in the question and cancel.	$= 1 + \frac{\cancel{342}^{171}}{\cancel{1000}^{500}}$
4 Write the answer.	$= 1\frac{171}{500}$
c 1 Write the question.	**c** −0.8
2 Rewrite as a fraction with the same number of zeros in the denominator as there are decimal places in the question. Simplify the fraction by cancelling.	$= -\frac{\cancel{8}^{4}}{\cancel{10}^{5}}$
3 Write the answer.	$= -\frac{4}{5}$

REMEMBER

1. When changing fractions to decimals, divide the numerator of the fraction by the denominator and round the answer to 2 decimal places if it is not otherwise specified.
2. When changing a mixed number to a decimal, write it as an improper fraction before dividing.
3. When changing a decimal to a fraction, rewrite the decimal as a fraction with the same number of zeros in the denominator as there are decimal places in the question.
4. Simplify the fraction by cancelling.
5. Terminating decimals have a fixed number of decimal places.
6. Recurring decimals that have one recurring digit are written with a dot above the recurring digit. Recurring decimals with more than one digit are written with a line above the recurring digits.
7. The same rules apply when converting negative fractions and decimals.

EXERCISE 4C

Terminating and recurring decimals

INDIVIDUAL PATHWAYS

eBook*plus*

Activity 4-C-1 Fractions and decimals doc-6871

Activity 4-C-2 More fractions and decimals doc-6872

Activity 4-C-3 Advanced fractions and decimals doc-6873

FLUENCY

1 WE11a Convert the following fractions to decimals, giving exact answers or using the correct notation for recurring decimals where appropriate.

a $\frac{4}{5}$ **b** $\frac{1}{4}$ **c** $\frac{3}{4}$ **d** $\frac{5}{12}$ **e** $\frac{9}{11}$

f $\frac{21}{25}$ **g** $\frac{7}{4}$ **h** $\frac{13}{6}$ **i** $\frac{7}{15}$ **j** $\frac{2}{3}$

2 WE11b Convert the following mixed numbers to decimal numbers, giving exact answers, or using the correct notation for recurring decimals where appropriate. Check your answers using a calculator.

a $1\frac{5}{6}$ **b** $1\frac{3}{4}$ **c** $3\frac{2}{5}$ **d** $8\frac{4}{5}$ **e** $12\frac{9}{10}$

f $6\frac{3}{4}$ **g** $5\frac{2}{3}$ **h** $11\frac{11}{15}$ **i** $6\frac{1}{2}$ **j** $4\frac{1}{3}$

3 WE11c Convert the following fractions to decimal numbers, giving exact answers, or correct to 2 decimal places where appropriate.

a $-\frac{4}{5}$ **b** $-\frac{7}{9}$ **c** $-\frac{8}{5}$ **d** $-\frac{4}{15}$ **e** $-\frac{3}{8}$

f $-2\frac{1}{4}$ **g** $-6\frac{3}{5}$ **h** $-3\frac{1}{7}$ **i** $-1\frac{5}{6}$ **j** $-5\frac{8}{9}$

eBook*plus*

Digital docs
Spreadsheet **Converting fractions to decimals** doc-2131
Spreadsheet **Converting decimals to fractions** doc-2132

4 WE12 Convert the following decimal numbers to fractions in simplest form.

a 0.4 **b** 0.8 **c** 1.2 **d** 3.2 **e** 5.6
f 0.75 **g** 1.30 **h** 7.14 **i** 4.21 **j** 10.04
k 1.333 **l** 8.05 **m** 7.312 **n** 9.940 **o** 12.045
p 84.126 **q** 73.90 **r** 0.0042

5 Of the people at a school social $\frac{3}{4}$ were boys. Write this fraction as a decimal number.

UNDERSTANDING

6 On a recent science test Katarina worked the bonus question correctly as well as everything else, and her score was $\frac{110}{100}$. What is this as a decimal value?

7 Alison sold the greatest number of chocolates in her Scouting group. She sold $\frac{5}{9}$ of all chocolates sold by the group. Write this as a decimal number, correct to 2 decimal places.

8 Alfonzo ordered a pizza to share with three friends, but he ate 0.6 of it. What fraction was left for his friends?

9 Using examples, explain the difference between rational and irrational numbers.

REFLECTION

How would you decide whether it is better to write a number as a fraction or a decimal?

4D Addition and subtraction of decimals

Addition and subtraction of positive decimals

- When decimals are being added or subtracted, the decimal points are lined up one underneath the other.

WORKED EXAMPLE 13

Find 4.622 + 38 + 210.07 + 21.309.

THINK	WRITE
Write the numbers one underneath the other with the decimal points lined up and fill the spaces with zeros. Then add as for whole numbers putting the decimal point in the answer directly under the decimal points in the question.	$$\begin{array}{r} 4.622 \\ 38.000 \\ 210.070 \\ +\ 2_1 1_1 . 3_1 0_1 9 \\ \hline 274.001 \end{array}$$

WORKED EXAMPLE 14

Find 37.6 – 12.043.

THINK	WRITE
Write the numbers one under the other with the larger number on top and the decimal points lined up. Add in the required zeros and subtract using the method shown.	$$\begin{array}{r} 37.{}^{5}8{}^{9}0{}^{1}0 \\ -12.\ 043 \\ \hline 25.\ 557 \end{array}$$

Addition and subtraction of positive and negative decimals

- The rules for addition and subtraction of negative numbers apply.
  - To add two numbers with the same sign, add and keep the sign.
  - To add two numbers with different signs, find the difference between the signed numbers, then use the sign of the number further from 0.
  - To subtract a number, add the opposite.

WORKED EXAMPLE 15

Calculate: a $-3.64 + -2.9$ b $-5.7 + 2.4$ and check each answer by using estimation.

THINK	WRITE
a 1 Write the question in columns with the decimal points directly beneath each other. Include the zeros.	**a** $\begin{array}{r} -3.64 \\ +-2.90 \\ \hline -6.54 \end{array}$
2 They have the same sign, so add and keep the sign.	
3 Check the answer by using estimation.	$-4 + -3 = -7$
b 1 Repeat step 1 of part **a**.	**b** $\begin{array}{r} 5.7 \\ -2.4 \\ \hline 3.3 \end{array}$
2 They have different signs, so subtract the smaller number from the larger number and use the sign of the number furthest from zero.	$-5.7 + 2.4 = -3.3$
3 Check the answer by using estimation.	$-6 + 2 = -4$

WORKED EXAMPLE 16

Calculate $-5.307 - 0.62$ and check the answer by using estimation.

THINK	WRITE
1 Write the question.	$-5.307 - 0.62$
2 Change to addition of the opposite.	$= -5.307 + -0.62$
3 Rewrite the question in columns with the decimal points directly beneath each other. Include the zeros.	$\begin{array}{r} -5.307 \\ +-0.620 \\ \hline -5.927 \end{array}$
4 Evaluate.	
5 Check the answer by using estimation.	$-5 - 1 = -6$

REMEMBER

1. When adding and subtracting decimals, be sure that the *decimal points* are *lined up* one underneath the other.
2. The rules for addition and subtraction of positive and negative numbers apply.

EXERCISE
4D Addition and subtraction of decimals

INDIVIDUAL PATHWAYS

eBookplus

Activity 4-D-1
Addition and subtraction of decimals
doc-6874

Activity 4-D-2
More addition and subtraction of decimals
doc-6875

Activity 4-D-3
Advanced addition and subtraction of decimals
doc-6876

FLUENCY

1 WE13 Find the following.

a $8.3 + 4.6$ b $7.2 + 5.8$ c $16.45 + 3.23$
d $7.9 + 12.4$ e $13.06 + 4.2$ f $5.34 + 2.80$
g $128.09 + 4.35$ h $5.308 + 33.671 + 3.74$ i $0.93 + 4.009 + 1.3$
j $5.67 + 3 + 12.002$ k $56.830 + 2.504 + 0.1$ l $306 + 5.2 + 6.032 + 76.9$
m $25.3 + 89 + 4.087 + 7.77$ n $34.2 + 7076 + 2.056 + 1.3$

2 WE14 Find the following.

a $4.56 - 2.32$ b $19.97 - 12.65$ c $124.99 - 3.33$
d $63.872 - 9.051$ e $43.58 - 1.25$ f $1709.53 - 34.6$
g $87.25 - 34.09$ h $125.006 - 0.04$ i $24.86 - 1.963$
j $35 - 8.97$ k $42.1 - 9.072$ l $482 - 7.896$

3 a MC The difference between 47.09 and 21.962 is:
A 17.253 B 26.93 C 25.932 D 26.128 E 25.128

b The sum of 31.5 and 129.62 is:
A 98.12 B 161.12 C 150.12 D 444.62 E 132.77

4 Calculate the following.

a $56.3 + 52.09 + 6.7$ b $7.9 + 3 + 21.053$
c $908.52 - 87.04$ d $53.091 + 6 + 1895.2$
e $1495.945 - 2.07$ f $439.98 - 6$
g $7.286 + 5.4 + 2.083 + 1538.82$ h $12.784 - 3.9$
i $603.9 - 5.882$ j $3965.09 + 3.2 + 256 + 0.006$

eBookplus

Digital docs
Spreadsheet
Adding decimals
doc-2133
Spreadsheet
Subtracting decimals
doc-2134

5 WE15 Calculate the following and check each answer by using estimation.

a $-0.4 + -0.5$ b $0.2 + -0.9$
c $-0.8 + 0.23$ d $-0.021 + -0.97$
e $13.69 + -6.084$ f $-0.0037 + 0.638$

6 WE16 Calculate the following and check each answer by using estimation.

a $0.8 - 1.5$ b $-0.6 - 0.72$
c $-3 - -6.4$ d $-2.6 - 1.7$
e $-3.2 - -0.65$ f $0.084 - 0.902$

UNDERSTANDING

7 Round to the nearest whole number to find an approximate answer to the following.

a $33.2 + 4.8 - 10.5$ b $59.62 - 17.71 + 3.6$
c $29.5 - 15.3 + 5.7$ d $99.9 + 35.3 - 5.5$

8 a On a recent shopping trip, Salmah spent the following amounts: \$45.23, \$102.78, \$0.56 and \$8.65. How much did he spend altogether?

b If Salmah started with \$200.00, how much did he have left after the trip?

9 Dagmar is in training for the school athletic carnival. The first time she ran the 400 m it took her 187.04 seconds. After a week of intensive training she had reduced her time to 145.67 seconds. By how much had she cut her time?

10 Kathie runs each morning before school. On Monday she ran 1.23 km, on Tuesday she ran 3.09 km, she rested on Wednesday and on both Thursday and Friday she ran 2.78 km. How many kilometres has she run for the week?

REASONING

11 Students in your school are planning to raise money for a needy cause by holding running days for different Year levels. They hope to run a total of 1946 km.

The Year 7s ran 278.2 km, the Year 8s ran 378.4 km and the Year 9s ran 526 km. How many more kilometres must the students run to reach their goal?

12 A group of bushwalkers — Alan, Brett, Chris and Dan — were staying at Wilson's Promontory. From their camp at Tidal River, they wanted to walk 8.2 km to Barry Creek. At the 5-km mark, Dan developed blisters because he had incorrect footwear and was accompanied back 3.8 km by Alan. There they met another walking group who had band aids with them. After fixing Dan's feet, Dan and Alan decided to walk back past their Tidal River camp and continue on another 2.1 km until they came to Three Mile Beach. How far did they have to walk to get back to Tidal River after Dan fixed his blisters? How far apart are Barry Creek and Three Mile Beach? Draw a strip map of the walks, indicating all relevant stops and information. If Alan and Dan had decided to meet Chris and Brett instead of going to Three Mile Beach, how far would they have walked in total to get to Barry Creek?

13 During 2007, international visitors to Australia spent \$58.3 billion. During 2008, international visitors spent \$47.8 billion. By how much did spending by international visitors increase or decrease from 2007 to 2008?

REFLECTION

When decimals are being added, why are the decimal points lined up one underneath the other?

4E Multiplication and division of decimals

Multiplication of positive decimals

- To multiply decimals, ignore the decimal point and multiply as for whole numbers. Count the number of digits after the decimal point in each of the multiplying numbers, then add these together to find the number of decimal places in the answer.
- It is a good idea to estimate the answer to make sure that your answer makes sense.

WORKED EXAMPLE 17

Calculate, giving an exact answer, 125.678 × 0.23.

THINK	WRITE
1 Write the numbers with the larger one on top. Multiply, starting with the last digit and ignoring the decimal point.	1 1 1 1 1 2 2 2 12 5678 × 023 37 7034 $251_1 3560$ 289 0594
2 Count the number of digits after the decimal point in each of the multiplying numbers and use this total as the number of decimal places in the answer. There are 3 decimal places in 125.678 and 2 in 0.23 so there will be 5 decimal places in the answer.	125.678 × 0.23 = 28.905 94

Division of positive decimals

- When dividing decimals, make sure that the divisor (the number you are dividing by) is a whole number.
- If the divisor is not a whole number, make it a whole number be either:
  - writing the question as a fraction and multiplying the numerator and denominator by an appropriate power of 10, or
  - multiplying the dividend and divisor by an appropriate power of 10.
- Once the divisor is a whole number, divide the numbers as usual, making sure the decimal point in the answer is directly above the decimal point in the question.
- Extra zeros can be placed after the decimal point in the dividend if needed.

WORKED EXAMPLE 18

Calculate:

a 54.6 ÷ 8

b 89.356 ÷ 0.06.

Give answers correct to 2 decimal places.

THINK		WRITE
a 1	Write the question as shown, adding zeros to one more decimal place than is required. Write the decimal point in the answer directly above the decimal point in the question and divide as for short division.	**a** $8\overline{)54.{}^{6}6{}^{2}0{}^{4}0}$ quotient 6. 8 2 5
2	Write the question and answer, rounded to the required number of decimal places.	54.6 ÷ 8 ≈ 6.83 (2 decimal places)
b 1	Write the question.	**b** 89.356 ÷ 0.06
2	Multiply both parts by an appropriate multiple of 10 so that the divisor is a whole number. (In this case, 100.)	= (89.356 × 100) ÷ (0.06 × 100) = 8935.6 ÷ 6
3	Divide, adding zeros to one more decimal place than required. Write the decimal point in the answer directly above the decimal point in the question and divide as for short division.	$6\overline{)8{}^{2}9{}^{5}3{}^{5}5.{}^{1}6{}^{4}0{}^{4}0}$ quotient 1 4 8 9. 2 6 6
4	Write the question and answer, rounded to the required number of decimal places.	89.356 ÷ 0.06 ≈ 1489.27 (2 decimal places)

Multiplication and division of positive and negative decimals

- When positive and negative decimals are being multiplied and divided, the rules for multiplying and dividing positive and numbers apply.
  - If both numbers are positive or negative, the result is positive.
  - If one number is positive and the other is negative, the result is negative.

WORKED EXAMPLE 19

Simplify -3.8×0.05.

THINK	WRITE
1 Multiply as for whole numbers.	$\begin{array}{r} {}^{4}3\ 8 \\ \times 5 \\ \hline 190 \end{array}$
2 Count the number of decimal places in the question and insert the decimal point. The signs are different, so insert a negative sign in the answer.	$-3.8 \times 0.05 = -0.190$ $= -0.19$

WORKED EXAMPLE 20

Find the quotient of $-0.015 \div -0.4$, giving an exact answer.

THINK	WRITE
1 Write the question.	$-0.015 \div -0.4$ $= -(0.015 \times 10) \div -(0.4 \times 10)$
2 Multiply both parts by 10 to produce a whole number divisor.	$= -0.15 \div -4$
3 Divide until an exact answer is achieved or until a recurring pattern is evident.	$\begin{array}{r} 0.03\ 7\ 5 \\ 4\overline{)0.15^{3}0^{2}0} \end{array}$
4 The signs are the same, so the answer is positive.	$-0.015 \div -0.4 = 0.0375$

REMEMBER

1. When multiplying decimals, count the number of digits after the decimal point in each of the numbers being multiplied and add these together to find the total number of decimal points in the answer.
2. When dividing, make sure that the divisor is a whole number.
3. When the divisor is a decimal, make it a whole number either by:
   (a) writing the question as a fraction and multiplying the numerator and denominator by a power of 10, or
   (b) multiplying both dividend and divisor by an appropriate power of ten.
4. When dividing decimals by a whole number, place the decimal point in the answer directly in line with the decimal point in the question.
5. When positive and negative decimals are being multiplied and divided, the rules for multiplying and dividing positive and negative integers apply.

EXERCISE
4E Multiplication and division of decimals

INDIVIDUAL PATHWAYS

eBook*plus*

Activity 4-E-1
Multiplication and division of decimals
doc-6877

Activity 4-E-2
More multiplication and division of decimals
doc-6878

Activity 4-E-3
Advanced multiplication and division of decimals
doc-6879

FLUENCY

1 WE17 Calculate the following giving an exact answer.

a 6.2×0.8 b 7.9×1.2 c 65.7×3.2
d 109.5×5.6 e 5.09×0.4 f 32.76×2.4
g 123.97×4.7 h 576.98×2 i 3.4×642.1
j 0.6×67.9 k 23.4×6.7 l 0.006×43.6
m 52.003×12 n 22.97×0.015 o 13.42×0.011

2 WE18a Calculate the following. Give answers correct to 2 decimal places.

a $43.2 \div 7$ b $523.9 \div 4$ c $6321.09 \div 8$
d $286.634 \div 3$ e $76.96 \div 12$ f $27.8403 \div 11$

3 WE18b Calculate the following. Give answers correct to 2 decimal places, where appropriate.

a $53.3 \div 0.6$ b $960.43 \div 0.5$ c $21.42 \div 0.004$
d $3219.09 \div 0.006$ e $478.94 \div 0.016$ f $76.327 \div 0.000\,08$
g $25.865 \div 0.004$ h $26.976 \div 0.0003$ i $0.0673 \div 0.0005$
j $12.000\,53 \div 0.007$ k $35.064 \div 0.005$ l $0.059 \div 0.009$

4 WE19 Simplify each of the following.

a 0.3×-0.2 b -0.8×0.9 c -0.4×-0.06
d $(-0.6)^2$ e $(-0.3)^2$ f -0.004×40
g 4000×-0.5 h -0.02×-0.4 i $(-0.05)^2$
j -4.9×0.06 k $(0.2)^2 \times -40$ l $(1.2)^2 \times (0.3)^2$

eBook*plus*

Digital docs
Spreadsheet
Multiplying decimals
doc-2135

Spreadsheet
Dividing decimals
doc-2136

5 WE20 Find the quotient of each of the following, giving an exact answer.

a $-8.4 \div 0.2$ b $0.15 \div -0.5$
c $-0.0405 \div -0.3$ d $-15 \div 0.5$
e $0.049 \div -0.07$ f $-3.2 \div -0.008$
g $-0.0036 \div 0.06$ h $270 \div -0.03$
i $-0.04 \div -800$ j $0.8 \div -0.16$
k $(1.2)^2 \div 0.04$ l $(1.5)^2 \div 0.05$

UNDERSTANDING

6 Evaluate the following, giving the answer correct to 1 decimal place.

a $4.6 \times 2.1 + 1.2 \times 3.5$ b $5.9 \times 1.8 - 2.4 \times 3.8$
c $6.2 + 4.5 \div 0.5 - 7.6$ d $11.4 - 7.6 \times 1.5 + 2$

7 a MC $\frac{1}{2}(3.6 + 1.4 \times 7.5)$ is equal to:

A 18.75 B 14.1 C 9.375
D 7.05 E 28.2

b Rounded to 2 decimal places, $\frac{3}{4}(10.5 - 5.8 \div 4 \times 1.2)$ is equal to:

A 1.06 B 6.57 C 0.73
D 11.68 E 2.19

8 Round each of the following to the nearest whole number to find an estimate.

a $3.5 \times 24.9 + 33.2$ b $4.8 \times 19.6 - 10.4$
c $15.6 + 50.1 \times 9.5 - 15.4$ d $49.8 - 20.3 \div 4.7$

9 A group of 21 Year 8 students were going on an excursion to the planetarium. If the total cost is \$111.30, how much would each student have to pay?

10 Simplify $\frac{0.16}{0.28} \times \frac{56}{3.2}$.

11 Your car's tank holds 55 litres of fuel. The car consumes 7.6 L of fuel for each 100 km travelled. You make a journey from Brisbane to Uki in northern NSW, a distance of 145 km. How much fuel is left in the tank after the journey?

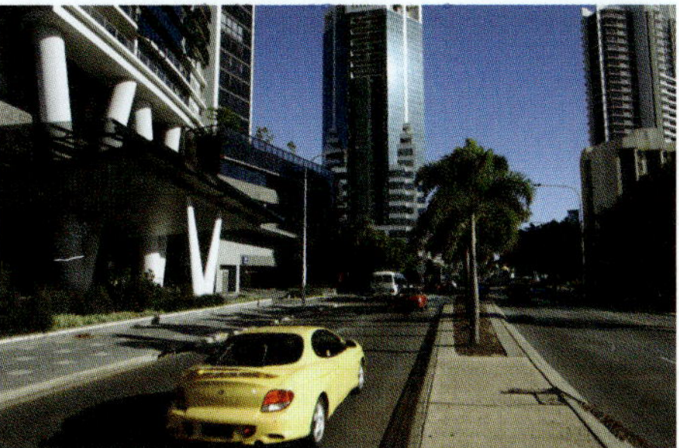

REFLECTION

Why is it a good idea to make an estimate of the answer when you are multiplying decimals?

12 Find the decimal exactly halfway between 2.01 and 2.02.

4F Percentages, fractions and decimals

See *Maths Quest 7* Chapter 10 for further examples of working with percentages.

- The term **per cent** means 'per hundred'.
- The symbol for percentage is %. For example, 60% means 60 parts out of 100 parts.
- Percentages, fractions and decimals are different ways of expressing the same quantity.
- Percentage is another way of writing a fraction with a denominator of 100, or of writing the number of hundredths in a decimal.

$$60\% = \frac{60}{100} = 0.60$$

- There are a number of common percentages, and their fraction and decimal equivalents, with which you should be familiar.

Percentage	Fraction	Decimal
50%	$\frac{1}{2}$	0.5
25%	$\frac{1}{4}$	0.25
75%	$\frac{3}{4}$	0.75
$33\frac{1}{3}\%$	$\frac{1}{3}$	$0.\dot{3}$
100%	1	1

WORKED EXAMPLE 21

Convert the following percentages to fractions and then decimals.

a 67% **b** 55%

THINK

a 1 To convert to a fraction, write the percentage, then change it to a fraction with a denominator of 100.

2 To convert 67% to a decimal, think of it as 67.0%, then divide it by 100 by moving the decimal point two places to the left.

WRITE

a $67\% = \frac{67}{100}$

$67\% = 0.67$

b 1 To convert 55% to a fraction, write the percentage, then change it to a fraction by adding a denominator of 100. | **b** $55\% = \frac{55}{100}$

2 This is not in simplest form, so cancel by dividing the numerator and the denominator by 5. | $55\% = \frac{55}{100} = \frac{11}{20}$

3 To convert 55% to a decimal, think of it as 55.0%, then divide it by 100 by moving the decimal point two places to the left. | $55\% = 0.55$

- The easiest method of comparing percentages, fractions and decimals is to convert all of them to their decimal form and use place values to compare them.

WORKED EXAMPLE 22

Place the following quantities in ascending order, and then place them on a number line.
$45\%, \frac{7}{10}, 0.36, 80\%, 2\frac{1}{2}, 110\%, 1.54$

THINK	WRITE
1 Convert all of the quantities into their decimal equivalents.	0.45, 0.7, 0.36, 0.80, 2.5, 1.10, 1.54
2 Place them in ascending order.	0.36, 0.45, 0.7, 0.80, 1.10, 1.54, 2.5
3 Place them in ascending order in their original form.	$0.36, 45\%, \frac{7}{10}, 80\%, 110\%, 1.54, 2\frac{1}{2}$
4 Draw a number line from 0 to 3, with increments of 0.25.	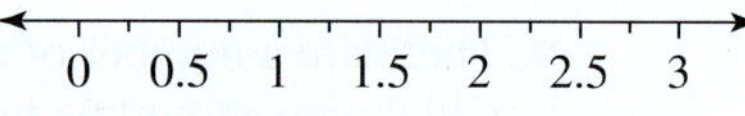
5 Place the numbers on the number line.	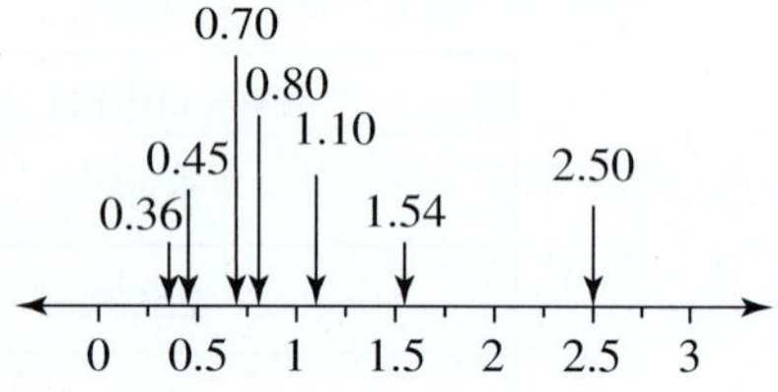

Percentage increases and decreases

- Percentage increases and decreases can be used to calculate and compare prices, mark ups, discounts, population changes, company profits and many other quantities.

WORKED EXAMPLE 23

Calculate the percentage increase when 52 increases to 72.

THINK	WRITE
1 The difference between 52 and 72 is 20.	$72 - 52 = 20$
2 The percentage increase can be calculated by creating the fraction 20 out of 52 and then multiplying by 100.	$\frac{20}{52} \times 100 = 10.4$
3 Write the answer.	The percentage increase is 10.4%.

WORKED EXAMPLE 24

Calculate the percentage decrease when the population of a town falls from 62 000 people to 48 000 people.

THINK	WRITE
1 The difference between 62 000 and 48 000 is 14 000.	$62\,000 - 48\,000 = 14\,000$
2 The percentage decrease can be calculated by creating the fraction 14 000 out of 62 000 and then multiplying by 100.	$\frac{14\,000}{62\,000} \times 100 = 22.58$
3 Write the answer.	The percentage decrease is 22.58%.

REMEMBER

1. The term *per cent* means 'per hundred'.
2. Percentage, fractions and decimals are different ways of expressing the same quantity.
3. Percentage is another way of writing a fraction with a denominator of 100, or of writing the number of hundredths in a decimal.
4. There are a number of common percentages and their fraction and decimal equivalent which should be familiar.
5. When comparing percentages, fractions and decimals, first convert them all to their decimal equivalent.
6. Percentage increases and decreases can be calculated on many different quantities.

EXERCISE

4F Percentages, fractions and decimals

INDIVIDUAL PATHWAYS

eBook*plus*

Activity 4-F-1 Review of percentages doc-6880

Activity 4-F-2 More percentages doc-6881

Activity 4-F-3 Advanced percentages doc-6882

FLUENCY

1 Express each of the following fractions as a percentage.

a $\frac{7}{8}$ **b** $\frac{3}{5}$ **c** $\frac{5}{6}$ **d** $2\frac{1}{3}$

2 Express each of the following decimals as a percentage.

a 0.15 **b** 0.85 **c** 3.10 **d** 0.024

3 WE21 Express the following percentages as fractions in simplest form.

a 20% **b** 35% **c** 61% **d** 105%

4 WE21 Express the following percentages as decimals.

a 24% **b** 13%

c 1.5% **d** 250%

UNDERSTANDING

5 WE22 For the following sets of numbers, write them in ascending order and then place them on a number line.

a 1.6, 25%, $\frac{7}{8}$, 75%, 10%, $3\frac{1}{2}$, 2.4

b $3\frac{4}{5}$, 330%, 4.5, 150%, 3, $2\frac{1}{3}$, 2.8

6 WE23 Calculate the percentage increase when 250 increases to 325.

7 WE24 Calculate the percentage decrease when the population of fish in a pond decreases from 1500 to 650.

8 Express \$120 as a percentage of \$400.

9 In a library, there are 24 children, 36 women and 42 men. What is the percentage of women visiting the library? Give your answer to two decimal places.

10 During a sale, a jacket originally priced at \$79.99 is given a discount of 30%. What is the new discounted price? Give your answer to two decimal places.

11 In a survey of 200 people, 28% of them chose A as the answer, $\frac{2}{5}$ of them chose B as the answer and the remainder chose C as the answer. Find the number of people who chose C as the answer.

12 Patrick, Jeremie, Charlotte and Alison had dinner at a restaurant. At the end of the meal, Patrick paid $\frac{2}{5}$ of the total bill, Jeremie paid 35% of the bill, Charlotte paid 0.2 of the bill and Alison paid $\frac{1}{10}$ of the bill. Did they leave a tip and if so what percentage of the bill was the tip?

13 A pair of shoes is marked down from \$150 to \$100. What is the percentage decrease on the original price?

4G Estimation

- Sometimes an **estimate** of the answer is all that is required (an estimate is answer close to the actual answer, but found using easier numbers).
- Some estimation methods are detailed in this section.

Clustering around a common value

- If the calculation involves similar values, the values can be rounded to the same number.

WORKED EXAMPLE 25

Marilyn and Kim disagree about the answer to the following calculation: 7.3 + 7.1 + 6.9 + 6.8 + 7.2 + 7.3 + 7.4 + 6.6. Marilyn says the answer is 56.6, but Kim thinks it is 46.6. Obtain an estimate for the calculation and determine who is correct.

THINK	WRITE
1 Carefully analyse the values and devise a method to estimate the total.	Each of the values can be approximated to 7 and there are 8 values.
2 Perform the calculation using the rounded numbers.	$7 \times 8 = 56$
3 Answer the question.	Marilyn is correct because the approximate value is very close to 56.6.

Rounding, rounding up, rounding down

- When we are **rounding** to a given place value:
  - If the next lower place value digit is less than 5, leave the place value digit as it is, and add zeros to all lower place values, if necessary.
  - If the next lower place value digit is 5 or greater, increase the given place value digit by 1 and add zeros to all lower place values, if necessary.
- When rounding 25 354:
  - to the nearest thousand, the result is 25 000
  - to the nearest hundred, the result is 25 400.
- When **rounding up**, the digit in the desired place value is increased by 1 regardless of the digits in the lower place positions (as long as they are not all zeros). Zeros are added to the lower place positions to retain the place value.
- When rounding up 3100:
  - to the nearest thousand, the result is 4000
  - to the nearest hundred, the result is 3100.
- When **rounding down**, all digits following the desired place value are replaced by zeros, leaving the given place value unchanged.
- When rounding down 635 to the nearest ten, the result in 630.

WORKED EXAMPLE 26

Consider the number 39 461 and perform the following.
a Round to the nearest thousand.
b Round up to the nearest hundred.
c Round down to the nearest ten.

THINK	WRITE
a 1 Consider the digit in the thousands place position and the digit in the next lower place position.	**a** The digit 9 lies in the thousands position. The digit 4, which is less than 5, lies in the hundreds position.
2 Write the answer, adding the required number of zeros.	The number 39 461 rounded to the nearest thousand is 39 000.
b 1 Consider the digit in the hundreds place position and the digit in the next lower place position.	**b** The digit 4 lies in the hundreds position. The digit 6 lies in the tens position. When rounding up to the nearest hundred, the 4 will increase to 5.
2 Write the answer, adding the required number of zeros.	The number 39 461 rounded up to the nearest hundred is 39 500.
c 1 Consider the digit in the tens place position and the digit in the next lower place position.	**c** The digit 6 lies in the tens position. The digit 1 lies in the units position. When rounding down to the nearest ten, the 1 will be converted to 0.
2 Write the answer, adding the required number of zeros.	The number 39 461 rounded down to the nearest ten is 39 460.

Rounding to the first digit

- When estimating answers to calculations, sometimes it is simplest to round all numbers in the calculation to the first digit and then perform the operation.

WORKED EXAMPLE 27

Provide an estimate to the following calculations by first rounding each number to its first digit. Check your estimate with a calculator. Comment on the accuracy of your estimate.

a $394 + 76 - 121$ **b** $\dfrac{692 \times 32}{19 \times 87}$

THINK	WRITE
a 1 Round each of the numbers to the first digit.	**a** Rounded to the first digit, 394 becomes 400, 76 becomes 80 and 121 becomes 100.
2 Perform the calculation using the rounded numbers.	$394 + 76 - 121 \approx 400 + 80 - 100$ ≈ 380
3 Check using a calculator. Comment on how the rounded result compares with the actual answer.	Using a calculator, the result is 349. The estimate compares well to the actual (calculator) value.
b 1 Round each of the numbers to the first digit.	**b** Rounded to the first digit, 692 becomes 700, 32 becomes 30, 19 becomes 20 and 87 becomes 90.
2 Perform the calculation using the rounded numbers.	$\dfrac{692 \times 32}{19 \times 87} \approx \dfrac{\cancel{700}^{35} \times \cancel{30}^{1}}{\cancel{20}_{1} \times \cancel{90}_{3}}$ $\approx \dfrac{35}{3}$ ≈ 12
3 Check using a calculator. Comment on how the rounded result compares with the actual answer.	Using a calculator, the result is 13.4 (rounded to 1 decimal place). The estimate is very close to the actual (calculator) value.

Rounding the dividend to a multiple of the divisor

- To make division easier, the dividend can be rounded to a multiple of the divisor. For example, in 20 532 ÷ 7, the 20 532 (the dividend) could be rounded to 21 000. Because we know that 21 is a multiple of 7, we could see, through mental approximation, that the answer is close to 3000 (the exact answer is 2933).

WORKED EXAMPLE 28

Provide estimates for the calculation $\frac{537}{40}$ by:
a rounding the dividend up to the nearest hundred **b rounding the dividend to the nearest ten**
c rounding the dividend to a multiple of the divisor.

THINK	WRITE
a 1 Round the dividend up to the nearest hundred.	**a** 537 rounded up to the nearest hundred is 600.
2 Perform the division. Write the estimation.	$\dfrac{537}{40} \approx \dfrac{\cancel{600}^{15}}{\cancel{40}_{1}}$ ≈ 15
b 1 Round the dividend to the nearest ten.	**b** 537 rounded up to the nearest ten is 540.
2 Perform the division. Write the estimation.	$\dfrac{537}{40} \approx \dfrac{\cancel{540}^{27}}{\cancel{40}^{2}}$ ≈ 13.5

c	1 Round the dividend to a multiple of the divisor.	**c** 52 is a multiple of 4.
	2 Perform the division. Write the estimation.	$\frac{537}{40} \approx \frac{\cancel{520}^{13}}{\cancel{40}_{1}}$ ≈ 13

■ Different methods will give slightly different estimates.

WORKED EXAMPLE 29

The exact answer to $\frac{132 \times 77}{55}$ has the digits 184.8. Use any estimation technique to locate the position of the decimal point.

THINK	WRITE
1 Round each of the numbers to the first digit.	Rounded to the first digit, 132 becomes 100, 77 becomes 80 and 55 becomes 60.
2 Perform the calculation using the rounded numbers and write the estimate ignoring the decimal.	$\frac{132 \times 77}{55} \approx \frac{100 \times \cancel{80}^{4}}{\cancel{60}_{3}}$ $\approx \frac{400}{3}$ ≈ 133
3 Use the estimate obtained to locate the position of the decimal point. Write the correct answer.	The estimate gives an answer between 100 and 200. This indicates that the decimal point should be between the last two digits. The correct answer is 184.8.

REMEMBER

1. Estimation is a method of checking the reasonableness of an answer or a calculator computation.
2. Clustering around a common value can be employed when a basic calculation involving similar values is required.
3. When estimating, numbers can be rounded, rounded up or rounded down.
4. Rounding involves increasing the value of the desired digit if the following digit is 5 or greater. If the following digit is less than 5, the value of the desired digit remains the same. Zeros are added to maintain the place value of the number, if necessary.
5. When rounding up, the desired digit is increased by 1 irrespective of the digits in the lower place value positions (as long as they are not all zeros). Zeros are added to maintain the place value of the number, if necessary.
6. If rounding down, the desired digit remains unchanged, irrespective of the digits in the lower place value positions. Zeros are added to maintain the place value of the number, if necessary.
7. When rounding to the first digit, apply the process of rounding to the first digit of the number.
8. Making the dividend a multiple of the divisor is another useful technique for estimating an answer involving division.

EXERCISE
4G Estimation

INDIVIDUAL PATHWAYS

eBook*plus*

Activity 4-G-1
Rounding
doc-6883

Activity 4-G-2
More rounding
doc-6884

Activity 4-G-3
Advanced rounding
doc-6885

FLUENCY

1 WE25 Marilyn and Kim disagree about the answer to the following calculation: $8.6 + 9.2 + 8.7 + 8.8 + 8.9 + 9.3 + 9.4 + 8.6$. Marilyn says the answer is 81.5, but Kim thinks it is 71.5. Obtain an estimate for the calculation and determine who is correct.

2 WE26 For each of the following numbers:

i round to the first digit
ii round up to the first digit
iii round down to the first digit.

a 239 **b** 4522
c 21 **d** 53 624
e 592 **f** 1044

3 Round each of the numbers in question **2** down to the nearest ten.

4 Round each of the numbers in question **1** up to the nearest hundred.

5 WE27 Find an estimate for each of the following.

a $78 \div 21$ **b** $297 + 36$
c $587 - 78$ **d** $235 + 67 + 903$
e $1256 - 678$ **f** 789×34
g 56×891 **h** $1108 \div 53$
i $345 + 8906 - 23 + 427$ **j** $907 \div 88$
k $326 \times 89 \times 4$ **l** $2378 \div 109$
m $(426 + 1076) \times 21$ **n** $7 \times 211 - 832$
o $977 \div 10 \times 37$ **p** $(12\,384 - 6910) \times (214 + 67)$

6 WE28 Provide estimates for each of the following by first rounding the dividend to a multiple of the divisor.

a $35\,249 \div 9$
b $2396 \div 5$
c $526\,352 \div 7$
d $145\,923 \div 12$
e $92\,487 \div 11$
f $5249 \div 13$

7 WE29 Use any of the estimation techniques to locate the position of the decimal point in each of the following calculations. The correct digits for each one are shown in brackets.

a $\dfrac{369 \times 16}{288}$ (205)

b $\dfrac{42\,049}{14 \times 20}$ (150 175)

c $\dfrac{99 \times 270}{1320}$ (2025)

d $\dfrac{285 \times 36}{16 \times 125}$ (513)

e $\dfrac{256 \times 680}{32 \times 100}$ (544)

f $\dfrac{7290 \times 84}{27 \times 350}$ (648)

8 If 127 people came to a school social and each paid \$5 admission, find an estimate for the amount of money collected.

UNDERSTANDING

9 Estimate the whole numbers between which each of the following will lie.

a $\sqrt{20}$ **b** $\sqrt{120}$ **c** $\sqrt{180}$ **d** $\sqrt{240}$

10 Complete the table below with the rounded question, the estimated answer and the exact answer. The first one has been completed.

	Question	Rounded question	Estimated answer	Exact answer
a	789×56	800×60	48 000	44 184
b	$124 \div 5$			
c	$678 + 98 + 46$			
d	235×209			
e	$7863 - 908$			
f	63×726			
g	$39\,654 \div 227$			
h	$1809 - 786 + 467$			
i	$21 \times 78 \times 234$			
j	$942 \div 89$			
k	$\dfrac{492 \times 94}{38 \times 49}$			
l	$\dfrac{54\,296}{97 \times 184}$			

REASONING

11 Find an approximate answer to each of the worded problems below. Remember to write your answer in a sentence.

a A company predicted that it would sell 13 cars in a month at \$28 999 each. About how much money would they take in sales?

b A tap was leaking 8 mL of water each hour. Approximately how many millilitres of water would be lost if the tap was allowed to leak for 78 hours?

c The Year 8 cake stall sold 176 pieces of cake for 95 cents each. How much money did they make?

d Steven swam 124 laps of a 50 m pool and, on average, each lap took him 47 seconds. If he swam non-stop, for approximately how many seconds was he swimming?

e An audience of 11 784 people attended a recent Kylie concert at Rod Laver Arena and paid $89 each for their tickets. How much money was taken at the door?

f A shop sold 4289 articles at $4.20 each. How much money was paid altogether?

g On Clean Up Australia Day, 19 863 people volunteered to help. If they each picked up 196 pieces of rubbish, how many pieces of litter were collected altogether?

eBook*plus*

Digital doc
WorkSHEET 4.2
doc-6886

REFLECTION

Can you think of some examples of when an estimate rather than the exact answer is required?

Summary

Addition and subtraction of fractions

- The real number system contains the set of rational and irrational numbers. It can be denoted by the symbol *R*. Fractions are rational numbers.
- *Addition*. Write all fractions with the same denominator, then add numerators. If the sign is the same, add and keep the sign. If the sign is different, then find the difference between the signless numbers and use the sign furthest from zero.
  Opposites add to zero.
- *Subtraction*. Write all fractions with the same denominator, then subtract numerators by adding the opposite.

Multiplication and division of fractions

- *Multiplication*. Cancel common factors in numerators and denominators then multiply numerators and multiply denominators. If the signs are the same, the result is positive. If the signs are different, the result is negative.
- *Division*. Change ÷ to × and invert the divisor, then follow the rules for multiplication.
  If mixed numbers are involved in multiplication and division of fractions, change them to improper fractions.

Terminating and recurring decimals

- When changing fractions to decimals, divide the numerator of the fraction by the denominator and round the answer to 2 decimal places if it is not otherwise specified.
- When changing a mixed number to a decimal, write it as an improper fraction before dividing.
- When changing a decimal to a fraction, rewrite the decimal as a fraction with the same number of zeros in the denominator as there are decimal places in the question.
- Simplify the fraction by cancelling.
- Terminating decimals have a fixed number of decimal places.
- Recurring decimals that have one recurring digit are written with a dot above the recurring digit. Recurring decimals with more than one digit are written with a line above the recurring digits.
- The same rules apply when we are converting negative fractions and decimals.

Addition and subtraction of decimals

- When adding and subtracting decimals, be sure that the *decimal points* are *lined up* one underneath the other.
- The rules for addition and subtraction of positive and negative numbers apply.

Multiplication and division of decimals

- When multiplying decimals, count the number of digits after the decimal point in each of the numbers being multiplied and add these together to find the total number of decimal points in the answer.
- When dividing, make sure that the divisor is a whole number.
- When the divisor is a decimal, make it a whole number either by:
  - writing the question as a fraction and multiplying the numerator and denominator by a multiple of 10, or
  - multiplying both dividend and divisor by an appropriate power of ten.
- When dividing decimals by a whole number, place the decimal point in the answer directly in line with the decimal point in the question.
- When multiplying and dividing positive and negative decimals, the rules for multiplying and dividing positive and numbers apply.

Percentages, fractions and decimals

- The term *per cent* means 'per hundred'.
- Percentage, fractions and decimals are different ways of expressing the same quantity.
- Percentage is another way of writing a fraction with a denominator of 100, or of writing the number of hundredths in a decimal.
- There are a number of common percentages and their fraction and decimal equivalent which should be familiar.
- When comparing percentages, fractions and decimals, first convert them all to their decimal equivalent.
- Percentage increases and decreases can be calculated on many different quantities.

Estimation

- Estimation is a method of checking the reasonableness of an answer or a calculator computation.
- Clustering around a common value can be employed when a basic calculation involving similar values is required.
- When estimating, numbers can be rounded, rounded up or rounded down.
- Rounding involves increasing the value of the desired digit if the following digit is 5 or greater. If the following digit is less than 5, the value of the desired digit remains the same. Zeros are added to maintain the place value of the number, if necessary.
- When rounding up, the desired digit is increased by 1 irrespective of the digits in the lower place value positions (as long as they are not all zeros). Zeros are added to maintain the place value of the number, if necessary.
- If rounding down, the desired digit remains unchanged, irrespective of the digits in the lower place value positions. Zeros are added to maintain the place value of the number, if necessary.
- When rounding to the first digit, apply the process of rounding to the first digit of the number.
- Making the dividend a multiple of the divisor is another useful technique for estimating an answer involving division.

MAPPING YOUR UNDERSTANDING

Using terms from the summary, and other terms if you wish, construct a concept map that illustrates your understanding of the key concepts covered in this chapter. Compare this concept map with the one that you created in *What do you know?* on page 73.

Have you completed the two *Homework sheets*, the *Rich task* and the two *Code puzzles* in your *Maths Quest 8 Homework Book*?

Chapter review

FLUENCY

1 Evaluate the following.
- **a** $-4 + 12 =$
- **b** $5 - 18 =$
- **c** $-25 - 61 =$
- **d** $-35 + 35 =$

2 Evaluate the following.
- **a** -6×-8
- **b** $24 \div -6$
- **c** $-72 \div -9$
- **d** -100×3
- **e** 50×-4

3 Simplify the following.
- **a** $\frac{2}{3} + \frac{6}{7}$
- **b** $\frac{3}{5} + 4\frac{1}{2}$
- **c** $2\frac{3}{4} - 1\frac{1}{8}$
- **d** $\frac{5}{6} + \frac{3}{12} + \frac{4}{15}$
- **e** $\frac{127}{64} - \frac{5}{8} + 2\frac{3}{4}$
- **f** $2\frac{1}{2} + 3\frac{1}{2} - 1\frac{3}{5}$

4 Write the next 3 numbers of the sequence.

$-3.6, -2.4, -1.2,$ ____, ____, ____

5 Describe the directed numbers graphed on each number line.

a 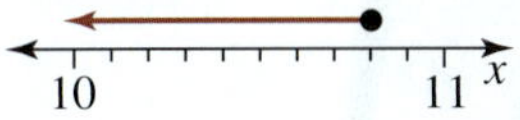

b 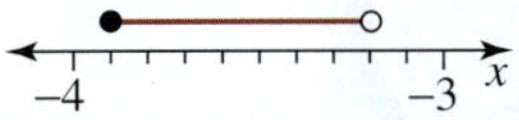

6 Graph the directed numbers $x > -2\frac{3}{4}$ on a number line.

7 Calculate the following.
- **a** $-1\frac{19}{60} + \frac{1}{4}$
- **b** $-\frac{3}{5} - \frac{7}{10}$

8 Simplify the following.
- **a** $\frac{2}{5} \times \frac{7}{8}$
- **b** $\frac{3}{4} \div \frac{7}{8}$
- **c** $\frac{22}{6} \times \frac{8}{11}$
- **d** $4\frac{1}{3} \times 9\frac{1}{2}$
- **e** $7\frac{1}{5} \div \frac{8}{20}$
- **f** $\frac{9}{4} \div 8\frac{1}{2}$
- **g** $-\frac{7}{8} \times \frac{5}{14}$
- **h** $-2\frac{3}{4} \div -\frac{3}{8}$

9 Convert the following fractions to decimals using correct notation.
- **a** $\frac{3}{4}$
- **b** $\frac{7}{5}$
- **c** $6\frac{1}{4}$
- **d** $\frac{9}{5}$
- **e** $4\frac{2}{3}$
- **f** $12\frac{3}{8}$

10 Convert the following decimals to fractions in simplest form.
- **a** 0.7
- **b** 0.45
- **c** 1.23
- **d** 3.08
- **e** 24.365
- **f** 17.04

11 Evaluate the following.
- **a** $2.4 + 3.7$
- **b** $11.62 - 4.89$
- **c** $12.04 + 2.9$
- **d** $5.63 - 0.07$
- **e** $34.2 - 4.008$
- **f** $34.09 + 1.2 + 3479.3 + 0.0003$
- **g** $-2.48 + 1.903$
- **h** $-1.63 - 2.54$

12 Evaluate the following, correct to 2 decimal places where appropriate.
- **a** 432.9×2
- **b** 78.02×3.4
- **c** $543.7 \div 0.12$
- **d** $9.65 \div 1.1$
- **e** $923.06 \times 0.000\,45$
- **f** $74.23 \div 0.0007$
- **g** $0.08 \div -0.4$
- **h** $-1.02 \div -0.5$

13 Express the following as percentages.
- **a** 0.26
- **b** $\frac{3}{4}$
- **c** $2\frac{1}{8}$
- **d** 4.35

14 For each of the following numbers:
- **i** round to the first digit
- **ii** round up to the first digit
- **iii** round down to the first digit.

- **a** 39 260
- **b** 222
- **c** 3001

15 Provide estimates for each of the following by first rounding the dividend to a multiple of the divisor.
- **a** $809 \div 11$
- **b** $7143 \div 9$
- **c** $13\,216 \div 12$

16 The answer to $\frac{99 \times 1560}{132 \times 312}$ contains the digits 375, in that order. Use an estimating technique to determine the position of the decimal point and write the true answer.

17 Use your estimation skills to find approximate answers for the following.
- **a** 306×12
- **b** $268 + 3075 + 28 + 98\,031$
- **c** $4109 \div 21$
- **d** $19\,328 - 4811$

PROBLEM SOLVING

1 In order to raise money for charity, a Year 8 class organised a cake stall. They started with 9 whole cakes, sold $2\frac{1}{4}$ cakes at recess and $4\frac{5}{8}$ at lunchtime.

a How much cake was left over?

b If there are 20 students in the class, would they be able to equally share the leftover cake if it had been cut up into eighths?

c This cake stall raised $150. If they plan to give $\frac{1}{5}$ to the Red Cross and $\frac{2}{3}$ to World Vision, how much will each group receive and how much is left over?

2 A number is rounded to give 2.15.

a What could the number have been?

b What is the smallest the number could have been?

c Is it possible to write down the largest number that can be rounded to give 2.15?

3 Find the fraction that is equivalent to $\frac{3}{4}$ and:

a the difference between the denominator and the numerator is 7

b the product of the denominator and numerator is 300.

4 At Teagan's Farm, there are 24 horses. One sixth of them are brown and one quarter of them are black. If half of the remaining horses are red and the other half grey, how many grey horses are there?

5 On this diagram, EFGH is half the area of ABCD, JKLM is half the area of EFGH and NPQR is half the area of JKLM. What fraction of ABCD is NPQR?

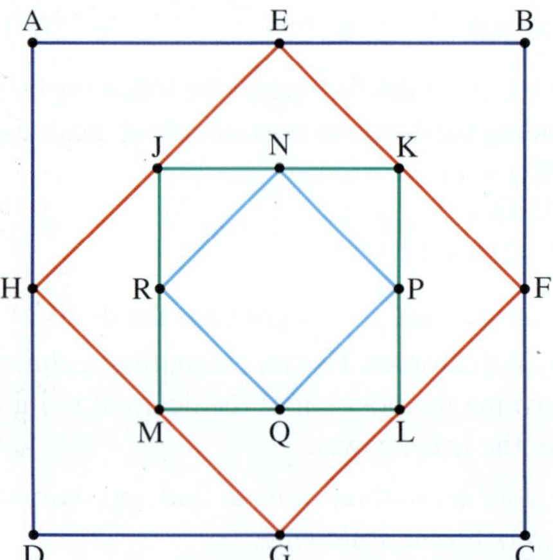

6 If a shend is 15.36 plombs (pl) long and 1 plomb is equivalent to 6.309 sharns (sh), find the length of 2.25 shends in sharns.

7 The five points shown on the number line are evenly spaced.
What is the value for B?

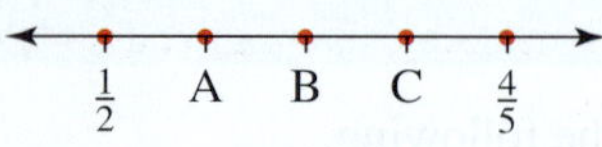

8 You and a friend have decided to test the combinations of cordial and water shown in the following table. The mixture with the highest cordial content will be the one you and your friend will give to 180 Year-8 students.

a Which mix will be used?

b If each student will drink $\frac{1}{2}$ cup each, how much will you need to make?

c How much water and how much cordial will be needed?

Mix A	Mix B
2 cups cordial 3 cups water	1 cup cordial 2 cups water
Mix C	**Mix D**
5 cups cordial 9 cups water	3 cups cordial 5 cups water

9 The skin of a banana weighs about $\frac{1}{8}$ the mass of the whole banana. The cost of a bundle of bananas was $5.12. They were peeled and the fruit was found to weigh 1.4 kg. What was the price/kg of the bananas?

Use mathematical reasoning to justify your answer.

10 James took a loan from a bank to pay a debt of $14 200. He pays $670.50 per month for 2 years. How much interest is the bank charging?

11 Magic squares show a grid of numbers which have the same sum horizontally, vertically and diagonally. It is not necessary for the numbers to be integers. Complete this magic square, indicating the magic sum.

1.7×0.2			$(0.4)^2$	$\frac{1}{10} + \frac{1}{5}$
$\frac{19}{25} - \frac{3}{10}$	$0.01 \div 0.1$		$0.14 \div 0.5$	$\frac{2^3}{5^2}$
	$\frac{8}{25} - \frac{1}{5}$	$\frac{1}{100} + \frac{1}{4}$		$\frac{33}{100} \div \frac{3}{4}$
	0.4×0.6	$\frac{39}{50} - \frac{2}{5}$	0.6×0.7	
$\frac{11}{100} \div \frac{1}{2}$	$\left(\frac{3}{5}\right)^2$			$\frac{17}{25} - \frac{1}{2}$

12 A unit fraction is one which has a numerator of 1. Two fractions are said to be *adjacent* if their difference is a unit fraction.

Find a fraction which is adjacent to $\frac{1}{2}$.

13 A fraction of the type $\cfrac{1}{a + \cfrac{1}{b + \cfrac{1}{c}}}$ is called a continued fraction. Study this method which converts $\frac{5}{9}$ into a continued fraction.

$$\frac{5}{9} = \frac{1}{\frac{9}{5}}$$

$$= \frac{1}{\frac{5}{5} + \frac{4}{5}}$$

$$= \frac{1}{1 + \cfrac{1}{\frac{5}{4}}}$$

$$= \frac{1}{1 + \cfrac{1}{\frac{4}{4} + \frac{1}{4}}}$$

$$= \frac{1}{1 + \cfrac{1}{1 + \cfrac{1}{4}}}$$

Use this method to show how $\frac{7}{16}$ can be written as a continued fraction.

14 Briony opened a packet of chocolate biscuits at lunch time and together with her friends she ate 30% of the pack. Later that afternoon, Briony ate 10% of the biscuits that were left. What percentage of the original pack of biscuits now remained?

15 The Year 8 maths class at Wilson High School completed a percentage test. Anna said she got 72% of the answers correct, Bill said he got $\frac{5}{7}$ of the answers correct, Sally said she got 0.717 of the answers correct and Jack said he beat them all because he got $\frac{8}{11}$ of the answers correct. Did Jack get the best result? Use mathematical reasoning to justify your answer.

16 A car purchased by a trader for \$25 000 was sold to a customer for \$32 000. What was the percentage profit on the purchase?

17 A family paid a total of \$75 for dinner at a local restaurant. If the GST on the dinner was 10%, what was the price of the dinner before the GST was added?

eBook*plus*

Interactivities
Test yourself
Chapter 4
int-2751

Word search
Chapter 4
int-2752

Crossword
Chapter 4
int-2753

eBookplus ACTIVITIES

Chapter opener

Digital doc *(page 73)*
- Hungry brain activity Chapter 4 (doc-6853)

Are you ready?

Digital docs *(page 74)*
- SkillSHEET 4.1 (doc-6854) Order of operations 1
- SkillSHEET 4.2 (doc-6855) Factors
- SkillSHEET 4.3 (doc-6856) Multiples
- SkillSHEET 4.4 (doc-6857) Adding and subtracting fractions 1
- SkillSHEET 4.5 (doc-6858) Multiplying and dividing fractions
- SkillSHEET 4.6 (doc-6859) Adding and subtracting decimals
- SkillSHEET 4.7 (doc-6860) Multiplying and dividing decimals
- SkillSHEET 4.8 (doc-6861) Rounding to the first (leading) digit
- SkillSHEET 4.9 (doc-6862) Operations with fractions
- SkillSHEET 4.10 (doc-6863) Operations with decimals

4A Addition and subtraction of fractions

Digital docs *(page 80)*
- Activity 4-A-1 (doc-6864) Addition and subtraction of fractions
- Activity 4-A-2 (doc-6865) More addition and subtraction of fractions
- Activity 4-A-3 (doc-6866) Advanced addition and subtraction of fractions

Interactivity *(page 81)*
- Adding and subtracting fractions (int-2357)

4B Multiplication and division of fractions

Digital docs *(page 83)*
- Activity 4-B-1 (doc-6867) Multiplication and division of fractions
- Activity 4-B-2 (doc-6868) More multiplication and division of fractions
- Activity 4-B-3 (doc-6869) Advanced multiplication and division of fractions
- Spreadsheet (doc-2130) Four operations with fractions *(page 84)*
- WorkSHEET 4.1 (doc-6870) *(page 84)*

Interactivity *(page 83)*
- Dividing fractions (int-2358)

4C Terminating and recurring decimals

Digital docs *(page 87)*
- Activity 4-C-1 (doc-6871) Fractions and decimals
- Activity 4-C-2 (doc-6872) More fractions and decimals
- Activity 4-C-3 (doc-6873) Advanced fractions and decimals
- Spreadsheet (doc-2131) Converting fractions to decimals
- Spreadsheet (doc-2132) Converting decimals to fractions

4D Addition and subtraction of decimals

Digital docs *(page 90)*
- Activity 4-D-1 (doc-6874) Addition and subtraction of decimals
- Activity 4-D-2 (doc-6875) More addition and subtraction of decimals
- Activity 4-D-3 (doc-6876) Advanced addition and subtraction of decimals
- Spreadsheet (doc-2133) Adding decimals
- Spreadsheet (doc-2134) Subtracting decimals

4E Multiplication and division of decimals

Digital docs *(page 94)*
- Activity 4-E-1 (doc-6877) Multiplication and division of decimals
- Activity 4-E-2 (doc-6878) More multiplication and division of decimals
- Activity 4-E-3 (doc-6879) Advanced multiplication and division of decimals
- Spreadsheet (doc-2135) Multiplying decimals
- Spreadsheet (doc-2136) Dividing decimals

4F Percentages, fractions and decimals

Digital docs *(page 97)*
- Activity 4-F-1 (doc-6880) Review of percentages
- Activity 4-F-2 (doc-6881) More percentages
- Activity 4-F-3 (doc-6882) Advanced percentages

4G Estimation

Digital docs *(page 102)*
- Activity 4-G-1 (doc-6883) Rounding
- Activity 4-G-2 (doc-6884) More rounding
- Activity 4-G-3 (doc-6885) Advanced rounding
- WorkSHEET 4.2 (doc-6886) *(page 104)*

Chapter review

Interactivities *(page 109)*
- Test yourself Chapter 4 (int-2751) Take the end-of-chapter test to test your progress.
- Word search Chapter 4 (int-2752)
- Crossword Chapter 4 (int-2753)

To access eBookPLUS activities, log on to

www.jacplus.com.au

Ratios and rates

5A Introduction to ratios
5B Simplifying ratios
5C Proportion
5D Comparing ratios
5E Dividing in a given ratio
5F Rates

WHAT DO YOU KNOW?

1 List what you know about ratios and rates. Create a concept map to show your list.
2 Share what you know with a partner and then with a small group.
3 As a class, create a large concept map that shows your class's knowledge of ratios and rates.

eBook*plus*

Digital doc
Hungry brain activity
Chapter 5
doc-6887

OPENING QUESTION

What is the ratio of the length of one of the frogs to the length of the leaf in the picture?

Are you ready?

Try the questions below. If you have difficulty with any of them, extra help can be obtained by completing the matching SkillSHEET located on your eBookPLUS.

Digital doc SkillSHEET 5.1 doc-6888

Converting units of length, capacity and time

1 Convert each of the following to the units shown in brackets.

a 3 m (cm) **b** 5.2 m (mm) **c** 4.25 km (m) **d** 2 kg (g)
e 0.5 t (kg) **f** 6.4 L (mL) **g** 8.2 kL (L) **h** 4 min (s)
i $2\frac{1}{2}$ hours (minutes) **j** 4 weeks (days) **k** 2 years (months) **l** 2 years (weeks)

eBook*plus*

Digital doc SkillSHEET 5.2 doc-6889

Highest common factor

2 Find the highest common factor of:

a 6 and 9 **b** 12 and 20 **c** 15 and 24 **d** 45 and 80.

eBook*plus*

Digital doc SkillSHEET 5.3 doc-6890

Simplifying fractions

3 Simplify each of the following fractions.

a $\frac{9}{12}$ **b** $\frac{20}{25}$ **c** $\frac{36}{60}$ **d** $\frac{72}{100}$

eBook*plus*

Digital doc SkillSHEET 5.4 doc-6891

Finding and converting to the lowest common denominator

4 Write each of the following fraction pairs over the lowest common denominator.

a $\frac{1}{3}$ and $\frac{3}{4}$ **b** $\frac{3}{8}$ and $\frac{7}{12}$ **c** $\frac{2}{3}$ and $\frac{5}{12}$ **d** $\frac{7}{10}$ and $\frac{3}{4}$

eBook*plus*

Digital doc SkillSHEET 5.5 doc-6892

Converting a mixed number to an improper fraction

5 Write the following mixed numbers as improper fractions.

a $1\frac{3}{4}$ **b** $2\frac{3}{5}$ **c** $3\frac{7}{10}$ **d** $10\frac{3}{8}$

eBook*plus*

Digital doc SkillSHEET 5.6 doc-6893

Multiplying decimals by 10, 100 and 1000

6 Perform each of the following multiplications.

a 1.237×10 **b** 0.084×10
c 0.284×100 **d** $0.000\,784 \times 1000$

eBook*plus*

Digital doc SkillSHEET 5.7 doc-6894

Multiplying a whole number by a fraction

7 Perform the following multiplications.

a $30 \times \frac{2}{3}$ **b** $60 \times \frac{4}{5}$ **c** $1\frac{1}{4} \times 120$ **d** $\frac{5}{8} \times 96$

eBook*plus*

Digital doc SkillSHEET 5.8 doc-6895

Converting minutes to a fraction of an hour

8 Write each of the following as a fraction of 1 hour.

a 15 min **b** 40 min **c** 36 min **d** 54 min

5A Introduction to ratios

- **Ratios** are used to compare quantities of the same kind.
- Ratios do not have a name or unit of measurement.
- The order of the numbers in a ratio is important. If the ratio of flour to water is 1 : 4, the 1 corresponds to the quantity of flour and the 4 corresponds to the quantity of water.
- Ratios can also be written in fractional form: $1:4 \Leftrightarrow \frac{1}{4}$.
- Ratios can also be written as percentages; for example if 20% of a class of Year 8 students walked to school then 80% did not walk to school — a ratio of 1 : 4.
- Before ratios are written, the numbers must be expressed in the *same* units of measurement. Once the units are the same, they can be omitted.
- Ratios contain only whole numbers.

WORKED EXAMPLE 1

Look at the completed game of noughts and crosses at right and write the ratios of:
a crosses to noughts
b noughts to unmarked spaces.

X	O	
X	X	X
O		O

THINK	WRITE
a Count the number of crosses and the number of noughts. Write the 2 numbers as a ratio (the number of crosses must be written first).	a 4 : 3
b Count the number of noughts and the number of unmarked spaces. Write the 2 numbers as a ratio, putting them in the order required (the number of noughts must be written first).	b 3 : 2

WORKED EXAMPLE 2

Rewrite the following statement as a ratio: 7 mm to 1 cm.

THINK	WRITE
1 Express both quantities in the same units. To obtain whole numbers, convert 1 cm to mm (rather than 7 mm to cm).	7 mm to 1 cm 7 mm to 10 mm
2 Omit the units and write the 2 numbers as a ratio.	7 : 10

REMEMBER

1. Ratios compare quantities of the same kind.
2. The ratios themselves do not have a name or unit of measurement.
3. The order of the numbers in a ratio is important.
4. Before ratios are written, the numbers must be expressed in the same units of measurement.
5. Ratios contain only whole numbers.

eBook*plus*

Weblink
Introducing ratios

EXERCISE

5A Introduction to ratios

INDIVIDUAL PATHWAYS

eBook*plus*

Activity 5-A-1
Ripper ratios
doc-2195

Activity 5-A-2
Radical ratios
doc-2196

Activity 5-A-3
Real ratios
doc-2197

eBook*plus*

Interactivity
Fruit salad ratio
int-0076

FLUENCY

1 WE1 Look at the completed game of noughts and crosses and write the ratios of:
  - a noughts to crosses
  - b crosses to noughts
  - c crosses to total number of spaces
  - d total number of spaces to noughts
  - e noughts in the top row to crosses in the bottom row.

X	X	O
O	O	X
X	X	O

2 Look at the coloured circles on the right and then write the following ratios.
  - a Black : red
  - b Red : black
  - c Aqua : black
  - d Black : aqua
  - e Aqua : red
  - f Black : (red and aqua)
  - g Aqua : (black and red)
  - h Black : total circles
  - i Aqua : total circles
  - j Red : total circles

3 For the diagram shown, write the following ratios.
  - a Shaded parts : unshaded parts
  - b Unshaded parts : shaded parts
  - c Shaded parts : total parts

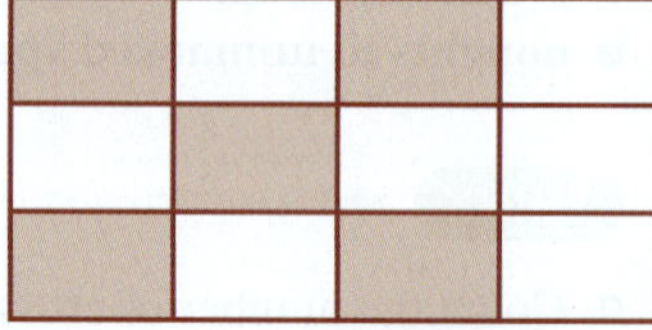

4 In the bag of numbers shown to the right, write the ratios of:
  - a even numbers to odd numbers
  - b prime numbers to composite numbers
  - c numbers greater than 3 to numbers less than 3
  - d multiples of 2 to multiples of 5
  - e numbers divisible by 3 to numbers not divisible by 3.

5 WE2 Rewrite each of the following statements as a ratio.
  - a 3 mm to 5 mm
  - b 6 s to 19 s
  - c $4 to $11
  - d 7 teams to 9 teams
  - e 1 goal to 5 goals
  - f 9 boys to 4 boys
  - g 3 weeks to 1 month
  - h 3 mm to 1 cm
  - i 17 seconds to 1 minute
  - j 53 cents to $1
  - k 11 cm to 1 m
  - l 1 g to 1 kg
  - m 1 L to 2 kL
  - n 7 hours to 1 day
  - o 5 months to 1 year
  - p 1 km to 27 m
  - q 7 apples to 1 dozen apples
  - r 13 pears to 2 dozen pears
  - s 3 females to 5 males
  - t 1 teacher to 22 students

6 Out of 100 people selected for a school survey, 59 were junior students, 3 were teachers and the rest were senior students. Write these ratios:
  - a teachers : juniors
  - b juniors : seniors
  - c seniors : teachers
  - d teachers : students
  - e juniors : other members of the survey.

7 Write each of the following, using a mathematical ratio.

- **a** In their chess battles, Lynda has won 24 games and Karen has won 17.
- **b** There are 21 first-division teams and 17 second-division teams.
- **c** Nathan could long jump twice as far as Rachel.
- **d** On the camp there were 4 teachers and 39 students.
- **e** In the mixture there were 4 cups of flour and 1 cup of milk.
- **f** Elena and Alex ran the 400 m in the same time.
- **g** The radius and diameter of a circle were measured.
- **h** The length of a rectangle is three times its width.
- **i** On Friday night 9 out of every 10 people enjoyed the movie.
- **j** The length of one side of an equilateral triangle compared to its perimeter.
- **k** The length of a regular hexagon compared to its perimeter.
- **l** The number of correct options compared to incorrect options in a multiple-choice question containing five options.

UNDERSTANDING

8 A pair of jeans originally priced at $215 was purchased for $179. What is the ratio of:

- **a** the original price compared to selling price?
- **b** the original price compared to the discount?

9 Matthew received a score of 97% for his Maths test. What is the ratio of:

- **a** the marks received compared to marks lost?
- **b** the marks lost compared to total marks possible?

10 For each comparison that follows, state whether a ratio could be written and give a reason for your answer. (*Remember:* Before ratios are written, numbers must be expressed in the same unit of measurement.)

- **a** Anna's mass is 55 kg. Her cat has a mass of 7 kg.
- **b** Brian can throw a cricket ball 40 metres, and John can throw the same ball 35 metres.
- **c** The cost of painting the wall was $55; its area is 10 m^2.
- **d** For a trip, the car's average speed was 85 km/h; the trip took 4 h.
- **e** Brett's height is 2.1 m. Matt's height is 150 cm.
- **f** Jonathon apples cost $2.40 per dozen; Delicious apples cost $3.20 per dozen.
- **g** Mary is paid $108; she works 3 days a week.
- **h** David kicked 5 goals and 3 behinds; his team scored 189 points.

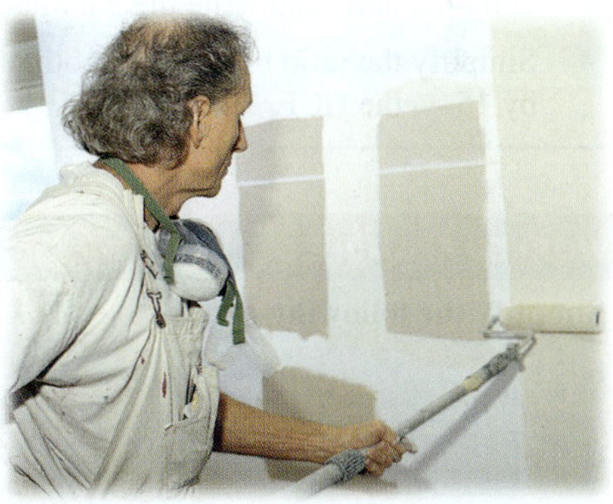

11 a If 17% of students in a class have sports training once a week, write as a ratio the number of students who have sports training once a week compared to the students who do not.

b A survey found that only 3% of workers take their lunch to work on a regular basis. Write as a ratio the number of workers who do not take their lunch to work compared to those who do.

REFLECTION

Why doesn't a simplified ratio have units?

5B Simplifying ratios

- When the numbers in a ratio are multiplied or divided by the same number to obtain another ratio, these two ratios are said to be **equivalent**. (This is a similar process to obtaining equivalent fractions).
- Like fractions, ratios are usually written in simplest form; that is, reduced to lowest terms.

WORKED EXAMPLE 3

Express the ratio 16 : 24 in simplest form.

THINK	WRITE
1 Write the ratio.	16 : 24
2 Determine the largest number by which both 16 and 24 can be divided (that is, what is the highest common factor)? It is 8.	÷ 8 ÷ 8
3 Divide both 16 and 24 by 8 to obtain an equivalent ratio in simplest form.	2 : 3

WORKED EXAMPLE 4

Write the ratio of 45 cm to 1.5 m in simplest form.

THINK	WRITE
1 Write the question.	45 cm to 1.5 m
2 Express both quantities in the same units by changing 1.5 m into cm. (1 m = 100 cm)	45 cm to 150 cm
3 Omit the units and write the 2 numbers as a ratio.	45 : 150
4 Simplify the ratio by dividing both 45 and 150 by 15 — the HCF.	÷ 15 ÷ 15 3 : 10

WORKED EXAMPLE 5

Simplify the following ratios.

a $\frac{2}{5} : \frac{7}{10}$

b $\frac{5}{6} : \frac{5}{8}$

THINK	WRITE
a 1 Write the fractions in ratio form.	a $\frac{2}{5} : \frac{7}{10}$
2 Write equivalent fractions using the lowest common denominator (in this case, 10).	$\frac{4}{10} : \frac{7}{10}$
3 Multiply both fractions by 10.	× 10 × 10
4 Check if the remaining whole numbers that form the ratio can be simplified. In this case they cannot.	4 : 7

	THINK	WRITE
b	1 Write the fractions in ratio form.	**b** $\frac{5}{6}:\frac{5}{8}$
	2 Write equivalent fractions using the lowest common denominator (in this case, 24).	
	3 Multiply both fractions by 24.	
	4 Check if the remaining whole numbers that form the ratio can be simplified. In this case divide each by the HCF of 5.	

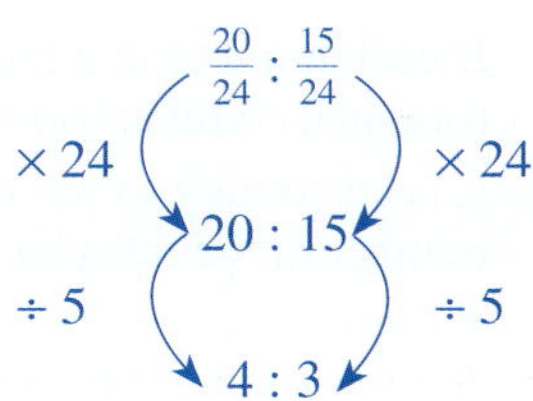

- If the ratio uses decimals, we multiply by the smallest power of 10 that will produce a whole number for both parts of the ratio.

WORKED EXAMPLE 6

Write the following ratios in simplest form.
a 2.1 to 3.5 **b 1.4 : 0.75**

	THINK	WRITE
a	1 Write the decimals in ratio form.	**a** 2.1 : 3.5
	2 Both decimals have one decimal place, so multiplying each by 10 will produce whole numbers.	
	3 Simplify by dividing both numbers by the HCF of 7.	

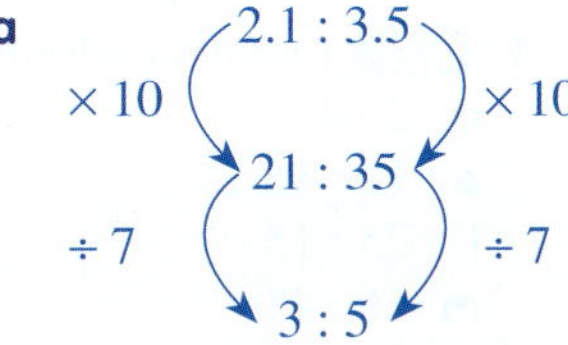

	THINK	WRITE
b	1 Write the decimals in ratio form.	**b** 1.4 : 0.75
	2 Because 0.75 has two decimal places, we multiply each decimal by 100 to produce whole numbers.	× 100 → 140 : 75
	3 Simplify by dividing both numbers by the HCF of 5.	÷ 5 → 28 : 15

- If the ratio contains algebraic terms, divide both parts of the ratio by the highest common factor (HCF) including common algebraic terms.

WORKED EXAMPLE 7

Simplify the ratios:
a $10a^2b : 15ab^2$ **b $3mn : 6mn$.**

	THINK	WRITE
a	1 Write the ratios.	**a** $10a^2b : 15ab^2$
	2 Simplify the ratio by dividing both sides by $5ab$ (the HCF).	$\frac{10a^2b}{5ab}:\frac{15ab^2}{5ab}$
	3 Cancel common factors to obtain the ratio in simplest form.	$2a : 3b$
b	1 Write the ratios.	**b** $3mn : 6mn$
	2 Simplify the ratio by dividing both sides by $3mn$ (the HCF).	$\frac{3mn}{3mn}:\frac{6mn}{3mn}$
	3 Cancel common factors to obtain the ratio in simplest form.	1 : 2

REMEMBER

1. If each number in a ratio is multiplied or divided by the same number, the equivalent (or equal) ratio is formed.
2. It is customary to write ratios in the simplest form. This is achieved by dividing each number in the ratio by the highest common factor (HCF).
3. To form a ratio using fractions, convert the fractions so that they have a common denominator and then write the ratio of the numerators.
4. Decimals can be easily changed into whole numbers if they are multiplied by powers of 10 (that is, 10, 100, 1000 and so on).
5. If the ratio contains algebraic terms, divide both parts of the ratio by the highest common factor (HCF) including common algebraic terms.

EXERCISE 5B

Simplifying ratios

INDIVIDUAL PATHWAYS

eBook plus

Activity 5-B-1 Simplifying ratios doc-2198

Activity 5-B-2 More simplifying of ratios doc-2199

Activity 5-B-3 Advanced simplifying of ratios doc-2200

eBook plus

Interactivity Converting percentages, decimals, fractions, ratios int-2740

FLUENCY

1 WE3 Express each ratio in simplest form.

a 2 : 4 **b** 3 : 9 **c** 5 : 10 **d** 6 : 18
e 12 : 16 **f** 15 : 18 **g** 24 : 16 **h** 21 : 14
i 25 : 15 **j** 13 : 26 **k** 15 : 35 **l** 27 : 36
m 36 : 45 **n** 42 : 28 **o** 45 : 54 **p** 50 : 15
q 56 : 64 **r** 75 : 100 **s** 84 : 144 **t** 88 : 132

2 Complete the patterns of equivalent ratios.

a	**b**	**c**	**d**	**e**
1 : 3	2 : 1	2 : 3	64 : 32	48 : 64
2 : 6	4 : 2	4 : 6	__ : 16	24 : __
_ : 9	_ : 4	6 : _	__ : 8	12 : __
_ : 12	_ : 8	_ : 12	8 : __	__ : 8
5 : __	20 : _	_ : 24	__ : 1	__ : __

3 WE4 Write the following ratios in simplest form.

a 8 cm to 12 cm **b** \$6 to \$18 **c** 50 s to 30 s
d 80 cm to 2 m **e** 75 cents to \$3 **f** 2 h to 45 min
g 300 mL to 4 L **h** 500 g to 2.5 kg **i** 45 mm to 2 cm
j \$4 to \$6.50 **k** 2500 L to 2 kL **l** 2500 m to 2 km
m 30 cents to \$1.50 **n** 2 h 45 min to 30 min **o** 200 m to 0.5 km
p 0.8 km to 450 m **q** $1\frac{1}{2}$ min to 300 s **r** 1.8 cm to 12 mm
s 3500 mg to 1.5 g **t** \$1.75 to \$10.50

4 Compare the following, using a mathematical ratio (in simplest form).

a The Hawks won 8 games and the Lions won 10 games.
b This jar of coffee costs \$4 but that one costs \$6.
c While Joanne made 12 hits, Holly made 8 hits.
d In the first innings, Ian scored 48 runs and Adam scored 12 runs.
e During the race, Rebecca's average speed was 200 km/h while Donna's average speed was 150 km/h.
f In the basketball match, the Tigers beat the Magic by 105 points to 84 points.
g The capacity of the plastic bottle is 250 mL and the capacity of the glass container is 2 L.
h Joseph ran the 600 m in 2 minutes but Maya ran the same distance in 36 seconds.
i In the movie audience, there were 280 children and 35 adults.
j On a page in the novel *Moby Dick* there are 360 words. Of these, 80 begin with a vowel.

5 A serving of Weet Biscuit Cereal contains:
3.6 g of protein 0.4 g of fat
20 g of carbohydrate 1 g of sugar
3.3 g of dietary fibre 84 mg of sodium.
Find the following ratios in simplest form:
- **a** sugar to carbohydrate
- **b** fat to protein
- **c** protein to fibre
- **d** sodium to protein.

6 **WE5** Write the following ratios in simplest form.

- **a** $\frac{1}{3}$ to $\frac{2}{3}$
- **b** $\frac{5}{7}$ to $\frac{6}{7}$
- **c** $\frac{1}{4} : \frac{1}{2}$
- **d** $\frac{2}{3} : \frac{5}{6}$
- **e** $\frac{4}{5}$ to $\frac{9}{20}$
- **f** $\frac{2}{3} : \frac{3}{5}$
- **g** $\frac{3}{10} : 1$
- **h** $1\frac{2}{3}$ to $\frac{1}{3}$
- **i** $1\frac{1}{4} : 1\frac{1}{2}$
- **j** $3\frac{1}{3}$ to $2\frac{1}{2}$
- **k** $1 : 1\frac{3}{5}$
- **l** $3\frac{1}{4}$ to $2\frac{4}{5}$

eBookplus

Digital doc
Spreadsheet
Simplifying ratios
doc-2213

7 **WE6** Write the following ratios in simplest form.

- **a** 0.7 to 0.9
- **b** 0.3 : 2.1
- **c** 0.05 to 0.15
- **d** 0.8 : 1
- **e** 0.25 : 1.5
- **f** 0.375 to 0.8
- **g** 0.95 : 0.095
- **h** 1 to 1.25
- **i** 0.01 : 0.1
- **j** 1.2 : 0.875
- **k** 0.004 to 0.08
- **l** 0.5 : 0.92

8 **WE7** Simplify these ratios.

- **a** $2a : 10b$
- **b** $6p : 3p$
- **c** $2x^2 : 3x$
- **d** $7xy^2 : 14xy$
- **e** $36m^3n^2 : 48m^2n^2$
- **f** $ab : 4ab^2$
- **g** $10^3x : 10x^3$
- **h** $50(cd)^2 : 25c$

UNDERSTANDING

9 In a primary school that has 910 students, 350 students are in the senior school and the remainder are in the junior school. Of the senior school students, 140 are females. There are the same number of junior males and junior females. Write the following ratios in simplest form:
- **a** senior students to junior students
- **b** senior females to senior males
- **c** senior males to total senior students
- **d** junior males to senior males
- **e** junior females to whole school population.

10 Compare the following, using a mathematical ratio (in simplest form):
- **a** Of the 90 000 people who attended the test match, 23 112 were females. Compare the number of males to females.
- **b** A Concorde jet cruises at 2170 km/h but a Cessna cruises at 220 km/h. Compare their speeds.
- **c** A house and land package is sold for $250 000. If the land was valued at $90 000, compare the land and house values.
- **d** In a kilogram of fertiliser, there are 550 g of phosphorus. Compare the amount of phosphorus to other components of the fertiliser.
- **e** Sasha saves $120 out of his take-home pay of $700 each fortnight. Compare his savings with his expenses.

11 The table at right represents the selling price of a house over a period of time.
- **a** Compare the price of the house purchased in December 2003 with the purchase price in April 2007 as a ratio in simplest form.
- **b** Compare the price of the house purchased in December 2003 with the purchase price in December 2007 as a ratio in simplest form.

Date of sale	Selling price
March 2010	$1.275 million
December 2007	$1.207 million
April 2007	$1.03 million
December 2003	$850 000

c Compare the price of the house purchased in December 2003 with the purchase price in March 2010 as a ratio in simplest form.

d **i** How much has the value of the house increased from December 2003 to March 2010?

ii Compare the increase obtained in part **d i** to the price of the house purchased in December 2003 as a ratio in simplest form.

e Comment on the results obtained in part **d**.

12 a MC Toowoomba's population is 80 000 and Brisbane's population is 1.8 million. The ratio of Toowoomba's population to that of Brisbane is:

A 2 : 45 B 4 : 9
C 1 : 1.8 D 9 : 4
E none of these

b When he was born, Samuel was 30 cm long. Now, on his 20th birthday, he is 2.1 m tall. The ratio of his birth height to his present height is:

A 3 : 7 B 1 : 21
C 7 : 10 D 1 : 7
E none of these

c The cost of tickets to two different concerts is in the ratio 3 : 5. If the more expensive ticket is $110, the cheaper ticket is:

A $180 B $80
C $50 D $45
E $66

d A coin was tossed 100 times and Tails appeared 60 times. The ratio of Heads to Tails was:

A 2 : 3 B 3 : 5
C 3 : 2 D 5 : 3
E 2 : 5

e Out of a 1.25 L bottle of soft drink, I have drunk 500 mL. The ratio of soft drink remaining to the original amount is:

A 2 : 3 B 3 : 5
C 3 : 2 D 5 : 3
E 2 : 5

REFLECTION
In what ways is simplifying ratios similar to simplifying fractions?

5C Proportion

- A **proportion** is a statement of equality of two ratios.
- In general, if $\frac{a}{b} = \frac{c}{d}$, then, using cross-multiplication, $a \times d = c \times b$.

WORKED EXAMPLE 8

Use the cross-multiplication method to determine whether the following pair of ratios is in proportion:
6 : 9; 24 : 36.

THINK	WRITE
1 Write the ratios in fraction form.	$\frac{6}{9}$ $\frac{24}{36}$
2 Perform a cross-multiplication.	$6 \times 36 = 216$ $24 \times 9 = 216$
3 Check whether the products are equal.	$216 = 216$ Therefore, the ratios are in proportion.

WORKED EXAMPLE 9

Find the value of a in the following proportion:
$\frac{a}{3} = \frac{6}{9}$.

THINK	WRITE
1 Write the proportion statement.	$\frac{a}{3} = \frac{6}{9}$
2 Cross-multiply and equate the products.	$a \times 9 = 6 \times 3$
3 Solve for a by dividing both sides of the equation by 9.	$9a = 18$ $\frac{9a}{9} = \frac{18}{9}$ $a = 2$

WORKED EXAMPLE 10

The ratio of girls to boys on the school bus was 4 : 3. If there were 28 girls, how many boys were there?

THINK	WRITE
1 Let the number of boys be b and write a proportion statement. (Since the first number in the ratio represents girls, place 28 (the number of girls) as the numerator.)	$\frac{4}{3} = \frac{28}{b}$
2 Cross-multiply and equate the products.	$4 \times b = 28 \times 3$
3 Solve for b by dividing both sides by 4.	$4b = 84$ $\frac{4b}{4} = \frac{84}{4}$ $b = 21$
4 Write the answer.	There are 21 boys.

REMEMBER

1. Proportion is a statement of equality of two ratios.
2. In any proportion, the products of the numbers, diagonally across from each other, are equal.
3. In general, if $\frac{a}{b} = \frac{c}{d}$, then, using cross-multiplication, $a \times d = c \times b$.

EXERCISE

5C Proportion

INDIVIDUAL PATHWAYS

eBook*plus*

Activity 5-C-1
Proportion
doc-2201

Activity 5-C-2
More proportion
doc-2202

Activity 5-C-3
Advanced proportion
doc-2203

FLUENCY

1 WE8 Use the cross-multiplication method to determine whether the following pairs of ratio are in proportion.

a 2 : 3; 8 : 12
b 4 : 7; 8 : 14
c 5 : 7; 10 : 14
d 5 : 8; 10 : 16
e $\frac{7}{9}; \frac{21}{25}$
f $\frac{3}{8}; \frac{12}{32}$
g $\frac{14}{16}; \frac{5}{9}$
h $\frac{11}{12}; \frac{7}{8}$
i $\frac{13}{15}; \frac{6}{7}$
j $\frac{8}{9}; \frac{24}{27}$
k $\frac{3}{5}; \frac{6}{8}$
l $\frac{21}{18}; \frac{49}{42}$

2 WE9 Find the value of a in each of the following proportions.

a $\frac{a}{2} = \frac{4}{8}$
b $\frac{a}{6} = \frac{8}{12}$
c $\frac{a}{9} = \frac{2}{3}$
d $\frac{3}{a} = \frac{9}{12}$
e $\frac{7}{a} = \frac{14}{48}$
f $\frac{10}{a} = \frac{3}{15}$
g $\frac{3}{7} = \frac{a}{28}$
h $\frac{12}{10} = \frac{a}{5}$
i $\frac{8}{12} = \frac{a}{9}$
j $\frac{35}{7} = \frac{5}{a}$
k $\frac{24}{16} = \frac{6}{a}$
l $\frac{30}{45} = \frac{2}{a}$

3 WE10 Solve each of the following, using a proportion statement and the cross-multiplication method.

a The ratio of boys to girls in a class is 3 : 4. If there are 12 girls, how many boys are in the class?
b In a room the ratio of length to width is 5 : 4. If the width is 8 m, what is the length?
c The team's win–loss ratio is 7 : 5. How many wins has it had if it has had 15 losses?
d A canteen made ham and chicken sandwiches in the ratio 5 : 6. If 20 ham sandwiches were made, how many chicken sandwiches were made?
e The ratio of concentrated cordial to water in a mixture is 1 : 5. How much concentrated cordial is needed for 25 litres of water?
f The ratio of chairs to tables is 6 : 1. If there are 42 chairs, how many tables are there?
g The ratio of flour to milk in a mixture is 7 : 2. If 14 cups of flour are used, how much milk is required?
h The ratio of protein to fibre in a cereal is 12 : 11. If there are 36 grams of protein, what is the mass of fibre?
i In a supermarket, the ratio of 600 mL cartons of milk to litre cartons is 4 : 5. If there are sixty 600 mL cartons, how many litre cartons are there?
j In a crowd of mobile-phone users, the ratio of men to women is 7 : 8. How many women are there if there are 2870 men?

eBook*plus*

Digital doc
Spreadsheet
Proportion
doc-2214

4 While we know that only whole numbers are used in ratios, sometimes in a proportion statement the answer can be a fraction or a mixed number. Consider the following proportion:

$$\frac{a}{6} = \frac{7}{4}$$

$$a \times 4 = 7 \times 6$$

$$4a = 42$$

$$a = 10.5 \text{ (or } 10\tfrac{1}{2}\text{)}$$

Calculate the value of a in each of the following proportion statements. Write your answer correct to 1 decimal place.

a $\frac{a}{7}=\frac{8}{5}$ **b** $\frac{a}{6}=\frac{4}{5}$ **c** $\frac{a}{3}=\frac{7}{10}$ **d** $\frac{a}{9}=\frac{9}{10}$ **e** $\frac{5}{a}=\frac{7}{10}$

f $\frac{8}{a}=\frac{6}{7}$ **g** $\frac{9}{7}=\frac{a}{6}$ **h** $\frac{13}{6}=\frac{a}{5}$ **i** $\frac{9}{15}=\frac{7}{a}$ **j** $\frac{7}{8}=\frac{9}{a}$

UNDERSTANDING

5 Write a proportion statement for each situation and then solve the problem. If necessary, write your answer correct to 1 decimal place.

a A rice recipe uses the ratio of 1 cup of rice to 3 cups of water. How many cups of rice can be cooked in 5 cups of water?

b Another recipe states that 2 cups of rice are required to serve 6 people. If you have invited 11 people, how many cups of rice will you need?

c In a chemical compound there should be 15 g of chemical A to every 4 g of chemical B. If my compound contains 50 g of chemical A, how many grams of chemical B should it contain?

d A saline solution contains 2 parts of salt to 17 parts of water. How much water should be added to 5 parts of salt?

e To mix concrete, 2 buckets of sand are needed for every 3 buckets of blue metal. For a big job, how much blue metal will be needed for 15 buckets of sand?

6 Decide whether a proportion statement could be made, using each of the following ratios:

a height : age **b** mass : age
c intelligence : age **d** distance : time
e cost : number **f** age : shoe size
g sausages cooked : number of people **h** eggs : milk (in a recipe)
i number of words : pages typed **j** length : area (of a square).

7 **a** **MC** If $\frac{p}{q}=\frac{l}{m}$, then:

A $p\times q=l\times m$ **B** $p\times l=q\times m$ **C** $p\times m=l\times q$
D $\frac{p}{m}=\frac{l}{q}$ **E** none of these is true.

b If $\frac{x}{3}=\frac{y}{6}$, then:

A $x=2$ and $y=4$ **B** $x=1$ and $y=2$ **C** $x=3$ and $y=6$
D $x=6$ and $y=12$ **E** all of these are true.

c If $\frac{23}{34}=\frac{x}{19}$ then, correct to the nearest whole number, x equals:

A 13 **B** 12 **C** 34
D 28 **E** 17

d The directions on a cordial bottle suggest mixing 25 mL of cordial with 250 mL of water. How much cordial should be mixed with 5.5 L of water?

A 0.55 mL **B** 5.5 mL **C** 55 mL
D 550 mL **E** 5500 mL

REASONING

8 In a family, 3 children receive their allowances in the ratio of their ages, which are 16 years, 14 years and 10 years. If the total of the allowances is $80, how much does each child receive?

9 In jewellery, gold is often combined with other metals. 'Pink gold' is a mixture of pure gold, copper and silver in the ratio of 15 : 4 : 1.

'White gold' is a mixture of pure gold and platinum in the ratio of 3 : 1.

a What fraction of both pink and white gold jewellery is pure gold?

Pure gold is 24 carats and is not mixed with other metals. For most jewellery, however, 18 carat gold is used.

b Using your answer to part **a**, show why jewellery gold is labelled 18 carats.

c If an 18 carat bracelet weighs 8 grams, what is the weight of gold in the bracelet?

d If the price of gold is $35 per gram, what is the cost of the gold in the bracelet?

eBook*plus*

Digital doc
WorkSHEET 5.1
doc-2216

10 Two classes each contain 8 boys. In one class, the ratio of boys to girls is 1 : 2; in the other it is 2 : 1. If the two classes combine, what will the new ratio be?

REFLECTION

Can you think of an example of how a proportion statement might be used?

5D Comparing ratios

- In some cases it is necessary to know which of two given ratios is the larger.
- In some cases it is necessary to know if two given ratios are equal.
- To compare ratios, write them as fractions with a common denominator.

WORKED EXAMPLE 11

Which is the larger ratio in the following pair?
3 : 5   2 : 3

THINK	WRITE
1 Write each ratio in fraction form.	$\frac{3}{5} \quad \frac{2}{3}$
2 Change each fraction to the lowest common denominator (which is 15).	$\frac{9}{15} \quad \frac{10}{15}$
3 Compare the fractions: since both fractions have a denominator of 15, the larger the numerator, the larger the fraction.	$\frac{9}{15} < \frac{10}{15}$
4 The second fraction is larger and it corresponds to the second ratio in the pair. State your conclusion.	Therefore, 2 : 3 is the larger ratio.

- When measuring the steepness of various slopes or hills, we need to compare the gradient.
- **Gradient** is calculated by finding the ratio

$$\frac{\text{vertical distance}}{\text{horizontal distance}}$$

between any 2 points on a hill. This is also known as calculating $\frac{\text{rise}}{\text{run}}$.

- The larger the gradient, the steeper the hill.

WORKED EXAMPLE 12

Find the gradient of the hill (AB) if AC = 2 m and BC = 10 m.

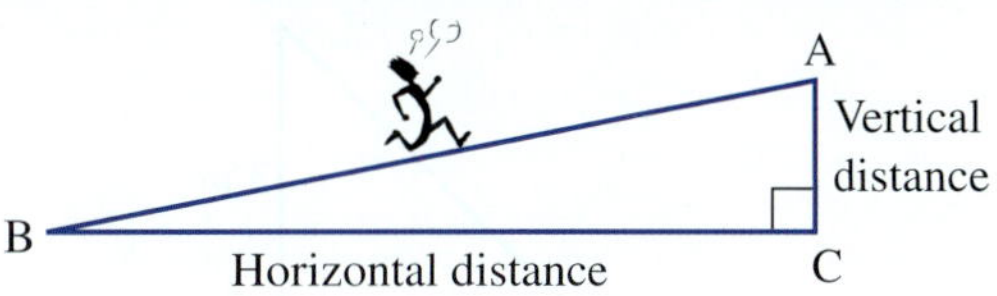

THINK	WRITE
1 Write the rule for finding the gradient.	$\text{Gradient} = \dfrac{\text{vertical distance}}{\text{horizontal distance}}$
2 Vertical distance is 2 m and horizontal distance is 10 m. Substitute these values into the formula.	$= \dfrac{2}{10}$
3 Simplify by dividing both numerator and denominator by 2.	$= \dfrac{1}{5}$

REMEMBER

1. To compare ratios, write them in fraction form first and then compare the 2 fractions by writing them with a common denominator.
2. Gradient is a measure of the steepness of the slope and is calculated by finding the ratio $\dfrac{\text{vertical distance}}{\text{horizontal distance}}$. (The distances are measured between any 2 points on the slope.)

EXERCISE 5D

Comparing ratios

INDIVIDUAL PATHWAYS

eBook*plus*

Activity 5-D-1 Comparing ratios doc-2204

Activity 5-D-2 More comparisons of ratios doc-2205

Activity 5-D-3 Advanced comparisons of ratios doc-2206

FLUENCY

1 WE11 Which is the greater ratio in each of the following pairs?

a 1 : 4, 3 : 4 **b** 5 : 9, 7 : 9
c 6 : 5, 2 : 5 **d** 3 : 5, 7 : 10
e 7 : 9, 2 : 3 **f** 2 : 5, 1 : 3
g 2 : 3, 3 : 4 **h** 5 : 6, 7 : 8
i 5 : 9, 7 : 12 **j** 9 : 8, 6 : 5

2 In each of the following cases, decide which netball team has the better record.

a St Marys won 2 matches out of 5. Colac won 5 out of 10.
b Bright 50 won 13 out of 18. Corio won 7 out of 12.
c Seymour won 12 out of 20. Geelong won 14 out of 25.
d Bell Post Hill won 8 out of 13. Bairnsdale won 13 out of 20.

3 In a cricket match, Jenny bowled 5 wides in her 7 overs and Lisa bowled 4 wides in her 6 overs. Which bowler had the higher wides per over ratio?

4 a WE12 Find the gradient of each of the hills represented by the following triangles.

i

ii

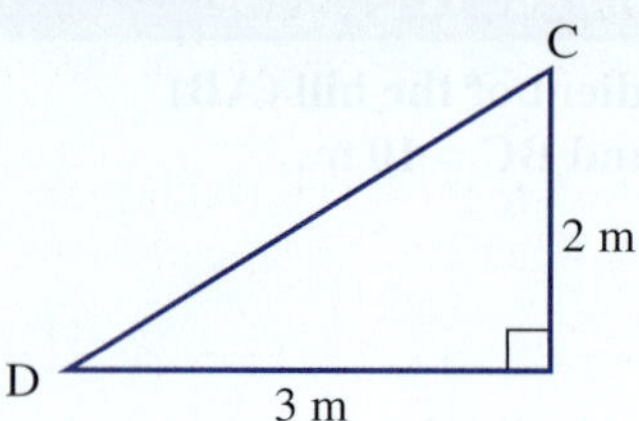

iii

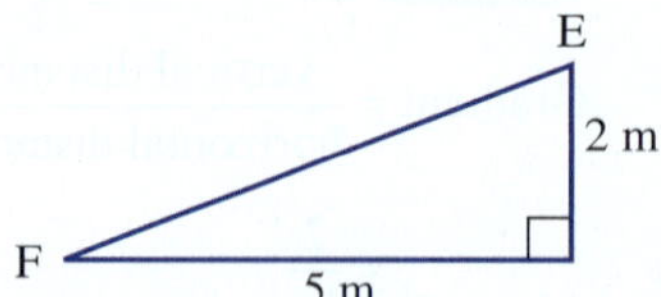

iv

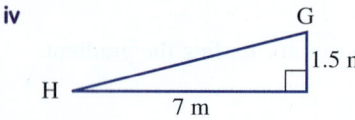

b Which slope has the largest gradient?

c Which slope has the smallest gradient?

d List the hills in order of increasing steepness.

5 Draw triangles that demonstrate a gradient of:

a $\frac{2}{1}$ **b** $\frac{3}{1}$ **c** $\frac{4}{3}$ **d** $\frac{3}{2}$ **e** $\frac{2}{5}$

eBook*plus*

Digital doc
Spreadsheet
Comparing ratios
doc-2215

UNDERSTANDING

6 a MC If the gradient of LN in the triangle at right is 1, then:

A $a > b$ **B** $a < b$ **C** $a = b$
D $a = 1$ **E** $b = 1$

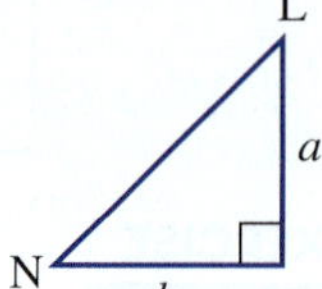

b If $\frac{5}{6} > \frac{a}{5}$, then a could be:

A 4 **B** 5 **C** 6
D 7 **E** all of these numbers.

c If $\frac{a}{b} < \frac{3}{5}$, then:

A $a < 3$ **B** $b < 5$ **C** $a < b$ **D** $b < a$ **E** $a = 2$

REASONING

7 Draw a right-angled triangle on a piece of graph paper so that the two sides at right-angles to each other are 6 cm and 8 cm. Measure the third side length of the triangle.

a What is the ratio of the three sides of this triangle?

b If you change the size of your triangle but keep the shape the same, what happens to the ratio of the three sides of the triangle?

c If you had 3 metres of string to mark out a triangle with its sides in the same ratio as the one you have drawn, what would be the length of each side marked out with string? Test your answer with a piece of string.

REFLECTION
What does it mean if the gradient is 0?

5E Dividing in a given ratio

When something is shared, we often use ratios to ensure that the sharing is fair.

Consider this situation. Two people buy a lottery ticket for $3. They win a prize of $60. How is the prize divided fairly?

eBook*plus*

eLesson
Dividing in ratios
eles-0041

Each person contributes $1.50	One person contributes $1 and the other $2
■ The contribution for the ticket is in the ratio 1 : 1. ■ The prize is divided in the ratio 1 : 1. ■ Each person receives $30.	■ The contribution for the ticket is in the ratio 1 : 2. ■ The prize is divided in the ratio 1 : 2. ■ The person who contributed $1 receives $20 and the other receives $40.

In the situation above:

- the 1 : 1 ratio has 1 + 1 = 2 total parts. Each person receives $\frac{1}{2}$ of the prize money ($30).
- the 1 : 2 ratio has 1 + 2 = 3 total parts. Person 1 paid for 1 part of the ticket so receives $\frac{1}{3}$ of the prize money ($20); person 2 paid for 2 parts of the ticket so receives $\frac{2}{3}$ of the prize money ($40).

WORKED EXAMPLE 13

Share the amount of $500 000 in the ratio 3 : 7.

THINK	WRITE
1 Determine how many shares (parts) are in the ratio.	Total number of parts $= 3 + 7$ $= 10$
2 The first share represents 3 parts out of a total of 10, so find $\frac{3}{10}$ of the total amount.	First share $= \frac{3}{10} \times \$500\,000$ $= \$150\,000$
3 The second share is the remainder, so subtract the first share amount from the total amount.	Second share $= \$500\,000 - \$150\,000$ $= \$350\,000$

- In Worked example 12, the second share represents 7 parts out of the total of 10. Another way to calculate the size of the second share would be to find $\frac{7}{10}$ of the total amount.

$$\text{Second share} = \frac{7}{10} \times \$500\,000$$
$$= \$350\,000$$

WORKED EXAMPLE 14

Concrete mixture for a footpath was made up of 1 part of cement, 2 parts of sand and 4 parts of blue metal. How much sand was used to make 4.2 m^2 of concrete?

THINK	WRITE
1 Find the total number of parts.	Total number of parts $= 1 + 2 + 4$ $= 7$
2 There are 2 parts of sand to be used in the mixture, so find $\frac{2}{7}$ of the total amount of concrete made.	Amount of sand $= \frac{2}{7} \times 4.2\ \text{m}^2$ $= 1.2\ \text{m}^2$

REMEMBER

To share a certain amount in a given ratio, find the total number of shares (parts) first. The size of each share is given by the fraction this share represents out of the total number of shares.

EXERCISE
5E Dividing in a given ratio

INDIVIDUAL PATHWAYS

eBook*plus*

Activity 5-E-1
Dividing in a given ratio
doc-2207

Activity 5-E-2
More dividing in a given ratio
doc-2208

Activity 5-E-3
Advanced dividing in a given ratio
doc-2209

FLUENCY

1 Write the total number of parts for each of the following ratios.

a 1 : 2 **b** 2 : 3 **c** 3 : 1 **d** 3 : 5 **e** 4 : 9
f 5 : 8 **g** 6 : 7 **h** 9 : 10 **i** 1 : 2 : 3 **j** 3 : 4 : 5

2 WE13 Share the amount of $1000 in the following ratios.

a 2 : 3 **b** 3 : 1 **c** 1 : 4 **d** 1 : 1 **e** 3 : 5
f 5 : 3 **g** 3 : 7 **h** 9 : 1 **i** 7 : 13 **j** 9 : 11

3 If Nat and Sam decided to share their lottery winnings of $10 000 in the following ratios, how much would each receive?

a 1 : 1 **b** 2 : 3 **c** 3 : 2 **d** 3 : 7 **e** 7 : 3
f 1 : 4 **g** 9 : 1 **h** 3 : 5 **i** 12 : 13 **j** 23 : 27

4 Rosa and Mila bought a lottery ticket costing $10. How should they share the first prize of $50 000 if their respective contributions were:

a $2 and $8?
b $3 and $7?
c $4 and $6?
d $5 and $5?
e $2.50 and $7.50?

5 WE14 Concrete mixture is made up of 1 part cement, 2 parts sand and 4 parts blue metal.

a How much sand is needed for 7 m^3 of concrete?
b How much cement is needed for 3.5 m^3 of concrete?
c How much blue metal is required for 2.8 m^3 of concrete?
d How much sand is used for 5.6 m^3 of concrete?
e How much cement is needed to make 8.4 m^3 of concrete?

6 Three of your teachers buy a Lotto ticket costing $20. How should they share the first prize of $600 000 if they each contribute:

a $3, $7 and $10?
b $6, $6 and $8?
c $1, $8 and $11?
d $5, $6 and $9?
e $5, $7.50 and $7.50?

eBook*plus*

Digital doc
Spreadsheet
Dividing in a given ratio
doc-2489

7 In a family, 3 children receive their allowances in the ratio of their ages, which are 15 years, 12 years and 9 years. If the total of the allowances is $60, how much does each child receive?

UNDERSTANDING

8 In a school, the ratio of girls in Years 8, 9 and 10 is 6 : 7 : 11. If there are 360 girls in the school:
- **a** how many Year 8 girls are there?
- **b** how many more Year 10 girls are there than Year 8 girls?

9 In a moneybox, there are 5 cent, 10 cent and 20 cent coins in the ratio 8 : 5 : 2. If there are 225 coins altogether:
- **a** how many 5 cent coins are there?
- **b** how many more 10 cent coins than 20 cent coins are there?
- **c** what is the total value of the 5 cent coins?
- **d** what is the total value of the coins in the moneybox?

10 **a** MC A square of side length 4 cm has its area divided into two sections in the ratio 3 : 5. The area of the larger section is:
A 3 cm^2 B 5 cm^2 C 8 cm^2 D 10 cm^2 E 16 cm^2

b A block of cheese is cut in the ratio 2 : 3. If the smaller piece is 150 g, the mass of the original block was:
A 75 g B 200 g C 300 g D 375 g E 450 g

c Contributions to the cost of a lottery ticket were $1.75 and $1.25. What fraction of the prize should the larger share be?
A $\frac{7}{12}$ B $\frac{5}{7}$ C $\frac{7}{5}$ D $\frac{3}{5}$ E $\frac{5}{12}$

d A television channel that telecasts only news, movies and sport does so in the ratio 2 : 3 : 4 respectively. How many movies, averaging a length of $1\frac{1}{2}$ hours, would be shown during a 24-hour period?
A 2 B 3 C 4 D 5 E 6

REASONING

11 Three angles of a triangle are in the ratio 1 : 2 : 3. What is the magnitude of each angle?

12 The angles of a quadrilateral are in the ratio 2 : 3 : 4 : 6. What is the difference in magnitude between the smallest and largest angles?

REFLECTION
Think of some examples of instances where you need to divide in a ratio other than 1 : 1.

5F Rates

- A rate is used to compare how quantities change.
- Unlike ratios, rates have units.
- An example of a rate is speed (measured in km/h or m/s)
- A rate is in its simplest form if it is per one unit.

WORKED EXAMPLE 15

Express the following statement using a rate in simplest form:
The 30 litre container was filled in 3 minutes.

THINK	WRITE
1 A suitable rate would be litres per minute (L/min). Put the capacity of the container in the numerator and the time in which it was filled in the denominator of the fraction.	Rate $= \frac{30 \text{ L}}{3 \text{ min}}$ $= \frac{10 \text{ L}}{1 \text{ min}}$
2 Simplify the fraction.	$= 10$ L/min

WORKED EXAMPLE 16

Joseph is paid $8.50 per hour as a casual worker. At this rate, how much does he receive for 6 hours of work?

THINK	WRITE
1 The rate is given in $ per hour. So it actually tells us the amount of money earned in each hour; that is, the hourly payment.	Payment per 1 hour = $8.50
2 State the number of hours worked.	Hours worked = 6
3 To find the total payment, multiply the hourly payment by the total number of hours worked.	Total payment = $8.50 × 6 = $51

REMEMBER

1. Rates are used to measure and compare the changes in different quantities.
2. Rates are usually written using 'per' or a slash (/).
3. Rates are considered to be in simplest form if they are expressed per one unit (for example, per minute, per hour, per kg and so on).

EXERCISE 5F Rates

INDIVIDUAL PATHWAYS

eBook*plus*

Activity 5-F-1 Rates doc-2210

Activity 5-F-2 More rates doc-2211

Activity 5-F-3 Advanced rates doc-2212

FLUENCY

1 WE15 Express each of the following statements using a rate in simplest form.

a A lawn of 600 m^2 was mown in 60 min.

b A tank of capacity 350 kL is filled in 70 min.

c A balloon of volume 4500 cm^3 was inflated in 15 s.

d The cost of 10 L of fuel was $13.80.

e A car used 16 litres of petrol in travelling 200 km.

f A 12 m length of material cost $30.

g There were 20 cows grazing in a paddock that was 5000 m^2 in area.

h The gate receipts for a crowd of 20 000 people were $250 000.

i The cost of painting a 50 m^2 area was $160.

j The cost of a 12 minute phone call was $3.00.

k The team scored 384 points in 24 games.

l Last year 75 kg of fertiliser cost $405.

m The winner ran the 100 m in 12 s.

n To win, Australia needs to make 260 runs in 50 overs.

o For 6 hours work, Bill received $159.

p The 5.5 kg parcel cost $19.25 to post.

q Surprisingly, 780 words were typed in 15 minutes.

r From 6 am to noon, the temperature changed from 10 °C to 22 °C.

s When Naoum was 10 years old he was 120 cm tall. When he was 18 years old he was 172 cm tall.

t A cyclist left home at 8.30 am and at 11.00 am had travelled 40 km.

2 WE16 Sima is paid \$15.50 per hour. At this rate, how much does she earn in a day on which she works 7 hours?

3 A basketball player scores, on average, 22 points per match. How many points will he score in a season in which he plays 18 matches?

4 A car's fuel consumption is 11 L/100 km. How much fuel would it use in travelling 550 km?

5 To make a solution of fertiliser, the directions recommend mixing 3 capfuls of fertiliser with 5 L of water. How many capfuls of fertiliser should be used to make 35 L of solution?

6 Anne can type 60 words per minute. How long will she take to type 4200 words?

7 Marie is paid \$42 per day. For how long will she have to work to earn \$504?

8 The rate of 1 teacher per 16 students is used to staff a school. How many teachers will be required for a school with 784 students?

9 Land is valued at \$42 per m^2. How much land could be bought for \$63 000?

10 On average, a test bowler took 1 wicket every 4.5 overs. How many wickets did he take in a season in which he bowled 189 overs?

UNDERSTANDING

11 What quantities (such as distance, time, volume) are changing if the units of rate are:

a km/h?
b cm^3/sec?
c L/km?
d \$ per h?
e \$ per cm?
f kL/min?
g cents/litre?
h \$ per dozen?
i kg/year?
j cattle/hectare?

12 What units would you use to measure the changes taking place in each of the following situations.

a A rainwater tank being filled.
b A girl running a sprint race.
c A boy getting taller.
d A snail moving across a path.
e An ink blot getting larger.
f A car consuming fuel.
g A batsman scoring runs.
h A typist typing a letter.

13 Water flows from a hose at a rate of 3 L/min. How much water will flow in 2 h?

14 Tea bags in a supermarket can be bought for \$1.45 per pack (pack of 10) or for \$3.85 per pack (pack of 25). Which is the cheaper way of buying the tea bags?

15

Car A uses 41 L of petrol in travelling 500 km. Car B uses 34 L of petrol in travelling 400 km. Which car is the more economical?

16 Coffee can be bought in 250 g jars for $9.50 or in 100 g jars for $4.10. Which is the cheaper way of buying the coffee and how large is the saving?

17 MC **a** A case containing 720 apples was bought for $180. The cost could be written as:

A 30 cents each **B** 20 cents each
C $3.00 per dozen **D** $2.00 per dozen
E $2.80 for 10

b Mark, a test cricketer, has a batting strike rate of 68, which means he has made 68 runs for every 100 balls faced. What is Steve's strike rate if he has faced 65 overs and has made 280 runs? (*Note:* Each over contains 6 balls.)

A 65 **B** 68.2 **C** 71.8
D 73.2 **E** 74.1

c A carport measuring 8 m × 4 m is to be paved. The paving tiles cost $36 per m^2 and the tradesperson charges $12 per m^2 to lay the tiles. How much will it cost to pave the carport (to the nearest $50)?

A $1400 **B** $1450 **C** $1500
D $1550 **E** $1600

d A tank of capacity 50 kL is to be filled by a hose whose flow rate is 150 L/min. If the tap is turned on at 8 am, when will the tank be filled?

A Between 1.00 pm and 1.30 pm **B** Between 1.30 pm and 2.00 pm
C Between 2.00 pm and 2.30 pm **D** Between 2.30 pm and 3.00 pm
E Between 3.00 pm and 3.30 pm

REASONING

18 A chiropractor sees 160 patients every week.

a What is his rate of seeing patients each hour if he works a 40-hour week?
b How long, on average, does he spend with each patient?
c Using these rates, if the chiropractor wants to make at least $10 000 every week, what is the minimum he must charge each patient?

19 If 4 monkeys eat 4 bananas in 4 minutes, how long does it take 12 monkeys to eat 12 bananas?

eBook*plus*
Digital doc
WorkSHEET 5.2
doc-2217

20 If Bill takes 3 hours to paint a room, and James takes 5 hours to paint a room, how long will it take to paint a room if they work together?

REFLECTION
Why do we need units with rates?

Summary

Introduction to ratios

- Ratios compare quantities of the same kind.
- The ratios themselves do not have a name or unit of measurement.
- The order of the numbers in a ratio is important.
- Before ratios are written, the numbers must be expressed in the same units of measurement.
- Ratios contain only whole numbers.

Simplifying ratios

- If each number in a ratio is multiplied or divided by the same number, the equivalent (or equal) ratio is formed.
- It is customary to write ratios in the simplest form. This is achieved by dividing each number in the ratio by the highest common factor (HCF).
- To form a ratio using fractions, convert the fractions so that they have a common denominator and then write the ratio of the numerators.
- Decimals can be easily changed into whole numbers if they are multiplied by powers of 10 (that is, 10, 100, 1000 and so on).
- If the ratio contains algebraic terms, divide both parts of the ratio by the highest common factor (HCF) including common algebraic terms.

Proportion

- Proportion is a statement of equality of two ratios.
- In any proportion, the products of the numbers, diagonally across from each other, are equal.
- In general, if $\frac{a}{b} = \frac{c}{d}$, then, using cross-multiplication, $a \times d = c \times b$.

Comparing ratios

- To compare ratios, write them in fraction form first and then compare the 2 fractions by writing them with a common denominator.
- Gradient is a measure of the steepness of the slope and is calculated by finding the ratio $\frac{\text{vertical distance}}{\text{horizontal distance}}$. (The distances are measured between any 2 points on the slope.)

Dividing in a given ratio

- To share a certain amount in a given ratio, find the total number of shares (parts) first. The size of each share is given by the fraction this share represents out of the total number of shares.

Rates

- Rates are used to measure and compare the changes in different quantities.
- Rates are usually written using 'per' or a slash (/).
- Rates are considered to be in simplest form if they are expressed per one unit (for example, per minute, per hour, per kg and so on).

MAPPING YOUR UNDERSTANDING

Using terms from the summary, and other terms if you wish, construct a concept map that illustrates your understanding of the key concepts covered in this chapter. Compare this concept map with the one that you created in *What do you know?* on page 111.

Have you completed the two *Homework sheets*, the *Rich task* and the two *Code puzzles* in your *Maths Quest 8 Homework Book*?

Chapter review

FLUENCY

1 On a farm there are 5 dogs, 3 cats, 17 cows and 1 horse. Write the following ratios.
- **a** cats : dogs
- **b** horses : cows
- **c** cows : cats
- **d** dogs : horses
- **e** dogs : other animals

2 Express each of the following ratios in simplest form.
- **a** 8 : 16
- **b** 24 : 36
- **c** 35 mm : 10 cm
- **d** \$2 : 60 cents
- **e** 20 s : $1\frac{1}{2}$ min
- **f** $\frac{1}{12} : \frac{1}{3}$
- **g** 4 : 10
- **h** 56 : 80
- **i** 2 hours : 40 min
- **j** 1.5 km : 400 m

3 Find the value of n in each of the following proportions.
- **a** $\frac{n}{3} = \frac{20}{15}$
- **b** $\frac{n}{28} = \frac{5}{7}$
- **c** $\frac{2}{3} = \frac{8}{n}$
- **d** $\frac{4}{5} = \frac{12}{n}$
- **e** $\frac{6}{n} = \frac{5}{8}$
- **f** $\frac{3}{10} = \frac{n}{4}$

4 The directions for making lime cordial require the mixing of 1 part cordial to 6 parts of water.
- **a** Express this as a ratio.
- **b** How much cordial would you have to mix with 9 L of water?

5 Which is the larger ratio?
- **a** $\frac{4}{5}, \frac{2}{3}$
- **b** $\frac{7}{12}, \frac{5}{8}$

6 Place a number in the box to make a ratio greater than 3 : 2 but less than 2 : 1.

□ : 6

7 The horizontal and the vertical distances between the top and bottom points of slide A are 3 m and 2 m respectively. For slide B the horizontal distance between the top and bottom points is 10 m, and the vertical distance is 4 m.
- **a** Calculate the gradients of slide A and slide B.
- **b** Which slide is steeper? Justify your answer.

8 **a** Divide \$25 in the ratio 2 : 3.
- **b** Share \$720 in the ratio 7 : 5.

9 Three people share a Lotto prize of \$6600 in the ratio 4 : 5 : 6. What is the difference between the smallest and largest shares?

10 A car travels 840 km on 72 litres of petrol. Find the fuel consumption of the car in L/100 km.

11 David's car has a fuel consumption rate of 12 km/L, and Susan's car has a fuel consumption rate of 11 km/L.
- **a** Which car is more economical?
- **b** How far can David's car travel on 36 L of fuel?
- **c** How much fuel (to the nearest litre) would Susan's car use in travelling 460 km?

12 A 1 kg packet of flour costs \$2.80 and a 750 g packet costs \$2.20. Which is the cheaper way of buying flour?

PROBLEM SOLVING

1 The sides of a triangle are in the ratio 3 : 4 : 5. If the longest side of the triangle measures 40 cm, what is the perimeter of the triangle?

2 A 747 airplane has a length of 70.7 m and a wingspan of 64.4 m. A model of this plane has a wingspan of 30 cm. How long is the model?

3 The triangle ABC at right is an isosceles right-angled triangle. The length of AC is 20 cm. If the lengths of AD and BD are the same and the lengths of CE and BE are the same, what is the length of DE?

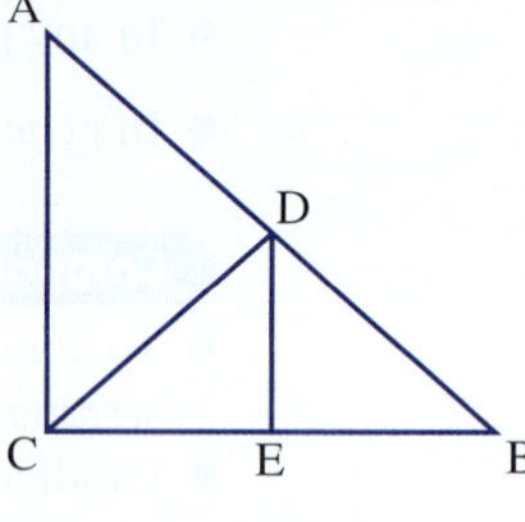

4 To make two $\frac{2}{3}$-cup servings of cooked rice, you add $\frac{3}{4}$ of a cup of rice, $\frac{1}{4}$ teaspoon of salt and 1 teaspoon of butter to $1\frac{1}{2}$ cups of water. How many $\frac{2}{3}$-cup servings of cooked rice can you make from a bag containing 12 cups of rice?

5 Lachlan was driven from Richmond to Kinglake National Park, a distance of 60 km, at an a verage speed of 80 km/h. He cycled back at an average speed of 20 km/h. What was his average speed for the whole journey? (*Hint:* It is not 50 km/h.)

6 The speed of the *Discovery* space shuttle while in orbit was 17 400 miles per hour. What is this in km/h? (1 kilometre = 0.62 miles)

7 The rate of ascent for the *Discovery* space shuttle is 71 miles in 8.5 minutes.
- **a** What speed is this in km/min?
- **b** What speed is this in km/h?

8 A cyclist riding at 12 km/h completes a race in 3 h 45 min.
  a What is the distance of the race?
  b At what speed would he have to ride to complete the race in 3 h?

9 You have a plastic bag that contains 80 tennis balls. This bag of balls weighs 4 kg (the weight of the plastic bag is insignificant). You add 10 more balls to your bag. How much does your bag of balls weigh now?

10 The steps of a staircase are to have a ratio of rise to run that is to be $\frac{2}{3}$. If the run is 30 cm, what is the rise?

11 Travelling from Noort to Bastion takes me 1 hour and 30 minutes by car at an average speed of 72 km per hour. I stop for 15 minutes in Bastion before travelling to Smoop, which is 163 km away. The trip from Bastion to Smoop takes me 2 hours and 12 minutes.
What is my average speed for the whole trip?

12 A sum of money is divided in the ratio 2 : 5 : 7. Given that the smallest share is $200, calculate the largest share.

13 It takes me 2 hours to mow my lawn. My son takes 2.5 hours to mow the same lawn. If we work together using two lawnmowers, how long will it take us to mow the lawn? Give your answer in hours, minutes and seconds.

eBook*plus*

Interactivities
Test yourself
Chapter 5
int-2364
Word search
Chapter 5
int-2623
Crossword
Chapter 5
int-2624

eBookplus ACTIVITIES

Chapter opener

Digital doc *(page 111)*
- Hungry brain activity Chapter 5 (doc-6887)

Are you ready?

Digital docs *(page 112)*
- SkillSHEET 5.1 (doc-6888) Converting units of length, capacity and time
- SkillSHEET 5.2 (doc-6889) Highest common factor
- SkillSHEET 5.3 (doc-6890) Simplifying fractions
- SkillSHEET 5.4 (doc-6891) Finding and converting to the lowest common denominator
- SkillSHEET 5.5 (doc-6892) Converting a mixed number to an improper fraction
- SkillSHEET 5.6 (doc-6893) Multiplying decimals by 10, 100 and 1000
- SkillSHEET 5.7 (doc-6894) Multiplying a whole number by a fraction
- SkillSHEET 5.8 (doc-6895) Converting minutes to a fraction of an hour

5A Introduction to ratios

Digital docs *(page 114)*
- Activity 5-A-1 (doc-2195) Ripper ratios
- Activity 5-A-2 (doc-2196) Radical ratios
- Activity 5-A-3 (doc-2197) Real ratios

Weblink *(page 113)*
- Introducing ratios

Interactivity *(page 114)*
- Fruit salad ratio (int-0076)

5B Simplifying ratios

Digital docs *(page 118)*
- Activity 5-B-1 (doc-2198) Simplifying ratios
- Activity 5-B-2 (doc-2199) More simplifying of ratios
- Activity 5-B-3 (doc-2200) Advanced simplifying of ratios
- Spreadsheet (doc-2213) Simplifying ratios *(page 119)*

Interactivity (int-2740) *(page 118)*
- Converting percentages, decimals, fractions, ratios

5C Proportion

Digital docs *(page 122)*
- Activity 5-C-1 (doc-2201) Proportion
- Activity 5-C-2 (doc-2202) More proportion
- Activity 5-C-3 (doc-2203) Advanced proportion
- Spreadsheet (doc-2214) Proportion
- WorkSHEET 5.1 (doc-2216) *(page 124)*

5D Comparing ratios

Digital docs *(page 125)*
- Activity 5-D-1 (doc-2204) Comparing ratios
- Activity 5-D-2 (doc-2205) More comparisons of ratios
- Activity 5-D-3 (doc-2206) Advanced comparisons of ratios
- Spreadsheet (doc-2215) Comparing ratios *(page 126)*

5E Dividing in a given ratio

Digital docs *(page 128)*
- Activity 5-E-1 (doc-2207) Dividing in a given ratio
- Activity 5-E-2 (doc-2208) More dividing in a given ratio
- Activity 5-E-3 (doc-2209) Advanced dividing in a given ratio
- Spreadsheet (doc-2489) Dividing in a given ratio

eLesson *(page 127)*
- Dividing in ratios (eles-0041)

5F Rates

Digital docs *(page 130)*
- Activity 5-F-1 (doc-2210) Rates
- Activity 5-F-2 (doc-2211) More rates
- Activity 5-F-3 (doc-2212) Advanced rates
- WorkSHEET 5.2 (doc-2217) *(page 132)*

Chapter review

Interactivities *(page 135)*
- Test yourself Chapter 5 (int-2364) Take the end-of-chapter test to test your progress.
- Word search Chapter 5 (int-2623)
- Crossword Chapter 5 (int-2624)

To access eBookPLUS activities, log on to

www.jacplus.com.au

Application of percentages

6A Common percentages and shortcuts
6B Discount
6C Profit and loss

WHAT DO YOU KNOW?

1 List what you know about percentages. Create a concept map to show your list.
2 Share what you know with a partner and then with a small group.
3 As a class, create a large concept map that shows your class's knowledge of percentages.

eBook*plus*

Digital doc
Hungry brain activity
Chapter 6
doc-6896

15% OFF
MARKED PRICE
FURTHER 5%
TRADE DISCOUNT

OPENING QUESTION

Will you get a 20% discount?

Are you ready?

Try the questions below. If you have difficulty with any of them, extra help can be obtained by completing the matching SkillSHEET located on your eBookPLUS.

eBook*plus*

Digital doc
SkillSHEET 6.1
doc-6897

Rounding money to the nearest 5 cents

1 Round the following amounts to the nearest 5 cents.

a $23.48 b $207.91

eBook*plus*

Digital doc
SkillSHEET 6.2
doc-6898

Converting a percentage to a decimal fraction

2 Convert each of the following percentages to a decimal fraction.

a 34% b 79% c 4%
d 67.2% e 8.25% f 17.5%

eBook*plus*

Digital doc
SkillSHEET 6.3
doc-6899

Decreasing a quantity by a percentage

3 Decrease 100% by the following percentages.

a 15% b 12.5% c 90% d 5.5%

eBook*plus*

Digital doc
SkillSHEET 6.4
doc-6900

Finding a percentage of a quantity (money)

4 Find each of the following.

a 10% of $350 b 25% of $1424 c 18% of $9000 d 12.5% of $4570

eBook*plus*

Digital doc
SkillSHEET 6.5
doc-6901

Expressing one quantity as a percentage of another

5 For each of the following pairs, express the first quantity as a percentage of the second quantity.

a $56, $400 b $13, $20 c $125, $625

eBook*plus*

Digital doc
SkillSHEET 6.6
doc-6902

Increasing a quantity by a percentage

6 Increase 100% by the following percentages.

a 25% b 5% c 100% d 12.5%

6A Common percentages and shortcuts

- Many money calculations involve the use of fractions or percentages. Some fractions are used more often than others; for example $\frac{1}{2}$, $\frac{1}{4}$, $\frac{3}{4}$, $\frac{1}{3}$ and $\frac{2}{3}$.
- Ten per cent is frequently used because it is one of the easiest percentages to calculate. For example:

10% of \$17.00	10% of \$89.90	10% of \$168.33
$= \frac{\cancel{10}^{1}}{\cancel{100}_{10}} \times \frac{17}{1}$	$= \frac{10}{100} \times 89.90$	$= \frac{10}{100} \times 168.33$
$= \frac{17}{10}$	$= 0.10 \times 89.90$	$= 0.10 \times 168.33$
= \$1.70	= 8.990	= 16.833
	= \$8.99	**= \$16.83**

Shortcut for finding 10%

- To find 10%, divide by 10 or move the decimal point one place to the left.
  10% of \$17.00 = \$1.70
  10% of \$89.90 = \$8.99 ≈ \$9 (to the nearest 5c)
  10% of \$168.33 = \$16.833 ≈ \$16.85 (to the nearest 5c)
- Remember: Round to 2 decimal places and then to the nearest 5c for cash.

WORKED EXAMPLE 1

Find 10% of each of the following, rounding the answer to the nearest 5 cents.
a \$37 b \$12.95

THINK	WRITE
a Write the question and move the position of the decimal point one place to the left for the answer. Remember that if there is no decimal point, put it at the end of the number. (\$17 = \$17.00)	a 10% of \$37 = \$3.70
b 1 Write the question and move the position of the decimal point one place to the left for the answer.	b 10% of \$12.95 = \$1.295
2 Round to the nearest 5 cents.	= \$1.30

- As you have just seen, finding 10% is easy without a calculator or a pen and paper. If you can find 10%, then a lot of other percentages are also easy to find. Some examples of these are:
  To find 5%, halve 10%.
  To find 20%, double 10%.
  To find 15%, add 10% and 5%.
  To find 25%, double 10% and add 5%.

WORKED EXAMPLE 2

Find: a 5% of \$180 b 20% of \$7
c 15% of \$52 d 25% of \$46.

THINK	WRITE
a 1 Find 10% of the amount.	a 10% of \$180 = \$18
2 Find 5% by halving the remaining amount.	5% of \$180 = \$9

b	1 Find 10% of the amount.	**b** 10% of \$7 = \$0.70
	2 Find 20% by doubling the amount.	20% of \$7 = 2 × \$0.70 = \$1.40
c	1 Find 10% of the amount.	**c** 10% of \$52 = \$5.20
	2 Find 5% of the amount by halving 10%.	5% of \$52 = \$5.20 ÷ 2 = \$2.60
	3 Find 15% of the amount by adding 10% and 5%.	15% of \$52 = \$5.20 + \$2.60 = \$7.80
d	1 Find 10% of the amount.	**d** 10% of \$46 = \$4.60
	2 Find 20% by doubling 10%.	20% = 2 × \$4.60 = \$9.20
	3 Find 5% of the original amount by halving 10%.	5% = \$4.60 ÷ 2 = \$2.30
	4 Find 25% by adding the 20% and the 5%.	25% = \$9.20 + \$2.30 = \$11.50

Shortcut method for using 10% and 1%

- Percentages such as 12% can be found using a combination of 10% and multiples of 1%.
- $1\% = \frac{1}{100}$ (one hundredth).
- To find 1%, divide by 100 or move the decimal point two places to the left.
- To calculate 12% of an amount, find 10% and add the product of 2 and 1%.
  12% = 10% + 2 × 1%

WORKED EXAMPLE 3

Find:

a 12% of \$53

b 43% of \$120. Round answers to the nearest 5c.

THINK		WRITE
a	1 Break up the percentage into lots of 10% and 1%.	**a** 12% = 10% + 2 × 1%
	2 Find 10% of the amount.	10% of \$53 = \$5.30
	3 Find 2% of the amount by finding 1% and doubling it.	2% of \$53 = 2 × 1% of \$53 = 2 × \$0.53 = \$1.06
	4 Find 12% of the amount by adding 10% and 2% of the amount.	12% of \$53 = \$5.30 + \$1.06 = \$6.36 Another way to write this solution would be: 12% of \$53 = 10% of \$53 + 2 × 1% of \$53 = \$5.30 + 2 × \$0.53 = \$6.36
	5 Round to the nearest 5c.	= \$6.35

b To find 43%, find $4 \times 10\% + 3 \times 1\%$.

b 43% of \$120 = $4 \times 10\%$ of \$120 + $3 \times 1\%$ of \$120
= $4 \times \$12 + 3 \times \$1.20$
= \$48 + \$3.60
= \$51.60

REMEMBER

1. To find 10% of an amount, move the position of the decimal point one place to the left.
2. To find 1% of an amount, move the position of the decimal point two places to the left.

EXERCISE 6A Common percentages and shortcuts

INDIVIDUAL PATHWAYS

eBook*plus*

Activity 6-A-1 Common percentages doc-6903

Activity 6-A-2 Shortcuts with percentages doc-6904

Activity 6-A-3 Advanced shortcuts with percentages doc-6905

FLUENCY

1 WE1 Find 10% of each of the following, rounding the answer to the nearest 5c.

a \$10.00	**b** \$18.00	**c** \$45.00	**d** \$81.00
e \$150.00	**f** \$112.00	**g** \$93.00	**h** \$79.00
i \$47.00	**j** \$22.00	**k** \$16.50	**l** \$17.20
m \$12.60	**n** \$1.50	**o** \$32.90	**p** \$47.80
q \$81.40	**r** \$192.40	**s** \$507.00	**t** \$4620.00
u \$1926.00	**v** \$3041.50	**w** \$7219.60	**x** \$1999.90

2 Find 10% of the following. Round your answers to the nearest 5c.

a \$15	**b** \$51	**c** \$17	**d** \$9
e \$137	**f** \$172	**g** \$4.29	**h** \$6.37
i \$8.12	**j** \$39.17	**k** \$74.81	**l** \$13.95
m \$102.75	**n** \$67.87	**o** \$42.96	**p** \$517.83
q \$304.77	**r** \$628.41	**s** \$100.37	**t** \$207.08

3 WE2a Find 5% of each of the following. Round the answers to the nearest 5c.

a \$8.20	**b** \$6.40	**c** \$1.60	**d** \$2.20
e \$140.20	**f** \$81.00	**g** \$42.40	**h** \$10.60
i \$242.60	**j** \$304.80	**k** \$1000	**l** \$642.75
m \$103.27	**n** \$31.70	**o** \$5.90	

4 WE2b Find 20% of the following. Round the answers to the nearest 5c.

a \$21.50	**b** \$42.30	**c** \$8.20	**d** \$3.30
e \$74.10	**f** \$0.90	**g** \$0.79	**h** \$16.40
i \$135.80	**j** \$261.70	**k** \$1237	**l** \$5069

5 For each of the following, express the percentage as a decimal first and then solve, remembering to round your answer to the nearest 5c.

a 15% of \$12	**b** 15% of \$8.00	**c** 15% of \$20.00	**d** 15% of \$60.00
e 25% of \$30.00	**f** 25% of \$45.00	**g** 25% of \$90.00	**h** 25% of \$220.00
i 30% of \$15.00	**j** 30% of \$25.00	**k** 30% of \$47.50	**l** 30% of \$102.20

6 Find 1% of the following. Round the answers to the nearest 5c.

a \$268	**b** \$713	**c** \$573	**d** \$604
e \$5.60	**f** \$12	**g** \$13	**h** \$14.80
i \$21.70	**j** \$81.75	**k** \$19.89	**l** \$429.50
m \$4.25	**n** \$6.49	**o** \$9.99	**p** \$0.24
q \$0.77	**r** \$1264.37		

7 WE3 Find the following. Round the answers to the nearest 5c.

a 12% of $11 b 21% of $50 c 11% of $30 d 3% of $22
e 6% of $40 f 22% of $10 g 13% of $14 h 35% of $210
i 12% of $150 j 9% of $17 k 2% of $53 l 7% of $29
m 45% of $71.50 n 33% of $14.50 o 42% of $3.80 p 31% of $1.45
q 64% of $22.50 r 41% of $1200

8 MC a 10% of $7.25 equals:

A $725 B $7.30 C $72.50 D $0.73 E $7250

b 1% of $31.48 equals:

A $3.14 B $0.31 C $0.32 D $31.50 E $0.03

c 15% of $124 equals:

A $18.60 B $1.24 C $6.20 D $13.64 E $15.24

d 22% of $5050 equals:

A $60.60 B $50.50 C $1111 D $43.56 E $1010

UNDERSTANDING

9 Maria is buying a new set of golf clubs. The clubs are marked at $950, but if Maria pays cash, the shop will take 10% off the marked price. How much will the clubs cost if Maria pays cash?

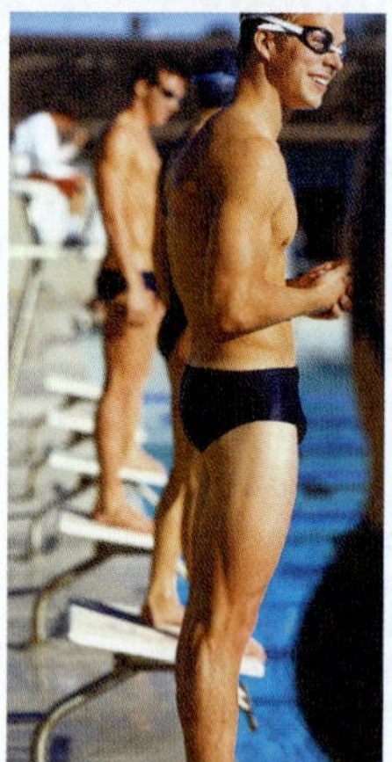

10 Thirty per cent of residents in the shire of Booroondara are over the age of 65. If there are 180 000 residents, how many are over the age of 65?

11 Jay is buying a new lounge suite worth $2150. Jay has to leave a 15% deposit and then pay the balance in monthly instalments. How much deposit does Jay have to pay?

12 Ninety per cent of students at a school were present for school photographs. If the school has 1100 students, how many were absent on the day the photographs were taken?

13 Jim can swim 50 m in 31 seconds. If he improves his time by 10%, what will Jim's time for 50 m be?

14 In a survey, 40 people were asked if they liked or disliked Vegemite. Of the people surveyed, 5% said they disliked Vegemite. How many people:

a disliked Vegemite?
b liked Vegemite?

15 Thirty-two thousand four hundred people went to the Gabba to watch a Brisbane versus Collingwood football match. Of the crowd, 42% went to the game by car and 55% caught public transport. How many people:

a arrived by car?
b caught public transport?

16 Explain how to use the shortcut method (that is, without using acalculator) to leave a $17\frac{1}{2}$% tip for a bill of $76.

17 The Geelong to Melbourne train fare of $12 was increased by 10%. How much will you pay for the return trip? (Assume that the fare is the same each way.)

18 The Goods and Services tax, known as GST, is charged at a rate of 10% in Australia. If the cost before tax for a jumper is $79.00, how much GST will be added to your bill?

19 A school receives a 10% discount on textbooks. How much discount will be given if it purchases 500 maths textbooks at $56 each?

REASONING

20 When I am 5% older than I am now, I will be 21 years old. How old am I now?

21 The price of bread has increased by 250% in the past 20 years. If a loaf of bread costs $2.00 now, how much would it have cost 20 years ago?

22 I am six months old. If I gain 10% of my current mass I will be three times my birth mass. If my birth mass was 3 kg, what is my mass now? Round your answer to one decimal place.

23 I am 33 years old. I have lived in England for 8 years. If I stay in England, how old will I be when the number of years I have lived there is 50% of my age?

24 My mother is four times older than I am. My sister is 75% of my age, and 10% of my grandfather's age. My father is 50, 2 years older than my mother. How old are my sister and grandfather?

eBook*plus*

Digital doc
WorkSHEET 6.1
doc-6912

REFLECTION

In what situations would it be useful to use the shortcut methods for common percentages?

6B Discount

- To get rid of old stock (for example out-of-date fashions at the end of a season), store managers often reduce prices by giving discounts.
- A discount is a reduction in price.
- A discount can be shown as an amount in dollars.

- A discount can be shown as a percentage of the marked price (that is, the price marked on the article).

- If the discount is expressed as a percentage, to find the actual amount of a discount, we calculate the percentage of the marked price by multiplying the marked price by the percentage. For example, a 10% discount on an item marked at \$120 gives a discount amount of \$12.

Calculating selling price of a discounted item

- Method 1
  - Use the percentage remaining after the percentage discounted has been subtracted from 100%; that is, if an item for sale has a 10% discount then the price must be 90% of the marked price.

WORKED EXAMPLE 4

Find the sale price on a hat marked \$72 if a 10% discount is given.

THINK	WRITE
1 Find the percentage of the marked price that is paid, by subtracting the percentage discount.	$100\% - 10\% = 90\%$
2 Find the sale price of the hat.	90% of \$72 $= 0.9 \times \$72$ $= \$64.80$
3 Write the answer in a sentence.	The sale price of the hat is \$64.80.

- Method 2
  - The new sale price of the item can be solved by calculating the amount of the discount, then subtracting the discount from the marked price.
  - Alternative solution:

$$\begin{aligned}\text{Discount} &= 10\% \text{ of } \$72.00\\ &= \$7.20\\ \text{Sale price} &= \text{marked price} - \text{discount}\\ &= \$72.00 - \$7.20\\ &= \$64.80\end{aligned}$$

WORKED EXAMPLE 5

Peddles is a bicycle store that has offered a discount of 15% on all goods.
Find:

a the cash discount allowed on a bicycle costing \$260
b the sale price of the bicycle.

THINK	WRITE
a Find the discount, which is 15% of the marked price.	**a** Discount = 15% of \$260 = 0.15 × \$260 = \$39 The cash discount allowed is \$39.
b 1 To find the sale price, subtract the discount from the marked price.	**b** Sale price = marked price − discount = \$260 − \$39 = \$221
2 Answer the question in a sentence.	The sale price of the bicycle is \$221.

- To calculate the percentage discount, write the monetary amount as a percentage of the original price.

$$\text{Percentage discount} = \frac{\text{cash discount}}{\text{original price}} \times \frac{100}{1}\%.$$

WORKED EXAMPLE 6

At Peddles, the price of a bicycle is reduced from \$260 to \$200. Calculate the percentage discount.

THINK	WRITE
1 Calculate the amount of the discount.	Discount = \$260 − \$200 = \$60
2 Write the discount as a percentage of the original price.	Percentage discount = $\frac{60}{260} \times 100\%$ = 23%
3 Answer the question in a sentence.	The percentage discount is about 23%.

REMEMBER

1. A discount is usually a percentage of the marked price.
2. To find the discounted price of an item, reduce the original price by the amount of the discount.
3. To find the percentage discount, write the discount as a percentage of the original price.

EXERCISE 6B Discount

INDIVIDUAL PATHWAYS

eBook*plus*

Activity 6-B-1 Discount doc-6906

Activity 6-B-2 More discounts doc-6907

Activity 6-B-3 Tricky discounts doc-6908

FLUENCY

1 Calculate the discount for each of the items in the table, using the percentage shown.

	Item	Marked price	Discount
a	MP3 player	\$210	20%
b	Skateboard	\$185	25%
c	Rollerblades	\$330	15%
d	Mobile phone	\$190	40%

2 Without the use of a calculator, calculate the percentage discount for each of the following.

	Marked price	Discount
a	\$100	\$10
b	\$250	\$125
c	\$90	\$30
d	\$80	\$20

3 **WE4** Find the sale price of each article when the marked price and discount are shown as in this table.

	Marked price (R.R.P.)	Discount
a	\$1000	15%
b	\$250	20%
c	\$95	12%
d	\$156	$33\frac{1}{3}\%$
e	\$69.95	$7\frac{1}{2}\%$

4 Decrease the amount by the percentages.

a \$50 by 10%

b \$90 by 50%

c \$45 by 20%

5 Find the percentage discount given on the items shown in the table. Round to the nearest per cent.

	Original price	Selling price
a	\$25	\$15
b	\$100	\$72
c	\$69	\$50
d	\$89.95	\$70

UNDERSTANDING

6 A PS3 player was advertised with a saving of \$148. Estimate the percentage discount being offered.

7 The following items are all discounted.

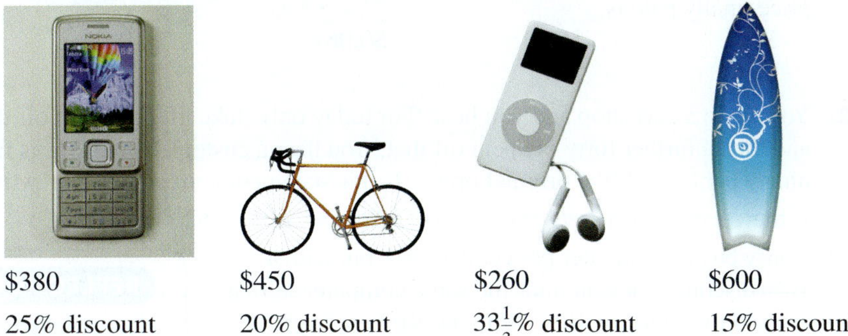

$380	$450	$260	$600
25% discount	20% discount	$33\frac{1}{3}$% discount	15% discount

a Which has the largest discount?
b Which have the same amount of discount?
c What is the difference between the largest and the smallest discount?
d If the surfboard had a discount of 20%, would $470 be enough to buy it?

8 WE5 A sale discount of 20% was offered by the music store Solid Sound. Find:
a the cash discount allowed on a $350 sound system
b the sale price of the system.

9 A calculator wristwatch is advertised at $69.95, less 10% discount. Find the sale price.

10 A store-wide clearance sale advertised 15% off everything.
a What would be the selling price of a pair of jeans marked at $49?
b If a camera marked at $189 was sold for $160.65, was the correct percentage deducted?

11 T-shirts are advertised at $15.95 less 5% discount. How much would Jim pay for five T-shirts?

12 WE6 Calculators were advertised at $20, discounted from $25. What percentage discount was given?

13 A tennis racquet marked at $79.95 sells for $60. What percentage discount is this, to the nearest whole number?

14 CDs normally selling for $28.95 were cleared for $23.95. What percentage discount was given?

15 A shirt was reduced from $90 to $63. Express the reduction as a percentage of the original price.

16 At a sale, Ann bought a $120 jacket for $48. What percentage of the original price did she save?

17 You bought a mobile phone priced $199.95 and signed up for a 1-year plan. You received a 10% discount on the telephone and 15% discount on the $75 connection fee. How much did you pay altogether (correct to the nearest 5 cents)?

18 Aanh bought two hairdryers for $128 each. She sold one at a loss of 5% and the other for a profit of 10%.
a Find the selling price of each.
b Will she have made a profit or a loss?

19 MC Kristen's car insurance was $670, but she had a 'No claim bonus' discount of 12%. Which of the following will not give the amount she must pay?
A First find 12% of $670 and add you answer to $670.
B Calculate $88 \div 100 \times 670$.
C Find 88% of $670.
D First find 12% of $670, and subtract your answer from $670.
E All of the above

REASONING

20 Movie tickets sell for $12.00 each, but if you buy 4 or more you get $1.00 off each ticket. What percentage discount is this? We figure $1 as a percentage of $11.

21 MC I am allowed a discount of 10% off the total price of 6 articles that cost $\$x$ each. The price finally paid is:
A $\$60x$ B $\$5.4x$ C $\$0.06x$
D $\$0.6x$ E $\$6x$

22 You are in a surf shop and you hear 'For today only: take fifty per cent off the original price and then a further forty per cent off that.' You hear a customer say 'This is fantastic! You get ninety per cent off the original price!' Is this statement correct? Explain why.

23 Is there a difference between 75% off $200 and 75% of $200? Explain.

24 Henry buys a computer priced at $1060, but with a 10% discount. Sancha finds the same computer selling at $840 plus a tax of 18%. Who has the best buy? Explain.

eBook*plus*
Digital doc
Investigation
Successive discounts
doc-2228

REFLECTION
How are discounts used to encourage people to purchase?

6C Profit and loss

- When a manufacturer produces a product, it is usually sold to a wholesaler who subsequently sells the product on to retail outlets. At each stage the product is marked up by a certain percentage.
- The price the retail shop owner pays for the product is the *cost price*.
- When a retailer calculates the price to be marked on an article (the *selling price*), many overhead costs must be taken into account (staff wages, rent, store improvements, electricity, advertising and so on).
- The *profit* is the difference between the total of the retailer's costs (cost price) and the price for which the goods actually sell (selling price).
  - If SP > CP then a profit is made.

$$\text{Profit} = \text{selling price} - \text{cost}$$

  - If SP < CP then a loss is made.

$$\text{Loss} = \text{cost} - \text{selling price}$$

Selling price

- To calculate the selling price of an item given the cost price and the percentage profit, increase the cost price by the given percentage.

$$\text{Selling price} = (100\% + \text{percentage profit}) \text{ of cost price}$$

- To calculate the selling price of an item given the cost price and the percentage loss, decrease the cost price by the given percentage.

$$\text{Selling price} = (100\% - \text{percentage loss}) \text{ of cost price}$$

WORKED EXAMPLE 7

Ronan operates a sports store at a fixed profit margin of 65%. For how much would he sell a pair of running shoes that cost him $40?

THINK	WRITE
1 Find the selling price by first adding the percentage profit to 100% then finding this percentage of the cost price.	Selling price = 165% of \$40 = 1.65 × \$40 = \$66
2 Write the answer in a sentence.	The running shoes would sell for \$66.

WORKED EXAMPLE 8

David bought a surfboard for \$300 and sold it at a 20% loss a year later. What was the selling price?

THINK	WRITE
1 Find the selling price by first subtracting the percentage loss from 100% then finding this percentage of the cost price.	Selling price = 80% of \$300 = 0.80 × \$300 = \$240
2 Write the answer in a sentence.	David sold the surfboard for \$240.

- Profit or loss is usually calculated as a percentage of the cost price.

$$\text{Percentage profit} = \frac{\text{profit}}{\text{cost}} \times 100\%$$

$$\text{Percentage loss} = \frac{\text{loss}}{\text{cost}} \times 100\%$$

WORKED EXAMPLE 9

A music store buys CDs at \$15 each and sells them for \$28.95 each. What is the percentage profit made on the sale of a CD?

THINK	WRITE
1 Calculate the profit on each CD: selling price – cost.	Profit = \$28.95 – \$15 = \$13.95
2 Calculate the percentage profit: $\frac{\text{profit}}{\text{cost}} \times 100\%$.	Percentage profit = $\frac{13.95}{15} \times 100\%$ = 93%
3 Write the answer in a sentence, rounding to the nearest per cent if applicable.	The profit is 93% of the cost price.

- Modern accounting practice favours calculating profit or loss as a percentage of the selling price. This is because commissions, discounts, taxes and other items of expense are commonly based on the selling price.

$$\text{Percentage profit} = \frac{\text{profit}}{\text{selling price}} \times 100\%$$

$$\text{Percentage loss} = \frac{\text{loss}}{\text{selling price}} \times 100\%$$

Weblink
Percent game

REMEMBER

1. (a) Profit = selling price – cost
   (b) Loss = cost – selling price
2. (a) Percentage profit = $\frac{\text{profit}}{\text{cost}} \times 100\%$ or Percentage profit = $\frac{\text{profit}}{\text{selling price}} \times 100\%$
   (b) Percentage loss = $\frac{\text{loss}}{\text{cost}} \times 100\%$ or Percentage loss = $\frac{\text{loss}}{\text{selling price}} \times 100\%$
3. (a) Selling price = (100% + percentage profit) of cost price
   (b) Selling price = (100% – percentage loss) of cost price

EXERCISE

6C Profit and loss

INDIVIDUAL PATHWAYS

eBook*plus*

Activity 6-C-1
Profit and loss
doc-6909

Activity 6-C-2
More profit and loss
doc-6910

Activity 6-C-3
Advanced profit and loss
doc-6911

Assume percentage profit or loss is calculated on the cost price unless otherwise stated.

FLUENCY

1 WE7,8 Find the selling price for each of the following:

	Cost price	%	Profit/loss
a	\$18	40%	profit
b	\$116	25%	loss
c	\$1300	30%	profit
d	\$213.00	75%	loss
e	\$699	$33\frac{1}{3}\%$	profit

2 WE9 For each of the following items, find the percentage profit or loss.

	Cost price	Selling price
a	\$15	\$20
b	\$40	\$50
c	\$40	\$30
d	\$75	\$85
e	\$38.50	\$29.95

UNDERSTANDING

3 A supermarket buys frozen chickens for \$3.50 each and sells them for \$5.60. What is the percentage profit made on the sale of each chicken?

4 A restored motorbike was bought for \$350 and later sold for \$895.
   a How much profit was made?
   b What percentage was profit? Give your answer correct to the nearest whole number.

5 James' Second Hand Bookshop buys second hand books for \$4.80 and sells them for \$6.00.
   a What is the ratio of the profit to the cost price?
   b What is the percentage profit on the cost price?
   c What is ratio of the profit to the selling price?
   d What is the percentage profit on the selling price?
   e Discuss how **a** and **b** are related.

6 A retailer bought a laptop for \$1200 and advertised it for \$1525.
   a How much profit was made?
   b What is the percentage profit on the cost price?
   c What is the percentage profit on the selling price?
   d Compare the differences between the answers to **b** and **c**.

7 Rollerblades bought for \$139.95 were sold after six months for \$60.

a How much was the loss?

b What was the percentage loss? Give your answer to the nearest whole number.

8 A sports card collection costing \$80 was sold for \$65. What was the percentage loss?

9 Running shoes bought by a sports store for \$30 per pair were sold at \$79.95. What percentage profit was made?

10 Kyle runs a jewellery business that uses a fixed profit margin of 98%. For how much would he sell a necklace that cost him \$830?

11 Find the selling price for each item.

a Jeans costing \$20 are sold with a profit margin of 95%.

b A soccer ball costing \$15 is sold with a profit margin of 80%.

c A sound system costing \$499 is sold at a loss of 45%.

d A skateboard costing \$30 is sold with a profit margin of 120%.

12 The *Cheapfruit shop* bought 500 kg of tomatoes for \$900 and sold them for \$2.80 per kg.

a What is the profit per kilogram?

b Calculate the profit as a percentage of the cost price (round to 1 decimal place).

c Calculate the profit as a percentage of the selling price (round to 1 decimal place).

d Compare the answers to parts **b** and **c**.

13 Sonja bought an old bike for \$20. She spent \$47 on parts and paint and renovated it. She then sold it for \$115 through her local newspaper. The advertisement cost \$10.

a What were her total costs?

b What percentage profit did she make on costs?

c What percentage profit was made on the selling price?

14 **MC** A clothing store operates on a profit margin of 150%. The selling price of an article bought for \$$p$ is:

A \$151p **B** \$150p **C** \$2.5p
D \$1.5p **E** \$0.15p

REASONING

15 A fruit and vegetable retailer buys potatoes by the tonne for \$180, and sells them in 5-kg bags for \$2.45. What percentage profit is made?

16 Two business partners bought a business for \$158 000 and sold it for \$213 000. The profit was to be shared between the two business partners in the ratio of 3 : 2.
What percentage share does each person receive?

17 What is the maximum discount a retailer can offer on her marked price of \$100 so that she ends up selling at no profit and no loss, if she had initially marked her goods up by \$50?

18 Four friends dine out at a restaurant. They calculate that their bill should be \$96. When they get the bill at the end of the night, the total is \$108, including GST of 10%. Was the bill correct? Use mathematical reasoning to justify your answer.

eBook*plus*

Digital doc
WorkSHEET 6.2
doc-6913

REFLECTION
How can you tell if an item is being sold for a profit or a loss?

Summary

Common percentages and shortcuts

- To find 10% of an amount, move the position of the decimal point one place to the left.
- To find 1% of an amount, move the position of the decimal point two places to the left.

Discount

- A discount is usually a percentage of the marked price.
- To find the discounted price of an item, reduce the original price by the amount of the discount.
- To find the percentage discount, write the discount as a percentage of the original price.

Profit and loss

- Profit = selling price − cost
  Loss = cost − selling price
- Percentage profit $= \dfrac{\text{profit}}{\text{cost}} \times 100\%$ or Percentage profit $= \dfrac{\text{profit}}{\text{selling price}} \times 100\%$

  Percentage loss $= \dfrac{\text{loss}}{\text{cost}} \times 100\%$ or Percentage loss $= \dfrac{\text{loss}}{\text{selling price}} \times 100\%$
- Selling price = (100% + percentage profit) of cost price
  Selling price = (100% − percentage loss) of cost price

MAPPING YOUR UNDERSTANDING

Using terms from the summary, and other terms if you wish, construct a concept map that illustrates your understanding of the key concepts covered in this chapter. Compare this concept map with the one that you created in *What do you know?* on page 137.

Have you completed the two *Homework sheets*, the *Rich task* and the two *Code puzzles* in your *Maths Quest 8 Homework Book*?

Chapter review

FLUENCY

1 Calculate these amounts.
   a $2.45 + $13.20 + $6.05
   b $304.60 − $126.25
   c $9.65 × 7

2 What is $65.50 ÷ 11? (Round your answer to the nearest 5 cents.)

3 Find 10% of each of the following by moving the position of the decimal point. Round your answer to the nearest 5 cents.
   a $63.00 b $42.00
   c $105.00 d $216
   e $3.45 f $42.68
   g $118.55 h $2125.85

4 Find 5% of the following by finding 10% and halving your answer. Round your answer to the nearest 5 cents.
   a $8.00 b $21.00
   c $64.00 d $104.00
   e $35.00 f $52.00
   g $205.50 h $77.30

5 Calculate the following using 'shortcuts'. Round your answer to the nearest 5 cents.
   a 1% of $16.00 b 1% of $28.00
   c 12% of $42.00 d 30% of $90.00
   e 22% of $220.00 f 43% of $27
   g 15% of $19.50 h 8% of $37

6 Mentally calculate 12% of $15.

7 Use a shortcut to calculate 1.5% of $20.

8 Use a shortcut to calculate 5.5% of $50.

9 Use a shortcut to calculate 10.1% of $18, rounding the answer to the nearest 5c.

10 Jill purchased a hand bag for $250 and later sold it on eBay for $330.
   a What is the percentage profit on the cost price?
   b What is the percentage profit on the selling price?
   c Compare the answers to **a** and **b**.

PROBLEM SOLVING

1 Natalie went shopping and bought a pair of bathers for $38.95, a football for $75.50, four pot plants at $8.75 each and a photograph album for $14.90. How much money did Natalie spend in total?

2 Sally bought a motorbike costing $2785. She paid a deposit of $160 then paid the remainder in 15 equal instalments. How much was each instalment?

3 Jacques' furniture shop had a sale with $\frac{1}{3}$ off the usual price of lounge suites. If the original price of a suite was $5689, what will the sale price be?

4 Heo buys a new television set marked $495. He pays a $100 deposit and 12 payments of $40 each. How much more than the marked price does he finally pay?

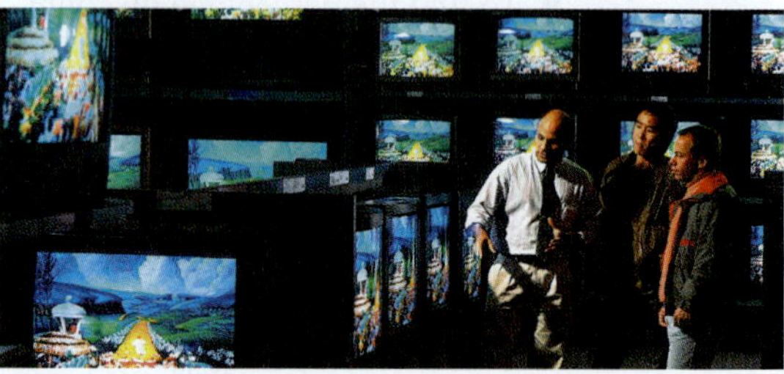

5 Estimate the total bill and change, then find the exact amounts when $150 is used to buy:

10 disks at $0.95 each

2 games at $59.95 each

1 file box at $8.95.

6 William owns a hairdressing salon and raises the price of haircuts from $26.50 to $29.95. By what percentage did he increase the price of haircuts?

7 The price of milk increased by 8%. If the original price was $1.84, what is the new price?

8 Goods listed at $180 were discounted by 22%.
   a What was the sale price?
   b If they had sold for $100, what would the percentage discount have been?

9 A discount of 18% on a tennis racquet reduced its price by $16.91. What was the sale price?

10 After a 5% discount, a telephone bill is $79.50. How much was the bill originally?

11 A portable CD player bought for $129 was later sold for $85. What percentage loss was made on the sale?

12 Find the percentage profit on a Mini Disc recorder purchased for $320 and later sold for $350.

13 A 15% discount reduced the price of a basketball by $4.83. What was the original price?

14 Tim works in a sports shop. He purchased wholesale golf shirts for $55 each. For how much did he sell the shirts, if he made 163% profit?

15 Shannon buys a used car for \$7500. The dealer requires a 15% deposit. Calculate the deposit Shannon has to pay.

16 Ricky Ponting buys a cricket bat for \$85, signs it and donates it for a sport's auction. If it sells for \$500:

- **a** what is the percentage increase in the bat's value?
- **b** what is the dollar value of the signature?

17 Sets of 90-minute CDs are sold as in the following packs. Which is the best buy?

Cost (\$)	Number of CDs
\$3.25	6
\$4.99	10
\$7.50	15

18 Which is a better buy — 400 g of biscuits costing \$2.98, or a pack of biscuits with 400 g + 25% extra, costing \$3.28?

19 Antwert buys a pair of jeans for \$59.95. The original price tag was covered by a 30% sticker but the sign on top of the rack said an 'Additional 15% off already reduced prices.'

- **a** How could Antwert work out how much he had saved?
- **b** What percentage of the original cost did he end up saving?

20 Ann has \$100 on March 30th. This increased by 10% on April 30th. The total amount increased by 10% again on May 30th.

- **a** How much did Ann have on May 30th?
- **b** Compare your answer with a 20% increase on \$100. Do they get the same answer?

eBook*plus*

Interactivities

Test yourself
Chapter 6
int-2366

Word search
Chapter 6
int-2625

Crossword
Chapter 6
int-2626

eBookplus ACTIVITIES

Chapter opener

Digital doc *(page 137)*
- Hungry brain activity Chapter 6 (doc-6896)

Are you ready?

Digital docs *(page 138)*
- SkillSHEET 6.1 (doc-6897) Rounding money to the nearest 5 cents
- SkillSHEET 6.2 (doc-6898) Converting a percentage to a decimal fraction
- SkillSHEET 6.3 (doc-6899) Decreasing a quantity by a percentage
- SkillSHEET 6.4 (doc-6900) Finding a percentage of a quantity (money)
- SkillSHEET 6.5 (doc-6901) Expressing one quantity as a percentage of another
- SkillSHEET 6.6 (doc-6902) Increasing a quantity by a percentage

6A Common percentages and shortcuts

Digital docs *(page 141)*
- Activity 6-A-1 (doc-6903) Common percentages
- Activity 6-A-2 (doc-6904) Shortcuts with percentages
- Activity 6-A-3 (doc-6905) Advanced shortcuts with percentages
- WorkSHEET 6.1 (doc-6912) *(page 143)*

6B Discount

Digital docs *(page 145)*
- Activity 6-B-1 (doc-6906) Discount
- Activity 6-B-2 (doc-6907) More discounts
- Activity 6-B-3 (doc-6908) Tricky discounts
- Investigation (doc-2228) Successive discounts *(page 148)*

6C Profit and loss

Digital docs *(page 150)*
- Activity 6-C-1 (doc-6909) Profit and loss
- Activity 6-C-2 (doc-6910) More profit and loss
- Activity 6-C-3 (doc-6911) Advanced profit and loss
- WorkSHEET 6.2 (doc-6913) *(page 152)*

Weblink *(page 149)*
- Percent game

Chapter review

Interactivities *(page 155)*
- Test yourself Chapter 6 (int-2366) Take the end-of-chapter test to test your progress.
- Word search Chapter 6 (int-2625)
- Crossword Chapter 6 (int-2626)

To access eBookPLUS activities, log on to

www.jacplus.com.au

7 Congruence and transformations

7A Congruent figures
7B Triangle constructions
7C Congruent triangles
7D Quadrilaterals

WHAT DO YOU KNOW?

1. List what you know about congruence and transformations. Create a concept map to show your list.
2. Share what you know with a partner and then with a small group.
3. As a class, create a large concept map that shows your class's knowledge of congruence and transformations.

eBook*plus*

Digital doc
Hungry brain activity
Chapter 7
doc-6914

OPENING QUESTION

The windows of this building are made up of repeating panes of glass. How many different shapes are in each window?

Are you ready?

Try the questions below. If you have difficulty with any of them, extra help can be obtained by completing the matching SkillSHEET located on your eBookPLUS.

eBook*plus*

Digital doc
SkillSHEET 7.1
doc-6915

Naming angles and shapes

1 Give two different names for the following angle.

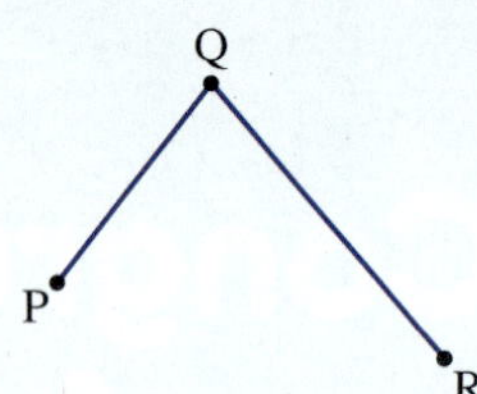

2 Name the following triangle in two different ways.

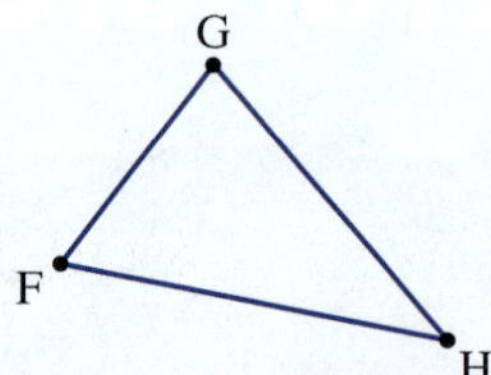

eBook*plus*

Digital doc
SkillSHEET 7.2
doc-6916

Calculating angles in triangles

3 Calculate the value of the variables.

a
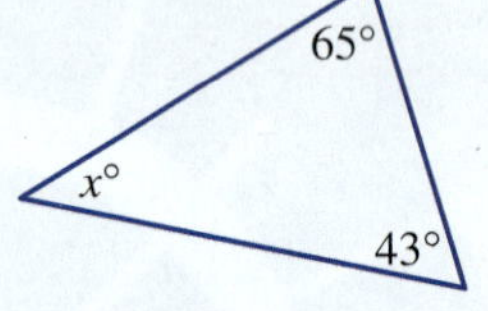

b
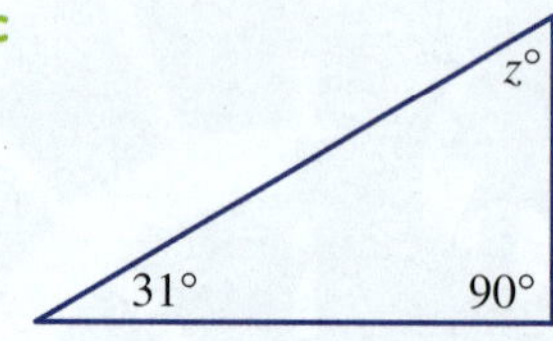

c

eBook*plus*

Digital doc
SkillSHEET 7.3
doc-6917

Angles and parallel lines

4 a Indicate whether the two angles given in each diagram are corresponding, alternate or co-interior.

i
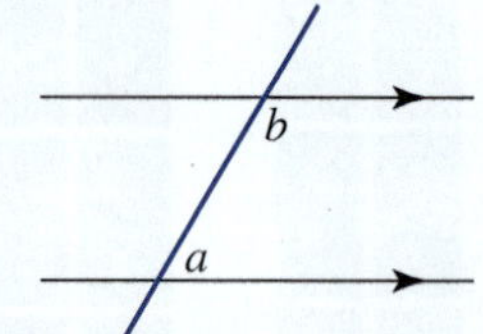

ii
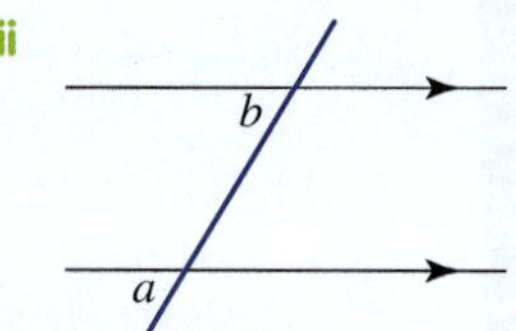

iii
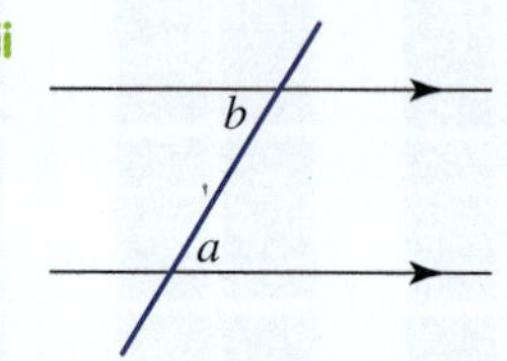

b Find the value of the variables in the diagram at right.

c State whether the line AB is parallel to line CD in this diagram. Give a reason for your answer.

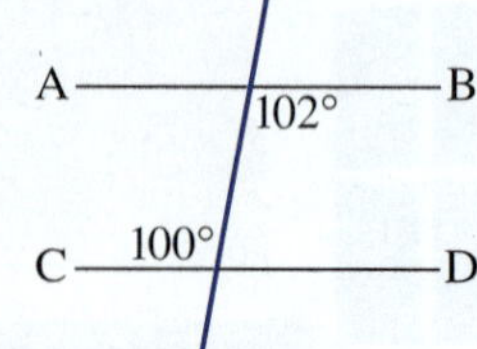

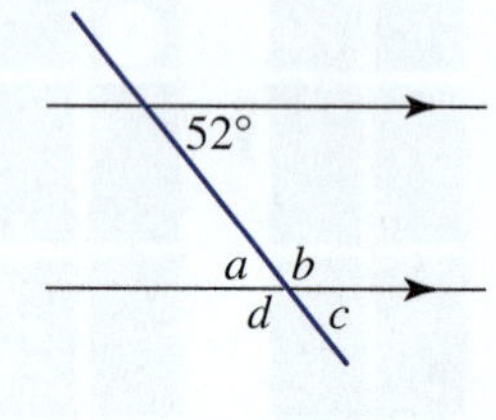

eBook*plus*

Digital doc
SkillSHEET 7.4
doc-6918

Reflections

5 What would the following letters look like in the mirror (reflection)?

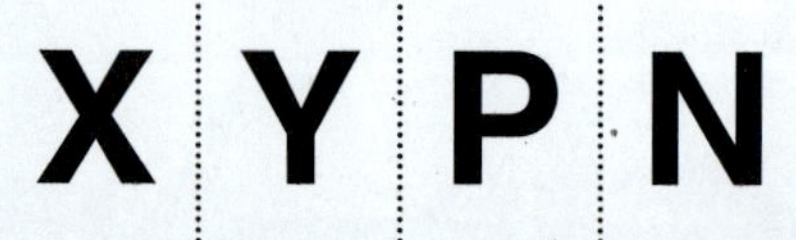

eBook*plus*

Digital doc
SkillSHEET 7.5
doc-6919

Rotations

6 Rotate the following shapes 90° clockwise about the origin.

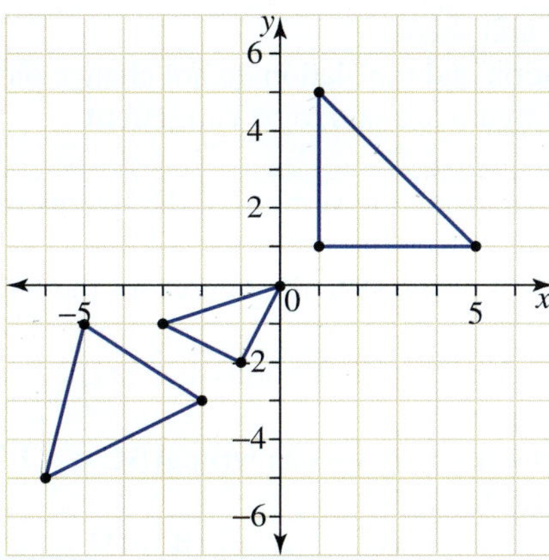

eBook*plus*

Digital doc
SkillSHEET 7.6
doc-6920

Translations

7 Move the following shapes up 2 and right 3.

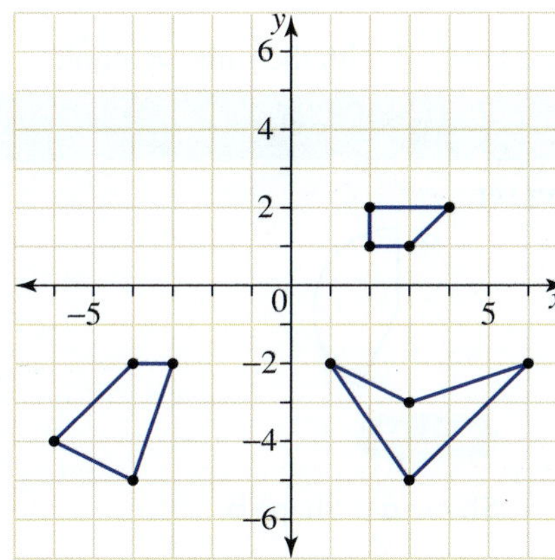

7A Congruent figures

- Congruent figures are identical in size and shape.
- The transformations of reflection, rotation and translation do not change the shape and size of a figure. The original and transformed figure are said to be **congruent**.
- The symbol used for congruence is ≡.
- When writing congruence statements, we name the vertices of the figures in corresponding (or matching) order.
- Sometimes you will need to rotate, reflect or translate the figures for them to be orientated the same way.
- If, through one or more translations, rotations and reflections, one shape lies exactly on top of the other, then these two figures are congruent.
- The figures below are congruent. For the triangle, we can write ABC ≡ A′B′C′; for the pentagon, we can write ABCDE ≡ PQRST.

B Mirror line B′

A C C′ A′

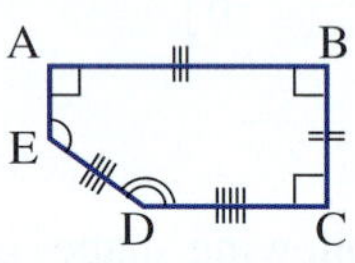

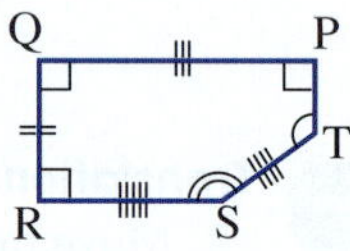

Note that equivalent sides and angles are labelled with the same symbol.

WORKED EXAMPLE 1

Select a pair of congruent shapes from the following set.

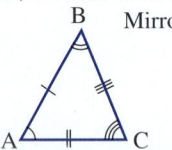

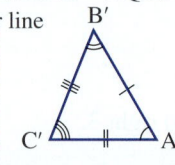

a **b** **c** **d**

THINK

Figures **a**, **b** and **c** have the same shape (that is, a semicircle). Figure **d** is not a semicircle and thus is not congruent to any other figures. Figure **c** is larger than figures **a** and **b** and so is not congruent to any one of them. Figures **a** and **b** are identical in shape and size (**b** is a reflection of **a**) and therefore, are congruent to each other.

WRITE

Shape **a** ≡ Shape **b**

WORKED EXAMPLE 2

Find the value of the variables in the pair of congruent triangles at right.

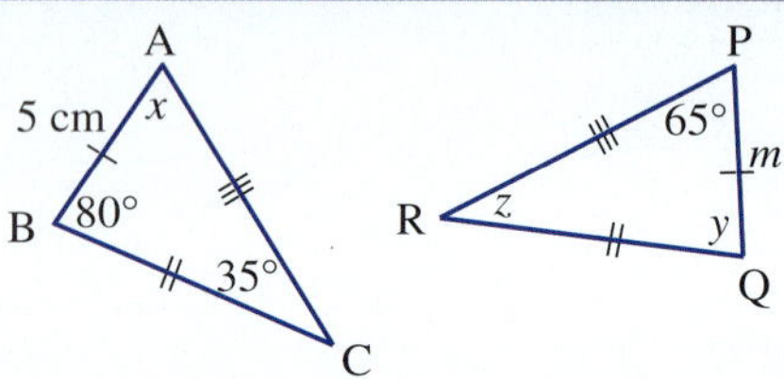

THINK

1 Since △ABC ≡ △PQR, the corresponding angles are equal in size. Corresponding angles are included between the sides of equal length.
So, by looking at the markings on the sides of the triangles, we can conclude that:
∠BAC corresponds to ∠RPQ
∠ABC corresponds to ∠PQR
∠ACB corresponds to ∠PRQ.
So, match the variables with the corresponding angles whose sizes are given.

WRITE

$x = 65°$
$y = 80°$
$z = 35°$

2 In congruent triangles, the corresponding sides are equal in length. Using the markings on the sides of the triangles, observe that the unknown side PQ corresponds to side AB. State the value of the variable (which represents the length of PQ).	$m = 5$ cm

REMEMBER

1. Congruent figures are identical figures; that is, they have the same shape and size.
2. When stating one figure is congruent to another, the vertices should be listed in corresponding (or matching) order.

EXERCISE 7A

Congruent figures

INDIVIDUAL PATHWAYS

eBook*plus*

Activity 7-A-1 Congruency doc-2238

Activity 7-A-2 More congruency doc-2239

Activity 7-A-3 Advanced congruency doc-2240

eBook*plus*

Interactivity **Transformations and the Cartesian plane** int-2368

FLUENCY

1 Plot the following coordinates on a Cartesian plane: (1, −1), (1, 0), (1, 1), (2, 1), (1, 2), (1, 3), (2, 3), (3, 3). Join the points with straight lines to make the shape of the letter F.

a Reflect this figure in the *y*-axis and describe the new location using the coordinate points.

b Translate the original figure by three units to the right and two units down, and describe the new location using the coordinate points.

c Rotate the original figure through 90° about the origin and describe the new location using the coordinate points.

d Look at the transformations in parts **a**, **b** and **c**. Are the shapes congruent? Why?

2 WE1 Select a pair of congruent shapes from each of the following sets.

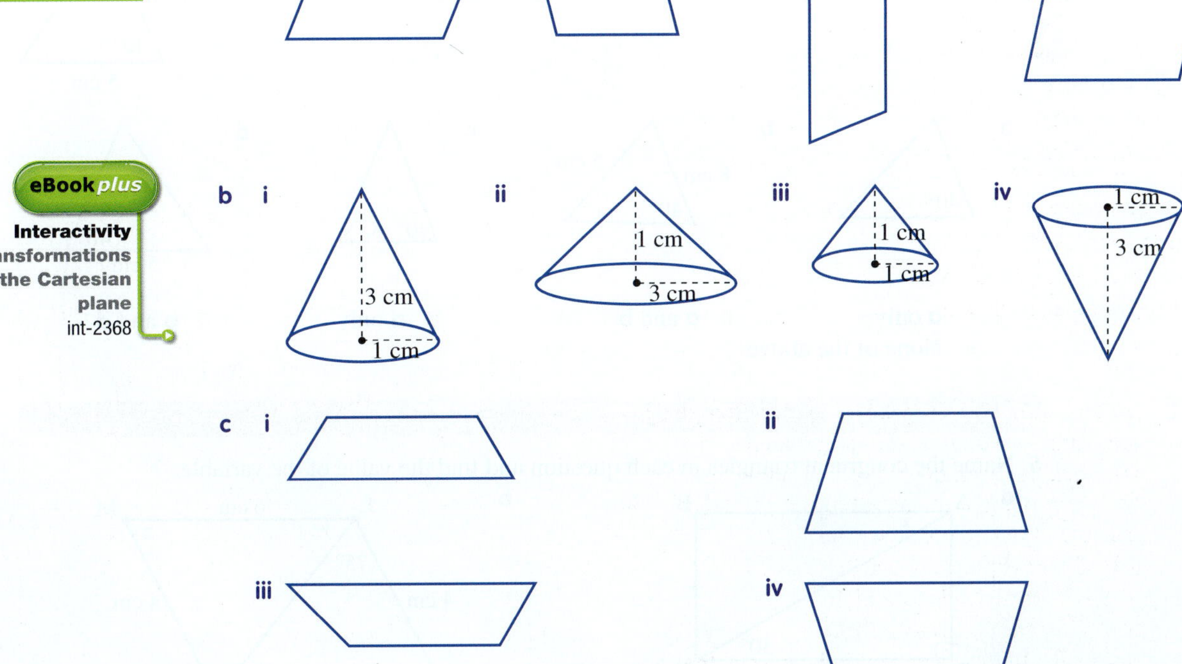

3 WE2 Name the congruent triangles in these figures and find the value of the variables in each case. (*Remember:* The vertices must be listed in corresponding order.)

a

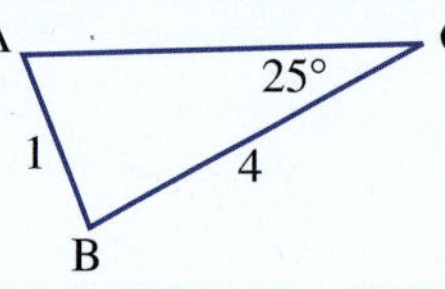

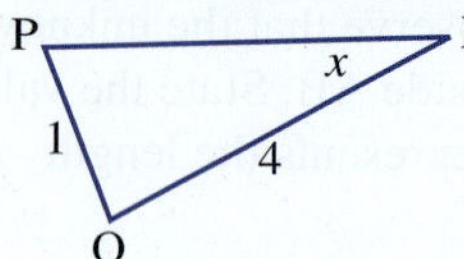

b

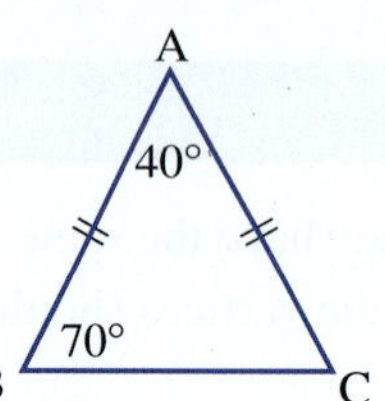

P
y
70°
x
Q
R

c

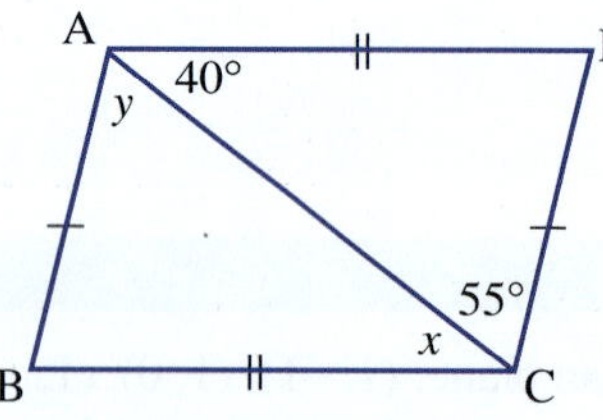

d

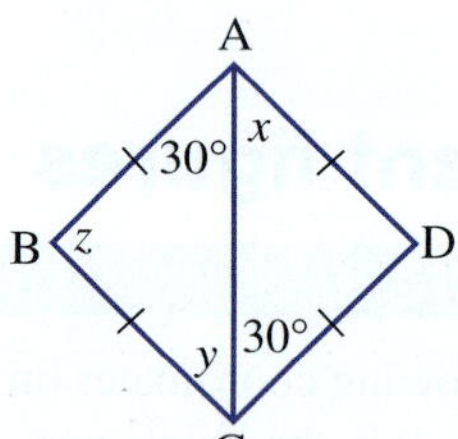

e

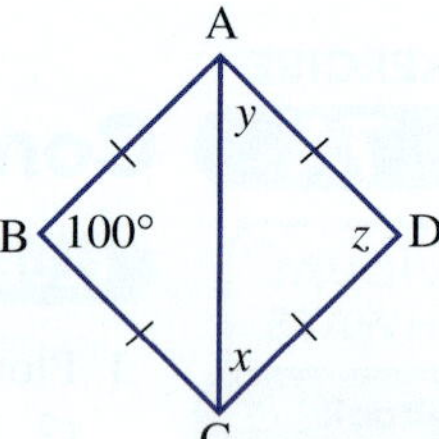

f

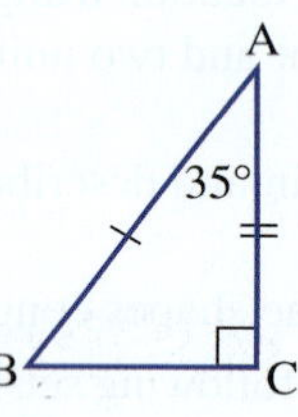

P
x
y
Q
R

4 MC Which of the following is congruent to the triangle shown?

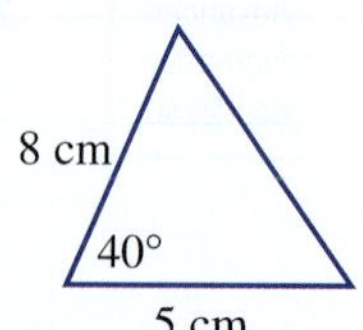

a

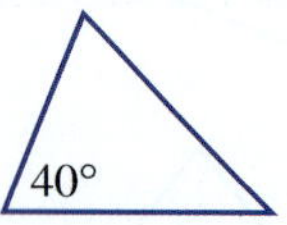

b

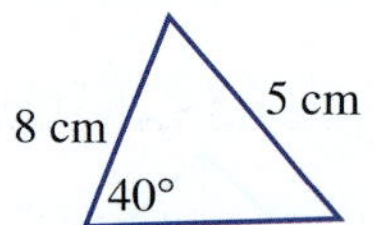

c

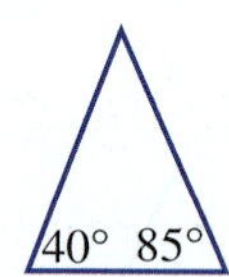

d

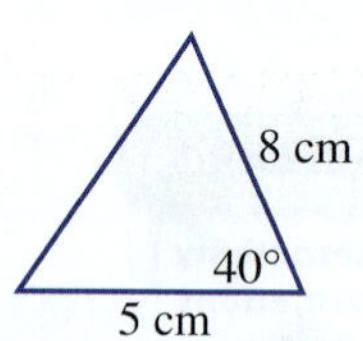

A a only **B** a and b **C** d only **D** b and d
E None of the above

UNDERSTANDING

5 Name the congruent triangles in each question and find the value of the variable.

a

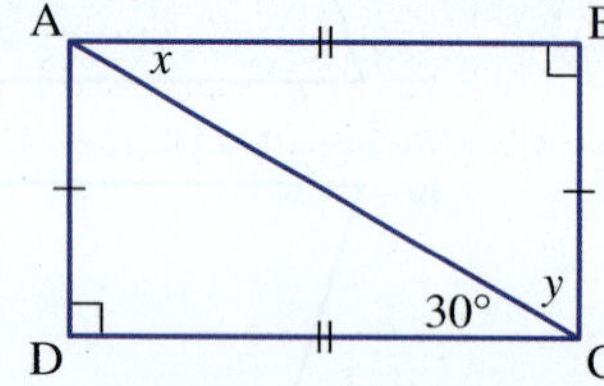

b

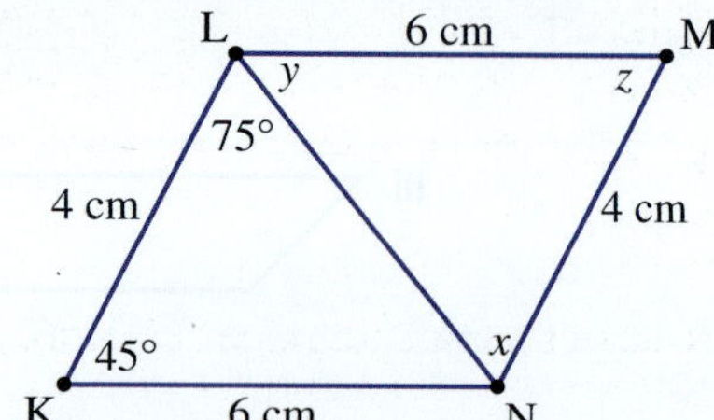

c

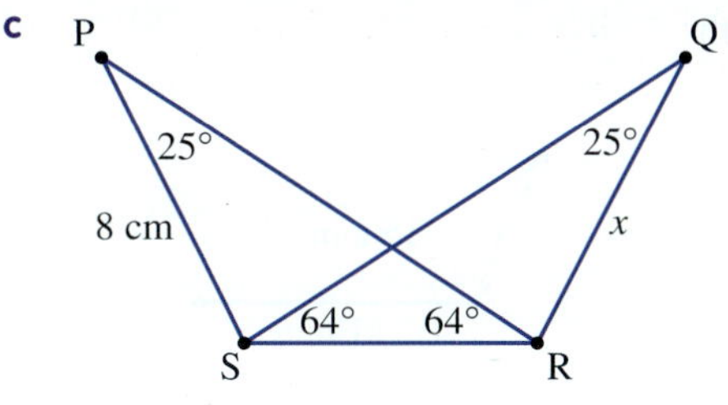

d

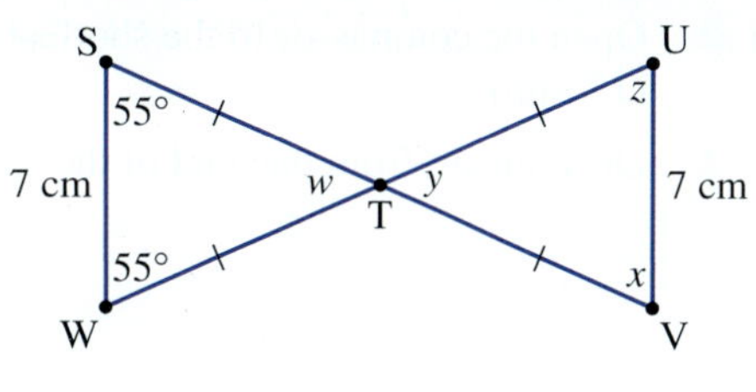

e

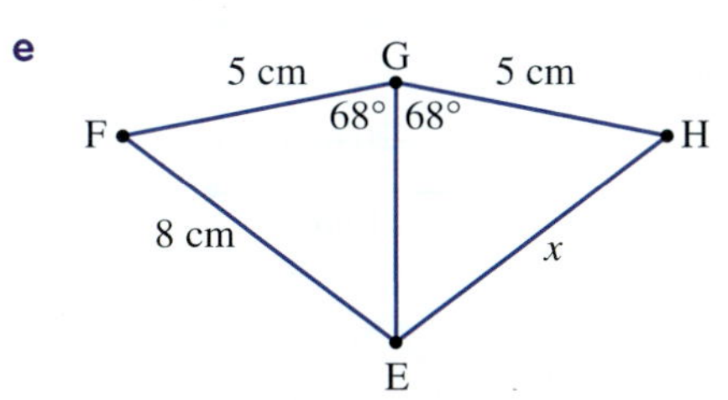

f

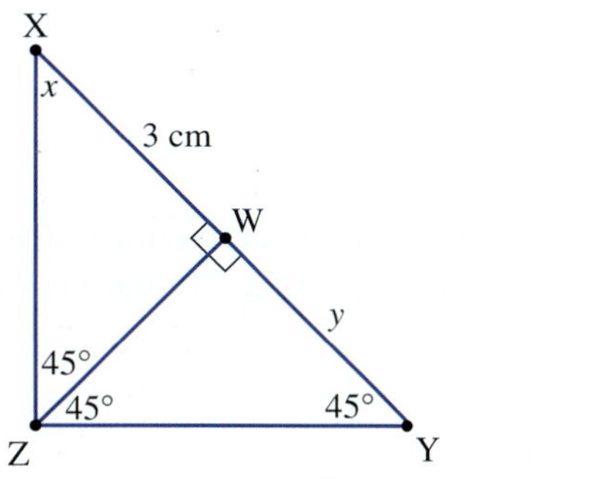

g

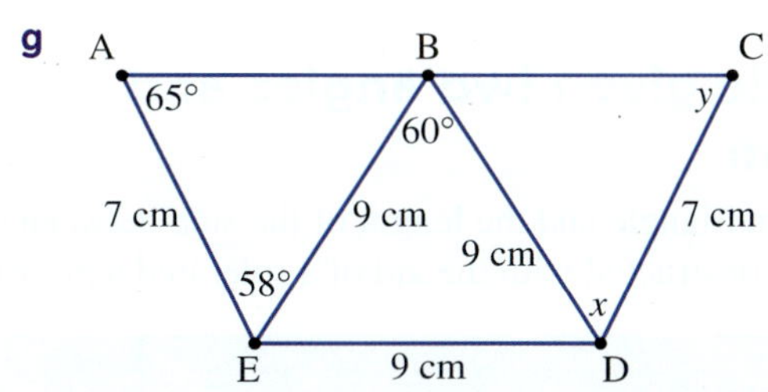

REASONING

6 Give an example to show that triangles with two angles of equal size and a pair of non-corresponding sides of equal length may not be congruent.

> **REFLECTION**
> When we write a congruence statement, why are the vertices listed in corresponding order?

7B Triangle constructions

- Using a ruler, protractor and a pair of compasses, you can construct any triangle from three pieces of information.
- Sometimes, only one triangle can be drawn from the information. Sometimes more than one triangle can be drawn.

Constructing a triangle given three side lengths

- If the lengths of the three sides of a triangle are known, it can be constructed with the help of a ruler and a pair of compasses.

WORKED EXAMPLE 3

Using a ruler and a pair of compasses, construct a triangle with side lengths 15 mm, 20 mm and 21 mm.

THINK	DRAW
1 Rule out the longest side (21 mm).	21 mm

2 Open the compasses to the shortest side length (15 mm).

3 Draw an arc from one end of the 21 mm side.

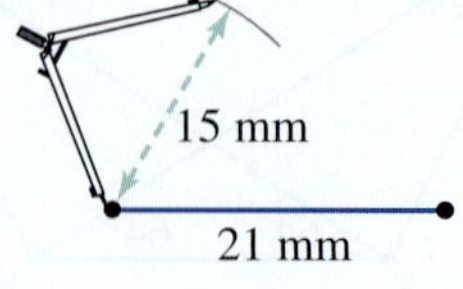

4 Open the compasses to the length of the third side (20 mm) and draw an arc from the other end of the 21 mm side.

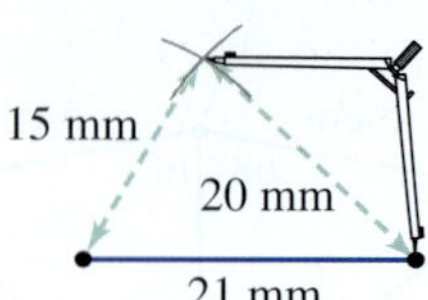

5 Join the point of intersection of the two arcs and the end points of the 21 mm side with lines.

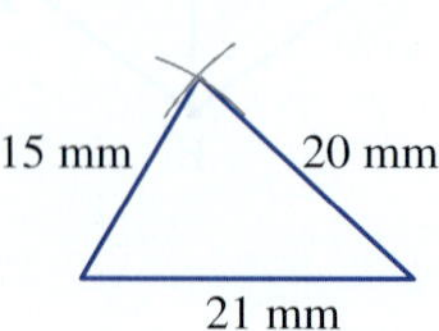

Constructing a triangle given two angles and the side between them

- If the size of any two angles of a triangle and the length of the side between these two angles are known, the triangle can be constructed with the aid of a ruler and a protractor.

WORKED EXAMPLE 4

Use a ruler and protractor to construct a triangle with angles 40° and 65°, and the side between them of length 2 cm.

THINK

DRAW

1 Rule a line of length 2 cm.

2 Place the centre of your protractor on one end point of the line and measure out a 40° angle. Draw a line so that it makes an angle of 40° with the 2 cm line.

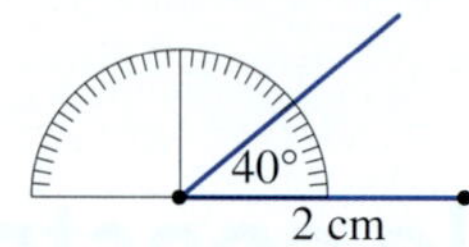

3 Place the centre of your protractor on the other end point of the 2 cm line and measure an angle of 65°. Draw a line so that it makes a 65° angle with the 2 cm line.

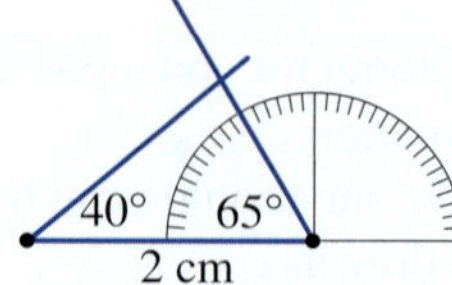

4 If necessary, continue the lines until they intersect each other to form a triangle.

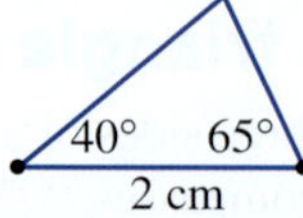

Constructing a triangle given two sides and the angle between them

- The angle between two sides is called the **included angle**.
- If the length of two sides and the size of the included angle are known, the triangle can be constructed with a protractor and a ruler.

WORKED EXAMPLE 5

Use a ruler and protractor to construct a triangle with sides 6 cm and 10 cm long, and an angle between them of 60°.

THINK | DRAW

1. Rule a line 10 cm long.
2. Place the centre of your protractor on one end point of the line and mark an angle of 60°. *Note:* These figures have been reduced.

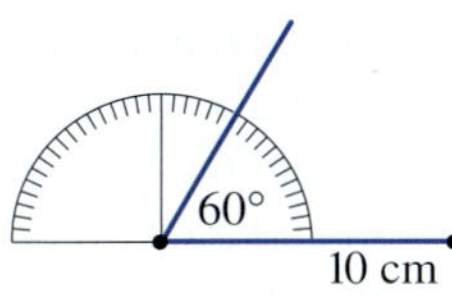

3. Join the 60° mark and the end point of the 10 cm side with the straight line. Extend the line until it is 6 cm long.

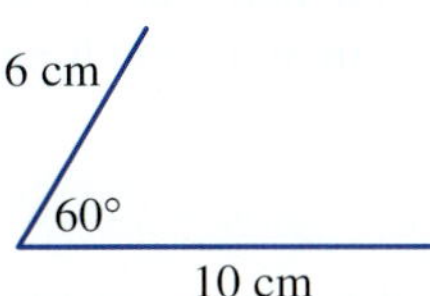

4. Join the end points of the two lines to complete the triangle.

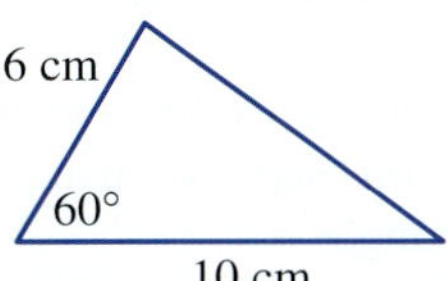

REMEMBER

1. A triangle can be constructed using a ruler and a pair of compasses if the three sides are known.
2. If two angles of a triangle and the side between them, or two sides and an angle between them are known, the triangle can be constructed using a protractor and a ruler.
3. When using a protractor:
   (a) make sure that the baseline of the protractor is exactly on the line, and the cross of the protractor is exactly on the point from which you are measuring the angle.
   (b) use the scale that begins from 0° (not 180°).

EXERCISE 7B

Triangle constructions

INDIVIDUAL PATHWAYS

eBook*plus*

Activity 7-B-1 Triangle constructions doc-2241

Activity 7-B-2 More triangle constructions doc-2242

Activity 7-B-3 Advanced triangle constructions doc-2243

FLUENCY

1 WE3 Using a ruler and a pair of compasses, construct 2 congruent triangles with the following side lengths:

a 7 cm, 6 cm, 4 cm
b 5 cm, 4 cm, 5 cm
c 6 cm, 5 cm, 3 cm
d 6 cm, 6 cm, 6 cm
e 7.5 cm, 4.5 cm, 6 cm
f 2 cm, 6.5 cm, 5 cm
g an equilateral triangle of side 3 cm
h an equilateral triangle of side 4.5 cm.

2 WE4 Use a ruler and protractor to construct these triangles:

a angles 60° and 60° with the side between them 5 cm long
b angles 50° and 50° with the side between them 6 cm long
c angles 30° and 40° with the side between them 4 cm long
d angles 60° and 45° with the side between them 3 cm long

eBook*plus*

Interactivity
Random triangles
int-2369

- **e** angles 30° and 60° with the side between them 4 cm long
- **f** angles 65° and 60° with the side between them 3.5 cm long
- **g** angles 60° and 90° with the side between them 5 cm long
- **h** angles 60° and 36° with the side between them 4.5 cm long.

3 WE5 Use a ruler and protractor to construct the following triangles:
- **a** two sides 10 cm and 5 cm long, angle of 30° between them
- **b** two sides 8 cm and 3 cm long, angle of 45° between them
- **c** two sides 6 cm and 6 cm long, angle of 60° between them
- **d** two sides 4 cm and 5 cm long, angle of 90° between them
- **e** two sides 7 cm and 6 cm long, angle of 80° between them
- **f** two sides 9 cm and 3 cm long, angle of 110° between them
- **g** two sides 6 cm and 6 cm long, angle of 50° between them
- **h** two sides 5 cm and 4 cm long, angle of 120° between them.

UNDERSTANDING

4 a Use your ruler and compass to draw an isosceles triangle with two sides 5 cm long and one side 7 cm.
- **b** Use your protractor to measure the size of the largest angle.
- **c** Complete this sentence using one of the words below: This triangle is an __________-angled triangle.
  i acute **ii** right **iii** obtuse

REASONING

5 a Construct a triangle with angles of 45°, 55° and 80°.
- **b** How many different triangles can be constructed from this information?

6 a Construct a right-angled triangle with a hypotenuse of 13 cm and a side of 5 cm.
- **b** How many different triangles can be constructed from this information?
- **c** What additional information is required to describe only one triangle?

7 Mike and Susan were constructing a triangle ABC where angle ABC = 30°, BC = 12 cm and AC = 8 cm. Mike's triangle was an acute-angled triangle and Susan's was an obtuse-angled triangle. Draw both triangles.

REFLECTION
When you are constructing a triangle and you know two angles and a side, do you need to know the side between the angles?

7C Congruent triangles

- From section 7B it can be seen that a triangle can be described with three pieces of information about side length and/or angle size.
- If three angles are known, an infinite number of triangles can be drawn. For example the triangles below have angle sizes of 60°, 40° and 80°.

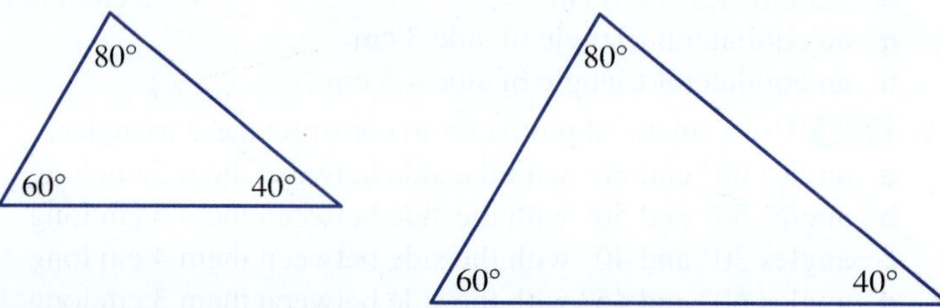

∴ If only three angles are known, this is not a test for congruence.

- There can be two possible triangles drawn from two sides and the non-included angle. In the diagram at right, angles ABC and ABD both have sides of 7 cm and 4 cm, and an angle of 30° between the 7-cm side and the unknown side.

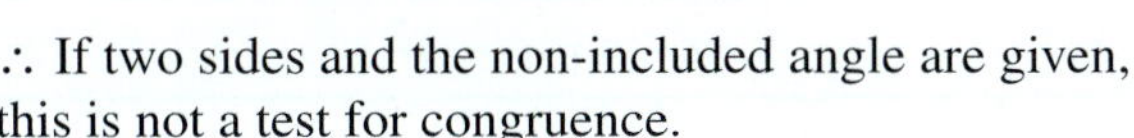

∴ If two sides and the non-included angle are given, this is not a test for congruence.

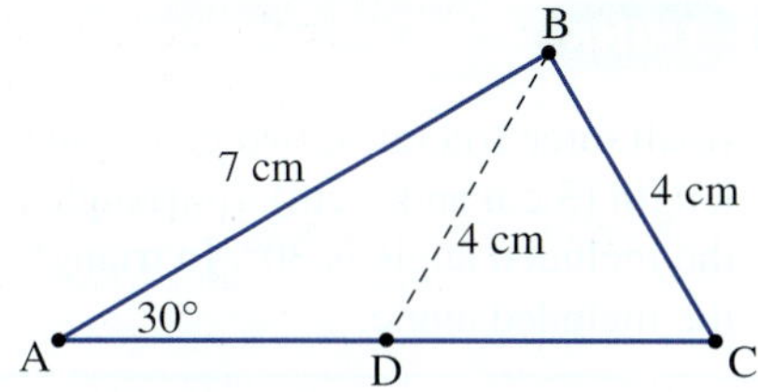

Congruency tests

- There are four tests that can be used to demonstrate that two triangles are congruent.
- It is not enough for the diagrams to look the same; you need evidence!
- Two triangles are congruent if:
  - three sides of one triangle are congruent to the three sides of the other (SSS)

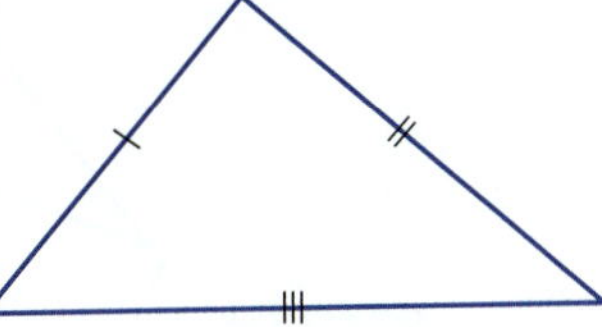
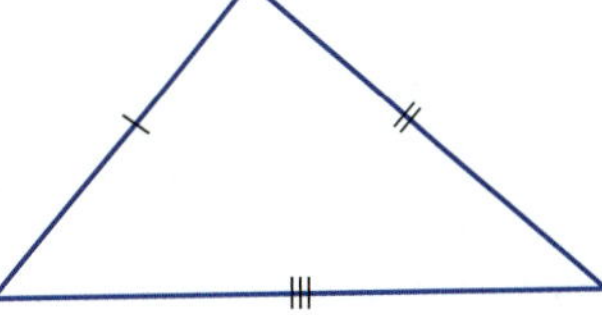

  - two sides and the included angle of one triangle are congruent to two sides and the included angle of the other (SAS)

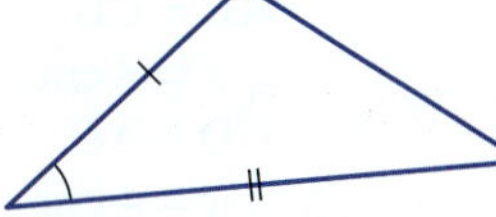
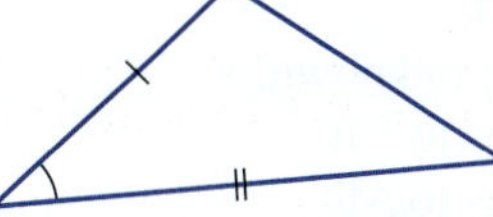

  - two angles and a side of one triangle are congruent to the two angles and the corresponding side of the other (ASA)

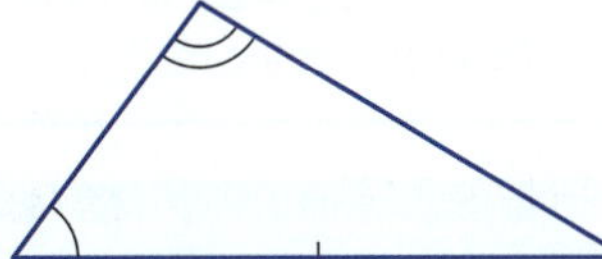
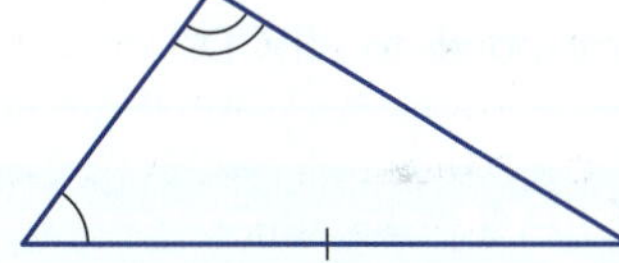

  - the triangles are right-angled and the hypotenuse and a side of one are congruent to the hypotenuse and a side of the other (RHS).

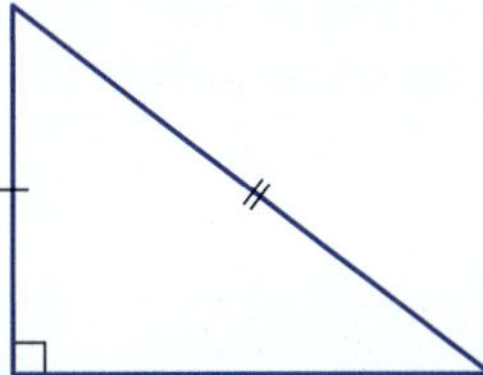
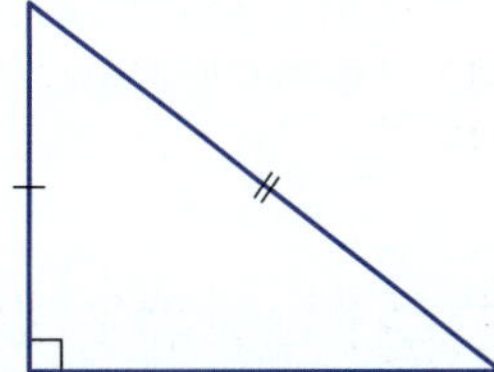

WORKED EXAMPLE 6

Which of the following triangles are definitely congruent? Give a reason for your answer.

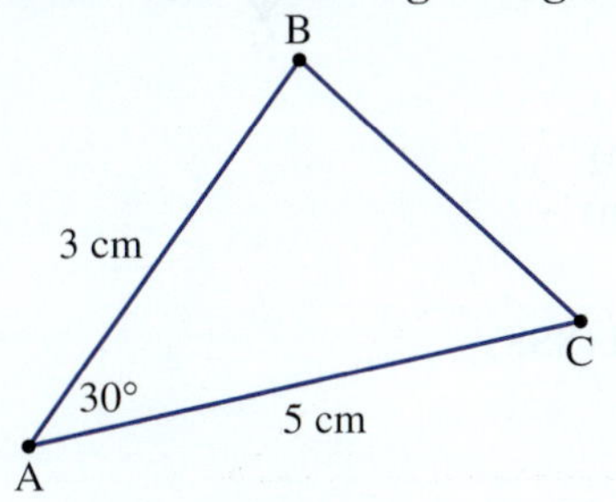

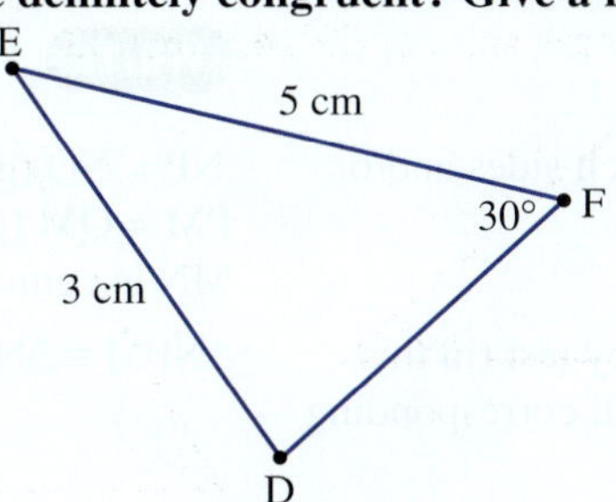

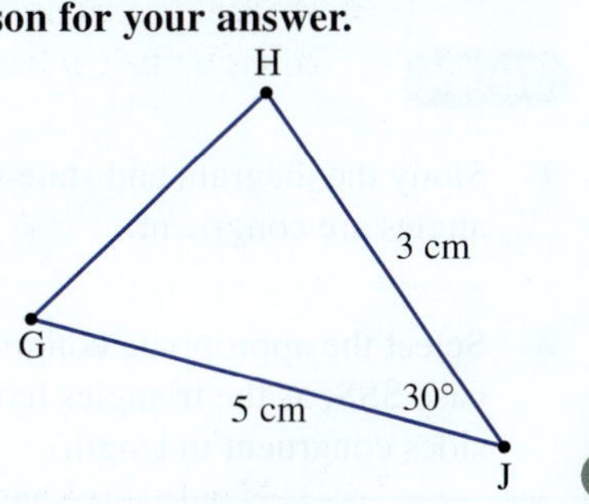

THINK	WRITE
In all three triangles, two given sides are of equal length (3 cm and 5 cm). In triangles ABC and JHG, the included angle is 30°. In triangle AFD, 30° is not the included angle.	$\Delta ABC \equiv \Delta JHG$ (SAS)

WORKED EXAMPLE 7

Given that $\Delta ABD \equiv \Delta CBD$, find the value of the variables.

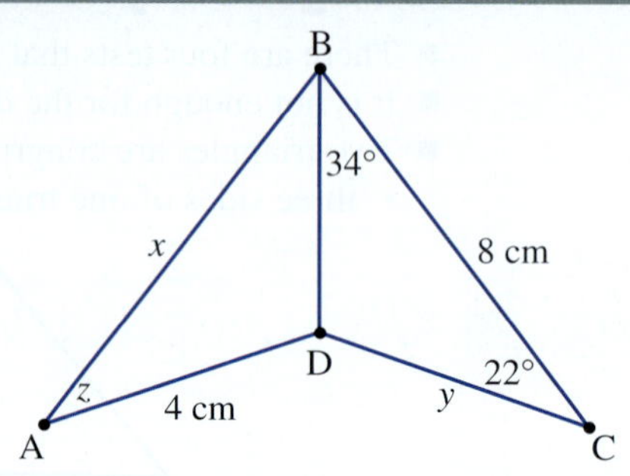

THINK	WRITE
1 The corresponding sides are equal in length. $\Delta ABD \equiv \Delta CBD$. AB and CD are unknown. AB corresponds to CB. CD corresponds to AD.	$\Delta ABD \equiv \Delta CBD$ AB = CB $x = 8$ cm CD = AD $y = 4$ cm
2 The corresponding angles are equal. $\angle BAD$ is unknown. $\angle BAD$ corresponds to $\angle BCD$.	$\angle BAD = \angle BCD$ $z = 22°$

WORKED EXAMPLE 8

Prove that ΔMNP is congruent to ΔMNQ.

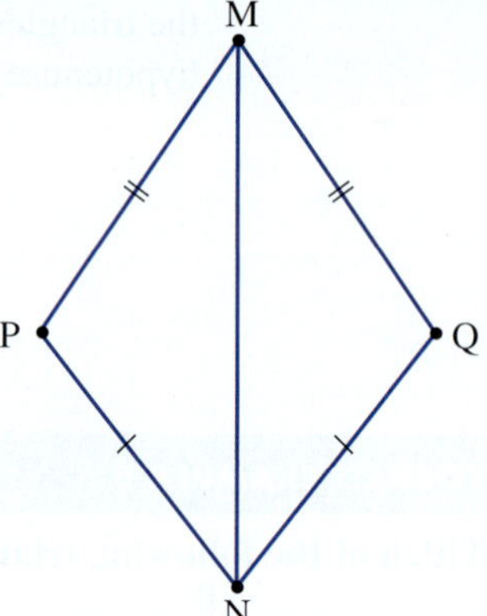

THINK	WRITE
1 Study the diagram and state which sides and/or angles are congruent.	NP = NQ (given) PM = QM (given) MN is common
2 Select the appropriate congruency test (in this case SSS, as the triangles have all corresponding sides congruent in length).	$\Delta NPM \equiv \Delta NQM$ (SSS)

REMEMBER

1. Triangles are congruent if any one of the following applies.
   (a) Corresponding sides are the same (SSS).
   (b) Two corresponding sides and the included angle are the same (SAS).
   (c) Two angles and a pair of corresponding sides are the same (ASA).
   (d) The hypotenuse and one pair of the other corresponding sides are the same in a right-angled triangle (RHS).
2. The following *do not* show congruence.
   (a) Three corresponding angles are the same (AAA).
   (b) Two corresponding sides and a non-included angle are the same (ASS).

EXERCISE

7C Congruent triangles

INDIVIDUAL PATHWAYS

eBook*plus*

Activity 7-C-1
Congruent triangles
doc-2244

Activity 7-C-2
More congruent triangles
doc-2245

Activity 7-C-3
Advanced congruent triangles
doc-2246

FLUENCY

1 WE6 In each part of the question, which of the triangles are congruent? Give a reason for your answer.

a

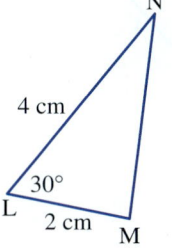

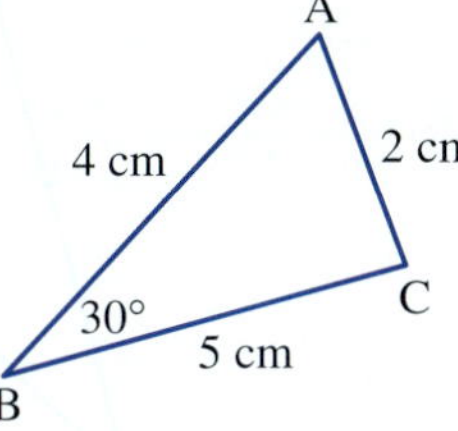

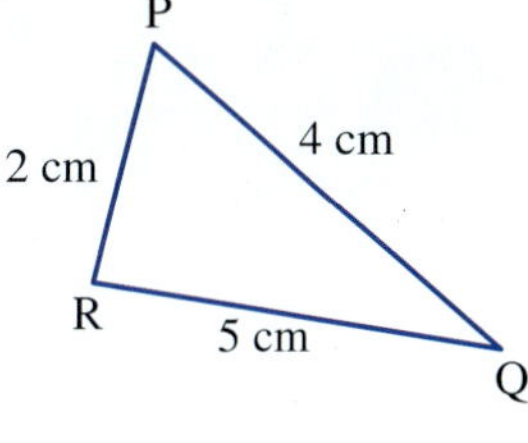

b

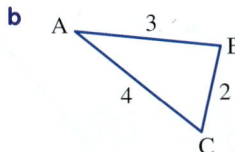

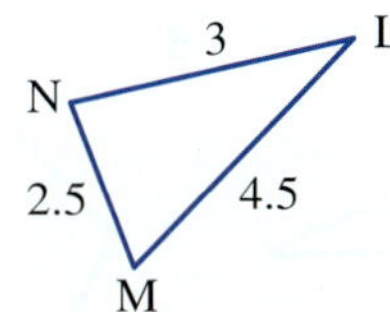

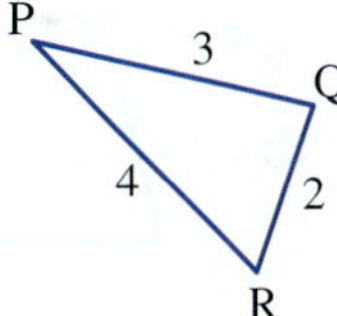

c

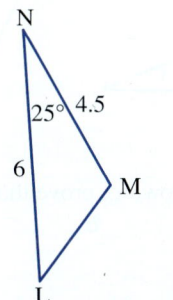

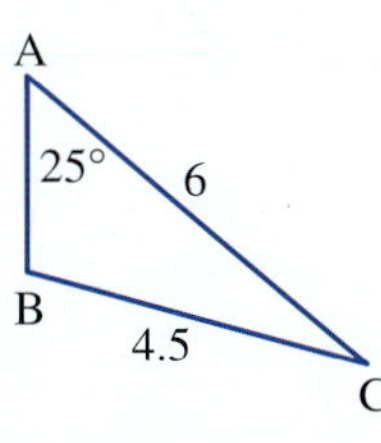

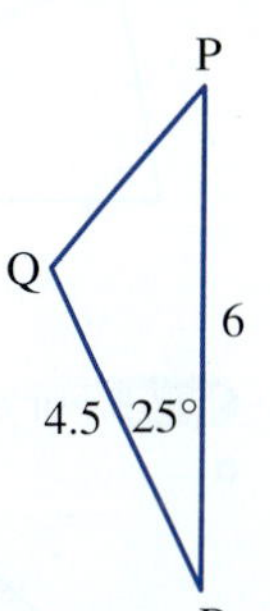

d

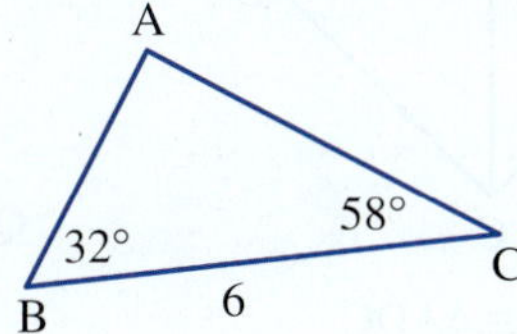

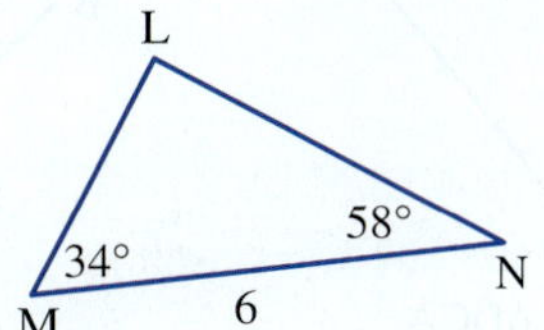

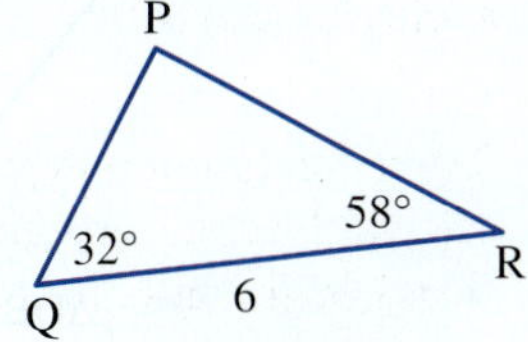

e

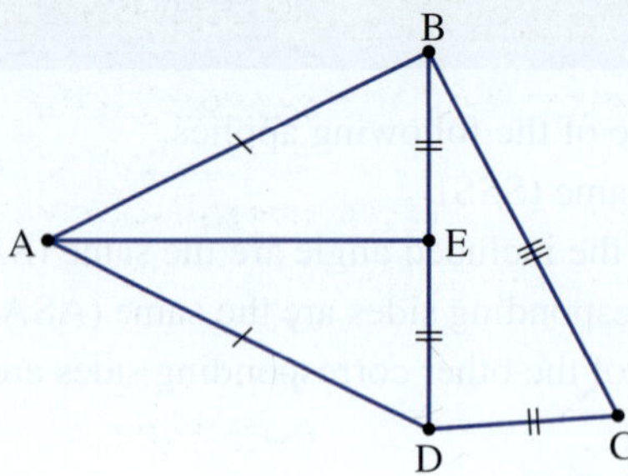

f

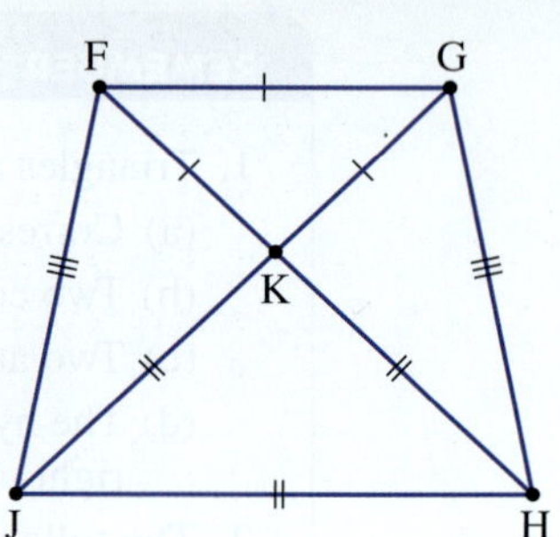

2 WE7 Find the values of the variables in each of the following pairs of congruent triangles. All side lengths are in centimetres.

a

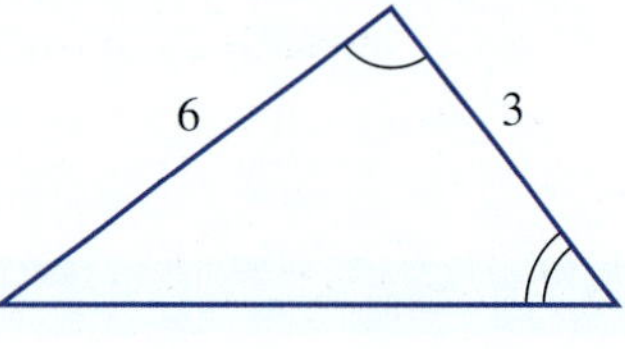

b

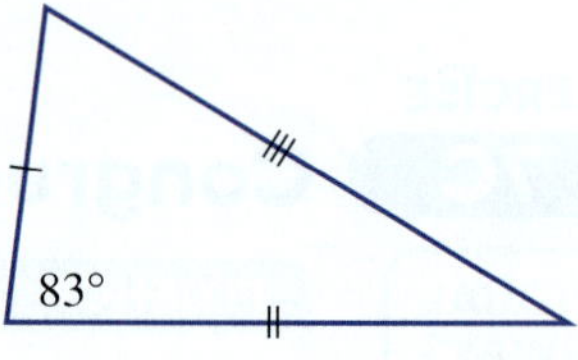

c

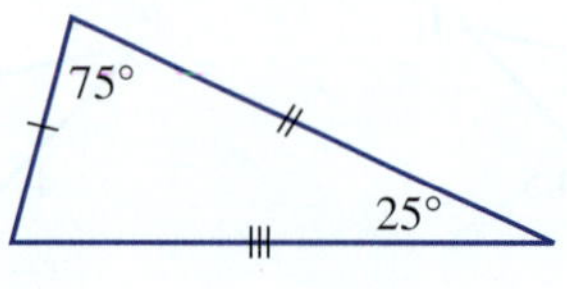

d

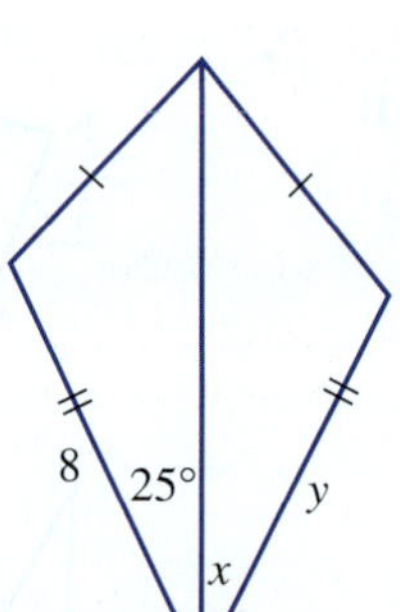

e

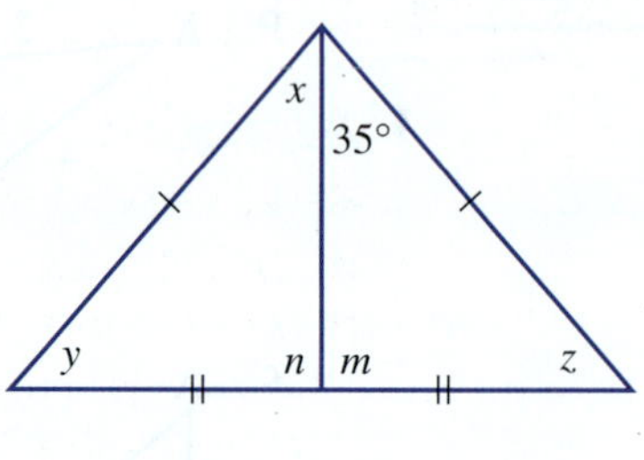

3 WE8 For each of the following, prove that:

a

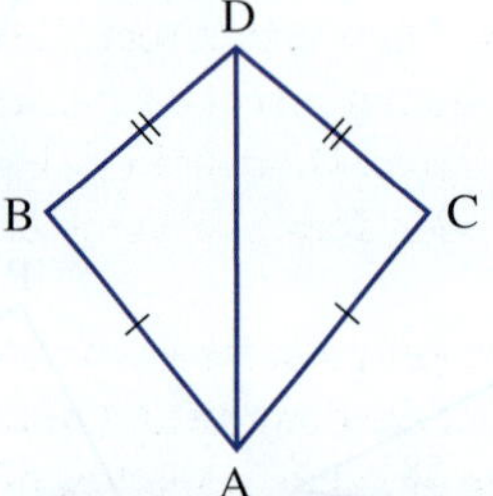

ΔDBA ≅ ΔDCA

b

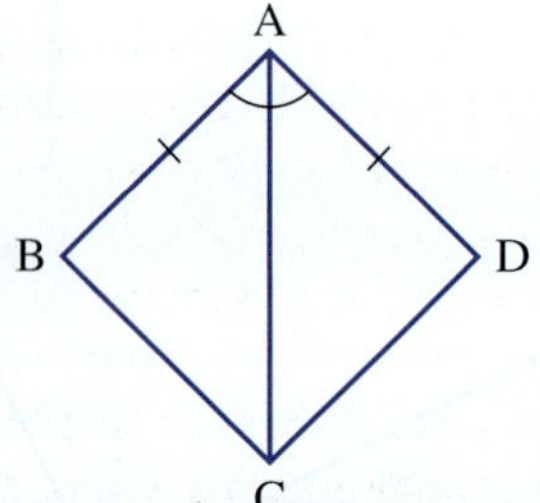

ΔABC ≅ ΔADC

c

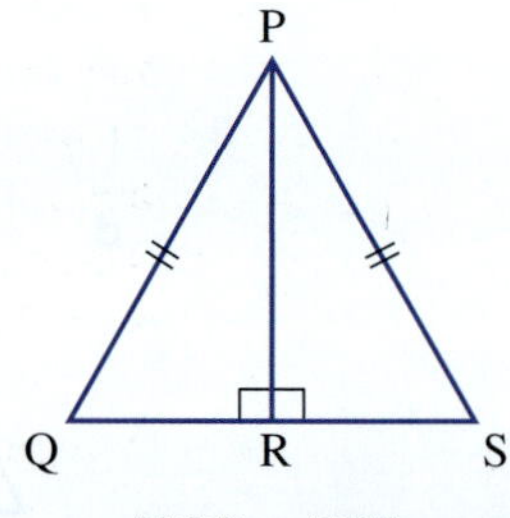

ΔPQR ≅ ΔPSR

UNDERSTANDING

4 Draw an example of two different triangles that have two corresponding sides equal and one pair of equal angles.

5 Draw an example of two different triangles that have three pairs of equal angles.

6 Are the following triangles congruent? Give a reason for your answer.

a

b

eBook*plus*

Digital doc
WorkSHEET 7.1
doc-2250

REASONING

7 In an equilateral triangle ABC, the midpoints of the sides are labelled D, E and F. Prove that triangle DEF is an equilateral triangle.

8 All triangles have three sides and three angles. Using mathematical reasoning, including examples, give the minimum information required to construct a unique triangle.

REFLECTION
When using the congruency rule ASA, why is it not necessary for the side to be between the two angles?

7D Quadrilaterals

Review of terms and rules

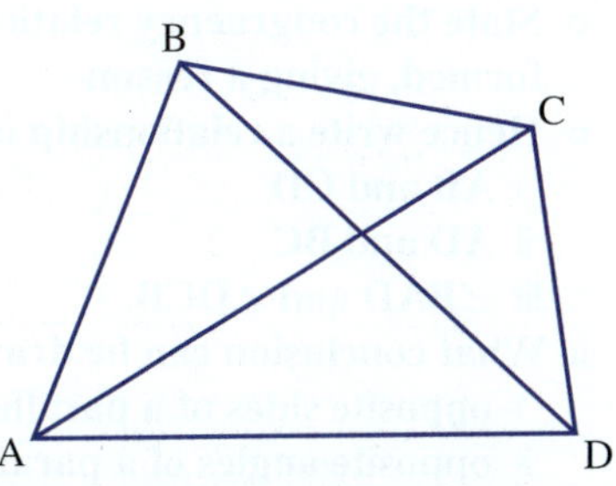

- The figure ABCD is a quadrilateral.
- A **quadrilateral** is a four-sided figure.
- **Opposite angles** do not have rays in common. ∠ABC and ∠ADC are opposite angles. ∠BCD and ∠BAD are also opposite angles.
- **Opposite sides** do not intersect. BC and AD are opposite sides. AB and CD are opposite sides.
- **Diagonals** connect opposite angles. AC is one diagonal and BD is the other.
- In some quadrilaterals, the *diagonals bisect each other*. In the diagram above, BD would bisect AC if it divided AC into two equal sections. AC would bisect BD if it divided it into two equal sections. In the diagram, the diagonals do not bisect each other.

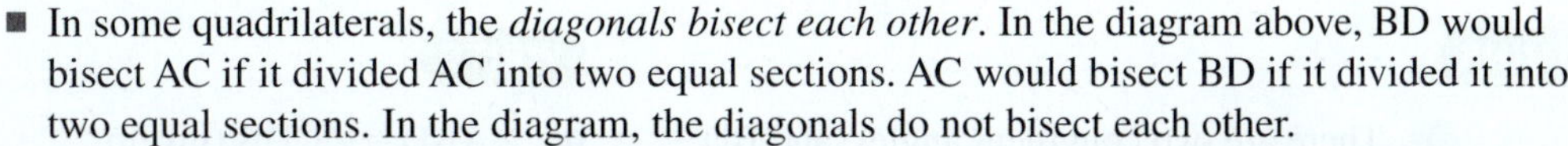

- In some quadrilaterals, the *diagonals bisect the angles*. Diagonal BD bisects ∠ABC if ∠ABD and ∠DBC are congruent. In the diagram, above, BD does not bisect ∠ABC.
- There are several special quadrilaterals.
  - A **parallelogram** is a quadrilateral where the opposite sides are parallel.
  - A **rhombus** is a parallelogram in which all sides are congruent. (Because it is a parallelogram, the properties of a parallelogram are also properties of a rhombus.)
  - A **rectangle** is a parallelogram in which all angles are 90°. (Because it is a parallelogram, the properties of a parallelogram are also properties of a rectangle.)

- A **square** is a rectangle with all sides congruent. (Because rectangles are parallelograms and a rhombus is a parallelogram with all sides congruent, a square is also a right-angled rhombus.)
- A **kite** is a quadrilateral in which adjacent pairs of sides are congruent.
- A **trapezium** is a quadrilateral with one pair of parallel sides.

Properties of quadrilaterals

- By finding congruent triangles in quadrilaterals, the properties of quadrilaterals can be determined.

Angles and parallel lines

(See *Maths Quest 7* for further details on angles and parallel lines.)

- Parallel lines are denoted by identical arrowheads.
- A straight line cutting a parallel line is called a **transversal**.
- **Corresponding angles** are equal in magnitude. For example, in the diagram, $a = e$, $c = g$, $b = f$ and $d = h$.
- **Vertically opposite angles** are equal in magnitude. For example, in the diagram, $a = d$, $b = c$, $f = g$ and $e = h$.
- **Alternate angles** are equal in magnitude. For example, in the diagram, $c = f$ and $d = e$.
- **Co-interior angles** (also known as allied angles) sum to 180°. For example, in the diagram, $c + e = 180°$ and $d + f = 180°$.
- Angles and parallel lines can be used to establish congruency in parallelograms.

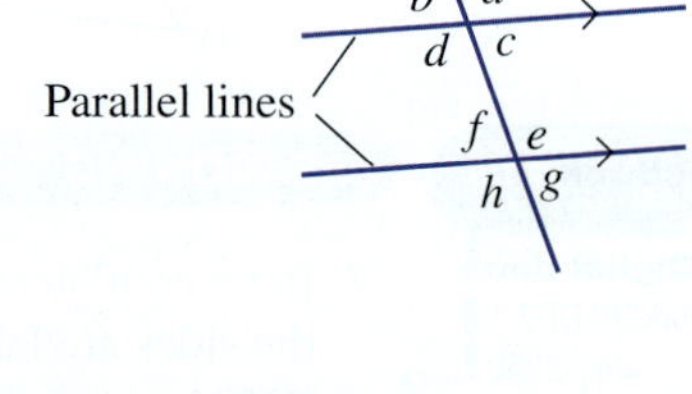

WORKED EXAMPLE 9

When a diagonal is drawn in a parallelogram, two pairs of congruent angles are formed, as shown (alternate angles).

a State the congruency relationship between the two triangles formed, giving a reason.

b Hence write a relationship between:

i AB and CD

ii AD and BC

iii ∠BAD and ∠DCB.

c What conclusion can be drawn about:

i opposite sides of a parallelogram?

ii opposite angles of a parallelogram?

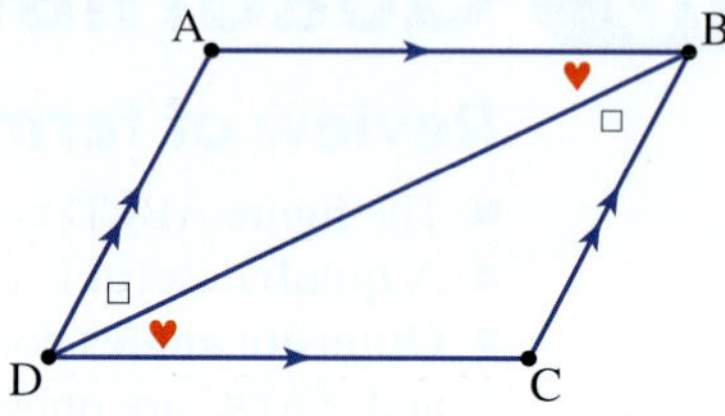

THINK		WRITE
a	1 There are two congruent angles, and BD is in both triangles.	a ∠ABD ≡ ∠CDB (given) ∠ADB ≡ ∠CBD (given) BD is common to both ∴ ΔABD ≡ ΔCDB (ASA)
b i	2 AB and CD are corresponding sides in the triangles.	b i AB ≡ CD
ii	3 AD and CB are corresponding sides in the triangles.	ii AD ≡ CB

	iii	4	∠BAD and ∠DCB are corresponding angles.		iii	∠BAD ≡ ∠DCB
c	i	5	AB and CD are opposite sides. AD and CB are opposite sides.	c	i	AB ≡ CD and AD ≡ CB; therefore, opposite sides are congruent.
	ii	6	∠BAD and ∠DCB are opposite angles. ∠ABD and ∠CDB are opposite angles.		ii	∠BAD ≡ ∠DCB ∠ABD ≡ ∠CDB (given) ∠ADB ≡ ∠CBD (given) ∴ ∠ABD ≡ ∠CDB Opposite angles are congruent.

REMEMBER

1. A quadrilateral is a four-sided figure.
2. Opposite angles do not have rays in common.
3. Opposite sides do not intersect.
4. Diagonals connect opposite angles.
5. In some quadrilaterals, the diagonals bisect each other.
6. In some quadrilaterals, the diagonals bisect angles.
7. A parallelogram is a quadrilateral where the opposite sides are parallel.
8. A rhombus is a parallelogram in which all sides are congruent. (Because it is a parallelogram, the properties of a parallelogram are also properties of a rhombus.)
9. A rectangle is a parallelogram in which all angles are 90°. (Because it is a parallelogram, the properties of a parallelogram are also properties of a rectangle.)
10. A square is a rectangle with all sides congruent. (Because rectangles are parallelograms and a rhombus is a parallelogram with all sides congruent, a square is also a right-angled rhombus.)
11. A kite is a quadrilateral in which adjacent pairs of sides are congruent.
12. A trapezium is a quadrilateral with one pair of parallel sides.
13. Congruent triangles can be used to investigate the properties of quadrilaterals.
14. Angles and parallel lines can be used to establish congruency in parallelograms.

EXERCISE 7D

Quadrilaterals

INDIVIDUAL PATHWAYS

eBook*plus*

Activity 7-D-1
Quadrilaterals
doc-2247

Activity 7-D-2
More quadrilaterals
doc-2248

Activity 7-D-3
Advanced quadrilaterals
doc-2249

FLUENCY

1 WE9a,b Consider the parallelogram WXYZ. From the worked example, we know that opposite sides are equal. Both diagonals are drawn giving 3 pairs of congruent angles as shown (alternate angles and opposite angles).

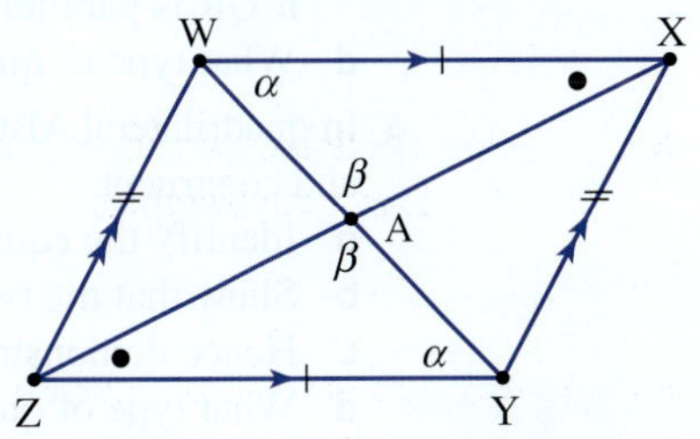

a State the congruency relationship between ΔWXA and ΔYZA, giving a reason.

b Hence state the relationship between:
 i WA and YA
 ii XA and ZA.

c Do the diagonals bisect each other?

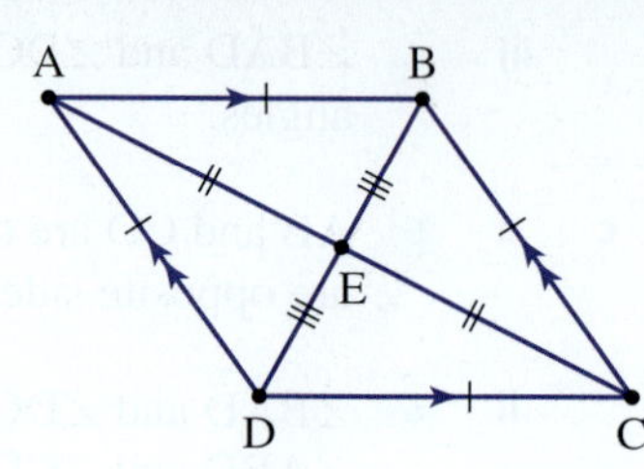

2 Consider the rhombus ABCD. Because the rhombus is also a parallelogram, we know that the diagonals bisect each other.

a State the congruency relationship between △ABE and △BEC, giving a reason.

b Hence state the relationship between:

i ∠AEB and ∠CEB

ii ∠ABE and ∠CBE.

c What is the magnitude of ∠AEB?

d Name all the triangles congruent to △ABE.

e Do the diagonals bisect the angles?

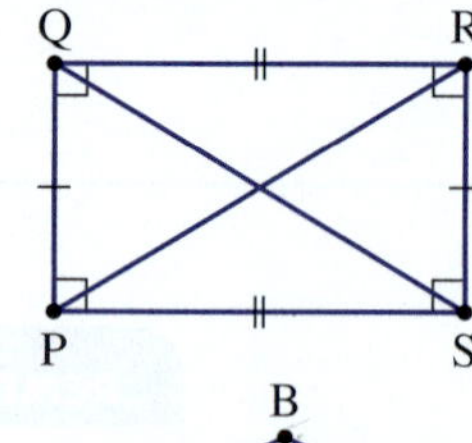

3 Consider the rectangle PQRS.

a Show that △PQR and △SRP are congruent.

b What can you say about the diagonals of a rectangle?

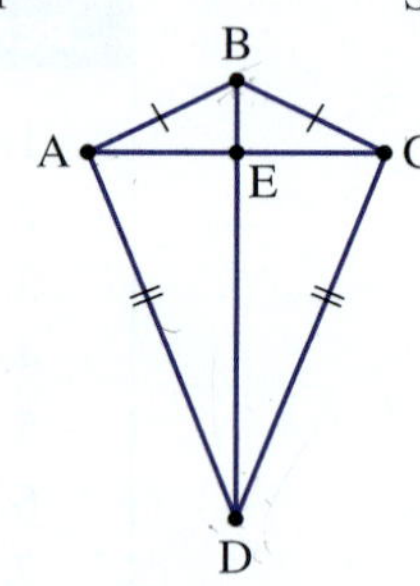

4 Consider the kite ABCD.

a Show that △ABD and △CBD are congruent.

b What can you say about:

i ∠ABD and ∠CBD?

ii ∠BAD and ∠BCD?

iii ∠BDA and ∠BDC?

c Use part **b** to show that △ABD ≡ △CBD.

d What can you say about:

i AE and CE?

ii ∠AEB and ∠CEB?

e Are △BEC and △DCE congruent?

f Use the above results to answer the following questions about kites.

i Are the opposite sides congruent?

ii Are the opposite angles congruent?

iii Do the diagonals bisect each other?

iv Do the diagonals intersect at 90°?

v Do the diagonals bisect the angles?

UNDERSTANDING

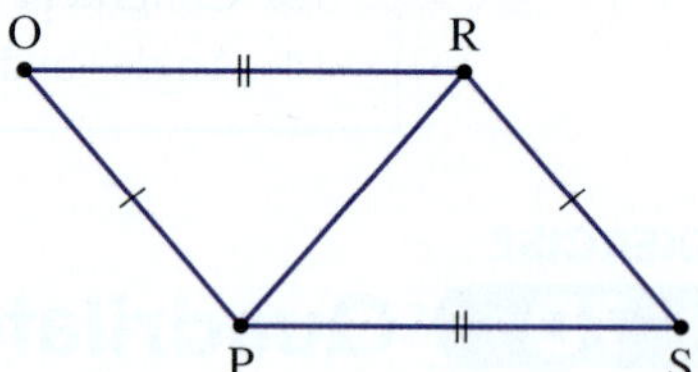

5 The quadrilateral PQRS has opposite sides that are congruent.

a Show that the triangles are congruent.

b Complete the following.

i ∠QPR = ________

ii ∠QRP = ________

c Complete the following.

i QP is parallel to ________.

ii QR is parallel to ________.

d What type of quadrilateral is PQRS?

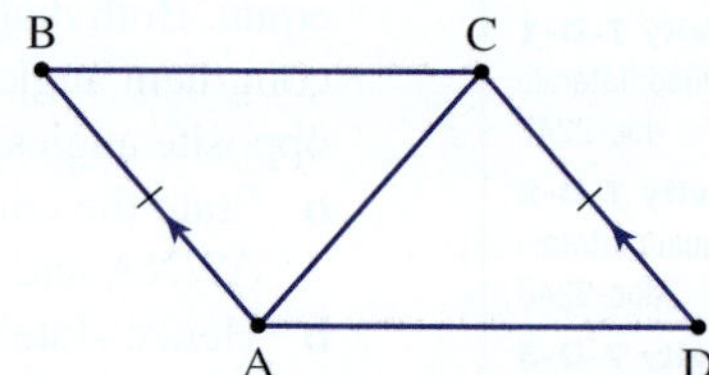

6 In quadrilateral ABCD, AB and CD are both parallel and congruent.

a Identify the equal alternate angles.

b Show that the two triangles are congruent.

c Hence demonstrate that BC and AD are parallel.

d What type of quadrilateral is ABCD?

eBook*plus*

Digital doc
WorkSHEET 7.2
doc-2251

REASONING

7 WXYZ is a quadrilateral, where ∠XYW = ∠YWZ. Use mathematical reasoning to determine the type of quadrilateral.

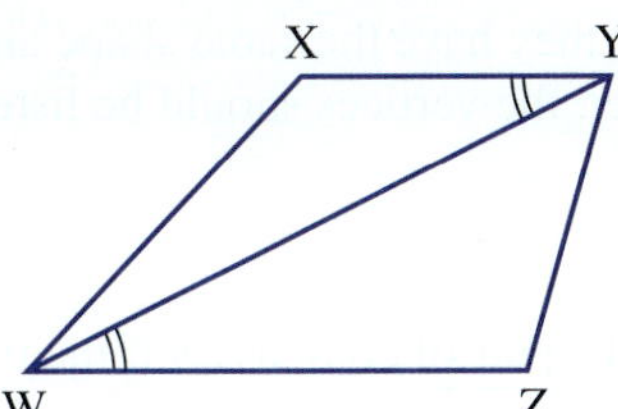

REFLECTION

Why is it important to be able to show congruency using mathematical reasoning?

Summary

Congruent figures

- Congruent figures are identical figures; that is, they have the same shape and size.
- When stating one figure is congruent to another, the vertices should be listed in corresponding (or matching) order.

Triangle constructions

- A triangle can be constructed using a ruler and a pair of compasses if the three sides are known.
- If two angles of a triangle and the side between them, or two sides and an angle between them are known, the triangle can be constructed using a protractor and a ruler.
- When using a protractor:
  (a) make sure that the baseline of the protractor is exactly on the line, and the cross of the protractor is exactly on the point from which you are measuring the angle.
  (b) use the scale that begins from 0° (not 180°).

Congruent triangles

- Triangles are congruent if any one of the following applies.
  (a) Corresponding sides are the same (SSS).
  (b) Two corresponding sides and the included angle are the same (SAS).
  (c) Two angles and a pair of corresponding sides are the same (ASA).
  (d) The hypotenuse and one pair of the other corresponding sides are the same in a right-angled triangle (RHS).
- The following *do not* show congruence.
  (a) Three corresponding angles are the same (AAA).
  (b) Two corresponding sides and a non-included angle are the same (ASS).

Quadrilaterals

- A quadrilateral is a four-sided figure.
- Opposite angles do not have rays in common.
- Opposite sides do not intersect.
- Diagonals connect opposite angles.
- In some quadrilaterals, the diagonals bisect each other.
- In some quadrilaterals, the diagonals bisect angles.
- A parallelogram is a quadrilateral where the opposite sides are parallel.
- A rhombus is a parallelogram in which all sides are congruent. (Because it is a parallelogram, the properties of a parallelogram are also properties of a rhombus.)
- A rectangle is a parallelogram in which all angles are 90°. (Because it is a parallelogram, the properties of a parallelogram are also properties of a rectangle.)
- A square is a rectangle with all sides congruent. (Because rectangles are parallelograms and a rhombus is a parallelogram with all sides congruent, a square is also a right-angled rhombus.)
- A kite is a quadrilateral in which adjacent pairs of sides are congruent.
- A trapezium is a quadrilateral with one pair of parallel sides.
- Congruent triangles can be used to investigate the properties of quadrilaterals.
- Angles and parallel lines can be used to establish congruency in parallelograms.

MAPPING YOUR UNDERSTANDING

Using terms from the summary, and other terms if you wish, construct a concept map that illustrates your understanding of the key concepts covered in this chapter. Compare this concept map with the one that you created in *What do you know?* on page 157.

Have you completed the two *Homework sheets*, the *Rich task* and the two *Code puzzles* in your *Maths Quest 8 Homework Book*?

Chapter review

FLUENCY

1 Which of the following pairs of shapes are congruent?

a

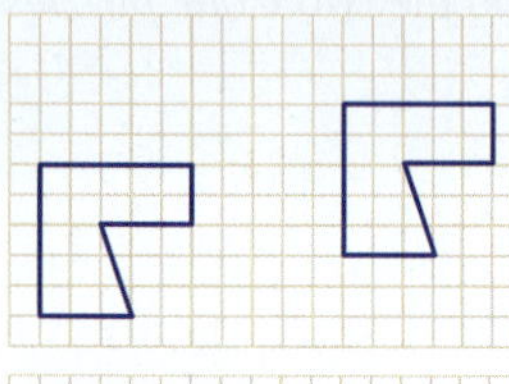

b

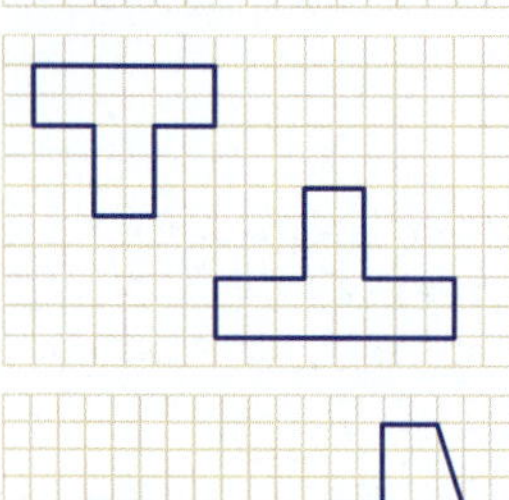

c

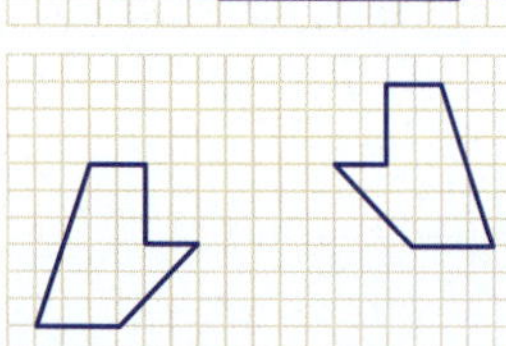

2 Draw a triangle with the following properties.

a three sides, 5 cm long

b two angles of 35° and 65° and a side of 6 cm between them

3 Name each pair of congruent triangles giving a reason. Hence, find the length of the side marked with the variables.

a

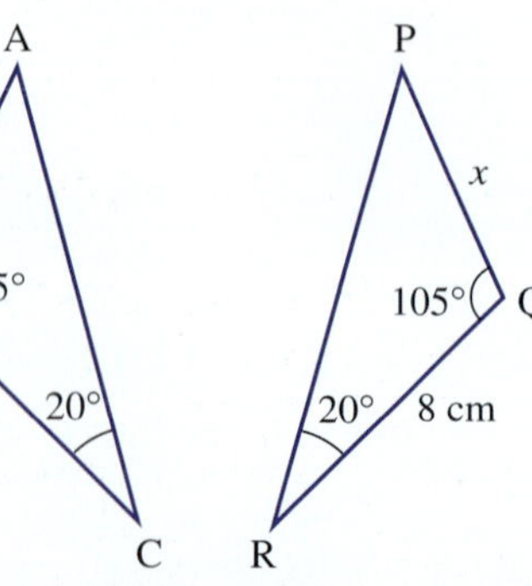

b

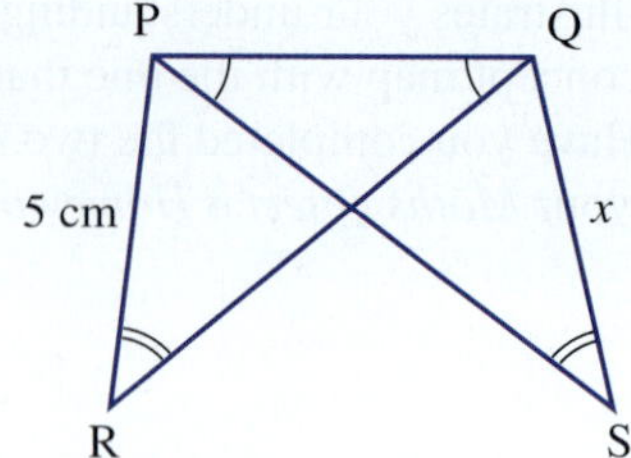

c

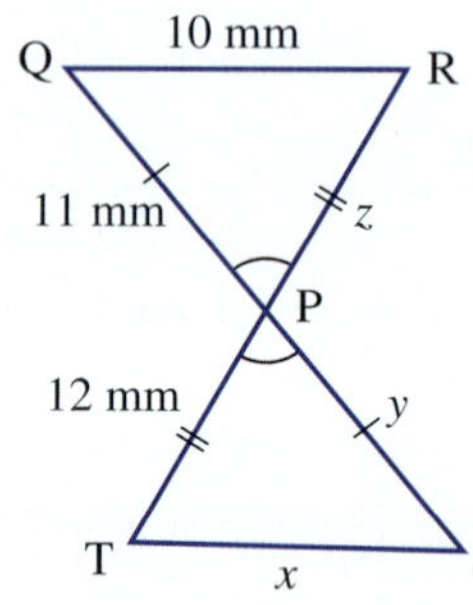

d

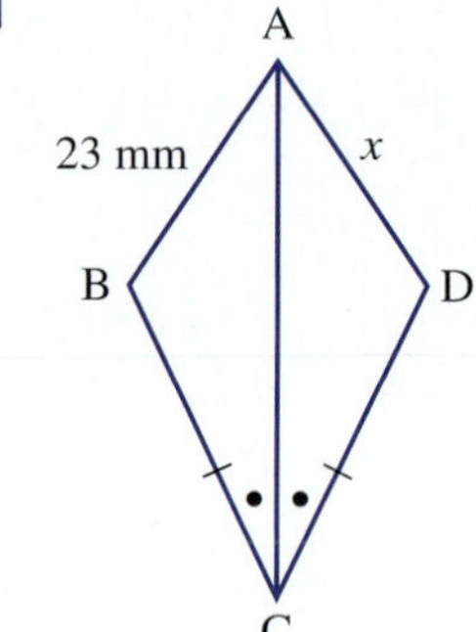

4 Complete the following property-of-quadrilaterals table.

Properties of quadrilaterals	Parallelogram	Rhombus	Rectangle	Square	Kite
Opposite sides parallel					
Opposite sides congruent					
All sides congruent					
All angles congruent (90°)					
Diagonals congruent					
Diagonals bisect each other					
Diagonals intersect at 90°					
Diagonals bisect angles					

PROBLEM SOLVING

1 Construct a rhombus ABCD where ∠DAB = 30° and diagonal BD is 5 cm.

2 Construct a rhombus with one diagonal 6 cm and the other diagonal 8 cm.

3 A kite has diagonals of 6 cm and 12 cm. If two of the sides are 5 cm, construct the kite.

4 In a quadrilateral PQRS, PQ ≡ RS and ∠PQR ≡ ∠RSP. Suzie claims that the quadrilateral must be a parallelogram. Is her claim correct? If yes, give evidence to justify the claim. If no, draw a diagram to demonstrate how her claim is wrong.

5 In a rectangle WXYZ, M is the midpoint of WX. Show that MZ ≡ MY.

6 ABCD is a square. E is a point on AB. F is a point on BC. G is a point on CD and H is a point on DA. If AE ≡ BF ≡ CG ≡ DH, what type of quadrilateral is EFGH? Justify your answer.

7 Are squares and rhombuses special examples of kites? Explain your answer using mathematical reasoning.

eBook*plus*

Interactivities

Test yourself
Chapter 7
int-2367

Word search
Chapter 7
int-2627

Crossword
Chapter 7
int-2628

eBookplus ACTIVITIES

Chapter opener

Digital doc *(page 157)*
- Hungry brain activity Chapter 7 (doc-6914)

Are you ready?

Digital docs *(pages 158–9)*
- SkillSHEET 7.1 (doc-6915) Naming angles and shapes
- SkillSHEET 7.2 (doc-6916) Calculating angles in triangles
- SkillSHEET 7.3 (doc-6917) Angles and parallel lines
- SkillSHEET 7.4 (doc-6918) Reflections
- SkillSHEET 7.5 (doc-6919) Rotations
- SkillSHEET 7.6 (doc-6920) Translations

7A Congruent figures

Digital docs *(page 161)*
- Activity 7-A-1 (doc-2238) Congruency
- Activity 7-A-2 (doc-2239) More congruency
- Activity 7-A-3 (doc-2240) Advanced congruency

Interactivity *(page 161)*
- Transformations and the Cartesian plane (int-2368)

7B Triangle constructions

Digital docs *(page 165)*
- Activity 7-B-1 (doc-2241) Triangle constructions
- Activity 7-B-2 (doc-2242) More triangle constructions
- Activity 7-B-3 (doc-2243) Advanced triangle constructions

Interactivity *(page 166)*
- Random triangles (int-2369)

7C Congruent triangles

Digital docs *(page 169)*
- Activity 7-C-1 (doc-2244) Congruent triangles
- Activity 7-C-2 (doc-2245) More congruent triangles
- Activity 7-C-3 (doc-2246) Advanced congruent triangles
- WorkSHEET 7.1 (doc-2250) *(page 171)*

7D Quadrilaterals

Digital docs *(page 173)*
- Activity 7-D-1 (doc-2247) Quadrilaterals
- Activity 7-D-2 (doc-2248) More quadrilaterals
- Activity 7-D-3 (doc-2249) Advanced quadrilaterals
- WorkSHEET 7.2 (doc-2251) *(page 175)*

Chapter review

Interactivities *(page 179)*
- Test yourself Chapter 7: (int-2367) Take the end-of-chapter test to test your progress.
- Word search Chapter 7 (int-2627)
- Crossword Chapter 7 (int-2628)

To access eBookPLUS activities, log on to
www.jacplus.com.au

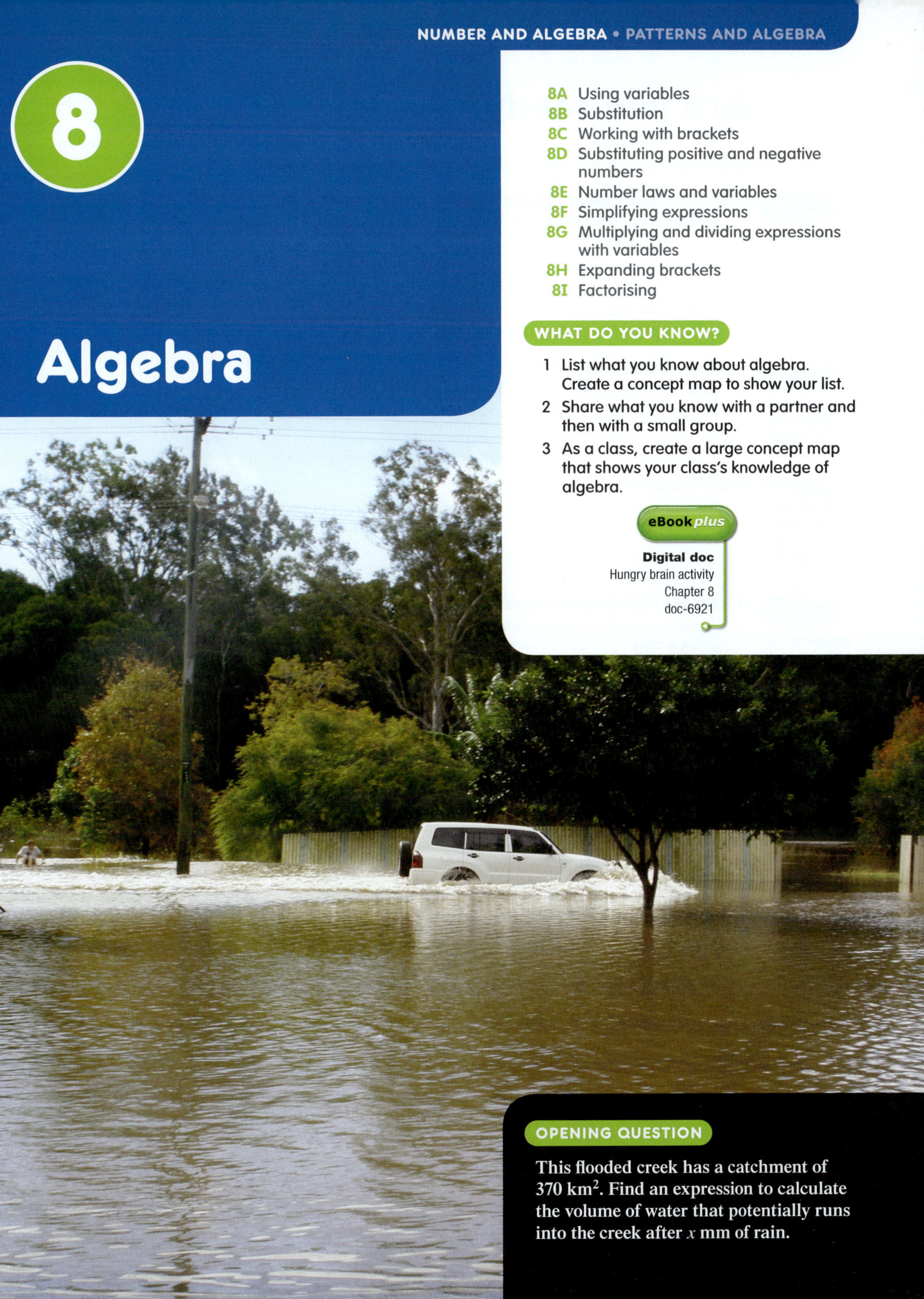

8 Algebra

8A Using variables
8B Substitution
8C Working with brackets
8D Substituting positive and negative numbers
8E Number laws and variables
8F Simplifying expressions
8G Multiplying and dividing expressions with variables
8H Expanding brackets
8I Factorising

WHAT DO YOU KNOW?

1 List what you know about algebra. Create a concept map to show your list.
2 Share what you know with a partner and then with a small group.
3 As a class, create a large concept map that shows your class's knowledge of algebra.

eBook*plus*

Digital doc
Hungry brain activity
Chapter 8
doc-6921

OPENING QUESTION

This flooded creek has a catchment of 370 km^2. Find an expression to calculate the volume of water that potentially runs into the creek after x mm of rain.

Are you ready?

Try the questions below. If you have difficulty with any of them, extra help can be obtained by completing the matching SkillSHEET located on your eBookPLUS.

eBook*plus*

Digital doc
SkillSHEET 8.1
doc-6922

Alternative expressions used to describe the four operations

1 Write expressions for the following:

a the difference between M and C
b the amount of money earned by selling B lamingtons for \$2 each
c the product of X and Y
d 12 more than H
e the cost of 10 oranges if each orange costs D cents.

eBook*plus*

Digital doc
SkillSHEET 8.2
doc-6923

Order of operations II

2 Find the value of each of the following using the order of operations rule.

a $12 + 18 \div 6$ **b** $14 - 16 \times 4 \div 8$ **c** $7 \times 3 - 5 \times 12$

eBook*plus*

Digital doc
SkillSHEET 8.3
doc-6924

Order of operations with brackets

3 Find the value of each of the following using the order of operations rule.

a $5 + (10 \times 2) - 13$ **b** $(2 \times 12) + (18 \div 6) - (2 + 7)$

eBook*plus*

Digital doc
SkillSHEET 8.4
doc-6925

Operations with directed numbers

4 Perform each of the calculations.

a $-8 + -10$ **b** $8 - -17$
c 26×-2 **d** $-32 \div -4$

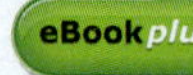

Digital doc
SkillSHEET 8.5
doc-6926

Combining like terms

5 Simplify the following expressions by adding or subtracting like terms.

a $3g + 4g$ **b** $y + 2y + 3y$ **c** $6gy - 3yg$
d $20x - 19x + 11$ **e** $7g + 8g + 8 + 9$ **f** $7h + 4t - 3h$

eBook*plus*

Digital doc
SkillSHEET 8.6
doc-6927

Simplifying fractions

6 Simplify the following.

a $\frac{7}{21}$ **b** $\frac{12}{30}$ **c** $\frac{15}{20}$

eBook*plus*

Digital doc
SkillSHEET 8.7
doc-6928

Highest common factor

7 Find the highest common factor for each of the following pairs of numbers.

a 8, 28 **b** 21, 35 **c** 18, 27

8A Using variables

eBookplus

eLesson
Using variables
eles-0042

- A **variable** (or **pronumeral**) is a letter or symbol that represents a value in an algebraic expression.
- In algebraic expressions such as $a + b$, the variables represent any number.
- In algebraic equations such as $x + 1 = 9$, variables are referred to as **unknowns** because the variable represents a specific value that is not yet known.
- When we write expressions with variables, the multiplication sign is omitted. For example, $8n$ means '$8 \times n$' and $12ab$ means '$12 \times a \times b$'.
- The division sign is rarely used. For example, $y \div 6$ is usually written as $\frac{y}{6}$.

WORKED EXAMPLE 1

Suppose we use b to represent the number of ants in a nest.

a **Write an expression for the number of ants in the nest if 25 ants died.**
b **Write an expression for the number of ants in the nest if the original ant population doubled.**
c **Write an expression for the number of ants in the nest if the original population increased by 50.**
d **What would it mean if we said that a nearby nest contained $b + 100$ ants?**
e **What would it mean if we said that another nest contained $b - 1000$ ants?**
f **Another nest in very poor soil contains $\frac{b}{2}$ ants. How much smaller than the original is this nest?**

THINK	WRITE
a The original number of ants (b) must be reduced by 25.	**a** $b - 25$
b The original number of ants (b) must be multiplied by 2. It is not necessary to show the × sign.	**b** $2b$
c 50 must be added to the original number of ants (b).	**c** $b + 50$
d This expression tells us that the nearby nest has 100 more ants.	**d** The nearby nest has 100 more ants.
e This expression tells us that the nest has 1000 fewer ants.	**e** This nest has 1000 fewer ants.
f The expression $\frac{b}{2}$ means $b \div 2$, so this nest is half the size of the original nest.	**f** This nest is half the size of the original nest.

REMEMBER

1. A variable is a letter or symbol that is used in place of a number.
2. Variables may represent a single number, or they may be used to show a relationship between two or more numbers.
3. When writing expressions with variables, it is important to remember the following points:
   (a) The multiplication sign is omitted.
   For example: $8n$ means '$8 \times n$' and $12ab$ means '$12 \times a \times b$'.
   (b) The division sign is rarely used.
   For example, $y \div 6$ is shown as $\frac{y}{6}$.

EXERCISE

8A Using variables

INDIVIDUAL PATHWAYS

eBook*plus*

Activity 8-A-1
Using variables
doc-2260

Activity 8-A-2
More variables
doc-2261

Activity 8-A-3
Advanced variables
doc-2262

FLUENCY

1 WE1 Suppose we use x to represent the number of ants in a nest.
 a Write an expression for the number of ants in the nest if 420 ants were born.
 b Write an expression for the number of ants in the nest if the original ant population tripled.
 c Write an expression for the number of ants in the nest if the original ant population decreased by 130.
 d What would it mean if we said that a nearby nest contained $x + 60$ ants?
 e What would it mean if we said that a nearby nest contained $x - 90$ ants?
 f Another nest in very poor soil contains $\frac{x}{4}$ ants. How much smaller than the original is this nest?

2 Suppose x people are in attendance at the start of a football match.
 a If a further y people arrive during the first quarter, write an expression for the number of people at the ground.
 b Write an expression for the number of people at the ground if a further 260 people arrive prior to the second quarter commencing.
 c At half-time 170 people leave. Write an expression for the number of people at the ground after they have left.
 d In the final quarter a further 350 people leave. Write an expression for the number of people at the ground after they have left.

3 The canteen manager at Browning Industries orders m Danish pastries each day. Write a paragraph that could explain the table below.

Time	Number of Danish pastries
9.00 am	m
9.15 am	$m - 1$
10.45 am	$m - 12$
12.30 pm	$m - 12$
1.00 pm	$m - 30$
5.30 pm	$m - 30$

4 Imagine that your cutlery drawer contains a knives, b forks and c spoons.
- a Write an expression for the total number of knives and forks you have.
- b Write an expression for the total number of items in the drawer.
- c You put 4 more forks in the drawer. Write an expression for the number of forks now.
- d Write an expression for the number of knives in the drawer after 6 knives are removed.

5 If y represents a certain number, write expressions for the following numbers.
- a A number 7 more than y.
- b A number 8 less than y.
- c A number that is equal to five times y.
- d The number formed when y is subtracted from 14.
- e The number formed when y is divided by 3.
- f The number formed when y is multiplied by 8 and 3 is added to the result.

6 Using a and b to represent numbers, write expressions for:
- a the sum of a and b
- b the difference between a and b
- c three times a subtracted from two times b
- d the product of a and b
- e twice the product of a and b
- f the sum of $3a$ and $7b$
- g a multiplied by itself
- h a multiplied by itself and the result divided by 5.

7 If tickets to a basketball match cost \$27 for adults and \$14 for children, write an expression for the cost of:
- a y adult tickets
- b d child tickets
- c r adult and h child tickets.

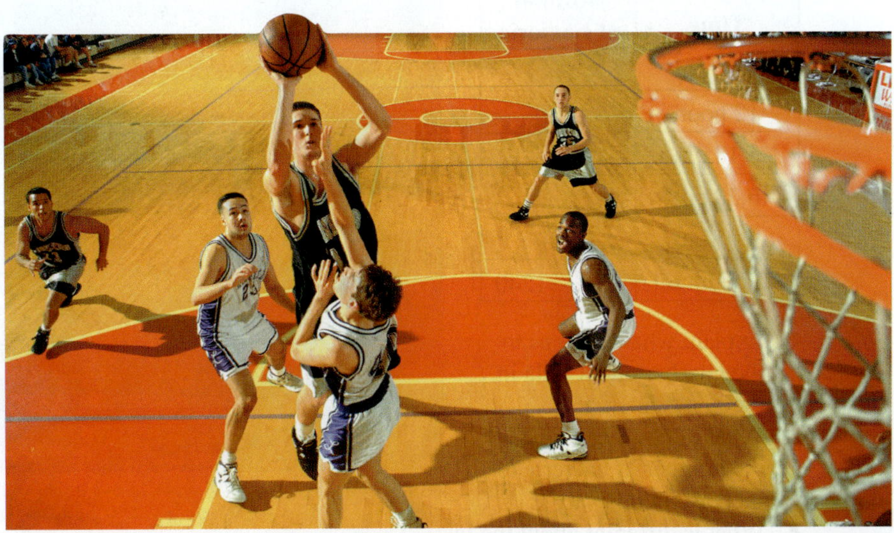

UNDERSTANDING

8 Naomi is now t years old.
- a Write an expression for her age in 2 years' time.
- b Write an expression for Steve's age if he is g years older than Naomi.
- c How old was Naomi 5 years ago?
- d Naomi's father is twice her age. How old is he?

9 James is travelling into town one particular evening and observes that there are t passengers in his carriage. He continues to take note of the number of people in his carriage each time the train departs from a station, which occurs every 3 minutes. The table at the top of the next page shows the number of passengers.

Time	Number of passengers
7.10 pm	t
7.13 pm	$2t$
7.16 pm	$2t + 12$
7.19 pm	$4t + 12$
7.22 pm	$4t + 7$
7.25 pm	t
7.28 pm	$t + 1$
7.31 pm	$t - 8$
7.34 pm	$t - 12$

a Write a paragraph explaining what happened.
b When did passengers first begin to alight the train?
c At what time did the carriage have the most number of passengers?
d At what time did the carriage have the least number of passengers?

REASONING

10 A microbiologist places m bacteria onto an agar plate. She counts the number of bacteria at approximately 3 hour intervals. The results are shown in the table below.

Time	Number of bacteria
9.00 am	m
12 noon	$2m$
3.18 pm	$4m$
6.20 pm	$8m$
9.05 pm	$16m$
12 midnight	$32m - 1240$

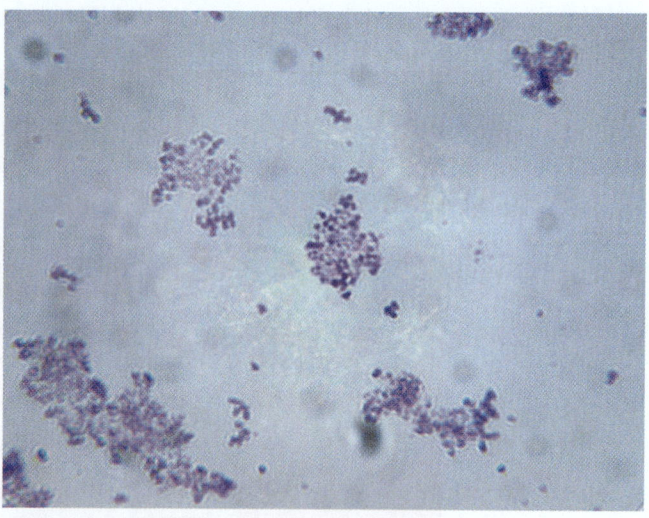

a Explain what happens to the number of bacteria in the first 5 intervals.
b What might be causing the number of bacteria to increase in this way?
c What is different about the last bacteria count?
d What may have happened to cause this?

11 n represents an even number.
a Is the number $n + 1$ odd or even?
b Is $3n$ odd or even?
c Write expressions for:
 i the next three even numbers that are greater than n
 ii the even number that is 2 less than n.

REFLECTION
List some reasons for using variables instead of numbers.

8B Substitution

- If the value of a variable (or variables) is known, it is possible to **evaluate** (work out the value of) an expression by using **substitution**. The variable is replaced with the number.
- Substitution can also be used with a formula or rule.

WORKED EXAMPLE 2

Find the value of the following expressions if $a = 3$ and $b = 15$.

a $6a$ **b** $7a - \frac{2b}{3}$

THINK	WRITE
a 1 Substitute the variable (a) with its correct value and replace the multiplication sign.	**a** $6a = 6 \times 3$
2 Evaluate and write the answer.	$= 18$
b 1 Substitute each variable with its correct value and replace the multiplication signs.	**b** $7a - \frac{2b}{3} = 7 \times 3 - \frac{2 \times 15}{3}$
2 Perform the first multiplication.	$= 21 - \frac{2 \times 15}{3}$
3 Perform the next multiplication.	$= 21 - \frac{30}{3}$
4 Perform the division.	$= 21 - 10$
5 Perform the subtraction and write the answer.	$= 11$

WORKED EXAMPLE 3

The formula for finding the area (A) of a rectangle of length l and width w is $A = l \times w$. Use this formula to find the area of the rectangle at right.

270 m

32 m

THINK	WRITE
1 Write the formula.	$A = l \times w$
2 Substitute each variable with its value.	$= 270 \times 32$
3 Perform the multiplication and state the correct units.	$= 8640 \text{ m}^2$

REMEMBER

Replacing a variable with a number is called substitution.

EXERCISE
8B Substitution

INDIVIDUAL PATHWAYS

eBook*plus*

Activity 8-B-1
Substitution
doc-2263

Activity 8-B-2
More substitution
doc-2264

Activity 8-B-3
Advanced substitution
doc-2265

FLUENCY

1 WE2 Find the value of the following expressions, if $a = 2$ and $b = 5$.

a $3a$ **b** $7a$ **c** $6b$ **d** $\frac{a}{2}$

e $a + 7$ **f** $b - 4$ **g** $a + b$ **h** $b - a$

i $5 + \frac{b}{5}$ **j** $3a + 9$ **k** $2a + 3b$ **l** $\frac{8}{a}$

m $\frac{25}{b}$ **n** ab **o** $2ab$ **p** $7b - 30$

q $6b - 4a$ **r** $\frac{ab}{5}$ **s** $\frac{15}{a} + \frac{7}{b}$ **t** $\frac{9}{a} - \frac{3}{b}$

2 Substitute $x = 6$ and $y = 3$ into the following expressions and evaluate.

a $6x + 2y$ **b** $\frac{x}{3} + \frac{y}{3}$ **c** $3xy$ **d** $\frac{24}{x} - \frac{9}{y}$

e $\frac{12}{x} + 4 + y$ **f** $3x - y$ **g** $2.5x$ **h** $\frac{7x}{2}$

i $3.2x + 1.7y$ **j** $11y - 2x$ **k** $\frac{13y}{3} - 2x$ **l** $\frac{4xy}{15}$

m $4.8x - 3.5y$ **n** $8.7y - 3x$ **o** $12.3x - 9.6x$ **p** $\frac{3x}{9} - \frac{y}{12}$

3 Evaluate the following expressions, if $d = 5$ and $m = 2$.

a $d + m$ **b** $m + d$ **c** $m - d$ **d** $d - m$

e $2m$ **f** md **g** $5dm$ **h** $\frac{md}{10}$

i $-3d$ **j** $-2m$ **k** $6m + 5d$ **l** $\frac{3md}{2}$

m $25m - 2d$ **n** $\frac{7d}{15}$ **o** $4dm - 21$ **p** $\frac{15}{d} - m$

4 WE3 The formula for finding the perimeter (P) of a rectangle of length l and width w is $P = 2l + 2w$. Use this formula to find the perimeter of the rectangular swimming pool at right.

5 The formula for the perimeter (P) of a square of side length l is $P = 4l$. Use this formula to find the perimeter of a square of side length 2.5 cm.

6 The formula $c = 0.1a + 42$ is used to calculate the cost in dollars (c) of renting a car for one day from Poole's Car Hire Ltd, where a is the number of kilometres travelled on that day. Find the cost of renting a car for one day if the distance travelled is 220 kilometres.

Digital doc
Spreadsheet
Substitution
doc-2287

7 The area (A) of a rectangle of length l and width w can be found using the formula $A = lw$. Find the area of the rectangles below:

a length 12 cm, width 4 cm
b length 200 m, width 42 m
c length 4.3 m, width 104 cm.

UNDERSTANDING

8 The formula $F = \frac{9}{5}C + 32$ is used to convert temperatures measured in degrees Celsius to an approximate Fahrenheit value. F represents the temperature in degrees Fahrenheit (°F) and C the temperature in degrees Celsius (°C).
- a Find F when $C = 100$ °C.
- b Convert 28 °C to Fahrenheit.
- c Water freezes at 0 °C. What is the freezing temperature of water in Fahrenheit?

9 The formula $D = 0.6T$ can be used to convert distances in kilometres (T) to the approximate equivalent in miles (D). Use this rule to convert the following distances to miles:
- a 100 kilometres
- b 248 kilometres
- c 12.5 kilometres.

REASONING

10 Ben says that $\frac{4x^2}{2x} = 2x$. Emma says that is not correct if $x = 0$. Explain Emma's reasoning.

REFLECTION

Can any value be substituted for a variable in every expression?

8C Working with brackets

- Brackets are grouping symbols. The expression $3(a + 5)$ can be thought of as 'three groups of $(a + 5)$', or $(a + 5) + (a + 5) + (a + 5)$.
- When substituting into an expression with brackets, remember to place a multiplication sign (×) next to the brackets. For example, $3(a + 5)$ is thought of as $3 \times (a + 5)$.
- Following operation order, evaluate the brackets first and then multiply by the value outside of the brackets.

WORKED EXAMPLE 4

a Substitute $r = 4$ and $s = 5$ into the expression $5(s + r)$ and evaluate.
b Substitute $t = 4$, $x = 3$ and $y = 5$ into the expression $2x(3t - y)$ and evaluate.

THINK	WRITE
a 1 Place the multiplication sign back into the expression.	a $5(s + r) = 5 \times (s + r)$
2 Substitute the variables with their correct values.	$= 5 \times (5 + 4)$
3 Evaluate the expression in the pair of brackets first.	$= 5 \times 9$
4 Perform the multiplication and write the answer.	$= 45$
b 1 Place the multiplication signs back into the expression.	b $2x(3t - y) = 2 \times x \times (3 \times t - y)$
2 Substitute the variables with their correct values.	$= 2 \times 3 \times (3 \times 4 - 5)$
3 Perform the multiplication inside the pair of brackets.	$= 2 \times 3 \times (12 - 5)$
4 Perform the subtraction inside the pair of brackets.	$= 2 \times 3 \times 7$
5 Perform the multiplication and write the answer.	$= 42$

REMEMBER

1. Brackets are grouping symbols.
2. When substituting into an expression with brackets, remember to place a multiplication (×) sign next to the brackets.
3. Work out the brackets first.

EXERCISE 8C Working with brackets

INDIVIDUAL PATHWAYS

eBook*plus*

Activity 8-C-1 Working with brackets doc-2266

Activity 8-C-2 More brackets doc-2267

Activity 8-C-3 Advanced use of brackets doc-2268

FLUENCY

1 WE4 Substitute $r = 5$ and $s = 7$ into the following expressions and evaluate.

a $3(r + s)$ **b** $2(s - r)$ **c** $7(r + s)$
d $9(s - r)$ **e** $s(r + 3)$ **f** $s(2r - 5)$
g $3r(r + 1)$ **h** $rs(3 + s)$ **i** $11r(s - 6)$
j $2r(s - r)$ **k** $s(4 + 3r)$ **l** $7s(r - 2)$
m $s(3rs + 7)$ **n** $5r(24 - 2s)$ **o** $5sr(sr + 3s)$
p $8r(12 - s)$

2 Evaluate each of the expressions below, if $x = 3$, $y = 5$ and $z = 9$.

a $xy(z - 3)$ **b** $\frac{12}{x}(z - y)$
c $\frac{z}{3}\left(\frac{2y}{10} + x - 2\right)$ **d** $(x + y)(z - y)$
e $(z - 3)4x$ **f** $zy(17 - xy)$
g $\frac{y}{5}(7 - x + 3)$ **h** $(8 - y)(z + x)$
i $\left(7 - \frac{12}{x}\right)4y$ **j** $\frac{6}{x}(xz + y - 3)$
k $(y + 2)\frac{z}{x}$ **l** $2x(xyz - 105)$
m $12(y - 1)(z + 3)$ **n** $(3x - 7)\left(\frac{27}{x} + 7\right)$
o $-2(4x + 1)\left(\frac{36}{z} - 3\right)$ **p** $-3(2y - 11)\left(\frac{z}{x} + 8\right)$

3 The formula for the perimeter (P) of a rectangle of length l and width w is $P = 2l + 2w$. This rule can also be written as $P = 2(l + w)$. Use the rule to find the perimeter of rectangular comic covers with the following measurements.

a $l = 20$ cm, $w = 11$ cm
b $l = 27.5$ cm, $w = 21.4$ cm

UNDERSTANDING

4 MC When $a = 8$ and $b = 12$ are substituted into the expression $\frac{a}{6}(15 - b + 9)$, the expression is equal to

A 32 B 16

C $21\frac{1}{3}$ D 24

E 27

5 A rule for finding the sum of the interior angles in a many-sided figure such as a pentagon is $S = 180(n - 2)$, where S represents the sum of the angles inside the figure and n represents the number of sides. The diagram at right shows the interior angles in a pentagon.

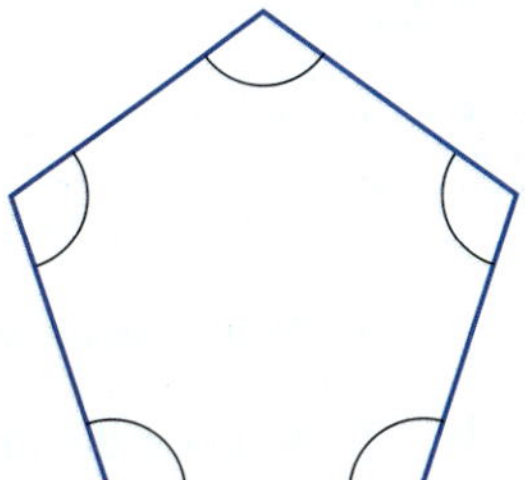

Use the rule to find the sum of the interior angles for the following figures:

a a hexagon (6 sides)
b a pentagon
c a triangle
d a quadrilateral (4 sides)
e a 20-sided figure.

REASONING

6 The dimensions of the figure on the right are given in terms of m and n. Write, in terms of m and n, an expression for:

a the length of CD
b the length of BC
c the perimeter of the figure.

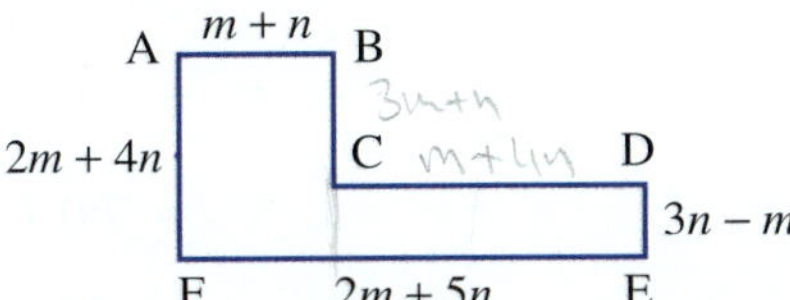

REFLECTION

Is operation order followed when substituting values for variables?

8D Substituting positive and negative numbers

- If the variable you are substituting has a negative value, simply remember the following rules for directed numbers:
  1. For addition and subtraction, signs that occur together can be combined.

Same signs positive	for example,	$7 + +3 = 7 + 3$
	and	$7 - -3 = 7 + 3$
Different signs negative	for example,	$7 - +3 = 7 - 3$
	and	$7 + -3 = 7 - 3$

  2. For multiplication and division.

Same signs positive	for example,	$+7 \times +3 = +21$
	and	$-7 \times -3 = +21$
Different signs negative	for example,	$+7 \times -3 = -21$
	and	$-7 \times +3 = -21$

WORKED EXAMPLE 5

a **Substitute $m = 5$ and $n = -3$ into the expression $m - n$ and evaluate.**
b **Substitute $m = -2$ and $n = -1$ into the expression $2n - m$ and evaluate.**
c **Substitute $a = 4$ and $b = -3$ into the expression $5ab - \frac{12}{b}$ and evaluate.**

THINK	WRITE
a 1 Substitute the variables with their correct value.	**a** $m - n = 5 - -3$
2 Combine the two negative signs and add.	$= 5 + 3$
3 Write the answer.	$= 8$
b 1 Replace the multiplication sign.	**b** $2n - m = 2 \times n - m$
2 Substitute the variables with their correct values.	$= 2 \times -1 - -2$
3 Perform the multiplication.	$= -2 - -2$
4 Combine the two negative signs and add.	$= -2 + 2$
5 Write the answer.	$= 0$
c 1 Replace the multiplication signs.	**c** $5ab - \frac{12}{b} = 5 \times a \times b - \frac{12}{b}$
2 Substitute the variables with their correct values.	$= 5 \times 4 \times -3 - \frac{12}{-3}$
3 Perform the multiplications.	$= -60 - \frac{12}{-3}$
4 Perform the division.	$= -60 - -4$
5 Combine the two negative signs and add.	$= -60 + 4$
6 Write the answer.	$= -56$

REMEMBER

When substituting, if the variable you are replacing has a negative value, simply remember the rules for directed numbers:

1. For addition and subtraction, signs that occur together can be combined.

Same signs positive	for example,	$7 + +3 = 7 + 3$
	and	$7 - -3 = 7 + 3$
Different signs negative	for example,	$7 - +3 = 7 - 3$
	and	$7 + -3 = 7 - 3$

2. For multiplication and division.

Same signs positive	for example,	$+7 \times +3 = +21$
	and	$-7 \times -3 = +21$
Different signs negative	for example,	$+7 \times -3 = -21$
	and	$-7 \times +3 = -21$

EXERCISE 8D Substituting positive and negative numbers

INDIVIDUAL PATHWAYS

eBook*plus*

Activity 8-D-1
What is the word? A
doc-2269

Activity 8-D-2
What is the word? B
doc-2270

Activity 8-D-3
What is the word? C
doc-2271

FLUENCY

1 WE5a Substitute $m = 6$ and $n = -3$ into the following expressions and evaluate.

a $m + n$ b $m - n$ c $n - m$ d $n + m$
e $3n$ f $-2m$ g $2n - m$ h $n + 5$
i $2m + n - 4$ j $11n + 20$ k $-5n - m$ l $\frac{m}{2}$
m $\frac{mn}{9}$ n $\frac{4m}{n-5}$ o $\frac{4m}{n}$ p $\frac{12}{2n}$
q $\frac{9}{n}+\frac{m}{2}$ r $6mn - 1$ s $-\frac{3n}{2}+1.5$ t $14-\frac{mn}{9}$

2 WE5b Substitute $x = 8$ and $y = -3$ into the following expressions and evaluate.

a $3(x - 2)$ b $x(7 + y)$ c $5y(x - 7)$ d $2(3 - y)$
e $(y + 5)x$ f $xy(7 - x)$ g $(3 + x)(5 + y)$ h $5(7 - xy)$
i $\frac{x}{2}(5-y)$ j $\left(\frac{x}{4}-1\right)\left(\frac{2y}{6}+4\right)$ k $\frac{9}{y}(6-x)$ l $3(x-1)\left(\frac{y}{3}+2\right)$

3 WE5c Substitute $a = -4$ and $b = -5$ into the following expressions and evaluate.

a $a + b$ b $a - b$ c $b - 2a$ d $2ab$
e $12 - ab$ f $-2(b - a)$ g $a - b - 4$ h $3a(b + 4)$
i $\frac{4}{b}$ j $\frac{8}{a}$ k $\frac{16}{4a}$ l $\frac{6b}{5}$
m $45 + 4ab$ n $8ab - 3b$ o $\frac{a}{2}+\frac{3b}{5}$ p $2.5b$
q $11a + 6b$ r $(a - 5)(8 - b)$ s $(9 - a)(b - 3)$ t $1.5b + 2a$

UNDERSTANDING

4 If $p = -2$ and $q = -3$, evaluate $\frac{3(-pq-p^2)}{q+2p}$.

REASONING

5 Consider the expression $1 - 5x$. If x is a negative integer, explain why the expression will have a positive value.

eBook*plus*

Digital doc
WorkSHEET 8.1
doc-2290

REFLECTION
What can you say about the sign of x^2?

8E Number laws and variables

- When dealing with any type of number, we must obey particular rules.

Commutative Law

- The **Commutative Law** refers to the order in which two numbers may be added, subtracted, multiplied or divided.
- The Commutative Law holds true for addition and multiplication because the order in which two numbers are added or multiplied does not affect the result.
  - $3 + 2 = 2 + 3$
  - $3 \times 2 = 2 \times 3$

- Since variables take the place of numbers, the Commutative Law holds true for the addition and multiplication of variables.
  - $x + y = y + x$
  - $x \times y = y \times x$
- The Commutative Law does not hold true for subtraction or division because the results obtained are different.
  - $3 - 2 \neq 2 - 3$
  - $3 \div 2 \neq 2 \div 3$
- Since variables take the place of numbers, the Commutative Law does not hold true for the subtraction and division of variables.
  - $x - y \neq y - x$
  - $x \div y \neq y \div x$

WORKED EXAMPLE 6

Find the value of the following expressions if $x = 4$ and $y = 7$. Comment on the results obtained.

a i $x + y$ **ii** $y + x$ **b i** $x - y$ **ii** $y - x$
c i $x \times y$ **ii** $y \times x$ **d i** $x \div y$ **ii** $y \div x$

THINK	WRITE
a i 1 Substitute each variable with its correct value.	**a i** $x + y = 4 + 7$
2 Evaluate and write the answer.	$= 11$
ii 1 Substitute each variable with its correct value.	**ii** $y + x = 7 + 4$
2 Evaluate and write the answer.	$= 11$
3 Compare the result with the answer obtained in part **a i**.	The same result is obtained; therefore, order is not important when adding two terms.
b i 1 Substitute each variable with its correct value.	**b i** $x - y = 4 - 7$
2 Evaluate and write the answer.	$= -3$
ii 1 Substitute each variable with its correct value.	**ii** $y - x = 7 - 4$
2 Evaluate and write the answer.	$= 3$
3 Compare the result with the answer obtained in part **b i**.	Two different results are obtained; therefore, order is important when subtracting two terms.
c i 1 Substitute each variable with its correct value.	**c i** $x \times y = 4 \times 7$
2 Evaluate and write the answer.	$= 28$
ii 1 Substitute each variable with its correct value.	**ii** $y \times x = 7 \times 4$
2 Evaluate and write the answer.	$= 28$
3 Compare the result with the answer obtained in part **c i**.	The same result is obtained; therefore, order is not important when multiplying two terms.
d i 1 Substitute each variable with its correct value.	**d i** $x \div y = 4 \div 7$
2 Evaluate and write the answer.	$= \frac{4}{7} (\approx 0.57)$

ii	**1** Substitute each variable with its correct value.	**ii** $y \div x = 7 \div 4$
	2 Evaluate and write the answer.	$= \frac{7}{4}(1.75)$
	3 Compare the result with the answer obtained in part **d i**.	Two different results are obtained; therefore, order is important when dividing two terms.

eBook*plus*

Interactivity
The Associative Law
int-2370

Associative Law

- The **Associative Law** refers to the order in which three numbers may be added, subtracted, multiplied or divided, taking two at a time.
  Note: The Associative Law refers to the order in which the addition (or other operation) is performed, and this order is indicated by the use of brackets. The order in which the variables are written does not change.
- Like the Commutative Law, the Associative Law holds true for addition and multiplication of numbers.
  - $5 + (10 + 3) = (5 + 10) + 3$
  - $5 \times (10 \times 3) = (5 \times 10) \times 3$
- Since variables take the place of numbers, the Associative Law holds true for the addition and multiplication of variables.
  - $x + (y + z) = (x + y) + z$
  - $x \times (y \times z) = (x \times y) \times z$
- Like the Commutative Law, the Associative Law does not hold for subtraction and division of numbers.
  - $5 - (10 - 3) \neq (5 - 10) - 3$
  - $5 \div (10 \div 3) \neq (5 \div 10) \div 3$
- Since variables take the place of numbers, the Associative law does not hold true for the subtraction and division of variables.
  - $x - (y - z) \neq (x - y) - z$
  - $x \div (y \div z) \neq (x \div y) \div z$

WORKED EXAMPLE 7

Find the value of the following expressions if $x = 12$, $y = 6$ and $z = 2$. Comment on the results obtained.

a i $x + (y + z)$ **ii** $(x + y) + z$ **b i** $x - (y - z)$ **ii** $(x - y) - z$
c i $x \times (y \times z)$ **ii** $(x \times y) \times z$ **d i** $x \div (y \div z)$ **ii** $(x \div y) \div z$

THINK		WRITE
a i	**1** Substitute each variable with its correct value.	**a i** $x + (y + z) = 12 + (6 + 2)$
	2 Evaluate the expression in the pair of brackets.	$= 12 + 8$
	3 Perform the addition and write the answer.	$= 20$
ii	**1** Substitute each variable with its correct value.	**ii** $(x + y) + z = (12 + 6) + 2$
	2 Evaluate the expression in the pair of brackets.	$= 18 + 2$
	3 Perform the addition and write the answer.	$= 20$
	4 Compare the result with the answer obtained in part **a i**.	The same result is obtained; therefore, order is not important when adding 3 terms.
b i	**1** Substitute each variable with its correct value.	**b i** $x - (y - z) = 12 - (6 - 2)$
	2 Evaluate the expression in the pair of brackets.	$= 12 - 4$
	3 Perform the subtraction and write the answer.	$= 8$

ii 1 Substitute each variable with its correct value.	**ii** $(x - y) - z = (12 - 6) - 2$
2 Evaluate the expression in the pair of brackets.	$= 6 - 2$
3 Perform the subtraction and write the answer.	$= 4$
4 Compare the result with the answer obtained in part **b i**.	Two different results are obtained; therefore, order is important when subtracting 3 terms.
c i 1 Substitute each variable with its correct value.	**c i** $x \times (y \times z) = 12 \times (6 \times 2)$
2 Evaluate the expression in the pair of brackets.	$= 12 \times 12$
3 Perform the multiplication and write the answer.	$= 144$
ii 1 Substitute each variable with its correct value.	**ii** $(x \times y) \times z = (12 \times 6) \times 2$
2 Evaluate the expression in the pair of brackets.	$= 72 \times 2$
3 Perform the multiplication and write the answer.	$= 144$
4 Compare the result with the answer obtained in part **c i**.	The same result is obtained; therefore, order is not important when multiplying 3 terms.
d i 1 Substitute each variable with its correct value.	**d i** $x \div (y \div z) = 12 \div (6 \div 2)$
2 Evaluate the expression in the pair of brackets.	$= 12 \div 3$
3 Perform the division and write the answer.	$= 4$
ii 1 Substitute each variable with its correct value.	**ii** $(x \div y) \div z = (12 \div 6) \div 2$
2 Evaluate the expression in the pair of brackets.	$= 2 \div 2$
3 Perform the division and write the answer.	$= 1$
4 Compare the result with the answer obtained in part **d i**.	Two different results are obtained; therefore, order is important when dividing 3 terms.

Identity Law

- The Identity Law for addition states that when zero is added to any number, the original number remains unchanged. For example, $5 + 0 = 0 + 5 = 5$.
- The Identity Law for multiplication states that when any number is multiplied by one, the original number remains unchanged. For example, $3 \times 1 = 1 \times 3 = 1$.
- Since variables take the place of numbers: $x + 0 = 0 + x = x$

$$x \times 1 = 1 \times x = x$$

Inverse Law

- The Inverse Law for addition states that when a number is added to its opposite, the result is zero. For example, $5 + -5 = 0$.
- The Inverse Law for multiplication states that when a number is multiplied by its reciprocal, the result is one. For example, $3 \times \frac{1}{3} = 1$.
- Since variables take the place of numbers:

$$x + -x = -x + x = 0$$

$$x \times \frac{1}{x} = \frac{1}{x} \times x = 1$$

REMEMBER

1. When dealing with numbers and variables, particular rules must be obeyed.
2. The Commutative Law holds true for addition (and multiplication) because the order in which two numbers or variables are added (or multiplied) does not affect the result. Therefore, in general,
   (a) $x + y = y + x$
   (b) $x - y \neq y - x$
   (c) $x \times y = y \times x$
   (d) $x \div y \neq y \div x$
3. The Associative Law holds true for addition (and multiplication) because the order in which three numbers or variables, taking two at a time, are added (or multiplied) does not affect the result. Therefore, in general,
   (a) $x + (y + z) = (x + y) + z$
   (b) $x - (y - z) \neq (x - y) - z$
   (c) $x \times (y \times z) = (x \times y) \times z$
   (d) $x \div (y \div z) \neq (x \div y) \div z$
4. The Identity Law states that, in general, $x + 0 = 0 + x = x$
   $x \times 1 = 1 \times x = x$
5. The Inverse Law states that, in general, $x + -x = -x + x = 0$
   $x \times \frac{1}{x} = \frac{1}{x} \times x = 1$

EXERCISE 8E

Number laws and variables

INDIVIDUAL PATHWAYS

eBook*plus*

Activity 8-E-1 Number laws and variables doc-2272

Activity 8-E-2 More number laws and variables doc-2273

Activity 8-E-3 Advanced number laws and variables doc-2274

FLUENCY

1 WE6a,b Find the value of the following expressions if $x = 3$ and $y = 8$. Comment on the results obtained.

a i $x + y$ ii $y + x$
b i $3x + 2y$ ii $2y + 3x$
c i $5x + 2y$ ii $2y + 5x$
d i $8x + y$ ii $y + 8x$
e i $x - y$ ii $y - x$
f i $2x - 3y$ ii $3y - 2x$
g i $4x - 5y$ ii $5y - 4x$
h i $3x - y$ ii $y - 3x$

2 WE6c,d Find the value of the following expressions if $x = -2$ and $y = 5$. Comment on the results obtained.

a i $x \times y$ ii $y \times x$
b i $6x \times 3y$ ii $3y \times 6x$
c i $4x \times y$ ii $y \times 4x$
d i $7x \times 5y$ ii $5y \times 7x$
e i $x \div y$ ii $y \div x$
f i $10x \div 4y$ ii $4y \div 10x$
g i $6x \div 3y$ ii $3y \div 6x$
h i $7x \div 9y$ ii $9y \div 7x$

3 Indicate whether each of the following is true or false for all values of the variables.

a $a + 5b = 5b + a$ **b** $6x - 2y = 2y - 6x$

c $7c + 3d = -3d + 7c$ **d** $5 \times 2x \times x = 10x^2$

e $4x \times -y = -y \times 4x$ **f** $4 \times 3x \times x = 12x \times x$

g $\frac{5p}{3r} = \frac{3r}{5p}$ **h** $-7i - 2j = 2j + 7i$

i $-3y \div 4x = 4x \div -3y$ **j** $-2c + 3d = 3d - 2c$

k $\frac{0}{3s} = \frac{3s}{0}$ **l** $15 \times -\frac{2x}{3} = \frac{2x}{3} \times -15$

4 WE7a,b Find the value of the following expressions if $x = 3$, $y = 8$ and $z = 2$. Comment on the results obtained.

a **i** $x + (y + z)$ **ii** $(x + y) + z$

b **i** $2x + (y + 5z)$ **ii** $(2x + y) + 5z$

c **i** $6x + (2y + 3z)$ **ii** $(6x + 2y) + 3z$

d **i** $x - (y - z)$ **ii** $(x - y) - z$

e **i** $x - (7y - 9z)$ **ii** $(x - 7y) - 9z$

f **i** $3x - (8y - 6z)$ **ii** $(3x - 8y) - 6z$

5 WE7c,d Find the value of the following expressions if $x = 8$, $y = 4$ and $z = -2$. Comment on the results obtained.

a **i** $x \times (y \times z)$ **ii** $(x \times y) \times z$

b **i** $x \times (-3y \times 4z)$ **ii** $(x \times -3y) \times 4z$

c **i** $2x \times (3y \times 4z)$ **ii** $(2x \times 3y) \times 4z$

d **i** $x \div (y \div z)$ **ii** $(x \div y) \div z$

e **i** $x \div (2y \div 3z)$ **ii** $(x \div 2y) \div 3z$

f **i** $-x \div (5y \div 2z)$ **ii** $(-x \div 5y) \div 2z$

UNDERSTANDING

6 Indicate whether each of the following is true or false for all values of the variables.

a $a - 0 = 0$ **b** $a \times 1\,000\,000 = 0$

c $15t \times -\frac{1}{15t} = 1$ **d** $3d \times \frac{1}{3d} = 1$

e $\frac{8x}{9y} \div \frac{8x}{9y} = 1$ **f** $\frac{11t}{0} = 0$

7 MC The value of the expression $x \times (-3y \times 4z)$ when $x = 4$, $y = 3$ and $z = -3$ is:

A 108 **B** −432

C 432 **D** 112

E −108

8 MC The value of the expression $(x - 8y) - 10z$ when $x = 6$, $y = 5$ and $z = -4$ is:

A −74 **B** 74

C −6 **D** 6

E −36

REFLECTION

The Commutative Law does not hold for subtraction. What can you say about the results of $x - a$ and $a - x$?

8F Simplifying expressions

- Expressions can often be written in a more simple form by collecting (adding or subtracting) like terms.
- **Like terms** are terms that contain exactly the same variables, raised to the same power.
  To understand why $2a + 3a$ *can* be added but $2a + 3ab$ can *not* be added, consider the following identical bags of lollies, each containing a lollies.

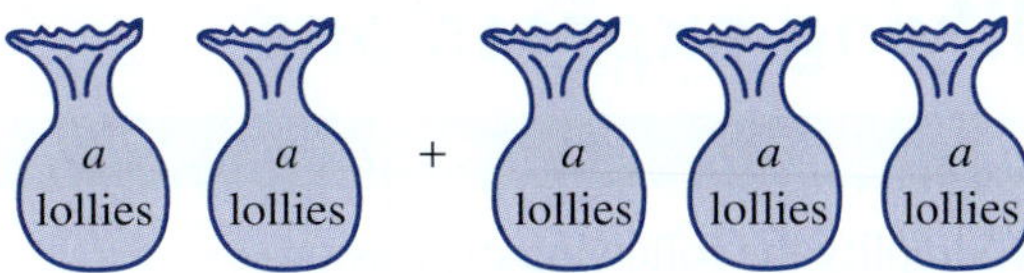

So, $2a + 3a = 5a$.
Then consider the following 2 bags containing a lollies and 3 bags containing $a \times b$ lollies.

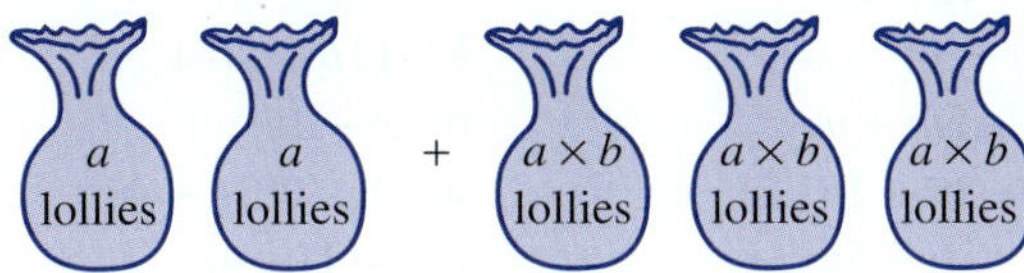

So $2a + 3ab$ cannot be added as they are not identical and we do not have any further information.
So, $2a + 3ab = 2a + 3ab$.
For example:

$3x$ and $4x$ are like terms.
$3ab$ and $7ab$ are like terms.
$2bc$ and $4cb$ are like terms.
$3g^2$ and $45g^2$ are like terms.

$3x$ and $3y$ are not like terms.
$7ab$ and $8a$ are not like terms.
$8a$ and $3a^2$ are not like terms.

WORKED EXAMPLE 8

Simplify the following expressions.

a $3a + 5a$ **b** $7ab - 3a - 4ab$ **c** $2c - 6 + 4c + 15$

THINK	WRITE
a 1 Write the expression and check that the two terms are like terms, that is, they contain the same variables.	**a** $3a + 5a$
2 Add the like terms and write the answer.	$= 8a$
b 1 Write the expression and check for like terms.	**b** $7ab - 3a - 4ab$
2 Rearrange the terms so that the like terms are together. Remember to keep the correct sign in front of each term.	$= 7ab - 4ab - 3a$
3 Subtract the like terms and write the answer.	$= 3ab - 3a$
c 1 Write the expression and check for like terms.	**c** $2c - 6 + 4c + 15$
2 Rearrange the terms so that the like terms are together. Remember to keep the correct sign in front of each term.	$= 2c + 4c - 6 + 15$
3 Simplify by collecting like terms and write the answer.	$= 6c + 9$

REMEMBER

1. When simplifying expressions, we can collect (add or subtract) only like terms.
2. Like terms are terms that contain the same variable parts.

EXERCISE 8F Simplifying expressions

INDIVIDUAL PATHWAYS

eBook*plus*

Activity 8-F-1 Simplifying expressions doc-2275

Activity 8-F-2 More simplifying expressions doc-2276

Activity 8-F-3 Advanced simplifying expressions doc-2277

FLUENCY

1 WE8a Simplify the following expressions.

- **a** $4c + 2c$
- **b** $2c - 5c$
- **c** $3a + 5a - 4a$
- **d** $6q - 5q$
- **e** $-h - 2h$
- **f** $7x - 5x$
- **g** $3a - 7a - 2a$
- **h** $-3f + 7f$
- **i** $4p - 7p$
- **j** $-3h + 4h$
- **k** $11b + 2b + 5b$
- **l** $7t - 8t + 4t$
- **m** $9m + 5m - m$
- **n** $x - 2x$
- **o** $7z + 13z$
- **p** $5p + 3p + 2p$
- **q** $9g + 12g - 4g$
- **r** $18b - 4b - 11b$
- **s** $13t - 4t + 5t$
- **t** $-11j + 4j$
- **u** $-12l + 2l - 5l$
- **v** $13m - 2m - 4m + m$
- **w** $m + 3m - 4m$
- **x** $t + 2t - t + 8t$

2 WE8b,c Simplify the following expressions.

- **a** $3x + 7x - 2y$
- **b** $3x + 4x - 12$
- **c** $11 + 5f - 7f$
- **d** $3u - 4u + 6$
- **e** $2m + 3p + 5m$
- **f** $-3h + 4r - 2h$
- **g** $11a - 5b + 6a$
- **h** $9t - 7 + 5$
- **i** $12 - 3g + 5$
- **j** $6m + 4m - 3n + n$
- **k** $5k - 5 + 2k - 7$
- **l** $3n - 4 + n - 5$
- **m** $2b - 6 - 4b + 18$
- **n** $11 - 12h + 9$
- **o** $12y - 3y - 7g + 5g - 6$
- **p** $8h - 6 + 3h - 2$
- **q** $11s - 6t + 4t - 7s$
- **r** $2m + 13l - 7m + l$
- **s** $3h + 4k - 16h - k + 7$
- **t** $13 + 5t - 9t - 8$
- **u** $2g + 5 + 5g - 7$
- **v** $17f - 3k + 2f - 7k$

UNDERSTANDING

3 Simplify the following expressions.

- **a** $x^2 + 2x^2$
- **b** $3y^2 + 2y^2$
- **c** $a^3 + 3a^3$
- **d** $d^2 + 6d^2$
- **e** $7g^2 - 8g^2$
- **f** $3y^3 + 7y^3$
- **g** $2b^2 + 5b^2$
- **h** $4a^2 - 3a^2$
- **i** $g^2 - 2g^2$
- **j** $a^2 + 4 + 3a^2 + 5$
- **k** $11x^2 - 6 + 12x^2 + 6$
- **l** $12s^2 - 3 + 7 - s^2$
- **m** $3a^2 + 2a + 5a^2 + 3a$
- **n** $11b - 3b^2 + 4b^2 + 12b$
- **o** $6t^2 - 6g - 5t^2 + 2g - 7$
- **p** $11g^3 + 17 - 3g^3 + 5 - g^2$
- **q** $12ab + 3 + 6ab$
- **r** $14xy + 3xy - xy - 5xy$
- **s** $4fg + 2s - fg + s$
- **t** $11ab + ab - 5$
- **u** $18ab^2 - 4ac + 2ab^2 - 10ac$

REASONING

4 Rose owns an art gallery and sells items supplied to her by various artists. She receives a commission for all items sold. She uses the following method to keep track of the money she owes the artists when their items are sold.

- Ask the artist how much they want for the item.
- Add 50% to that price, then mark the item for sale at this new price.
- When the item sells, take one-third of the sale price as commission, then return the balance to the artist.

Use algebra to show that this method does return the correct amount to the artist.

5 Explain, using mathematical reasoning and with diagrams if necessary, why the expression $2x + 2x^2$ cannot be simplified.

REFLECTION

What do you need to remember when checking for like terms?

8G Multiplying and dividing expressions with variables

Multiplying variables

- When we multiply variables (as already stated) the Commutative Law holds, so order is not important. For example:

$$3 \times 6 = 6 \times 3$$
$$6 \times w = w \times 6$$
$$a \times b = b \times a$$

- The multiplication sign (×) is usually omitted for reasons of convention.

$$3 \times g \times h = 3gh$$
$$2 \times x^2 \times y = 2x^2y$$

- Although order is not important, conventionally the variables in each term are written in alphabetical order. For example,

$$2 \times b^2 \times a \times c = 2ab^2c$$

WORKED EXAMPLE 9

Simplify the following.

a $5 \times 4g$ **b** $-3d \times 6ab \times 7$

THINK			WRITE
a	1	Write the expression and replace the hidden multiplication signs.	a $5 \times 4g$ $= 5 \times 4 \times g$
	2	Multiply the numbers.	$= 20 \times g$
	3	Remove the multiplication sign.	$= 20g$
b	1	Write the expression and replace the hidden multiplication signs.	b $-3d \times 6ab \times 7$ $= -3 \times d \times 6 \times a \times b \times 7$
	2	Place the numbers at the front.	$= -3 \times 6 \times 7 \times d \times a \times b$
	3	Multiply the numbers.	$= -126 \times d \times a \times b$
	4	Remove the multiplication signs and place the variables in alphabetical order.	$= -126abd$

Dividing expressions with variables

- When dividing expressions with variables, rewrite the expression as a fraction and simplify by cancelling.
- Remember that when the same variable appears as a factor on both the numerator and denominator, it may be cancelled.

WORKED EXAMPLE 10

a Simplify $\frac{16f}{4}$.

b Simplify $15n \div 3n$.

THINK	WRITE
a 1 Write the expression.	**a** $\frac{16f}{4} = \frac{{}^{4}\cancel{16}f}{\cancel{4}_{1}}$
2 Simplify the fraction by cancelling 16 with 4 (divide both by 4).	$= \frac{4f}{1}$
3 No need to write the denominator since we are dividing by 1.	$= 4f$
b 1 Write the expression and then rewrite it as a fraction.	**b** $15n \div 3n = \frac{15n}{3n}$ $= \frac{{}^{5}\cancel{15}\cancel{n}}{{}_{1}\cancel{3}\cancel{n}}$
2 Simplify the fraction by cancelling 15 with 3 and n with n.	$= \frac{5}{1}$
3 No need to write the denominator since we are dividing by 1.	$= 5$

WORKED EXAMPLE 11

Simplify $-12xy \div 27y$.

THINK	WRITE
a 1 Write the expression and then rewrite it as a fraction.	**a** $-12xy + 27y = -\frac{12xy}{27y}$ $= -\frac{{}^{4}\cancel{12}x\cancel{y}}{{}_{9}\cancel{27}\cancel{y}}$
2 Simplify the fraction by cancelling 12 with 27 (divide both by 3) and y with y.	$= -\frac{4x}{9}$

WORKED EXAMPLE 12

Simplify the following.

a $3m^3 \times 2m$ **b** $5p^{10} \times 3p^3$

c $36x^7 \div 12x^4$ **d** $\frac{6y^3 \times 4y^8}{12y^4}$

THINK	WRITE
a 1 Write the problem.	**a** $3m^3 \times 2m$

	2	The order is not important when multiplying, so place the numbers first.	$= 3 \times 2 \times m^3 \times m$
	3	Multiply the numbers.	$= 6 \times m^3 \times m$
	4	Check to see if the bases are the same. They are both m.	
	5	Simplify by adding the indices.	$= 6 \times m^{3+1}$ $= 6m^4$
b	1	Write the problem.	**b** $5p^{10} \times 3p^3$
	2	The order is not important when multiplying, so place the numbers first.	$= 5 \times 3 \times p^{10} \times p^3$
	3	Multiply the numbers.	$= 15 \times p^{10} \times p^3$
	4	Check to see if the bases are the same. They are both p.	
	5	Simplify by adding the indices.	$= 15 \times p^{10+3}$ $= 15p^{13}$
c	1	Write the problem and express it as a fraction.	**c** $36x^7 \div 12x^4$ $= \dfrac{36x^7}{12x^4}$
	2	Divide the numbers.	$= \dfrac{3x^7}{x^4}$
	3	Check to see if the bases are the same. They are both x.	
	4	Subtract the powers.	$= 3x^3$
d	1	Write the problem.	**d** $\dfrac{6y^3 \times 4y^8}{12y^4}$
	2	Multiply the numbers in the numerator. Simplify the numbers in index form in the numerator.	$= \dfrac{24y^{11}}{12y^4}$
	3	Divide the numbers and subtract the powers.	$= 2y^7$

REMEMBER

1. When multiplying variables:
   (a) the order is not important. For example, $d \times e = e \times d$.
   (b) place the numbers at the front of the expression and leave out the $\times$ sign.
2. When dividing variables, rewrite the expression as a fraction and simplify it by cancelling.
3. When the same variable appears on both the top and bottom lines of the fraction, it may be cancelled.

EXERCISE 8G

Multiplying and dividing expressions with variables

INDIVIDUAL PATHWAYS

eBook*plus*

Activity 8-G-1 Who invented algebra? doc-2278

Activity 8-G-2 Who is the father of algebra? doc-2279

Activity 8-G-3 Mathematician's riddle doc-2280

FLUENCY

1 WE9 Simplify the following.

a $4 \times 3g$ **b** $7 \times 3h$ **c** $4d \times 6$ **d** $3z \times 5$
e $6 \times 5r$ **f** $5t \times 7$ **g** $4 \times 3u$ **h** $7 \times 6p$
i $7gy \times 3$ **j** $2 \times 11ht$ **k** $4x \times 6g$ **l** $10a \times 7h$
m $9m \times 4d$ **n** $3c \times 5h$ **o** $9g \times 2x$ **p** $2.5t \times 5b$
q $13m \times 12n$ **r** $6a \times 12d$ **s** $2ab \times 3c$ **t** $4f \times 3gh$
u $2 \times 8w \times 3x$ **v** $11ab \times 3d \times 7$ **w** $16xy \times 1.5$ **x** $3.5x \times 3y$
y $11q \times 4s \times 3$ **z** $4a \times 3b \times 2c$

2 WE10 Simplify the following.

a $\frac{8f}{2}$ **b** $\frac{6h}{3}$ **c** $\frac{15x}{3}$ **d** $9g \div 3$
e $10r \div 5$ **f** $4x \div 2x$ **g** $8r \div 4r$ **h** $\frac{16m}{8m}$
i $14q \div 21q$ **j** $\frac{3x}{6x}$ **k** $\frac{12h}{14h}$ **l** $50g \div 75g$
m $\frac{8f}{24f}$ **n** $35x \div 70x$ **o** $24m \div 36m$ **p** $y \div 34y$
q $27h \div 3h$ **r** $\frac{20d}{48d}$ **s** $\frac{64q}{44q}$ **t** $81l \div 27l$

3 Simplify the following.

a $\frac{15fg}{3}$ **b** $12cd \div 4$ **c** $\frac{8xy}{12}$ **d** $24cg \div 24$
e $\frac{11xy}{11x}$ **f** $\frac{9pq}{18q}$ **g** $\frac{21ab}{28b}$ **h** $\frac{9dg}{12g}$
i $\frac{5jk}{kj}$ **j** $55rt \div 77t$ **k** $\frac{10mxy}{35mx}$ **l** $36bc \div 27c$
m $13xy \div x$ **n** $\frac{16cd}{40cd}$ **o** $14abc \div 7bc$ **p** $3gh \div 6h$
q $\frac{132mnp}{60np}$ **r** $\frac{11ad}{66ad}$ **s** $18adg \div 45ag$ **t** $\frac{bh}{7h}$

4 Simplify the following.

a $3 \times -5f$ **b** $-6 \times -2d$ **c** $11a \times -3g$
d $-9t \times -3g$ **e** $-5t \times -4dh$ **f** $6 \times -3st$
g $-3 \times -2w \times 7d$ **h** $-4a \times -3b \times 2c \times e$ **i** $11ab \times -3f$
j $3as \times -3b \times -2x$ **k** $-5h \times -5t \times -3q$ **l** $4 \times -3w \times -2 \times 6p$
m $-7a \times 3b \times g$ **n** $17ab \times -3gh$ **o** $-3.5g \times 2h \times 7$
p $5h \times 8j \times -k$ **q** $75x \times 1.5y$ **r** $12rt \times -3z \times 4p$
s $2ab \times 3c \times 5$ **t** $-4w \times 34x \times 3$ **u** $-3ab \times -5cd \times -6ae$

5 WE11 Simplify the following.

a $\frac{-4a}{8}$ **b** $\frac{-11ab}{33b}$ **c** $60jk \div -5k$

d $-3h \div -6dh$ **e** $\frac{-32g}{40gl}$ **f** $-12xy \div 48y$

g $\frac{12ab}{-14ab}$ **h** $\frac{6fgh}{30ghj}$ **i** $-4xyz \div 6yz$

j $\frac{-rt}{6rt}$ **k** $-5mn \div 20n$ **l** $-14st \div -28$

m $34ab \div -17ab$ **n** $\frac{-ab}{-3a}$ **o** $\frac{-7dg}{35gh}$

p $-60mn \div 55mnp$ **q** $\frac{28def}{18d}$ **r** $-72xyz \div 28yz$

s $\frac{54pq}{36pqr}$ **t** $-\frac{121oc}{132oct}$

UNDERSTANDING

6 WE12 Simplify the following.

a $2a \times a$ **b** $-5p \times -5p$ **c** $-5 \times 3x \times 2x$

d $ab \times 7a$ **e** $3b^2 \times 2cd$ **f** $-5xy \times 4 \times 8x$

g $7pq \times 3p \times 2q$ **h** $5m \times n \times 6nt \times -t$ **i** $-3 \times xyz \times -3z \times -2y$

j $-7a \times -3b \times -2c^2$ **k** $2mn \times -3 \times 2n \times 0$ **l** $w^2x \times -9z^2 \times 2xy^2$

m $2a^4 \times 3a^7$ **n** $2x^2y^3 \times x^3$ **o** $20m^{12} \div 2m^3$

p $\frac{25p^{12} \times 4q^7}{15p^2 \times 8q^2}$ **q** $\frac{8x^3 \times 7y^2 \times 2z^2}{6x \times 14y}$ **r** $\frac{a \times ab \times 3b^2}{5a^2b^2}$

7 Simplify the following.

a $\frac{3}{a} \times \frac{2}{a}$ **b** $\frac{5b}{2} \times \frac{4b}{3}$ **c** $w \times \frac{5}{w^2}$

d $\frac{3rk}{2s} \times \frac{6st}{5rt}$ **e** $-\frac{15gt}{10ag} \times \frac{2g}{5t}$ **f** $-\frac{4ht}{3dk} \times \frac{-12hk}{9dt}$

g $\frac{5t}{gn} \div \frac{1}{g}$ **h** $\frac{-9th}{4g} \div \frac{tg}{6h}$

i $\frac{4xy}{7wz} \div \frac{x}{14z}$ **j** $\frac{-10f}{3w} \div \frac{5}{-9wz}$

REFLECTION

How is multiplication and division of expressions with variables similar to multiplication and division of numbers?

8H Expanding brackets

The Distributive Law

- The **Distributive Law** is the name given to the following process.

$$3(5 + 8) = 3 \times 5 + 3 \times 8$$

This is because the number out in front is *distributed* to each of the terms in the bracket.

- Since variables take the place of numbers, the Distributive Law also holds true for algebraic expressions.

$$a(b + c) = ab + ac$$

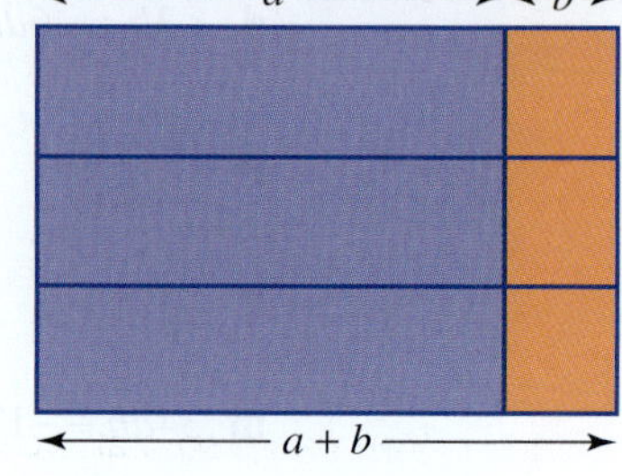

- The Distributive Law can be demonstrated using the concept of area. As can be seen in the diagram at right, $3(a + b) = 3a + 3b$
- We can think of $3(a + b) = (a + b) + (a + b) + (a + b)$
  Collecting like terms, $3(a + b) = a + a + a + b + b + b = 3a + 3b$
- An expression containing a bracket multiplied by a number can be written in expanded or factorised form.

$$\underbrace{3(a + b)}_{\text{Factorised form}} = \underbrace{3a + 3b}_{\text{Expanded form}}$$

  Expanding and factorising are the inverse of each other.
- The Distributive Law can be used when the terms inside the brackets are either added or subtracted.

$$a(b - c) = ab - ac$$

- The Distributive Law is not used when the terms inside the brackets are multiplied or divided. You can see this with numbers $2(4 \times 5) = 2 \times 4 \times 5$; *not* $(2 \times 4) \times (2 \times 5)$.
- When simplifying expressions, we can leave the result in either factorised form or expanded form, but not a combination of both.

WORKED EXAMPLE 13

Use the Distributive Law to expand the following expressions.

a $3(a + 2)$ **b** $-x(x - 5)$

THINK	WRITE
a 1 Write the expression.	**a** $3(a + 2) = 3(a + 2)$
2 Use the Distributive Law to expand the brackets.	$= 3 \times a + 3 \times 2$
3 Simplify by multiplying.	$= 3a + 6$
b 1 Write the expression.	**b** $x(x - 5) = x(x - 5)$
2 Use the Distributive Law to expand the brackets.	$= x \times x + x \times -5$
3 Simplify by multiplying.	$= x^2 - 5x$

- Some expressions can be simplified further by collecting like terms after any brackets have been expanded.

WORKED EXAMPLE 14

Expand the expressions below and then simplify by collecting any like terms.

a $3(x - 5) + 4$ **b** $4(3x + 4) + 7x + 12$ **c** $2x(3y + 3) + 3x(y + 1)$ **d** $4x(2x - 1) - 3(2x - 1)$

THINK	WRITE
a 1 Write the expression.	**a** $3(x - 5) + 4$
2 Expand the brackets.	$= 3 \times x + 3 \times -5 + 4$ $= 3x - 15 + 4$
3 Collect the like terms (−15 and 4).	$= 3x - 11$
b 1 Write the expression.	**b** $4(3x + 4) + 7x + 12$
2 Expand the brackets.	$= 4 \times 3x + 4 \times 4 + 7x + 12$ $= 12x + 16 + 7x + 12$

3 Rearrange so that the like terms are together. (Optional) $= 12x + 7x + 16 + 12$

4 Collect the like terms. $= 19x + 28$

c 1 Write the expression. **c** $2x(3y + 3) + 3x(y + 1)$

2 Expand the brackets. $= 2x \times 3y + 2x \times 3 + 3x \times y + 3x \times 1$
$= 6xy + 6x + 3xy + 3x$

3 Rearrange so that the like terms are together. (Optional) $= 6xy + 3xy + 6x + 3x$

4 Simplify by collecting the like terms. $= 9xy + 9x$

d 1 Write the expression. **d** $4x(2x - 1) - 3(2x - 1)$

2 Expand the brackets. Take care with negative terms. $= 4x \times 2x + 4x \times -1 - 3 \times 2x - 3 \times -1$
$= 8x^2 - 4x - 6x + 3$

3 Simplify by collecting the like terms. $= 8x^2 - 10x + 3$

REMEMBER

1. Brackets are grouping symbols.
2. Removing brackets from an expression is called expanding the expression.
3. When expanding brackets, put the × sign before the bracket.
4. The rule that is used to expand brackets is called the Distributive Law.
5. After expanding brackets, collect any like terms.

EXERCISE **8H**

Expanding brackets

INDIVIDUAL PATHWAYS

eBook*plus*

Activity 8-H-1 Snap doc-2281

Activity 8-H-2 More snap doc-2282

Activity 8-H-3 Advanced snap doc-2283

FLUENCY

1 WE13 Use the Distributive Law to expand the following expressions.

a $3(d + 4)$ **b** $2(a + 5)$ **c** $4(x + 2)$ **d** $5(r + 7)$
e $6(g + 6)$ **f** $2(t + 3)$ **g** $7(d + 8)$ **h** $9(2x + 6)$
i $12(4 + c)$ **j** $7(6 + 3x)$ **k** $45(2g + 3)$ **l** $1.5(t + 6)$
m $11(t - 2)$ **n** $3(2t - 6)$ **o** $t(t + 3)$ **p** $x(x + 4)$
q $g(g + 7)$ **r** $2g(g + 5)$ **s** $3f(g + 3)$ **t** $6m(n - 2m)$

2 Expand the following.

a $3(3x - 2)$ **b** $3x(x - 6y)$ **c** $5y(3x - 9y)$ **d** $50(2y - 5)$
e $-3(c + 3)$ **f** $-5(3x + 4)$ **g** $-5x(x + 6)$ **h** $-2y(6 + y)$
i $-6(t - 3)$ **j** $-4f(5 - 2f)$ **k** $9x(3y - 2)$ **l** $-3h(2b - 6h)$
m $4a(5b + 3c)$ **n** $-3a(2g - 7a)$ **o** $5a(3b + 6c)$ **p** $-2w(9w - 5z)$
q $12m(4m + 10)$ **r** $-3k(-2k + 5)$

3 WE14 Expand the expressions below and then simplify by collecting any like terms.

a $7(5x + 4) + 21$ **b** $3(c - 2) + 2$ **c** $2c(5 - c) + 12c$
d $6(v + 4) + 6$ **e** $3d(d - 4) + 2d^2$ **f** $3y + 4(2y + 3)$
g $24r + r(2 + r)$ **h** $5 - 3g + 6(2g - 7)$ **i** $4(2f - 3g) + 3f - 7$
j $3(3x - 4) + 12$ **k** $-2(k + 5) - 3k$ **l** $3x(3 + 4r) + 9x - 6xr$
m $12 + 5(r - 5) + 3r$ **n** $12gh + 3g(2h - 9) + 3g$ **o** $3(2t + 8) + 5t - 23$
p $24 + 3r(2 - 3r) - 2r^2 + 5r$

eBook*plus*

Digital doc
Spreadsheet
Expanding brackets
doc-2288

4 Expand the following and then simplify by collecting like terms.

a $3(x + 2) + 2(x + 1)$ **b** $5(x + 3) + 4(x + 2)$ **c** $2(y + 1) + 4(y + 6)$
d $4(d + 7) - 3(d + 2)$ **e** $6(2h + 1) + 2(h - 3)$ **f** $3(3m + 2) + 2(6m - 5)$
g $9(4f + 3) - 4(2f + 7)$ **h** $2a(a + 2) - 5(a^2 + 7)$ **i** $3(2 - t^2) + 2t(t + 1)$
j $m(n + 4) - mn + 3m$

UNDERSTANDING

5 Simplify the following expressions by removing the brackets and then collecting like terms.

a $3h(2k + 7) + 4k(h + 5)$ **b** $6n(3y + 7) - 3n(8y + 9)$ **c** $4g(5m + 6) - 6(2gm + 3)$
d $11b(3a + 5) + 3b(4 - 5a)$ **e** $5a(2a - 7) - 5(a^2 + 7)$ **f** $7c(2f - 3) + 3c(8 - f)$
g $7x(4 - y) + 2xy - 29$ **h** $11v(2w + 5) - 3(8 - 5vw)$ **i** $3x(3 - 2y) + 6x(2y - 9)$
j $8m(7n - 2) + 3n(4 + 7m)$

REASONING

6 a Using the concept of area as shown above, explain with diagrams and mathematical reasoning why $5(6 - 2) = 5 \times 6 - 5 \times 2$.

b Using the concept of area as shown above, explain with diagrams and mathematical reasoning why $4(x - y) = 4 \times x - 4 \times y$.

7 Expressions of the form $(a + b)(c + d)$ can be expanded by using the Distributive Law twice. Distribute one of the factors over the other; for example, $(a + b)(c + d)$. The expression can then be fully expanded following Worked example 13.

a $(x + 1)(x + 2)$ **b** $(a + 3)(a + 4)$
c $(c + 2)(c - 3)$ **d** $(y + 4)(y - 4)$
e $(u - 2)(u - 3)$ **f** $(k - 5)(k - 2)$

REFLECTION
Why doesn't the Distributive Law apply when there is a multiplication sign inside the brackets, that is for $a(b \times c)$?

8I Factorising

- **Factorising** is the opposite process to expanding.
- Factorising involves identifying the highest common factors of the algebraic terms.
- To find the highest common factor of the algebraic terms:
  1. Find the highest common factor of the number parts.
  2. Find the highest common factor of the variable parts.
  3. Multiply these together.

WORKED EXAMPLE 15

Find the highest common factor of 6*x* and 10.

THINK	WRITE
1 Find the highest common factor of the number parts.	
Break 6 down into factors.	$6 = 3 \times 2$
Break 10 down into factors.	$10 = 5 \times 2$
The highest common factor is 2.	HCF = 2
2 Find the highest common factor of the variable parts. There isn't one, because only the first term has a variable part.	The HCF of $6x$ and 10 is 2.

WORKED EXAMPLE 16

Find the highest common factor of 14*fg* and 21*gh*.

THINK	WRITE
1 Find the highest common factor of the number parts.	
Break 14 down into factors.	$14 = 7 \times 2$
Break 21 down into factors.	$21 = 7 \times 3$
The highest common factor is 7.	HCF = 7
2 Find the highest common factor of the variable parts.	
Break *fg* down into factors.	$fg = f \times g$
Break *gh* down into factors.	$gh = g \times h$
Both contain a factor of *g*.	HCF = g
3 Multiply these together.	The HCF of $14fg$ and $21gh$ is $7g$.

- To factorise an expression, place the highest common factor of the terms outside the brackets and the remaining factors for each term inside the brackets.

WORKED EXAMPLE 17

Factorise the expression $2x + 6$.

THINK	WRITE
1 Break down each term into its factors.	$2x + 6$ $= 2 \times x + 2 \times 3$
2 Write the highest common factor outside the brackets. Write the other factors inside the brackets.	$= 2 \times (x + 3)$
3 Remove the multiplication sign.	$= 2(x + 3)$

WORKED EXAMPLE 18

Factorise $12gh - 8g$.

THINK	WRITE
1 Break down each term into its factors.	$12gh - 8g$ $= 4 \times 3 \times g \times h - 4 \times 2 \times g$
2 Write the highest common factor outside the brackets. Write the other factors inside the brackets.	$= 4 \times g \times (3 \times h - 2)$
3 Remove the multiplication signs.	$= 4g(3h - 2)$

REMEMBER

1. Factorising is the opposite process to expanding.
2. Factorising a number or expression involves breaking it down into smaller factors.
3. To find the highest common factor (HCF) of algebraic terms, follow these steps.
   (a) Find the highest common factor of the number parts.
   (b) Find the highest common factor of the variable parts.
   (c) Multiply these together.
4. To factorise an expression we place the highest common factor of the terms outside the brackets and the remaining factors for each term inside the brackets.

EXERCISE
8I Factorising

INDIVIDUAL PATHWAYS

eBook*plus*

Activity 8-I-1 Factorising doc-2284

Activity 8-I-2 More factorising doc-2285

Activity 8-I-3 Tricky factorising doc-2286

FLUENCY

1 WE15 Find the highest common factor of the following.

a 4 and 6 **b** 6 and 9 **c** 12 and 18 **d** 13 and 26
e 14 and 21 **f** $2x$ and 4 **g** $3x$ and 9 **h** $12a$ and 16

2 WE16 Find the highest common factor of the following.

a $2gh$ and $6g$ **b** $3mn$ and $6mp$ **c** $11a$ and $22b$ **d** $4ma$ and $6m$
e $12ab$ and $14ac$ **f** $24fg$ and $36gh$ **g** $20dg$ and $18ghq$ **h** $11gl$ and $33lp$
i $16mnp$ and $20mn$ **j** $28bc$ and $12c$ **k** $4c$ and $12cd$ **l** x and $3xz$

3 WE17 Factorise the following expressions.

a $3x + 6$ **b** $2y + 4$ **c** $5g + 10$
d $8x + 12$ **e** $6f + 9$ **f** $12c + 20$
g $2d + 8$ **h** $2x - 4$ **i** $12g - 18$
j $11h + 121$ **k** $4s - 16$ **l** $8x - 20$
m $12g - 24$ **n** $14 - 4b$ **o** $16a + 64$
p $48 - 12q$ **q** $16 + 8f$ **r** $12 - 12d$

4 WE18 Factorise the following.

a $3gh + 12$ **b** $2xy + 6y$ **c** $12pq + 4p$
d $14g - 7gh$ **e** $16jk - 2k$ **f** $12eg + 2g$
g $12k + 16$ **h** $7mn + 6m$ **i** $14ab + 7b$
j $5a - 15abc$ **k** $8r + 14rt$ **l** $24mab + 12ab$
m $4b - 6ab$ **n** $12fg - 16gh$ **o** $ab - 2bc$
p $14x - 21xy$ **q** $11jk + 3k$ **r** $3p + 27pq$
s $12ac - 4c + 3dc$ **t** $4g + 8gh - 16$ **u** $28s + 14st$
v $15uv + 27vw$

eBook*plus*

Digital doc Spreadsheet **Finding the HCF** doc-2289

UNDERSTANDING

5 Find the highest common factor of $4ab$, $6a^2b^3$ and $12a^3b$.

6 Find the lowest common multiple of $3ab$, $4a^3bc$ and $6a^2b^2$.

7 Simplify: $\dfrac{4x-4}{10x-20} \times \dfrac{15x+15}{3x-3} \times \dfrac{6x-12}{20x+20}$.

8 Simplify: $\dfrac{3x+6}{x-1} \div \dfrac{12x+24}{6(x+1)}$.

9 Factorise and hence simplify: $\dfrac{2x^2y-6xy^2}{a+2b} \times \dfrac{4a+8b}{3xy} \div \dfrac{2x-6y}{7}$.

eBook*plus*

Digital doc WorkSHEET 8.2 doc-2291

REASONING

10 Simplify $(5ax^2y - 6bxy + 2ax^2y - bxy) \div (ax^2 - bx)$.

REFLECTION
What strategies will you use to find the highest common factor?

Summary

Using variables

- A variable (or pronumeral) is a letter or symbol that is used in place of a number.
- Variables may represent a single number, or they may be used to show a relationship between two or more numbers.
- When writing expressions with variables, it is important to remember the following points:
  - The multiplication sign is omitted.
    For example: $8n$ means '$8 \times n$' and $12ab$ means '$12 \times a \times b$'.
  - The division sign is rarely used.
    For example, $y \div 6$ is shown as $\frac{y}{6}$.

Substitution

- Replacing a variable with a number is called substitution.

Working with brackets

- Brackets are grouping symbols.
- When substituting into an expression with brackets, remember to place a multiplication (×) sign next to the brackets.
- Work out the brackets first.

Substituting positive and negative numbers

- When substituting, if the variable you are replacing has a negative value, simply remember the rules for directed numbers:
  - For addition and subtraction, signs that occur together can be combined.

Same signs positive	for example,	$7 + +3 = 7 + 3$
	and	$7 - -3 = 7 + 3$
Different signs negative	for example,	$7 - +3 = 7 - 3$
	and	$7 + -3 = 7 - 3$

  - For multiplication and division.

Same signs positive	for example,	$+7 \times +3 = +21$
	and	$-7 \times -3 = +21$
Different signs negative	for example,	$+7 \times -3 = -21$
	and	$-7 \times +3 = -21$

Number laws and variables

- When dealing with numbers and variables, particular rules must be obeyed.
- The Commutative Law holds true for addition (and multiplication) because the order in which two numbers or variables are added (or multiplied) does not affect the result. Therefore, in general,
  - $x + y = y + x$
  - $x - y \neq y - x$
  - $x \times y = y \times x$
  - $x \div y \neq y \div x$
- The Associative Law holds true for addition (and multiplication) because the order in which three numbers or variables, taking two at a time, are added (or multiplied) does not affect the result. Therefore, in general,
  - $x + (y + z) = (x + y) + z$
  - $x - (y - z) \neq (x - y) - z$
  - $x \times (y \times z) = (x \times y) \times z$
  - $x \div (y \div z) \neq (x \div y) \div z$

- The Identity Law states that, in general, $x + 0 = 0 + x = x$
  $x \times 1 = 1 \times x = x$
- The Inverse Law states that, in general, $x + -x = -x + x = 0$
  $x \times \frac{1}{x} = \frac{1}{x} \times x = 1$

Simplifying expressions

- When simplifying expressions, we can collect (add or subtract) only like terms.
- Like terms are terms that contain the same variable parts.

Multiplying and dividing expressions with variables

- When multiplying variables:
  (a) the order is not important. For example, $d \times e = e \times d$.
  (b) place the numbers at the front of the expression and leave out the × sign.
- When dividing variables, rewrite the expression as a fraction and simplify it by cancelling.
- When the same variable appears on both the top and bottom lines of the fraction, it may be cancelled.

Expanding brackets

- Brackets are grouping symbols.
- Removing brackets from an expression is called expanding the expression.
- When expanding brackets, put the × sign before the bracket.
- The rule that is used to expand brackets is called the Distributive Law.
- After expanding brackets, collect any like terms.

Factorising

- Factorising is the opposite process to expanding.
- Factorising a number or expression involves breaking it down into smaller factors.
- To find the highest common factor (HCF) of algebraic terms, follow these steps.
  (a) Find the highest common factor of the number parts.
  (b) Find the highest common factor of the variable parts.
  (c) Multiply these together.
- To factorise an expression we place the highest common factor of the terms outside the brackets and the remaining factors for each term inside the brackets.

MAPPING YOUR UNDERSTANDING

Using terms from the summary, and other terms if you wish, construct a concept map that illustrates your understanding of the key concepts covered in this chapter. Compare this concept map with the one that you created in *What do you know?* on page 181.

Have you completed the two *Homework sheets*, the *Rich task* and the two *Code puzzles* in *Maths Quest 8 Homework Book*?

Chapter review

FLUENCY

1 Using x and y to represent numbers, write expressions for:
- **a** the sum of x and y
- **b** the difference between y and x
- **c** five times y subtracted from three times x
- **d** the product of 5 and x
- **e** twice the product of x and y
- **f** the sum of $6x$ and $7y$
- **g** y multiplied by itself
- **h** twice a number is decreased by 7
- **i** the sum of p and q is tripled.

2 If tickets to the school play cost $15 for adults and $9 for children, write an expression for the cost of:
- **a** x adult tickets
- **b** y child tickets
- **c** k adult tickets and m child tickets.

3 Jake is now m years old.
- **a** Write an expression for his age in 5 years' time.
- **b** Write an expression for Jo's age if she is p years younger than Jake.
- **c** Jake's mother is 5 times his age. How old is she?

4 Find the value of the following expressions if $a = 2$ and $b = 6$.

a $2a$ **b** $6a$ **c** $5b$
d $\frac{a}{2}$ **e** $a + 8$ **f** $b - 2$
g $a + b$ **h** $b - a$ **i** $5+\frac{b}{2}$
j $3a + 7$ **k** $2a + 3b$ **l** $\frac{20}{a}$
m $3b - 2a$ **n** $\frac{b}{a}$ **o** $\frac{a}{b}$
p $-3ab$ **q** $\frac{5a}{b}$ **r** $\frac{2b}{9a}$

5 The formula $C = 2.2k + 4$ can be used to calculate the cost in dollars, C, of travelling by taxi for a distance of k kilometres. Find the cost of travelling 4.5 km by taxi.

6 The area (A) of a rectangle of length l and width w can be found using the formula $A = lw$. Find the width of a rectangle if $A = 65\text{ cm}^2$ and $l = 13$ cm.

7 Substitute $r = 3$ and $s = 5$ into the following expressions and evaluate.

a $2(r + s)$ **b** $2(s - r)$ **c** $5(r + s)$
d $8(s - r)$ **e** $s(r + 4)$ **f** $s(2r - 3)$
g $2r(r + 1)$ **h** $rs(7 + s)$ **i** $r^2(5 - r)$
j $s^2(s + 15)$ **k** $4r(s + r)$ **l** $12r(r - s)$

8 Find the value of the following expressions if $a = 2$ and $b = -5$.

a $a + b$ **b** $b + a$
c ab **d** $\frac{ab}{5}$
e $2ab$ **f** $5 - a$
g $12 - ab$ **h** $a^2 - 2$
i $3(a + 2)$ **j** $b(a - 4)$
k $12 - a(b - 3)$ **l** $5a + 6b$

9 Indicate whether each of the following is true or false for all values of the variables.
- **a** $3a + 5b = 5b + 2a$
- **b** $7x - 10y = 10y - 7x$
- **c** $8c + d = d + 8c$
- **d** $16 \times 2x \times x = 32x^2$
- **e** $9x \times -y = -y \times 9x$
- **f** $-4 \times 3x \times x = 12x \times x$
- **g** $\frac{11p}{5r} = \frac{5r}{11p}$
- **h** $7i + 2j = 2j + 7i$
- **i** $-3y \div 7x = 7x \div -3y$
- **j** $-8c + 5d = 5d - 8c$
- **k** $\frac{0}{5k} = \frac{5k}{0}$
- **l** $21\times-\frac{7x}{3}=\frac{7x}{3}\times-21$

10 Simplify the following by collecting like terms.

a $4d + 3d$ **b** $3c - 5c$
c $3d + 5a - 4a$ **d** $6g - 4g$
e $4x + 11 - 2x$ **f** $2g + 5 - g - 6$
g $2xy + 7xy$ **h** $12t^2 + 3t + 3t^2 - t$

11 Simplify the following.

a $3 \times 7g$ **b** $6 \times 3y$
c $7d \times 6$ **d** $-3z \times 8$

12 Simplify the following.

a $\frac{2a}{8}$ **b** $\frac{11b}{44b}$
c $6rt \div -2t$ **d** $-3gh \div -6g$
e $\frac{32t}{40stv}$ **f** $-36xy \div -12y$
g $\frac{12ab}{-14ab}$ **h** $\frac{5egh}{30ghj}$

13 Use the Distributive Law to expand the following expressions.

a $2(x + 3)$ **b** $5(2x - 1)$
c $-2(f + 7)$ **d** $3m(b - m)$
e $-3y(7 - y)$ **f** $9b(c - 2)$

14 Expand the following and then simplify by collecting like terms.

a $3(4v + 5) - 15$
b $6t + 5(2t - 7)$
c $23 + 5(3p - 4) + 2p$
d $2(x + 5) + 5(x + 1)$
e $2g(g - 6) + 3g(g - 7)$
f $3(3t - 4) - 6(2t - 9)$

15 Factorise the following expressions.

a $3g + 12$ **b** $xy + 5y$
c $5n - 20$ **d** $12mn + 4pn$
e $12g - 6gh$ **f** $12xy - 36yz$

16 Show that the Distributive Law holds for the following.

$$10(16 - 6) = 10 \times 16 - 10 \times 6$$

PROBLEM SOLVING

1 Using only +, –, ×, ( ), complete the following equations to demonstrate the Distributive Law.

a 3 2 1 = 3 2 3 1
b –10 8 –6 –10 = –10 8 –6
c 8 6 5 = 8 5 6 8
d –4 7 1 7 = –4 1 7
e 2 *x* *y* = 2 *x* 2 *y*
f 3 *a* *a* *b* = 3 *a* *a* 3 *a* *b*

2 A builder has a 120-cm section of wood and wants to cut it into two unequal pieces.

a If the length of one of the sections is a cm, what is the length of the other piece?
He has a second section of wood that is b cm long, and he cuts it into four unequal pieces: one is 36 cm, another 60 cm and another is $12a$ cm. (*Hint:* Draw a diagram.)

b What is the length of the fourth part of this second section of wood?

c If the total length of four of the six sections of wood is $(96 + 13a)$ cm, what is the total length of the other two pieces in terms of a and b?

3 The base of a box has a length of $(x + 4)$ cm and a width of x cm.

a Draw a diagram, labelling the length and the width.
b Write an expression for the area of the base of the box.
c Expand part **b**.
d If $x = 3$, what is the area of the base of the box?
e If the height of the box is x cm, find an expression for the volume of the box.
f Find the volume of the box if x is 3 cm.

4 Aussie Rules Football is played in many Australian states. The scoring for the game is in Goals (G) and Behinds (B). Each Goal (G) scores six points and each behind (B) scores one point. To calculate the total number of points (P) scored by a team use the following rule: $P = 6G + B$

a Name the variables in the rule.
b State the expression in the rule.
c A team scored 11 goals and 10 behinds. How many points is this?
d A second team scored nine goals and 18 behinds. How many points is this?
e How many goals and behinds might a team have scored if its total points score was 87 points and the team scored more than six goals?

5 Stephanie bought some clothes from Target during their annual sale. She spent \$79.00. She bought a skirt, a T-shirt and a pair of shorts. She paid \$9 more for the T-shirt than for the shorts, and \$7 more for the skirt than for the T-shirt. How much did the skirt cost her?

6 a If the pattern below continues, how many barrels are needed to make 8 layers? *Note:* The top barrel is sitting on the next two and the layers go straight up.

Layer	1	2	3
Barrels	1	3	6

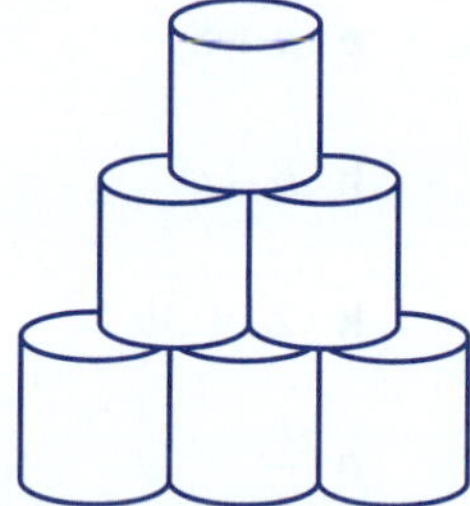

b If the pattern below continues, how many barrels are needed to make 8 layers? *Note:* Each layer forms a triangle.

Layer	1	2	3
Barrels	1	4	10

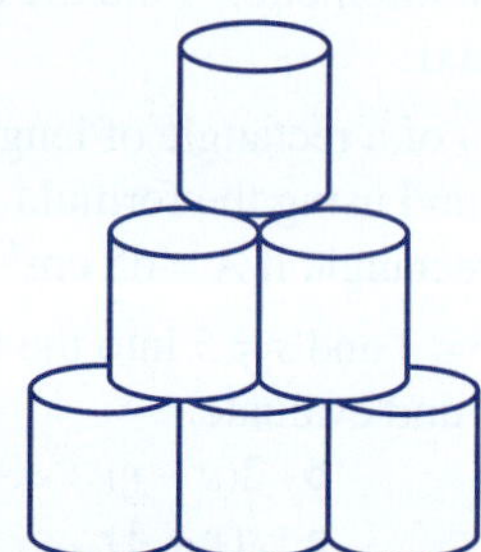

7 Bobby the painter has two partially used 10-L tins of paint, A and B. There is more paint in Tin A than in Tin B. He mixes the paint in the following fashion.
- He pours paint from Tin A into Tin B until the volume of paint in Tin B is doubled.
- He pours paint from Tin B into Tin A until the volume of paint in Tin A is doubled.
- He pours paint from Tin A into Tin B until the volume of paint in Tin B is doubled.

When he's finished, the tins both contain 4 L of paint. How much paint was in the tins before Bobby began mixing?

8 Two numbers have a sum of 7 and a product of 12. Find the sum of their reciprocals.

9 Given $3a + 2b = 3(2a - b)$, find the value of $\frac{a^3}{b^3}$.

10 If you add the first and last of any three consecutive integers together, can you find a relationship to the middle number?

11 The Flesch-Kincaid Grade Level formula is used to determine the readability of a piece of text. It produces a 0 to 100 score that can be used to determine the number of years of education generally required to understand a particular piece of text. The formula is as follows:

$$0.39\left(\frac{\text{Total words}}{\text{Total sentences}}\right) + 11.8\left(\frac{\text{Total syllables}}{\text{Total words}}\right) - 15.59$$

Text suitable for a Year 8 student should have a value of roughly 8.
A passage of text contains 30 sentences, with 500 words and 730 syllables. Would it be suitable for a Year 8 student? Explain your answer.

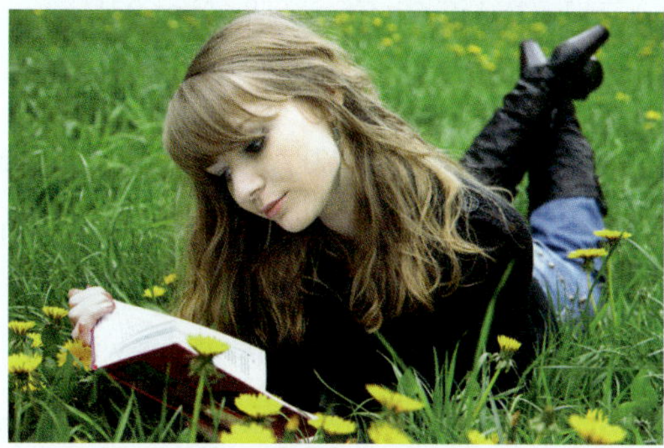

12 Consider the expression

$$x^{(x+1)^{(x+2)}}$$

This is called a *power tower*.
What is the value of the last digit of this expression when $x = 2$?
Note: You will have to look at patterns to determine the answer, as a calculator will not give you an exact answer to the power.

eBook*plus*

Interactivities

Test yourself
Chapter 8
int-2371

Word search
Chapter 8
int-2629

Crossword
Chapter 8
int-2630

eBookplus ACTIVITIES

Chapter opener

Digital doc *(page 181)*
- Hungry brain activity Chapter 8 (doc-6921)

Are you ready?

Digital docs *(page 182)*
- SkillSHEET 8.1 (doc-6922) Alternative expressions used to describe the four operations
- SkillSHEET 8.2 (doc-6923) Order of operations II
- SkillSHEET 8.3 (doc-6924) Order of operations with brackets
- SkillSHEET 8.4 (doc-6925) Operations with directed numbers
- SkillSHEET 8.5 (doc-6926) Combining like terms
- SkillSHEET 8.6 (doc-6927) Simplifying fractions
- SkillSHEET 8.7 (doc-6928) Highest common factor

8A Using variables

Digital docs *(page 184)*
- Activity 8-A-1 (doc-2260) Using variables
- Activity 8-A-2 (doc-2261) More variables
- Activity 8-A-3 (doc-2262) Advanced variables

eLesson *(page 183)*
- Using variables (eles-0042)

8B Substitution

Digital docs *(page 188)*
- Activity 8-B-1 (doc-2263) Substitution
- Activity 8-B-2 (doc-2264) More substitution
- Activity 8-B-3 (doc-2265) Advanced substitution
- Spreadsheet (doc-2287) Substitution

8C Working with brackets

Digital docs *(page 190)*
- Activity 8-C-1 (doc-2266) Working with brackets
- Activity 8-C-2 (doc-2267) More brackets
- Activity 8-C-3 (doc-2268) Advanced use of brackets

8D Substituting positive and negative numbers

Digital docs *(page 193)*
- Activity 8-D-1 (doc-2269) What is the word? A
- Activity 8-D-2 (doc-2270) What is the word? B
- Activity 8-D-3 (doc-2271) What is the word? C
- WorkSHEET 8.1 (doc-2290)

8E Number laws and variables

Digital docs *(page 197)*
- Activity 8-E-1 (doc-2272) Number laws and variables
- Activity 8-E-2 (doc-2273) More number laws and variables
- Activity 8-E-3 (doc-2274) Advanced number laws and variables

Interactivity *(page 195)*
- The Associative Law (int-2370)

8F Simplifying expressions

Digital docs *(page 200)*
- Activity 8-F-1 (doc-2275) Simplifying expressions
- Activity 8-F-2 (doc-2276) More simplifying expressions
- Activity 8-F-3 (doc-2277) Advanced simplifying expressions

8G Multiplying and dividing expressions with variables

Digital docs *(page 204)*
- Activity 8-G-1 (doc-2278) Who invented algebra?
- Activity 8-G-2 (doc-2279) Who is the father of algebra?
- Activity 8-G-3 (doc-2280) Mathematician's riddle

8H Expanding brackets

Digital docs *(page 207)*
- Activity 8-H-1 (doc-2281) Snap
- Activity 8-H-2 (doc-2282) More snap
- Activity 8-H-3 (doc-2283) Advanced snap
- Spreadsheet (doc-2288) Expanding brackets *(page 208)*

8I Factorising

Digital docs *(page 210)*
- Activity 8-I-1 (doc-2284) Factorising
- Activity 8-I-2 (doc-2285) More factorising
- Activity 8-I-3 (doc-2286) Tricky factorising
- Spreadsheet (doc-2289) Finding the HCF
- WorkSHEET 8.2 (doc-2291)

Chapter review

Interactivities *(page 215)*
- Test yourself Chapter 8 (int-2371) Take the end-of-chapter test to test your progress.
- Word search Chapter 8 (int-2629)
- Crossword Chapter 8 (int-2630)

To access eBookPLUS activities, log on to

www.jacplus.com.au

Problem solving I

9A Introduction to problem solving — create a table
9B Draw a diagram
9C Look for a pattern
9D Work backwards from the answer
9E Elimination
9F Simplify the problem
9G Guess and check
9H Mixed problems I
9I Mixed problems II
9J Mixed problems III

OPENING QUESTION

When this house was going up for sale, two real estate agents were asked to quote. The first said that they could sell the house for $180 000 and would charge 2.5% commission on the sale. The second said that they could sell the house for $178 000 and would charge 2.3% commission. If all other costs were equal, which company was offering the better deal?

9A Introduction to problem solving — create a table

Weblink
More Maths problems

Introduction to problem solving

- When solving problems, the main processes that we can use are as follows:
  1. Read the question at least twice and take note of all the important facts.
  2. Identify the solution required.
  3. Solve the problem using an appropriate strategy.
  4. Communicate the solution using appropriate language and mathematical terms.
  5. Support the solution with mathematical reasoning.
  6. Reflect on the solution. Does it answer the question and does it make sense? Could it have been solved a better way?
- The problem solving processes are interrelated. The importance of each process will depend on the problem being solved. By practising the skills involved in using all processes, you will learn to tackle new mathematics problems with confidence and arrive at the correct and complete solution using the most appropriate methods.
- **READ THE QUESTION** at least twice. Make sure you know what the question is asking you to do. Do you have enough information to solve the problem?
- **IDENTIFY THE SOLUTION REQUIRED**: What is the question asking you to do?
- **SOLVE THE PROBLEM** using an appropriate strategy. Decide on a suitable strategy to solve the problem. Examples of strategies that could be used are as follows:
  - Create a table
  - Draw a diagram
  - Look for a pattern — using technology
  - Work backwards from the answer
  - Elimination
  - Simplify the problem
  - Guess and check
- **COMMUNICATE THE SOLUTION**: Another person reading your work needs to be able to follow your method or strategy. You need to present your data, explanation and solutions in a clear and concise form, using correct mathematical terms and appropriate diagrams.
- **SUPPORT THE SOLUTION** with mathematical reasoning. When you think you've solved the problem, use mathematical reasoning to verify that your answer is correct and your method is justified.
- **REFLECT ON THE SOLUTION**: Have you answered the question? Think back over how you solved the problem. Could it have been solved in a different or better way? Learn from the experience, and use this knowledge to solve problems in the future.

Create a table

- A table is a way of organising or grouping numbers.
- Think about the number of rows or columns that will be needed and label them appropriately.
- A table can help you see patterns in the numbers you have organised.
- A table can demonstrate to others how you arrived at your solution.
- There are many different ways of presenting information in a table.

WORKED EXAMPLE 1

Sallie makes long telephone calls to her relatives overseas. The duration of each call made last week is listed below. Use a table to calculate the total time spent on the telephone, expressed in hours and minutes.

2 h 23 min, 1 h 57 min, 3 h 16 min, 59 min, 3 h 21 min, 44 min, 52 min

THINK	WRITE/DISPLAY
1 Read the question at least twice and take note of all the important facts.	The duration of each of the seven individual calls is listed.
2 Identify the solution required.	The question asks to determine the total time, expressed in hours and minutes, spent on the phone.
3 Decide how the 'amounts' of time can be arranged in a table. Set up a spreadsheet and enter each 'amount' of time into separate columns. Enter the hours in cells **A2**, **A3**, **A4**, **A5**, **A6**, **A7**, **A8**; enter the minutes in cells **C2**, **C3**, **C4**, **C5**, **C6**, **C7**, **C8**. Place the heading 'Hours' in cell **A1** and 'Minutes' in cell **C1**.	
4 We need to total the hours column and the minutes column. In the cell at the bottom of the **A** column, cell **A9**, enter **=sum(A2:A8)**. This will total the hours. Similarly, for the minutes column in cell **C9**, enter **=sum(C2:C8)**.	
5 For the total of the minutes column, in cell **C9**, we need to calculate the number of whole hours (integer value of hours). Alongside the total of the minutes, in cell **E9**, enter **=int(C9/60)**.	
6 We need to know what's left from the amount in cell **C9** when the whole hours, expressed as minutes, are subtracted from the current total of the minutes. In cell **G9** enter **=C9–60*int(C9/60)**, and then in cells **D9**, **F9**, **H9** enter **=**, **hours**, **minutes**.	
7 We need to add all the hours and then make a conclusion about time spent on the telephone this week. In cell **A12** enter **=A9+E9&'HOURS'&G9&'MINUTES' spent on the telephone this week.** Your spreadsheet should appear as shown. Notice that your table is an active spreadsheet; if you change an amount in columns **A** or **C**, the final values will adjust accordingly.	(spreadsheet below)
8 Answer the question.	The total time spent on the telephone this week is 13 hours and 32 minutes.

	A	B	C	D	E	F	G	H
1	HOURS		MINUTES					
2	2		23					
3	1		57					
4	3		16					
5	0		59					
6	3		21					
7	0		44					
8	0		52					
9	9		272	=	4	hours	32	minutes
10								
11								
12	13hours32minutes spent on the telephone this week							
13								

- Note this problem could be solved without a spreadsheet. The spreadsheet just made the repetitive task faster.

REMEMBER

1. The five main processes used to solve problems are:
   (a) questioning
   (b) applying strategies
   (c) communicating
   (d) reasoning
   (e) reflecting.
2. One strategy that can be used is to create a table. This strategy allows you to organise or group numbers. It can help you see patterns in the numbers and can demonstrate to others how you arrived at your solution.

EXERCISE 9A

Introduction to problem solving — create a table

PROBLEM SOLVING

1 A small drapery store had a stocktake. The lengths of cloth in the store were recorded in feet and inches as shown below. We are advised that 12 inches equals 1 foot. Use a table to calculate the total length of material in the store. Express your answer in feet and inches.

14 feet 56 inches	9 feet 64 inches	12 feet 36 inches
24 feet	22 feet 56 inches	14 feet 53 inches
5 feet 8 inches	16 feet 23 inches	4 feet 54 inches
98 inches	5 feet 20 inches	5 feet 62 inches

2 Peta is a great cook and buys her flour in 20 kg bags. Over the last few weeks she has had a baking spree and recorded the quantities of flour used in her dishes.
1.2 kg, 750 g, 1.25 kg, 275 g, 125 g, 1 kg, 800 g, 2.2 kg, 950 g, 1.3 kg, 950 g, 1.8 kg
How much flour is left in her 20 kg bag? Express your answer in kilograms and grams.

3 My friend and I are trying to work out whether it is it is better to take a million dollars now or to collect the money after 21 days by doing the following. Put in a dollar on the first day, double that dollar the next day, then double the previous day's dollars and continue this for 21 days. What would you advise? (Use mathematics to explain your answer.)

4 On a multiple choice test of 20 questions, each correct answer scores 5 points, each incorrect answer scores –2 points, and each question left unanswered scores 0 points. If you answer all questions on the test, what is the least number of questions you must answer correctly to still get a positive score? Use algebra to explain your answer.

5 The Goods and Services Tax or GST rate is 10%. This means that when a business sells something or provides a service it must charge an extra $\frac{1}{10}$ more than what it is asking for. That extra money then must be sent to the tax office. For example, an item that would otherwise be worth \$100 now has GST of \$10 added. So the price tag will show \$110. The business will then send to the tax office that \$10 and all the other GST it has collected on behalf of the government.

a Suppose a shopkeeper made sales totalling \$15 400. How much GST must he put aside?

b Is there a number he can quickly divide by to figure out the GST?

6 Goldilocks and the three bears relate to each other with Baby bear being $\frac{1}{2}$ the height of Papa bear and Mama bear being $\frac{3}{4}$ the height of Papa bear. Their possessions are all in proportion too. This means that Mama bear's bed is $\frac{3}{4}$ the length of Papa bear's bed. The items belonging to Goldilocks do not fit this pattern. Some of her things are almost as big as Papa bear's and some are almost as small as baby bear's. The height of the bowls is $\frac{2}{3}$ the diameter. Can you work out the owners of the items on the next page?

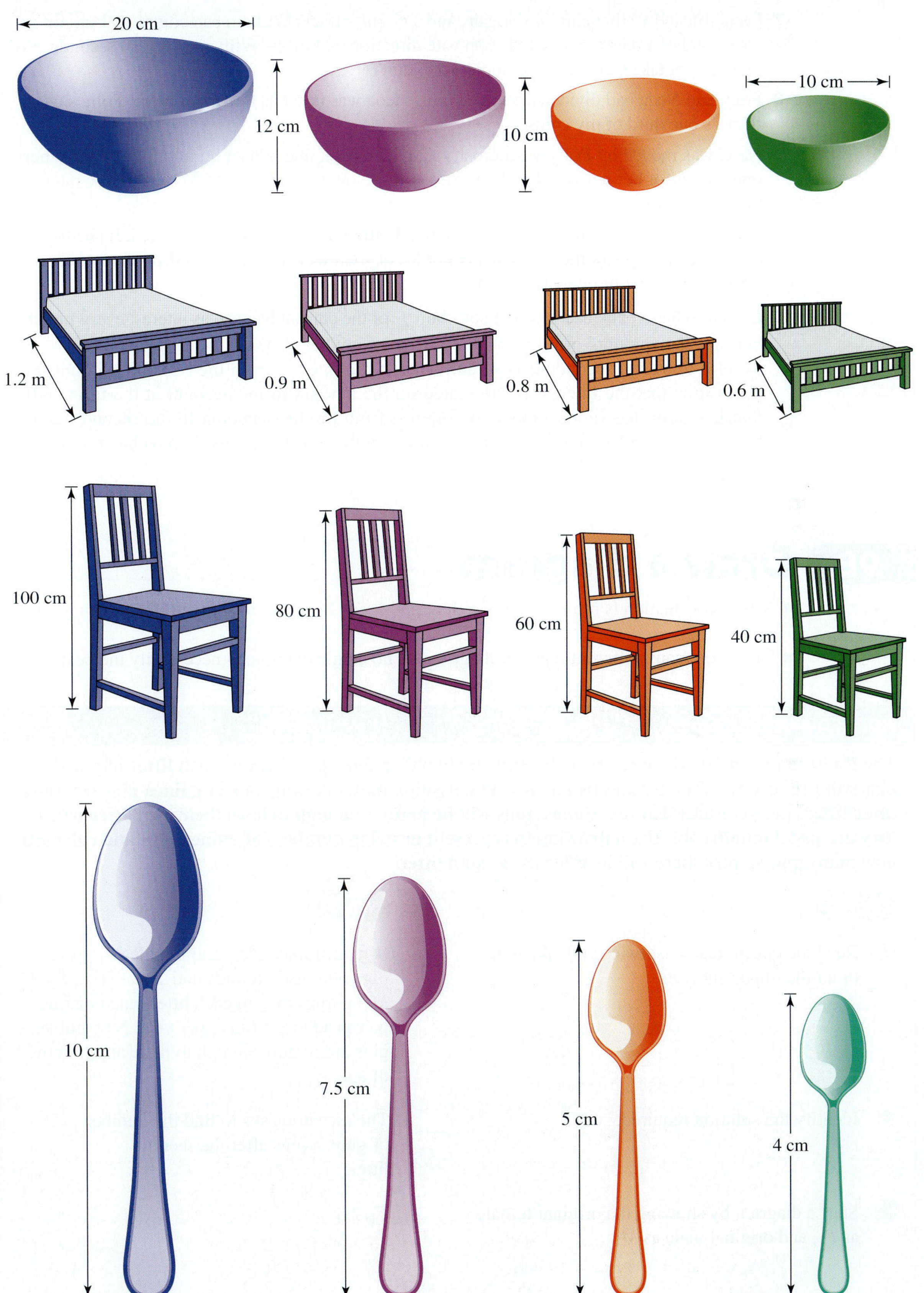
20 cm
12 cm
10 cm
10 cm
1.2 m
0.9 m
0.8 m
0.6 m
100 cm
80 cm
60 cm
40 cm
10 cm
7.5 cm
5 cm
4 cm

7 Cameron and William are running around a circular track. William can complete 1 circuit in 45 seconds. Cameron runs in the opposite direction and meets William every 20 seconds. How long does it take Cameron to complete a circuit?

8 Polly and Neda had divided up some coins. Neda was upset as Polly had more. Polly said 'Here's one third of my coins'.

Neda was moved by Polly's generosity and gave back one half of her total. Polly gave her one quarter of her new total and an extra coin. 'Now we both have 62 coins'. How many did they start with?

9 Gwen likes soda. Her local store gives a free bottle for every 5 bottles recycled. If she has collected 77 empty bottles, how many bottles of soda will she be able to drink free of charge? (It might take her more than 1 day.)

10 Leonardo has a bank account that pays him $\frac{1}{10}$ of the current balance as interest every month, but only on amounts of up to \$25 000. He already has \$25 000 in the account and decides to start a second account and deposit the interest from the \$25 000 account into it. Assume that the interest is calculated on the amount in the account at the time and that Leonardo has time to move the interest from the first account to the second before the interest is calculated there. How many months will it take for him to have at least \$25 000 in the second account.

9B Draw a diagram

- When information is represented as a diagram, it can be easier to study all the information at once.
- There are many different types of diagram, so no single diagram is necessarily the best.

WORKED EXAMPLE 2

The Rowe family currently have one male and one female guinea pig. Assume each litter of guinea pigs will produce two females and two males. Also assume that a mating pair of guinea pigs will have three litters per year and that new guinea pigs will be mature enough to have their own litter when they are just 3 months old. Use a drawing to represent growing numbers of guinea pigs and calculate how many guinea pigs there will be after the second litter.

THINK	WRITE
1 Read the question at least twice and take note of all the important facts.	A pair of male (M_1) and female (F_1) guinea pigs produce 2 female and 2 male (F_2, F_3, M_2, M_3) guinea pigs in each litter. Each mating pair produces 3 litters per year. New guinea pigs are mature enough to mate at 3 months of age.
2 Identify the solution required.	The question asks to find the number of guinea pigs after the second litter.
3 Start a diagram by showing the original female as F_1, and original male as M_1.	F_1, M_1

4 Connect F_1, M_1 to each member of the litter, F_2, F_3, M_2, M_3.

5 Start a new diagram because now there are three mating pairs, each producing another litter of four.

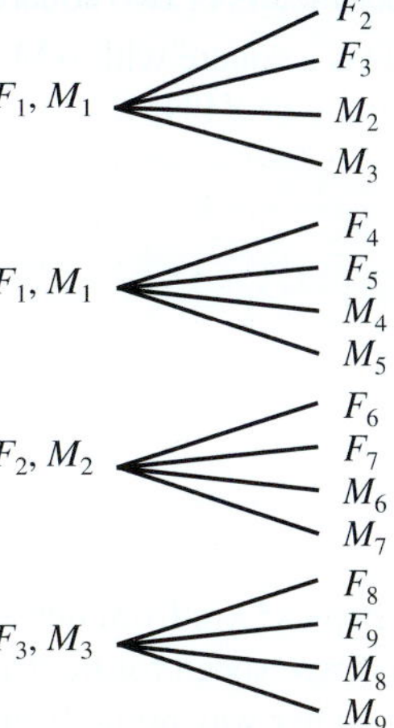

6 The total number of guinea pigs must be counted for a conclusion to be made. Remember to include F_1 and M_1.

There are 18 guinea pigs after two litters.

7 Answer the question.

REMEMBER

Drawing a diagram can help to solve the problem.

EXERCISE 9B

Draw a diagram

PROBLEM SOLVING

1 Nigel has one mating pair of rabbits. Assume that each litter of rabbits produces three males and three females. Rabbits are mature enough to have their own litter by the time their parents have another litter. How many rabbits will Nigel have after the second litter?

2 If the rabbits in question **1** produce only two males and two females per litter, how many rabbits would Nigel have after the third litter?

3 Our Earth is just a mere speck in our solar system. The sun is our nearest star and is 150 000 000 km away. Light from the sun travels to us (and the other planets) at 300 000 km/s. It takes about 12.5 minutes for light to reach Mars from the sun. Use this information to calculate the distance between Earth and Mars when the sun, Earth and Mars are aligned.

4 Local time in Brisbane (there is no daylight saving) is 3 hours behind Auckland (NZ) and one hour ahead of Tokyo (Japan). Auckland is 11 hours ahead of Paris (France) time. What is the time difference between:

a Brisbane and Paris?

b Tokyo and Auckland?

5 At Miami High School there are 600 students. Three per cent of them wear one earring. Of the other 97%, half wear 2 earrings and half do not wear any. What is the total number of earrings being worn at Miami High School?

6 In a school of 600 students, 390 study Mathematics, 300 study Science and 185 study both. Show this information on:

a a Venn diagram **b** a Karnaugh map.

c What is the ratio of students who study Mathematics only to students who study Science only?

7 The perimeters of two squares are in the ratio 4 to 9. What is the ratio of their areas?

8 ABCD is a square with NM bisecting both AD and BC and PN = NQ = NM. Determine the magnitude of ∠PNM.

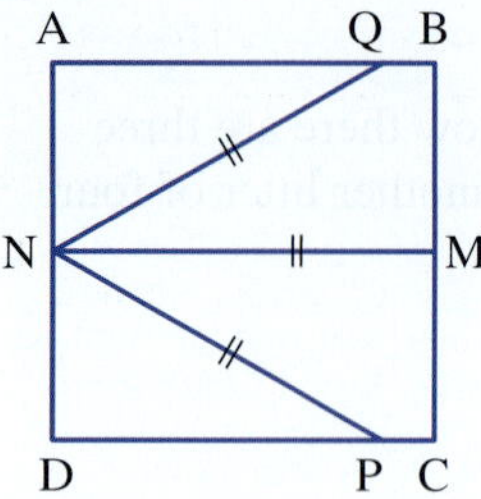

9 Sally lives 35 km from her work. On her way to work this morning she averaged 60 km/h. Her average speed for her trip to and from work today was 56 km/h. What was Sally's average speed on her way home from work?

10 The ratio of black to white balls in a bag is 3 : 4. There are 48 white balls. How many white balls must be removed to make the ratio of black to white balls 4 : 3?

9C Look for a pattern

- Repetitive tasks are suited to a spreadsheet.
- A spreadsheet can list patterns of numbers from which a result can be found.

WORKED EXAMPLE 3

Paul has been asked to demonstrate that the decimal number 5.462 multiplied by 29 can be calculated by repeated addition using a spreadsheet.

THINK	WRITE/DISPLAY
1 Read the question at least twice and take note of all the important facts.	Using a spreadsheet, calculate 5.462 × 29 by repeated addition; that is, add 29 amounts of 5.462.
2 Identify the solution required.	The question asks to obtain a spreadsheet solution to 5.462 × 29 using repeated addition.
3 Set up a spreadsheet and write a heading in the first cell. In cell **A1** enter **repeated addition**.	
4 We need to enter **5.462** in 29 cells from **A2** to **A30** and add them up. In cells **A2, A3, A4** enter **5.462** then select these cells and drag the mouse down all the way to **A30**.	
5 Add the numbers in the cells automatically. In cell **A31**, enter **=sum(A2:A30)**.	
6 We need to multiply 5.462 and 29 automatically on the spreadsheet. In cell **C31** enter **=5.462*29**.	
7 We need a heading for this cell. In cell **C30** enter **Multiplication 5.462 × 29**.	
8 Answer the question.	5.462 × 29 = 158.398

	A	B	C	D	E
4	5.462				
5	5.462				
6	5.462				
7	5.462				
8	5.462				
9	5.462				
10	5.462				
11	5.462				
12	5.462				
13	5.462				
14	5.462				
15	5.462				
16	5.462				
17	5.462				
18	5.462				
19	5.462				
20	5.462				
21	5.462				
22	5.462				
23	5.462				
24	5.462				
25	5.462				
26	5.462				
27	5.462				
28	5.462				
29	5.462				
30	5.462		multiplication 5.462 x 29		
31	158.398		158.398		
32					

REMEMBER

1. Repetitive tasks are suited to a spreadsheet.
2. If a pattern of numbers is listed in a spreadsheet, the result can be found.

EXERCISE

9C Look for a pattern

PROBLEM SOLVING

1 Verity wants to use a spreadsheet to show that \$783.57 × 43 can be calculated by repeated addition using a spreadsheet. Use a spreadsheet to calculate the answer.

2 Phillip wants to use a spreadsheet to show that $\frac{3}{57} \times 43$ can be calculated by repeated addition using a spreadsheet. (*Hint:* First format the cells to accept fractions with three digits in numerator and denominator, and enter the fraction by typing **3/57**.) Use a spreadsheet to calculate the answer.

3 Amelia wants to use a spreadsheet to show that 144 ÷ 3 can be calculated by repeated subtraction of 3 from 144 using a spreadsheet. (*Hint:* Enter **144** in a cell **A1**, then enter **=A1–3** in cell **A2**, and enter **=A2–3** in cell **A3**. Carefully select just cells **A2** and **A3** and then drag downwards.) Use a spreadsheet to calculate the answer.

4 Sonja wants to use a spreadsheet to show that $\left(\frac{1}{2}\right)^8$ can be calculated using repeated multiplication by $\frac{1}{2}$. (*Hint:* Enter **1/2** in cell **A1**; then enter **=A1*(1/2)** in cell **A2**. Drag this formula down from **A2** to **A8**.) Use a spreadsheet to calculate the answer.

5 It is common to use shortcuts when performing calculations. Consider the following case: $6.293 \times 9 = 6.293 \times 10 - 6.293 \times 1$.

Use a spreadsheet to calculate the first term of the right-hand side by repeated addition; then subtract the second term. Confirm that your answer is the same as the left-hand side value. Set out your spreadsheet so that it is logical and clear.

6 If this pattern continues, how many cubes will it take to make 10 layers?

7 If today is Monday, what day will it be 50 days from now?

8 In the song *The Twelve Days of Christmas* the person receives gifts on each of the 12 days leading up to Christmas — 1 the first day, 2 the second day, 3 the third day and so on. How many gifts did the person receive altogether?

9 **a** Calculate the values of the following pairs of expressions:

i $\frac{1}{2} + \frac{1}{4} + \frac{1}{8}; 1 - \frac{1}{8}$

ii $\frac{1}{2} + \frac{1}{4} + \frac{1}{8} + \frac{1}{16}; 1 - \frac{1}{16}$

iii $\frac{1}{2} + \frac{1}{4} + \frac{1}{8} + \frac{1}{16} + \frac{1}{32}; 1 - \frac{1}{32}$

b Consider this sum: $\frac{1}{2} + \frac{1}{4} + \frac{1}{8} + \frac{1}{16} + \frac{1}{32} + \frac{1}{64} + \frac{1}{128} + \ldots$ It goes on forever. To express it we could include as many terms as we like as long as we add the dashes to indicate a never ending series.

i What are the next two terms?

ii This sum cannot be done in the same fashion as ordinary fraction sums but there are various ways to determine its value. Can you explain why it equals 1?

10 In Mathville, there are no house numbers that are either a multiple of 3 or a multiple of 4. If the highest number is a street is 67, how many houses are there?

9D Work backwards from the answer

- If there is a sequence of steps for which we know the final answer, then a useful strategy is to work backwards from this final result or answer.

WORKED EXAMPLE 4

Milo arrived at his desk on Monday morning to find that his in-tray was full of reports. He spent all day processing and filing 25 of these reports. Overnight the clerical staff added an extra 7 reports. On Tuesday Milo processed and filed 19 reports, but there were still 56 reports left in his in-tray. How many reports were in Milo's in-tray on Monday morning?

THINK	WRITE
1 Read the question at least twice and take note of all the important facts.	Milo filed 25 reports on Monday. Seven reports were then added to the in-tray that evening. Nineteen reports were filed Tuesday, leaving 56 reports in the in-tray that evening.
2 Identify the solution required.	The question asks to determine how many reports were originally in the in-tray Monday morning.
3 The last facts we know are that on Tuesday, Milo took 19 reports from his in-tray and there were 56 reports left. This means that 56 + 19 gives the number at the start of Tuesday.	$56 + 19 = 75$ at the start of Tuesday
4 Overnight from Monday to Tuesday, the clerical staff added 7 reports. Before that there must have been 7 fewer reports in the in-tray.	$75 - 7 = 68$ at the end of the day on Monday
5 Milo removed, processed and filed 25 reports on Monday.	$68 + 25 = 93$ at the start of Monday
6 Answer the question.	There were 93 reports in the in-tray at the start of Monday.

REMEMBER

If there is a sequence of steps for which we know the final answer, then a useful strategy is to work backwards from this final result or answer.

EXERCISE 9D Work backwards from the answer

PROBLEM SOLVING

1 Mike works on a cattle station. At the start of the year 2010 there were a certain number of cattle. Due to the drought, 15 cattle perished during summer. Fortunately there were 18 healthy calves born that year. Just before the cattle were rounded up to be counted, 3 strayed on to a major highway and were killed. When the cattle were finally counted later in 2010, there were 245 animals. How many were there at the start of the year 2010?

2 Rae opened a savings account with a certain amount of money earning interest monthly. During October, \$2.65 interest was added. In November, Rae withdrew \$450 for Christmas gifts and other expenses. The November interest added was \$2.44. Rae was paid \$1048 for a week's work during December and this money was deposited into the account. By Christmas, Rae had \$1393 in the account. How much was there when the account was opened?

3 Grace sells tropical fish. Last week Grace counted the fish and then she added 3 dozen new fish. She sold 17 fish the next day. Over the following week fin rot claimed 13 fish, which had to be thrown away. The next week Grace added another 10 fish. When she then counted the fish in the tank there were 223. How many were in the tank when she first counted them?

4 Diana had always wanted to have a large rose garden. When the local garden nursery had a special on roses, she purchased as many as she could fit in her car. Unfortunately, 4 of the plants died during the first week. In anticipation of further losses, Diana purchased another dozen. A harsh winter claimed the life of another 5 roses. Her six children came to the rescue by each giving her a rosebush for her birthday. The number of roses in the garden now totalled 57. How many plants did Diana buy initially?

5 Dan constantly struggled to deal with all his email at work, trying to answer his client's queries as quickly as possible. Monday morning he arrived at work to find his inbox needing urgent attention. He started by deleting all the spam email — 57 in all. By the end of the day he had answered 35 genuine work enquiries. He also answered 10 personal emails. During the day he received another 15 emails, 5 of which were spam emails, which he immediately deleted. Tuesday morning he arrived at work to find another 18 emails had been received overnight. Dan now had 38 emails in his inbox. If Dan removes emails from his inbox once he's answered them, how many emails were in Dan's inbox on Monday morning?

6 Craig has bought shares in CSL which have a value \$34.56 per share one week after he bought them. Each day the change in share price was given as –0.45, +1.23, –2.56, +0.07 and –0.75. What did Craig pay for the shares?

7 Give an example of a set of 5 numbers that have a mean of 7, a median of 8 and a range of 5.

8 Sean has passed 20 out of 25 tasks. He has 15 tasks left to complete. He needs to pass a minimum of 75% of the tasks. What is the minimum number of the remaining tasks he needs to pass?

9 Charles took a maths exam with 20 questions. For every correct question, Charles received 10 marks. For every incorrect or unanswered question, he lost 5 marks. If his final score was 140 marks, how many questions were answered correctly?

10 James had 18 litres of water shared unequally between three buckets. Then he:

a Poured three quarters of the water in bucket 1 into bucket 2.

b Poured half the water that was now in bucket 2 into bucket 3.

c Poured a third of the water that was now in bucket 3 into bucket 1.

After the pouring, all the buckets contained equal amounts of water.

How much water did each bucket start with?

9E Elimination

- When using a process of elimination we remove or eliminate possible solutions that do not match the given information.
- We first write down all the possible combinations or solutions in a grid or table. From the information supplied, we cross out (eliminate) those combinations that do not match.

WORKED EXAMPLE 5

Harvey is solving a riddle. He needs to find a number between 20 and 30 that is not odd, is not a multiple of 4, and is not a multiple of 13.

THINK	WRITE
1 Read the question at least twice and take note of all the important facts.	The clues concerning the required number are: it is between 20 and 30; it is not odd; it is neither a multiple of 4 nor a multiple of 13.
2 Identify the solution required.	The question asks to find the required number.
3 List the numbers from between 20 and 30.	21, 22, 23, 24, 25, 26, 27, 28, 29
4 Eliminate (strike through) the odd number(s) that are odd.	~~21~~, 22, ~~23~~, 24, ~~25~~, 26, ~~27~~, 28, ~~29~~
5 Eliminate the number(s) that are multiples of 4; that is, 24, 28.	~~21~~, 22, ~~23~~, ~~24~~, ~~25~~, 26, ~~27~~, ~~28~~, ~~29~~
6 Eliminate the number(s) that are multiples of 13; that is, 26.	~~21~~, 22, ~~23~~, ~~24~~, ~~25~~, ~~26~~, ~~27~~, ~~28~~, ~~29~~
7 The remaining number is the answer.	The answer is 22.
8 Answer the question.	

REMEMBER

1. When using a process of elimination we remove or eliminate possible solutions that do not match the given information.
2. We first write down all the possible combinations or solutions in a grid or table. From the information supplied, we cross out (eliminate) those combinations that do not match.

EXERCISE 9E Elimination

PROBLEM SOLVING

1 Mr Bateaux will give away a diamond ring to the first person that correctly guesses its value. Here are the clues. The amount is a multiple of \$50 and is more than \$500 but less than \$2000. It is not a multiple of \$200, and it is not a multiple of \$350. The first digit is a prime number. One of the digits is repeated.

2 Find the terminating decimal that has three digits after the decimal point and lies between 0.5 and 0.6. No digits are repeated. The first two digits are prime. The digits are increasing in value from left to right. The third digit is a multiple of 3.

3 Find an integer between 50 and 80 that is both a perfect square and a perfect cube.

4 What two numbers multiply to give -12 and add to give -11?

5 Triangular numbers are those whose dots form the pattern of a triangle, for example 1, 3, 6, 10, ... Find a triangular number below 50 that is also a square number.

6 The number 15 can be represented as the sum of two or more consecutive positive integers in three different ways. One of them begins with 1, that is, $1 + 2 + 3 + 4 + 5$. What do the other sequences begin with?

7 There is a number.
If it is not a multiple of 4, it is between 60 and 69.
If it is a multiple of 3, it is between 50 and 59.
If it is not a multiple of 6, it is between 70 and 79.
What is the number?

8 Identify the following shape:
Four of the sides are equal.
The angles add to 360°.
It is not a square.

9 Place the following numbers in the grid below. (There may be more than one way to do this.)

1	2	3	4	5
6	7	9	10	11
12	15	16	18	20
21	23	24	25	30
35	36	45	55	60

	Prime	**Triangular**	**Square**	**Multiple of 3**	**Multiple of 5**
Odd					
Even					
Less than 20					
Greater than 20					
Factor of 60					

10 Emily bought a 5-scoop ice-cream. Her brother wanted to know what she'd bought. Can you figure it out from the clues she gave him?
The flavours are Bubblebum, Chocolate, Pistachio, Strawberry and Vanilla.
The flavour on the bottom does not have 9 letters in the name.
Strawberry touches both Chocolate and Vanilla.
Bubblegum is not on top.

9F Simplify the problem

- If you are overwhelmed by the size of the numbers involved in a question, try to solve a similar but simpler question. This can be achieved by changing the numbers in the original question to smaller numbers.
- After finding the answer to the simpler question, the same method can be used to solve the original problem.

WORKED EXAMPLE 6

After 57 days, a team installed 153.6 km of fibre-optic cable. How much longer would it take to reach the target of 170 km?

THINK	WRITE
1 Read the question at least twice and take note of all the important facts.	It takes 57 days to install 153.6 km of cable; a total of 170 km must be installed.
2 Identify the solution required.	The question asks to find the time taken to reach the target length of 170 km.
3 Consider a similar but much easier question.	Consider a team that takes 2 days to install 6 km of cable with a target of completing 8 km.
4 Calculate the time taken to install 1 km of cable in the simplified problem.	Time to install 1 km of cable $= \frac{2}{6}$ day $= \frac{1}{3}$ day
5 Calculate the remaining length of cable still to be installed.	Remaining length of cable to install $= 8 - 6$ $= 2$ km
6 Use the time taken to install 1 km of cable to calculate the time needed to install the remaining length of cable.	Time to install 2 km of cable $= \frac{1}{3} \times 2$ $= \frac{2}{3}$ day
7 Repeat the same method to work out the answer for the original question. First list the given information.	In 57 days, 153.6 km of cable is installed. Need to install a total of 170 km of cable.
8 Calculate the time taken to install 1 km of cable.	Time to install 1 km of cable $= \frac{57}{153.6}$ day $= \frac{570}{1536}$ day $= \frac{95}{256}$ (or approximately 0.37 day)
9 Calculate the remaining length of cable still to be installed.	Remaining length of cable to install $= 170 - 153.6$ $= 16.4$ km
10 Use the time taken to install 1 km of cable to calculate the time needed to install the remaining length of cable.	Time to install 16.4 km of cable $= \frac{95}{256} \times 16.4$ $= 6.085\,937\,5$ days
11 Answer the question.	To reach the target of installing 170 km of cable, approximately 6 more days are needed.

REMEMBER

1. If you are overwhelmed by the size of the numbers involved in a question, try to solve a similar but simpler question. This can be achieved by changing the numbers in the original question to smaller numbers.
2. After finding the answer to the simpler question, the same method can be used to solve the original problem.

EXERCISE

9F Simplify the problem

PROBLEM SOLVING

1 After 73 days, a sailing boat had travelled 1264 nautical miles. How much longer would it take to reach the target of 2000 nautical miles?

2 The school's Building Fund hopes to raise \$2 000 000 for a new swimming pool and sporting complex. During one month \$24 892 was raised. How long would it take to raise the \$2 000 000 at this contribution rate?

3 If you calculated the following sum $9 + 99 + 999 + 9\,999 + 99\,999 + \ldots$, where the last number consists of ten digits of 9, how many times would the number 1 appear in your answer? (*Hint:* $9 = 10 - 1$, $99 = 100 - 1$)

4 A chess board is made up of 64 small squares.

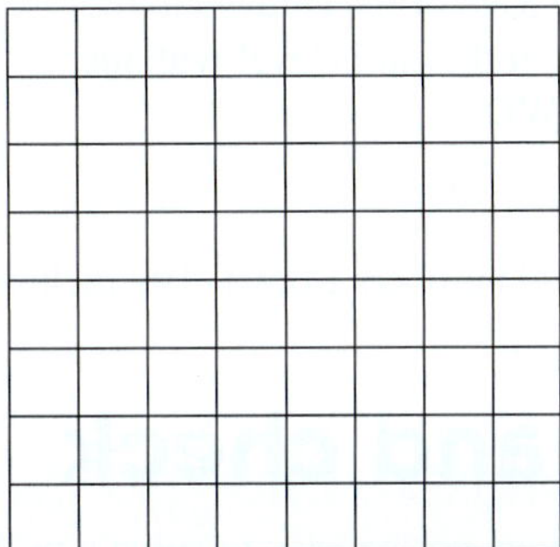

There are many more than 64 squares in total on the board.

a Use this board to investigate the total number of squares on an 8×8 chess board.

b Explain how you could deduce a formula to determine the total number of squares on a board with 12 rows and 12 columns, and hence find the number of squares on a board with 12 rows and 12 columns.

5 A motorist was driving in the rain at a steady speed of 72 km/h. As the car passed under a bridge, the rain stopped falling on the car for 2.7 seconds. How wide was the bridge in metres?

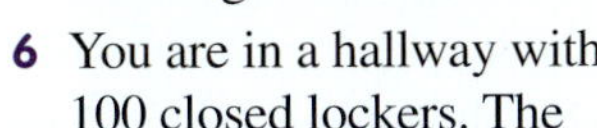

6 You are in a hallway with 100 closed lockers. The first time you walk through the hallway, you open every locker. The second time you walk through, you close every second locker. The third time through, you change every third locker, this means that you open it (if it's closed) or close it (if it's open). The fourth time through, you change every fourth locker. This pattern continues until the 100th walk through the hallway, where the 100th locker is changed. How many lockers are left open?

7 Mrs Mather won \$25 and decided to share her winnings with her 5 children.

The first child received \$1 plus $\frac{1}{6}$ of the money remaining.

The second child received \$2 plus $\frac{1}{6}$ of the money remaining.

The third child received \$3 plus $\frac{1}{6}$ of the money remaining and so on.

a How much money did each child receive?

When Mrs Smith won some money, she divided the money in a similar manner (but she only had 4 children):

The first child received \$1 plus $\frac{1}{5}$ of the money remaining.

The second child received $2 plus $\frac{1}{5}$ of the money remaining and so on.

b If each child received the same amount of money, how much did Mrs Smith win?

c Mrs Brown has 8 children. If she wants to share money using a method similar to Mrs Mather and Mrs Smith, how much money does she need and what fraction would she use?

8 Is the number $4^{33} + 3^{44}$ divisible by 5?

9 A motorist, travelling at 100 km/h, overtakes an 4WD towing a caravan. The 4WD and caravan together are 13 metres long and have a speed of 64 km/h. The car is 5 metres long. How many seconds will it take from the time the front of the car is level with the back of the caravan to the time the back of the car is level with the front of the 4WD?

10 If all of the odd numbers from 1–199 inclusive are added together, what is the total?

9G Guess and check

- Sometimes is may not be easy to solve a problem directly, in this case we can use a strategy in which we guess at the solution. We test this guess by using the available information supplied in the problem to check whether it is the solution. We continue to guess and check until the solution is found.
- Technology, such as a spreadsheet, can be used to give instant feedback about the guess.

WORKED EXAMPLE 7

Chocolates were distributed among three groups of children. The second group received 4 times the number of chocolates of the first group. The third group received 10 more chocolates than the second group. One hundred and nine chocolates were distributed altogether. How many chocolates did the first, the second and the third group receive?

THINK	WRITE/DISPLAY
1 Read the question at least twice and take note of all the important facts.	Three groups of children receive chocolates. Group 2 receives 4 times as many chocolates as group 1. Group 3 receives 10 more chocolates than group 2. In total 109 chocolates are distributed.
2 Identify the solution required.	The question asks to find the number of chocolates group 1, group 2 and group 3 have received.
3 Since the number of chocolates received by the first group is an unknown value, guess any number (say 20). In a spreadsheet, type the heading **1st group chocolates** in cell **A1**. Enter **20** in cell **A2**.	(see spreadsheet below)

	A	B	C	D
1	First group chocolates	Second group chocolates	Third group chocolates	Sum of chocolates
2		= A2*4	= B2 + 10	= A2 + B2 + C2
3	20	80	90	190
4	10	40	50	100
5	11	44	54	109

REMEMBER

1. Sometimes it may not be easy to solve a problem directly, in this case we can use a strategy in which we guess at the solution. We test this guess by using the available information supplied in the problem to check whether it is the solution. We continue to guess and check until the solution is found.
2. Technology, such as a spreadsheet, can be used to give instant feedback about the guess.

EXERCISE

9G Guess and check

PROBLEM SOLVING

1 Chocolates were distributed among three groups of children. The second group received 4 more chocolates than the first group. The third group received 3 times the number of chocolates of the second group. One hundred and one chocolates were distributed altogether. How many chocolates did the first, the second and the third group receive?

2 Toula observed the number of times she saw a red car, white car or blue car pass through an intersection. She kept a tally of these colours. She ignored all other colours. Out of 219 cars, there were 13 more white cars than red cars, and the number of blue cars was $\frac{2}{3}$ the number of white cars. What was the most popular colour, and how many did Toula see of that colour?

3 Four people, Max, Kim, Lilla and Harvey, decided to pool their money and hire a taxi. They each contributed \$1 or \$2 coins. Together they had \$66. Kim had \$5 less than Max. Lilla had \$3 more than Max and Harvey had half as much as Lilla. How much did Harvey contribute?

4 Three integers have a sum of 50. The second integer is four times as large as the first integer and the third integer is 4 less than the second integer. What are the three integers?

5 Each digit in a four-digit number is a prime number. The first digit is the smallest digit. The third digit is two smaller than the last digit and the number is a multiple of 5. What is the four-digit number?

6 The Puregold Jewellery company makes bracelets and necklaces. A bracelet has 6 links of gold and no gem stone. A necklace has 12 links of gold and 3 gem stones. A marketing review found that they use 5 times as many links as gemstones and 60 links were used. What is the ratio of bracelets to necklaces made by the Puregold Jewellery company. Explain your answer.

7 Using the numbers 1, 2, 3, 4, in that order, generate the numbers from -1 to -10. You may use any of the operations ($+, -, \times, \div, \sqrt{}$).

8 There are two integers whose square root is the last 2 digits of the integer. Find the integers.

9 A two-digit number is such that if the digits are added together and divided by 5, the result is the same as placing a decimal point between the digits of the original number. Find the two-digit number.

10 Fill in the blanks in the following addition sum using all the digits 1 to 9 only once each.

```
  _ _ _
+ _ _ _
  _ _ _
```

9H Mixed problems I

Communicating, reasoning and reflecting

- It is important to understand that solving problems involves much more than just writing numbers on a page. Words should accompany the mathematics and these words should be in the form of appropriate English and use correct mathematical terms.

- Care should be taken that when the equals (=) sign is used, the mathematics following is indeed equal.
- After providing a solution to a question, it is good practice to review your solution to see whether another person could understand your work without first reading the question.
- Finally, if you take the time to reflect on your work, you may increase your understanding of the problem and the strategies you used to solve it. You may be able to connect this to previous experiences as well as to future problems you will have to tackle.

WORKED EXAMPLE 8

Abdul is updating prices on all the stationery items in the shop. He adds a 20% profit margin and a further 10% GST. How can he easily update the price in one calculation?

THINK	WRITE
1 Read the question at least twice and take note of all the important facts.	A 20% profit margin is to be added on all items followed by a further 10% GST.
2 Identify the solution required.	The question asks to find the percentage equivalent to these two percentages.
3 Consider an appropriate strategy. In this case, define a variable to be used to represent the original price.	Let x = original price of a stationery item.
4 Perform the first of the two separate calculations.	Adding a 20% profit margin: $x + 20\%$ of x or 120% of $x = \frac{120}{100} \times x$ $= x + \frac{20}{100} \times x$; $= 1.2 \times x$ $= x + 0.2x$; $= 1.2x$ $= 1.2x$
5 Perform the second of the two separate calculations.	Adding a further 10% GST: $1.2x + 10\%$ of $1.2x$ or 110% of $1.2x = \frac{110}{100} \times 1.2x$ $= 1.2x + \frac{10}{100} \times 1.2x$; $= 1.1 \times 1.2x$ $= 1.2x + 0.1 \times 1.2x$; $= 1.32x$ $= 1.2x + 0.12x$ $= 1.32x$
6 Devise a question that will lead Abdul to the required equivalent single calculation.	How can I relate $1.32x$ as a percentage increase?
7 First express 1.32 as an improper fraction and then as an equivalent percentage. Hence, find the required percentage increase.	$1.32 = \frac{132}{100}$ $= 132\%$ so $1.32x = 132\%$ of x. This means that x has been increased by 32%.

8 Communicate the answer with reasoning.	Abdul can easily update the price of any stationery item by increasing the price by 32%. This he can do by multiplying the price by 1.32. We can check this by considering an item that costs \$5.00. Applying a 20% increase gives $1.2 \times \$5.00 = \$6.00$; then a further increase of 10% gives $1.1 \times \$6.00 = \$6.60$. A single calculation of applying a 32% increase gives $1.32 \times \$5.00 = \$6.60$.
9 Reflect on the solution.	It would be tempting to think that successive increases of 20% and then 10% would be the same as increasing by 30%. Performing each calculation separately with a variable to represent the original price lets us work back to the single calculation shortcut.

REMEMBER

1. It is important to communicate your solution clearly.
2. Take care with how equals (=) signs are used.
3. After you have written your solution, review your work.
4. Reflect on your work.

EXERCISE

9H Mixed problems I

PROBLEM SOLVING

1 A sports reporter was researching the physical characteristics of football players. As she was writing for an English newspaper, she reported their weights in the English system of stones and pounds. (In that system, 14 pounds equal one stone.) From the following records, construct a table to find the total weight of the 12 players. Express your answer in stones and pounds.

18 stone 8 pounds	19 stone 4 pounds	13 stone 12 pounds
18 stone 13 pounds	17 stone 8 pounds	17 stone 4 pounds
18 stone 5 pounds	14 stone 11 pounds	18 stone 10 pounds
18 stone 2 pounds	14 stone 11 pounds	17 stone 13 pounds

2 There are six faces on a normal die, numbered 1 to 6. If such a die is rolled twice, how many different combinations of numbers can result?

3 In a random sample of 64 823 cars, exactly 1741 had defective brake lights. How many cars would you expect to have defective brake lights in a sample of 68 cars?

4 Ten children were using buckets to fill a drum with water from a creek. On their first trip they brought the following quantities.
6.8 L, 8.5 L, 7.7 L, 8.9 L, 9.5 L, 7.6 L, 8.4 L, 9.3 L, 8.1 L, 7.9 L
They tipped their buckets of water into the drum. Use a spreadsheet to determine the volume of water in the drum at this stage. Express your answer in litres and millilitres.

5 The canteen sells sandwiches on white, brown or grain bread. The filling can be either egg, cheese, chicken or ham. These can be served with tomato sauce, BBQ sauce or no sauce. How many different types of sandwiches are available at the canteen?

6 Use a spreadsheet to show that 4^8 can be calculated by repeated multiplication.

7 At the beginning of the year, Sue noticed that her cupboard was overflowing with shoes, many of which she hadn't worn for some time. This prompted her to clear out eight pairs of unwanted summer shoes and buy two pairs in the latest style. As winter approached, Sue purchased two new pairs of boots and discarded four pairs of old winter shoes. With the Christmas holidays approaching, Sue treated herself to three new pairs of sandals. She now had eleven pairs of shoes. How many shoes were in Sue's cupboard at the beginning of the year?

8 Ken's house number is a number between 50 and 100. It is a multiple of 3 and has a prime number as one of its factors. The sum of its digits is 15 and the first digit is larger than the second digit. Use a spreadsheet to determine Ken's house number.

9 John's pedometer showed that he had taken 65 423 paces and travelled a distance of 42.5 km. At this rate, how far would John travel every 100 paces?

10 Three numbers have a product of 400. The second number is the cube of the first and the third number is a square number between 20 and 30. Use a spreadsheet to determine the three numbers.

9I Mixed problems II

EXERCISE

9I Mixed problems II

PROBLEM SOLVING

1 A popular website has been visited a total of 15 670 234 times in 28 hours. How many times might the website be visited every 5 seconds?

2 Jocelyn and Bernard have three children. They are all married and each has a daughter and a son. The daughters are all married, each with one child. The sons are not married and do not have children as yet. How many people are in Jocelyn and Bernard's extended family?

3 Your school is taking part in a community 'Get fit' campaign. Students are organised into groups of 12. Each student wears a pedometer and records the distance walked in a week. The results for one group are recorded as follows. Find the total distance this group walked, expressing your answer in kilometres and metres.

6.8 km	10.3 km	12.4 km
5.9 km	8.8 km	16.5 km
8.4 km	11.9 km	9.3 km
13.7 km	15.7 km	10.2 km

4 Julius was asked to use a single calculation that will increase the selling price by 5% and then add GST of 10%. How can he easily update the price in one calculation?

5 Gemma was asked to use a single calculation that will decrease the pre-GST selling price of a car by 10% and then add GST of 10%. Find this single calculation.

6 Alfie had $\$x$ in the bank. He was given 5% interest and then charged \$1. How can a single calculation be made to obtain the final balance?

7 Jeff left a sum of money in a bank for exactly 3 years. The interest (8% p.a.) was added to the account at the end of each 12 months. How can a single calculation be made to obtain the final balance?

8 Write a simple formula to use on a house plan for converting millimetres on the plan (d) into metres on the land (m). You are told that the plan has a scale of 1 : 2000.

9 Write a simple formula to calculate the number of pages (p) of writing that can be stored on a writable CD with memory (d) (assume that one writable CD can store approximately 750 megabytes). Assume 1 page uses approximately 40 kilobytes of memory.

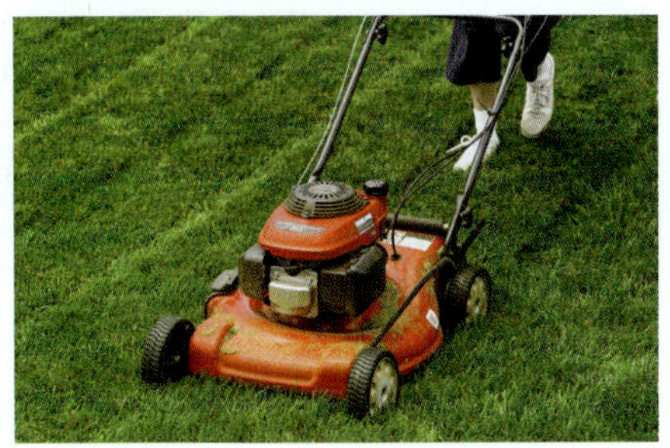

10 Write a simple formula to calculate the number of millilitres of oil (m) to add to the number of litres of petrol (p) when mixing lawnmower petrol. You are told that the ratio of oil to petrol is 1 to 250.

9J Mixed problems III

EXERCISE 9J Mixed problems III

PROBLEM SOLVING

1 In a retirement village there are 9 residents who are over the age of 90. Their ages are:

90 years 6 months	92 years 1 month	94 years 3 months
91 years 2 months	96 years 4 months	90 years 5 months
90 years 11 months	95 years 10 months	97 years 7 months

What is the total age of these residents? Express your answer in years and months.

2 On a charity walk, Gordon covered the 150 km distance in 22 hours 12 minutes. At this rate, how far did Gordon walk every 15 minutes?

3 A medical laboratory is studying the growth of a bacterium. A single bacterium splits into two bacteria in 30 seconds. These two cells then each split in two in 30 seconds. If this pattern continues, how many bacteria will there be after 5 minutes?

4 Write a formula to calculate V (the value in dollars and cents of a quantity of coins) if we know the number of A (of 5 cent coins) and B (of 10 cent coins) and C (of 20 cent coins) and D (of 50 cent coins).

5 The sides of a triangles are in the ratio 5 : 12 : 15. If the longest side measures 60 cm, what is the perimeter of the triangle?

6 A garden sunshade viewed from above looks like the diagram below. Four metal arms hold up the material of the sunshade. Each arm is 1 m long. Supporting wires are also wrapped around the arms to support the material. What length of wire is required to make the outer perimeter? Give your answer in exact form. How much material is required to make the sunshade (in square metres)? If you had 6 m^2 of material, how long would the arms need to be to support this sunshade if its shape is similar?

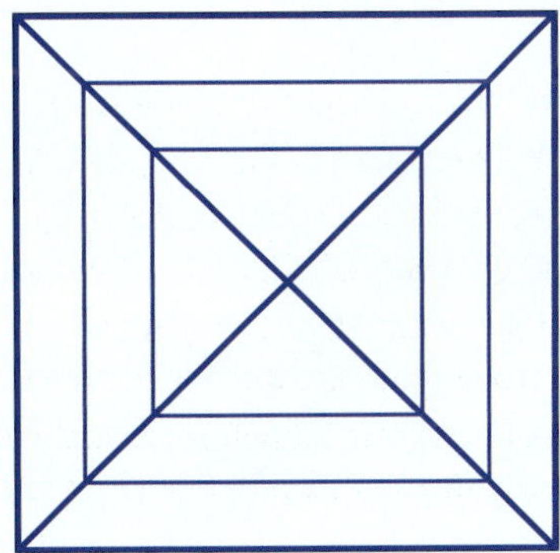

7 A household of five used 84 kilolitres of water during the quarter October–December.

a Find the average daily water use for the family.
b Find the average daily water use per person.
c If there is a target of 155 L per person per day, how much water should this family have used in this quarter?
d If the first 14 kL is charged at a rate of $1.05/kL and the rest is at $1.35/kL, what is the household water charge?

8 The square base of a tent has an area of $6\frac{1}{4}$ square metres.
a How long is one side of the tent?
b What is the perimeter?

9 You are using a natural spray to feed the flowers in your garden. The instructions are to mix 15 mL with every 2 litres of water. Your bottle is 200 mL. How many litres of water will you mix up if you if you use the entire bottle?

10 A car uses $\frac{3}{4}$ of a tank of petrol to travel 504 km. The tank holds 52 litres. How far can the car go on one litre?

Measurement

10A Perimeter
10B Circumference
10C Area of rectangles, triangles, parallelograms, rhombuses and kites
10D Area of a circle
10E Area of trapeziums
10F Volume of prisms and other solids
10G Time
10H 24-hour clock and time zones

WHAT DO YOU KNOW?

1. List what you know about measurement. Create a concept map to show your list.
2. Share what you know with a partner and then with a small group.
3. As a class, create a large concept map that shows your class's knowledge of measurement.

eBook*plus*

Digital doc
Hungry brain activity
Chapter 10
doc-6955

OPENING QUESTION

Will the one-bedroom unit, whose floor plan is shown, fit on the available area of 60 m^2?

Are you ready?

Try the questions below. If you have difficulty with any of them, extra help can be obtained by completing the matching SkillSHEET located on your eBookPLUS.

eBook*plus*
Digital doc
SkillSHEET 10.1
doc-6956

Multiplying and dividing by powers of 10

1 Calculate each of the following.

a $32 \div 100$ b 0.04×1000.

eBook*plus*
Digital doc
SkillSHEET 10.2
doc-6957

Converting units of length

2 Convert each of the following measurements.

a 34 mm to cm b 1.6 m to mm c 4500 cm to km

eBook*plus*
Digital doc
SkillSHEET 10.3
doc-6958

Area of squares, rectangles and triangles

3 Find the area of each of the following shapes.

a 1.3 cm

4.5 cm

b 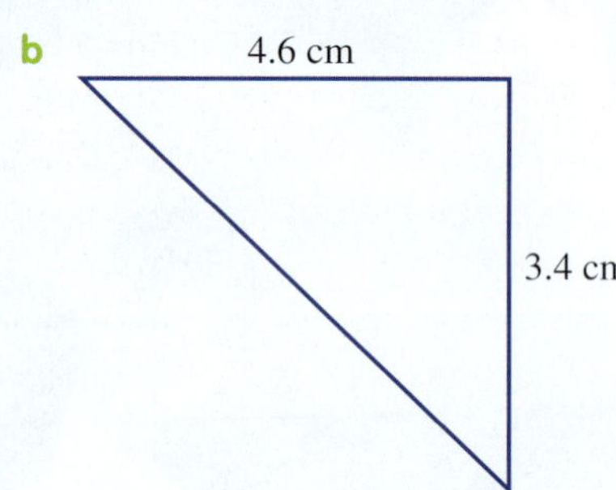

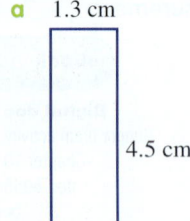

eBook*plus*
Digital doc
SkillSHEET 10.4
doc-6959

Volume of cubes and rectangular prisms

4 Find the volume of the following solid.

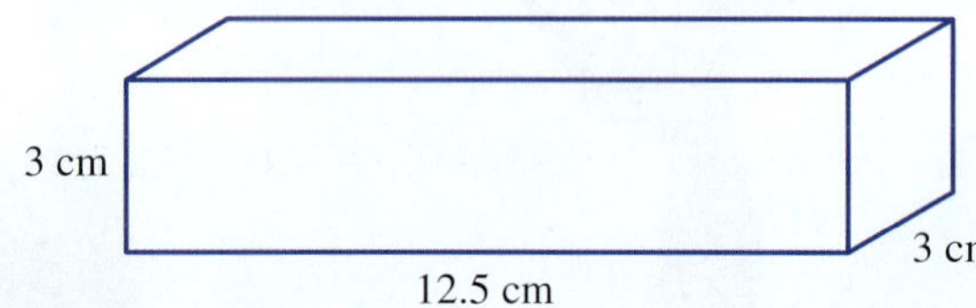

eBook*plus*
Digital doc
SkillSHEET 10.5
doc-6960

Reading the time (from analogue clocks)

5 What is the time shown on each of the following analogue clocks?

a 

b 

eBook*plus*
Digital doc
SkillSHEET 10.6
doc-6961

24-hour clock

6 Match the following 12-hour times to the corresponding 24-hour times.

12-hour time	24-hour time
a 9.00 pm	1000
b 10.00 am	2100
c 2.00 pm	1400

10A Perimeter

Units of length

- Metric units of length include millimetres (mm), centimetres (cm), metres (m) and kilometres (km).
- To convert between the units of length, we use the following conversion chart:

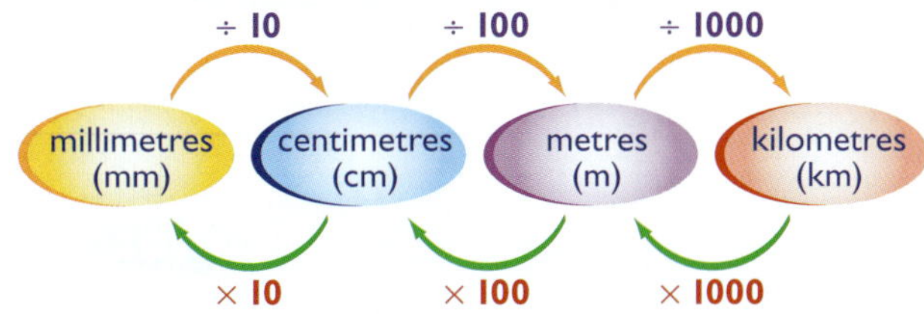

- When converting from a large unit to a smaller unit, multiply by the conversion factor; when converting from a smaller unit to a larger unit, divide by the conversion factor.

WORKED EXAMPLE 1

Complete the following metric length conversions.

a **1.027 m = ____ cm** **b** **0.0034 km = ____ m**
c **76 500 m = ____ km** **d** **3.069 m = ____ mm**

THINK	WRITE
a Look at the conversion table. To convert metres to centimetres, we need to multiply by 100. So, move the decimal point two places to the right.	**a** $1.027 \times 100 = 102.7$ cm
b To convert kilometres to metres, we need to multiply by 1000. So, move the decimal point three places to the right.	**b** $0.0034 \times 1000 = 3.4$ m
c To convert metres to kilometres, divide by 1000. This can be done by moving the decimal point three places to the left.	**c** $76\,500 \div 1000 = 76.5$ km
d Look at the conversion table. To convert metres to millimetres, we need to multiply by 100 and then by 10. This is the same as multiplying by 1000, so move the decimal point three places to the right.	**d** $3.069 \times 100 \times 10 = 3069$ mm

The perimeter

- The **perimeter** of a shape is the total distance around the shape.
- To find the perimeter of a shape:
  - identify the length of each side
  - ensure that all measurements are in the same units
  - add all side lengths together and include units with your answer.

WORKED EXAMPLE 2

Find the perimeter of each of the shapes below.

a A kite

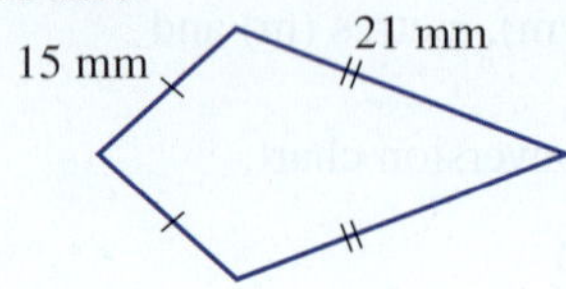

b A trapezium

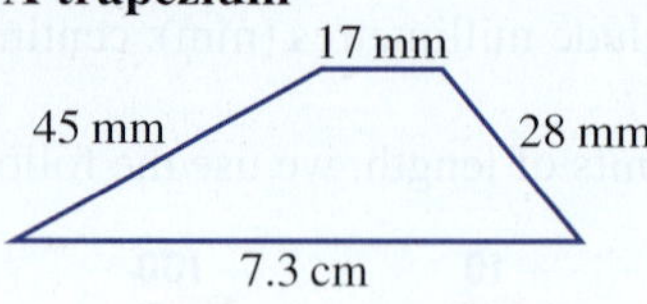

c An irregular shape

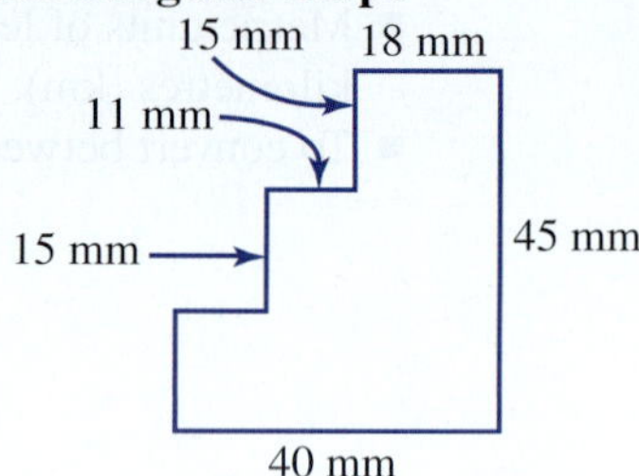

THINK	WRITE
a 1 Make sure that all the measurements are in the same units and add them together.	**a** $P = 21 \times 2 + 15 \times 2$ $= 72$
2 Write the answer in words, including the units.	The perimeter of the kite shown is 72 mm.
b 1 Notice that the measurements are not all in the same metric units. Convert to the smaller unit (in this case convert 7.3 cm to mm).	**b** 7.3 cm = 73 mm
2 Add the measurements.	$P = 45 + 17 + 28 + 73$ $= 163$
3 Write the answer in words, including the units.	The perimeter of the trapezium shown is 163 mm.
c 1 Make sure that given measurements are in the same units.	**c** 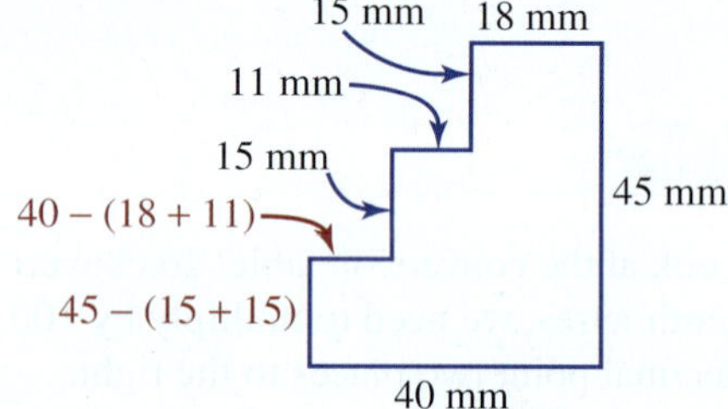
2 Determine the lengths of the unknown sides and label them on the diagram.	
3 Add the measurements.	$P = 45 + 18 + 15 + 11 + 15 + [40 - (18 + 11)] + [45 - (15 + 15)] + 40$ $= 45 + 18 + 15 + 11 + 15 + 11 + 15 + 40$ $= 170$ mm
4 Write the answer in words, including the units.	The perimeter of the irregular shape shown is 170 mm.

Finding the perimeter of a square and a rectangle

- The perimeter (P) of a rectangle is given by the formula $P = 2(l + w)$, where l is the length and w is the width of the rectangle.

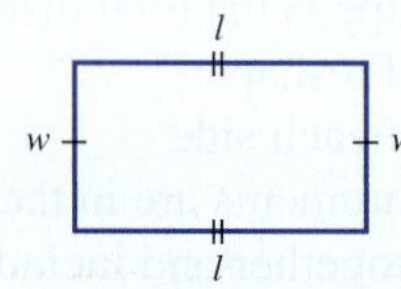

- The perimeter (P) of a square is given by the formula $P = 4l$, where l is the side length of the square.

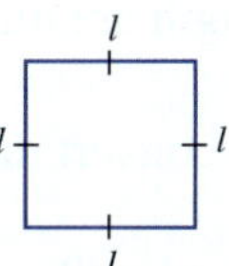

WORKED EXAMPLE 3

Find the perimeter of a rectangular block of land that is 20.5 m long and 9.8 m wide.

THINK	WRITE
1 Draw a diagram of the block of land and write in the measurements.	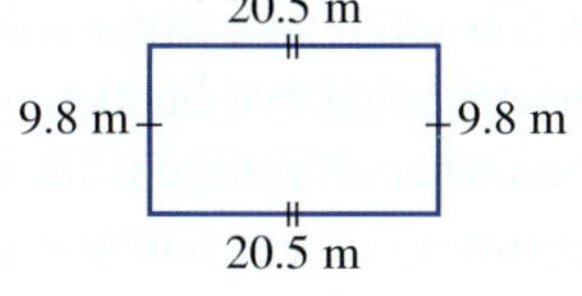
2 Write the formula for the perimeter of a rectangle.	$P = 2(l + w)$
3 Substitute the values of l and w into the formula, and calculate.	$P = 2 \times (20.5 + 9.8)$ $= 2 \times 30.3$ $= 60.6$ m
4 Write the worded answer with the correct units.	The perimeter of the block of land is 60.6 m.

WORKED EXAMPLE 4

A rectangular billboard advertising country Victoria has a perimeter of 16 m. Calculate its width if the length is 4.5 m.

THINK	WRITE
1 Draw a diagram of the rectangular billboard and write in the measurements.	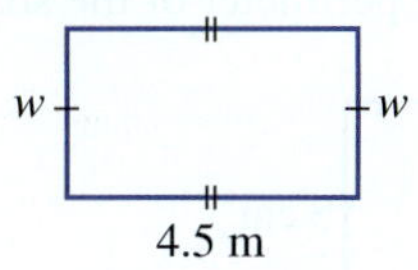
	$P = 16$ m
2 Write the formula for the perimeter of a rectangle.	$P = 2(l + w)$ $= 2l + 2w$
3 Substitute the values of P and l into the formula, and solve the equation: (a) subtract 9 from both sides (b) divide both sides by 2 (c) simplify if appropriate.	$16 = 2 \times 4.5 + 2w$ $16 = 9 + 2w$ $16 - 9 = 9 - 9 + 2w$ $7 = 2w$ $\frac{7}{2} = \frac{2w}{2}$ $3.5 = w$ $w = 3.5$
4 Write the worded answer with the correct units.	The width of the rectangular billboard is 3.5 m.

REMEMBER

1. The metric units of length are millimetres (mm), centimetres (cm), metres (m) and kilometres (km).
2. Use the table below to convert metric units of length.

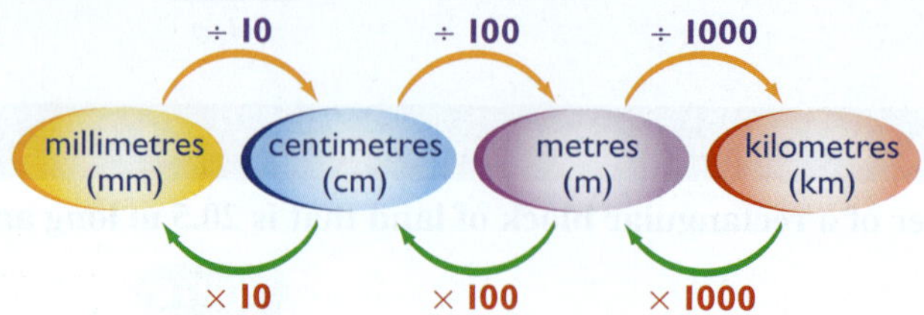

3. When converting to a larger unit, divide.
4. When converting to a smaller unit, multiply.
5. The perimeter of a shape is the total distance around that shape.
6. The perimeter of a rectangle is given by the rule $P = 2(l + w)$.
7. The perimeter of a square is given by the rule $P = 4l$.

EXERCISE

10A Perimeter

INDIVIDUAL PATHWAYS

eBook*plus*

Activity 10-A-1 Perimeters doc-2297

Activity 10-A-2 More perimeters doc-2298

Activity 10-A-3 Tricky perimeters doc-2299

FLUENCY

1 WE1 Fill in the gaps for each of the following.

a 20 mm = ________ cm
b 13 mm = ________ cm
c 130 mm = ________ cm
d 1.5 cm = ________ mm
e 0.03 cm = ________ mm
f 2.8 km = ________ m
g 0.034 m = ________ cm
h 2400 mm = ________ cm = ________ m
i 1375 mm = ________ cm = ________ m
j 2.7 m = ________ cm = ________ mm
k 0.08 m = ________ mm
l 6.071 km = ________ m
m 670 cm = ________ m
n 0.0051 km = ________ m

2 WE2 Find the perimeter of the shapes below.

a

4 cm, 3 cm

b

5 cm, 1 cm

c

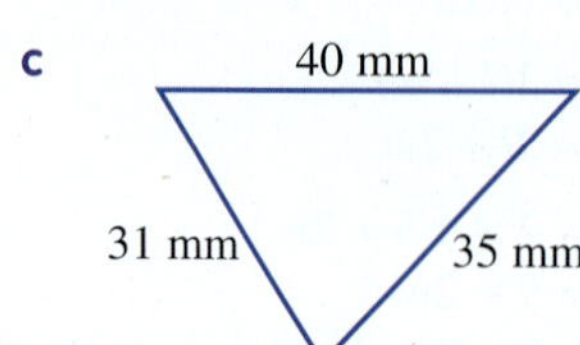

d

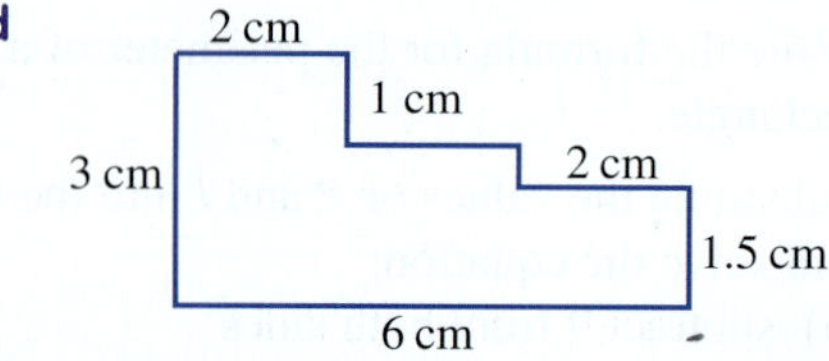

e

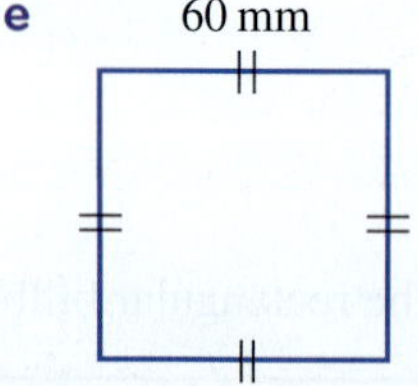

f

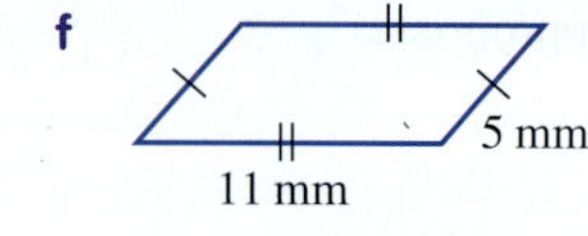

g

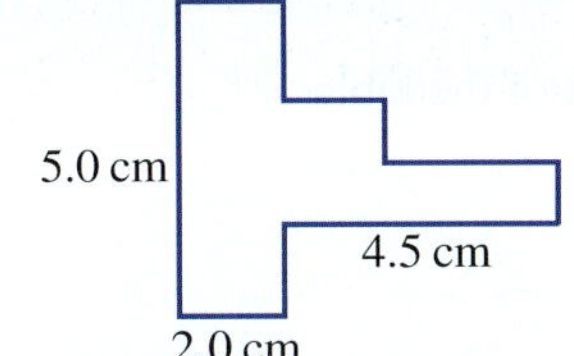

h

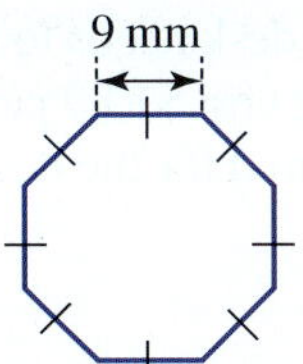

i

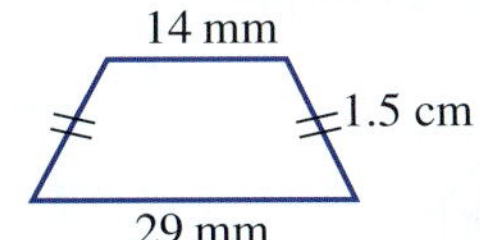

j

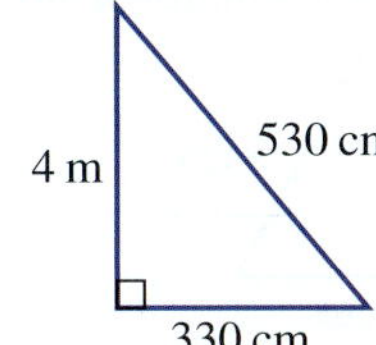

k

l

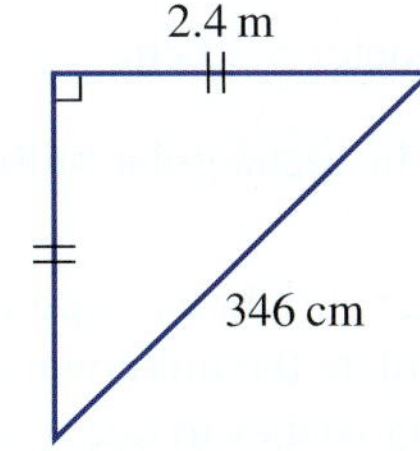

UNDERSTANDING

Weblink
Length conversions

3 Chipboard sheets are sold in three sizes. Convert each of the measurements below into centimetres and then into metres:
- **a** 1800 mm × 900 mm
- **b** 2400 mm × 900 mm
- **c** 2700 mm × 1200 mm.

4 A particular type of chain is sold for $2.25 per metre. What is the cost of 2.4 m of this chain?

5 Fabric is sold for $7.95 per metre. How much will 4.8 m of this fabric cost?

6 The standard marathon distance is 42.2 km. If a marathon race starts and finishes with one lap of Stadium Australia, seen at right, which is 400 m in length, what distance is run on the road outside the stadium?

7 Maria needs 3 pieces of timber of lengths 2100 mm, 65 cm and 4250 mm to construct a clothes rack.
- **a** What is the total length of timber required, in metres?
- **b** How much will the timber cost at $3.80 per metre?

8 WE3 Find the perimeter of a basketball court, which is 28 m long and 15 m wide.

9 A woven rectangular rug is 175 cm wide and 315 cm long. Find the perimeter of the rug.

10 A line is drawn to form a border 2 cm from each edge of a piece of A4 paper. If the paper is 30 cm long and 21 cm wide, what is the length of the border line?

11 A rectangular paddock 144 m long and 111 m wide requires a new three-strand wire fence.
- **a** What length of fencing wire is required to complete the fence?
- **b** How much will it cost to rewire the fence if the wire cost $1.47 per metre.

12 A computer desk needs to have table edging. If the edging cost $1.89 per metre, find the cost of the table edging required for the desk.

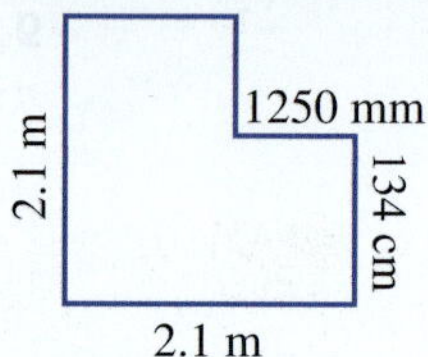

13 Calculate the unknown side lengths in each of the given shapes.

a

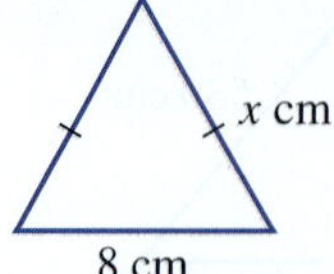

Perimeter = 30 cm

b

Perimeter = 176 cm

c

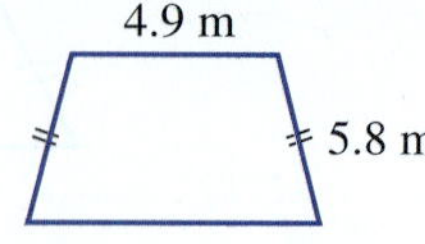

Perimeter = 23.4 m

14 WE4 The rectangular billboard has a perimeter of 25 m. Calculate its width if the length is 7 m.

15 The ticket at right has a perimeter of 42 cm.

a Calculate the unknown side length.

b Olivia wishes to decorate the ticket by placing a gold line along the slanted sides. How long is the line on each ticket?

c A bottle of gold ink will supply enough ink to draw 20 m of line. How many bottles of ink should be purchased if 200 tickets are to be decorated?

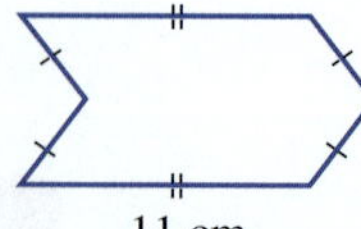

REASONING

16 A square and an equilateral triangle have the same perimeter. The side of the triangle is 3 cm longer than the side of the square. How long is the side of the square?

> **REFLECTION**
> What is the best way to remember the units conversion chart?

10B Circumference

- The **circumference** (C) is another term for the perimeter of a circle.
- The **diameter** (D) of a circle is the name given to the straight-line distance across a circle though its centre.
- The straight-line distance from the centre of the circle to the circumferences is called the **radius**.
- There is a relationship between the diameter and the circumference of a circle.
- The ratio $\frac{C}{D}$ is approximately 3. When this ratio is calculated exactly, it is called *pi* or π.
- The symbol π represents the ratio of the circumference of a circle to its diameter. It is an infinite, non-recurring and non-terminating decimal that begins as 3.1415926535 . . . For problem-solving purposes, 3.14 is a good approximation for π. For better accuracy, use a special button on your calculator, labelled π.
- The circumference of a circle is given by the formula $C = \pi D$.

Circumference
Diameter
Radius

- A diameter of a circle is twice as long as its radius, that is, $D = 2r$. Therefore, the other way to write the formula for the circumference is $C = 2\pi r$, where r is the radius of a circle.

WORKED EXAMPLE 5

Find the circumference of each of the following circles, giving answers i in terms of π ii correct to 2 decimal places.

a

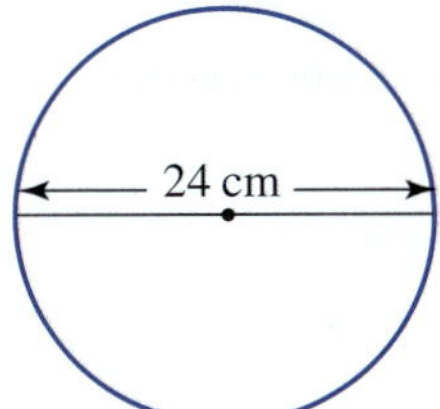

b

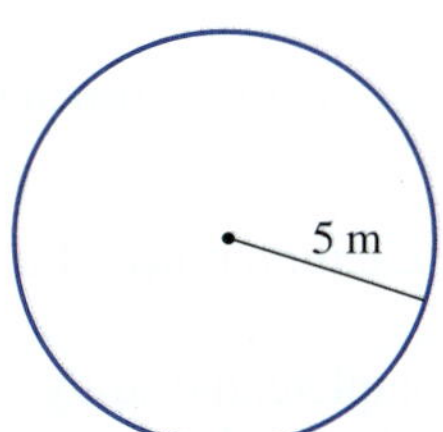

THINK	WRITE
a i 1 Write the formula for the circumference of a circle. *Note:* Since the diameter of the circle is given, use the formula that relates the circumference to the diameter.	**a i** $C = \pi D$
2 Substitute the value $D = 24$ into the formula.	$= \pi \times 24$
3 Write the answer and include the correct units.	$= 24\pi$ cm
ii 1 Write the formula for the circumference of a circle.	**ii** $C = \pi D$
2 Substitute the values $D = 24$ and $\pi = 3.14$ into the formula.	$= 3.14 \times 24$
3 Evaluate and include the correct units.	$= 75.36$ cm
b i 1 Write the formula for the circumference of a circle. *Note:* Since the radius of the circle is given, use the formula that relates the circumference to the radius.	**b i** $C = 2\pi r$
2 Substitute the value $r = 5$ into the formula.	$= 2 \times \pi \times 5$
3 Write the answer and include the correct units.	$= 10\pi$ m
ii 1 Write the formula for the circumference of a circle.	**ii** $C = 2\pi r$
2 Substitute the values $r = 5$ and $\pi = 3.14$ into the formula.	$= 2 \times 3.14 \times 5$
3 Evaluate and include the correct units.	$= 31.40$ m

WORKED EXAMPLE 6

Find the perimeter of the shape at right, correct to 2 decimal places.

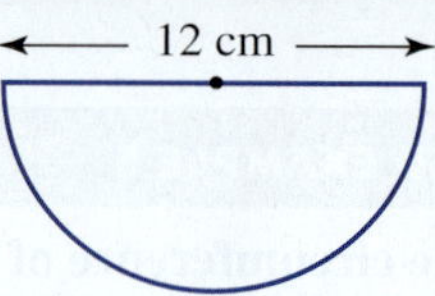

THINK	WRITE
1 Identify the parts that constitute the perimeter of the given shape.	$P = \frac{1}{2}$ circumference + straight-line section
2 Write the formula for the circumference of a circle. *Note:* If the circle were complete, the straight-line segment shown would be its diameter. So the formula that relates the circumference to the diameter is used.	$P = \frac{1}{2}\pi D$ + straight-line section
3 Substitute the values $D = 12$ and $\pi = 3.14$ into the formula.	$= \frac{1}{2} \times 3.14 \times 12 + 12$
4 To find the perimeter of the given shape, halve the value of the circumference and add the length of the straight section.	$= 18.84 + 12$
5 Evaluate and include the correct units.	$= 30.84$ cm

REMEMBER

1. The radius (r), diameter (D) and circumference (C) of a circle are shown at right.
2. The circumference of a circle, C, is given by the formula $C = \pi D$, or $C = 2\pi r$, where D is the diameter and r is the radius of a circle.
3. π represents the ratio of the circumference of a circle to its diameter, that is, $\frac{C}{D}$.
4. The numerical approximation for π is 3.14.

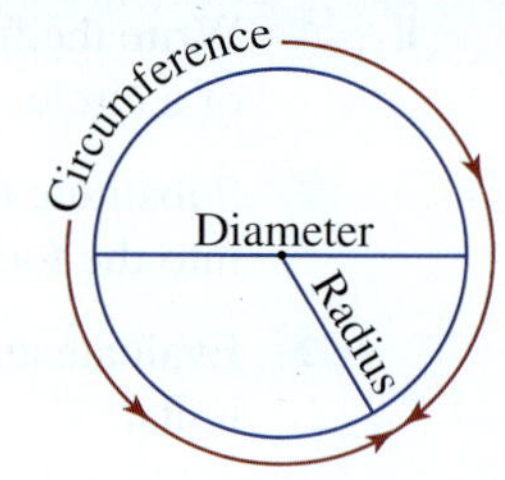

EXERCISE 10B Circumference

FLUENCY

1 WE5a Find the circumference of each of these circles, giving answers **i** in terms of π **ii** correct to 2 decimal places.

a

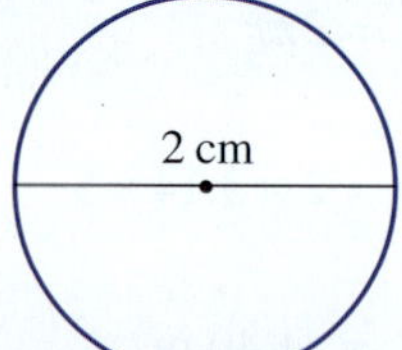

b

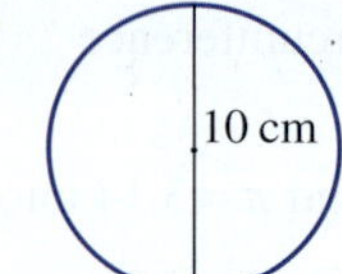

c

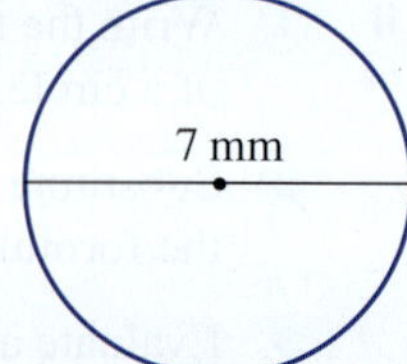

INDIVIDUAL PATHWAYS

eBook*plus*

Activity 10-B-1 Circumference doc-2300

Activity 10-B-2 More circumference doc-2301

Activity 10-B-3 Advanced circumference doc-2302

eBook*plus*

Interactivity **Finding pi** int-0079

eBook*plus*

Digital doc Investigation **The diameter of a circle and its circumference — any connection?** doc-2318

d
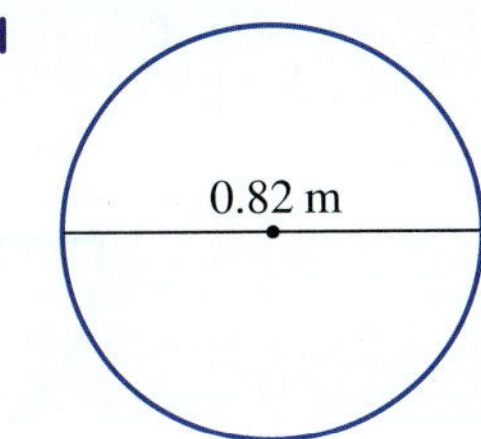

e
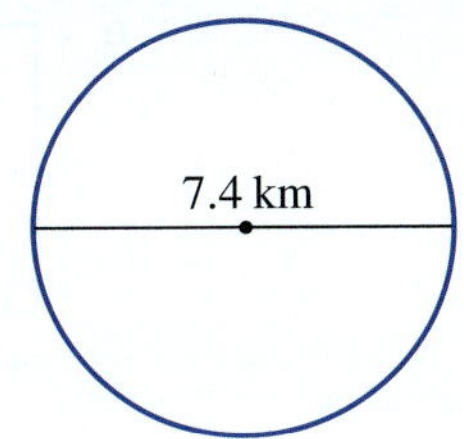

f
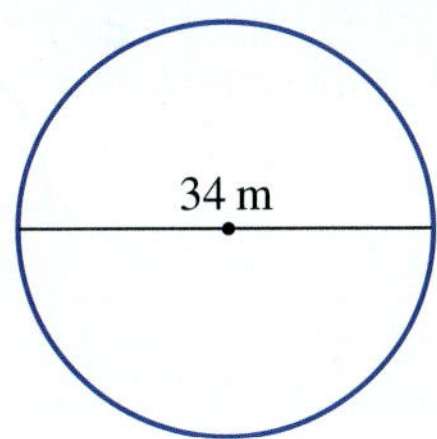

2 WE5b Find the circumference of each of the following circles, giving answers **i** in terms of π **ii** correct to 2 decimal places.

a
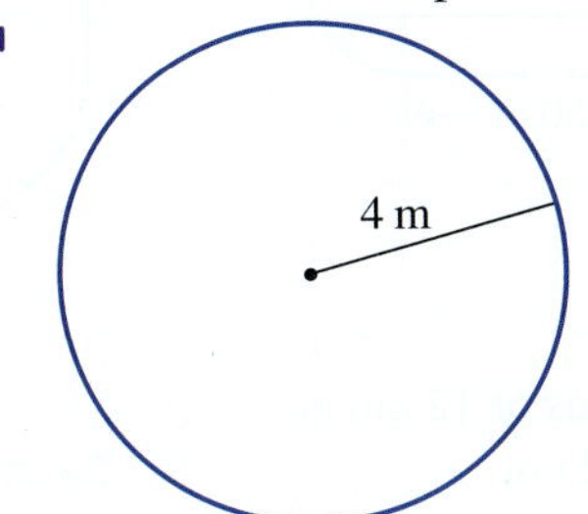

b
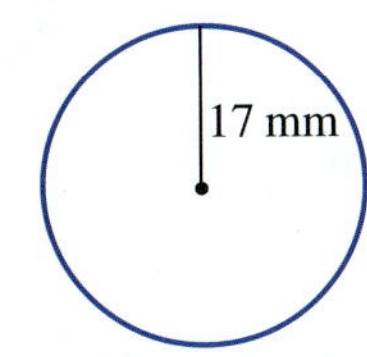

c
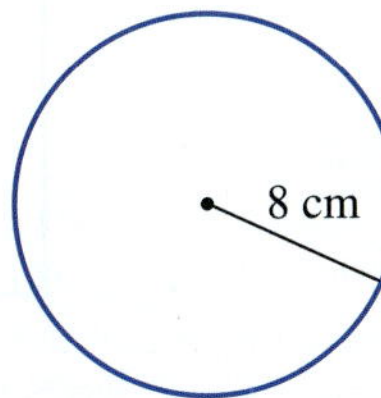

d

e
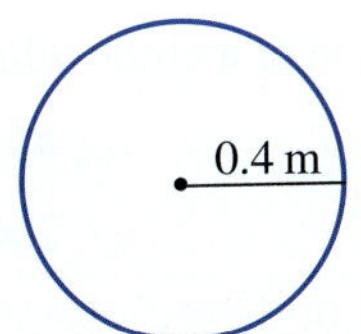

f
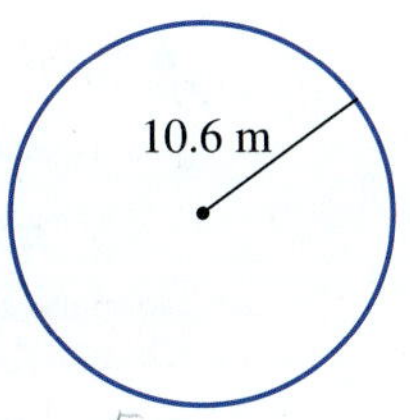

3 Choose the appropriate formula and find the circumference of these circles.

a
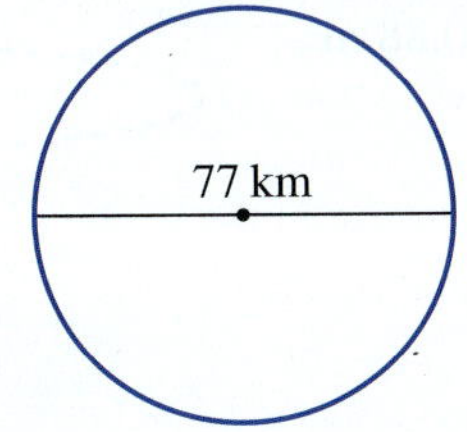

b
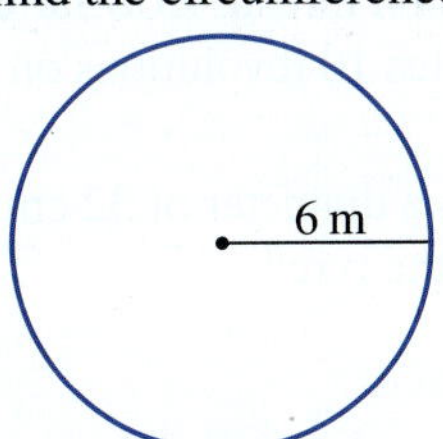

c
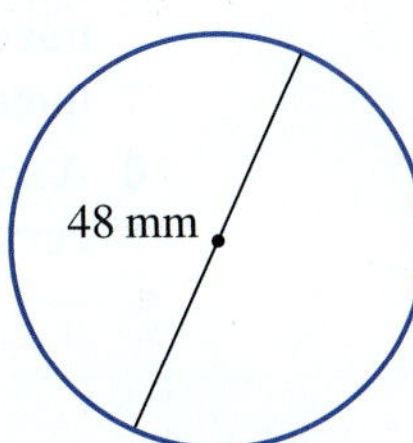

d
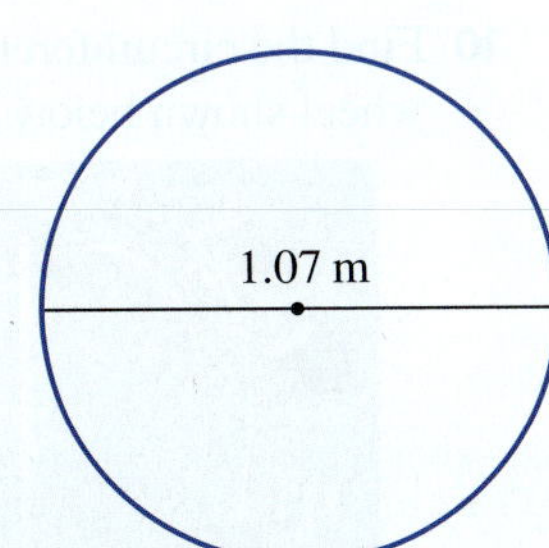

e
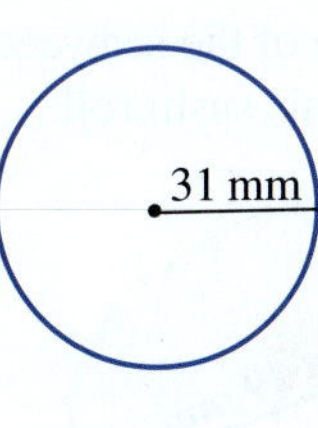

f
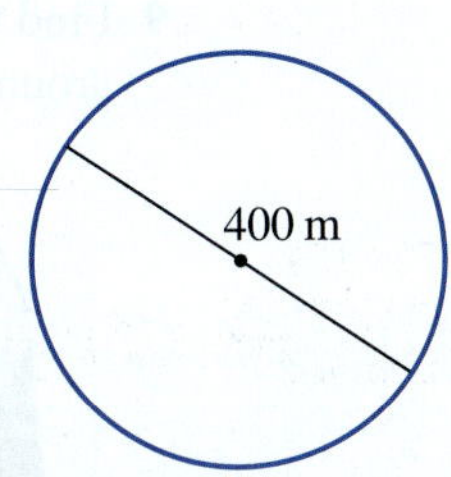

4 WE6 Find the perimeter of each of the shapes below. (Remember to add the lengths of the straight sections.)

a
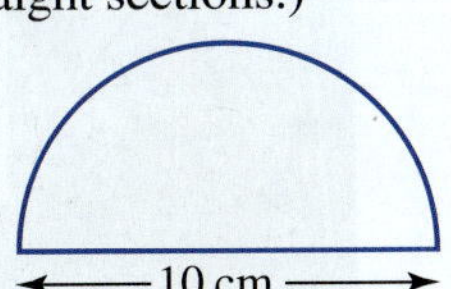

b
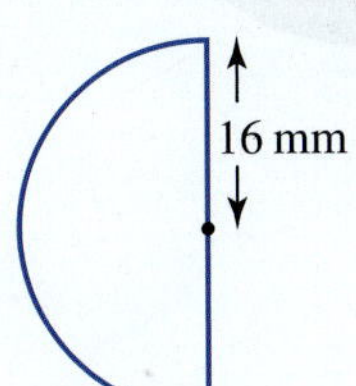

c
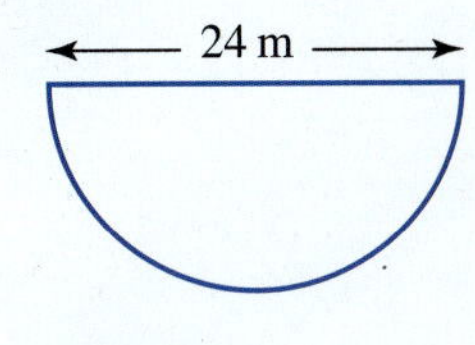

(continued)

d
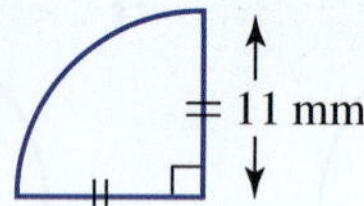

e
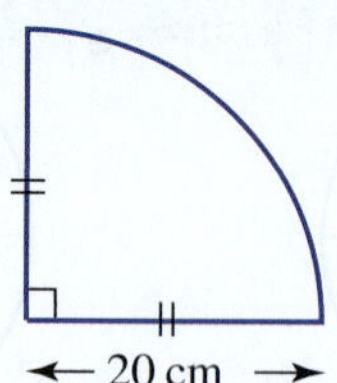

f
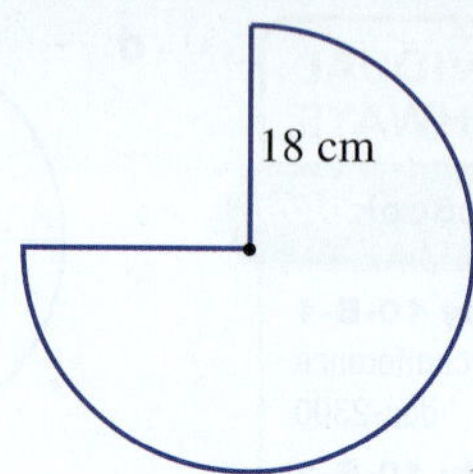

g
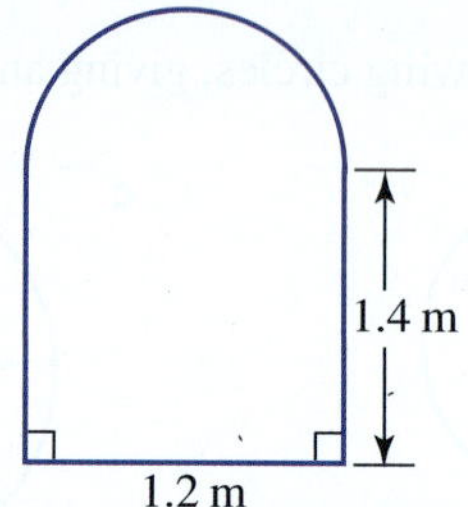

h
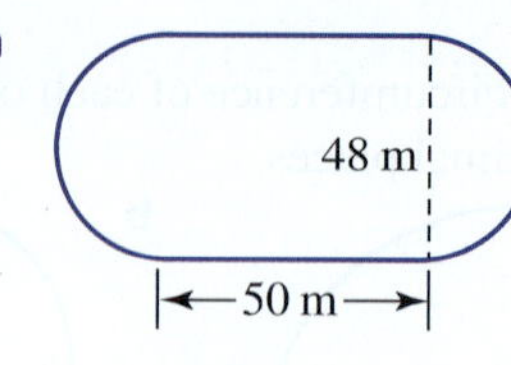

i
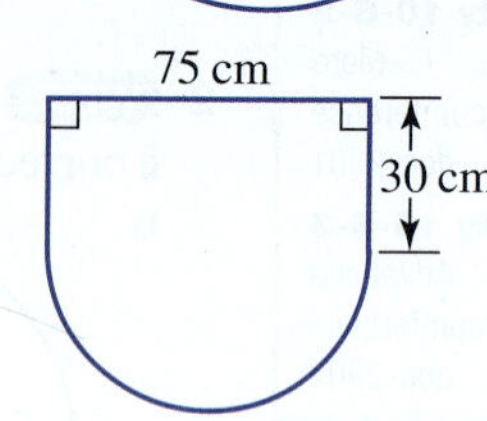

5 MC The circumference of a circle with a radius of 12 cm is:

A $\pi \times 12$ cm B $2 \times \pi \times 12$ cm C $2 \times \pi \times 24$ cm
D $\pi \times 6$ cm E $\pi \times 18$ cm

6 MC The circumference of a circle with a diameter of 55 m is:

A $2 \times \pi \times 55$ m B $\pi \times \frac{55}{2}$ m C $\pi \times 55$ m
D $\pi \times 110 \times 2$ m E $2 \times \pi \times 110$ m

UNDERSTANDING

7 In a Physics experiment, students spin a metal weight around on the end of a nylon thread. How far does the metal weight travel if it completes 10 revolutions on the end of a 0.88 m thread?

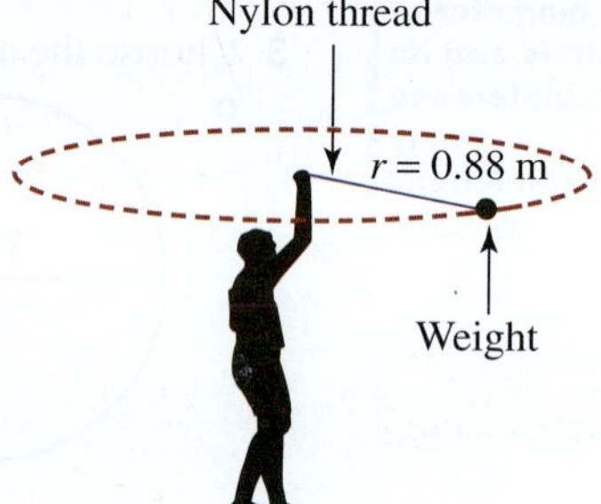

8 A scooter tyre has a diameter of 32 cm. What is the circumference of the tyre?

9 Find the circumference of the seaweed around the outside of this sushi roll.

10 Find the circumference of the Ferris wheel shown below.

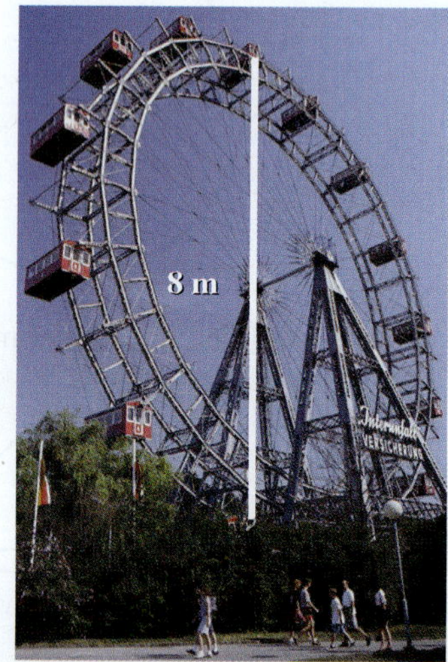

11 Calculate the diameter of a circle (correct to 2 decimal places where appropriate) with a circumference of:

a 18.84 m

b 64.81 cm

c 74.62 mm.

12 Calculate the radius of a circle (correct to 2 decimal places where appropriate) with a circumference of:

a 12.62 cm

b 47.35 m

c 157 mm.

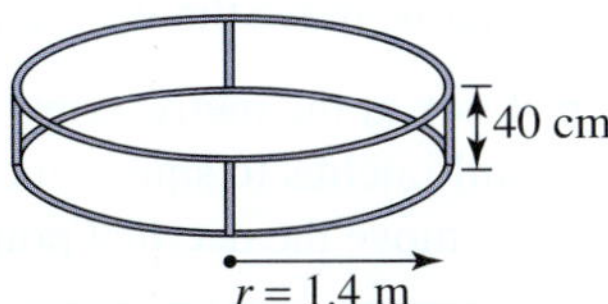

13 Calculate the radius of a tyre with a circumference of 135.56 cm.

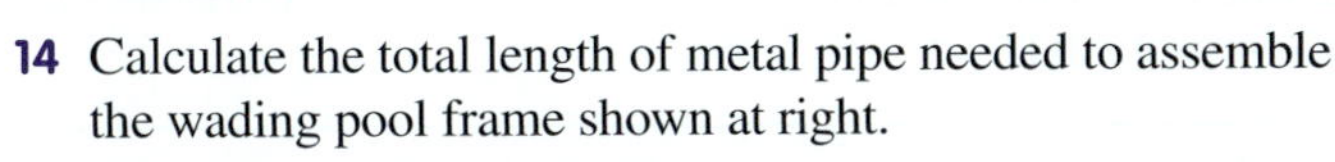

14 Calculate the total length of metal pipe needed to assemble the wading pool frame shown at right.

15 Nathan runs around the inside lane of a circular track that has a radius of 29 m. Rachel runs in the outer lane, which is 2.5 m further from the centre of the track. How much longer is the distance Rachel runs each lap?

REASONING

16 In *Around the world in eighty days* by Jules Verne, Phileas Fogg boasts that he can travel around the world in 80 days or fewer. This was in the 1800s, so he couldn't take a plane. What average speed is needed to go around the Earth at the equator in 80 days? Assume you travel for 12 hours each day and that the radius of the Earth is approximately 6390 km.

17 Liesel's bicycle covers 19 m in 10 revolutions of her bicycle wheel while Jared's bicycle covers 20 m in 8 revolutions of his bicycle wheel. What is the difference between the radii of the two bicycle wheels?

REFLECTION

If you needed to estimate the value of π using any round object, how would you do it?

10C Area of rectangles, triangles, parallelograms, rhombuses and kites

Area

- The area of a shape is the amount of flat surface enclosed by the shape.
- Area is measured in square units, such as square millimetres (mm^2), square centimetres (cm^2), square metres (m^2) and square kilometres (km^2)
- Area units can be converted using the chart below.

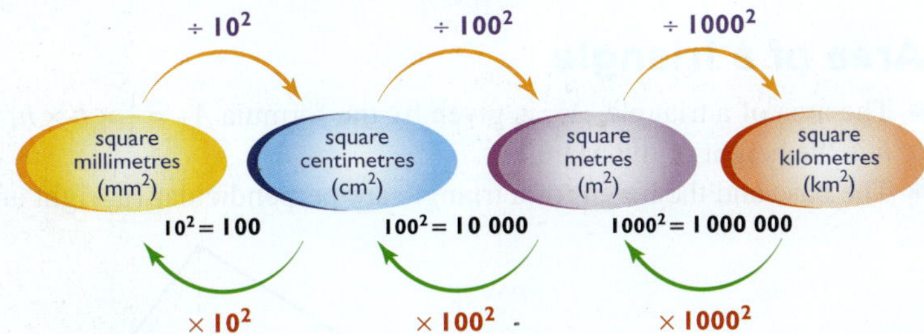

- Area units are the squares of those for the corresponding linear units.
- Large areas of land can be measured in hectares (ha). 1 ha = 10 000 m^2.

WORKED EXAMPLE 7

Complete the following metric conversions.

a $0.081 \text{ km}^2 =$ ______ m^2

b $19\,645 \text{ mm}^2 =$ ______ m^2

THINK	WRITE
a Look at the metric conversion chart. To convert square kilometres to square metres, multiply by 1 000 000; that is, move the decimal point 6 places to the right.	**a** $0.081 \text{ km}^2 = 0.081 \times 1\,000\,000 \text{ m}^2$ $= 81\,000 \text{ m}^2$
b Look at the metric conversion chart. To convert square millimetres to square metres, divide by 1 000 000; that is, move the decimal point 6 places to the left.	**b** $19\,645 \text{ mm}^2 = 19\,645 \div 1\,000\,000 \text{ m}^2$ $= 0.019\,645 \text{ m}^2$

Area of a rectangle

- The area of a rectangle can be found using the formula $A_R = l \times w$, where l is the length and w is the width of the rectangle.
- The area of a square can be found using the formula $A_S = l^2$, where l is the side length of the square.

WORKED EXAMPLE 8

Find the area of a rectangle with dimensions shown below.

8 cm

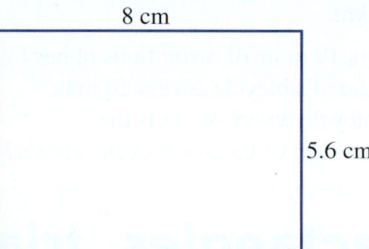

5.6 cm

THINK	WRITE
1 Write the formula for the area of a rectangle.	$A = l \times w$
2 Identify the values of l and w.	$l = 8$ and $w = 5.6$
3 Substitute the values of l and w into the formula and evaluate. Include the appropriate units.	$A = 8 \times 5.6$ $= 44.8 \text{ cm}^2$

Area of a triangle

- The area of a triangle, A_T, is given by the formula $A_T = \frac{1}{2} \times b \times h$, where b is the base and h is the height of the triangle.
- The base and the height of a triangle are perpendicular (at right angles) to each other.

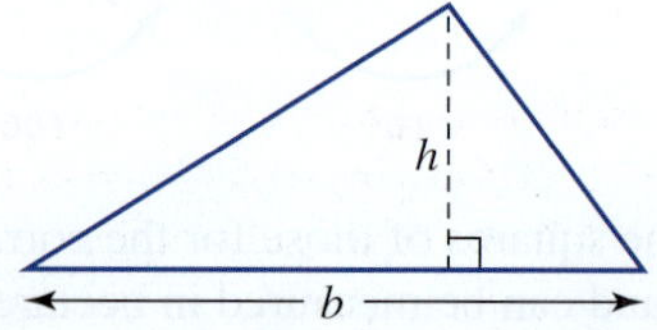

WORKED EXAMPLE 9

Find the area of each of these triangles in the smaller unit.

a

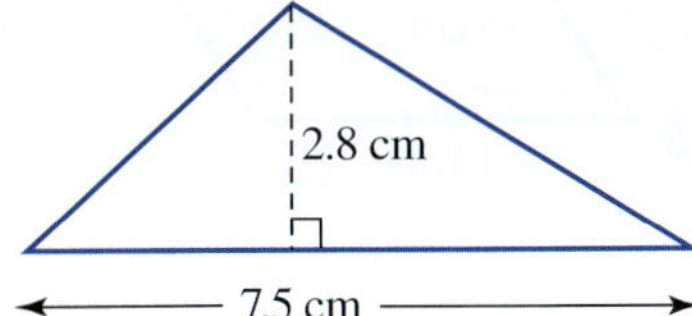

b

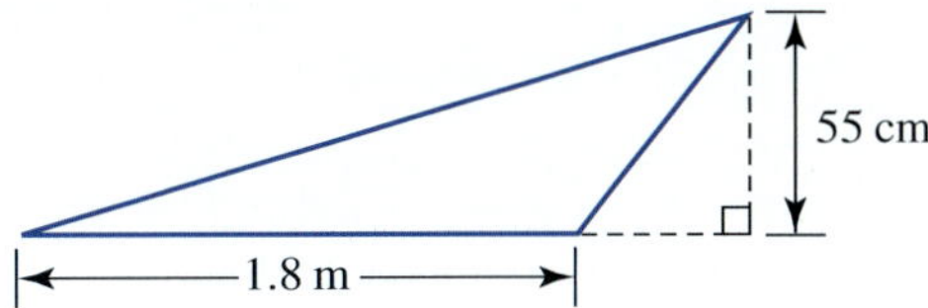

THINK		WRITE
a	1 Write the formula for the area of a triangle.	**a** $A = \frac{1}{2}bh$
	2 Identify the values of b and h.	$b = 7.5, h = 2.8$
	3 Substitute the values of b and h into the formula.	$A = \frac{1}{2} \times 7.5 \times 2.8$
	4 Evaluate. Remember to include the correct units (cm²).	$= 3.75 \times 2.8$ $= 10.5 \text{ cm}^2$
b	1 Write the formula for the area of a triangle.	**b** $A = \frac{1}{2}bh$
	2 Convert measurements to cm.	$1.8 \text{ m} = 1.8 \times 100 \text{ cm}$ $= 180 \text{ cm}$
	3 Identify the values of b and h.	$b = 180, h = 55$
	4 Substitute the values of b and h into the formula.	$A = \frac{1}{2} \times 180 \times 55$
	5 Evaluate. Remember to include the correct units (cm²).	$= 90 \times 55$ $= 4950 \text{ cm}^2$

Area of a parallelogram

eBook*plus*

Digital doc
Investigation
Area of a parallelogram
doc-2319

- A **parallelogram** is a quadrilateral with two pairs of parallel sides. Each pair is of equal length.
- It can be divided into two triangles by drawing a diagonal.
  In the parallelogram PQRS below, are ΔPQR and ΔRSP congruent?
  As their corresponding sides are of equal length, then $\Delta PQR \equiv \Delta RSP$ (SSS congruency condition).

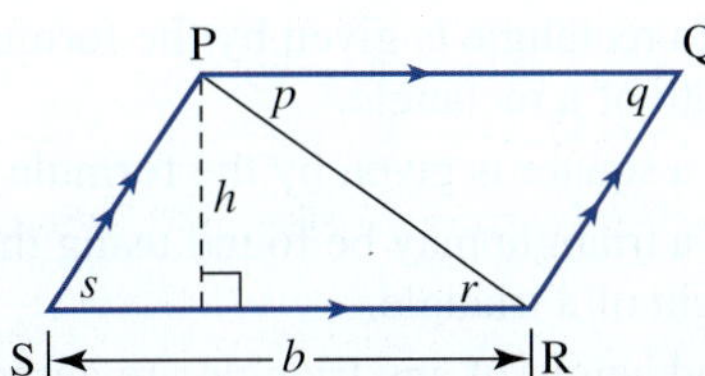

- As the area of a triangle is given as $A_T = \frac{1}{2} \times b \times h$, then the area of a parallelogram must be twice the area of each triangle, so A_P, area of a parallelogram is given by the formula $A_P = b \times h$, where b is the base and h is the height of a parallelogram.
- The base and the height of a parallelogram are perpendicular to each other.

WORKED EXAMPLE 10

Find the area of the parallelogram shown.

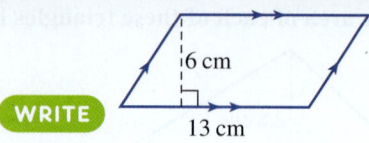

THINK	WRITE
1 Write the formula for the area of a parallelogram.	$A = bh$
2 Identify the values of b and h.	$b = 13, h = 6$
3 Substitute 6 for h and 13 for b.	$A = 13 \times 6$
4 Multiply the numbers together and include the correct units.	$= 78 \text{ cm}^2$

Area of a rhombus

- A **rhombus** is a parallelogram with all four sides of equal length and each pair of opposite sides parallel.
- The area of a rhombus, A_{RH}, is given as $A_{RH} = b \times h$.

Area of a kite

- A **kite** is a quadrilateral with two pairs of equal, adjacent sides and one pair of equal angles.
- The area of a kite can be determined by dividing the kite into two equal triangles and using the formula for the area of a triangle.

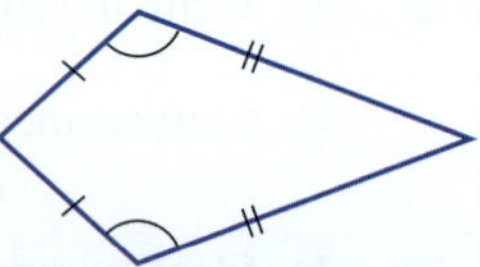

REMEMBER

1. The area of a shape is the amount of flat surface enclosed by the shape.
2. Area is measured in units based on the square metre, as shown in this conversion chart.

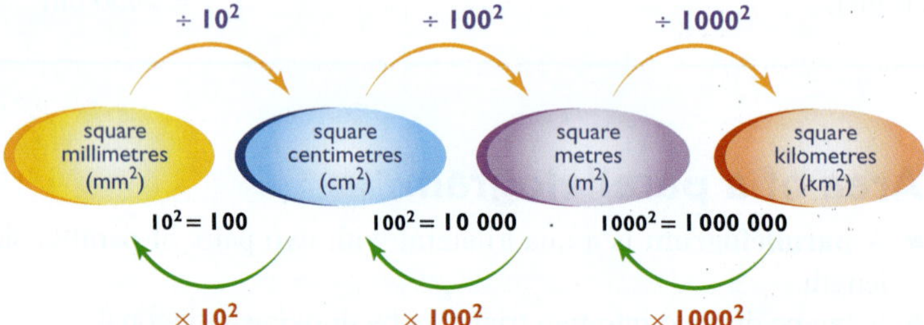

Recall $10\,000 \text{ m}^2 = 1$ hectare
$= 1$ ha

Note: The conversion is the square of the equivalent linear conversion.

3. The area of a rectangle is given by the formula $A = l \times w$, where l is the length and w is the width of a rectangle.
4. The area of a square is given by the formula $A = l^2$.
5. The area of a triangle may be found using the rule $A = \frac{1}{2}bh$, where b is the base and h is the height of a triangle.
6. The base and height of any triangle are perpendicular to each other.
7. A parallelogram is a quadrilateral with two pairs of parallel sides.
8. The area of a parallelogram is given by the formula $A = bh$, where b is the length of the base of the parallelogram and h is its vertical height.
9. The base and the height of any parallelogram are perpendicular to each other.

EXERCISE **10C**

Area of rectangles, triangles, parallelograms, rhombuses and kites

INDIVIDUAL PATHWAYS

eBook*plus*

Activity 10-C-1
Area of rectangles, triangles and parallelograms
doc-2303

Activity 10-C-2
More area of rectangles, triangles and parallelograms
doc-2304

Activity 10-C-3
Advanced area of rectangles, triangles and parallelograms
doc-2305

FLUENCY

1 WE7 Complete the following metric conversions.

a $0.53\ \text{km}^2 = $ ________ m^2
b $235\ \text{mm}^2 = $ ________ cm^2
c $2540\ \text{cm}^2 = $ ________ mm^2
d $542\,000\ \text{cm}^2 = $ ________ m^2
e $74\,000\ \text{mm}^2 = $ ________ m^2
f $3\,000\,000\ \text{m}^2 = $ ________ km^2
g $98\,563\ \text{m}^2 = $ ________ ha
h $1.78\ \text{ha} = $ ________ m^2
i $0.987\ \text{m}^2 = $ ________ mm^2
j $0.000\,127\,5\ \text{km}^2 = $ ________ cm^2

2 WE8 Find the area of each of the rectangles below.

a
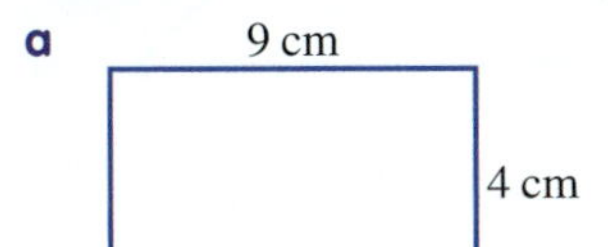

b
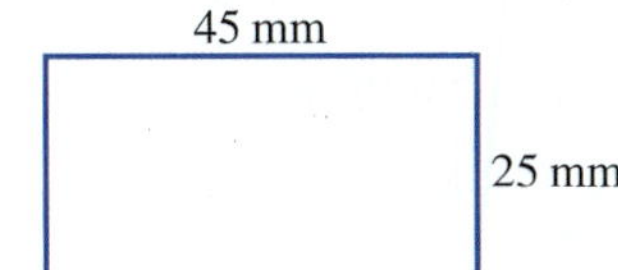

c
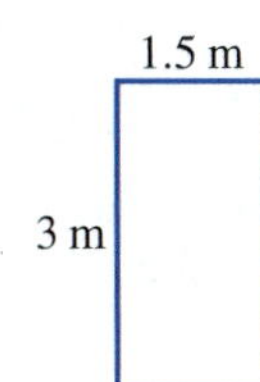

d
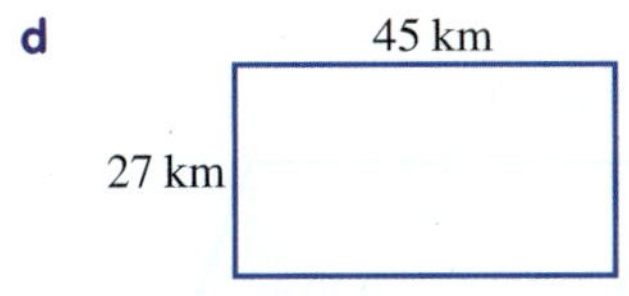

e
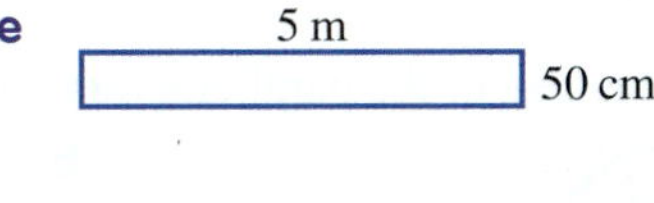

f
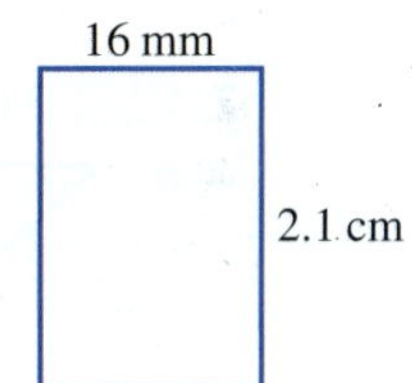

3 Find the area of each of the squares below.

a
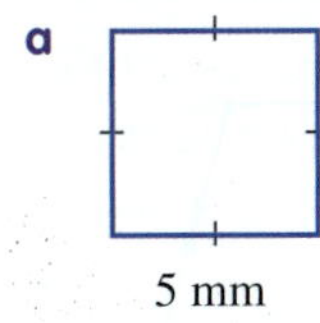

b
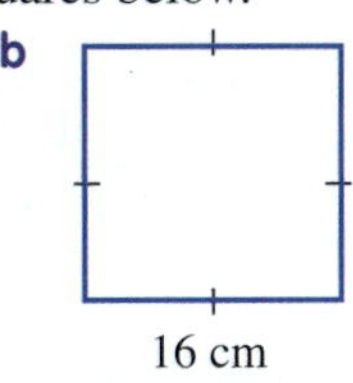

c
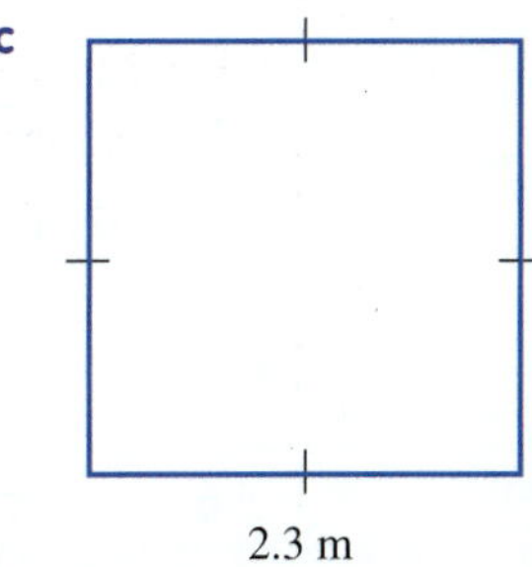

Questions **4** and **5** relate to the diagram at right.

62 mm
134 mm
32 mm
187 mm

4 MC The height and base respectively of the triangle are:

A 32 mm and 62 mm
B 32 mm and 134 mm
C 32 mm and 187 mm
D 62 mm and 187 mm
E 134 mm and 187 mm

5 MC The area of the triangle is:

A 2992 mm
B $2992\ \text{mm}^2$
C 5984 mm
D $5984\ \text{mm}^2$
E $6128\ \text{mm}^2$

6 WE9 Find the area of the following triangles in smaller units.

a
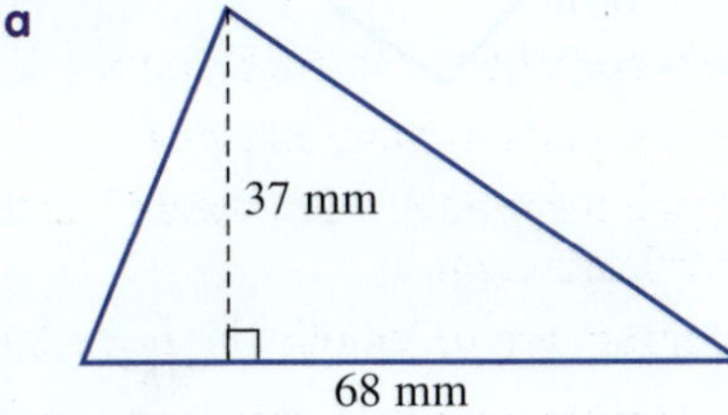

b
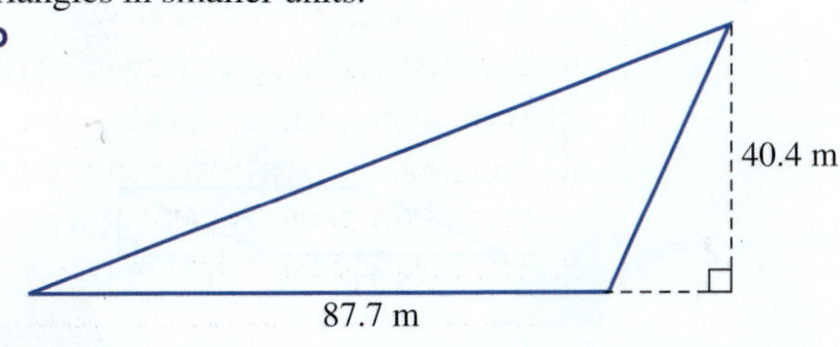

c

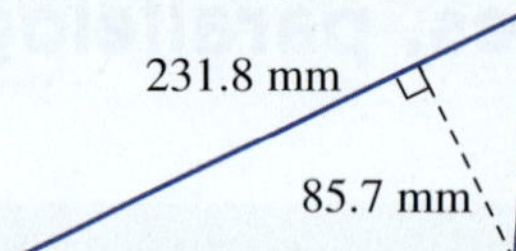

d

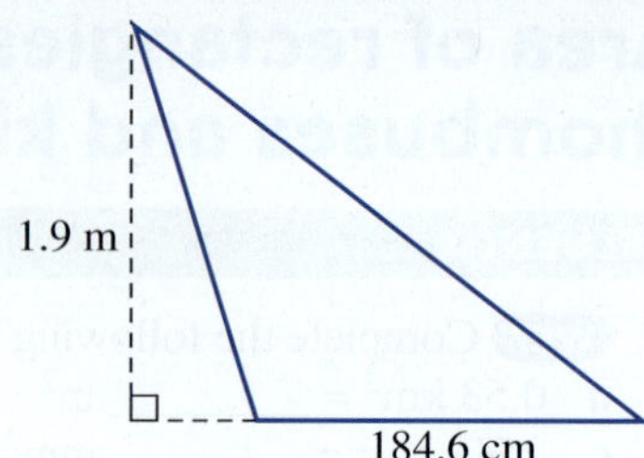

e

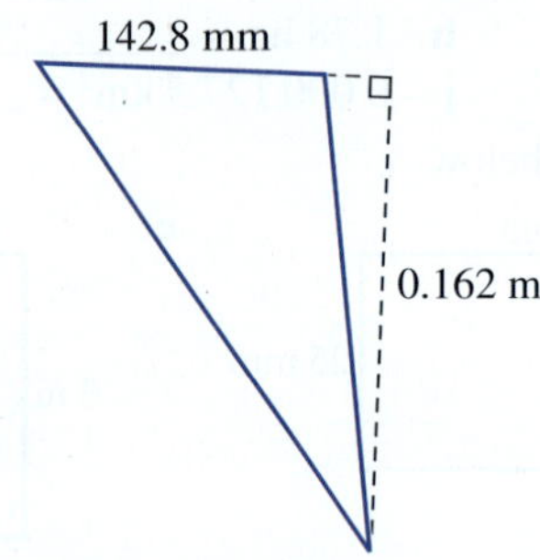

f

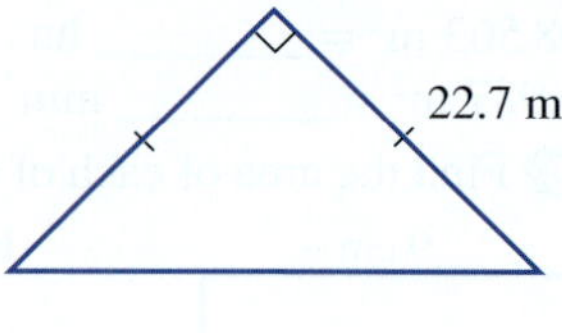

7 WE10 Find the area of the parallelograms shown below.

a

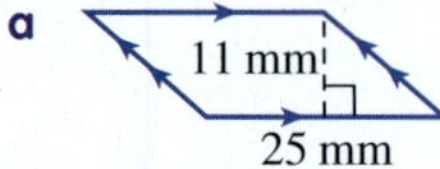

b

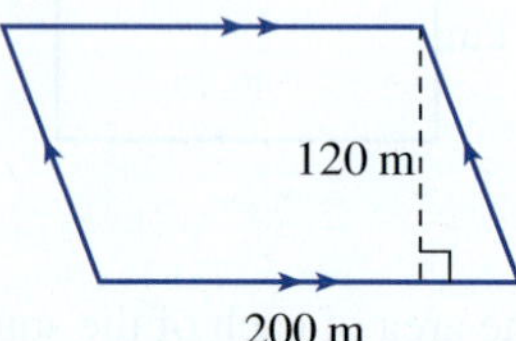

c

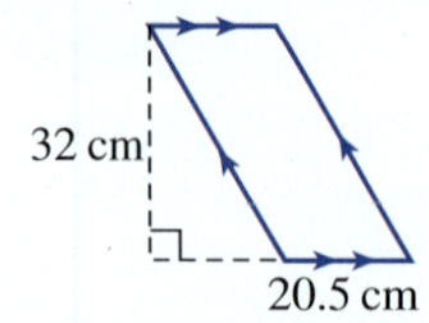

d

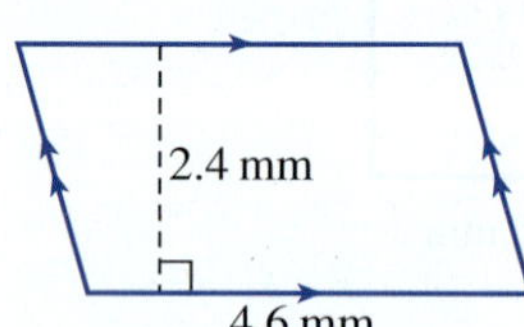

e

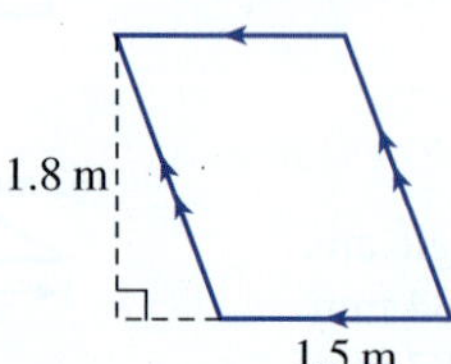

f

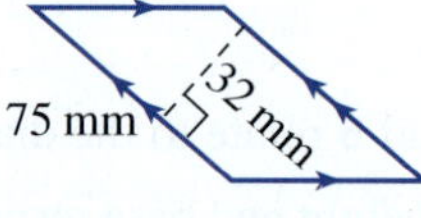

g

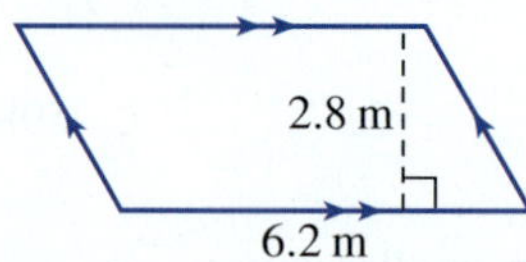

h

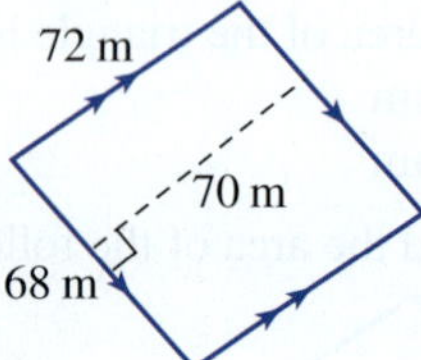

i

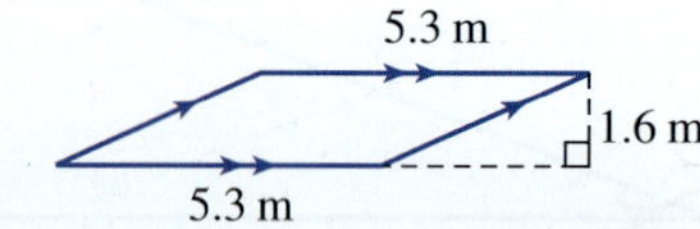

UNDERSTANDING

8 Zorko has divided his vegetable patch, which is in the shape of a regular (all sides equal) pentagon, into 3 sections as shown in the diagram at right.

a Calculate the area of each individual section, correct to 2 decimal places.

b Calculate the area of the vegetable patch, correct to 2 decimal places.

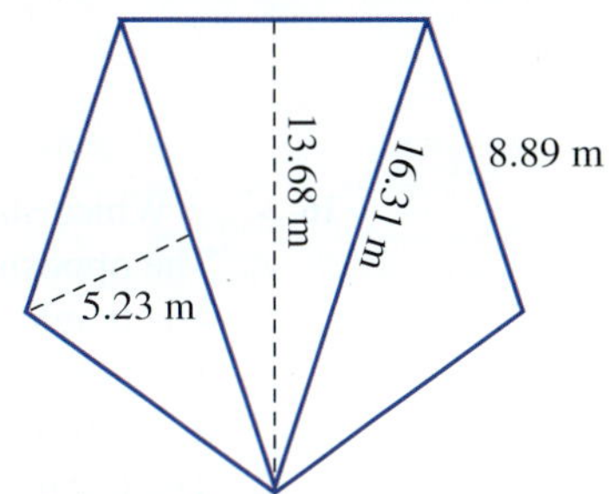

9 Find the area of the triangle used to rack up the billiard balls at right.

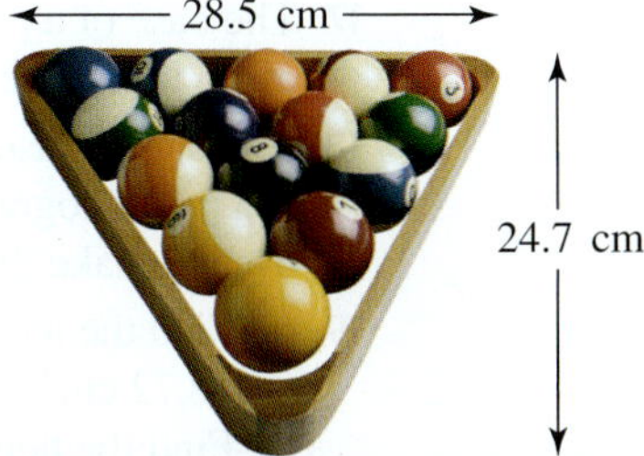

10 The pyramid at right has 4 identical triangular faces with the dimensions shown. Calculate:

a the area of one of the triangular faces

b the total area of the 4 faces.

150 m

200 m

11 Georgia is planning to create a feature wall in her lounge room by painting it a different colour. The wall is 4.6 m wide and 3.4 m high.

a Calculate the area of the wall to be painted.

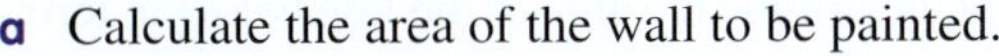

b Georgia knows that a 4 litre can of paint is sufficient to cover 12 square metres of wall. How many cans must she purchase if she needs to apply two coats of paint?

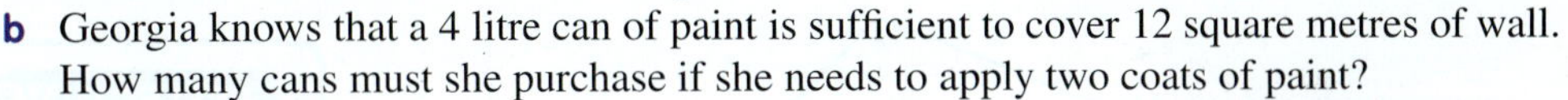

12 Calculate the base length of the give-way sign at right.

13 **a** Calculate the width of a rectangular sportsground if it has an area of 30 ha and a length of 750 m.

b The watering system at the sportsground covers 8000 square metres in 10 minutes. How long does it take to water the sportsground?

14 Find the area of gold braid needed to make the four military stripes shown.

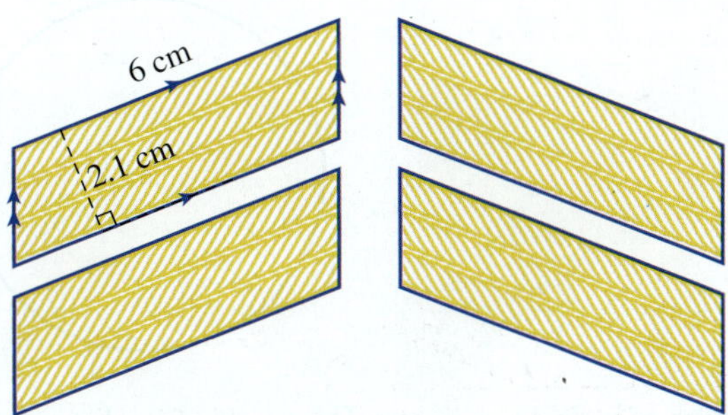

15 What is the area of the block of land in the figure at right?

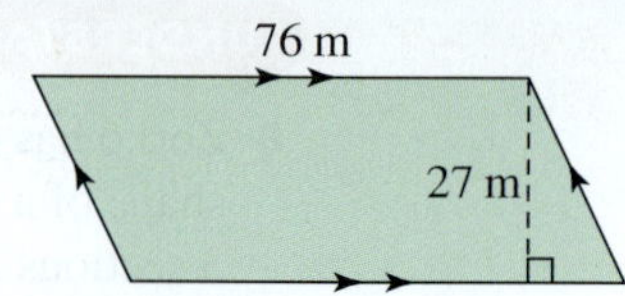

16 MC Which statement about a parallelogram is false?

A The opposite sides of a parallelogram are parallel.
B The height of the parallelogram is perpendicular to its base.
C The area of a parallelogram is equal to the area of the rectangle whose length is the same as the base and whose width is the same as the height of the parallelogram.
D The perimeter of the parallelogram is given by the formula $P = 2(b + h)$.
E The area of a parallelogram is given by the formula $A = bh$.

17 The base of a parallelogram is 3 times as long as its height. Find the area of the parallelogram, given that its height is 2.4 cm long.

18 A designer vase has a square base of side length 12 cm and four identical sides, each of which is a parallelogram. If the vertical height of the vase is 30 cm, find the total area of the glass used to make this vase. (Assume no waste and do not forget to include the base.)

19 **a** Find the length of the base of a parallelogram whose height is 5.2 cm and whose area is 18.72 cm^2.
b Find the height of a parallelogram whose base is 7.5 cm long and whose area is 69 cm^2.

20 The length of the base of a parallelogram is equal to its height. If the area of the parallelogram is 90.25 cm^2, find its dimensions.

eBook*plus*

Weblink
Area of a rhombus

REASONING

21 If the diagonals of a rhombus bisect each other and intersect at right angles, use mathematical reasoning to show and explain that $A_{RH} = \frac{1}{2} \times x \times y$, where x and y are the lengths of the diagonals of the rhombus.

22 Using mathematical reasoning, determine the area of the kite below in terms of a and b.

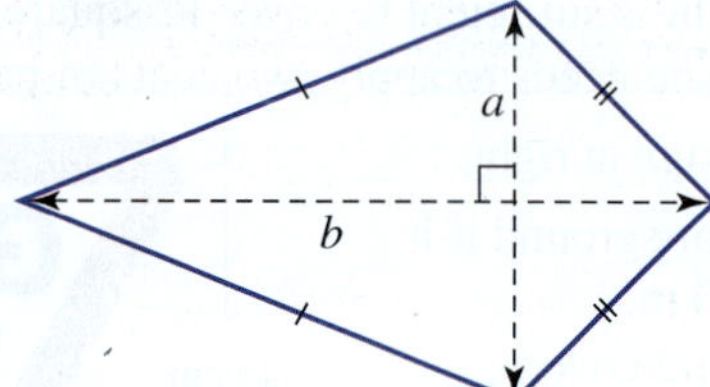

REFLECTION
Why is it important to know that the height and the base of any triangle and any parallelogram are perpendicular?

10D Area of a circle

eBook*plus*

Digital doc
Investigation
Area of a circle
doc-2321

- The area of a circle, A, can be found using the formula $A = \pi r^2$, where r is the radius of the circle.

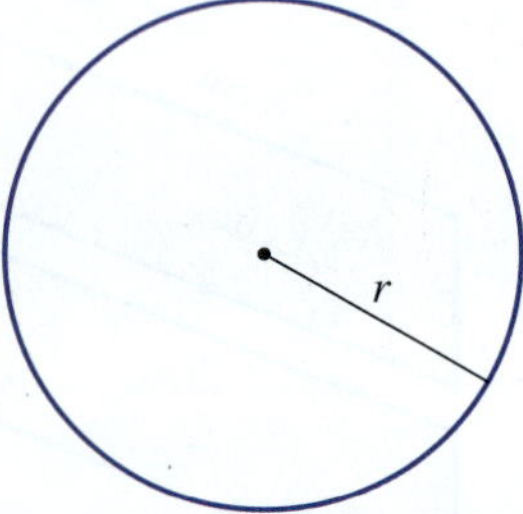

- The radius of a circle, r, is equal to a half of its diameter, D: $r = \frac{D}{2}$.

WORKED EXAMPLE 11

Find the area of each of the following circles.

a

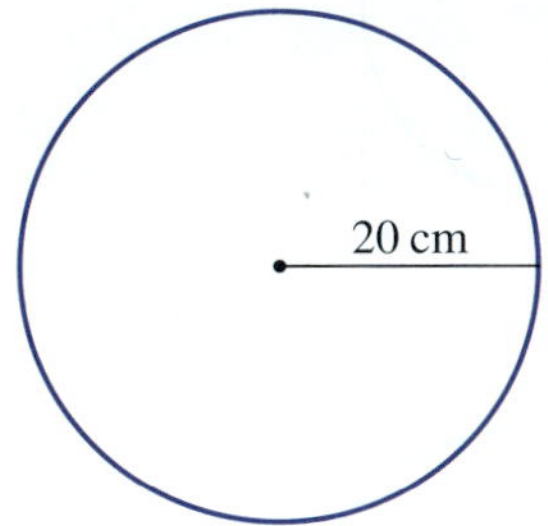

b

18 cm

THINK / **WRITE**

a
1. Write the formula for the area of a circle. — $A = \pi r^2$
2. Substitute 20 for r and 3.14 for π. — $A = 3.14 \times 20^2$
3. Evaluate (square the radius first) and include the correct units. — $= 3.14 \times 400$
   $= 1256\text{ cm}^2$

b
1. Write the formula for the area of a circle. — $A = \pi r^2$
2. We need radius, but are given the diameter. State the relation between the radius and the diameter. — $D = 18;\ r = D \div 2$
3. Halve the value of the diameter to get the radius. — $r = 18 \div 2$
   $= 9$
4. Substitute 9 for r and 3.14 for π. — $A = 3.14 \times 9^2$
   $= 3.14 \times 81$
5. Evaluate (square the radius first) and include the correct units. — $= 254.34\text{ cm}^2$

REMEMBER

1. The area of a circle is given by the formula $A = \pi r^2$, where r is the radius of a circle and π has an approximate value of 3.14.
2. The radius of a circle, r, is equal to a half of its diameter, D: $r = \dfrac{D}{2}$.

EXERCISE 10D Area of a circle

INDIVIDUAL PATHWAYS

eBook*plus*

Activity 10-D-1
Area of a circle
doc-2306

Activity 10-D-2
More circles
doc-2307

Activity 10-D-3
Advanced calculations involving areas of circles
doc-2308

FLUENCY

1 WE11 Find the area of each of the following circles.

a

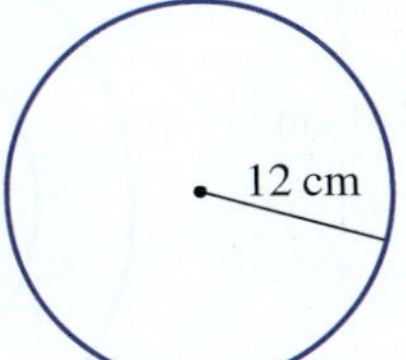

b

2.5 km

c

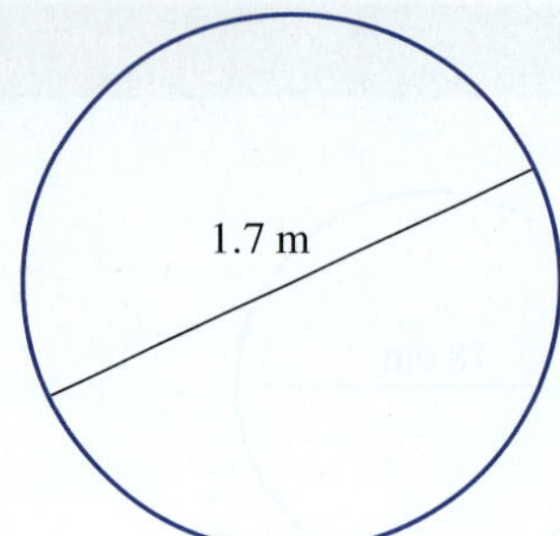

d

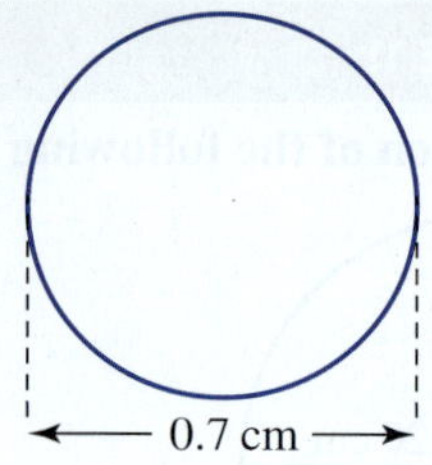

e

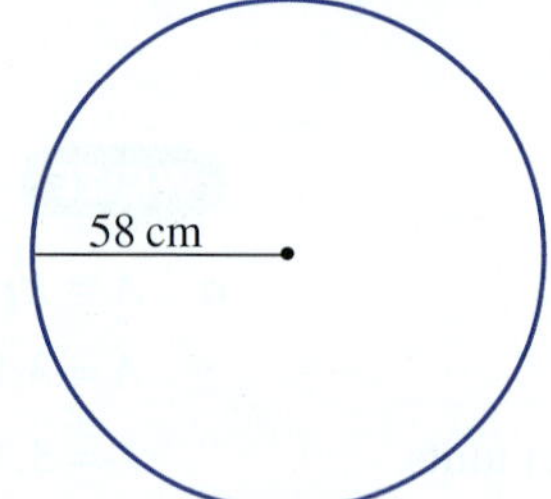

f

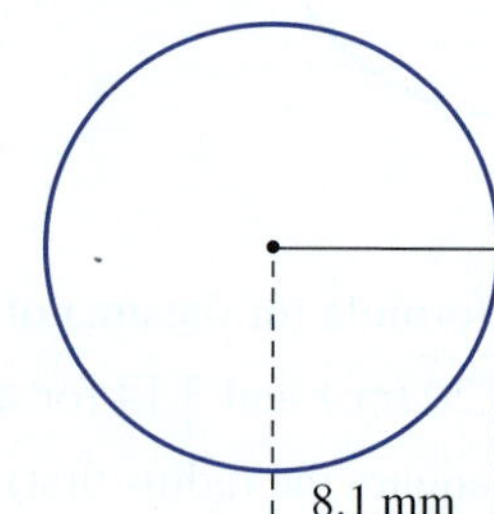

2 Find the area of:

a a circle of radius 5 cm

b a circle of radius 12.4 mm

c a circle of diameter 28 m

d a circle of diameter 18 cm.

UNDERSTANDING

3 The word **annulus** is the Latin word for *ring*. An annulus is the shape formed between two circles with a common centre (called concentric circles). To find the area of an annulus, calculate the area of the smaller circle and subtract it from the area of the larger circle. Find the area of the annulus for the following sets of concentric circles.

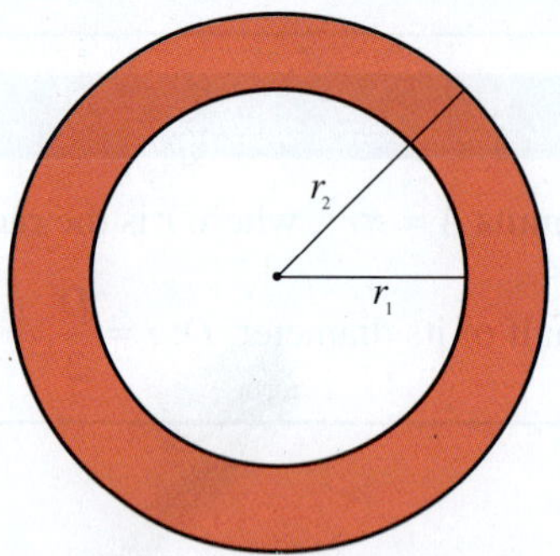

An annulus is the shaded area between the concentric circles.

r_1 = radius of smaller circle
r_2 = radius of larger circle
$\text{Area}_{\text{annulus}} = \pi r_2^2 - \pi r_1^2$

a

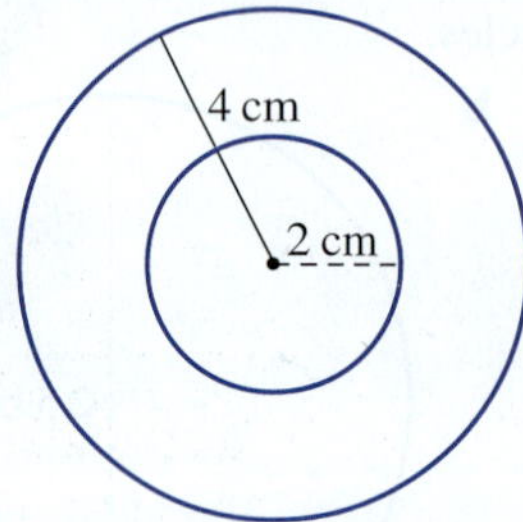

b

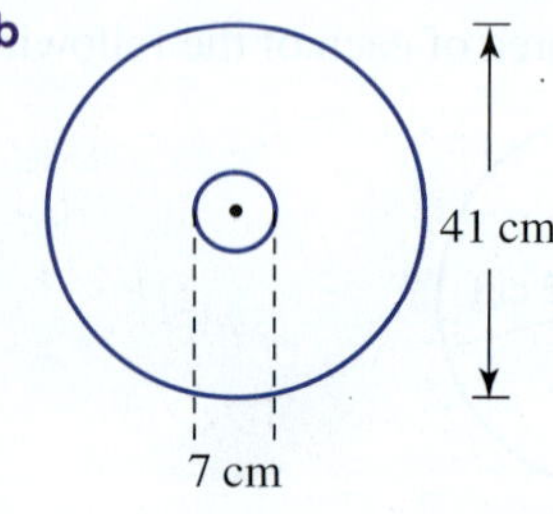

c

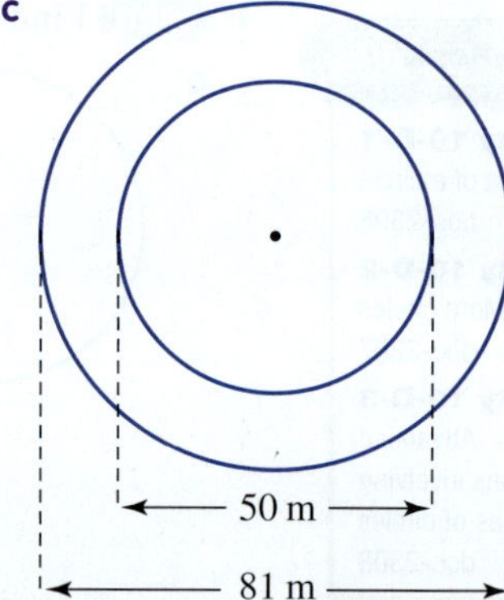

4 Find the area of each of the following shapes.

a

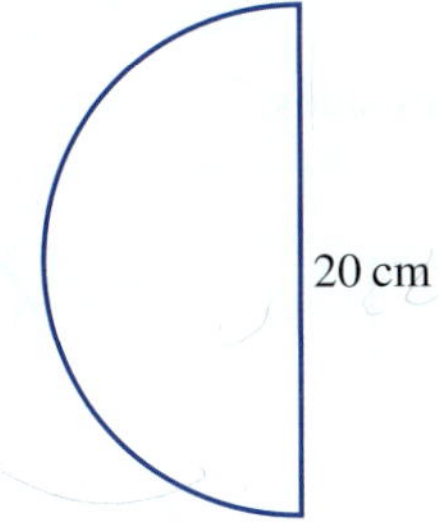

b

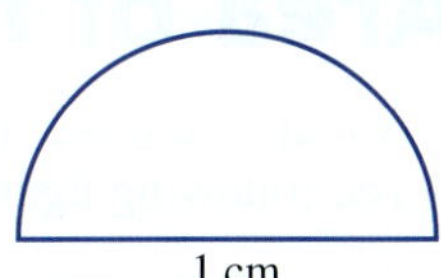

c

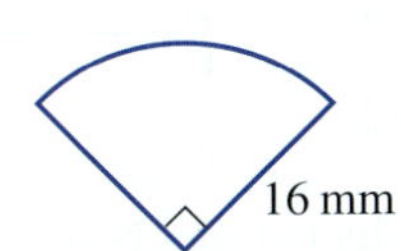

d

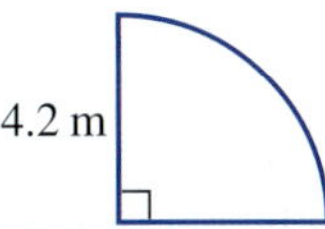

e

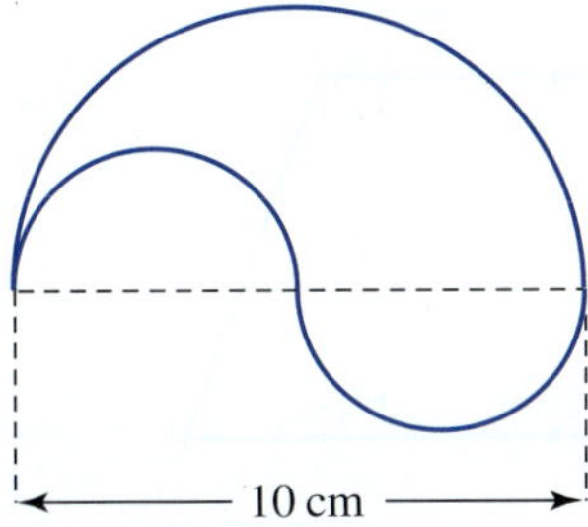

f

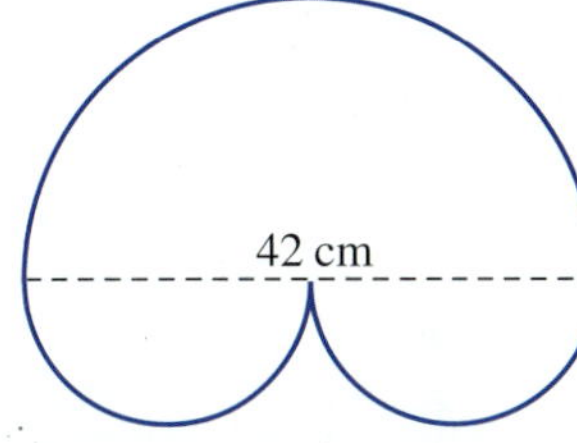

g

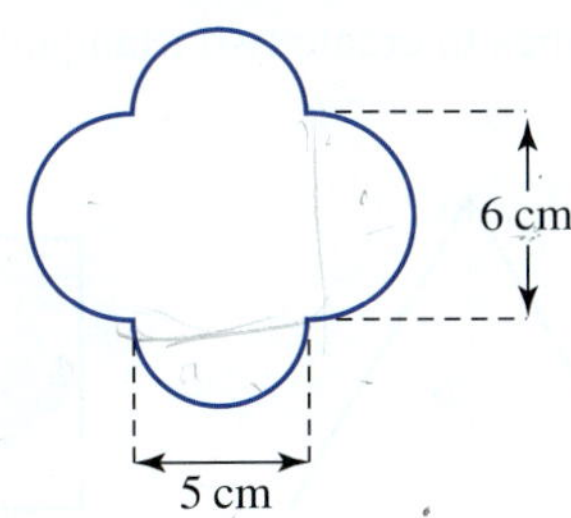

h

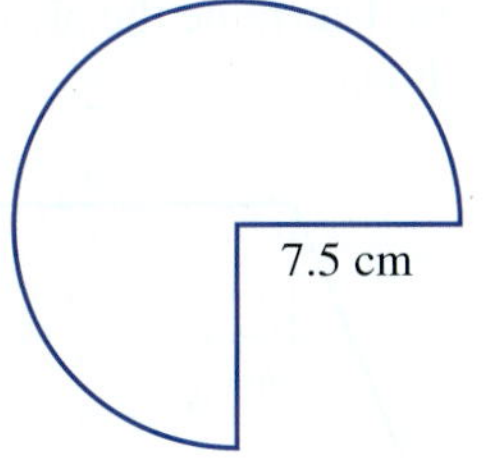

i

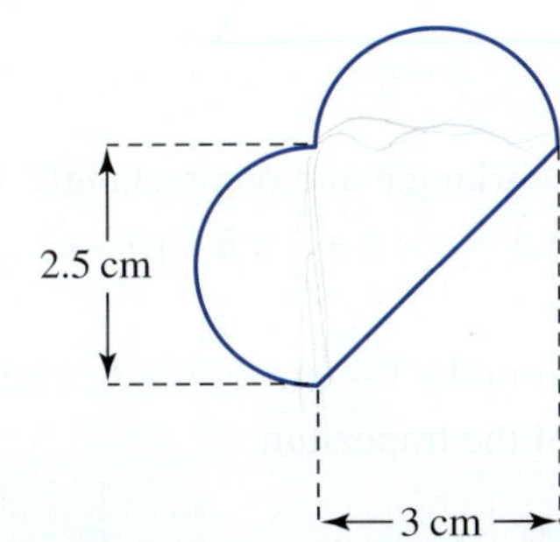

5 Find the minimum area of aluminium foil that could be used to cover the top of the circular tray with diameter 38 cm.

6 What is the area of material in a circular mat of diameter 2.4 m?

7 How many packets of lawn seed should Joanne buy to sow a circular bed of diameter 27 m, if each packet of seed covers 23 m^2?

8 A landscape gardener wishes to spread fertiliser on a semicircular garden bed that has a diameter of 4.7 m. How much fertiliser is required if the fertiliser is applied at the rate of 20 g per square metre?

REFLECTION

Think of a way to remember the difference between the formula for the circumference and that for the area of a circle.

10E Area of trapeziums

eBook*plus*

Digital doc
Investigation
Area of a trapezium
doc-2320

- A **trapezium** is a quadrilateral with one pair of parallel sides. The following figures are all trapeziums.

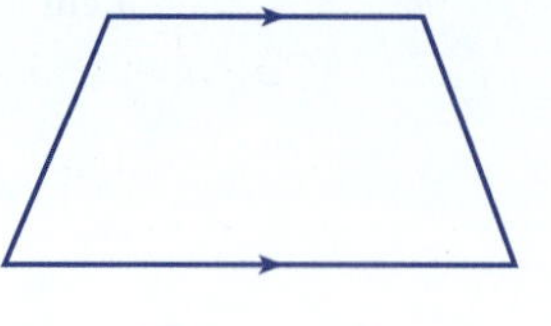
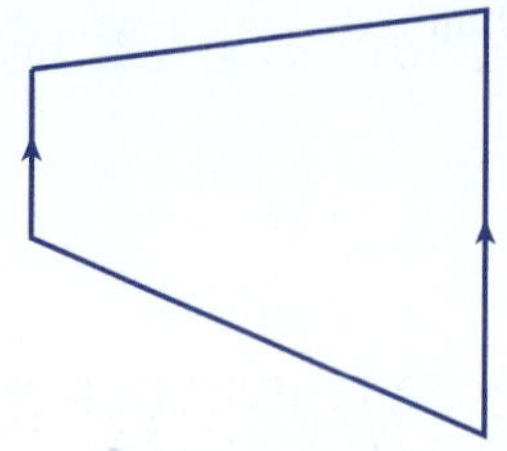
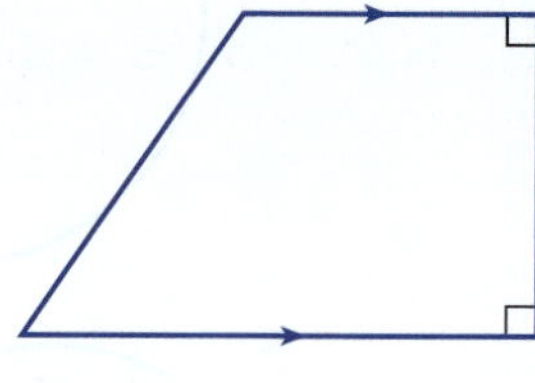

- The height of the trapezium is perpendicular to each of its parallel bases.

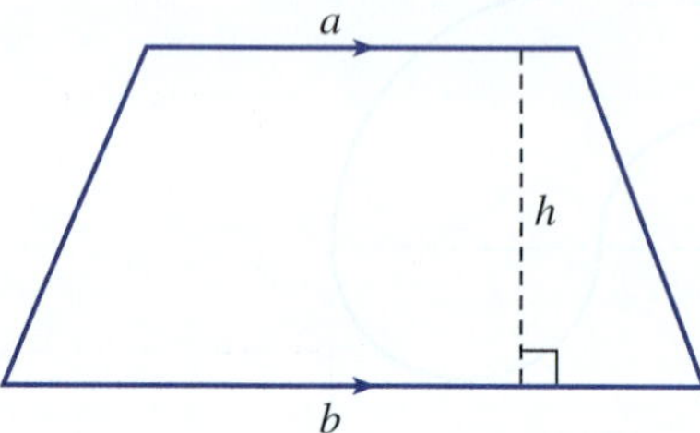

To determine the area of a trapezium, draw two lines to create two triangles and one rectangle as shown.

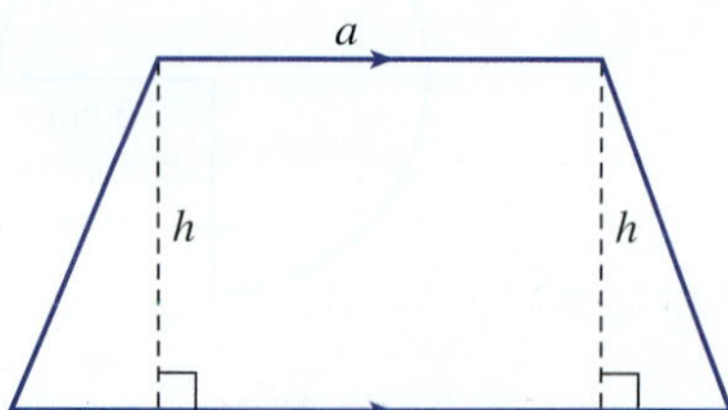

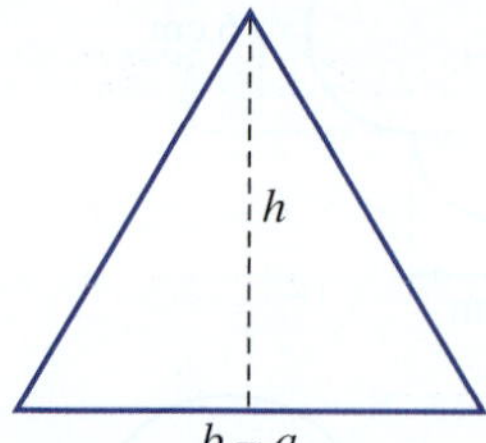

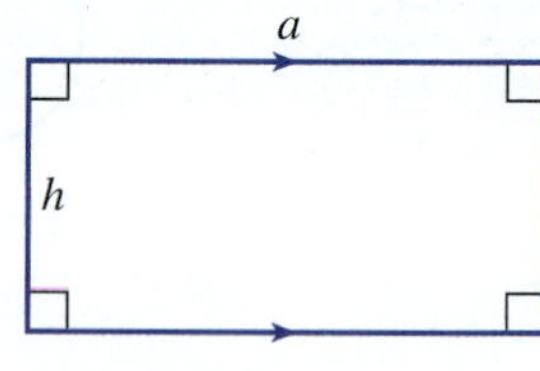

Placing the two triangles together creates one triangle and one rectangle.
The total area of the two shapes, A, will give $A = a \times h + \frac{1}{2} \times h \times (b - a)$.
Simplifying this gives $A = \frac{1}{2}(a + b) \times h$.

- The area of a trapezium, A, is given by the formula $A = \frac{1}{2}(a + b) \times h$, where a and b are the lengths of parallel sides and h is the height of the trapezium.

WORKED EXAMPLE 12

Find the area of the trapezium at right.

6 cm
4 cm
10 cm

THINK	WRITE
1 Write the formula for the area of the trapezium.	$A = \frac{1}{2}(a + b) \times h$

2	Identify the values of a, b and h. *Note:* It does not matter which of the parallel sides is a and which one is b, since we will need to add them together.	$a = 10$, $b = 6$ and $h = 4$
3	Substitute the values of a, b and h into the formula.	$A = \frac{1}{2} \times (10 + 6) \times 4$
4	Evaluate (work out the brackets first) and include the correct units.	$A = \frac{1}{2} \times 16 \times 4$ $= 32 \text{ cm}^2$

REMEMBER

The area of a trapezium is given by the formula $A = \frac{1}{2}(a + b) \times h$, where a and b are parallel sides and h is the height of a trapezium.

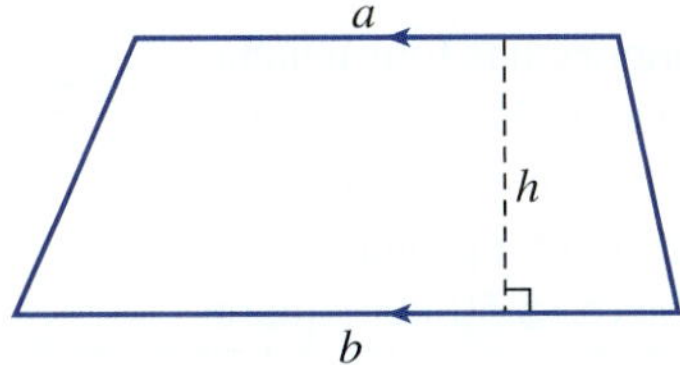

The height of the trapezium is always perpendicular to the parallel sides.

EXERCISE

10E Area of trapeziums

INDIVIDUAL PATHWAYS

eBook*plus*

Activity 10-E-1
Area of a trapezium
doc-2309

Activity 10-E-2
More trapeziums
doc-2310

Activity 10-E-3
Advanced trapeziums
doc-2311

FLUENCY

1 WE12 Find the area of each of the following trapeziums.

a 3 cm; 2 cm; 6 cm

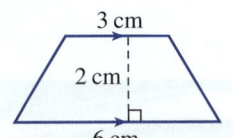

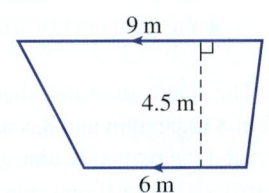

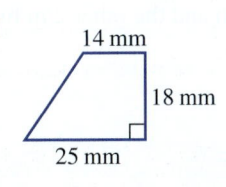

b 9 m; 4.5 m; 6 m

c 5.0 m; 3.0 m; 3.5 m

d 14 mm; 18 mm; 25 mm

e

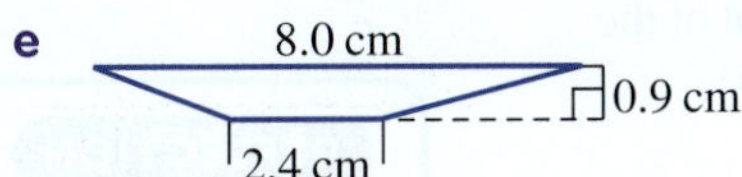

f

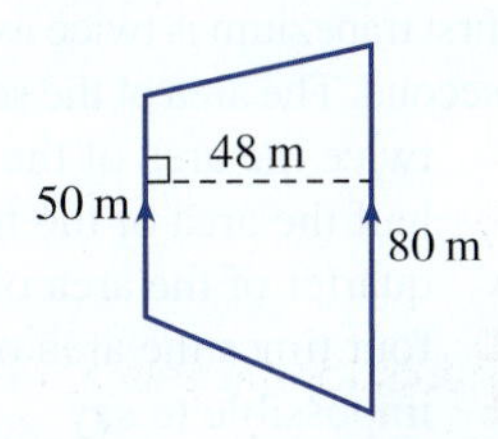

2 MC Which of the following is the correct way to calculate the area of the trapezium shown?

A $\frac{1}{2} \times (3 + 5) \times 11$ **B** $\frac{1}{2} \times (3 + 5 + 11)$ **C** $\frac{1}{2} \times (11 - 3) \times 5$
D $\frac{1}{2} \times (11 + 5) \times 3$ **E** $\frac{1}{2} \times (3 + 11) \times 5$

3 cm
5 cm
11 cm

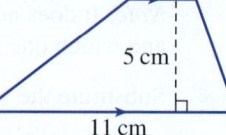

UNDERSTANDING

3 A dress pattern contains these two pieces.

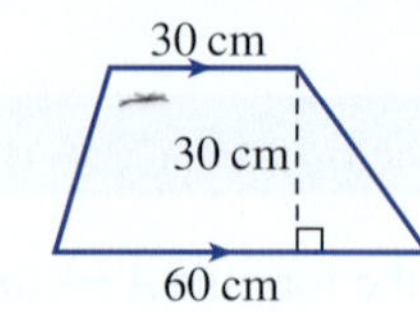

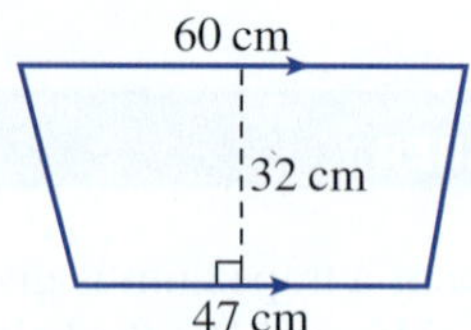

Find the total area of material needed to make both pieces.

4 A science laboratory has four benches with the dimensions shown at right.

What would be the cost of covering all four benches with a protective coating that costs $38.50 per square metre?

0.84 m
0.39 m
2.1 m

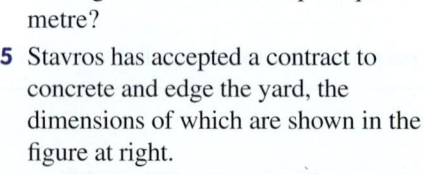

5 Stavros has accepted a contract to concrete and edge the yard, the dimensions of which are shown in the figure at right.

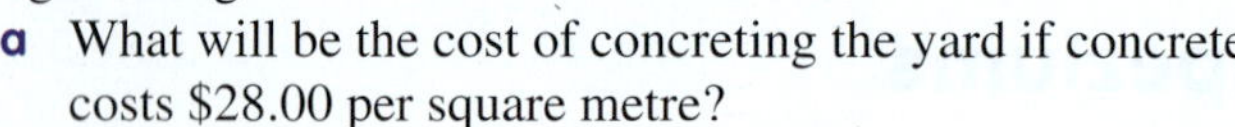

a What will be the cost of concreting the yard if concrete costs $28.00 per square metre?

b The yard must be surrounded by edging strips, which cost $8.25 per metre. Find:

i the cost of the edging strips

ii the total cost of materials for the job.

12.4 m
10 m
9.2 m
8.8 m

6 The side wall of this shed is in the shape of a trapezium and has an area of 4.6 m^2. Find the perpendicular distance between the parallel sides if one side of the wall is 2.6 m high and the other 2 m high.

eBook*plus*

Digital doc
WorkSHEET 10.1
doc-2322

7 MC Two trapeziums have corresponding parallel sides of equal length. The height of the first trapezium is twice as large as the height of the second. The area of the second trapezium is:

A twice the area of the first trapezium
B half the area of the first trapezium
C quarter of the area of the first trapezium
D four times the area of the first trapezium
E impossible to say

REFLECTION

Can you think of a strategy to help you remember the formula for finding the area of a trapezium?

10F Volume of prisms and other solids

Volume

- Volume is the amount of space inside a three-dimensional object.
- Volume is measured in cubic units such as mm^3, cm^3 or m^3.
- Volume units can be converted using the chart below.

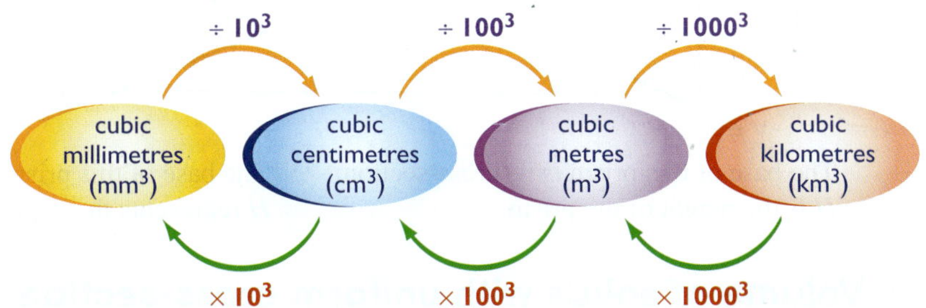

Prisms

- Prisms are solid shapes with identical opposite ends joined by straight edges. They are three-dimensional objects that can be cut into identical 'slices', called cross-sections.
- Prisms are named according to the shape of their cross-section. The objects below are all prisms.

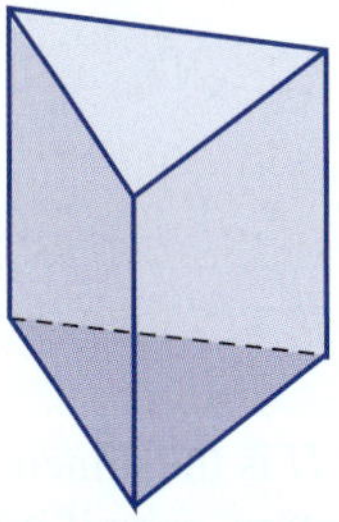
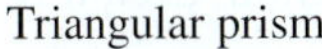
Triangular prism

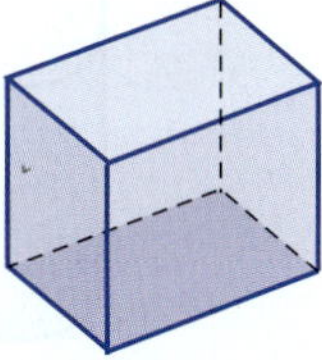
Rectangular prism

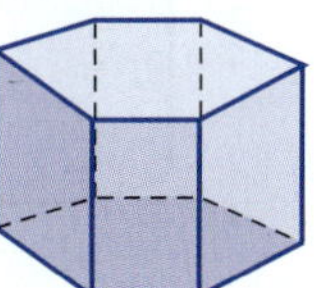
Hexagonal prism

- Objects that do not have a uniform cross-section can not be classified as prisms. For example, the objects below are not prisms.

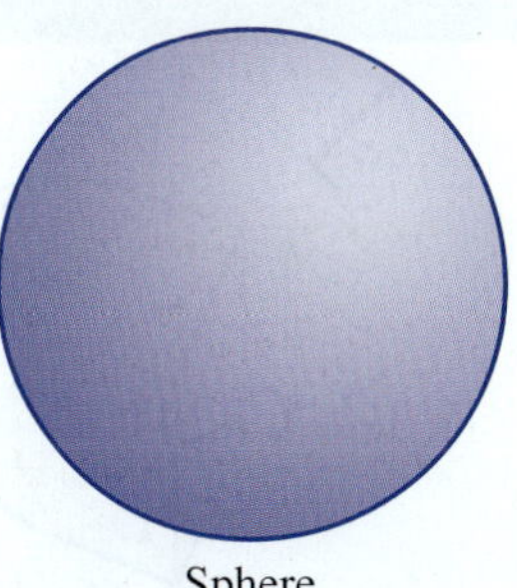
Sphere

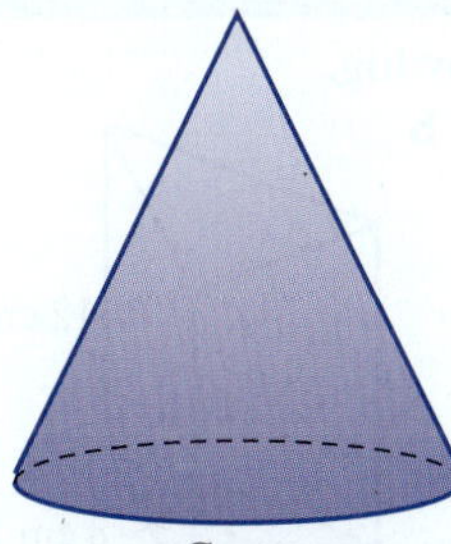
Cone

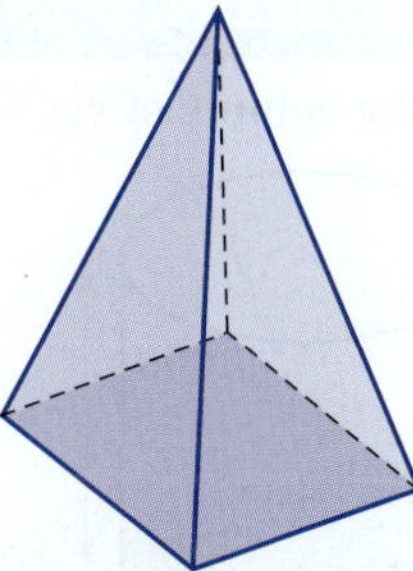
Square pyramid

- The volume of a rectangular prism is given by the formula $V = lwh$, where l is the length, w is the width and h is the height of the prism.
- A rectangular prism can be cut to form two equal triangular prisms.
- The volume of a cube is given by the formula $V = l^3$, where l is the side length of a cube.
- The volume of any prism is given by the formula $V = A \times H$, where A is the cross-sectional area of a prism and H is the height of a prism.

- The height of the prism is not necessarily the height of the object in a true sense of the word. It is just the dimension perpendicular to the cross-section.

eBook*plus*

Interactivity
Volumes of prisms
int-2754

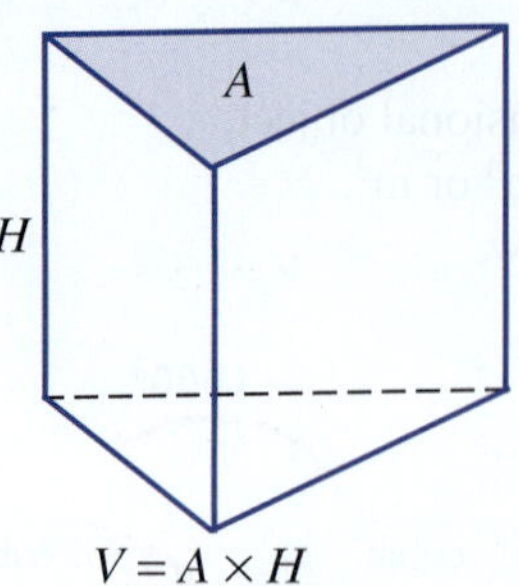

The base of this prism *is* its cross-section; H *is* the height of the prism.

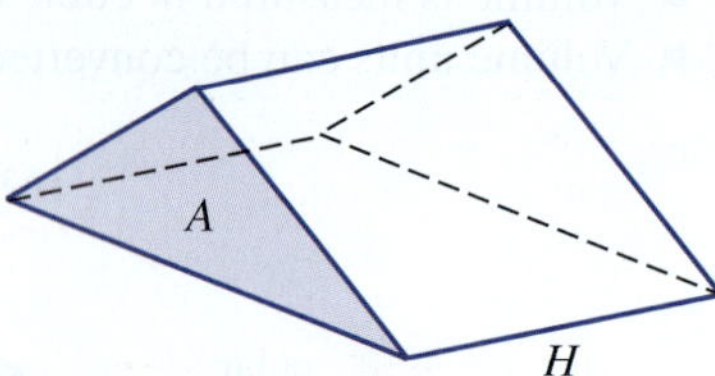

The base of this prism *is not* its cross-section; H represents the depth (or length) of the prism.

Volume of solids with uniform cross-section that are not prisms

- The objects with a uniform cross-section, whose ends are not joined by straight edges, can not be classified as prisms. For example, the shapes below are not prisms, even though they have uniform cross-sections.

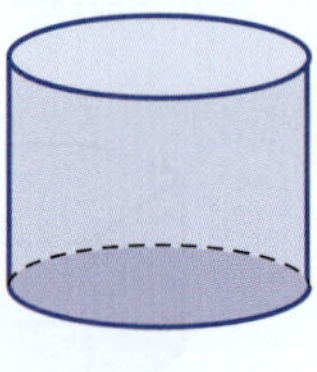

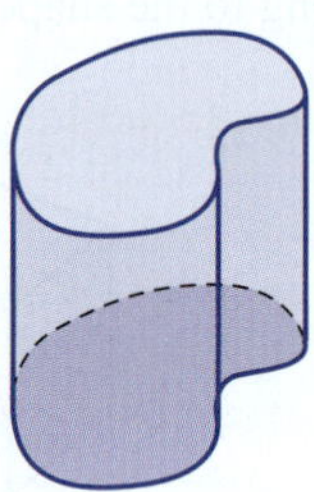

- The formula $V = AH$, where A is the cross-sectional area and H is the dimension perpendicular to it, will give the volume of any solid with uniform cross-section, even if it is not a prism.

WORKED EXAMPLE 13

Find the volume of each of the following.

a

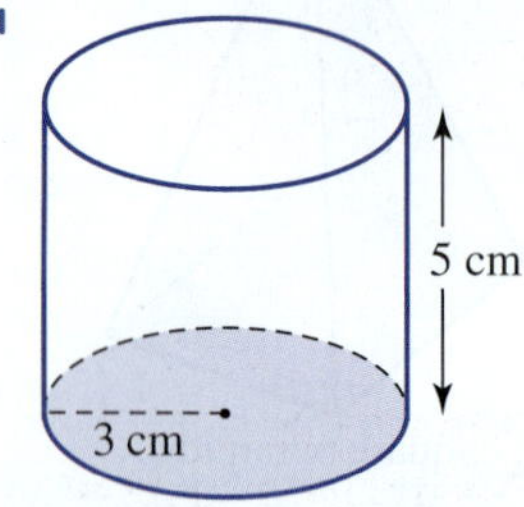

b

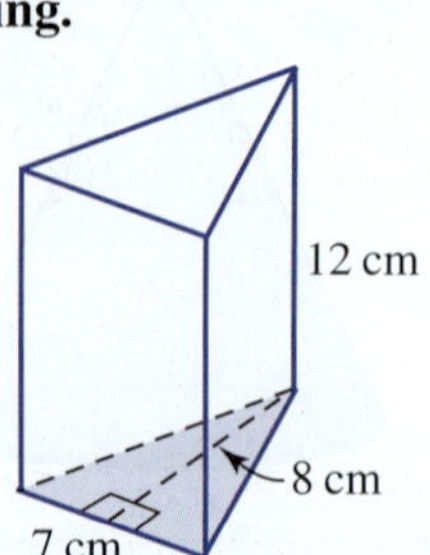

c

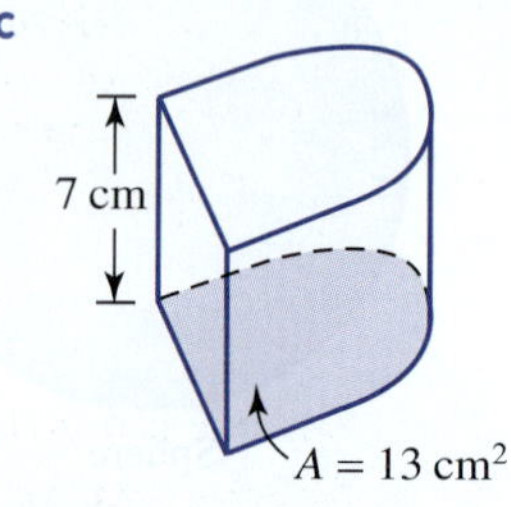

THINK		WRITE
a 1	Write the formula for the volume of the given shape.	**a** $V = A \times H$
2	Identify the shape of the cross-section and, hence, write the formula to find its area	$A_{circle} = \pi r^2$

	3	State the value of r.	$r = 3$
	4	Substitute the value of r into the formula and evaluate.	$A = 3.14 \times 3^2$ $= 28.26\text{ cm}^2$
	5	State the value of H.	$H = 5$
	6	To find the volume, multiply the cross-sectional area by the height and include the correct units.	$V = 28.26 \times 5$ $= 141.3\text{ cm}^3$
b	1	Write the formula for the volume of a prism.	**b** $V = A \times H$
	2	Identify the shape of the cross-section and, hence, write the formula to find its area.	$A_{\text{triangle}} = \frac{1}{2}bh$
	3	State the values of the variables. (*Note: h* is the height of the triangle, *not* of the prism.)	$b = 7, h = 8$
	4	Substitute the values of b and h into the formula and evaluate.	$A = \frac{1}{2} \times 7 \times 8$ $= 28\text{ cm}^2$
	5	State the value of H, the height of the prism.	$H = 12$
	6	To find the volume of the prism, multiply the cross-sectional area by the height and include the correct units.	$V = 28 \times 12$ $= 336\text{ cm}^3$
c	1	Write the formula for the volume of the given shape.	**c** $V = A \times H$
	2	State the values of the cross-sectional area and the height of the shape.	$A = 13, H = 7$
	3	Multiply the cross-sectional area by the height and include the correct units.	$V = 13 \times 7$ $= 91\text{ cm}^3$

REMEMBER

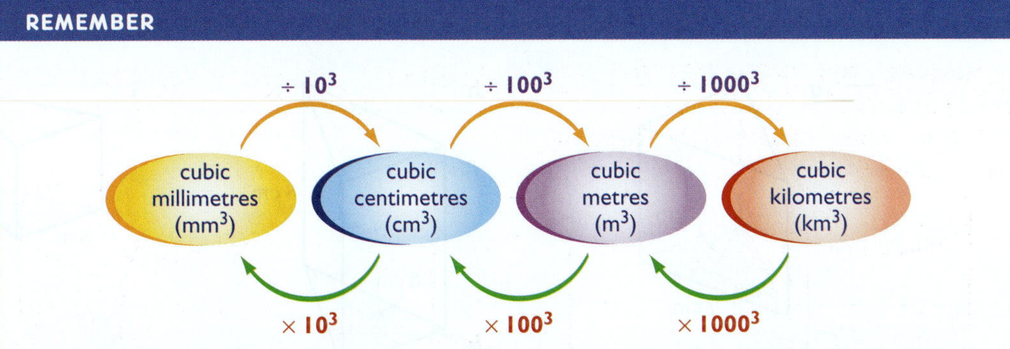

1. Volume is a measure of the amount of space inside a three-dimensional object.
2. Volume is measured in cubic units, such as cubic centimetres (cm^3) and cubic metres (m^3).
3. Prisms are solid shapes with identical opposite ends joined by straight edges. They are three-dimensional figures with identical layers or cross-sections.
4. The volume of a prism is given by the formula $V = A \times H$, where A is the cross-sectional area and H is the height of the prism (a dimension, perpendicular to the cross-section).
5. Use an area formula appropriate to each object to find the cross-sectional area.

EXERCISE
10F Volume of prisms and other solids

INDIVIDUAL PATHWAYS

eBook*plus*

Activity 10-F-1 Volume of prisms and other solids doc-6929

Activity 10-F-2 More volume doc-6930

Activity 10-F-3 Capacity doc-6931

FLUENCY

1 Which of the three-dimensional shapes below are prisms?

a
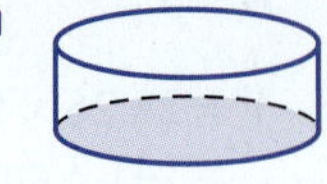

b
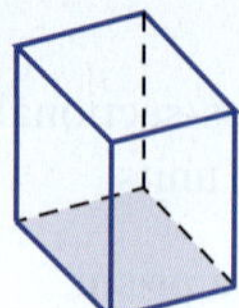

c
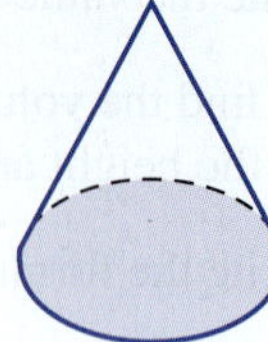

d
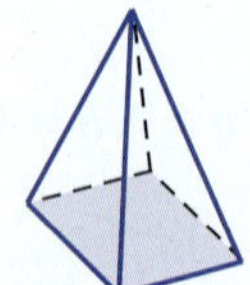

e
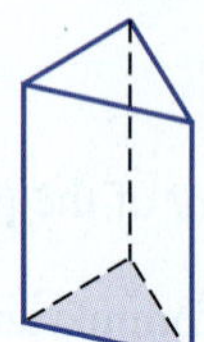

eBook*plus*

Digital doc Spreadsheet **Volume of a prism** doc-2324

2 WE13 Find the volume of each of the following.

a
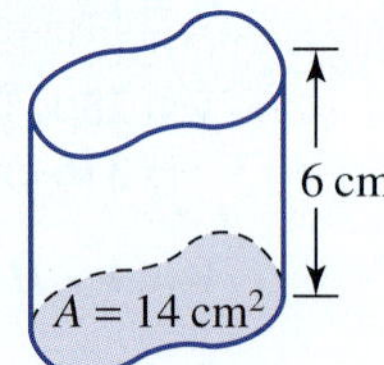

b
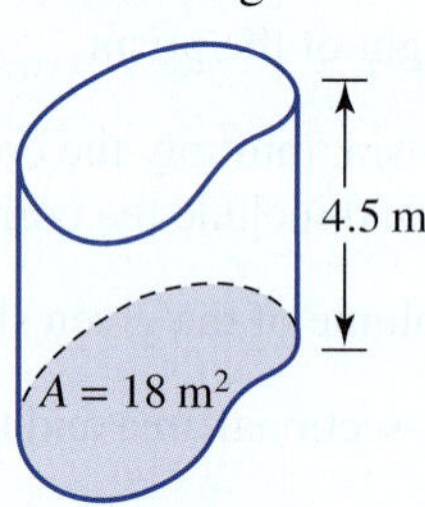

c
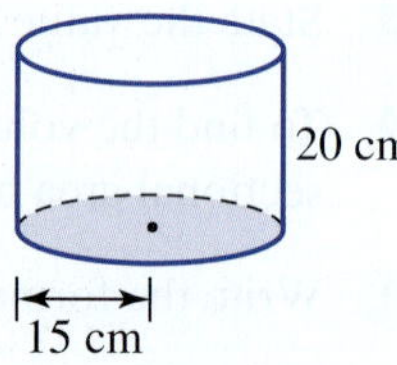

d
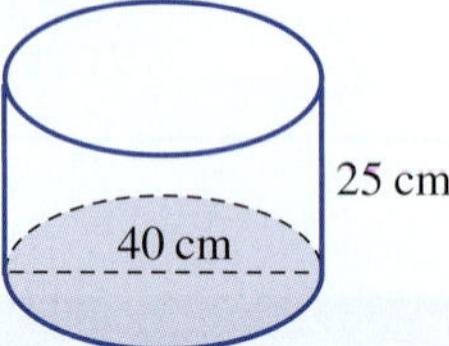

e
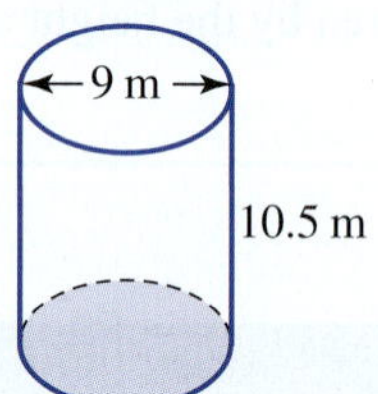

f
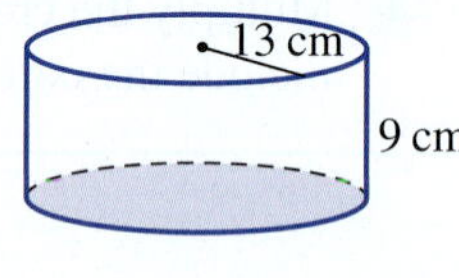

g
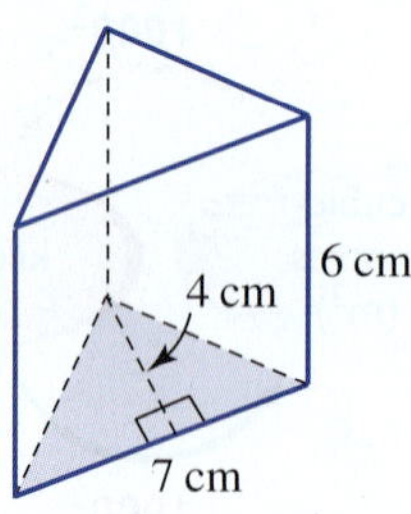

h
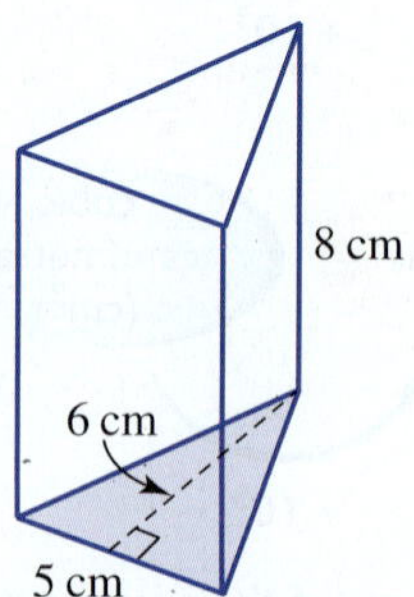

i
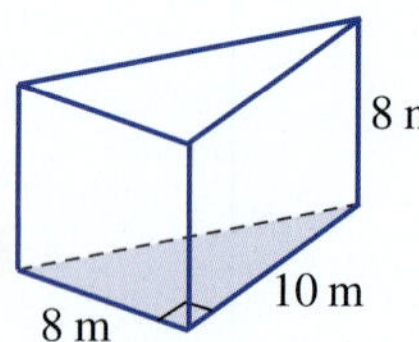

j
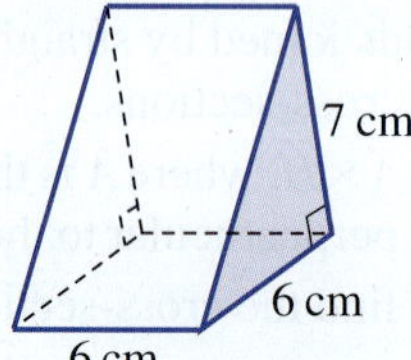

k
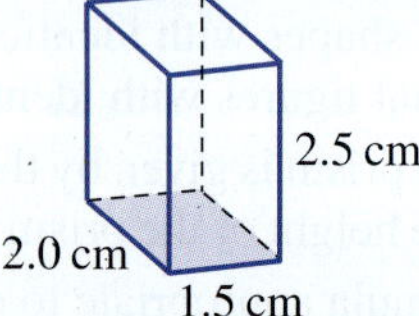

l
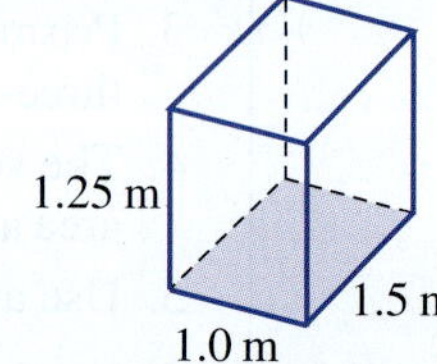

UNDERSTANDING

3 What volume of water will a rectangular swimming pool with dimensions shown in the photograph below hold if it is completely filled? The pool has no shallow or deep end. It is all the same depth.

4 How many cubic metres of cement will be needed to make the cylindrical foundation shown in the figure at right?

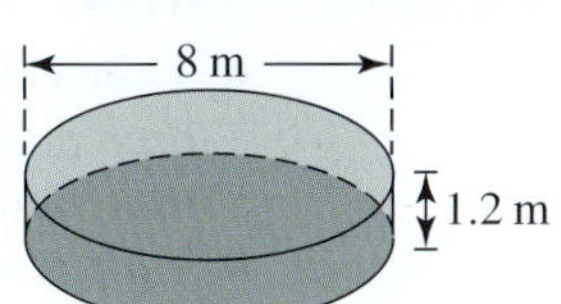

5 What are the volumes of these pieces of cheese?

a

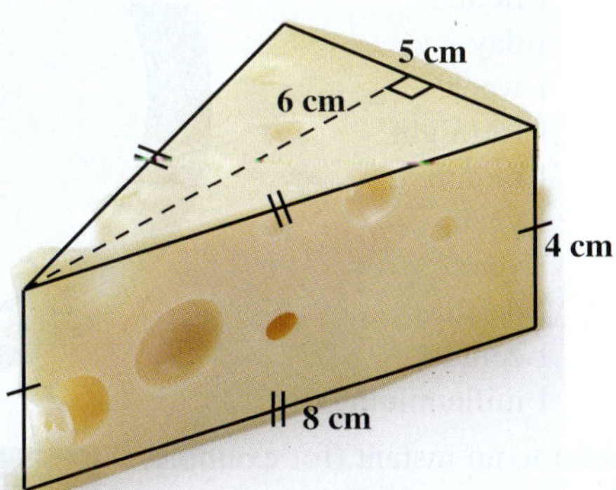

b

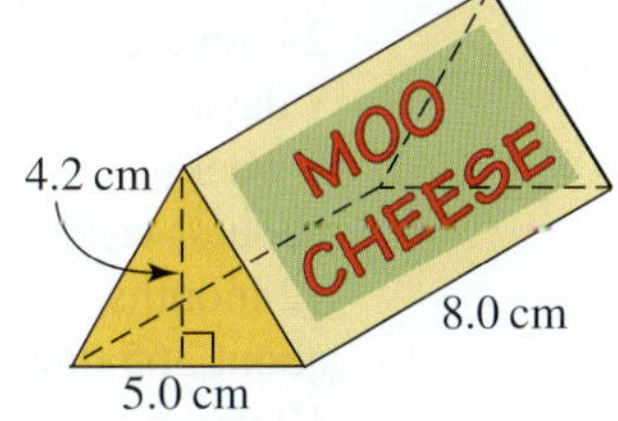

6 What is the volume of the bread bin shown at right?

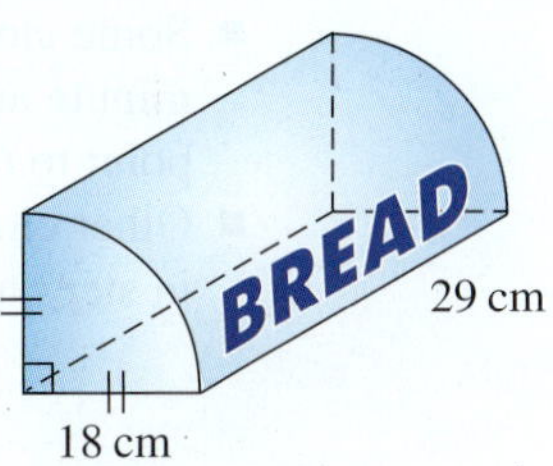

7 How much water will this pig trough, with dimensions shown in the figure at right, hold if it is completely filled?

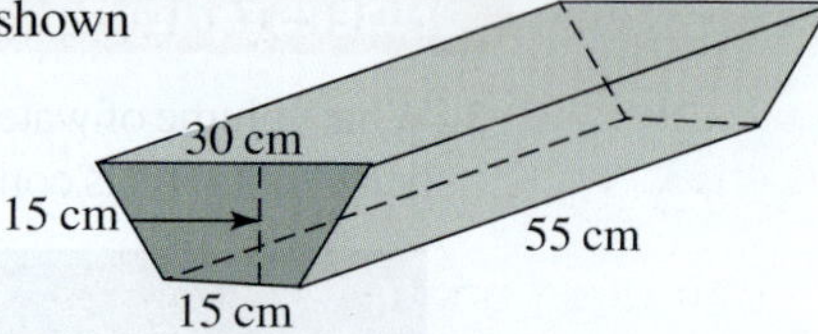

REASONING

8 The areas of the three sides of a rectangular box are as shown in the figure. What is the volume of the box?

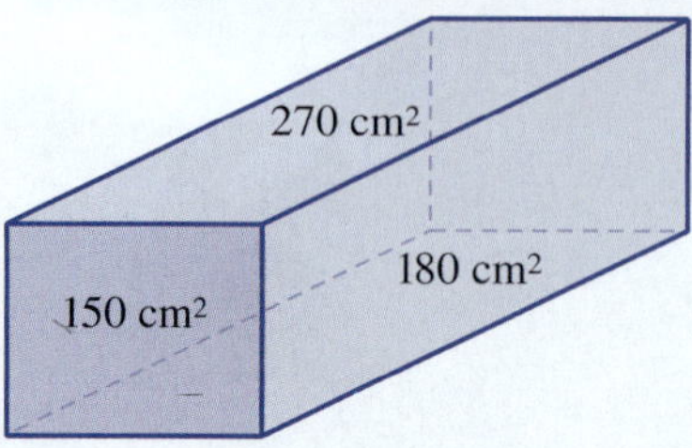

9 A vase is shaped like a rectangular prism with a square base of length 11 cm. It has 2 litres of water poured into it. To what height does the water reach in the vase? (*Hint:* 1 litre = 1000 cm^3.)

REFLECTION

How can you say if a solid has a uniform cross-section?

10G Time

Time — an introduction

- **Time** is one of our most useful measurements. We can use it to work out how long we have been doing something, or how long we have until we must do something. We can use it to make future arrangements.
- Time is something we all use, every day.

Time is divided into units. There are:

60 seconds	in	1 minute
60 minutes	in	1 hour
24 hours	in	1 day
7 days	in	1 week
2 weeks	in	1 fortnight
about 4 weeks	in	1 month
12 months	in	1 year
about 365 days	in	1 year
10 years	in	1 decade
100 years	in	1 century
1000 years	in	1 millennium.

- We also use the word time to refer to an instant (for example, 3 o'clock) rather than a period.
- A clock or watch can display the time in one of two ways.
- Some clocks display the time in analogue form using hour, minute and second hands that move continuously as they point to numbers on the clock face.
- Other clocks and watches display a set of digits that change in steps as time passes.

Time calculations

WORKED EXAMPLE 14

How many minutes are there in $4\frac{1}{4}$ hours?

THINK	WRITE
1 Convert the mixed number to an improper fraction.	$4\frac{1}{4}$ hours $= \frac{4 \times 4 + 1}{4}$ $= \frac{17}{4}$ hours
2 Multiply the improper fraction by the number of minutes in 1 hour.	$\frac{17}{4}$ hours $= \frac{17}{4} \times 60$ minutes $= \frac{1020}{4}$ minutes
3 Evaluate.	$= 255$ minutes

WORKED EXAMPLE 15

How many minutes are there in 5 days?

THINK	WRITE
1 Convert the number of days to hours, that is, multiply 5 by 24 hours.	5 days $= 5 \times 24$ hours
2 Evaluate.	$= 120$ hours
3 Convert the number of hours to minutes, that is, multiply 120 by 60 minutes.	120 hours $= 120 \times 60$
4 Evaluate.	$= 7200$ minutes

WORKED EXAMPLE 16

Change the following into hours and minutes.
a 300 minutes
b 425 minutes

THINK	WRITE
a 1 Convert minutes to hours, that is, divide 300 by 60.	a 300 minutes $= 300 \div 60$
2 Evaluate.	$= 5$ hours
b 1 Convert minutes to hours, that is, divide 425 by 60.	b 425 minutes $= 425 \div 60$ $= \frac{425}{60}$
2 Evaluate.	$= 7$ remainder 5
3 Write the answer in hours and minutes.	425 minutes $= 7$ hours 5 minutes

- The suffixes am and pm are used to indicate morning and afternoon, and are derived from 'ante meridiem' (meaning before midday), and 'post meridiem' (after midday).

  Note: 12 noon may be written as 12.00 pm, and 12 midnight may be written as 12.00 am.
- One way to find time differences is to mentally calculate how long it is to the next hour, then to the next 12.00 noon or 12.00 midnight. The following worked example illustrates this technique.

WORKED EXAMPLE 17

Find the time difference between:

a 7.15 pm and 10.25 pm **b 2.50 am and 8.20 pm**

c 3.40 am on Tuesday and 5.10 pm the following Wednesday.

THINK

a
1. Construct a vertical column starting at 7.15 pm and ending at 10.25 pm. Set up two columns with the headings 'hours' and 'minutes' next to the first time.
2. Write 'key' times between the start and finish times.
3. Calculate the times added to get each key time, and write them under the hours and minutes headings as shown.
4. Add the time differences to find the total time difference.
5. Convert any minute values over 60 to hours and minutes and adjust the answer.
6. Answer the question.

b Repeat steps 1 to 6 in part **a**.

c Repeat steps 1 to 6 in part **a**.

WRITE

a

	Hours	Minutes
7.15 pm		
8.00 pm		45
10.25 pm	2	25
Total time	2	70
	= 3	10

The time difference is 3 hours 10 minutes.

b

	Hours	Minutes
2.50 am		
3.00 am		10
12.00 noon	9	00
8.20 pm	8	20
Total time	17	30

The time difference is 17 hours 30 minutes.

c

	Hours	Minutes
3.40 am Tuesday		
4.00 am Tuesday		20
4.00 am Wednesday	24	00
12.00 noon Wednesday	8	00
5.10 pm Wednesday	5	10
Total time	37	30

The time difference is 37 hours 30 minutes.

REMEMBER

When finding time differences:
1. use a vertical column
2. work to the next key time (exact hours, 12.00 am and 12.00 pm) until the final time is reached
3. 12 noon is 12 pm and 12 midnight is 12 am.

EXERCISE

10G Time

INDIVIDUAL PATHWAYS

eBook*plus*

Activity 10-G-1
Silly snake A
doc-6962

Activity 10-G-2
Silly snake B
doc-6963

Activity 10-G-3
Super silly snake
doc-6964

FLUENCY

1 Match the following activities with the most likely amount of time.

	Activity	Time
a	a cricket test match	1 year
b	writing your name	10 seconds
c	eating breakfast	15 minutes
d	building a house	5 days
e	flying time from Melbourne to Hong Kong	7 hours
f	being in Year 7	6 months

2 What are the times shown on each of the following analogue clocks?

a

b

c

d

e

f

3 For each of the following, draw a 12-hour clock face and show the time.

a 8.20 am **b** 8.45 pm **c** 10.50 am
d 12.00 midnight **e** 11.05 pm **f** 5.11 pm
g 7.32 pm **h** 9.24 am **i** 11.16 am

4 Today we use clocks and watches to tell the time. Name two other devices that have been used in the past to measure time.

5 Explain the difference between 2 hours 25 minutes and 2.25 hours.

6 WE14,15 How many minutes are there in each of the following periods?

a 2 hours **b** $2\frac{1}{2}$ hours **c** $3\frac{1}{4}$ hours
d $\frac{1}{2}$ hour **e** $\frac{3}{4}$ hour **f** $7\frac{3}{4}$ hours
g 1 day **h** 9 days

7 WE16 Change the following to hours and minutes.

a 200 minutes **b** 185 minutes **c** 160 minutes
d 230 minutes **e** 405 minutes **f** 95 minutes
g 610 minutes **h** 72 minutes **i** 305 minutes

8 Change the following to minutes.

a 1 hour 15 minutes **b** 2 hours 10 minutes **c** 1 hour 50 minutes
d 4 hours 25 minutes **e** 7 hours 35 minutes **f** 3 hours 12 minutes
g $16\frac{3}{4}$ hours **h** $5\frac{1}{2}$ hours **i** $6\frac{1}{4}$ hours

9 How many:

a days in a week? **b** weeks in a year? **c** seconds in a minute?
d seconds in an hour? **e** seconds in a day? **f** hours in a day?
g hours in a year? **h** minutes in a day? **i** minutes in a year?

Note: Assume 1 year = 365 days.

10 What is the time:

a 1 hour after 4.00 pm?
b 1 hour before 4.00 pm?
c 1 hour after 5.30 am?
d 1 hour 20 minutes after half past 10 am?
e 1 hour 20 minutes before 10.00 am?
f 3 hours 18 minutes after 2.00 pm?
g 2 hours 30 minutes before 4.30 am?
h 4 hours 35 minutes after quarter to 10 am?
i 4 hours 35 minutes before 10.05 pm?
j 5 hours 27 minutes after 1.08 am?
k 5 hours 27 minutes before 1.08 am?
l 1 hour 10 minutes before 11.30 am?

11 WE17a,b Find the time difference between:

a 8.20 pm and 8.35 pm **b** 4.15 pm and 5.20 pm **c** 7.15 am and 8.28 am
d 5.17 am and 6.32 am **e** 9.15 pm and 10.08 pm **f** 3.16 pm and 5.09 pm

g 11.28 pm and 12 midnight
h 9.21 am and 1.06 pm
i 11.10 am and 4.25 pm
j 6.05 am and 6.05 pm
k half past 6 pm and quarter to 3 am.

12 WE17c Find the time difference between:
a 7.20 am on Monday and 6.30 pm the following Tuesday
b 4.38 am on Saturday and 1.25 pm the following Sunday
c 8.45 pm on Wednesday and 10.16 am the following Thursday
d 1.20 pm on Wednesday and 9.09 am the following Friday.

eBook*plus*

Digital doc
Spreadsheet
Time differences
doc-3445

13 MC 225 minutes is the same as:
A 2 hours 25 minutes
B 2 hours 15 minutes
C 3 hours 45 minutes
D 3 hours 25 minutes
E 2 hours 45 minutes

14 MC If the time was 8.45 pm, what would be the time 5 hours 20 minutes later?
A 1.05 am
B 1.05 pm
C 2.05 pm
D 2.05 am
E 1.10 pm

15 MC If a train takes 2 hours and 18 minutes to arrive at its destination and it arrives at 6.03 pm, at what time did it leave?
A 3.45 pm
B 8.21 pm
C 4.15 pm
D 3.21 pm
E 3.45 am

UNDERSTANDING

16 If it takes Joanne 16 minutes to write one page of a letter, how long will it take her to write a letter of three pages?

17 Mathew spends half an hour doing homework each week night. How many hours of homework has he done after 3 weeks?

18 If the time is now 7.55 am in Melbourne, what is the time in Adelaide if South Australian time is half an hour behind Victorian time?

19 If the time is now 8.30 am in Melbourne, what is the time in Perth if Western Australia is two hours behind Victoria?

20 If the time is 9.45 pm in Perth, what is the time in Melbourne? (See question **19**.)

21 If the time is 10.05 pm in Adelaide, what is the time in Melbourne? (See question **18**.)

22 If Susan takes 25 minutes to walk to the station, waits for the train for 7 minutes, travels on the train for 12 minutes and then takes 8 minutes to walk to her friend's house, how long has she taken altogether?

23 If James spends 35 minutes on Friday, 2 hours and 12 minutes on Saturday and $1\frac{1}{4}$ hours on Sunday to complete his assignment, how much time did he take altogether?

REASONING

24 In a mirror reflection, the time on an analogue clock face appears to be 25 minutes to 2. What time is it?

25 When would an analogue clock and its mirror image appear exactly the same?

REFLECTION
What strategies will you use to help you remember how to convert between different units of time?

10H 24-hour clock and time zones

- Sometimes the time is given using a 24-hour system or 24-hour clock.
- The hours are numbered from 1 to 24, beginning at midnight.
- The times from midnight to 12.59 pm look very similar to the 12-hour time. At 1.00 pm you need to add 12 hours, making the time 1300 hours.
- Times in the 24-hour system are written as 'fourteen hundred hours' (1400) or 'twenty-three thirty hours' (2330).

- Notice that in 24-hour time, we always use 4 digits. Some examples are given in the table below.

12-hour time	24-hour time
6.00 am	0600 hours
10.00 am	1000 hours
12.30 pm	1230 hours
2.00 pm	1400 hours (add 12 hours to 2.00)
8.00 pm	2000 hours (add 12 hours to 8.00)
11.30 pm	2330 hours (add 12 hours to 11.30)

WORKED EXAMPLE 18

Find the difference in hours and minutes between the following 24-hour times:
a 0635 and 2150
b 1055 and 1543.

THINK		WRITE
a	1 Set up two columns with the headings 'hours' and 'minutes'.	a Hours Minutes
	2 Write the values, putting the highest hour value first.	21 50 06 35
	3 Calculate by subtraction.	15 15
	4 Write as hours and minutes.	15 hours 15 minutes
b	1 Set up two columns with the headings 'hours' and 'minutes'.	b Hours Minutes
	2 Write the values, putting the highest hour value first.	15 43 10 55
	3 You cannot take 55 minutes from 43 minutes. Convert 1 hour into 60 minutes and add it to the minutes column. Then rewrite 15 43 as 14 103. (Using 14 103 helps us to do the subtraction, but it is not a real time.)	14 103 10 55
	4 Calculate by subtraction.	4 48
	5 Write as hours and minutes.	4 hours 48 minutes

Time zones

- Time changes as we travel around the world. In Europe it is night time when in Australia it is day and it is day time in Europe when we have night.
- To help everyone know what time it is in different countries, the world is divided into 24 **time zones**. (See the map showing world time zones on page 281.)
- If we travel east, we need to set our watches ahead.

Time in Perth	Time in Melbourne	Time in Jakarta
3.00 pm	5.00 pm	2.00 pm
6.00 pm	8.00 pm	5.00 pm
10.00 am	12 midday	9.00 am
10.00 pm	12 midnight	9.00 pm

- If we travel west, we need to set our watches back.
- Australia is divided into three time zones.
  - Queensland, New South Wales, the ACT, Victoria and Tasmania observe Eastern Standard Time (EST).
  - The Northern Territory and South Australia observe Central Standard Time (CST), which is $\frac{1}{2}$ hour behind EST.
  - Western Australia observes Western Standard Time (WST), which is 2 hours behind EST.
- The time in England is called Greenwich Mean Time (GMT) and is 10 hours behind EST.

eBook*plus*

Digital doc
Spreadsheet
Time zones
doc-3449

Time in London (GMT)	Time in Jakarta	Time in Perth	Time in Melbourne (EST)
8.00 am	3.00 pm	4.00 pm	6.00 pm
4.00 pm	4.00 pm	12 midnight	2.00 am (next day)
12 midday	7.00 pm	8.00 pm	10.00 pm
12 midnight	7.00 am	8.00 am	10.00 am
3.00 am	10.00 am	11.00 am	1.00 pm

WORKED EXAMPLE 19

a What is the time in Melbourne if the time in London (GMT) is 8.00 am?
b What is the time in London (GMT) if the time in Melbourne is 8.00 am?

THINK	WRITE
a 1 Melbourne is 10 hours ahead of London. Add 10 hours to the London time.	**a** London time: 8.00 am Melbourne time: 8.00 am + 10 hours
2 Calculate.	It is 6.00 pm
b 1 London is 10 hours behind Melbourne. Subtract 10 hours from the Melbourne time.	**b** Melbourne time: 8.00 am London time: 8.00 am – 10 hours
2 Calculate.	It is 10.00 pm the previous day.

Daylight-saving time

- Many countries around the world have daylight-saving time during summer so that people can make the most of the warm weather.
- When daylight-saving time begins, clocks are turned forward by 1 hour at 2.00 am.
- At the end of daylight-saving time, the clocks are then turned back by 1 hour at 3.00 am.
- In Australia, the states Queensland and Western Australia, and the Northern Territory do not observe daylight-saving time, while the ACT and other states do.
- During daylight-saving, the time in Tasmania, Victoria, New South Wales and ACT is known as Eastern Daylight-Saving Time (EDT). The time in South Australia is known as Central Daylight-Saving Time (CDT).
- During daylight-saving time:
  - Queensland (EST) is 1 hour behind EDT
  - Northern Territory (CST) is $1\frac{1}{2}$ hours behind EDT
  - South Australia (CDT) is $\frac{1}{2}$ hour behind EDT
  - Western Australia (WST) is 3 hours behind EDT.

WORKED EXAMPLE 20

You call your friend in Darwin on Christmas Day from your home in Sydney. It is 7 pm in Sydney. What time is it in Darwin?

THINK	WRITE
1 Because it is Christmas Day (the middle of summer), Sydney time will be at EDT, which is $1\frac{1}{2}$ hours ahead of Darwin time (CST).	Sydney time is EDT and Darwin time is CST. The time in Sydney is $1\frac{1}{2}$ hours ahead of the time in Darwin.
2 Subtract $1\frac{1}{2}$ hours from the Sydney time to give the time in Darwin.	Time in Darwin = 7 pm − 1 h 30 min = 5.30 pm

REMEMBER

1. 24-hour time is expressed as four-digit numbers, for example, 0300, 2300, 1530.
2. To convert 'pm' times between 1.00 pm and 12.00 midnight to 24-hour time, add 12 hours and write the four digits.
3. The world is divided into 24 one-hour time zones.
4. Places to the east are ahead of those to the west.
5. Australia is divided into three different time zones (EST, CST and WST).
6. During daylight-saving time, Australia has five different time zones (EST, EDT, CST, CDT and WST).

EXERCISE 10H 24-hour clock and time zones

INDIVIDUAL PATHWAYS

eBook*plus*

Activity 10-H-1 Time triangles doc-6965

Activity 10-H-2 Tempting time triangles doc-6966

Activity 10-H-3 Advanced time triangles doc-6967

FLUENCY

1 Write each time from the first column and match it with the 24-hour time from the second column.

10.12 am	1212	12 midday	1120
12.12 pm	1200	11.20 pm	0000
12 midnight	1012	11.20 am	2320

2 Write each of the following times using the 24-hour clock.

a 10.20 am **b** 11.30 am **c** 5.10 am
d 4.15 am **e** 5.15 pm **f** 6.30 pm
g 8.30 am **h** 8.40 pm **i** 12.00 midday
j 11.30 pm **k** 4.35 am **l** 2.30 pm

3 Convert each of the following 24-hour times to 12-hour time.

a 2315 **b** 1310 **c** 0815
d 0115 **e** 1818 **f** 1220
g 0005 **h** 1005 **i** 2005
j 1135 **k** 1520 **l** 1414

4 WE18 Find the difference between each of the following times. (The first time is the earlier time in each case.)

a 1023 and 2312 **b** 1000 and 1215
c 1430 and 1615 **d** 1530 and 1615
e 1005 and 2315 **f** 1135 and 1440
g 0820 and 1550 **h** 0712 and 2008
i 1455 and 0015

eBook*plus*

Digital docs
Spreadsheet
12-h to 24-h time
doc-3447
Spreadsheet
24-h to 12-h time
doc-3448

5 Mary-Jane always arrived at school at 0855 and left at 1526. How long was she at school?

6 Peter wished to record a movie on video. He had a 180-minute tape and a 240-minute tape. The film he wished to record started at 2030 and finished at 2345.
  a How long was the movie?
  b Which tape should Peter use?

7 An aircraft left the airport at 0920 and arrived at its destination at 1305. How long was the flight?

8 MC A clock shows the time as 1543. What is the correct time if it is known that the clock is 33 minutes slow?
  A 1576 B 1616 C 1510 D 1516 E 1606

9 MC A clock shows the time as 2345. What is the correct time if it is known that the clock is 27 minutes slow?
  A 2318 B 2372 C 2412 D 0042 E 0012

10 MC A clock shows the time 0857. What is the correct time if it is known that the clock is 48 minutes fast?
  A 0809 B 0811 C 0945 D 0805 E 0905

11 MC A clock shows the time 1004. What is the correct time if it is known that the clock is 31 minutes fast?
  A 1035 B 0935 C 0973 D 1013 E 0933

12 WE19a What is the time in Melbourne if the time in London (GMT) is as given below?
  a 11.00 am b 12.30 pm c 10.20 am
  d 12.00 midnight e 12.00 noon f 2.15 am
  g 3.30 pm h 5.45 pm i 8.10 am
  j 9.35 pm k 1.12 pm l 1.12 am?

13 WE19b What is the time in London (GMT) if the time in Melbourne is as given below?
  a 3.30 am b 12 noon c 12 midnight
  d 5.50 pm e 6.40 am f 7.20 pm
  g 11.10 am h 1325 i 1550
  j 0615 k 1855 l 1935?

14 WE20 You call your friend in Adelaide on Christmas Day from your home in Cairns, Queensland. It is 5 pm in Cairns. What time is it in Adelaide?

UNDERSTANDING

15 Jamie has made a schedule for football training. He will start exercising at 0615 and stop at 0705. He will also train from 1600 until 1810. For how long will Jamie train each day?

16 A chart supplied with your bread-making machine shows the program process and the time it takes at each stage.

Program process	Basic light	Basic medium	Basic dark
First knead	5 min	5 min	5 min
Second knead	20 min	20 min	20 min
Dispenser activates at	2 min 33 s	2 min 43 s	2 min 53 s
First rise	39 min	39 min	39 min
First punch down	10 s	10 s	10 s
Second rise	25 min 50 s	25 min 50 s	25 min 50 s
Shape (use pause button)	15 s	15 s	15 s
Third rise	49 min 45 s	49 min 45 s	49 min 45 s
Bake	30 min	40 min	50 min
Total cycle time			

a Calculate the total cycle time for the 3 types of loaves shown.

b You can preset the timer on your bread-making machine so that the bread will be ready at a specific time. The timer uses the 24-hour clock format. You decide to bake a basic light loaf so that it will be ready when you arrive home from school at 4.30 pm. At what time should the machine start the process? To what value should the timer be preset to begin the process?

17 MC If Suzie wanted to telephone her friend in England before he went to work for the day, what would be the best time for her to ring from Melbourne, Australia?

A 0700 B 1700 C 1900
D 2100 E 2300

18 If the time was 5.00 am in London, what would the time be in:

a Perth? **b** Melbourne? **c** Jakarta?

19 If the time was 8.00 pm in Perth, what would the time be in:

a London? **b** Melbourne? **c** Jakarta?

20 If the time was 3.30 pm in Jakarta, what would the time be in:

a London? **b** Perth? **c** Melbourne?

eBook*plus*

Digital doc
WorkSHEET 10.2
doc-6932

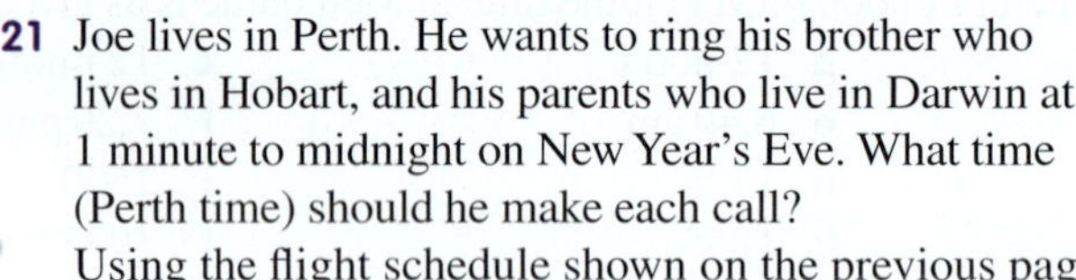

21 Joe lives in Perth. He wants to ring his brother who lives in Hobart, and his parents who live in Darwin at 1 minute to midnight on New Year's Eve. What time (Perth time) should he make each call?

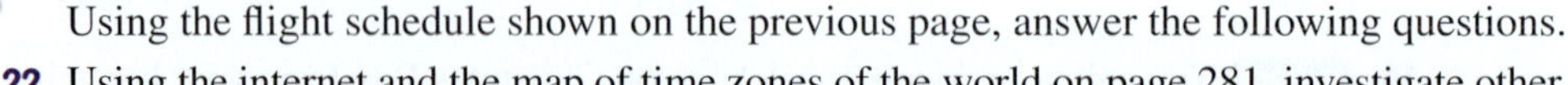

Using the flight schedule shown on the previous page, answer the following questions.

22 Using the internet and the map of time zones of the world on page 281, investigate other countries in the world that are in the same time zones as Australia. List three cities in other countries that are in the same time zone as Australian capital cities.

REASONING

23 Jessica and Connor have to catch the airport train at 8.20 am so they will be on time to catch their plane at the airport. Jessica's watch is 10 minutes fast, but she thinks it is 5 minutes slow. Connor's watch is 10 minutes slow, but he thinks it is 10 minutes fast. Each leaves home expecting to arrive at the station just in time to catch the train. Do they both catch the train?

REFLECTION

Why is it important that arrival and departure times at airports are in 24-hour time?

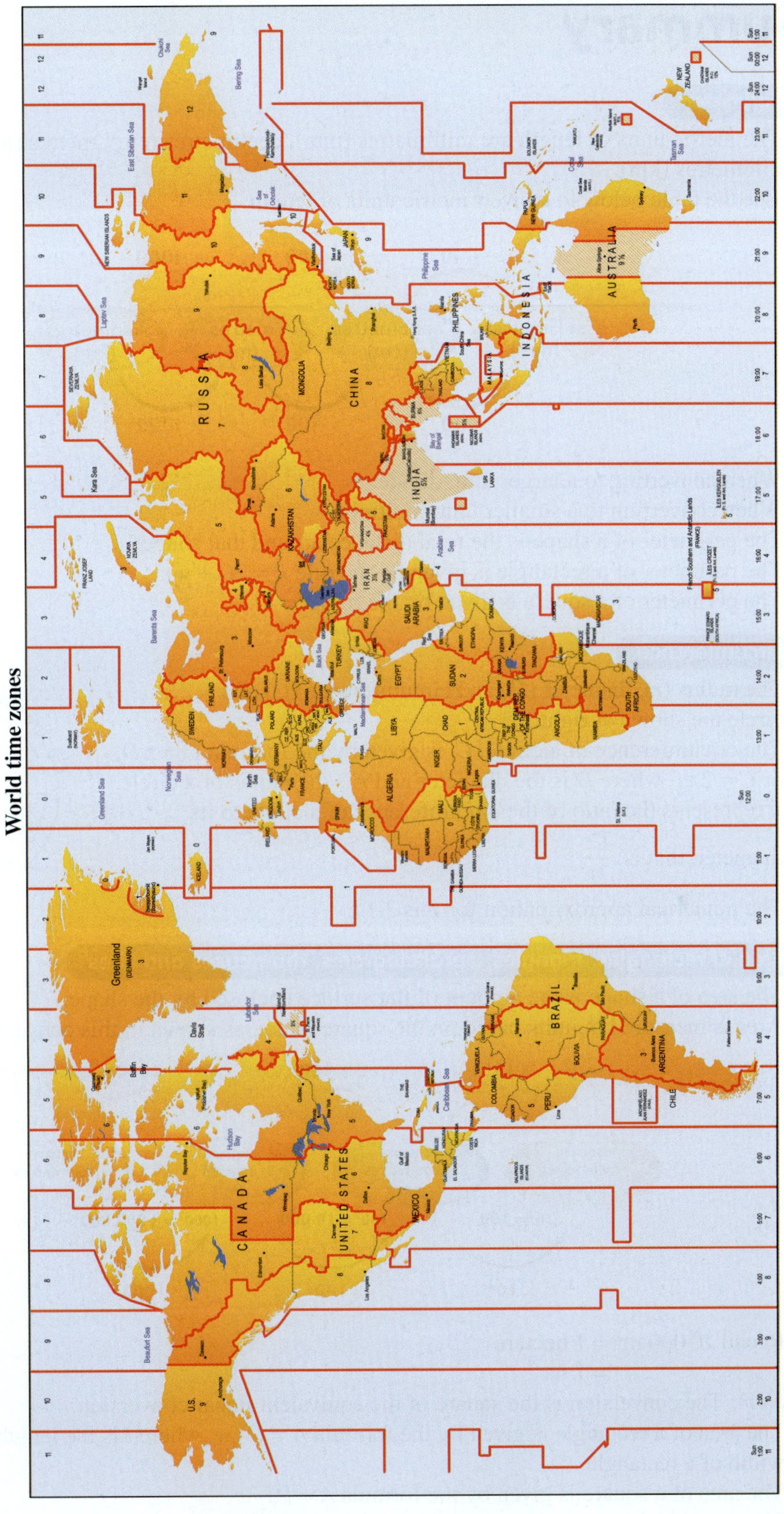

World time zones

Summary

Perimeter

- The metric units of length are millimetres (mm), centimetres (cm), metres (m) and kilometres (km).
- Use the table below to convert metric units of length.

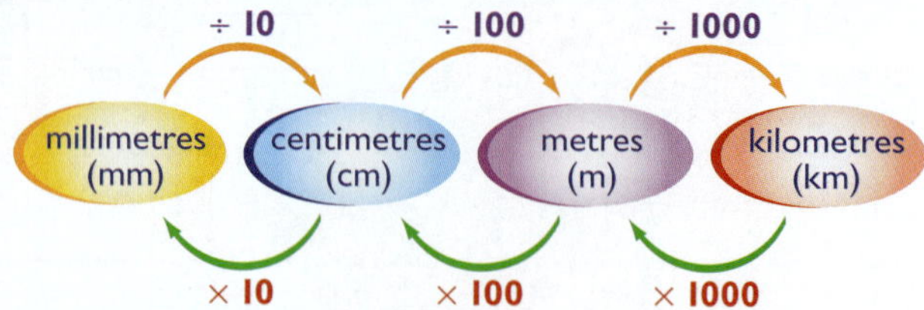

- When converting to a larger unit, divide.
- When converting to a smaller unit, multiply.
- The perimeter of a shape is the total distance around that shape.
- The perimeter of a rectangle is given by the rule $P = 2(l + w)$.
- The perimeter of a square is given by the rule $P = 4l$.

Circumference

- The radius (r), diameter (D) and circumference (C) of a circle are shown at right.
- The circumference of a circle, C, is given by the formula $C = \pi D$, or $C = 2\pi r$, where D is the diameter and r is the radius of a circle.
- π represents the ratio of the circumference of a circle to its diameter, that is, $\dfrac{C}{D}$.
- The numerical approximation for π is 3.14.

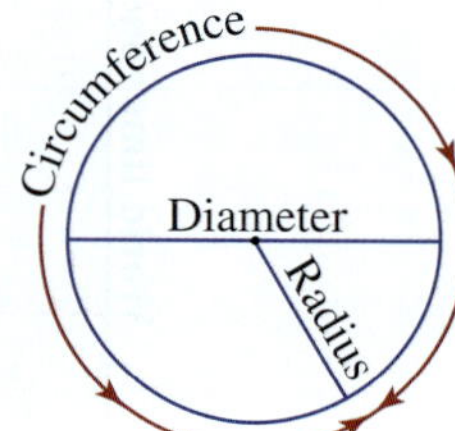

Area of rectangles, triangles, parallelograms, rhombuses and kites

- The area of a shape is the amount of flat surface enclosed by the shape.
- Area is measured in units based on the square metre, as shown in this conversion chart.

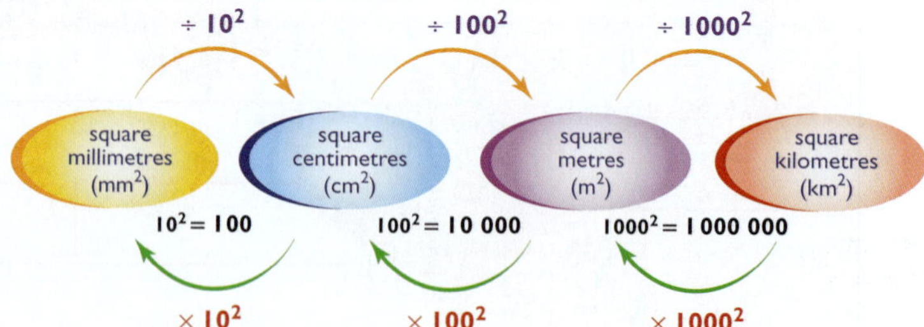

Recall $10\,000 \text{ m}^2 = 1$ hectare
$= 1$ ha

Note: The conversion is the square of the equivalent linear conversion.

- The area of a rectangle is given by the formula $A = l \times w$, where l is the length and w is the width of a rectangle.
- The area of a square is given by the formula $A = l^2$.
- The area of a triangle may be found using the rule $A = \frac{1}{2}bh$, where b is the base and h is the height of a triangle.
- The base and height of any triangle are perpendicular to each other.

- A parallelogram is a quadrilateral with two pairs of parallel sides.
- The area of a parallelogram is given by the formula $A = bh$, where b is the length of the base of the parallelogram and h is its vertical height.
- The base and the height of any parallelogram are perpendicular to each other.

Area of a circle

- The area of a circle is given by the formula $A = \pi r^2$, where r is the radius of a circle and π has an approximate value of 3.14.
- The radius of a circle, r, is equal to a half of its diameter, D: $r = \frac{D}{2}$.

Area of trapeziums

- The area of a trapezium is given by the formula $A = \frac{1}{2}(a + b) \times h$, where a and b are parallel sides and h is the height of a trapezium.

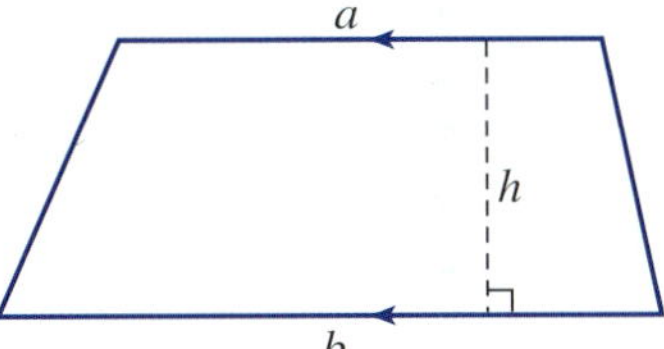

- The height of the trapezium is always perpendicular to the parallel sides.

Volume of prisms and other solids

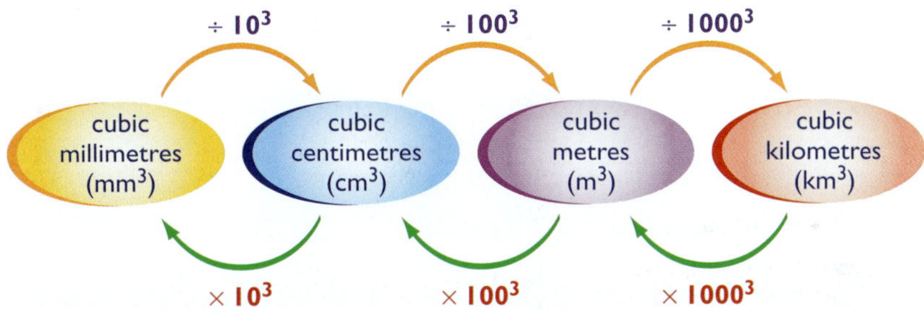

- Volume is a measure of the amount of space inside a three-dimensional object.
- Volume is measured in cubic units, such as cubic centimetres (cm^3) and cubic metres (m^3).
- Prisms are solid shapes with identical opposite ends joined by straight edges. They are three-dimensional figures with identical layers or cross-sections.
- The volume of a prism is given by the formula $V = A \times H$, where A is the cross-sectional area and H is the height of the prism (a dimension, perpendicular to the cross-section).
- Use an area formula appropriate to each object to find the cross-sectional area.

Time

- When finding time differences:
  (a) use a vertical column
  (b) work to the next key time (exact hours, 12.00 am and 12.00 pm) until the final time is reached
  (c) 12 noon is 12 pm and 12 midnight is 12 am.

24-hour clock and time zones

- 24-hour time is expressed as four-digit numbers, for example, 0300, 2300, 1530.
- To convert ‘pm’ times between 1.00 pm and 12.00 midnight to 24-hour time, add 12 hours and write the four digits.
- The world is divided into 24 one-hour time zones.

- Places to the east are ahead of those to the west.
- Australia is divided into three different time zones (EST, CST and WST).
- During daylight-saving time, Australia has five different time zones (EST, EDT, CST, CDT and WST).

MAPPING YOUR UNDERSTANDING

Using terms from the summary, and other terms if you wish, construct a concept map that illustrates your understanding of the key concepts covered in this chapter. Compare this concept map with the one that you created in *What do you know?* on page 239.

Have you completed the two *Homework sheets*, the *Rich task* and the two *Code puzzles* in your *Maths Quest 8 Homework book*?

Chapter review

FLUENCY

1 Convert each of the following to the units shown in brackets.
- **a** 5.3 mm (cm)
- **b** 7.6 cm (mm)
- **c** 15 cm (m)
- **d** 4.6 m (cm)
- **e** 250 m (km)
- **f** 6.5 km (m)
- **g** 1.5 m (mm)
- **h** 12 500 cm (km)

2 Find the perimeter of the shapes below. Where necessary, change to the smaller unit.

a
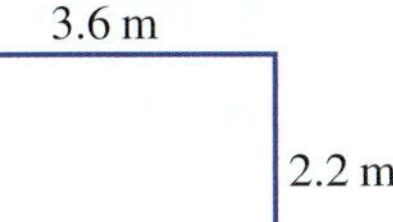

b
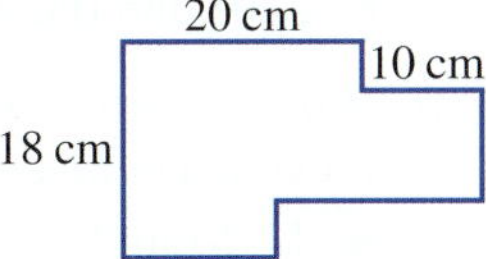

c
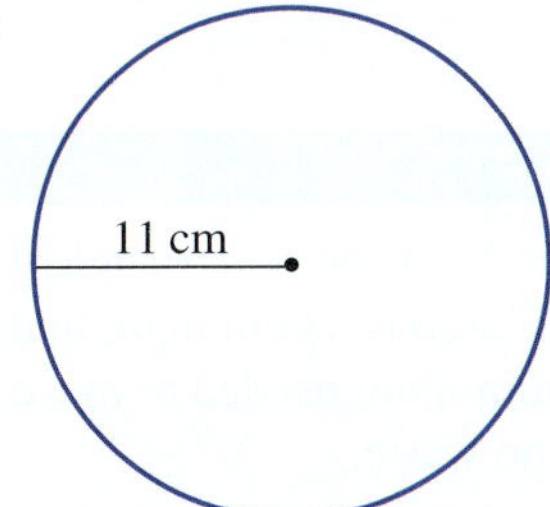

3 Find the circumference of each of these circles.

a
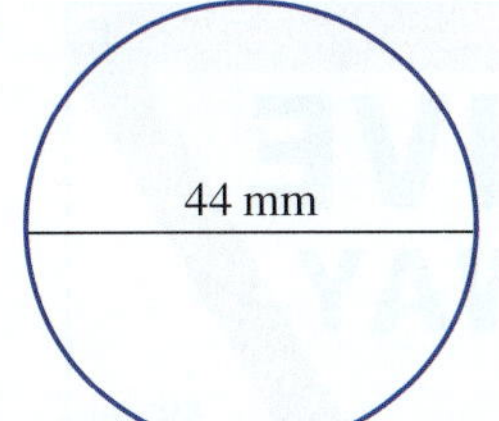

b
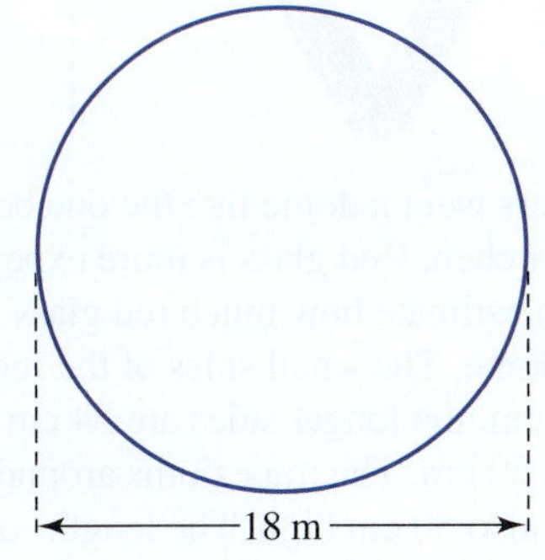

c

4 Find the perimeter of these shapes.

a
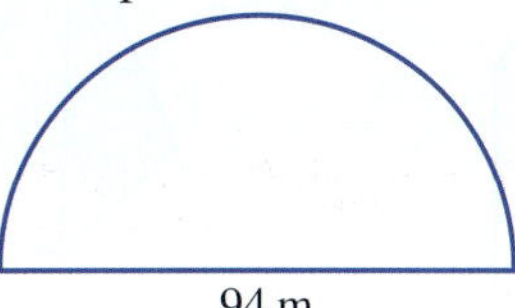

b
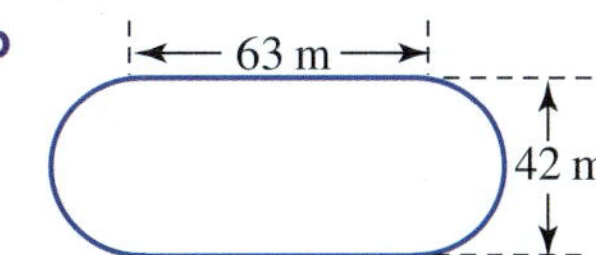

c
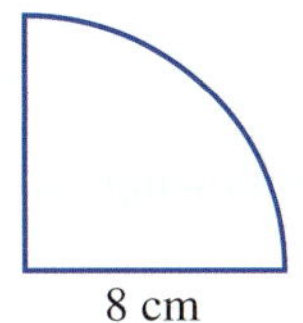

5 Find the area of the following triangles.

a
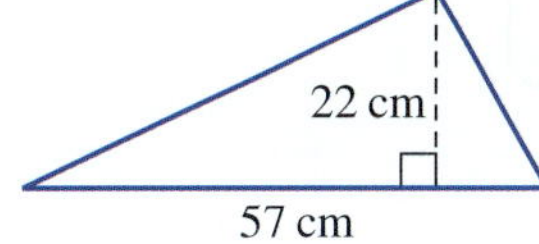

b
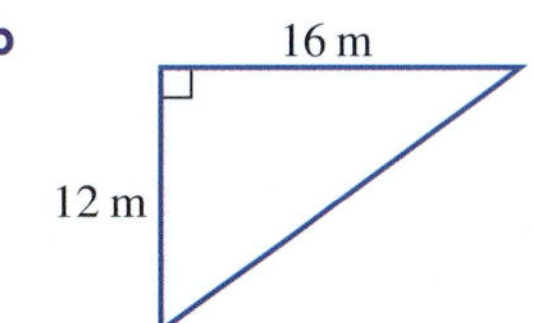

c
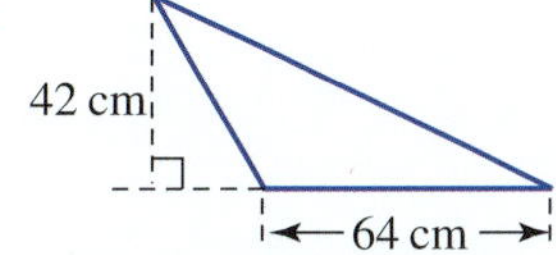

6 Find the area of this parallelogram.

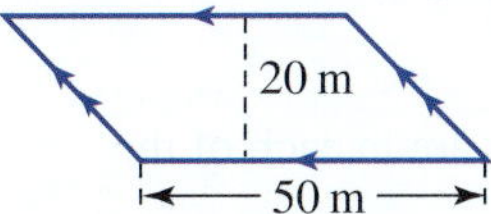

7 Find the area of these trapeziums.

a
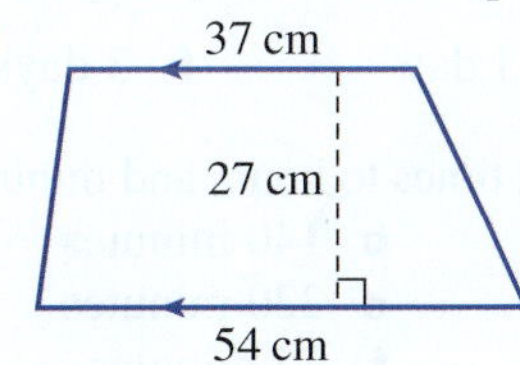

b
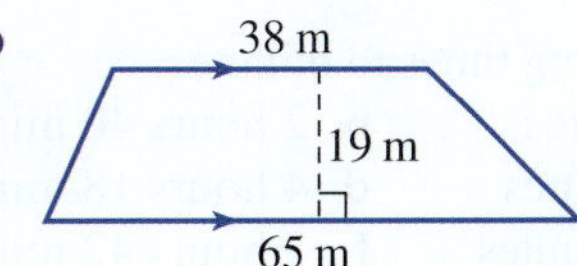

8 Find the total surface area (TSA) of the following three-dimensional objects.

a

2.5 cm

b

5.6 cm

3 cm

c

8.5 cm

9 Find the volume of each of the following.

a

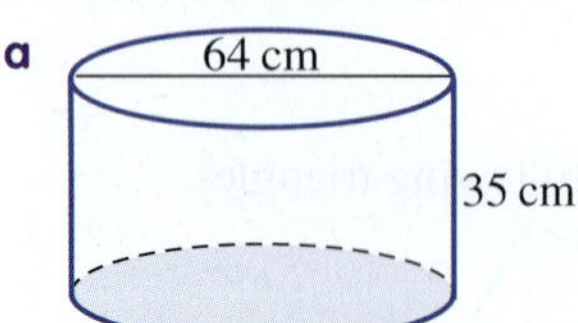

b

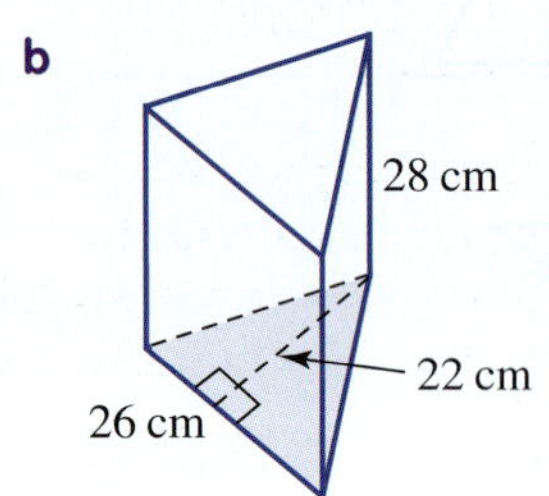

c

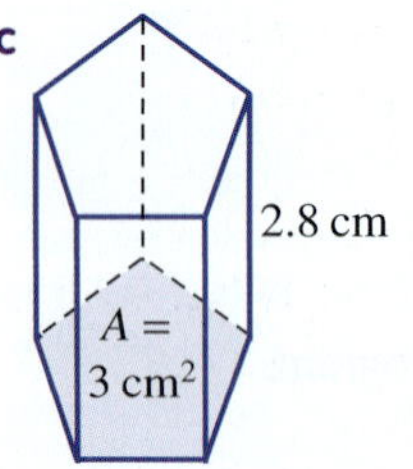

10 State how many minutes are in each of the following times.

a 3 hours **b** $5\frac{1}{4}$ hours **c** $7\frac{1}{2}$ hours

d $1\frac{3}{4}$ hours **e** 1 day **f** 3 days

11 Change the following times to hours and minutes.

a 165 minutes **b** 140 minutes
c 210 minutes **d** 220 minutes
e 800 minutes **f** 75 minutes

12 Change the following times to minutes.

a 1 hour 20 minutes **b** 2 hours 40 minutes
c 3 hours 10 minutes **d** 4 hours 18 minutes
e 10 hours 35 minutes **f** 3 hours 42 minutes

13 Jamie and his family are preparing to visit relatives in Canberra. They begin their journey at 8.15 am and arrive at their destination at 4.30 pm. For how long did they travel?

14 Write each of the following using 24-hour clock time.

a 10.35 pm **b** 7.15 am
c 3.20 am **d** 4.42 pm
e 9.50 pm **f** 1.05 am

15 Convert each of the following 24-hour times to 12-hour times.

a 1240 **b** 0725
c 1550 **d** 0909
e 2121 **f** 1120

16 Find the difference between the following 24-hour times.

a 1840 and 0920 **b** 2112 and 1115
c 2205 and 0627 **d** 1833 and 1158

17 What is the time in Melbourne if the GMT (Greenwich Mean Time) is:

a 11.20 am? **b** 3.30 pm?
c 9.15 pm? **d** 6.23 am?

18 What is the GMT (Greenwich Mean Time) when the time in Melbourne is:

a 11.30 pm? **b** 11.30 am?
c 1450 hours? **d** 0835 hours?

PROBLEM SOLVING

1 A give-way sign is in the shape of a triangle with a base of 0.5 m. If the sign is 58 cm high, find the amount (in m^2) of aluminium needed to make 20 such signs. Assume no waste.

2 Restaurant owners want a dome like the one below over their new kitchen. Red glass is more expensive and they want to estimate how much red glass is needed for the dome. The small sides of the red triangles are 40 cm, the longer sides are 54 cm and their heights are 50 cm. The trapeziums around the central light are also 50 cm high. The lengths of their parallel sides are 30 cm and 20 cm. Calculate the area of:

a the red triangles

b the red trapeziums

c the total area of red glass in m^2.

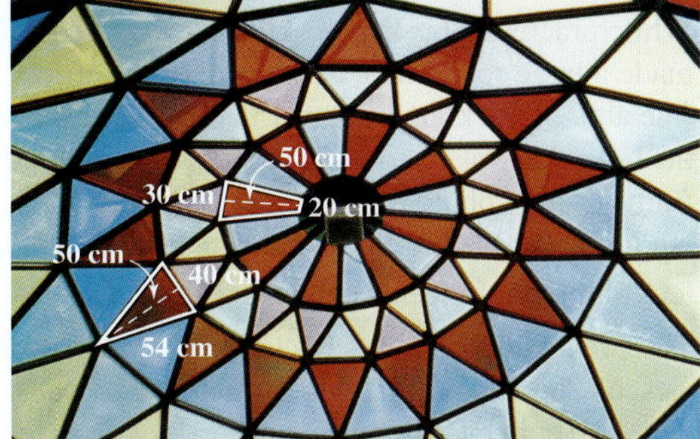

3 What area of cardboard would be required to make the poster shown below?

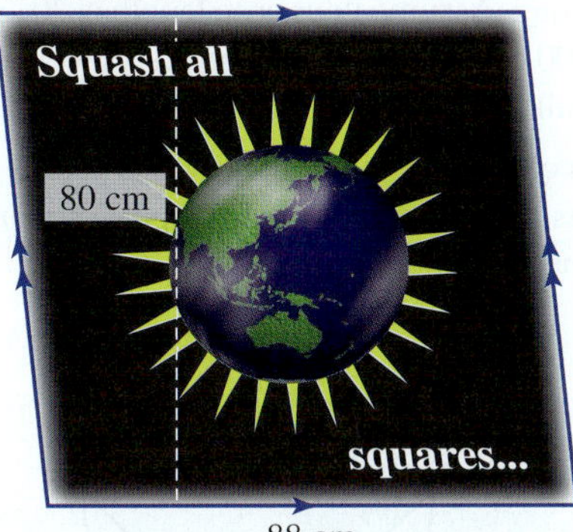

4 Find the area of each of the circles in question **3** in the Fluency section.

5 Find the area that the 12-mm-long minute hand of a watch sweeps out in one revolution.

6 Of the two parallel sides of a trapezium, one is 5 cm longer than the other. Find the height of the trapezium if the longer side is 12 cm and its area is 57 cm^2.

7 The diagram shows a design for a brooch.

a What is the total area of the brooch in square millimetres?

b If the brooch were to be edged with gold, what length of gold strip would be needed for the edge?

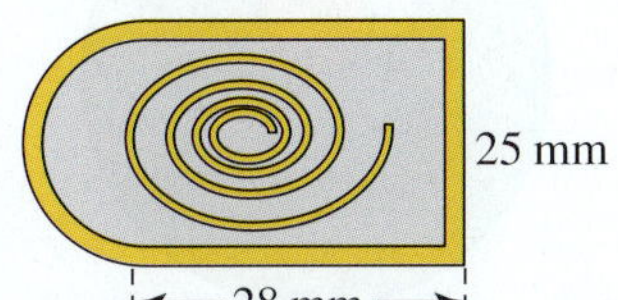

8 A rectangular toy box with no lid is to be painted all over (inside and outside). If the box is 1.2 m long, 60 cm wide and 80 cm tall, find the total area that needs to be painted.

9 A narrow cylindrical vase is 33 cm tall and has the volume of 2592 cm^2. Find (to the nearest cm) the radius of the base of the vase.

10 Nathan and Rachel ride around a circular track that has an inner radius of 30 m. The track is 2 m wide and Rachel rides along the outer lane.

a How much further does Rachel ride than Nathan in one lap?

b The track area needs to be repaved before the next big race. How much bitumen will need to be laid (in m^2)?

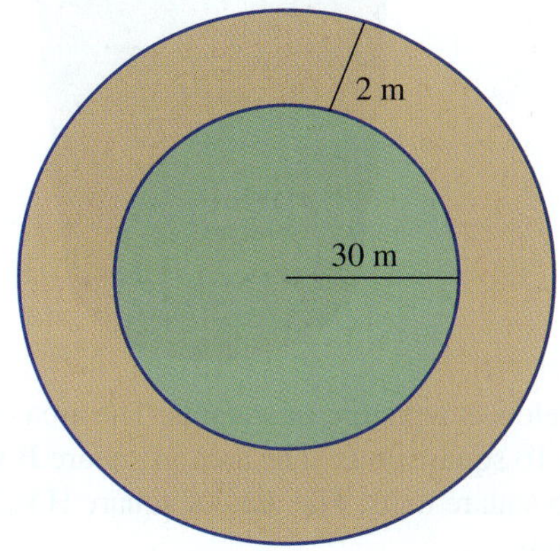

c The centre of the circular field will be grass except for a rectangular area in the centre, which will be a large shed used to store extra bikes and equipment. If the shed sits on a slab of concrete that is 18 m by 10 m, how much area will be grass?

d How many packets of lawn seed will be required if each packet covers 25 m^2.

11 A sand pit is to be built in the grounds of a kindergarten. As the garden already has various play equipment in it, the sand pit is shaped as shown below.

a Calculate the perimeter of the sand pit.

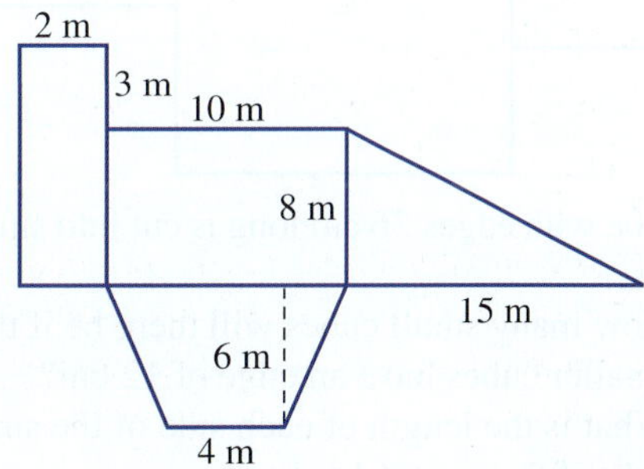

b Find the area of the sandpit.

c How much sand (in m^3) will be needed if the sandpit is to be 30 cm deep?

12 A cylindrical petrol drum has a base diameter of 40 cm and is 80 cm high. The drum was full on Friday morning but then 30 L of petrol was used for the mower and 5 L was used for the whipper snipper. Find the height of the petrol left in the drum. (*Hint:* 1 cm^3 = 1 mL)

13 Below is a picture of squares. The area of square F is 16 square units. The area of square B is 25 square units. The area of square H is 25 square units.

- **a** Find the area of all the other squares and explain how you got your answer.
- **b** Find the area of the total shape.
- **c** Find the perimeter of the shape.

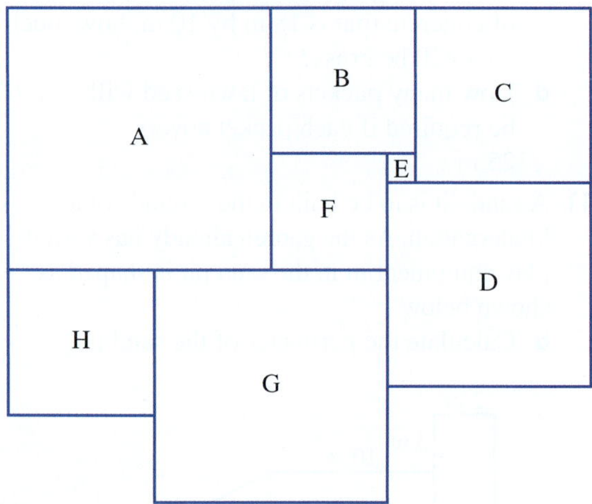

14 A cube with edges 36 cm long is cut into smaller cubes.

- **a** How many small cubes will there be if the smaller cubes have an edge of 12 cm?
- **b** What is the length of each side of the smaller cube if there are 64 cubes?

15 Elena is 162 cm tall. If she could walk around the earth along the equator (and the equator can be approximated as a circle), then the top of Elena's head would travel further than her feet would travel. How much further is this? Round your answer to 1 decimal place.

16 The width of a rectangle is 6 cm and its perimeter is 26 cm. What is the area of the rectangle?

17 While practising his karate skills, Alex accidentally made a large round hole in the wall of his office. The area of the hole is about 154 cm^2. To cover up the hole, Alex plans to use a square shaped photo frame (with a photo of himself in full uniform including his black belt). What is the smallest side length the photo frame can have? (Use $\pi = \frac{22}{7}$.)

18 The Great Wall of China stretches from the east to the west of China. It is the largest of a number of walls that were built bit by bit over thousands of years to serve as protection against military invasions. Some estimates are that the Great Wall itself is about 6300 km long. Assume your pace length is 70 cm. At 10 000 paces a day, how many days would it take you to walk the length of the Great Wall?

19 This clock face is circular, with a radius of 10 cm. It has a decorative mother-of-pearl square inset, connecting the numbers 12, 3, 6 and 9.

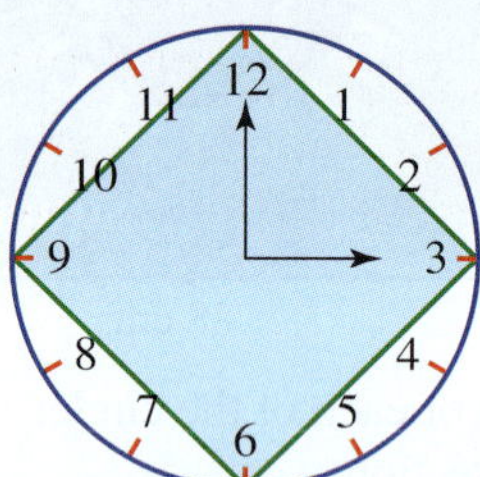

What fraction of the circular face does the square inset represent? Give your answer as an exact fraction in terms of π.

20 The two smaller circles in this diagram have a diameter that is equal to the radius of the medium-sized circle. The diameter of the medium-sized circle is equal to the radius of the large circle. What fraction of the large circle do the two small circles represent?

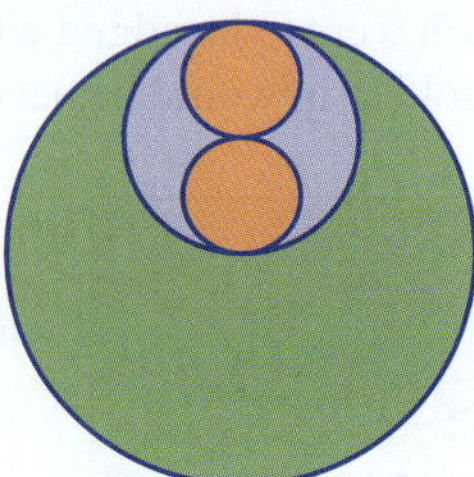

21 A square field is enclosed by a square fence, using 48 posts. The posts are 5 m apart, with one at each corner of the field. Determine the area bounded by the fence.

22 Pete's Pizzas come in four sizes:
small (12 cm diameter) \$8
medium (25 cm diameter) \$19
large (30 cm diameter) \$23.50
party size (22 cm by 40 cm) \$27.
Which one is the better buy?

23 Cameron was mowing his back yard, when he stubbed his toe and had to come inside. If he'd mowed a 2 m strip around the outside before he stopped, what area did his sister need to mow when she finished the job for him?

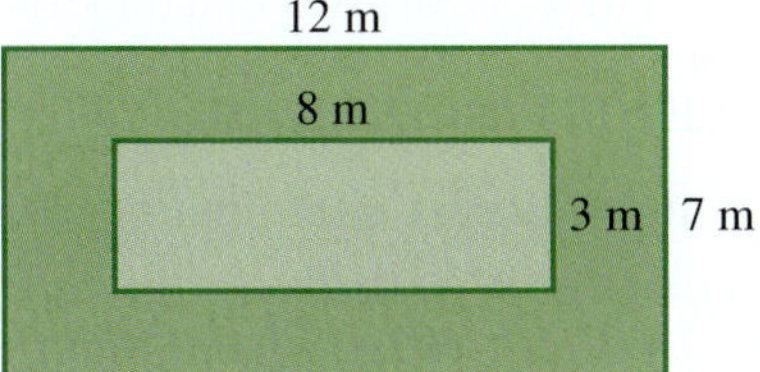

24 Polly divided her rectangular vegetable garden into four plots as shown. Three of the plots were rectangular and one was square. Find the area of the shaded plot.

15 m²	9 m²
	12 m²

25 Joe wants to make a kite. He has 0.5625 m^2 of material and wants to use it all. What lengths should Joe make his cross rods for his kite, if he wants them to be in the ratio 2:1? Explain.

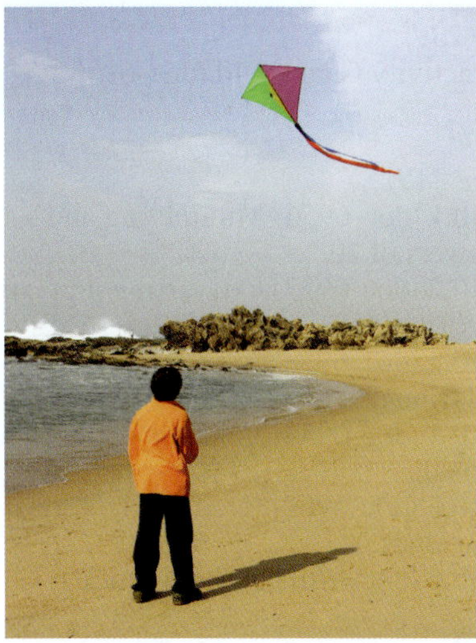

eBook*plus*

Interactivities
Test yourself
Chapter 10
int-2755
Word search
Chapter 10
int-2756
Crossword
Chapter 10
int-2757

eBook*plus* **ACTIVITIES**

Chapter opener

Digital doc *(page 239)*
- Hungry brain activity Chapter 10 (doc-6955)

Are you ready?

Digital docs *(page 240)*
- SkillSHEET 10.1 (doc-6956) Multiplying and dividing by powers of 10
- SkillSHEET 10.2 (doc-6957) Converting units of length
- SkillSHEET 10.3 (doc-6958) Areas of squares, rectangles and triangles
- SkillSHEET 10.4 (doc-6959) Volumes of cubes and rectangular prisms
- SkillSHEET 10.5 (doc-6960) Reading the time (from analogue clocks)
- SkillSHEET 10.6 (doc-6961) 24-hour clock

10A Perimeter

Digital docs *(page 244)*
- Activity 10-A-1 (doc-2297) Perimeters
- Activity 10-A-2 (doc-2298) More perimeters
- Activity 10-A-3 (doc-2299) Tricky perimeters

Weblink *(page 245)*
- Length conversions

10B Circumference

Digital docs *(page 249)*
- Activity 10-B-1 (doc-2300) Circumference
- Activity 10-B-2 (doc-2301) More circumference
- Activity 10-B-3 (doc-2302) Advanced circumference
- Investigation (doc-2318) The diameter of a circle and its circumference — any connection?

Interactivity *(page 249)*
- Finding pi (int-0079)

10C Area of rectangles, triangles, parallelograms, rhombuses and kites

Digital docs *(page 255)*
- Activity 10-C-1 (doc-2303) Area of rectangles, triangles and parallelograms
- Activity 10-C-2 (doc-2304) More area of rectangles, triangles and parallelograms
- Activity 10-C-3 (doc-2305) Advanced area of rectangles, triangles and parallelograms
- Investigation (doc-2319) Area of a parallelogram *(page 253)*

Weblink *(page 258)*
- Area of a rhombus

10D Area of a circle

Digital docs *(page 259)*
- Activity 10-D-1 (doc-2306) Area of a circle
- Activity 10-D-2 (doc-2307) More circles
- Activity 10-D-3 (doc-2308) Advanced calculations involving areas of circles
- Investigation (doc-2321) Area of a circle *(page 258)*

10E Area of trapeziums

Digital docs *(page 263)*
- Activity 10-E-1 (doc-2309) Area of a trapezium
- Activity 10-E-2 (doc-2310) More trapeziums
- Activity 10-E-3 (doc-2311) Advanced trapeziums
- Investigation (doc-2320) Area of a trapezium *(page 262)*
- WorkSHEET 10.1 (doc-2322) *(page 264)*

10F Volume of prisms and other solids

Digital docs *(page 268)*
- Activity 10-F-1 (doc-6929) Volume of prisms and other solids
- Activity 10-F-2 (doc-6930) More volume
- Activity 10-F-3 (doc-6931) Capacity
- Spreadsheet (doc-2324) Volume of a prism

Interactivity *(page 266)*
- Volume of prisms (int-2754)

10G Time

Digital docs *(page 273)*
- Activity 10-G-1 (doc-6962) Silly snake A
- Activity 10-G-2 (doc-6963) Silly snake B
- Activity 10-G-3 (doc-6964) Super silly snake
- Spreadsheet (doc-3445) Time differences *(page 275)*

10H 24-hour clock and time zones

Digital docs *(page 278)*
- Activity 10-H-1 (doc-6965) Time triangles
- Activity 10-H-2 (doc-6966) Tempting time triangles
- Activity 10-H-3 (doc-6967) Advanced time triangles
- WorkSHEET 10.2 (doc-6932) *(page 280)*
- Spreadsheet (doc-3447) 12-h to 24-h time
  Spreadsheet (doc-3448) 24-h to 12-h time *(page 279)*
- Spreadsheet (doc-3449) Time zones *(page 277)*

Chapter review

Interactivities *(page 289)*
- Test yourself Chapter 10 (int-2755) Take the end-of-chapter test to test your progress.
- Word search Chapter 10 (int-2756)
- Crossword Chapter 10 (int-2757)

To access eBookPLUS activities, log on to
www.jacplus.com.au

Linear equations

11A Identifying patterns
11B Backtracking and inverse operations
11C Keeping equations balanced
11D Using algebra to solve problems
11E Equations with the unknown on both sides

WHAT DO YOU KNOW?

1 List what you know about equations. Create a concept map to show your list.
2 Share what you know with a partner and then with a small group.
3 As a class, create a large concept map that shows your class's knowledge equations.

eBook*plus*

Digital doc
Hungry brain activity
Chapter 11
doc-6977

OPENING QUESTION

A plane uses an average of 40 L of fuel an hour. Write an equation that will enable a pilot to input the speed and output the number of hours of flight.

Are you ready?

Try the questions below. If you have difficulty with any of them, extra help can be obtained by completing the matching SkillSHEET located on your eBookPLUS.

eBookplus
Digital doc
SkillSHEET 11.1
doc-6978

Number patterns

1 For each of the following sequences of numbers, describe the pattern in words and then write down the next three numbers in the pattern.

a 7, 9, 11, 13, …
b 28, 24, 20, 16, …
c 3, 6, 12, 24, …
d 100 000, 10 000, 1000, …

eBookplus
Digital doc
SkillSHEET 11.2
doc-6979

Using tables to show number patterns

2 a Complete the table shown, using the diagrams at right as a guide.

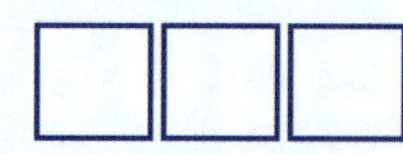

1 square　　2 squares　　3 squares

Number of squares	1	2	3	4	5	6
Number of sides	4	8				

b How many sides are there for 10 squares?

eBookplus
Digital doc
SkillSHEET 11.3
doc-6980

Describing a number pattern from a table

3 Describe each number pattern shown in the tables.

a

First number	1	2	3	4	5
Second number	7	8	9	10	11

b

First number	1	3	5	7	9
Second number	3	9	15	21	27

eBookplus
Digital doc
SkillSHEET 11.4
doc-6981

Flowcharts

4 Complete these flowcharts to find the output number.

a
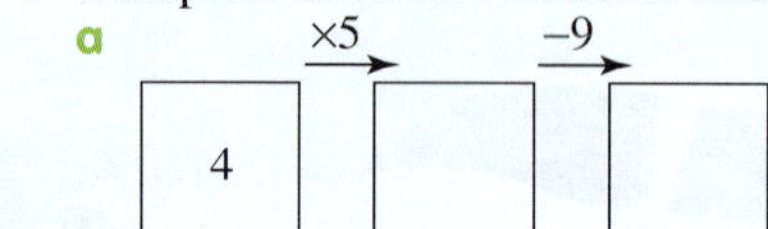

b
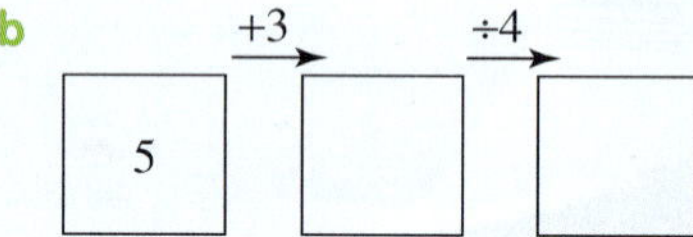

eBookplus
Digital doc
SkillSHEET 11.5
doc-6982

Inverse operations

5 Write the inverse operation for each of the following.

a $\times 2$
b $+8$
c -17
d $\div -5$

eBookplus
Digital doc
SkillSHEET 11.6
doc-6983

Solving equations by backtracking

6 Solve each of the following equations by first completing the flowcharts below. Remember to show the operations needed to backtrack to x.

a $7(x-4) = 35$

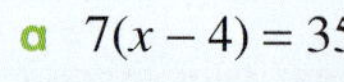
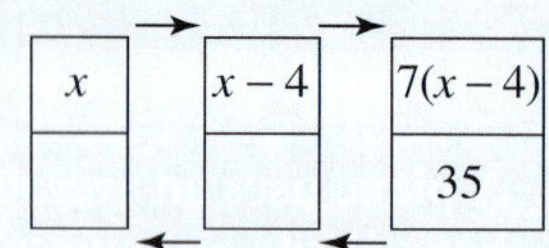

b $\dfrac{x+9}{5} = 3$

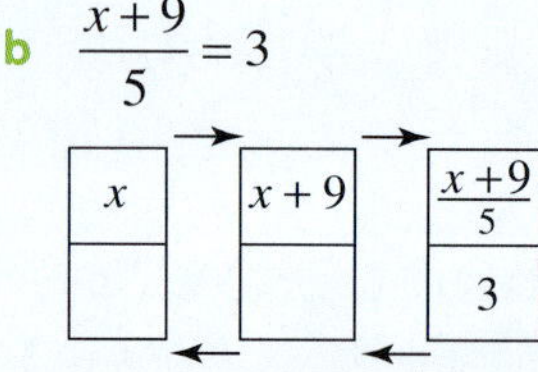

eBookplus
Digital doc
SkillSHEET 11.7
doc-6984

Combining like terms

7 Simplify each of the following expressions by combining like terms.

a $7v + 3 + 3v + 4$

b $6c + 15 - 5c - 8$

eBookplus
Digital doc
SkillSHEET 11.8
doc-6985

Expanding expressions containing brackets

8 Expand each of the following expressions containing brackets.

a $2(3x + 5)$

b $-7(m - 1)$

eBookplus
Digital doc
SkillSHEET 11.9
doc-6986

Checking solutions by substitution

9 For each equation below there is a solution given. Is the solution correct?

a $5x - 7 = 2x + 2 \qquad x = 3$

b $\dfrac{x + 9}{2} = 2x - 7 \qquad x = 5$

eBookplus
Digital doc
SkillSHEET 11.10
doc-6987

Writing equations from worded statements

10 Write an equation for each of the following statements, using x to represent the unknown number.

a When 2 is added to a certain number, the result is 9.

b Eight times a certain number is 40.

c When 11 is subtracted from a certain number, the result is 3.

d Dividing a certain number by 6 gives a result of 2.

11A Identifying patterns

- Mathematics is used to describe *relationships* in the world around us.
- Mathematicians study *patterns* in numbers and shapes found in nature to discover rules.
- These rules can then be applied to other, more general situations.
- Looking at the number pattern 1, 4, 7, 10, . . . we can see that by adding 3 to any of these numbers, we obtain the next number.
- This number pattern is called a **sequence**.
- Each number in the sequence is called a **term**.
- Each sequence has a *rule* that describes the pattern. For the sequence above, the rule is 'add 3'.

WORKED EXAMPLE 1

Describe the following number patterns in words then write down the next three numbers in the pattern.
a 4, 8, 12, . . .   b 4, 8, 16, . . .

THINK	WRITE
a 1 The next number is found by adding 4 to the previous number.	**a** Next number = previous number + 4
2 Add 4 each time to get the next three numbers.	
3 Write down the next three numbers.	Next three numbers are 16, 20, 24.
b 1 The next number is found by multiplying the previous number by 2.	**b** Next number = previous number × 2
2 Multiply by 2 each time to get the next three numbers.	
3 Write the next three numbers.	Next three numbers are 32, 64, 128.

WORKED EXAMPLE 2

Using the following rules, write down the first five terms of the number pattern.
a Start with 32 and divide by 2 each time.
b Start with 2, multiply by 4 and subtract 3 each time.

THINK	WRITE
a 1 Start with 32 and divide by 2.	**a** $32 \div 2 = 16$
2 Keep dividing the previous answer by 2 until five numbers have been calculated.	$16 \div 2 = 8$ $8 \div 2 = 4$ $4 \div 2 = 2$ $2 \div 2 = 1$
3 Write the answer.	The first five numbers are 16, 8, 4, 2 and 1.
b 1 Start with 2 then multiply by 4 and subtract 3.	**b** $2 \times 4 - 3 = 5$ $5 \times 4 - 3 = 17$
2 Continue to apply this rule to the answer until five numbers have been calculated.	$17 \times 4 - 3 = 65$ $65 \times 4 - 3 = 257$ $257 \times 4 - 3 = 1025$
3 Write the five numbers.	The first five numbers are 5, 17, 65, 257, 1025.

WORKED EXAMPLE 3

Describe the pattern that occurs in the final digit of the number set represented by: $7^1, 7^2, 7^3, \ldots$

THINK	WRITE
1 Calculate a few of these powers.	$7^1 = 7$
2 Continue until a pattern in the last digit is noticed. When the number becomes large, be concerned with only the last digit.	$7^2 = 49$ $7^3 = 49 \times 7 = 343$ $7^4 = 343 \times 7 = 2401$ $7^5 = 2401 \times 7 = 16\,807$ $7^6 = \ldots 7 \times 7 = \ldots 9$
3 Write the pattern.	The pattern in the last digit is 7, 9, 3, 1 repeated.

Geometric patterns

- Patterns can be found in geometric shapes.
- If we examine the three shapes below, we can see patterns by investigating the changes from one shape to the next. For example, look at the number of matchsticks in each set of triangles.

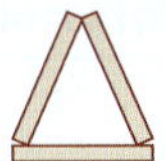 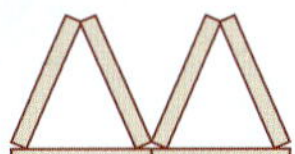 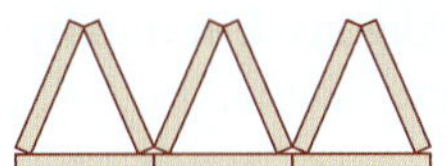

By using a table of values we can see a number pattern developing:

Number of triangles	Number of matchsticks
1	3
2	6
3	9
4	12
5	15
6	18

The pattern in the bottom row is 3, 6, 9, . . .; we can see that the rule here is 'add 3'.

We can also look for a relationship between the number of triangles and the number of matchsticks in each shape. If you examine the table, you will see that a relationship can be found. In words, the relationship is 'the number of matchsticks equals 3 times the number of triangles'.

WORKED EXAMPLE 4

Consider a set of hexagons constructed according to the pattern shown below.

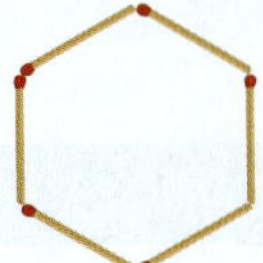 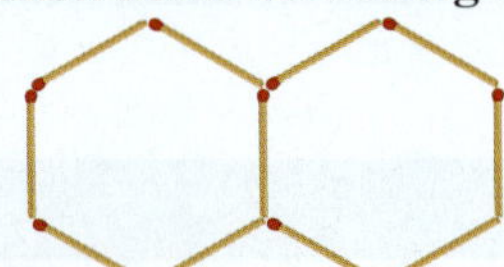 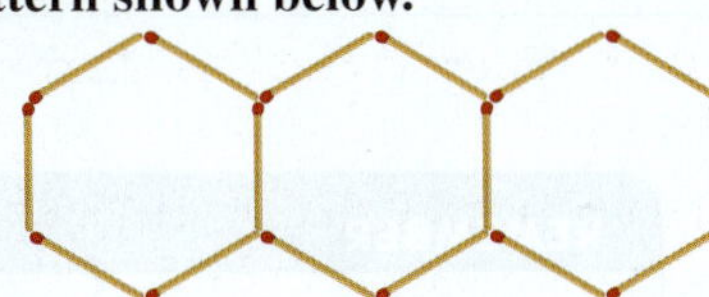

a Using matches, pencils or similar objects, construct the above figures. Draw the next two figures in the series.

b Draw up a table showing the relationship between the number of hexagons in the figure and the number of matches used to construct the figure.

c Devise a rule to describe the number of matches required for each figure in terms of the number of hexagons in the figure.

d Use your rule to determine the number of matches required to make a figure consisting of 20 hexagons.

THINK

WRITE

a 1 Construct the given figures with matches. Note the number of additional matches it takes to progress from one figure to the next — 5 in this case.

a The next two figures are

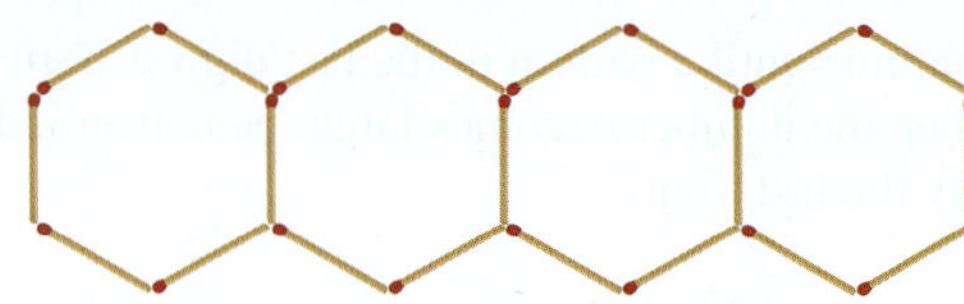

2 Draw the next two figures, adding another 5 matches each time.

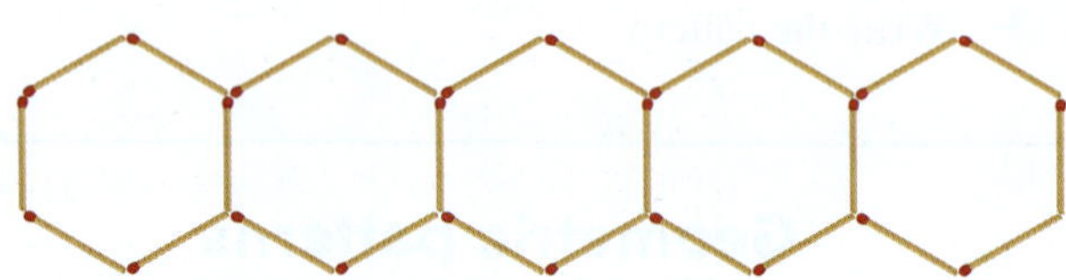

b Draw up a table showing the number of matches needed for each figure in terms of the number of hexagons. Fill it in by looking at the figures.

b

Number of hexagons	1	2	3	4	5
Number of matches	6	11	16	21	26

c 1 Look at the pattern in the number of matches going from one figure to the next. It is increasing by 5 each time.

c The number of matches increased by 5 in going from one figure to the next.

2 If we take the number of hexagons and multiply this number by 5, it does not give us the number of matches. However, if we add 1 to this number, it does give us the number of matches in each shape.

Number of matches
$= \text{number of hexagons} \times 5 + 1$

d 1 Use the rule to find the number of matches to make a figure with 20 hexagons.

d Number of matches for 20 hexagons
$= 20 \times 5 + 1$
$= 101$

2 Work out the answer and write it down.

So 101 matches would be required to construct a figure consisting of 20 hexagons.

REMEMBER

1. A number pattern has a rule that can describe the pattern.
2. Geometric patterns have a rule that can describe the pattern.
3. The rule can be used to make predictions.

EXERCISE

11A Identifying patterns

INDIVIDUAL PATHWAYS

eBook*plus*

Activity 11-A-1
Identifying patterns
doc-2336

Activity 11-A-2
More patterns
doc-2337

Activity 11-A-3
Advanced patterns
doc-2338

FLUENCY

1 WE1 Copy the patterns below, describe the pattern in words and then write down the next three numbers in the pattern.

a 2, 4, 6, 8, … **b** 3, 8, 13, 18, … **c** 27, 24, 21, 18, …
d 1, 3, 9, 27, … **e** 128, 64, 32, 16, … **f** 1, 4, 9, 16, …

2 Fill in the missing numbers in the following number patterns.

a 3, …, 9, 12, …, … **b** 8, …, …, 14, … **c** 4, 8, …, 32, …
d …, …, 13, 15, … **e** 66, 77, …, 99, … 121 **f** 100, …, …, 85, 80, …

3 WE2 Using the following rules, write down the first five terms of the number patterns.

a Start with 1 and add 4 each time.
b Start with 5 and multiply by 3 each time.
c Start with 50 and take away 8 each time.
d Start with 64 and divide by 2 each time.
e Start with 1, multiply by 2 and add 2 each time.
f Start with 1, add 2 then multiply by 2 each time.

UNDERSTANDING

4 Each of the following represents a special number set. What is common to the numbers in the set?

a 2, 4, 6, 8, 10 **b** 1, 8, 27, 64 **c** 2, 3, 5, 7, 11
d 1, 1, 2, 3, 5, 8 **e** 1, 2, 3, 4, 6, 12 **f** 3, 9, 27, 81

5 WE3 Investigate the pattern that occurs in the final digit of the following sets. Describe the pattern in each case.

a $2^1, 2^2, 2^3, \ldots$ **b** $3^1, 3^2, 3^3, \ldots$ **c** $4^1, 4^2, 4^3, \ldots$
d $5^1, 5^2, 5^3, \ldots$ **e** $8^1, 8^2, 8^3, \ldots$

6 WE4 For each of the sets of shapes below:

i Construct the shapes using matches. Draw the next two shapes in the series.
ii Construct a table to show the relationship between the number of shapes in each figure and the number of matchsticks used to construct it.
iii Devise a rule in words that describes the pattern relating the number of shapes in each figure and the number of matchsticks used to construct it.
iv Use your rule to work out the number of matchsticks required to construct a figure made up of 20 such shapes.

a
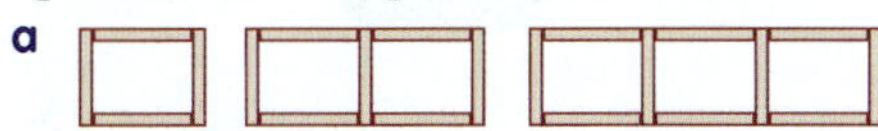

b
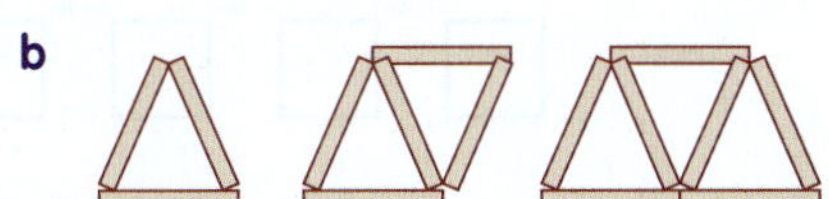

c
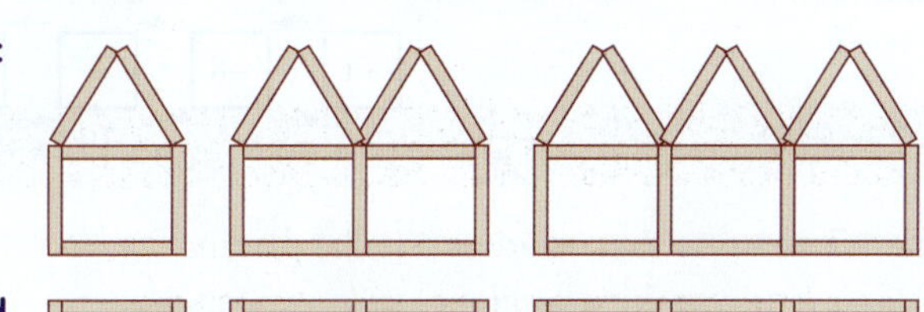

d
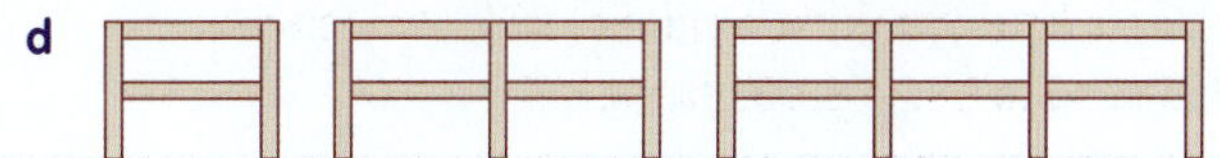

REASONING

7 Consider the triangular pattern of even numbers shown below.

2
4 6
8 10 12

a Complete the next three lines of the triangle using this pattern.
b Complete the triangle as far as necessary to find the position of the number 60.
c Explain how, without completing any more of the triangle, you could find the position of the number 100.
d Study the triangle you have created in part **2** and write down as many patterns as you can find. Illustrate each pattern with numbers from the triangle.
e Create a similar triangle using odd numbers. Look for the patterns in this triangle. Are they the same as or different from those for the triangle of even numbers? Justify your answers by illustrations from the triangle.

REFLECTION
What should you look for when trying to determine number patterns?

11B Backtracking and inverse operations

- An equation links two expressions with an equals sign.
- Adding and subtracting are inverse operations.
- Multiplying and dividing are inverse operations.
- A flowchart can be used to represent a series of operations.
- In a flowchart, the starting number is called the input number and the final number is called the output number.
- By using inverse operations, it is possible to reverse the flowchart and work from the output number to the input number.

WORKED EXAMPLE 5

Find the input number for this flowchart.

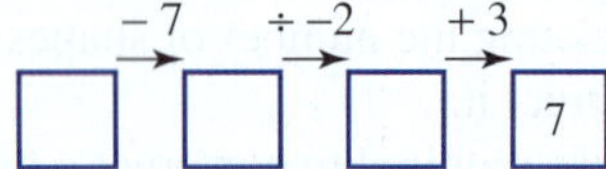

THINK

1 Copy the flowchart.

2 Backtrack to find the input number.
The inverse operation of +3 is −3
(7 − 3 = 4).
The inverse operation of ÷ −2 is × −2
(4 × −2 = −8).
The inverse operation of −7 is +7
(−8 + 7 = −1).
Fill in the missing numbers.

WRITE

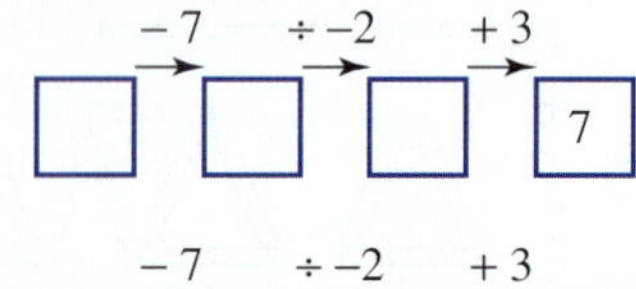

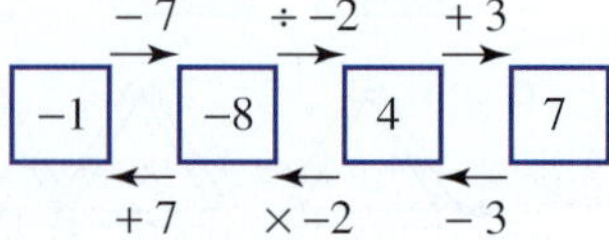

WORKED EXAMPLE 6

Find the output expression for this flowchart.

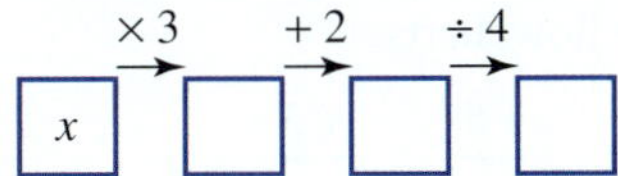

THINK

1. Copy the flowchart and look at the operations that have been performed.

WRITE

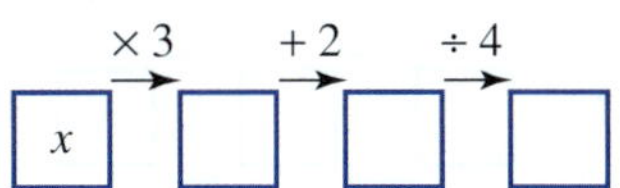

THINK

2. Multiplying x by 3 gives $3x$.

WRITE

× 3 → + 2 → ÷ 4

x → $3x$ → ☐ → ☐

THINK

3. Adding 2 gives $3x + 2$.

WRITE

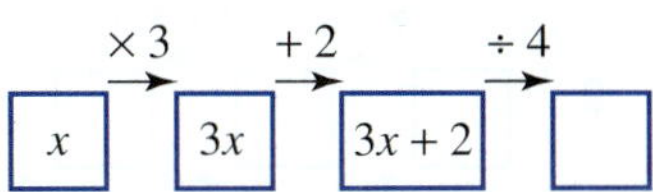

THINK

4. Now place a line beneath all of $3x + 2$ and divide by 4.

WRITE

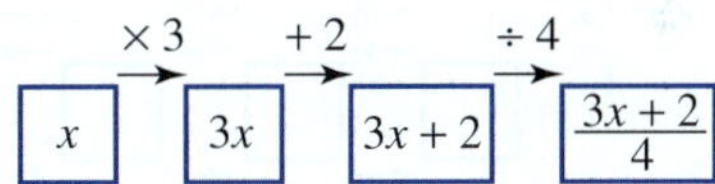

WORKED EXAMPLE 7

Starting with x, draw the flowchart whose output number is given by the expressions:

a $6 - 2x$

b $-2(x + 6)$.

THINK

a
1. Rearrange the expression.
Note: $6 - 2x$ is the same as $-2x + 6$.
2. Multiply x by -2, and then add 6.

b
1. The expression $x + 6$ is grouped in a pair of brackets, so we must obtain this part first. Therefore, add 6 to x.
2. Multiply the whole expression by -2.

WRITE

a

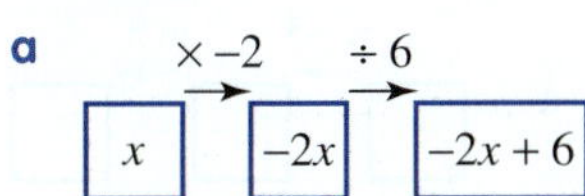

b

÷ 6 → × − 2

x → $x + 6$ → $-2(x + 6)$

REMEMBER

1. To work backwards through a flowchart we use inverse operations.
2. Adding and subtracting are inverse operations.
3. Multiplying and dividing are inverse operations.

EXERCISE

11B Backtracking and inverse operations

INDIVIDUAL PATHWAYS

eBook*plus*

Activity 11-B-1
Sudoku challenge A
doc-2339

Activity 11-B-2
Sudoku challenge B
doc-2340

Activity 11-B-3
Sudoku challenge C
doc-2341

FLUENCY

1 WE5 Find the input number for each of the following flowcharts.

a 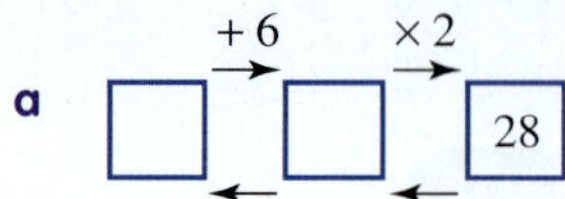
$+6$, $\times 2$ → 28

b 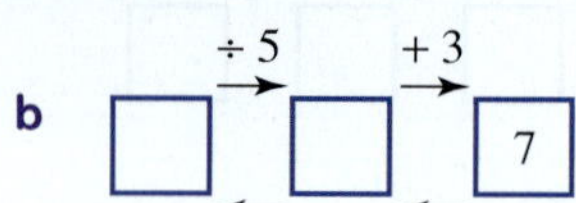
$\div 5$, $+3$ → 7

c 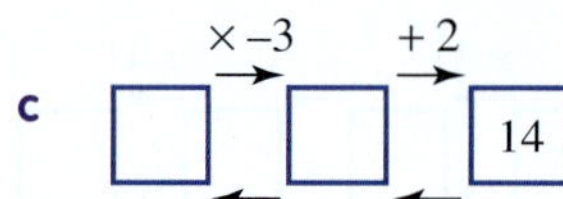
$\times -3$, $+2$ → 14

d 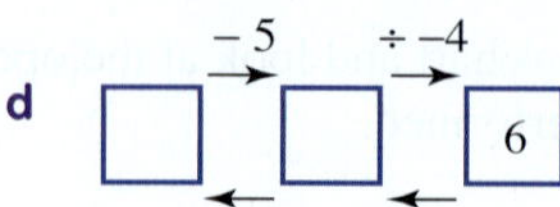
-5, $\div -4$ → 6

e 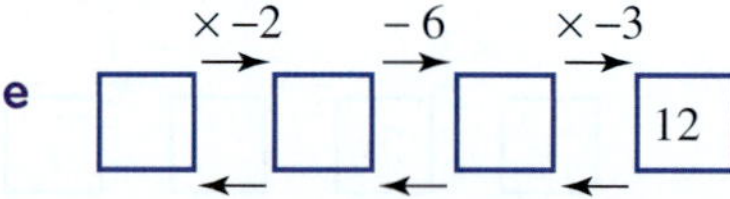
$\times -2$, -6, $\times -3$ → 12

f 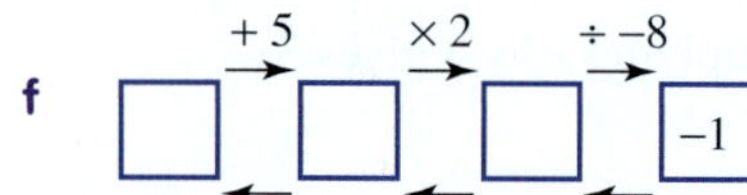
$+5$, $\times 2$, $\div -8$ → -1

g 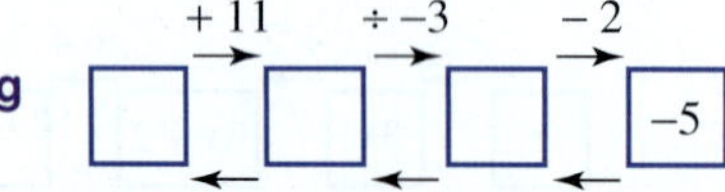
$+11$, $\div -3$, -2 → -5

h 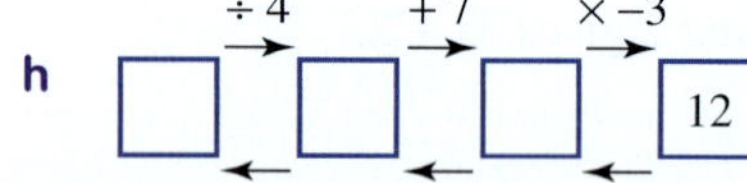
$\div 4$, $+7$, $\times -3$ → 12

i 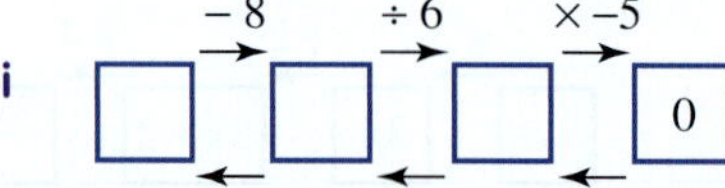
-8, $\div 6$, $\times -5$ → 0

j 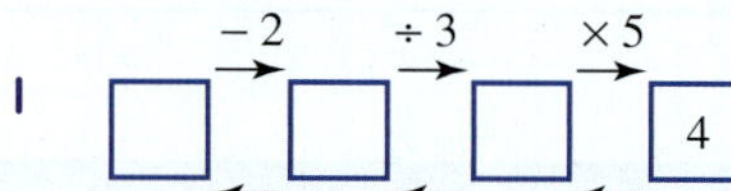
-7, $\times 2$, -5 → -11

k $+0.5$, $\times 4$, -5.1 → 1.2

l -2, $\div 3$, $\times 5$ → 4

2 WE6 Find the output expression for each of the following flowcharts.

a x → $\times 2$, -7

b w → -7, $\times 2$

c s → $\times -5$, $+3$

d n → $+3$, $\times -5$

e m → $\div 2$, $+7$

f y → $+7$, $\div 2$

g z → $\times 6$, -3, $\div 2$

h d → $+5$, $\times -3$, $\div 4$

i e → $\times 2$, $\div 5$, $+1$

j 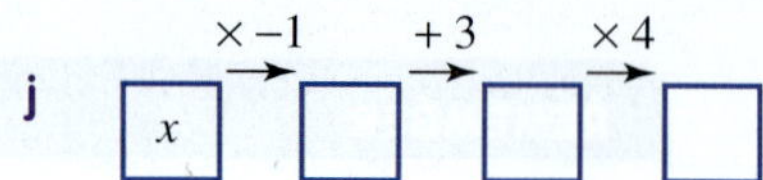
x → $\times -1$, $+3$, $\times 4$

k w → -5, $\times -2$, $\div 7$

l z → $+6$, $\times -3$, -11

m 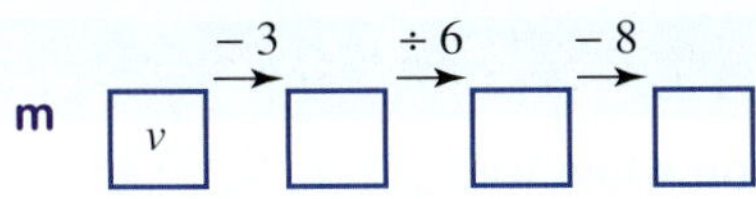

n 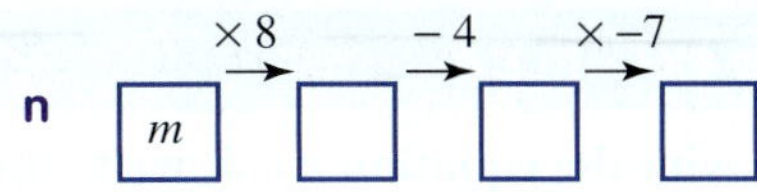

o 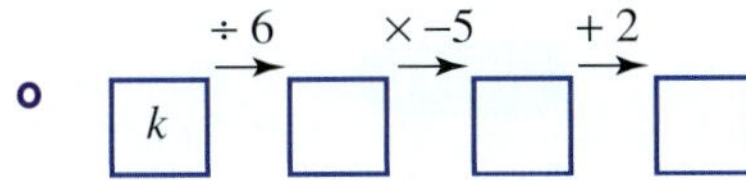

p 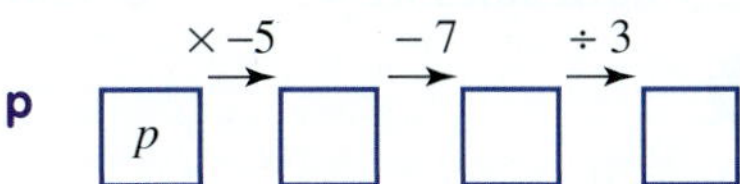

3 WE7 Starting with x, draw the flowchart whose output number is:

a $2(x + 7)$
b $-2(x - 8)$
c $3m - 6$
d $-3m - 6$
e $\frac{x-5}{8}$
f $\frac{x}{8} - 5$
g $-5x + 11$
h $-x + 11$
i $-x - 13$
j $5 - 2x$
k $\frac{3x-7}{4}$
l $\frac{-3(x-2)}{4}$
m $\frac{x+5}{8} - 3$
n $-7\left(\frac{x}{5} - 2\right)$
o $3\left(\frac{2x}{7} + 4\right)$
p $\frac{1}{4}\left(\frac{6x}{11} - 3\right)$

REFLECTION
What do you need to be careful of when you are backtracking equations?

11C Keeping equations balanced

- As an equation can be thought of as two expressions with an equals sign between them, an equation can be thought of as a balanced scale. The diagram at right represents the simple equation $x = 3$.

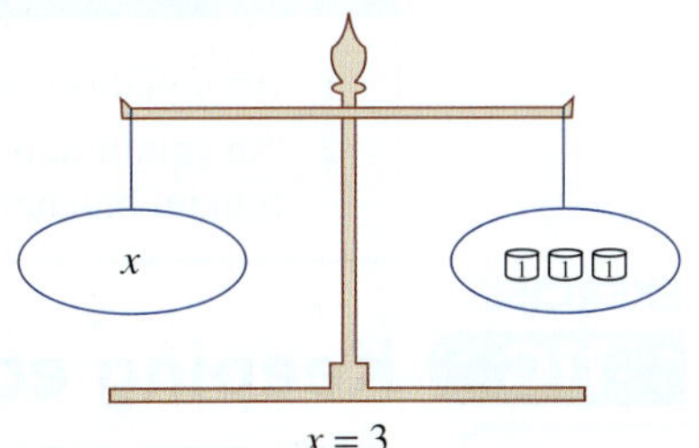

$x = 3$

- If the amount of the left-hand side (LHS) is doubled, the scale will stay balanced provided that the amount on the right-hand side (RHS) is doubled.

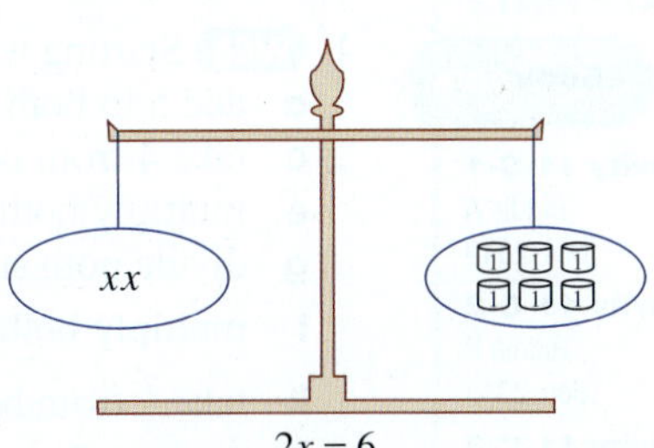

$2x = 6$

- Similarly, the scale will stay balanced if we add a quantity to both sides.
- The scales will remain balanced as long as we do the same to both sides.

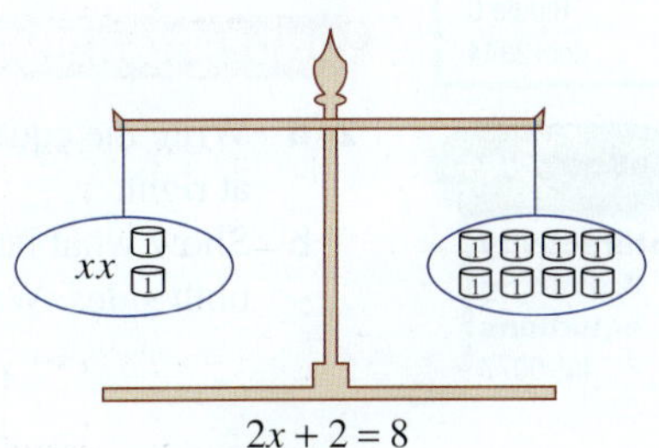

$2x + 2 = 8$

WORKED EXAMPLE 8

Starting with the equation $x = 4$, write the new equation when we:

a multiply both sides by 4 **b** take 6 from both sides **c** divide both sides by $\frac{2}{5}$.

THINK		WRITE
a	1 Write the equation.	**a** $x = 4$
	2 Multiply both sides by 4.	$x \times 4 = 4 \times 4$
	3 Simplify by removing the multiplication signs. Write numbers before variables.	$4x = 16$
b	1 Write the equation.	**b** $x = 4$
	2 Subtract 6 from both sides.	$x - 6 = 4 - 6$
	3 Simplify.	$x - 6 = -2$
c	1 Write the equation.	**c** $x = 4$
	2 Dividing by a fraction is the same as multiplying by its reciprocal. Multiply both sides by $\frac{5}{2}$.	$x \div \frac{2}{5} = 4 \div \frac{2}{5}$ $x \times \frac{5}{2} = 4 \times \frac{5}{2}$
	3 Simplify.	$\frac{5x}{2} = \frac{20}{2}$ $\frac{5x}{2} = 10$

REMEMBER

1. An equation links two expressions with an equals sign.
2. An equation is like a pair of balanced scales (or a seesaw). The scales (or seesaw) will remain balanced as long as we do the same to both sides.

EXERCISE 11C Keeping equations balanced

INDIVIDUAL PATHWAYS

eBook*plus*

Activity 11-C-1 Riddle A doc-2342

Activity 11-C-2 Riddle B doc-2343

Activity 11-C-3 Riddle C doc-2344

FLUENCY

1 WE8 Starting with the equation $x = 6$, write the new equation when we:

a add 5 to both sides
b multiply both sides by 7
c take 4 from both sides
d divide both sides by 3
e multiply both sides by -4
f multiply both sides by -1
g divide both sides by -1
h take 9 from both sides
i multiply both sides by $\frac{2}{3}$
j divide both sides by $\frac{2}{3}$
k take $\frac{2}{3}$ from both sides.

UNDERSTANDING

eBook*plus*

Interactivity Balancing equations int-0077

2 **a** Write the equation that is represented by the diagram at right.
b Show what happens when you halve the amount on both sides. Write the new equation.

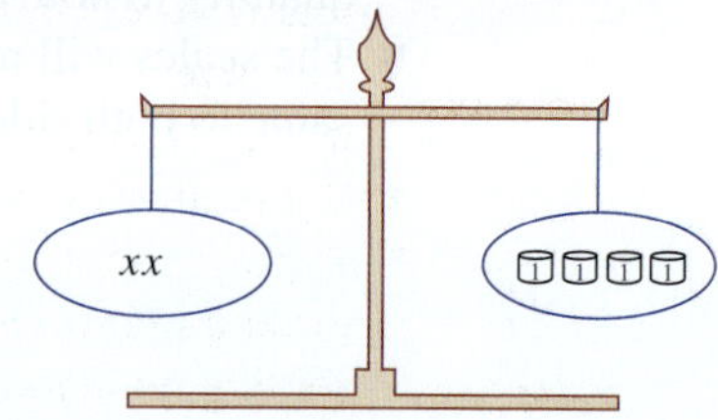

3 **a** Write the equation that is represented by the diagram at right.

b Show what happens when you take three from both sides. Write the new equation.

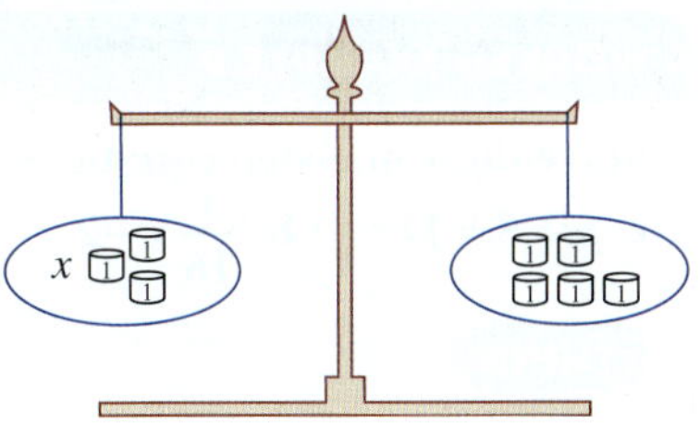

4 **a** Write the equation that is represented by the diagram at right.

b Show what happens when you add three to both sides. Write the new equation.

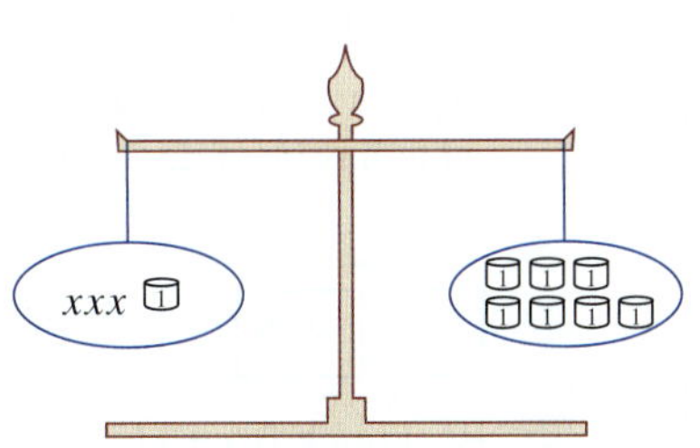

5 **a** Write the equation that is represented by the diagram at right.

b Show what happens when you double the amount on each side. Write the new equation.

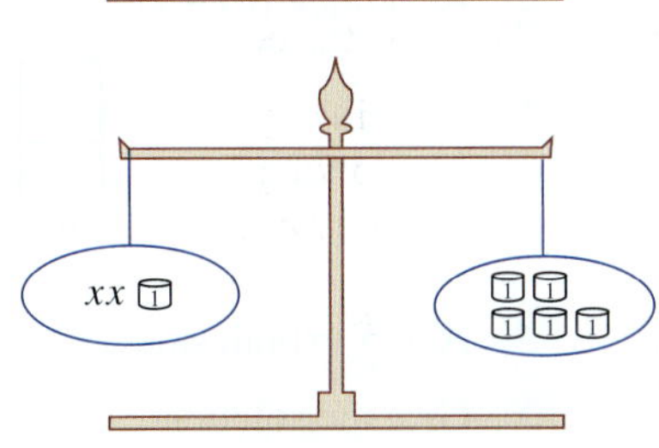

6 **MC** If we start with $x = 5$, which of these equations is not true?

A $x + 2 = 7$ **B** $3x = 8$ **C** $-2x = -10$

D $\frac{x}{5} = 1$ **E** $x - 2 = 3$

7 **MC** If we start with $x = 3$, which of these equations is not true?

A $\frac{2x}{3} = 2$ **B** $-2x = -6$ **C** $2x - 6 = 0$

D $\frac{x}{5} = \frac{3}{5}$ **E** $x - 5 = 2$

8 **MC** If we start with $x = -6$, which of these equations is not true?

A $-x = 6$ **B** $2x = -12$ **C** $x - 6 = 0$

D $x + 4 = -2$ **E** $x - 2 = -8$

eBook*plus*

Digital doc
WorkSHEET 11.1
doc-2351

9 **MC** If we start with $2x = 12$, which of these equations is not true?

A $\frac{2x}{3} = 4$ **B** $-2x = -12$ **C** $2x - 6 = 2$

D $4x = 24$ **E** $2x + 5 = 17$

REFLECTION
How does using inverse operations keep the equations balanced?

11D Using algebra to solve problems

- A **linear equation** is an equation where the variable has an index (power) of 1. This means that it never contains terms like x^2 or $\sqrt{x}$.
- To solve a linear equation, perform the same operations on both sides until the variable or unknown is left by itself.
- Sometimes the variable or unknown is called a pronumeral.
- A flowchart is useful to show you the order of operations applied to x, so that the reverse order and inverse operation can be used to solve the equation. As you become confident with solving equations algebraically, you can leave out the flowchart steps.

WORKED EXAMPLE 9

Solve these one-step equations by doing the same to both sides.

a $p - 5 = 11$ **b** $\dfrac{x}{16} = -2$

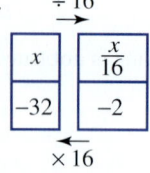

THINK		WRITE
a	1 Write the equation.	**a** $p - 5 = 11$
	2 Draw a flowchart and fill in the arrow to show what has been done to p. $\xrightarrow{-5}$ p → $p - 5$	
	3 Backtrack from 11. 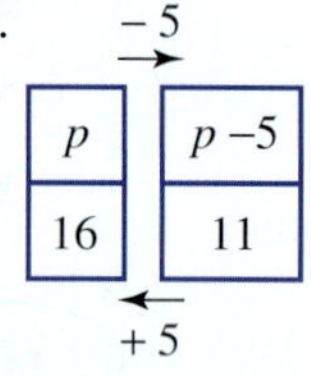	
	4 Add 5 to both sides.	$p - 5 + 5 = 11 + 5$
	5 Give the solution.	$p = 16$
b	1 Write the equation.	**b** $\dfrac{x}{16} = -2$
	2 Draw a flowchart and fill in the arrow to show what has been done to x. $\xrightarrow{16}$ x → $\dfrac{x}{16}$	
	3 Backtrack from -2. $\xrightarrow{\div 16}$ x → $\dfrac{x}{16}$ -32 ← -2 $\xleftarrow{\times 16}$	
	4 Multiply both sides by 16.	$\dfrac{x}{16} \times 16 = -2 \times 16$
	5 Give the solution.	$x = -32$

- The equations in Worked example 9 are called one-step equations because only one operation needs to be undone to obtain the value of the unknown.

WORKED EXAMPLE 10

Solve these two-step equations by doing the same to both sides.

a $2(x + 5) = 18$ **b** $\dfrac{x}{3} + 1 = 7$

THINK		WRITE
a	1 Write the equation.	**a** $2(x + 5) = 18$

2 Draw a flowchart and fill in the arrow to show what has been done to x.

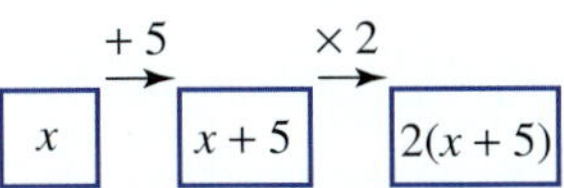

3 Backtrack from 18.

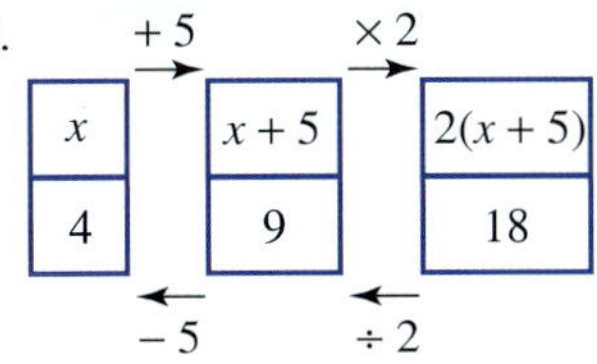

4 Divide both sides by 2.

$$\frac{2(x+5)}{2} = \frac{18}{2}$$
$$x + 5 = 9$$

5 Subtract 5 from both sides.

$$x + 5 - 5 = 9 - 5$$

6 Give the solution.

$$x = 4$$

b 1 Write the equation.

b $$\frac{x}{3} + 1 = 7$$

2 Draw a flowchart and fill in the arrows to show what has been done to x.

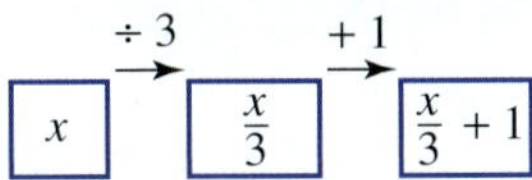

3 Backtrack from 7.

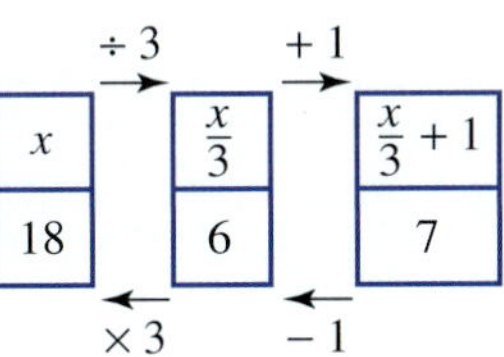

4 Subtract 1 from both sides.

$$\frac{x}{3} + 1 - 1 = 7 - 1$$
$$\frac{x}{3} = 6$$

5 Multiply both sides by 3.

$$\frac{x}{3} \times 3 = 6 \times 3$$

6 Give the solution.

$$x = 18$$

- The equations in Worked example 10 are called two-step equations because two operations need to be undone to obtain the value of the unknown.

WORKED EXAMPLE 11

Solve the following equations by doing the same to both sides.

a $3(m - 4) + 8 = 5$ **b** $6\left(\frac{x}{2} + 5\right) = -18$

THINK

WRITE

a 1 Write the equation.

a $3(m - 4) + 8 = 5$

2 Draw a flowchart and fill in the arrows to show what has been done to m.

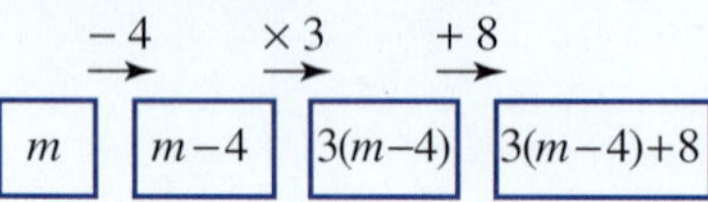

3 Backtrack from 5.

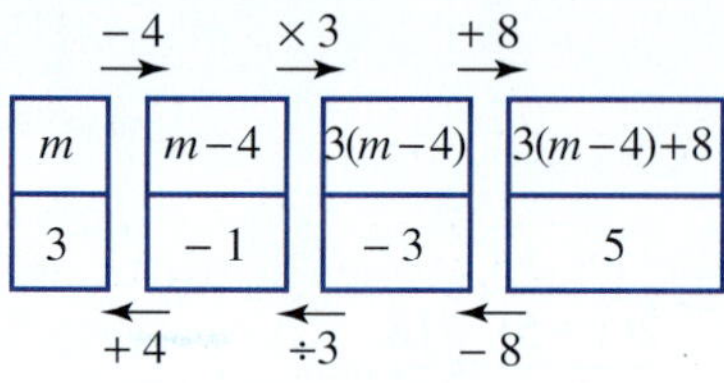

4 Subtract 8 from both sides.

$$3(m-4)+8-8=5-8$$
$$3(m-4)=-3$$

5 Divide both sides by 3.

$$\frac{3(m-4)}{3}=\frac{-3}{3}$$
$$m-4=-1$$

6 Add 4 to both sides.

$$m-4+4=-1+4$$

7 Give the solution.

$$m=3$$

b 1 Write the equation.

b $6\left(\frac{x}{2}+5\right)=-18$

2 Draw a flowchart and fill in the arrows to show what has been done to x.

x	$\xrightarrow{\div 2}$	$\frac{x}{2}$	$\xrightarrow{+5}$	$\frac{x}{2}+5$	$\xrightarrow{\times 6}$	$6(\frac{x}{2}+5)$

3 Backtrack from −18.

x	$\xrightarrow{\div 2}$	$\frac{x}{2}$	$\xrightarrow{+5}$	$\frac{x}{2}+5$	$\xrightarrow{\times 6}$	$6(\frac{x}{2}+5)$
−16	$\xleftarrow{\times 2}$	−8	$\xleftarrow{-5}$	−3	$\xleftarrow{\div 6}$	−18

4 Divide both sides by 6.

$$\frac{6\left(\frac{x}{2}+5\right)}{6}=\frac{-18}{6}$$
$$\frac{x}{2}+5=-3$$

5 Subtract 5 from both sides.

$$\frac{x}{2}+5-5=-3-5$$
$$\frac{x}{2}=-8$$

6 Multiply both sides by 2.

$$\frac{x}{2}\times 2=-8\times 2$$

7 Give the solution.

$$x=-16$$

REMEMBER

1. A linear equation is an equation where the variable has an index (power) of 1.
2. When solving linear equations, perform the same operations on both sides of the equation until the unknown is left by itself.
3. You can draw a flowchart to help you to decide what to do next.

EXERCISE 11D

Using algebra to solve problems

INDIVIDUAL PATHWAYS

eBook*plus*

Activity 11-D-1 Using algebra to solve problems doc-2345

Activity 11-D-2 More problems using algebra doc-2346

Activity 11-D-3 Advanced problems using algebra doc-2347

eBook*plus*

Digital doc Spreadsheet **2-step equations** doc-2353

FLUENCY

1 WE9a Solve these one-step equations by doing the same to both sides.

a $x+8=7$ **b** $12+r=7$ **c** $31=t+7$ **d** $w+4.2=6.9$
e $\frac{5}{8}=m+\frac{1}{8}$ **f** $\frac{2}{7}=j+3$ **g** $q-8=11$ **h** $-16+r=-7$
i $21=t-11$ **j** $y-5.7=8.8$ **k** $-\frac{11}{7}=z-\frac{2}{3}$ **l** $-\frac{9}{13}=f-1$

2 WE9b Solve these one-step equations by doing the same to both sides.

a $11d=88$ **b** $7p=-98$ **c** $5u=4$ **d** $2.5g=12.5$
e $8m=\frac{1}{4}$ **f** $-\frac{3}{5}=9j$ **g** $\frac{t}{8}=3$ **h** $\frac{k}{5}=-12$
i $-5.3=\frac{l}{4}$ **j** $\frac{v}{6}=\frac{2}{3}$ **k** $\frac{c}{9}=-\frac{5}{27}$ **l** $-\frac{7}{12}=\frac{h}{5}$

3 WE10a Solve these two-step equations by doing the same to both sides.

a $3m+5=14$ **b** $-2w+6=16$ **c** $-5k-12=8$ **d** $4t-3=-15$
e $2(m-4)=-6$ **f** $-3(n+12)=18$ **g** $5(k+6)=-15$ **h** $-6(s+11)=-24$
i $2m+3=10$ **j** $40=-5(p+6)$ **k** $5-3g=14$ **l** $11-4f=-9$
m $2q-4.9=13.2$ **n** $7.6+5r=-8.4$ **o** $13.6=4t-0.8$ **p** $-6k+7.3=8.5$
q $-4g-\frac{1}{5}=\frac{4}{5}$ **r** $-\frac{3}{8}=2f-\frac{18}{8}$

4 WE10b Solve these two-step equations by doing the same to both sides.

a $\frac{x}{3}+2=9$ **b** $\frac{x-5}{4}=1$ **c** $\frac{m+3}{2}=-7$ **d** $\frac{h}{-3}+1=5$
e $\frac{-m}{5}-3=1$ **f** $\frac{2w}{5}=-4$ **g** $\frac{-3m}{7}=-1$ **h** $\frac{c-7}{3}=-2$
i $\frac{-5m}{4}=10$ **j** $\frac{t+2}{7}=-5$ **k** $\frac{c-21}{9}=-4.5$ **l** $\frac{x}{8}-3.2=-5.8$

5 WE11 Solve these equations by doing the same to both sides. They will need more than two steps.

a $2(m+3)+7=3$ **b** $\frac{-2(x+5)}{5}=6$ **c** $\frac{5m+6}{3}=4$ **d** $\frac{3x-2}{7}=1$
e $\frac{4-2x}{3}=6$ **f** $\frac{-x+3}{2}=-4$ **g** $\frac{3x}{7}-2=1$ **h** $\frac{4b}{5}-3=5$
i $\frac{7f}{9}+2=-5$ **j** $6-\frac{4z}{3}=-2$ **k** $8-\frac{6m}{5}=2$ **l** $-9-\frac{5u}{11}=-4$
m $\frac{3m-5}{-2}=7$ **n** $-7(5w+3)=35$ **o** $5\left(\frac{x}{2}-6\right)=-10$ **p** $\frac{d-7}{2}+10=8$
q $\frac{3n+1}{4}-5=2$ **r** $\frac{3(t-5)}{7}+9=6$

UNDERSTANDING

eBook*plus*

Digital doc
Spreadsheet
3-step equations
doc-2354

6 Below is Alex's working to solve the equation $2x + 3 = 14$.

$$2x + 3 = 14$$
$$\frac{2x}{2} + 3 = \frac{14}{2}$$
$$x + 3 = 7$$
$$x + 3 - 3 = 7 - 3$$
$$x = 4$$

a Is the solution correct?
b If not, can you find where the error is and correct it?

7 Simplify the left-hand side of the following equations by collecting like terms, and then solve.

a $3x + 5 + 2x + 4 = 19$
b $13v - 4v + 2v = -22$
c $-3m + 6 - 5m + 1 = 15$
d $-3y + 7 + 4y - 2 = 9$
e $-3y - 7y + 4 = 64$
f $5t + 4 - 8t = 19$
g $5w + 3w - 7 + w = 13$
h $w + 7 + w - 15 + w + 1 = -5$
i $7 - 3u + 4 + 2u = 15$
j $7c - 4 - 11 + 3c - 7c + 5 = 8$

REASONING

8 A repair person calculates his service fee using the equation $F = 40t + 55$, where F is the service fee in dollars and t is the number of hours spent on the job.
a How long did a particular job take if the service fee was $155?
b Explain what the numbers 40 and 55 could represent as costs in the service fee equation.

9 Lyn and Peta together raised $517 from their cake stalls at the school fete. If Lyn raised l dollars and Peta raised $286, write an equation that represents the situation and determine the amount Lyn raised.

10 a Write an equation that represents the perimeter of the figure at right and then solve for x.

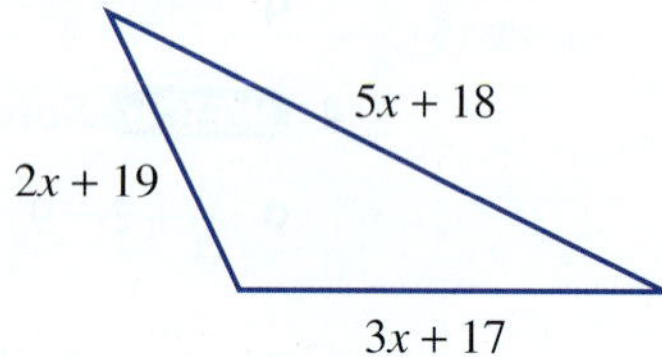

b Write an equation that represents the perimeter of the figure at right and then solve for x.

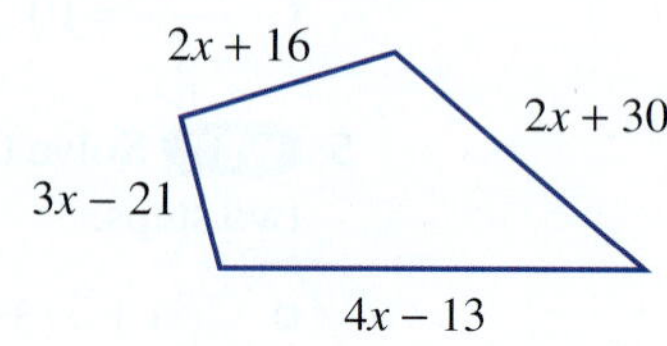

11 Two positive integers have a difference of 5 and a sum of 13. Find the two numbers.

12 If four times a certain number equals nine minus a half of the number, find the number.

13 Tom is 5 years old and his dad is 10 times his age, being 50 years old. Is it possible, at any stage, for Tom's dad to be twice the age of his son? Explain your answer.

14 Laurie earns the same amount for mowing the four of the neighbour's lawns every month. Each month he saves all his pay except $30, which he spends on his mobile phone. If he has $600 at the end of the year, how much did he earn each month? (Write an equation to solve for this situation first.)

15 The linear relationship between two variables x and y is displayed in this table.

x	$\frac{1}{8}$	$\frac{1}{4}$	$\frac{3}{8}$	$\frac{1}{2}$
y	$\frac{7}{12}$	$\frac{5}{6}$	$\frac{13}{12}$	$\frac{4}{3}$

Write the linear relationship as an equation.

REFLECTION

How do you decide on the order to undo the operations?

11E Equations with the unknown on both sides

- Some equations have unknowns on both sides of the equation.
- If an equation has unknowns on both sides, eliminate the unknowns from one side and then solve as usual.
- Consider the equation $4x + 1 = 2x + 5$.
  - Drawing the equation on a pair of scales, looks like this:

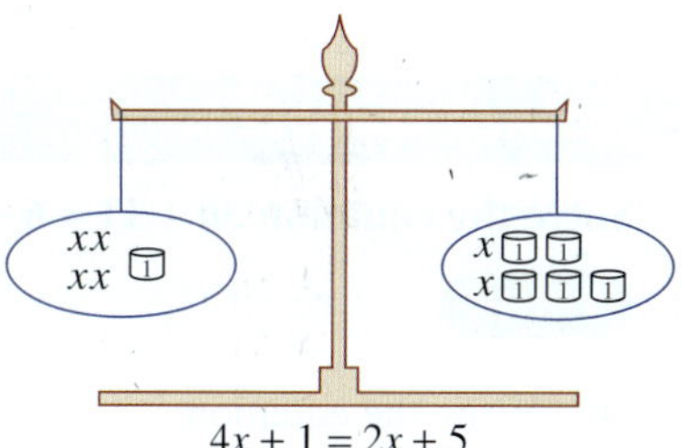

$4x + 1 = 2x + 5$

  - The scales remain balanced if $2x$ is eliminated from both sides:

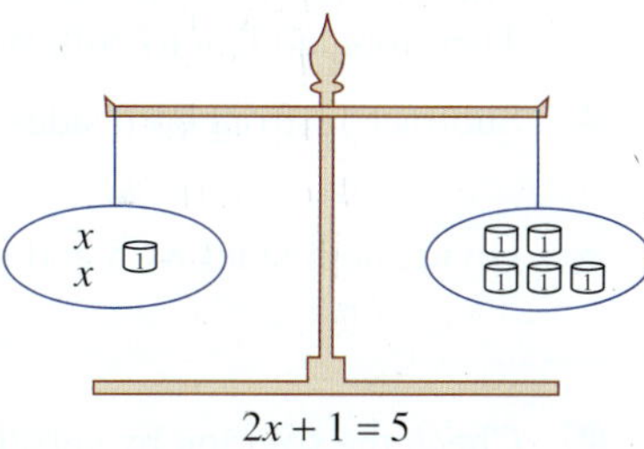

$2x + 1 = 5$

  - Writing this algebraically, we have

$$\begin{aligned} 4x + 1 &= 2x + 5 \\ 4x + 1 - 2x &= 2x + 5 - 2x \\ 2x + 1 &= 5 \\ 2x + 1 - 1 &= 5 - 1 \\ 2x &= 4 \\ \frac{2x}{2} &= \frac{4}{2} \\ x &= 2 \end{aligned}$$

WORKED EXAMPLE 12

Solve the equation $5t - 8 = 3t + 12$ and check your solution.

THINK	WRITE
1 Write the equation.	$5t - 8 = 3t + 12$
2 Subtract the smaller unknown (that is, $3t$) from both sides and simplify.	$5t - 8 - 3t = 3t + 12 - 3t$ $2t - 8 = 12$

3 Add 8 to both sides and simplify.

$$2t - 8 + 8 = 12 + 8$$
$$2t = 20$$

4 Divide both sides by 2 and simplify.

$$\frac{2t}{2} = \frac{20}{2}$$
$$t = 10$$

5 Check the solution by substituting $t = 10$ into the left-hand side and then the right-hand side of the equation.

If $t = 10$,

$$\begin{aligned} \text{LHS} &= 5t - 8 \\ &= 50 - 8 \\ &= 42 \end{aligned}$$

If $t = 10$,

$$\begin{aligned} \text{RHS} &= 3t + 12 \\ &= 30 + 12 \\ &= 42 \end{aligned}$$

6 Comment on the answers obtained.

Since the LHS and RHS are equal, the equation is true when $t = 10$.

WORKED EXAMPLE 13

Solve the equation $3n + 11 = 6 - 2n$ and check your solution.

THINK

WRITE

1 Write the equation.

$$3n + 11 = 6 - 2n$$

2 The inverse of $-2n$ is $+2n$.
Therefore, add $2n$ to both sides and simplify.

$$3n + 11 + 2n = 6 - 2n + 2n$$
$$5n + 11 = 6$$

3 Subtract 11 from both sides and simplify.

$$5n + 11 - 11 = 6 - 11$$
$$5n = -5$$

4 Divide both sides by 5 and simplify.

$$\frac{5n}{5} = \frac{-5}{5}$$
$$n = -1$$

5 Check the solution by substituting $n = -1$ into the left-hand side and then the right-hand side of the equation.

If $n = -1$,

$$\begin{aligned} \text{LHS} &= 3n + 11 \\ &= -3 + 11 \\ &= 8 \end{aligned}$$

If $n = -1$,

$$\begin{aligned} \text{RHS} &= 6 - 2n \\ &= 6 - -2 \\ &= 6 + 2 \\ &= 8 \end{aligned}$$

6 Comment on the answers obtained.

Since the LHS and RHS are equal, the equation is true when $n = -1$.

WORKED EXAMPLE 14

Expand the brackets and then solve the following equation, checking your solution.

a $3(s + 2) = 2(s + 7) + 4$
b $4(d + 3) - 2(d + 7) + 4 = 5(d + 2) + 7$

THINK	WRITE
a 1 Write the equation.	**a** $3(s+2)=2(s+7)+4$
2 Expand the brackets on each side of the equation first and then simplify.	$3s+6=2s+14+4$ $3s+6=2s+18$
3 Subtract the smaller unknown term (that is, $2s$) from both sides and simplify.	$3s+6-2s=2s+18-2s$ $s+6=18$
4 Subtract 6 from both sides and simplify.	$s+6-6=18-6$ $s=12$
5 Check the solution by substituting $s=12$ into the left-hand side and then the right-hand side of the equation.	If $s=12$, $\text{LHS}=3(s+2)$ $=3(12+2)$ $=3(14)$ $=42$ If $s=12$, $\text{RHS}=2(s+7)+4$ $=2(12+7)+4$ $=2(19)+4$ $=38+4$ $=42$
6 Comment on the answers obtained.	Since the LHS and RHS are equal, the equation is true when $s=12$.
b 1 Write the equation.	**b** $4(d+3)-2(d+7)+4=5(d+2)+7$
2 Expand the brackets on each side of the equation first, and then simplify.	$4d+12-2d-14+4=5d+10+7$ $2d+2=5d+17$
3 Subtract the smaller unknown term (that is, $2d$) from both sides and simplify.	$2d-2d+2=5d-2d+17$ $2=3d+17$
4 Rearrange the equation so that the unknown is on the left-hand side of the equation.	$3d+17=2$
5 Subtract 17 from both sides and simplify.	$3d+17-17=2-17$ $3d=-15$
6 Divide both sides by 3 and simplify.	$\frac{3d}{3}=-\frac{15}{3}$ $d=-5$
7 Check the solution by substituting $d=-5$ into the left-hand side and then the right-hand side of the equation.	If $d=-5$, $\text{LHS}=4(d+3)-2(d+7)+4$ $=4(-5+3)-2(-5+7)+4$ $=4(-2)-2(2)+4$ $=-8-4+4$ $=-8$ If $d=-5$, $\text{RHS}=5(-5+2)+7$ $=5(-3)+7$ $=-15+7$ $=-8$
8 Comment on the answers obtained.	Since the LHS and RHS are equal, the equation is true when $d=-5$.

■ *Note:* When solving equations with the unknown on both sides, it is good practice to remove the unknown with the smaller coefficient from the relevant side.

REMEMBER

1. When a unknown appears on both sides of an equation, remove the unknown term from one side. It is good practice to remove the smaller unknown from the relevant side.
2. For a positive term we can remove by subtraction. For example, $7x + 7 = 5x - 3$ (subtract $5x$ from both sides).
3. For a negative term we can remove by addition. For example, $3x + 11 = 7 - 2x$ (add $2x$ to both sides).

EXERCISE 11E Equations with the unknown on both sides

INDIVIDUAL PATHWAYS

eBook*plus*

Activity 11-E-1 Rocket A doc-2348

Activity 11-E-2 Rocket B doc-2349

Activity 11-E-3 Rocket C doc-2350

FLUENCY

1 WE12 Solve the following equations and check your solutions.

- a $8x + 5 = 6x + 11$
- b $5y - 5 = 2y + 7$
- c $11n - 1 = 6n + 19$
- d $6t + 5 = 3t + 17$
- e $2w + 6 = w + 11$
- f $4y - 2 = y + 9$
- g $3z - 15 = 2z - 11$
- h $5a + 2 = 2a - 10$
- i $2s + 9 = 5s + 3$
- j $k + 5 = 7k - 19$
- k $4w + 9 = 2w + 3$
- l $7v + 5 = 3v - 11$

2 WE13 Solve the following equations and check your solutions.

- a $3w + 1 = 11 - 2w$
- b $2b + 7 = 13 - b$
- c $4n - 3 = 17 - 6n$
- d $3s + 1 = 16 - 2s$
- e $5a + 12 = -6 - a$
- f $7m + 2 = -3m + 22$
- g $p + 7 = -p + 15$
- h $3 + 2d = 15 - 2d$
- i $5 + m = 5 - m$
- j $7s + 3 = 15 - 5s$
- k $3t - 7 = -17 - 2t$
- l $16 - 2x = x + 4$

eBook*plus*

Digital doc Spreadsheet **Unknowns on both sides** doc-2355

3 WE14 Expand the brackets and then solve the following equations, checking your solutions.

- a $3(2x + 1) + 3x = 30$
- b $2(4m - 7) + m = 76$
- c $3(2n - 1) = 4(n + 5) + 1$
- d $t + 4 = 3(2t - 7)$
- e $3d - 5 = 3(4 - d)$
- f $4(3 - w) = 5w + 1$
- g $2(k + 5) - 3(k - 1) = k - 7$
- h $4(2 - s) = -2(3s - 1)$
- i $-3(z + 3) = 2(4 - z)$
- j $5(v + 2) = 7(v + 1)$
- k $2m + 3(2m - 7) = 4 + 5(m + 2)$
- l $3d + 2(d + 1) = 5(3d - 7)$
- m $4(d + 3) - 2(d + 7) + 5 = 5(d + 12)$
- n $5(k + 11) + 2(k - 3) - 7 = 2(k - 4)$
- o $7(v - 3) - 2(5 - v) + 25 = 4(v + 3) - 8$
- p $3(l - 7) + 4(8 - 2l) - 7 = -4(l + 2) - 6$

UNDERSTANDING

4 Solve the equation:

$$\frac{-3(x+4)}{7} - \frac{5(1-3x)}{3} = 3x - 4$$

5 Solve the equation: $\frac{(x-2)}{3} + 5 = 2x$

6 Find the value of x given the perimeter of the rectangle is 48 cm.

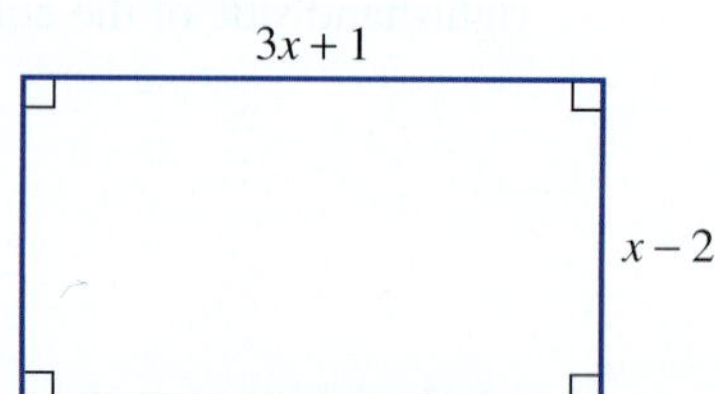

7 The two shapes below have the same area.

- a Write an equation to show that the parallelogram and the trapezium have the same area.
- b Solve the equation for x.
- c State the dimensions of the shapes.

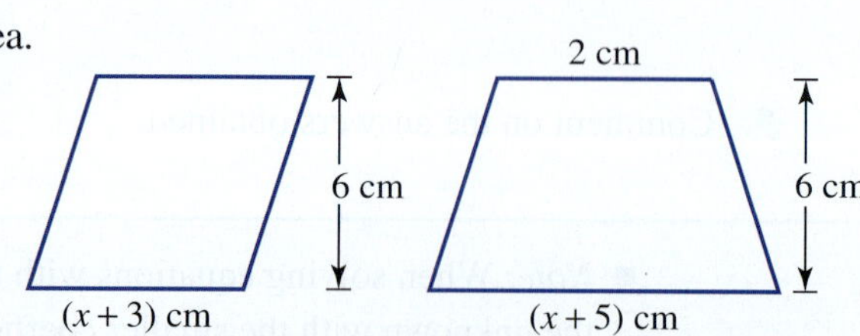

eBook*plus*

Digital doc
WorkSHEET 11.2
doc-2352

eBook*plus*

Weblink
Solving equations

eBook*plus*

Interactivity
Solving equations
int-2373

REASONING

8 A maths class has equal numbers of boys and girls. Eight of the girls left early to play in a netball match. This left 3 times as many boys in the class as girls. How many students are in the class?

9 Judy is thinking of a number. First she doubles it and adds 2. She realizes that if she multiplies it by 3 and subtracts 1, she gets the same result. Find the number.

10 Mick's father was 28 years old when Mick was born. If his father is now 3 times as old as Mick is, how old are they both now?

11 Given the following number line for a line segment PR, determine the length of PR?

$3x + 8$

P $2x$ Q $4x$ R

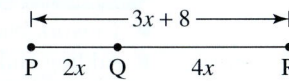

12 In 8 years' time, Tess will be 5 times as old as her age 8 years ago. How old is Tess now?

REFLECTION

Does it matter to which side of the equation the unknowns are moved?

Summary

Identifying patterns

- A number pattern has a rule that can describe the pattern.
- Geometric patterns have a rule that can describe the pattern.
- The rule can be used to make predictions.

Backtracking and inverse operations

- To work backwards through a flowchart we use inverse operations.
- Adding and subtracting are inverse operations.
- Multiplying and dividing are inverse operations.

Keeping equations balanced

- An equation links two expressions with an equals sign.
- An equation is like a pair of balanced scales (or a seesaw). The scales (or seesaw) will remain balanced as long as we do the same to both sides.

Using algebra to solve problems

- A linear equation is an equation where the variable has an index (power) of 1.
- When solving linear equations, perform the same operations on both sides of the equation until the unknown is left by itself.
- You can draw a flowchart to help you to decide what to do next.

Equations with the unknown on both sides

- When an unknown appears on both sides of an equation, remove the unknown term from one side. It is good practice to remove the smaller unknown from the relevant side.
- For a positive term we can remove by subtraction.
  For example, $7x + 7 = 5x - 3$ (subtract $5x$ from both sides).
- For a negative term we can remove by addition.
  For example, $3x + 11 = 7 - 2x$ (add $2x$ to both sides).

MAPPING YOUR UNDERSTANDING

Using terms from the summary, and other terms if you wish, construct a concept map that illustrates your understanding of the key concepts covered in this chapter. Compare this concept map with the one that you created in *What do you know?* on page 291.

Have you completed the two *Homework sheets*, the *Rich task* and the two *Code puzzles* in your *Maths Quest 8 Homework Book*?

Chapter review

FLUENCY

1 Find the output number for each of these flowcharts.

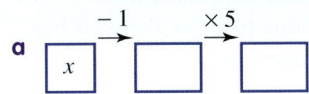

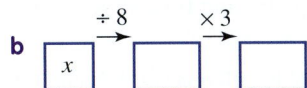

a x $\xrightarrow{-1}$ ☐ $\xrightarrow{\times 5}$ ☐

b x $\xrightarrow{\div 8}$ ☐ $\xrightarrow{\times 3}$ ☐

c x $\xrightarrow{+8}$ ☐ $\xrightarrow{\div 5}$ ☐ $\xrightarrow{+3}$ ☐

d x $\xrightarrow{\times 3}$ ☐ $\xrightarrow{-7}$ ☐ $\xrightarrow{\div 2}$ ☐

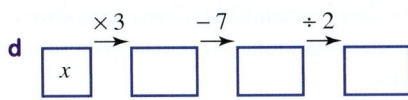

2 Draw the flowchart whose output number is given by the following expressions.

a $-3(m+4)$

b $\dfrac{n}{3}+5$

c $\dfrac{m-7}{5}-4$

d $7-15w$

3 a Write an equation that is represented by the diagram below.

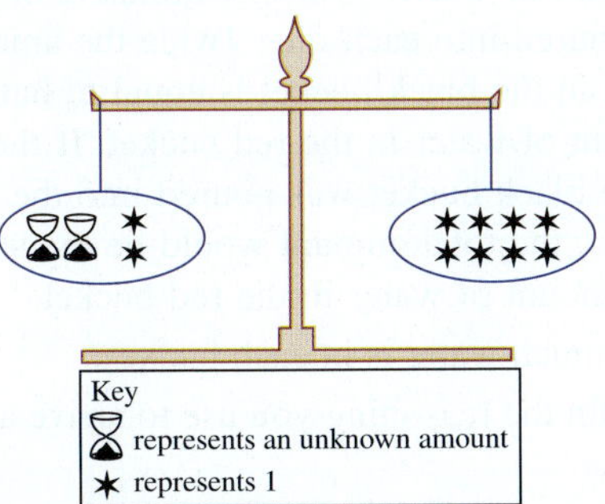

b Show what happens when you take 2 from both sides, and write the new equation.

4 MC If we start with $x = 5$, which of these equations is not true?

A $x+2=7$
B $3x=12$
C $-2x=-10$
D $\dfrac{x}{5}=1$
E $x-2=3$

5 MC If we start with $x = 3$, which of these equations is not true?

A $\dfrac{2x}{3}=2$
B $-2x=-6$
C $2x-6=0$
D $\dfrac{x}{5}=\dfrac{3}{5}$
E $x-5=2$

6 Solve these equations by doing the same to both sides.

a $z+7=18$
b $-25+b=-18$
c $-\frac{8}{9}=z-\frac{4}{3}$
d $9t=\frac{1}{3}$
e $-8.7=\dfrac{l}{5}$
f $-\frac{6}{13}=\dfrac{h}{8}$

7 Solve these equations by doing the same to both sides.

a $5v+3=18$
b $5(s+11)=35$
c $\dfrac{d-7}{4}=10$
d $-2(r+5)-3=5$
e $\dfrac{2y-3}{7}=9$
f $\dfrac{x}{5}-3=2$

8 Solve the following equations and check each solution.

a $5k+7=k+19$
b $4s-8=2s-12$
c $3t-11=5-t$
d $5x+2=-2x+16$

9 Expand the brackets first and then solve the following equations.

a $5(2v+3)-7v=21$
b $3(m-4)+2m=m+8$

PROBLEM SOLVING

1 Ray the electrician charges $80 for a call-out visit and then $65 per half hour.

a Write an equation for his fees, where C is his cost and t is the number of 30-minute periods he spent on the job.

b How long did a particular job take if he charged $275.00?

c Ray's brother Roger is a plumber and uses the equation $C = 54t + 86$ to calculate his costs. He also charged $275 for one job. How long did Roger spend at this particular job?

d Explain what the number 54 and 86 could mean.

2 At the end of the term, Katie's teacher gave the class their average scores. They had done four tests for the term. Katie's average was 76%. She had a mark of 83% for Probability, 72% for Geometry and 91% for Measurement but had forgotten what she got for Algebra. Write an equation to show how Katie would work out her Algebra test score and then solve this equation.

3 My three daughters were each born 2 years apart. Their combined ages come to 63 years. What is the age of the eldest?

4 A truck carrying 50 bags of cement weighs 5.2 tonnes. After delivering 15 bags of cement, the truck weighs 5.173 tonnes. How much would an empty truck weigh?

5 You are 4 times as old as your sister. In 8 years time you will be twice as old as your sister. What are your ages now?

6 What whole number must be added to both the numerator and the denominator of a fraction of $\frac{1}{4}$ to obtain an answer of $\frac{2}{3}$?

7 You lend three friends a total of $45. You lend the first friend x dollars. To the second friend you lend $5 more than you do for the first friend. To the third friend you lend three times as much as for the second friend. How much does each person receive?

8 What is the greatest possible perimeter of a triangle with sides $5x + 20$, $3x + 76$, $x + 196$, given that the triangle is isosceles? All sides are in mm.

9 Penny was looking at the following phone plans to see which one would be the most economical for her phone habits. Penny's average phone conversation was approximately 2 minutes long.

1. 15 cents connection fee and 30 cents per minute
2. No connection fee and 40 cents per minute
3. 40 cents connection fee and 19 cents per minute

a Help Penny by writing an algebraic equation for each phone plan.

b Use the equations to find the most economical phone plan for Penny if her conversations average:
1 minute, 2 minutes, 3 minutes

c At what average talking time should you switch to Plan 3?

10 A rectangular vegetable patch is $(3x + 4)$ metres long and $(2x - 5)$ metres wide. Its perimeter is 58 metres. What are the dimensions of the vegetable plot?

11 Knitting involves following patterns, often with outstanding designs resulting. Consider a simple pattern to knit a triangular scarf. The pattern might read like this.

- Start with 3 stitches.
- Increase by 1 stitch at both ends of each row.
- Continue in this manner until the scarf is as long as you would like.

a If r represents the row number, and n the number of stitches in that row, write an equation showing the relationship between n and r.

b Use your equation to calculate the number of rows you would have to knit to have 65 stitches.

12 Three buckets (one black, one white and one red) each hold a maximum of 5 L. Different volumes of water (in whole numbers of litres) are poured into each one. Twice the amount of water in the black bucket is equal to half the amount of water in the red bucket. If the water in the black bucket was poured into the white bucket, the total amount would be the same as the amount of water in the red bucket.

How much water is in each bucket?

Explain the reasoning you use to arrive at your answer.

13 While on holidays Amy hired a bicycle for $9 an hour and $3 for the use of a helmet. Her brother, Ben, found a cheaper hire place, which charged $6 per hour; but the hire of the helmet was $5 and he had to pay $5 for insurance. Both places measured the time in 20-minute increments. They both ended up paying the same amount and were gone for the same number of hours. Construct a table of values to determine how long they were gone and how much it cost?

14 Michael checked his bank balance before going shopping. He had \$450. While shopping he paid with his bank card. He bought two suits, which cost the same, and three pairs of shoes, each of which cost half the price of a suit. He also had lunch for \$12. When he checked his balance again he was \$33 overdrawn. What did one suit cost?

15 Shannon is saving to buy a new computer, which costs \$3299. So far he has \$449 in the bank and he wants to make regular deposits each month until he reaches his target of \$3299. If he wants to buy the computer in 8 months time, how much does he need to save as a monthly deposit?

eBook*plus*

Interactivities

Test yourself
Chapter 11
int-2374

Word search
Chapter 11
int-2633

Crossword
Chapter 11
int-2634

eBookplus ACTIVITIES

Chapter opener

Digital doc *(page 291)*

- Hungry brain activity Chapter 11 (doc-6977)

Are you ready?

Digital docs *(pages 292–93)*

- SkillSHEET 11.1 (doc-6978) Number patterns
- SkillSHEET 11.2 (doc-6979) Using tables to show number patterns
- SkillSHEET 11.3 (doc-6980) Describing a number pattern from a table
- SkillSHEET 11.4 (doc-6981) Flowcharts
- SkillSHEET 11.5 (doc-6982) Inverse operations
- SkillSHEET 11.6 (doc-6983) Solving equations by backtracking
- SkillSHEET 11.7 (doc-6984) Combining like terms
- SkillSHEET 11.8 (doc-6985) Expanding expressions containing brackets
- SkillSHEET 11.9 (doc-6986) Checking solutions by substitution
- SkillSHEET 11.10 (doc-6987) Writing equations from worded statements

11A Identifying patterns

Digital docs *(page 297)*

- Activity 11-A-1 (doc-2336) Identifying patterns
- Activity 11-A-2 (doc-2337) More patterns
- Activity 11-A-3 (doc-2338) Advanced patterns

11B Backtracking and inverse operations

Digital docs *(page 300)*

- Activity 11-B-1 (doc-2339) Sudoku challenge A
- Activity 11-B-2 (doc-2340) Sudoku challenge B
- Activity 11-B-3 (doc-2341) Sudoku challenge C

11C Keeping equations balanced

Digital docs *(page 302)*

- Activity 11-C-1 (doc-2342) Riddle A
- Activity 11-C-2 (doc-2343) Riddle B
- Activity 11-C-3 (doc-2344) Riddle C
- WorkSHEET 11.1 (doc-2351) *(page 303)*

Interactivity *(page 302)*

- Balancing equations (int-0077)

11D Using algebra to solve problems

Digital docs *(page 307)*

- Activity 11-D-1 (doc-2345) Using algebra to solve problems
- Activity 11-D-2 (doc-2346) More problems using algebra
- Activity 11-D-3 (doc-2347) Advanced problems using algebra
- Spreadsheet (doc-2353) 2-step equations *(page 307)*
- Spreadsheet (doc-2354) 3-step equations *(page 308)*

11E Equations with the unknown on both sides

Digital docs *(page 312)*

- Activity 11-E-1 (doc-2348) Rocket A
- Activity 11-E-2 (doc-2349) Rocket B
- Activity 11-E-3 (doc-2350) Rocket C
- Spreadsheet (doc-2355) Unknowns on both sides
- WorkSHEET 11.2 (doc-2352) *(page 313)*

Weblink *(page 313)*

- Solving equations

Interactivity *(page 313)*

- Solving equations (int-2373)

Chapter review

Interactivities *(page 317)*

- Test yourself Chapter 11 (int-2374) Take the end-of-chapter test to test your progress.
- Word search Chapter 11 (int-2633)
- Crossword Chapter 11 (int-2634)

To access eBookPLUS activities, log on to

www.jacplus.com.au

Representing and interpreting data

12A Samples and populations
12B Organising and displaying data
12C Measures of centre
12D Measures of spread
12E Analysing data

WHAT DO YOU KNOW?

1 List what you know about data. Create a concept map to show your list.
2 Share what you know with a partner and then with a small group.
3 As a class, create a large concept map that shows your class's knowledge of data.

eBook*plus*

Digital doc
Hungry brain activity
Chapter 12
doc-6988

OPENING QUESTION

If you took handfuls of M&M's from this plate, what would be the average number of red ones you would get each time?

Are you ready?

Try the questions below. If you have difficulty with any of them, extra help can be obtained by completing the matching SkillSHEET located on your eBookPLUS.

eBookplus

Digital doc
SkillSHEET 12.1
doc-6989

Presenting data in a frequency table

1 Copy and complete the following frequency table for the scores listed below.
1, 3, 2, 6, 4, 4, 3, 5, 2, 3, 1, 3, 4, 2, 5, 3, 6, 2, 3, 6, 1, 3, 2, 4

Score (x)	Tally	Frequency (f)
1	|||	3
2		
3		
4		
5		
6		

eBookplus

Digital doc
SkillSHEET 12.2
doc-6990

Reading scales

2 How much is each interval worth in the following scales?

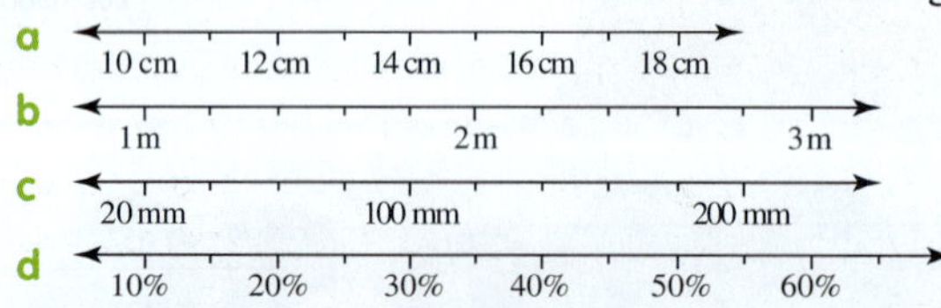

eBookplus

Digital doc
SkillSHEET 12.3
doc-6991

Finding the mean of ungrouped data

3 Find the average of the following scores.
a 1, 2, 3, 4, 5
b 11, 12, 13, 14, 15
c 1, 7, 9, 4, 2
d 180, 426, 392, 874

eBookplus

Digital doc
SkillSHEET 12.4
doc-6992

Arranging a set of data in ascending order

4 Arrange each of the following sets of data in ascending order.
a 25, 20, 22, 21, 29, 34, 25
b 215, 381, 276, 345, 298, 277, 325, 400, 304
c 4.6, 0.3, 3.6, 5.8, 2.9, 1.8, 3.5, 5.8, 3.1, 2.8, 3.6

eBookplus

Digital doc
SkillSHEET 12.5
doc-6993

Finding the median

5 Arrange the following scores in ascending order, then state the middle score.
a 4, 8, 3, 9, 2
b 27, 16, 2, 9, 11
c 5, 6, 4, 8, 2, 9, 4
d 9, 9, 8, 7, 8, 4, 9

eBookplus

Digital doc
SkillSHEET 12.6
doc-6994

Finding the middle score for data arranged in a dot plot

6 Find the middle score of each of the following data sets.

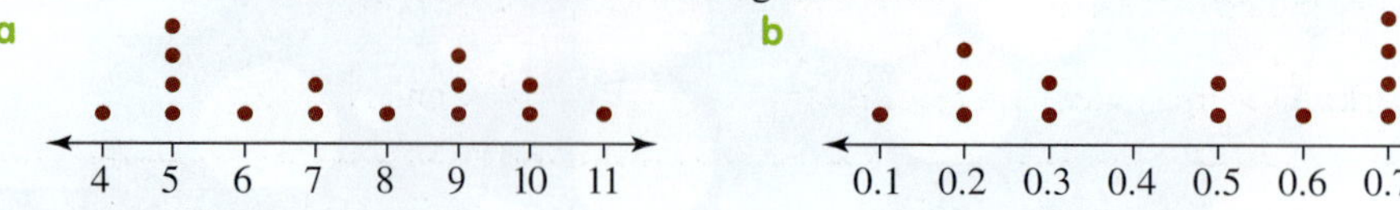

eBookplus

Digital doc
SkillSHEET 12.7
doc-6995

Finding the score in a data set that occurs most frequently

7 For each of the following data sets, find the score that occurs most frequently.
a 1, 1, 2, 2, 2, 2, 3, 4, 4, 5, 5
b 23, 29, 25, 24, 23, 21, 25, 26, 25, 29
c 7, 12, 8, 3, 5, 11, 8, 4, 2, 1, 6, 10, 13

12A Samples and populations

Collecting data

- Information or **data** is constantly being collected.
- Different organisations collect different types of data. For example, at a cricket match, some of the **statistics** gathered for a batsman are: time spent batting, the number of balls faced, the runs off a particular delivery, where the ball was hit, the number of 4s or 6s hit, and so on.
- Once the data is collected, it can be organised, analysed and interpreted.
- A *survey* is the process of collecting data. If every member of a target population is surveyed, the process is called a **census**.
- A census is conducted in Australia every 5 years to obtain an accurate profile of Australians. On census night each person in Australia is required to complete a detailed booklet containing a series of questions relating to age, marital status, employment, income, housing, education, modes of transport and so on. This allows the government to analyse the population and make decisions on how to improve services.
- Due to limitations in time, cost and practicality, in many cases a **sample** of the population is selected at **random** (not in any particular order or pattern) to prevent biased (leaning in a favoured direction) results.

eBook*plus*

Digital docs
Investigation **Data and the Olympics** doc-7013
Spreadsheet **Data and the Olympics** doc-7106

WORKED EXAMPLE 1

In each of the following, state if the information was obtained by census or survey.

a A school uses a roll to count the number of students absent each day.
b The television ratings, in which 2000 families complete a questionnaire on the programs they watch over a one-week period.
c A battery manufacturer tests every hundredth battery off the production line.
d A teacher records the examination marks of her class.

THINK	WRITE
a Every student is counted at roll call each morning.	a Census
b Not every family is asked to complete a ratings questionnaire.	b Survey
c Not every battery is tested.	c Survey
d The marks of every student are recorded.	d Census

- Data can be collected using a variety of techniques. Three common methods are:
  - observation
  - survey
  - experiment.

Surveys

- Collecting data by survey is the form most frequently used. The survey is administered with the aid of a questionnaire. The success of obtaining meaningful and relevant data from a questionnaire depends largely on the care taken in designing the questions. Methods used to collect data include:
  - personal interviews, where the interviewer usually asks prepared questions, then records the replies from the respondent
  - telephone interviews, where the interview is conducted over the telephone
  - self-administered questionnaires, which are usually mailed to individuals who complete the questionnaire, then return it in a pre-paid envelope, or hold it for collection.

Questionnaires

- When a **questionnaire** is designed, we must keep in mind that the collected data should be in a form that is easy to analyse. Questions can be **open** or **closed**.
- Open questions are those where the respondent has no guided boundaries within which to answer. Questions that belong to this class include:

  'Who is your favourite singer?'

  'What is your favourite food?'

  The main problem with open questions is that their answers are often difficult to classify and analyse.
- Closed questions are of the type where the respondent must answer within a category. The question about food above could be rewritten as:

  'Which one of the following foods do you prefer most?'
  - Meat
  - Seafood
  - Poultry
  - Vegetables
  - Fruit

  These types of answers are easier to analyse than answers to open questions. It must be noted that options such as:
  - None of the above or
  - Don't know

  should be avoided, if possible, as they provide the respondent with a 'way out'.

WORKED EXAMPLE 2

Ten students were asked the open question:
'What do you dislike about your school uniform?'
These were their responses.

1. **It's too old-fashioned.**
2. **It costs too much.**
3. **It's just yucky.**
4. **It's a dreadful colour.**
5. **The girls aren't allowed to wear slacks.**
6. **The colour is drab.**
7. **The skirt is too long.**
8. **It would be better to have it all one colour rather than three different colours.**
9. **The shoes are too uncomfortable.**
10. **We should be allowed to wear leggings in winter.**

Classify the responses into categories to identify the two main reasons given.

THINK	WRITE
1 Since two main reasons have to be identified, look for, say, 3 categories which could be used to classify the data.	Two main categories are apparent: 1 Style 2 Colour A third category is not apparent.
2 Classify the responses.	**Style** Responses 1, 5, 7, 9, 10 **Colour** Responses 4, 6, 8 Responses 2 and 3 can be in a miscellaneous category.
3 Identify the main reasons.	The main reasons students dislike the uniform are its style and colour.

It can be seen from this worked example that it is probably worth taking the time to write closed questions for a questionnaire, as this reduces the incidence of answers that are difficult to classify.

Planning a questionnaire

- To prepare good questions you should keep the following points in mind.
  1. The questions should flow smoothly from one to the next.
  2. Introductory remarks should be included, outlining the aim and purpose of the questionnaire, along with any necessary instructions.
  3. Jargon, slang and abbreviations should be avoided.
  4. Do not ask questions that are vague or ambiguous.
  5. Avoid bias and emotional language.
  6. Avoid double-barrel questions.
  7. Do not ask leading questions (those that lead to an expected response).
  8. Make sure your questions are capable of being answered by your respondents.
  9. Avoid questions with double negatives.
  10. At the conclusion, thank the respondent for answering.

WORKED EXAMPLE 3

Identify the areas of concern with the following questions, then rewrite each so that the meaning is clear, unbiased and understandable.

a Don't you agree that the school uniform should be changed?

b Didn't you know that students are not allowed to go to the school canteen at morning tea?

c Those poor, distraught animals in the zoo should be running wild and not restricted in cages. Don't you agree?

d How old are you?

THINK	WRITE
a This is a leading question — leading the respondent to agree.	a This is a leading question. Are you in favour of a change in the school uniform?
b This question has two negative parts causing confusion for the respondent.	b This is a double negative question. Are you aware of the rule banning students from the school canteen at morning tea?

c This question plays on the emotions of the respondent.

c This question raises an emotional issue. What's your opinion about keeping animals in cages at zoos?

d People (particularly older people) often don't like disclosing personal details.

d This is a personal question. To which age group do you belong?

- Less than 10 years
- 10–20 years
- 21–50 years
- Over 50 years of age

Selecting samples

- When a sample is selected from a population, care must be taken to ensure that the composition of the sample is as close as possible to that of the population.
- One of the simplest ways to select a reliable sample is by using a random sampling technique.
- A way in which this can be achieved is by numbering each element of the population, then randomly selecting items for the sample by using random digit tables, the random function on a calculator or (without looking) drawing numbers from a container.

WORKED EXAMPLE 4

As part of their quality control program, staff members at Perplexing Puzzles select 5 puzzles from a batch of 50 coming off a production line, for testing. Use the following table of random numbers to select the 5 puzzles to be tested.

94, 01, 54, 68, 74	**32, 44, 44, 82, 77**	**59, 82, 09, 61, 63**	**64, 65, 42, 58, 43**
71, 10, 88, 82, 22	**88, 57, 07, 40, 15**	**25, 70, 49, 10, 35**	**01, 75, 51, 47, 50**
62, 88, 08, 78, 73	**95, 16, 05, 92, 21**	**22, 30, 49, 03, 14**	**75, 87, 71, 73, 34**
11, 74, 81, 21, 02	**80, 58, 01, 18, 67**	**18, 71, 05, 96, 21**	**06, 55, 40, 78, 50**
17, 94, 40, 56, 00	**60, 47, 80, 33, 43**	**25, 85, 02, 89, 05**	**57, 21, 63, 96, 18**

THINK	WRITE
1 Assign each puzzle on the production line a number, according to its order, ranging from 1 to 50. *Note:* 01 will represent the first puzzle on the production line.	01 — First puzzle on the production line. 02 — Second puzzle on the production line. 03 — Third puzzle on the production line. . . . . . . 50 — Fiftieth puzzle on the production line.
2 Randomly select a starting point and move in a systematic order, jotting down 5 pairs of digits that range from 01 to 50. *Note:* Reject any values that equal 00 or are greater than 50. Reject any repeated values.	Starting position: fourth row, first block, fourth pair of digits; that is, 21. 21 accept 02 accept 80 reject since value is greater than 50 58 reject since value is greater than 50 01 accept 18 accept 67 reject since value is greater than 50 18 reject since value is repeated 71 reject since value is greater than 50 05 accept
3 List the puzzles whose numbers correspond to those selected in step 2 and interpret the results.	The puzzles numbered 21, 02, 01, 18 and 05 will be selected for testing.

eBook*plus*

Digital doc
Investigation
Bias
doc-2473

Biased samples

- If a sample is not representative of the population, it is said to be **biased**.
- To avoid bias, the size of the sample should be about $\sqrt{\text{Population size}}$.

eBook*plus*

Digital doc
Investigation
Collecting data for surveys and questionnaires
doc-2167

WORKED EXAMPLE 5

Comment on the selection of the sample in the following cases.
a Members of the men's basketball team were interviewed regarding the height of the mirrors in the gym changing room.
b Spectators at a music concert were interviewed regarding the sporting facilities in the town.
c Of the 100 people in the bush walking group, 5 were interviewed regarding increasing the club's fees.

THINK	WRITE
a Are those in the men's basketball team of typical height compared with those who use the gym?	**a** Those in the men's basketball team would be taller than most of the people who use the gym change room. They would prefer the mirrors to be higher. This is a biased sample.
b Those at a music concert probably would not use the sporting facilities very frequently.	**b** This is a biased sample as it does not include those who would make greatest use of the sporting facilities.
c This sample is too small.	**c** This sample of 5 from the group of 100 is too small to represent the views of the whole group.

REMEMBER

1. A census collects data from a population, while a survey collects data from a sample.
2. Surveys can be conducted through personal interviews, telephone interviews or self-administered questionnaires.
3. The questions in questionnaires can be open-ended or closed.
4. Care must be taken in preparing questions that are clear, unbiased and easily understood.
5. When a sample is selected from a population, be careful to ensure that the composition of the sample is as close as possible to that of the population.
6. A random sampling technique can be used to select an appropriate sample from a population.
7. The sample should be sufficiently large and not biased.

eBook*plus*

Interactivity
Random numbers
int-0089

EXERCISE 12A Samples and populations

FLUENCY

1 Copy and complete the following.
When we obtain data from the whole population, we conduct a ____________; however, a survey obtains data from a ____________ of the population.

2 A school conducts an election for a new school captain. Every teacher and student in the school casts a vote. Is this an example of a census or a survey? Explain your answer.

INDIVIDUAL PATHWAYS

eBook*plus*

Activity 12-A-1 Populations and samples doc-6996

Activity 12-A-2 More populations and samples doc-6997

Activity 12-A-3 Advanced populations and samples doc-6998

3 A questionnaire is conducted by the school council to see what library facilities the community needs. If 500 people who live in the community participate, is this an example of a census or a survey?

4 WE1 For each of the following, state whether a census or a survey has been used.

a Fifty people at a shopping centre are asked to nominate the supermarket where they do most of their grocery shopping.

b To find the most popular new car on the road, 300 new-car buyers are asked what make and model they purchased.

c To find the most popular new car on the road, the make and model of every new car registered are recorded.

d To test the life of a light bulb, every 100th bulb is tested.

5 For each of the following, recommend whether you would use a census or a survey to find:

a the most popular TV program on Sunday night at 8.30 pm

b the number of 4-wheel-drive cars sold in a year

c the number of cars travelling on a toll road each day

d the percentage of defective SIM cards produced by a mobile phone manufacturing company.

6 Explain what you understand by the terms 'open' and 'closed' questions. Give an example of an open question, then rewrite your question in a closed format.

7 WE2 Ten students were asked their opinions about the cause of congestion at the school's front gate. Analyse their responses below, suggest categories into which they could be classified and identify the most commonly stated reasons for the congestion.

1. The cars shouldn't come up the front driveway.
2. The front entrance is too small.
3. There should be another entrance.
4. The buses are the problem.
5. Bike riders should have a separate entrance.
6. Parents don't care where they park.
7. Kids just sit around there talking.
8. The buses all arrive at the same time.
9. The road is not wide enough.
10. There should be a traffic control officer there to direct the traffic.

8 Fifteen students were asked to identify the one thing in their Maths class that they particularly didn't like.

Classify the responses below into appropriate categories, then identify the main reasons.

1. It's too hard.
2. There's too much homework.
3. I can't understand the teacher.
4. It's boring.
5. The boys are too distracting.
6. The teacher favours the boys.
7. It's too much work.
8. I can't concentrate for that length of time.
9. We do something new every lesson.
10. The teacher expects too much.
11. I don't like working in groups.
12. Our teacher is too strict.
13. Our class is too big.

14. The work is not interesting.
15. I don't like doing presentations to the class.

9 WE3 Identify the areas of concern with the following questions, then rewrite each so that the meaning is clear, unbiased and understandable.
- **a** How much money do you earn?
- **b** Do you exercise regularly?
- **c** Which venue do you prefer — the MCG, the SCG, the Gabba or the WACA?
- **d** Do you support the Premier's policy on wildlife preservation?
- **e** How tall are you in feet and inches?
- **f** Did you buy your sneakers for comfort and quality?

10 WE4 As part of their quality control program, staff members at Perplexing Puzzles select 5 puzzles from a batch of 50 coming off a production line, for testing. Use the following table of random numbers to select the 5 puzzles to be tested.

94, 01, 54, 68, 74	32, 44, 44, 82, 77	59, 82, 09, 61, 63	64, 65, 42, 58, 43
71, 10, 88, 82, 22	88, 57, 07, 40, 15	25, 70, 49, 10, 35	01, 75, 51, 47, 50
62, 88, 08, 78, 73	95, 16, 05, 92, 21	22, 30, 49, 03, 14	75, 87, 71, 73, 34
11, 74, 81, 21, 02	80, 58, 01, 18, 67	18, 71, 05, 96, 21	06, 55, 40, 78, 50
17, 94, 40, 56, 00	60, 47, 80, 33, 43	25, 85, 02, 89, 05	57, 21, 63, 96, 18

11 Use the table of random numbers given in question **10** to select at random the following samples:
- **a** 3 people from a population of 99 (work horizontally from top left)
- **b** 4 students from a class of 60 (work horizontally from the bottom row of the second block)
- **c** 3 raffle tickets from a book of 50 (diagonally in the third block, starting at bottom left).

12 MC Using the table of random numbers from question **10**, the sample '5 students from a group of 50' (working horizontally and beginning from the first pair of digits in row 2, block 3) would correspond to:

A 25, 70, 49, 10, 35 **B** 95, 16, 05, 92, 21 **C** 16, 05, 21, 22, 30
D 25, 49, 10, 35, 01 **E** 09, 42, 43, 10, 22

13 WE5 Comment on the selection of the sample in the following cases.
- **a** The choir members were interviewed regarding the opening hours of the school swimming pool.
- **b** Spectators at a football match were interviewed after the match to get their views on the Prime Minister's new health package.
- **c** Visitors arriving at the Sydney international airport were interviewed regarding the transport system from there into the city.
- **d** Twenty spectators at the Australian Tennis Open championships were interviewed regarding an appropriate time of the year to hold the event.

UNDERSTANDING

14 An opinion poll is conducted to try to predict the outcome of an election. People are asked to ring one number if they would vote for the current political party, and a different number if they favour the opposition. Comment on this method of collecting data.

15 Rewrite the following open questions in closed format.
- **a** How much pocket money do you get each week?
- **b** How do you travel to school?
- **c** What type of destination do you prefer for a holiday?

16 Use technology to select at random the following samples:
- **a** 6 shoppers from 75 in a store
- **b** 4 babies from 30 born on a particular day
- **c** 6 products from 100 coming off a production line.

17 Describe how you could use a standard pack of cards to select a random sample from a small population.

REFLECTION

Are the random numbers generated by a computer or calculator truly random?

12B Organising and displaying data

Examining data

- Once collected, the data must be organised.
- When this has been done, any anomalies in the data will be highlighted.
- Before we rush into doing calculations, we must consider how to treat any anomalies. These could have occurred because of:
  - recording errors
  - unusual responses.
- Sometimes a decision is made just to disregard these anomalies, which are regarded as **outliers**.
- Outliers can greatly affect the results of calculations, as we shall see later.

Frequency tables

- Organising the raw data into a frequency table is the first step in allowing us to see trends in the data.

WORKED EXAMPLE 6

In a suburb of 350 houses, a sample of 20 households was surveyed to find the number of children in them. The data were collected and recorded as follows:
0, 2, 3, 2, 1, 3, 5, 2, 0, 1, 2, 0, 2, 1, 2, 1, 2, 3, 1, 0.

a Organise the data into a frequency table.
b Comment on the distribution of the data.
c What could you say about the number of children per household in the suburb?

THINK | WRITE

a Draw up a frequency table and complete the entries.

a

Children per household	Frequency
0	4
1	5
2	7
3	3
4	0
5	1

b Look at how the data are distributed.

b The data value of 5 appears to be an outlier. This is probably not a recording error, but it is not typical of the number of children per household. Most households seem to have 1 or 2 children.

c Does this sample seem to reflect the population characteristics?

c The sample is an appropriate size, and would probably reflect the characteristics of the population. It would be reasonably safe to say that most houses in the suburb contained 1 or 2 children.

- Sometimes there is too much data to treat as single entries, and it is necessary to group the data into **class intervals**.
- The choice for the size of class intervals should lead to between 5 and 10 groups being formed.
- Class intervals are set so that each score belongs to one group only.
- This means that it is not possible to have intervals such as 5–10, 10–20, . . ., because an entry of 10 would then be in two class intervals.

WORKED EXAMPLE 7

A sample of 40 people was surveyed about the number of hours per week they spent watching TV. The results, rounded to the nearest hour, are listed below.
12, 18, 9, 17, 20, 7, 24, 16, 9, 27, 7, 16, 26, 15, 7, 28, 11, 20, 9, 11, 23, 19, 29, 12, 19, 12, 16, 21, 8, 4, 16, 20, 17, 10, 24, 21, 5, 13, 29, 26
a Organise the data into a frequency table using class intervals of 5–<10, 10–<15 etc. Show the midpoint of each class interval.
b Comment on the distribution of the data.

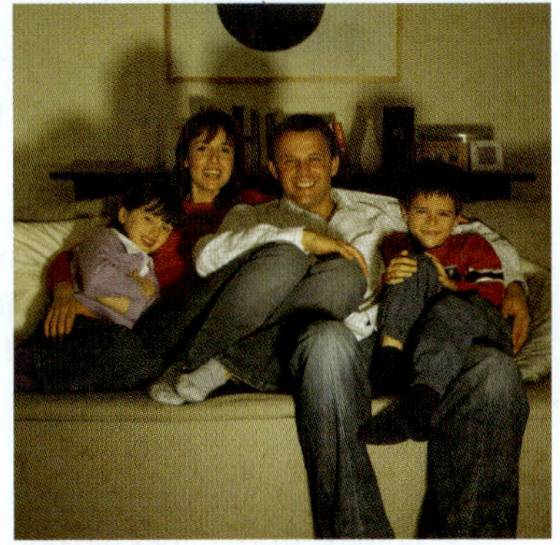

THINK

a 1 Draw up a frequency table with three columns: class interval (hours of TV), midpoint and frequency.

2 The midpoint is calculated by adding the two extremes of the class interval and dividing by 2. For example, the midpoint of the first class interval is $\frac{5+10}{2} = 7.5$.

3 Systematically go through the list, determine how many times each score occurs and enter the information into the frequency column.

b Look at how the data are distributed.

WRITE

a

Hours of TV	Midpoint	Frequency
5–<10	7.5	9
10–<15	12.5	7
15–<20	17.5	10
20–<25	22.5	8
25–<30	27.5	6

b The TV viewing times are fairly evenly distributed, but the most-frequent number of hours per week viewing was about 15 to 20 hours.

Column graphs

- Once a frequency table has been constructed from the data, it can be displayed in graphical form. The most important statistical displays are column graphs. A special type of column graph is called a **histogram**. It has the following characteristics.
  1. All columns are of equal width.
  2. No gaps are left between columns.

3. Each column 'straddles' an x-axis score; that is, the column starts and finishes halfway between scores.
4. Usually a half-interval is left at the beginning and end of the graph. That is, the first score is one unit in from the frequency (y)-axis.

WORKED EXAMPLE 8

Consider the frequency table created in Worked example 6.

Children per household	Frequency
0	4
1	5
2	7
3	3
4	0
5	1

a Display the data as a histogram.
b Comment on the shape of the graph.
c Are these comments consistent with those in Worked example 6?

THINK

a 1 Rule a set of axes on graph paper. Give the graph a title. Label the horizontal axis 'Number of children per household' and the vertical axis 'Frequency'.

2 Leaving a $\frac{1}{2}$ unit space at the beginning, draw the first column so that it starts and finishes halfway between each household, and reaches a vertical height of 4 units. Repeat this technique for the other scores.

WRITE/DRAW

a

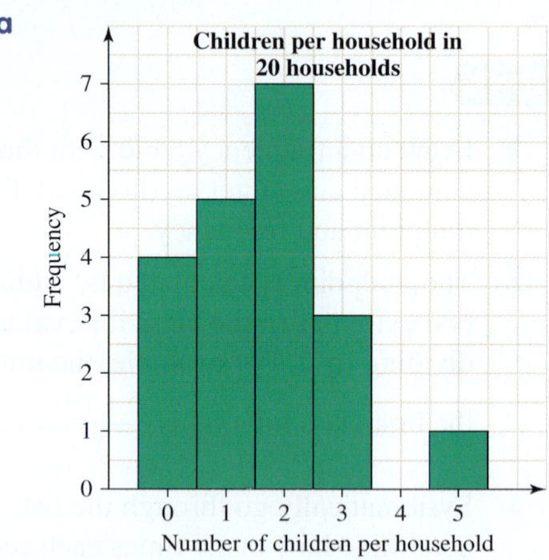

b Look at how the data are distributed.

b The data show that the score of '5 children per household' seems to be an outlier, and that the majority of households seem to have 1 or 2 children.

c Look for any similarities or differences between the observations in Worked example 6 and those made here.

c These comments are consistent with those made in Worked example 6.

- When presenting grouped data graphically, we label the horizontal axis (score) with either:
  - the class interval, or
  - the midpoint of each class interval.

WORKED EXAMPLE 9

Consider the grouped frequency table created in Worked example 7.

a Display the data as a histogram.

b Comment on the shape of the graph.

Hours of TV	Midpoint	Frequency
5–<10	7.5	9
10–<15	12.5	7
15–<20	17.5	10
20–<25	22.5	8
25–<30	27.5	6

THINK

a 1 Rule a set of axes on graph paper. Give the graph a title. Label the horizontal axis 'Number of hours of television watched' and the vertical axis 'Frequency'.

2 Leaving a $\frac{1}{2}$ unit space at the beginning, draw the first column so that it starts and finishes halfway between class intervals, and reaches a vertical height of 9 units. Repeat this technique for the other scores.

b Look at how the data are distributed.

WRITE/DRAW

a

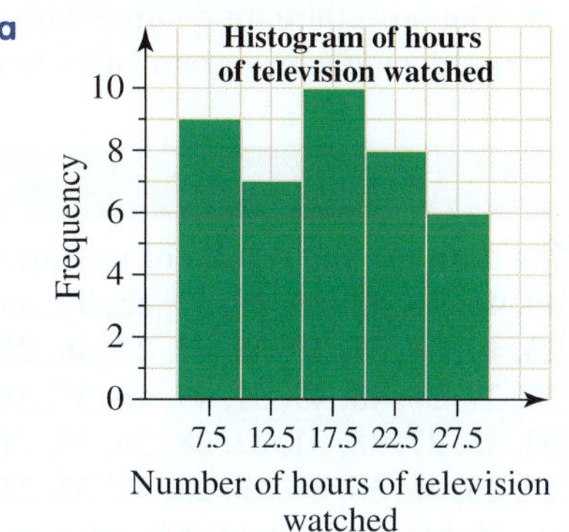

b The hours of TV watching is fairly consistent throughout the week. A maximum number of people watch about 15 to 20 hours per week.

- If we join the midpoints of the tops of the columns of a histogram, then extend the ends to the x-axis, we form what is called a **frequency polygon**.

WORKED EXAMPLE 10

Use the histogram created in Worked example 9 to draw a frequency polygon of the data.

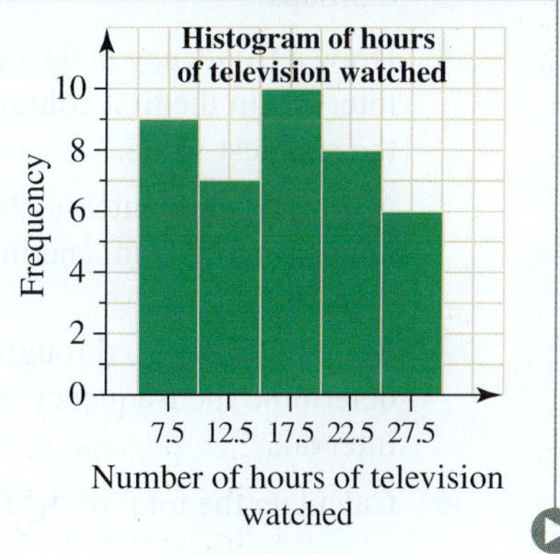

THINK

1. Mark the midpoints of the tops of the columns of the histogram.
2. Join the midpoints with straight lines.
3. Close the polygon by drawing lines at each end down to the x-axis.

WRITE/DRAW

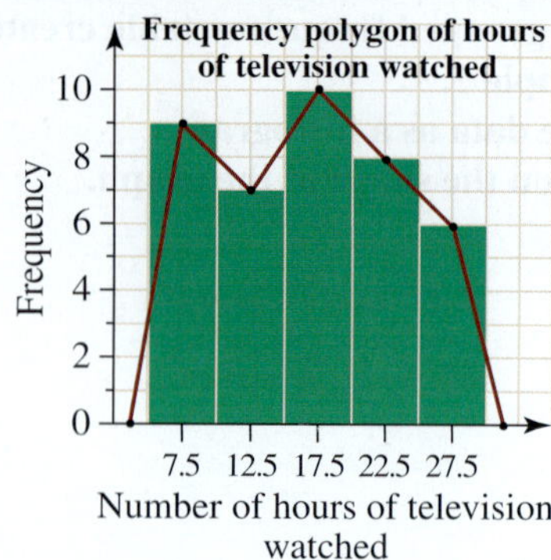

- The procedure for dealing with a large amount of data, organising it into class intervals, then producing a histogram and a frequency polygon can be seen in this next example.

WORKED EXAMPLE 11

The following data are the results of testing the lives (in hours) of 100 torch batteries.
20, 31, 42, 49, 46, 36, 42, 25, 28, 37, 48, 49, 45, 35, 25, 42, 30, 23, 25, 26, 29, 31, 46, 25, 40, 30, 31, 49, 38, 41, 23, 46, 29, 38, 22, 26, 31, 33, 34, 32, 41, 23, 29, 30, 29, 28, 48, 49, 31, 49, 48, 37, 38, 47, 25, 43, 38, 48, 37, 20, 38, 22, 21, 33, 35, 27, 38, 31, 22, 28, 20, 30, 41, 49, 41, 32, 43, 28, 21, 27, 20, 39, 40, 27, 26, 36, 36, 41, 46, 28, 32, 33, 25, 31, 33, 25, 36, 41, 28, 33

a Choose a suitable class interval for the given data and present the results in a frequency distribution table.
b Draw a histogram of the data.
c Add a polygon to the histogram.

THINK | WRITE

a 1. Choose a suitable size for the class interval.

2. Obtain the range for the given data; that is, subtract the smallest value from the largest.

Range = largest value − smallest value
= 49 − 20
= 29

3. Divide the results obtained for the range by 5 and round to the nearest whole number.

Note: A class interval of 5 hours will result in 6 groups.

Number of class intervals: $\frac{29}{5} = 5.8$
$= 6$

4. Draw a frequency table and list the class intervals in the first column, beginning with the smallest value.

Note: The class interval 20–<25 includes hours ranging from and including 20 to less than 25.

5. Systematically go through the data and determine the frequency of each class interval.

6. Calculate the total of the frequency column.

Life time (hours)	Tally	Frequency (f)
20–<25	ﾃ ﾃ ‖	12
25–<30	ﾃ ﾃ ﾃ ﾃ |||	23
30–<35	ﾃ ﾃ ﾃ ﾃ	20
35–<40	ﾃ ﾃ ﾃ		16
40–<45	ﾃ ﾃ |||	13
45–<50	ﾃ ﾃ ﾃ		16
	Total	100

b 1 Rule and label a set of axes on graph paper. Give the graph a title.

2 Add scales to the horizontal and vertical axes.

Note: Leave a half interval at the beginning and end of the vertical axis.

3 Draw in the first column so that it starts and finishes halfway between class intervals and reaches a vertical height of 12 units.

4 Repeat step 3 for each of the other scores.

b

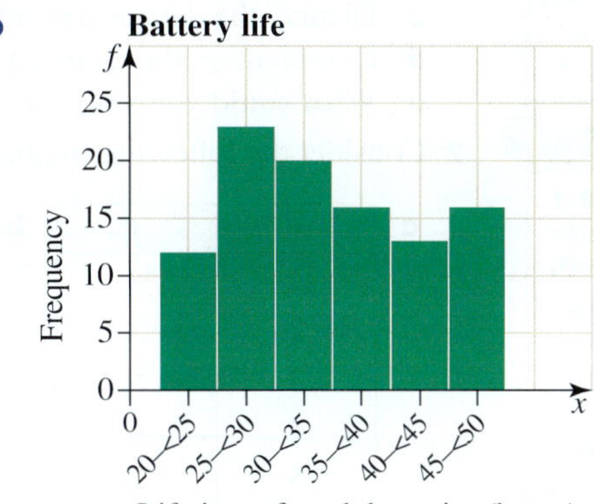

c 1 Mark the midpoints of the tops of the columns obtained in the histogram from part **b**.

2 Join the midpoints by straight line intervals.

3 Close the polygon by drawing lines at each end down to the class interval (x) axis.

c

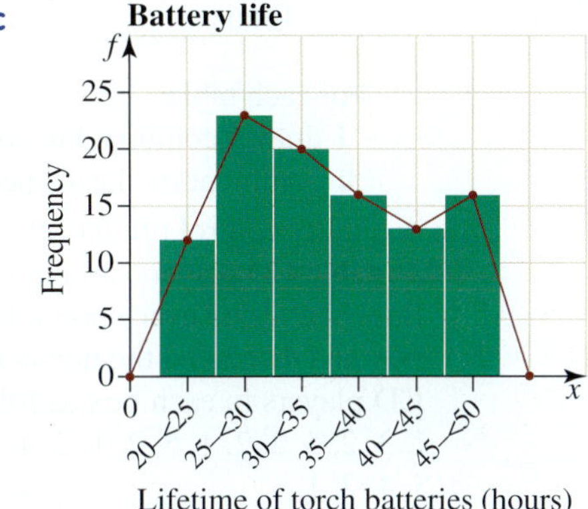

REMEMBER

1. After being collected, data should be examined to determine if there are any values that appear to be anomalies.
2. Data can be organised into frequency tables.
3. Large amounts of data can be organised into class intervals in a frequency table. The choice for the size of a class interval should lead to the formation of 5 to 10 groups.
4. Histograms are used to display numerical data. These are simply column graphs with no gaps between the bars. A half-interval is left at each end of the x-axis.
5. A frequency polygon can be formed from a histogram by joining the midpoints of the tops of the columns with straight lines, then completing the polygon by drawing a line to the x-axis at either end.

EXERCISE

12B Organising and displaying data

FLUENCY

1 WE6, 8, 10 In a suburb of roughly 1500 houses, a random sample of 40 households were chosen, and surveyed to find the number of children in each of them. The data were collected and recorded as follows.

0, 3, 2, 4, 1, 2, 3, 2, 2, 2, 2, 1, 3, 4, 5, 2, 3, 1, 1, 1,
0, 0, 2, 3, 4, 1, 3, 4, 2, 2, 0, 1, 2, 3, 2, 0, 2, 4, 5, 1.

a Comment on the sample.
b Organise the data into a frequency table.

INDIVIDUAL PATHWAYS

eBook*plus*

Activity 12-B-1
Data and graphs
doc-6999

Activity 12-B-2
More data and graphs
doc-7000

Activity 12-B-3
Advanced data and graphs
doc-7001

c Display the data as a combined histogram and frequency polygon.

d Comment on the distribution of the data and the shape of the graph.

e What could you say about the number of children per household in the suburb?

2 Consider the following frequency tables.

a

x	f
1	4
2	3
3	5
4	0
5	2
6	6
Total	

b

x	f
150	2
151	6
152	9
153	18
154	11
155	3
Total	

c

x	f
50	3
52	3
54	2
56	2
58	1
60	5
Total	

For each table:

i draw a combined histogram and frequency polygon to suit the data

ii comment on the shape of the graph.

3 A quality control officer selected 25 boxes of portable CD players at random from a production line. She tested every portable CD player in each box and displayed the number of defective portable CD players in each box as follows:

1, 3, 2, 5, 2, 2, 1, 5, 2, 1, 2, 4, 3, 0, 5, 3, 2, 1, 3, 2, 1, 3, 4, 2, 1.

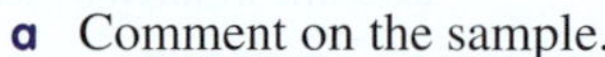

a Comment on the sample.

b Organise the data into a frequency table.

c Comment on the distribution of the data.

d What could you say about the population of CD players?

4 This table shows the number of hours of sport played per week by a group of Year 8 students.

Score (hours of sport played)	Frequency (f)
1	3
2	8
3	10
4	12
5	16
6	8
7	7
Total	64

a Draw a histogram and frequency polygon to display the data.

b Comment on the shape of the graph.

c Discuss whether you feel this sample reflects the sporting habits of Year 8 students generally.

5 WE7, 9, 10 A block of houses in a suburb was surveyed to find the size of each house (in m^2). These are the results.

Size of house (m^2)	Frequency
100–<150	13
150–<200	18
200–<250	19
250–<300	17
300–<350	14
350–<400	11
Total	92

a Draw a histogram and frequency polygon to display the data.
b Comment on the shape of the graph.
c Discuss whether you feel this sample reflects the size of the houses in the suburb.

6 Forty people joined a weight-loss program. Their mass (in kg) was recorded at the beginning of the program and is shown in this frequency table.

Class interval	Frequency
60–<70	2
70–<80	5
80–<90	9
90–<100	12
100–<110	7
110–<120	3
120–<130	2
Total	40

a Draw a histogram and frequency polygon to display the data.
b Comment on the shape of the graph.
c Discuss whether you feel this sample reflects the mass of people in the community.

7 WE11 Forty people in a shopping centre were asked about the number of hours per week they spent watching TV. The result of the survey is shown below.

10, 13, 7, 12, 16, 11, 6, 14, 6, 11, 5, 14, 12, 8, 27, 17, 13, 8, 14, 10,
13, 7, 15, 10, 16, 8, 18, 14, 21, 28, 9, 12, 11, 13, 9, 13, 29, 5, 24, 11

a Organise the data into class intervals of 5–<10 hours etc., and draw up a frequency table.
b Draw a histogram and frequency polygon to display the data.
c Comment on the shape of the graph.
d Discuss whether you feel this sample reflects the TV viewing habits of the community.

UNDERSTANDING

8 A Year 8 class sat for a 10-question multiple-choice test. These are their results.

2, 6, 5, 9, 8, 7, 3, 6, 9, 4, 8, 8, 6, 7, 6, 4, 7, 8, 7, 8, 6, 7, 8, 5, 3, 9, 2, 6, 5, 8

a Organise the data into a frequency table.
b Display the data as a combined histogram and frequency polygon.
c Comment on the performance of the class in the test.

9 The number of hours of sleep during school week nights for a Year 8 class are recorded below.

$6, 9, 7, 8, 7, 8\frac{1}{2}, 6\frac{1}{2}, 8, 7\frac{1}{2}, 7\frac{1}{2}, 8, 8\frac{1}{2}, 6\frac{1}{2}, 8, 8, 7, 7\frac{1}{2}, 8, 9, 8$

a Organise the data into a frequency table.
b Display the data as a histogram.
c Comment on the sleeping habits of the Year 8 students.
d Discuss whether you feel these sample results reflect those of Year 8 students generally.

10 The amount of pocket money (in dollars) available to a random sample of 13-year-olds each week was found to be as shown below.

10, 15, 5, 4, 8, 10, 4, 15, 5, 6, 10, 6, 5, 10, 8, 10, 5, 10, 10, 6

a Organise the data into a frequency table.
b Display the data as a histogram.
c Comment on the shape of the histogram.
d Discuss whether you feel these sample results reflect those of 13-year-olds generally.

11 The following data give the results of testing the lives (in hours) of 100 torch batteries.

25, 36, 30, 34, 21, 40, 36, 46, 29, 38, 20, 41, 34, 45, 25, 40, 31, 39, 24, 45, 27, 44, 23, 35, 47, 49, 20, 37, 43, 26, 35, 28, 48, 30, 20, 36, 41, 26, 32, 42, 21, 31, 45, 42, 26, 37, 33, 24, 45, 38, 36, 43, 21, 34, 38, 35, 28, 41, 30, 22, 29, 32, 39, 25, 44, 21, 35, 38, 41, 35, 30, 23, 37, 43, 33, 34, 28, 39, 22, 31, 35, 42, 38, 27, 36, 46, 28, 34, 37, 29, 24, 30, 39, 44, 31, 24, 36, 28, 47, 21

eBook*plus*

Digital doc
Spreadsheet
Histograms and frequency polygons
doc-2183

a Choose a suitable class interval for the given data, and present the results in a frequency distribution table.
b Draw a histogram and frequency polygon of the data.
c Comment on the trends shown by the histogram.
d Discuss whether you feel these results reflect those of the battery population.

12 A random sample of 30 students in Year 9 undertook a survey to investigate the height of Year 9 students. These were their measured heights (in cm).

146, 163, 156, 168, 159, 170, 152, 174, 156, 163, 157, 161, 178, 151, 148, 167, 162, 157, 166, 154, 150, 166, 160, 155, 164, 157, 171, 168, 158, 162

a Organise the data into class intervals 145–<150 cm etc., and draw up a frequency distribution table.
b Draw a histogram displaying the data.
c Reorganise the class intervals to be 145–<148 cm etc., and construct a new frequency distribution table.
d Draw a new histogram displaying the data in part **c**.
e Comment on the similarities and differences between the two histograms.

eBook*plus*

Digital doc
WorkSHEET 12.1
doc-7005

REFLECTION
How does a column graph for categorical data differ from a histogram for numerical data?

12C Measures of centre

- Simple calculations based on collected data can help give us typical values, or values that show how the data cluster.
- These typical values are commonly referred to as averages.
- We will look at 3 different types of averages used in interpreting data: **mean**, **median** and **mode**.

Mean

- The mean or average of a set of scores is the sum of all the scores divided by the number of scores.
- It is denoted by the symbol $\bar{x}$ (pronounced x bar).

WORKED EXAMPLE 12

Jan's basketball scores were: 18, 24, 20, 22, 14, 12. What was his mean score? Calculate your answer, correct to 1 decimal place.

THINK	WRITE
1 Calculate the total of the basketball scores.	Total score = 18 + 24 + 20 + 22 + 14 + 12 = 110
2 Count the number of basketball scores.	Number of scores = 6
3 Define the rule for the mean.	$\text{Mean} = \dfrac{\text{total score}}{\text{number of scores}}$
4 Substitute the known values into the rule.	$\bar{x} = \dfrac{110}{6}$
5 Evaluate, rounding to 1 decimal place. *Note:* The mean is often not one of the given scores.	= 18.33333... = 18.3

- Sometimes calculations need to be performed from a frequency distribution table.

WORKED EXAMPLE 13

Calculate the mean of the frequency distribution data given below.

Score (x)	1	2	3	4	5	6
Frequency (f)	3	2	4	0	1	5

THINK

1 Rearrange the rows as columns and include an extra column headed: 'Score × frequency ($x \times f$)'.

2 Enter the information into the third column; that is, the score of 1 occurred 3 times. Therefore, $x \times f = 1 \times 3 = 3$. The score of 2 occurred 2 times. Therefore, $x \times f = 2 \times 2 = 4$. Continue this process for each pair of data.

3 Determine the total of the 'Frequency' column. This shows how many scores there are altogether.

4 Determine the total of the 'Score × frequency' column. This shows the overall value of all the scores.

5 Define the rule for the mean.

6 Substitute the known values into the rule.

7 Evaluate the answer to 1 decimal place.
Note: The mean is often not one of the given scores.

WRITE

Score (x)	Frequency (f)	Score × Frequency ($x \times f$)
1	3	$1 \times 3 = 3$
2	2	$2 \times 2 = 4$
3	4	$3 \times 4 = 12$
4	0	$4 \times 0 = 0$
5	1	$5 \times 1 = 5$
6	5	$6 \times 5 = 30$
Total	15	54

$$\text{Mean} = \frac{\text{total of score} \times \text{frequency values}}{\text{total frequency values}}$$

$$\bar{x} = \frac{54}{15}$$
$$= 3.6$$

Median

- The median is the middle score for an odd number of scores and the average of the two middle scores for an even number of scores.
- Alternatively, if a set of data contains n scores, the median is given by the $\frac{n+1}{2}$ th score.
- To obtain the median, the scores must be arranged in numerical order.

WORKED EXAMPLE 14

Find the median of the scores:

a 10, 8, 11, 5, 17 **b 9, 3, 2, 6, 3, 5, 9, 8.**

THINK

a 1 Arrange the values in ascending order.

2 Select the middle value.
Note: There are an odd number of scores, that is, 5. Hence, the third value is the middle number or median. Alternatively, use the rule $\frac{n+1}{2}$, where $n = 5$ gives the position of the median. The location of the median is $\left(\frac{5+1}{2} = 3\right)$; that is, the 3rd score.

3 Answer the question.

WRITE

a 5, 8, (10), 11, 17

The median of the scores is 10.

b 1 Arrange the values in ascending order. | b 2, 3, 3, ⑤, ⑥, 8, 9, 9

2 Select the middle values.
Note: There are an even number of scores that is, 8. Hence, the fourth and fifth values are the middle numbers, or median.
Again the rule $\frac{n+1}{2}$ could be used to locate the position of the median.

3 Obtain the average of the two middle values.

$$\text{Median} = \frac{5+6}{2} = \frac{11}{2} = 5\tfrac{1}{2} \text{ (or 5.5)}$$

4 Answer the question.
Note: The median in this case is not one of the actual scores.

The median of the score is $5\frac{1}{2}$ or 5.5.

Note: For sets of data containing an odd number of scores, the median will be one of the actual scores, while for the sets with an even number of scores, the median will be positioned halfway between the two scores.

Mode

- The mode is the most common score in a set of data.
- It is the score with the highest frequency. It measures clustering of scores.
- Some sets of scores have more than one mode or no mode at all; that is, there is no score that corresponds to the highest frequency, as all values occurred once only.

WORKED EXAMPLE 15

Find the mode of the following scores:
a 5, 7, 9, 8, 5, 8, 5, 6
b 10, 8, 11, 5, 17
c 9, 3, 2, 6, 3, 5, 9, 8.

THINK | WRITE

a 1 Look at the set of data and circle any values that have been repeated. | a ⑤, 7, 9, ⑧, ⑤, ⑧, ⑤, 6

2 Choose the values that have been repeated the most. | The number 5 occurs 3 times.

3 Answer the question. | The mode for the given set of values is 5.

b 1 Look at the set of data and circle any values that have been repeated. | b 10, 8, 11, 5, 17
No values have been repeated.

2 Answer the question.
Note: No mode is not the same as having a mode which equals 0. | The following set of data has no mode, since none of the scores correspond to a highest frequency. Each of the numbers occur only once.

c 1 Look at the set of data and circle any values that have been repeated. | c ⑨, ③, 2, 6, ③, 5, ⑨, 8

2 Choose the values that have been repeated the most.	The number 3 occurs twice. The number 9 occurs twice.
3 Answer the question.	The modes for the given set of values are 3 and 9.

The effect of outliers on measures of centre

- An **outlier** is a data value that is considerably different from the rest of the values in a set of data.
- The presence of one or more outliers may have a considerable effect on the measures of centre of a particular set of data.

Consider a netball team where the team scored the following in 10 games:
17, 23, 31, 19, 50, 29, 16, 23, 30, 32.
Rearrange the scores in order:
16, 17, 19, 23, 23, 29, 30, 31, 32, 50

$$\text{Mean} = \frac{16+17+19+23+23+29+30+31+32+50}{10} = 27$$

$$\text{Median} = \frac{23+29}{2} = 26$$

Mode = 23

The following Saturday, the regular goal shooter was ill, and Lauren, who plays in a higher division, was asked to play. The team's score for that game was 200.
When the measures of centre were recalculated for 11 games, the following results were obtained:
16, 17, 19, 23, 23, 29, 30, 31, 32, 50, 200

$$\text{Mean} = \frac{16+17+19+23+23+29+30+31+32+50+200}{10} = 43$$

Median = 29
Mode = 23

The inclusion of an extreme value or outlier has dramatically increased the mean of the data, marginally increased the median and left the mode unchanged.
The important point to learn from this illustration is that when a set of data includes extreme values, the mean may not be truly representative of the data.

Which measure of centre is most useful?

- Now that we have discussed the three measures of central tendency, it is important to know which measure will be most useful in a given situation.
  - The mean is appropriate when no extreme values or outliers distort the picture.
  - The median is appropriate when outliers are present.
  - The mode is appropriate when the most common result is significant.

Summary of measures of centre		
Mode	**Median**	**Mean**
The most common value or category. It tells us nothing about the rest of the data. Data may have no mode, one mode or more than one mode.	The score in the exact middle of the values placed in numerical order. It tells us nothing about other values. It is unaffected by exceptionally large or small values.	Uses all the scores as a total, divided by the number of scores. It is affected by exceptionally large or small scores.

REMEMBER

1. Measures of centre represent a typical value around which the data are centred. These are the mean, median and mode.
2. The mean represents the average of the scores, and is calculated by dividing the sum of the scores by the number of scores.
3. The median is the middle score of a data set, where the scores have been arranged in order.
4. The mode is the most common score in the data set.
5. When outliers are present, the median is the most appropriate measure of centre.

EXERCISE 12C Measures of centre

INDIVIDUAL PATHWAYS

eBook*plus*

Activity 12-C-1
Measures of centre
doc-7002

Activity 12-C-2
More measures of centre
doc-7003

Activity 12-C-3
Advanced measures of centre
doc-7004

eBook*plus*

Interactivity
Measures of centre
int-2362

FLUENCY

1 WE12 Caroline's basketball scores were: 28, 25, 29, 30, 27, 22. What was her mean score? Give the answer correct to 1 decimal place.

2 Find the mean (average) of each set of the following scores. Give the answers correct to 2 decimal places.

a 1, 2, 3, 4, 7, 9
b 2, 7, 8, 10, 6, 9, 11, 4, 9
c 3, 27, 14, 0, 2, 104, 36, 19, 77, 81
d 4, 8.4, 6.6, 7.0, 7.5, 8.0, 6.9

3 Francesca's soccer team has the following goals record this season: 2, 0, 1, 3, 1, 2, 4, 0, 2, 3.

a What total number of goals have they scored?
b How many games have they played?
c Find the team's average score.

4 MC Frisco's athletics coach timed 5 consecutive 200 m training runs. He recorded times of 25.1, 23.9, 24.8, 24.5 and 27.3 seconds. His mean 200 m time (in seconds) is:

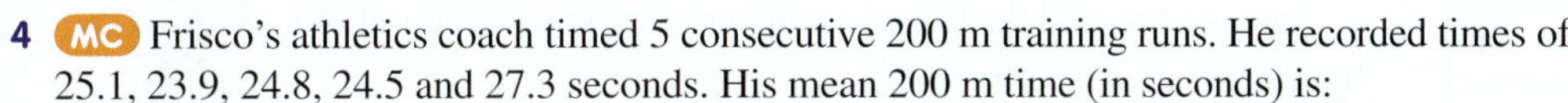

A 24.60 **B** 25.20
C 25.12 **D** 25.42
E 26.12

5 An Olympic figure skater was given these scores by the panel of judges: 4.8, 4.6, 4.5, 4.7, 4.8, 4.9, 4.2, 4.0, 4.8.
Find the average score correct to 1 decimal place.

6 Two Year 8 groups did the same mathematics test. Their results out of 10 were:
Group A: 5, 8, 7, 9, 6, 7, 8, 5, 4, 2
Group B: 5, 6, 4, 5, 9, 7, 8, 8, 9, 7

a Which group had the highest mean?
b Compare the spread of the marks for the groups.

7 WE13 Calculate the mean of this frequency distribution.

Score (x)	1	2	3	4	5
Frequency (f)	4	3	2	1	0

8 Calculate the mean of this frequency distribution.

Score (x)	6	7	8	9	10
Frequency (f)	2	8	3	4	2

9 These scores show the number of people in each apartment in a block of flats. Use a frequency table to calculate the mean number of people per unit, correct to 1 decimal place.
1, 3, 2, 4, 2, 1, 3, 5, 3, 2, 4, 1, 3, 2, 1, 2

10 The mean of 10 scores is 8. What is the total of all the scores?

11 WE14a Find the median of the following scores.
- **a** 5, 5, 7, 12, 13
- **b** 28, 13, 17, 21, 18, 17, 14

12 WE14b Find the median of the following scores.
- **a** 2, 52, 46, 52, 48, 52, 48
- **b** 4, 1.5, 1.7, 2.0, 1.8, 1.5, 1.7, 1.8, 1.9

13 WE15 For each set of scores in questions **11** and **12**, find the mode.
Questions **14** and **15** refer to the following set of scores.
1, 1, 1, 4, 4, 5, 5, 6, 3, 3, 7, 6, 5, 4, 6, 2, 1, 8

14 MC The median of the given scores is:
A 1 **B** 4.5 **C** 4 **D** 5 **E** 8

15 MC The mode of the given scores is:
A 5 **B** 6 **C** 4 **D** 3 **E** 1

UNDERSTANDING

eBook*plus*

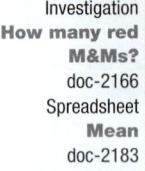

Digital docs
Investigation **How many red M&Ms?** doc-2166
Spreadsheet **Mean** doc-2183
Spreadsheet **Median** doc-2185
Spreadsheet **Mode** doc-2187

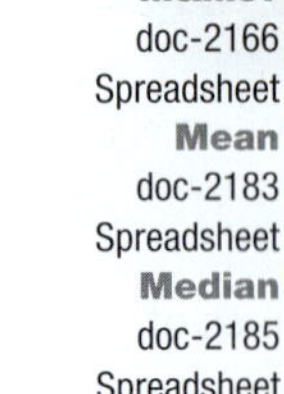

16 A third Year 8 group had the following results in the same test as in question **6**:
5, 7, 8, 4, 6, 8, 5, 9, 8.
- **a** What is the average score of this group?
- **b** What must a tenth student (who was originally absent) score to bring this group's average to 7?

17 A survey of the number of occupants in each house in a street gave the following data:
2, 5, 1, 6, 2, 3, 2, 4, 1, 2, 0, 2, 3, 2, 4, 5, 4, 2, 3, 4.
Prepare a frequency distribution table with an $x \times f$ column and use it to find the average number of people per household.

18 The mean of 5 scores is 7.2.
- **a** What is the sum of the scores?
- **b** If four of the scores are 9, 8, 7 and 5, what is the fifth?

19 Over 10 matches, a soccer team scored the following number of goals:
2, 3, 1, 0, 4, 5, 2, 3, 3, 4.
- **a** What was the most common number of goals scored?
- **b** What was the median number of goals scored?
- **c** In this case, does the mode or the median give a score that shows a typical performance?

20 Here are Tiger Woods's scores (numbers of strokes) hole by hole for the first 9 holes of a major golf tournament.

Hole number	1	2	3	4	5	6	7	8	9
Score	4	4	3	2	4	3	3	2	4

- **a** How many strokes were most commonly hit?
- **b** What was his median score?
- **c** As Woods prepares to tee off towards the next hole, how many strokes could the crowd expect him to take to complete the hole? Discuss factors which could influence the outcome.

21 The following scores represent the number of museli bars sold in a school canteen each day over two weeks.
54, 64, 51, 58, 56, 59, 10, 34, 48, 56

a Calculate the mean.
b Calculate the median.
c Calculate the mode.
d Which of the mean, median or mode best represents a typical day's sales in the school canteen? Explain.

22 A small business pays the following annual wages (in thousands of dollars) to its employees:
18, 18, 18, 18, 26, 26, 26, 40, 80.

a What is the mode of the distribution?
b What is the median wage?
c What is the mean wage?
d Which measure would you expect the employee's union to use in wage negotiations?
e Which might the boss use in such negotiations?

REASONING

23 Find five numbers that have a mean of 10 and a median of 12.

24 The mean of 5 different test scores is 15. What are the largest and smallest possible test scores, given that the median is 12? All test scores are whole numbers.

25 The mean of 5 different test scores is 10. What are the largest and smallest possible values for the median? All test scores are whole numbers.

26 The mean of 9 different test scores that are whole numbers and range from 0 to 100 is 85. The median is 80. What is the greatest possible range between the highest and lowest possible test scores?

REFLECTION
Why is the mean affected more by an outlier than the median or the mode?

12D Measures of spread

- In analysing a set of scores, it is helpful to see not only how the scores tend to cluster, or how the middle of the set looks, but also how they spread or scatter.
- Two classes may have the same average mark, but the spread of scores may differ considerably.

Range

- The **range** of a set of scores is the difference between the highest and lowest scores.

WORKED EXAMPLE 16

Find the range of the following sets of data.

a 7, 3, 5, 2, 1, 6, 9, 8.

b

x	7	8	9	10
f	1	3	5	2

THINK	WRITE
a 1 Obtain the highest and lowest values.	**a** Highest value = 9 Lowest value = 1
2 Define the range.	Range = highest value − lowest value
3 Substitute the known values into the rule.	= 9 − 1
4 Evaluate.	= 8
5 Answer the question.	The set of values has a range of 8.
b 1 Obtain the highest and lowest values. *Note:* Consider the values only, not the frequencies.	**b** Highest value = 10 Lowest value = 7

2	Define the range.	Range = highest value − lowest value
3	Substitute the known values into the rule.	= 10 − 7
4	Evaluate.	= 3
5	Answer the question.	The frequency distribution table data have a range of 3.

- Although the range identifies both the lowest and highest scores, the spread of the scores within the range is frequently not uniform.

Skewness

- The mean and median are measures of centre.
- They represent typical values around which the data are centred.
- In a symmetrical distribution, values of the mean, median and mode are very close, and any of these measures could be used to describe a 'central' value of the data set.
- In reality, not many data sets have a symmetrical distribution; they are said to be **skewed**.
- Consider the graph that has been drawn at right. This graph is symmetrical, and we can see that the mean, median and mode are all equal to 3.
- The majority of scores are clustered around the mean. This is an example of a **normal distribution**.
- The second graph shows a data set in which the scores are not clustered and there are two modes at either end of the distribution. In this example, although it is still symmetrical there are two modes, 1 and 5, while the mean and median are still 3.

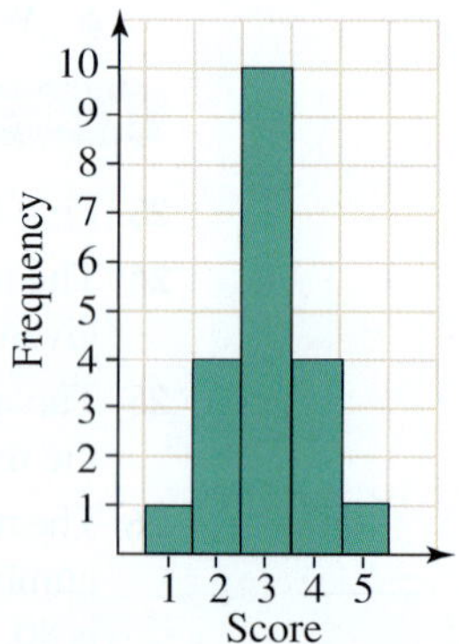

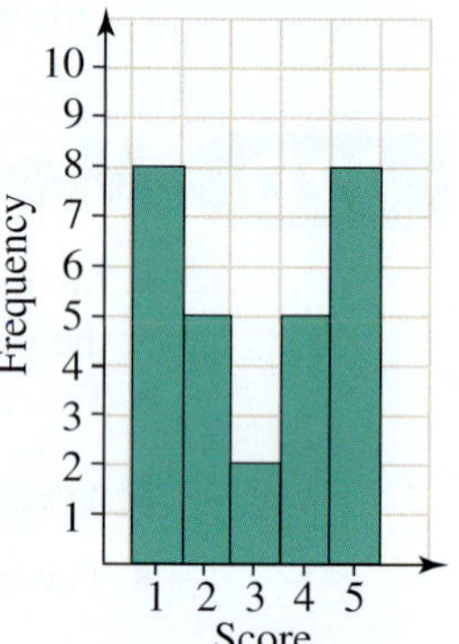

WORKED EXAMPLE 17

The figure at right shows the distribution of a set of scores on an exam.

a Is the graph symmetrical?

b What is the mode?

c Can the mean and median be seen from the graph and, if so, what are their values?

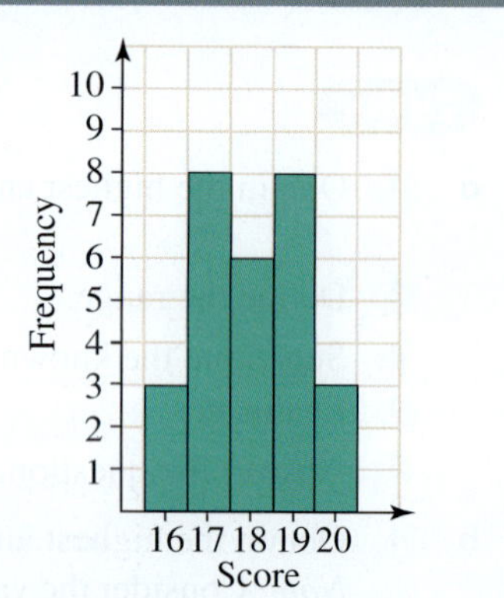

THINK	WRITE
a Consider the columns either side of the middle. If they are equal, then the graph is symmetrical.	**a** The graph is symmetrical.
b Look for the score or scores that occur the most often.	**b** Mode = 17 and 19
c Since the graph is symmetrical, the middle score will be the mean and the median.	**c** Mean = 18 Median = 18

- When a graph is not symmetrical, the mean and median cannot be easily seen from the graph.
- Consider the graph at right where the scores are gathered to the lower end of the distribution.
- The way in which the data are gathered to one end of the distribution is called the **skewness**.
- When a greater number of scores are distributed at the lower end of the distribution, the data are said to be positively skewed.

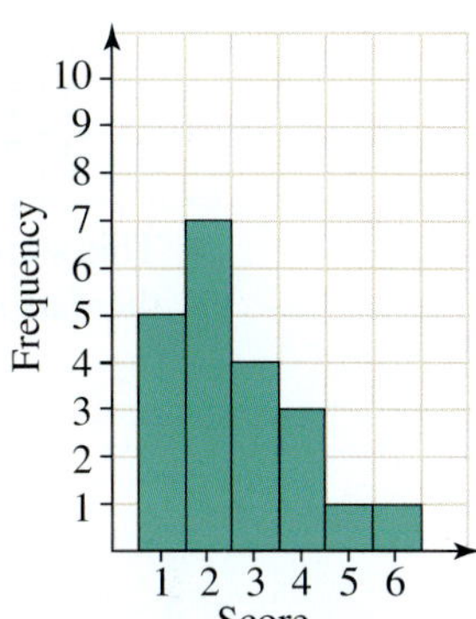

- Similarly, when most of the scores are distributed at the upper end, the data are said to be negatively skewed, as shown at right.

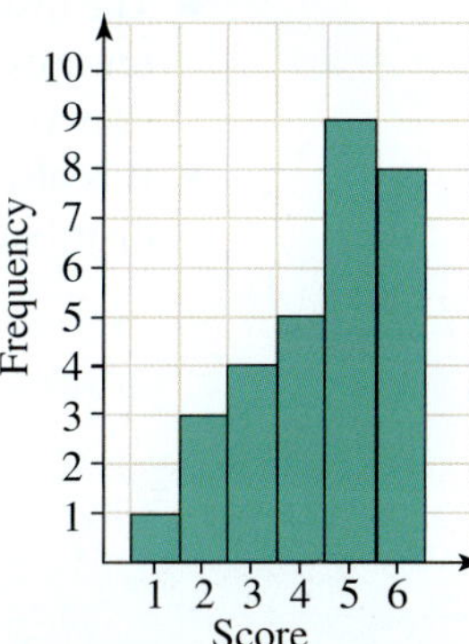

WORKED EXAMPLE 18

The distribution at right shows the results of the Mathematics exam at a certain school.
a What is the modal class?
b Describe the skewness of the data set.

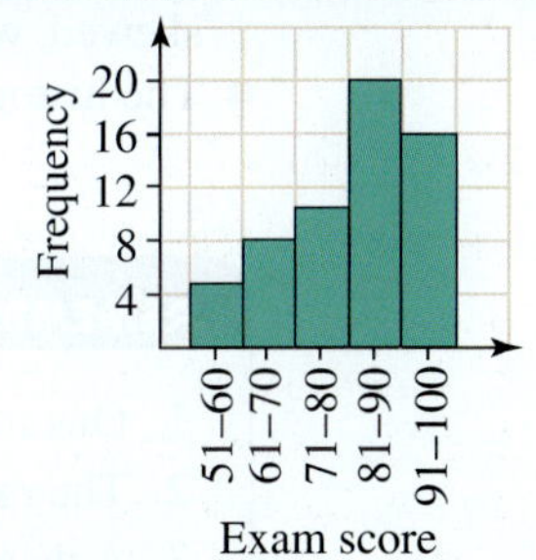

THINK	WRITE
a Locate the modal class by considering which class occurs most often. Which column is the largest?	**a** Modal class = 81 – 90
b Observe where the majority of data are located. In this case it is at the upper end of the distribution.	**b** The data are negatively skewed.

- There are many reasons why a data set may be skewed.
- In the case of an exam, an easier exam may lead to negatively skewed data with more students obtaining a higher mark, while a more difficult exam may lead to more students at the lower end of the distribution and hence the data will be positively skewed.
- The skewness of a distribution is also evident in other graphical forms.

Key: 1|6 = 16 people

Stem	*Leaf*
0	2 4
0	7 7 9
1	0 1 4 4 4 4
1	5 6 6 7 8 8 9
2	1 2 2 3 3 3
2	7

- This stem plot shows the data concentrated towards the upper end of the distribution, making the data set negatively skewed.

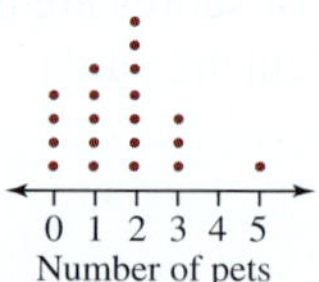

- The distribution of this dot plot is concentrated towards the lower end, making it positively skewed.
- It is also possible to see the skewness of a distribution from a frequency table.

Children per household	Frequency
0	4
1	5
2	7
3	3
4	0
5	1

- This frequency table produced in Worked example 6 shows that the distribution is positively skewed, with the scores being concentrated at the lower end of the distribution.
- The histogram displaying the data also confirms this.

REMEMBER

1. One measure used to determine the spread of a data set is the range.
2. The range measures the difference between the highest and lowest scores.
3. A distribution is symmetrical when the data are equally distributed around the mean.
4. When the data are symmetrical, the median and the mean will both be the middle score.
5. When the majority of scores are at the lower end of a distribution, it is said to be positively skewed.
6. When the majority of scores are at the upper end of the distribution, it is said to be negatively skewed.

EXERCISE
12D Measures of spread

INDIVIDUAL PATHWAYS

eBook*plus*

Activity 12-D-1
Measures of spread
doc-7006

Activity 12-D-2
More measures of spread
doc-7007

Activity 12-D-3
Advanced measures of spread
doc-7008

FLUENCY

1 WE16a Find the range of the following scores.
  a 5, 5, 7, 12, 13
  b 28, 13, 17, 21, 18, 17, 14
  c 2, 52, 46, 52, 48, 52, 48
  d 4, 1.5, 1.7, 2.0, 1.8, 1.5, 1.7, 1.8, 1.9

2 WE16b Find the range of the following sets of data.

a

x	6	7	8	9	10
f	1	5	10	7	3

b

x	1	2	3	4	5	6
f	7	9	6	8	10	10

c

x	5	10	15	20
f	1	5	10	7

d

x	110	111	112	113	114
f	2	2	2	3	3

3 WE17 The figure at right shows the distribution of a set of scores.
  a Is the graph symmetrical?
  b What is the mode?
  c Can the mean and median be seen from the graph and, if so, what are their values?

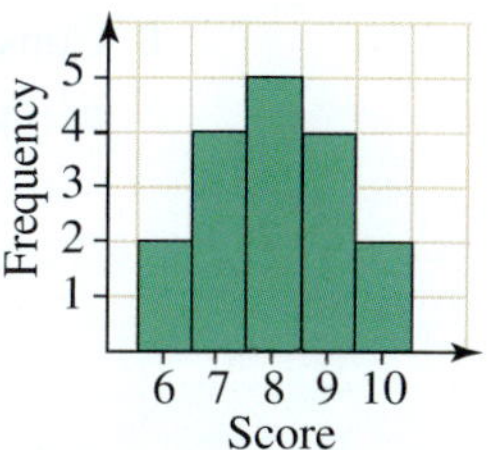

4 Consider the distribution shown at right.
  a Are the data symmetrical?
  b What is the modal class?
  c Can the mean and median be seen from the graph and, if so, what are their values?

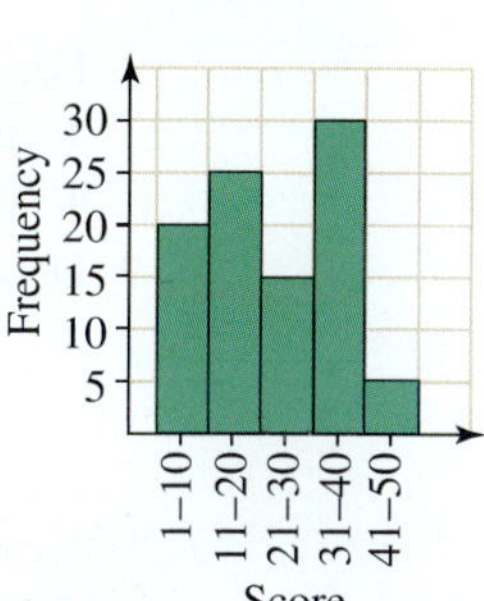

5 WE18 Consider the distribution shown at right.
  a What is the modal class?
  b Describe the skewness of the distribution.

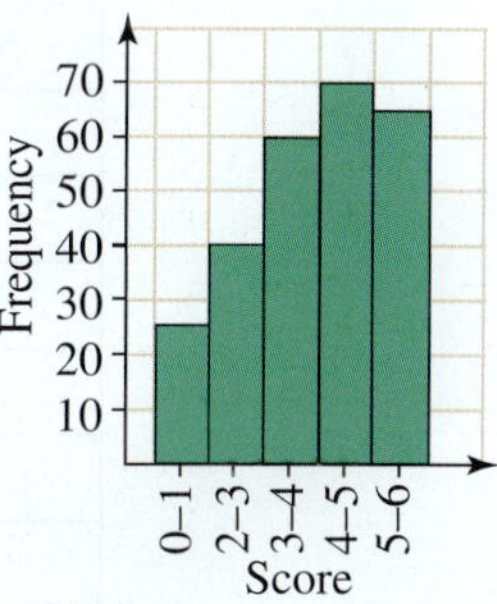

6 The table below shows the number of goals scored by a netball team throughout a season.

Number of goals	Frequency
1–10	13
11–20	16
21–30	27
31–40	33
41–50	31

a Draw a frequency histogram of the data.
b Describe the data set in terms of its skewness.

7 MC The distribution represented by the graph at right is:
A positively skewed
B negatively skewed
C symmetrical
D normally distributed
E none of the above.

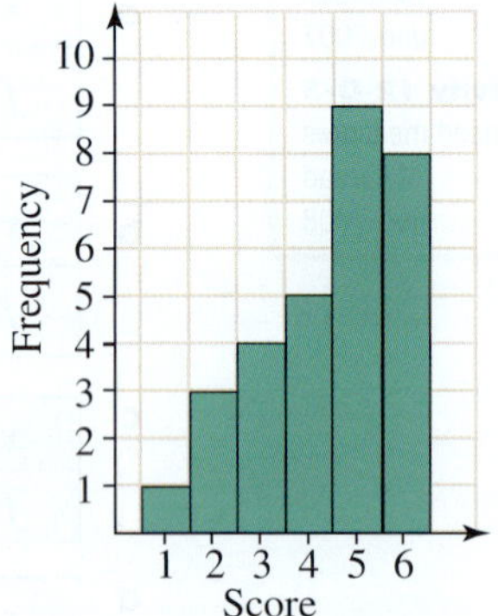

UNDERSTANDING

8 Consider the stem plots below.

a Key: 1 | 5 = 15

Stem	*Leaf*
1	1 2 7 8 9
2	2 8
3	1 3 7 9
4	0 1 2 6

b Key: 24 | 7 = 247

Stem	*Leaf*
24	2 7
25	2 4 6 6 8
26	0 1 3 5 9
28	5 6 6 8

c Key: 17 | 4 = 174

Stem	*Leaf*
15	6 2 4
16	8 6 1 3 9
17	0 2 1 8 6 7 3 4
18	4 1 5 2 7 1

For each stem plot:
i give the range
ii describe the skewness of the distribution.

9 Describe the skewness of the distribution in this dot plot.

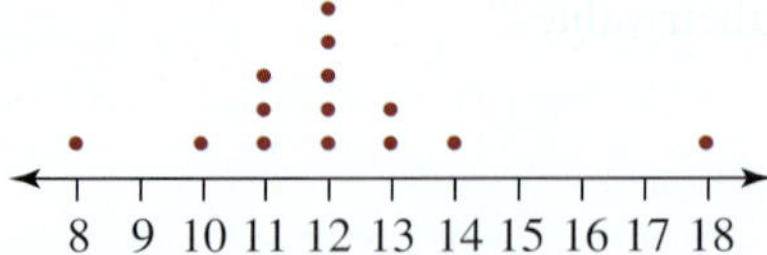

10 The table shows the number of goals scored by a soccer team throughout a season.

Number of goals	Frequency
0	5
1	7
2	7
3	7
4	7
5	5

a Show this information in a frequency histogram.
b Are the data symmetrical?
c What is the mode?
d Can the mean and median be seen for this distribution and, if so, what are their values?

11 A movie is shown at 30 cinemas across Sydney on its opening day. The number of people attending at each cinema is shown in the table below.

Number of people	Frequency
1–50	3
51–100	2
101–150	6
151–200	9
201–250	10

a Present the data in a frequency histogram.
b Are the data symmetrical?
c What is the modal class?
d Describe the skewness of the distribution and explain possible reasons for the skewness.

12 Year 10 students at Merrigong High School sit exams in Science and Maths. The results are shown in the table below.

Mark	Number of students (Science)	Number of students (Maths)
51–60	7	6
61–70	10	7
71–80	8	12
81–90	8	9
91–100	2	6

a Is either distribution symmetrical?
b If either distribution is not symmetrical, state whether it is positively or negatively skewed.
c Discuss the possible reasons for any skewness.
d State the modal class of each distribution.
e In which subject is the standard deviation greater? Explain your answer.

13 Draw an example of a graph that is:
a symmetrical
b positively skewed with one mode
c negatively skewed with two modes.

REFLECTION

Could a distribution be symmetrical and have three modes?

12E Analysing data

- You are now armed with the skills to calculate measures of centre and spread for a data set, and to construct and analyse various forms of graphs.
- It must be remembered that most of the data we analyse is the result of a survey conducted on a sample of the population.

- It is appropriate, then, that we consider the results of data collected from surveys in light of the population from which it originated.
- To understand what information the data give, and perhaps to draw conclusions from it, we must appreciate what each statistical measure does.

Statistical measures	Definition and purpose
Mode	The most common score or category. It tells us nothing about the rest of the data. Data may have no mode, one mode or more than one mode.
Median	The score in the exact middle of the values placed in numerical order. It tells us nothing about the rest of the data. It is unaffected by exceptionally large or small scores.
Mean	The sum of all the scores divided by the number of scores. It is affected by exceptionally large or small scores.
Range	The difference between the highest score and the lowest score. It shows how far the scores are spread apart. It is particularly useful when combined with the mean or the median.

WORKED EXAMPLE 19

Explain which statistical measure is referred to in these statements.
a The majority of people surveyed prefer Activ-8 sports drink.
b The ages of fans at the Rolling Stones concert varied from 8 to 80.
c The average Australian family has 2.5 children.

THINK	WRITE
a 1 Write the statement and highlight the key word(s).	**a** The majority of people surveyed prefer Activ-8 sports drink.
2 Relate the highlighted word to one of the statistical measures.	Majority implies most, which refers to the mode.
3 Answer the question.	This statement refers to the mode.
b 1 Write the statement and highlight the key word(s).	**b** The ages of fans at the Rolling Stones concert varied from 8 to 80.
2 Relate the highlighted word to one of the statistical measures.	The statement refers to the range of fans' ages at the concert.
3 Answer the question.	This statement refers to the range.
c 1 Write the statement and highlight the key word(s).	**c** The average Australian family has 2.5 children.

2 Relate the highlighted word to one of the statistical measures.

The statement deals with surveying the population (census) and finding out how many children are in each family.

3 Answer the question.

This statement refers to the mean.

Using sample properties to predict those of the population

- Once survey data has been collated and analysed, we can use it to predict the characteristics of the population from which it was taken. Consider this example.

WORKED EXAMPLE 20

The 153 students in Year 8 all sat for a 10-question multiple-choice test as a practice test for an upcoming exam. A random sample of the results of 42 of the students gave this distribution.

Score (x)	1	2	3	4	5	6	7	8	9	10
Frequency (f)	2	3	6	7	11	8	4	0	0	1

a Calculate the mean mark.
b Determine the median mark.
c Give the modal mark.
d Which measure of centre best represents the data?
e Describe the distribution.
f Comment on any prediction about the properties of the population from this sample.

THINK

a Add a third column to the table to calculate the total of all the marks. Use the total to then calculate the mean.

WRITE

a

Mark (x)	Frequency (f)	$f \times x$
1	2	2
2	3	6
3	6	18
4	7	28
5	11	55
6	8	48
7	4	28
8	0	0
9	0	0
10	1	10
Total	42	195

$$\text{Mean} = \frac{\text{Total of all scores}}{\text{Number of scores}}$$
$$= \frac{195}{42}$$
$$= 4.6$$

b The median is the score in the middle, i.e. the $\frac{42+1}{2}$th score — the average of the 21st and 22nd score. Add a cumulative frequency column to the original frequency distribution. (Find the total frequency at that point for each mark.) Look in the cumulative frequency column to see where the 21st and 22nd scores lie.

b

Mark (x)	Frequency (f)	Cumulative frequency
1	2	2
2	3	$2+3=5$
3	6	$5+6=11$
4	7	$11+7=18$
5	11	$18+11=29$
6	8	$29+8=37$
7	4	$37+4=41$
8	0	$41+0=41$
9	0	$41+0=41$
10	1	$41+1=42$
Total	42	42

The 21st and 22nd scores are both 5. The median is 5.

c The modal mark is the one that occurs most frequently. Look for the one with the highest frequency.

c The mode is 5.

d Compare the results for the mean, median and mode. Look for similarities and differences.

d The mean is 4.6, the median is 5 and the mode is 5. It seems that any of these measures of centre would be appropriate to use as a measure of centre of the data. However, check the outlier of 10. When the outlier is disregarded, the mean is calculated to be $185 \div 41 = 4.5$. It seems that the outlier in this case does not have a great effect on the mean. So, the mean, median or mode could be used as a measure of the centre of the data.

e Look for skewness of the data.

e The score of 10 seems to be an outlier. It is most likely not due to a recording error. The remaining scores form a cluster towards the higher end of the data set, indicating that the distribution is negatively skewed.

f Consider whether these results from the sample would reflect those of the population.

f It seems likely that these results would reflect those of the whole population. The sample is random, and of sufficient size. The outlier of 10 indicates that there would be a few students with full marks, and at least half the students passed the test.

REMEMBER

1. This is a summary of what each statistical measure does.
   Mean: Uses all the scores as a total, divided by the number of scores
   Median: The score in the middle of a data set that is arranged in order
   Mode: The most common score or category
   Range: The highest score minus the lowest score
2. A decision should be made as to which measure of centre best represents the data.
3. A distribution can be symmetrical, negatively skewed, or positively skewed.
4. Consider how well the sample statistical measures reflect those of the population from which they were taken.

EXERCISE 12E

Analysing data

INDIVIDUAL PATHWAYS

eBook*plus*

Activity 12-E-1 Data distributions doc-7009

Activity 12-E-2 More data distributions doc-7010

Activity 12-E-3 Advanced data distributions doc-7011

FLUENCY

1 WE19 Explain which statistical measure is referred to in these statements.

a There was a 15° temperature variation during the day.
b Children at this school are absent 3.4 days per semester, on average.
c Most often you have to pay $79.95 for those sports shoes.
d The average Australian worker earns about $470 per week.
e A middle-income family earns about $35 000 per annum.

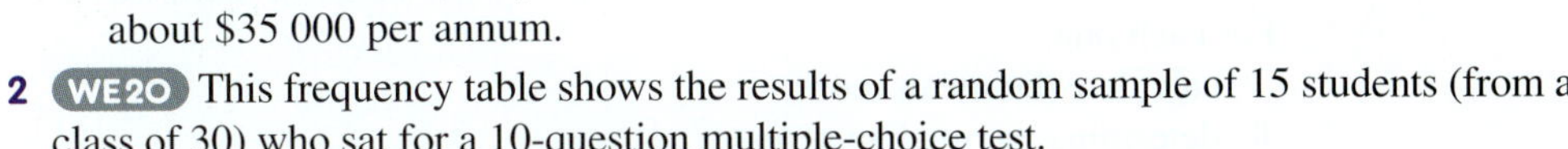

2 WE20 This frequency table shows the results of a random sample of 15 students (from a class of 30) who sat for a 10-question multiple-choice test.

Score (x)	Frequency (f)
4	1
5	2
6	5
7	4
8	3
Total	15

a Calculate the mean mark.
b Determine the median mark.
c Give the modal mark.
d Which measure of centre best represents the data?
e Describe the distribution.
f Comment on any prediction of properties of the population from this sample.

3 Consider the following frequency distribution tables.

a

x	1	2	3	4	5
f	4	3	2	1	0

b

x	6	7	8	9	10
f	2	8	3	4	2

For each one:

i calculate the mean score
ii determine the median score
iii give the modal score
iv indicate which measure of centre best describes the distribution
v describe the skewness of the distribution.

4 Consider the following frequency stem plots.

a Key: 1 | 0 = 10

Stem	Leaf
1	0 2
2	1 3 3 5
3	
4	4

b Key: 10 | 0 = 100

Stem	Leaf
10	0
11	0 2 2 2
12	0 4 6 6
13	3

For each one:

i calculate the mean score
ii determine the median score
iii give the modal score
iv indicate which measure of centre best describes the distribution
v describe the skewness of the distribution.

5 a

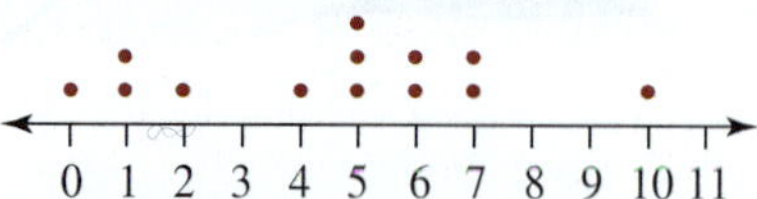

b

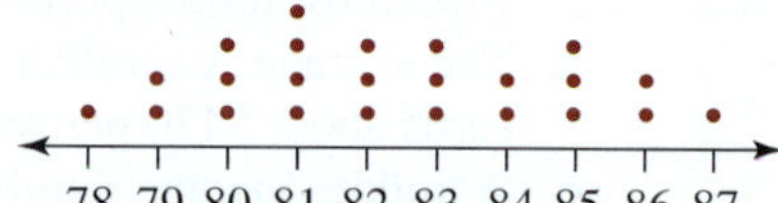

For each one:

i calculate the mean score
ii determine the median score
iii give the modal score
iv indicate which measure of centre best describes the distribution
v describe the skewness of the distribution.

UNDERSTANDING

6 A survey of the number of people in each house in a street produced these data:
2, 5, 1, 6, 2, 3, 2, 1, 4, 3, 4, 3, 1, 2, 2, 0, 2, 4.

a Prepare a frequency distribution table with an $f \times x$ column and use it to find the average (mean) number of people per household.
b Draw a dot plot of the data and use it to find the median number per household.
c Find the modal number per household.
d Which of the measures would be most useful to:
 i a real estate agent renting out houses?
 ii a government population survey?
 iii an ice-cream mobile vendor?

7 A small business pays these wages (in thousands of dollars) to its employees:
18, 18, 18, 18, 26, 26, 26, 35, 80 (boss).

a What is the wage earned by most workers?
b What is the 'average' wage?
c Find the median of the distribution.
d Which measure might be used in wage negotiations by:
  i the union, representing the employees (other than the boss)?
  ii the boss?
Explain each answer.

8 The contents of 20 packets of matches were counted after random selection and the following numbers obtained:
138, 139, 139, 141, 137, 140, 137, 141, 139, 142, 140, 141, 141, 139, 141, 138, 139, 140, 141, 138.

a Compile a frequency distribution table, including an $f \times x$ column.
b Find the mode, median and mean of the distribution.
c Which of the 3 measures best supports the manufacturer's claim that there are 140 matches per box?
d Display the data as a combined histogram and frequency polygon.

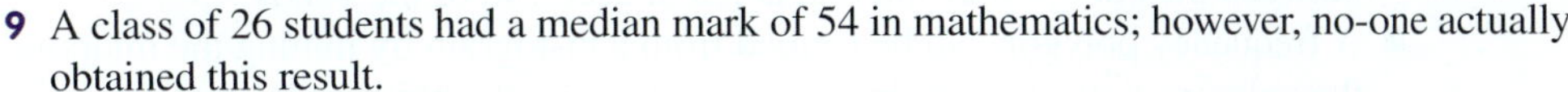

9 A class of 26 students had a median mark of 54 in mathematics; however, no-one actually obtained this result.

a Explain how this is possible.
b Explain how many must have scored below 54.

10 A soccer team had averaged 2.6 goals per match after 5 matches. After their sixth match, the average had dropped to 2.5. How many goals did they score in that latest match?

11 A tyre manufacturer selects 48 tyres at random from the production line for testing. The total distance travelled during the safe life of each tyre is shown in the table.

Distance in km ('000)	82	78	56	52	50	46
Number of tyres	2	4	10	16	12	4

a Calculate the mean, median and mode.
b Which measure best describes 'average' tyre life? Explain.
c Recalculate the mean with the 6 longest-lasting tyres removed. By how much is it lowered?
d If you selected a tyre at random, what tyre life would it most likely have?
e In a production run of 10 000 tyres, how many could be expected to last for a maximum of 50 000 km?
f As the manufacturer, for what distance would you be prepared to guarantee your tyres? Why?

REFLECTION
Why are measures of centre important statistical measures for businesses?

eBook*plus*

Digital doc
WorkSHEET 12.2
doc-7012

Summary

Samples and populations

- A census collects data from a population, while a survey collects data from a sample.
- Surveys can be conducted through personal interviews, telephone interviews or self-administered questionnaires.
- The questions in questionnaires can be open-ended or closed.
- Care must be taken in preparing questions that are clear, unbiased and easily understood.
- When a sample is selected from a population, be careful to ensure that the composition of the sample is as close as possible to that of the population.
- A random sampling technique can be used to select an appropriate sample from a population.
- The sample should be sufficiently large and not biased.

Organising and displaying data

- After being collected, data should be examined to determine if there are any values that appear to be anomalies.
- Data can be organised into frequency tables.
- Large amounts of data can be organised into class intervals in a frequency table. The choice for the size of a class interval should lead to the formation of 5 to 10 groups.
- Histograms are used to display numerical data. These are simply column graphs with no gaps between the bars. A half-interval is left at each end of the x-axis.
- A frequency polygon can be formed from a histogram by joining the midpoints of the tops of the columns with straight lines, then completing the polygon by drawing a line to the x-axis at either end.

Measures of centre

- Measures of centre represent a typical value around which the data are centred. These are the mean, median and mode.
- The mean represents the average of the scores, and is calculated by dividing the sum of the scores by the number of scores.
- The median is the middle score of a data set, where the scores have been arranged in order.
- The mode is the most common score in the data set.
- When outliers are present, the median is the most appropriate measure of centre.

Measures of spread

- One measure used to determine the spread of a data set is the range.
- The range measures the difference between the highest and lowest scores.
- A distribution is symmetrical when the data are equally distributed around the mean.
- When the data are symmetrical, the median and the mean will both be the middle score.
- When the majority of scores are at the lower end of a distribution, it is said to be positively skewed.
- When the majority of scores are at the upper end of the distribution, it is said to be negatively skewed.

Analysing data

- This is a summary of what each statistical measure does.
  Mean: Uses all the scores as a total, divided by the number of scores
  Median: The score in the middle of a data set that is arranged in order
  Mode: The most common score or category
  Range: The highest score minus the lowest score

- A decision should be made as to which measure of centre best represents the data.
- A distribution can be symmetrical, negatively skewed, or positively skewed.
- Consider how well the sample statistical measures reflect those of the population from which they were taken.

MAPPING YOUR UNDERSTANDING

Using terms from the summary, and other terms if you wish, construct a concept map that illustrates your understanding of the key concepts covered in this chapter. Compare this concept map with the one that you created in *What do you know?* on page 319.

Have you completed the two *Homework sheets*, the *Rich task* and the two *Code puzzles* in your *Maths Quest 8 Homework Book?*

Chapter review

FLUENCY

1 For each of the following statistical investigations, state whether a census or a survey has been used.
 a The average price of petrol in Sydney was estimated by averaging the price at 40 petrol stations.
 b The Australian Bureau of Statistics has every household in Australia complete an information form every five years.
 c The performance of a cricketer is measured by looking at his performance in every match he has played.
 d Public opinion on an issue is sought by a telephone poll of 2000 homes.

2 MC Which of the following is an example of a census?
 A A newspaper conducts an opinion poll of 2000 people.
 B A product survey of 1000 homes to determine what brand of washing powder is used.
 C Every 200th jar of Vegemite is tested to see if it is the correct mass.
 D A federal election is held.
 E At a shopping centre, 500 people are questioned regarding the parking facilities at the centre.

3 MC Which of the following is an example of a random sample?
 A The first 50 students who arrive at school take a survey.
 B Fifty students' names are drawn from a hat, and those drawn take the survey.
 C Ten students from each year level in the school are asked to complete a survey.
 D One class in the school is asked to complete the survey.
 E Those who catch the bus to school are asked to complete the survey.

4 Discuss how bias can be introduced into statistics through:
 a questionnaire design
 b sample selection.

5 How can you determine an appropriate sample size from a population of known size?

6 A number of people were asked to rate a video on a scale of 0 to 5. Here are their scores:
1, 0, 2, 1, 0, 0, 1, 0, 2, 3, 0, 0, 1, 0, 1, 2, 5, 3, 1, 0.
 a Sort the data into a frequency distribution table.
 b Display the data as a histogram, with a frequency polygon overlay.
 c Comment on the shape of the graph.
 d Determine the mode.
 e Find the median.
 f Calculate the range.

7 Weekly earnings from casual work performed by a sample of 50 high school students were rounded to the nearest dollar, as follows:
35, 19, 46, 54, 57, 24, 62, 08, 58, 28,
57, 53, 65, 51, 24, 60, 43, 56, 71, 50,
09, 65, 16, 38, 24, 38, 53, 68, 56, 64,
49, 49, 27, 55, 46, 79, 58, 16, 59, 62,
47, 27, 38, 47, 61, 64, 44, 34, 58, 44.
 a Organise the data into a frequency distribution with class intervals 0–9, 10–19, etc.
 b Display the data as a histogram and frequency polygon.
 c Comment on the shape of the graph.

8 Calculate the mean of the following scores 1, 2, 2, 2, 3, 3, 5, 4 and 6.

9 The mean of 10 scores was 5.5; nine of the scores were: 4, 5, 6, 8, 2, 3, 4, 6 and 9; what was the tenth score?

Questions **10** and **11** refer to the following distribution table.

x	2	3	5	6
f	3	2	8	2

10 Calculate the mean of the given frequency distribution table.

11 For the given frequency distribution table, determine:
 a the mode
 b the median
 c the range.

12 a Determine the mode of the following values: 3, 2, 6, 5, 9, 8, 1, 7. Explain your answer.
 b Determine the median of the following values: 10, 6, 1, 9, 8, 5, 17, 3.
 c Calculate the range of the following values: 1, 6, 15, 7, 21, 8, 41, 7.

13 Consider the data set represented by the frequency histogram at right.

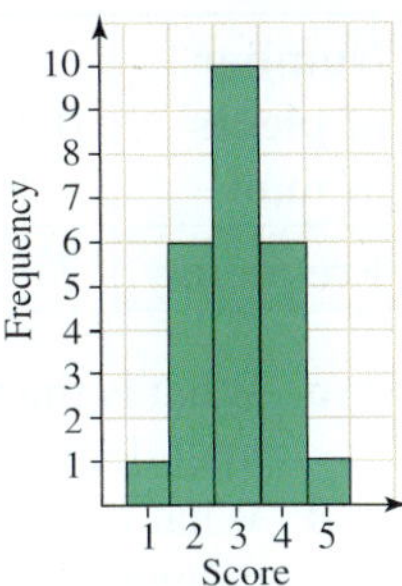

a Are the data symmetrical?

b Can the mean and median of the data be seen? If so, what are their values?

c What is the mode of the data?

14 The table below shows the number of cars that are garaged at each house in a certain street each night.

Number of cars	Frequency
1	9
2	6
3	2
4	1
5	1

a Show these data in a frequency histogram.

b Are the data positively or negatively skewed?

15

x	1.5	2.0	2.5	3.0	3.5
f	10	20	8	5	6

For this frequency distribution:

a calculate the mean score

b determine the median score

c give the modal score

d indicate which measure of centre best describes the distribution

e describe the skewness of the distribution.

16 Key: 6.1 | 8 = 6.18

Stem	*Leaf*
6.1	8 8 9
6.2	0 5 6 8
6.3	0 1 2 4 4 4

For this stem plot:

a calculate the mean score

b determine the median score

c give the modal score

d indicate which measure of centre best describes the distribution

e describe the skewness of the distribution.

17 For this dot plot:

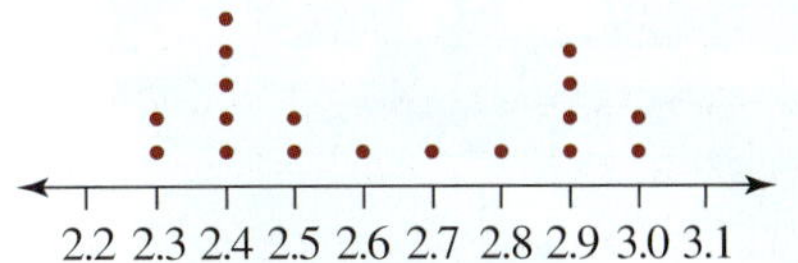

a calculate the mean score

b determine the median score

c give the modal score

d indicate which measure of centre best describes the distribution

e describe the skewness of the distribution.

PROBLEM SOLVING

1 A frozen goods section manager recorded the following sales of chickens by size during a sample week.

16, 14, 13, 12, 15, 14, 13, 11, 12, 14, 14, 16, 15, 13, 11, 12, 14, 13, 15, 17, 13, 12, 14, 16, 13, 11, 15, 14, 12, 11, 15, 12, 13, 12, 12, 15, 13, 11, 11, 13, 16, 13, 12, 15, 17, 13, 14, 16, 12, 15

a Construct a frequency distribution table showing x, f, and $x \times f$ columns. You may include a tally column if you wish.

b Draw a histogram to display the data.

c Identify the mode of the distribution.

d Calculate the mean and median sizes of the chickens sold.

e Of which size should the manager order most? Explain.

f What is the range of sizes?

g What percentage of total sales are in the size 12 to 14 group?

h Is the mean a useful measure to the manager? Explain.

2 The following table displays the results of the number of pieces of mail delivered in a week to a number of homes.

Number of pieces of mail	0	1	2	3	4	5	6	7	8	9
Frequency	7	25	34	11	8	2	4	5	3	1

a What is the most common number of pieces of mail delivered?

b What is the mean number of pieces of mail delivered?

c Calculate the range.

d Explain what this shows about the mail delivery service to these homes.

eBook*plus*

Interactivities

Test yourself
Chapter 12
int-2758

Word search
Chapter 12
int-2759

Crossword
Chapter 12
int-2760

eBookplus ACTIVITIES

Chapter opener

Digital doc *(page 319)*
- Hungry brain activity Chapter 12 (doc-6988)

Are you ready?

Digital docs *(page 320)*
- SkillSHEET 12.1 (doc-6989) Presenting data in a frequency table
- SkillSHEET 12.2 (doc-6990) Reading scales
- SkillSHEET 12.3 (doc-6991) Finding the mean of ungrouped data
- SkillSHEET 12.4 (doc-6992) Arranging a set of data in ascending order
- SkillSHEET 12.5 (doc-6993) Finding the median
- SkillSHEET 12.6 (doc-6994) Finding the middle score for data arranged in a dot plot
- SkillSHEET 12.7 (doc-6995) Finding the score in a data set that occurs most frequently

12A Samples and populations

Digital docs *(page 326)*
- Activity 12-A-1 (doc-6996) Populations and samples
- Activity 12-A-2 (doc-6997) More populations and samples
- Activity 12-A-3 (doc-6998) Advanced populations and samples
- Investigation (doc-2473) Bias *(page 325)*
- Investigation (doc-2167) Collecting data for surveys and questionnaires *(page 325)*
- Investigation (doc-7013) Data and the Olympics *(page 321)*
- Spreadsheet (doc-7106) Data and the Olympics *(page 321)*

Interactivity *(page 325)*
- Random numbers (int-0089)

12B Organising and displaying data

Digital docs *(page 334)*
- Activity 12-B-1 (doc-6999) Data and graphs
- Activity 12-B-2 (doc-7000) More data and graphs
- Activity 12-B-3 (doc-7001) Advanced data and graphs
- Spreadsheet (doc-2183) Histograms and frequency polygons *(page 336)*
- WorkSHEET 12.1 (doc-7005) *(page 336)*

12C Measures of centre

Digital docs *(page 341)*
- Activity 12-C-1 (doc-7002) Measures of centre
- Activity 12-C-2 (doc-7003) More measures of centre
- Activity 12-C-3 (doc-7004) Advanced measures of centre
- Investigation (doc-2166) How many red M&Ms? *(page 342)*
- Spreadsheet (doc-2183) Mean *(page 342)*
- Spreadsheet (doc-2185) Median *(page 342)*
- Spreadsheet (doc-2187) Mode *(page 342)*

Interactivity *(page 341)*
- Measures of centre (int-2362)

12D Measures of spread

Digital docs *(page 347)*
- Activity 12-D-1 (doc-7006) Measures of spread
- Activity 12-D-2 (doc-7007) More measures of spread
- Activity 12-D-3 (doc-7008) Advanced measures of spread

12E Analysing data

Digital docs *(page 353)*
- Activity 12-E-1 (doc-7009) Data distributions
- Activity 12-E-2 (doc-7010) More data distributions
- Activity 12-E-3 (doc-7011) Advanced data distributions
- WorkSHEET 12.2 (doc-7012) *(page 355)*

Chapter review

Interactivities *(page 360)*
- Test yourself Chapter 12 (int-2758) Take the end-of-chapter test to test your progress.
- Word search Chapter 12 (int-2759)
- Crossword Chapter 12 (int-2760)

To access eBookPLUS activities, log on to

www.jacplus.com.au

eBook*plus* ICT ACTIVITY

projects*plus*

How to burglar-proof your bedroom

SEARCHLIGHT ID: PRO-0097

Scenario

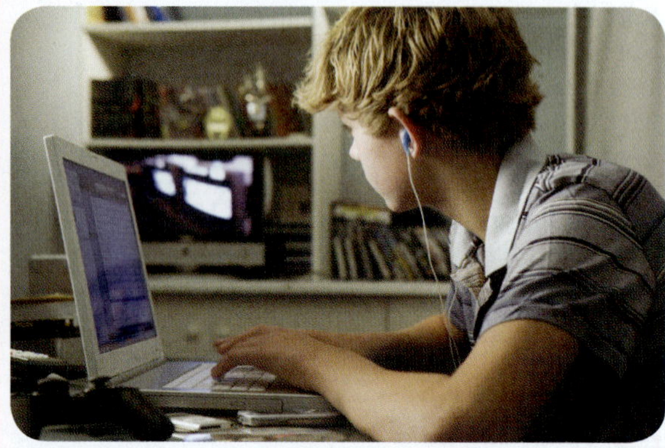

As new employees of *Kidnapper Nappers*, you and your team have been asked to design a burglar alarm for Alvin's bedroom. Alvin is a little tired of his younger brother, Michael, going into his bedroom and using Alvin's electronic equipment whenever he chooses. Alvin wants a simple alarm installed to deter anyone entering his bedroom without permission.

Alvin has asked that both his door and window be alarmed as added security.

Your brief is to design the circuitry that will then be built by the development team. This will involve:

1. learning the three basic building blocks of logic — NOT, AND and OR — using truth tables
2. learning the concept of a logic circuit, which consists of INPUTS (0's or 1's), OUTPUTS (0's or 1's) and GATES that control the logic
3. learning how to design a simple burglar alarm to meet Alvin's needs
4. learning how to design a logic circuit for the alarm consisting of a series of INPUTS, GATES and OUTPUTS.

This is your team's first big project and it is very important that your presentation is first class.

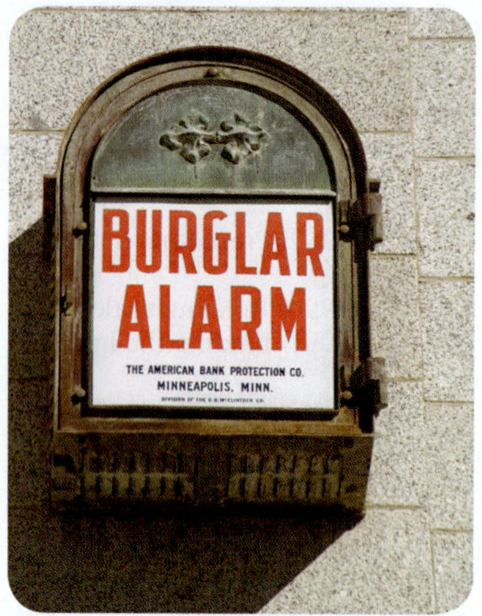

Task

You will produce a PowerPoint presentation to be shown to Alvin and your manager, clearly explaining the features of the circuit you have designed, and the problems it will solve. It is important that you use appropriate circuit diagrams and terminology.

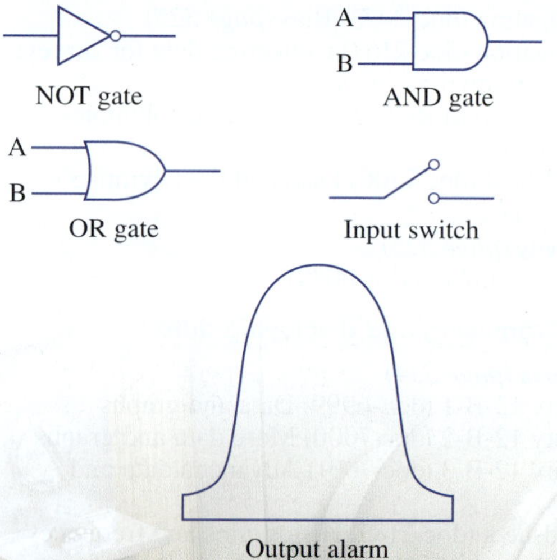

As your manager understands your inexperience with this type of project, he has provided an Interactivity to help you understand and also a series of Learning tasks to be completed to start your team on its way.

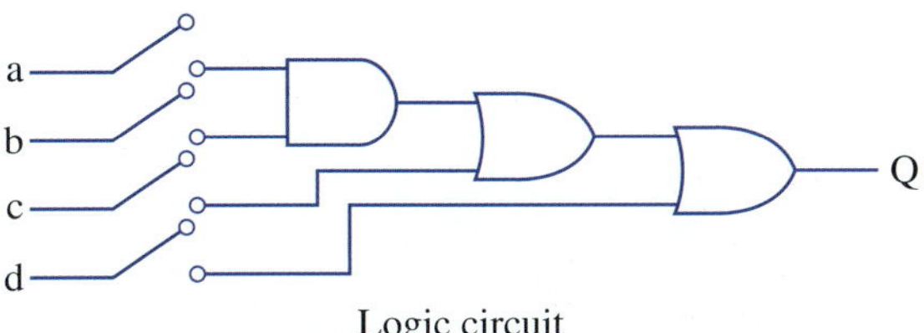

Logic circuit

Process

- Open the ProjectsPLUS application for this chapter in your eBookPLUS. Watch the introductory video lesson, click the Start project button and then set up your project group. You can complete this project individually or invite other members of your class to form a group. Save your settings, and the project will be launched.
- Go to your Media centre and find the Interactivity-Logic gates int-2448 to determine how Logic gates can be used.
- Navigate to your Media Centre. Here you will find a series of learning tasks (Worksheets) that will help you to complete the project. These must be completed and submitted to your teacher before you commence the next step.
- Research: Navigate again to your Research forum and make notes of important facts and ideas that you discover during your research. Enter your findings as articles under your topics in the Research forum. Each of your team members should find at least three different sources. You can view and comment on other group members' research, and rate the information they have entered. When your research is complete, print your Research report to hand in to your teacher.
- Visit the Media Centre and download the PowerPoint template (alarm template.ppt), to help you prepare your presentation. Your Media centre also includes images that can help to liven up your presentations.
- Use the Powerpoint template (alarm template.ppt) to develop your presentation. Remember that you are trying to convince Alvin and your manager that your design and proposal will be simple and easy to construct. Make sure that you include all the information they requested, and that your presentation will grab their attention.

SUGGESTED SOFTWARE

- ProjectsPLUS
- Microsoft PowerPoint
- Microsoft Excel

Your ProjectsPLUS application is available in this chapter's Student Resources tab inside your eBookPLUS. Visit www.jacplus.com.au to locate your digital resources.

Interactivity

LOGIC GATES

SEARCHLIGHT ID: INT-2448

Boolean logic is at the heart of the digital age. It was developed by George Boole in the 1800s. Logic gates are the basic building blocks of a digital circuit. Using different combinations of these gates, it is possible to implement any digital component. Use this interactivity to investigate the input and output functions of logic gates.

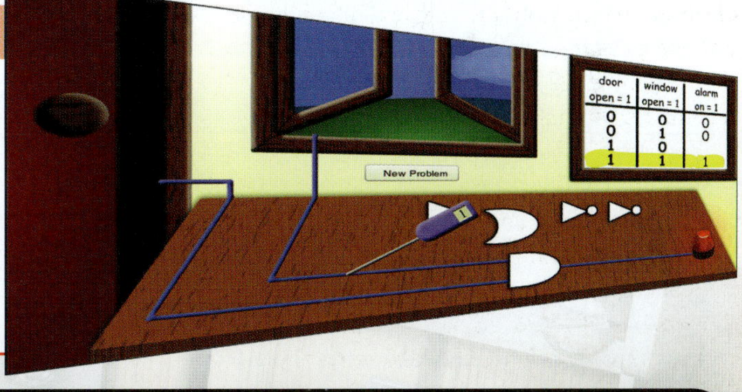

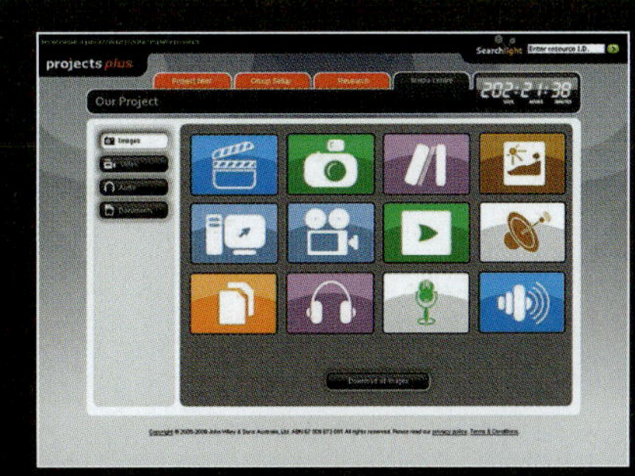

MEDIA CENTRE

Your Media Centre contains:

- a Document section with worksheets
- a Template section with presentation guidelines and circuit templates
- some images you can use in your presentation
- an assessment rubric.

Probability

13A Probability scale
13B Experimental probability
13C Sample spaces and theoretical probability
13D Complementary events
13E Venn diagrams
13F Tree diagrams and two-way tables

WHAT DO YOU KNOW?

1 List what you know about probability. Create a concept map to show your list.
2 Share what you know with a partner and then with a small group.
3 As a class, create a large concept map that shows your class's knowledge of probability.

eBook*plus*

Digital doc
Hungry brain activity
Chapter 13
doc-6968

OPENING QUESTION

If a button was tossed onto this quilt, what is the probability that it lands on a white section?

Are you ready?

Try the questions below. If you have difficulty with any of them, extra help can be obtained by completing the matching SkillSHEET located on your eBookPLUS.

eBook*plus*

Digital doc
SkillSHEET 13.1
doc-6969

Understanding chance words

1 For each of the following events, specify whether the chance of the event occurring is certain, fifty–fifty or impossible.

a Two dice are rolled and a total of 14 is obtained.
b A coin is tossed and it lands on Tails.
c The month of July will follow June.
d The maximum temperature on a summer's day in Melbourne will be less than 0°C.
e A fair die is rolled and a number less than 4 is obtained.

eBook*plus*

Digital doc
SkillSHEET 13.2
doc-6970

Understanding a deck of playing cards

2 For a standard deck of 52 playing cards, state the number of:

a red cards
b jacks
c black queens
d kings of diamonds
e eights
f number of cards with face value greater than 7.

eBook*plus*

Digital doc
SkillSHEET 13.3
doc-6971

Simplifying fractions

3 Simplify each of the following fractions.

a $\frac{4}{8}$ b $\frac{12}{15}$ c $\frac{36}{100}$ d $\frac{5}{20}$

eBook*plus*

Digital doc
SkillSHEET 13.4
doc-6972

Converting a fraction into a decimal

4 Convert the following fractions into decimals.

a $\frac{1}{5}$ b $\frac{3}{4}$ c $\frac{3}{10}$ d $\frac{17}{20}$

eBook*plus*

Digital doc
SkillSHEET 13.5
doc-6973

Converting a fraction into a percentage

5 Convert the following fractions into percentages.

a $\frac{1}{4}$ b $\frac{3}{5}$ c $\frac{7}{10}$ d $\frac{7}{20}$

eBook*plus*

Digital doc
SkillSHEET 13.6
doc-6974

Multiplying a fraction by a whole number

6 Calculate each of the following.

a $\frac{4}{5} \times 20$ b $\frac{8}{11} \times 99$ c $\frac{3}{10} \times 35$ d $\frac{1}{6} \times 96$

eBook*plus*

Digital doc
SkillSHEET 13.7
doc-6975

Listing the sample space

7 List the sample space (possible outcomes) for each of the following.

a Rolling a die
b Tossing a coin
c Spinning a circular spinner numbered from 1 to 5

eBook*plus*

Digital doc
SkillSHEET 13.8
doc-6976

Multiplying proper fractions

8 Calculate each of the following.

a $\frac{4}{7} \times \frac{3}{8}$ b $\frac{1}{3} \times \frac{8}{9}$ c $\frac{5}{8} \times \frac{7}{15}$ d $\frac{6}{13} \times \frac{4}{9}$

13A Probability scale

- **Probability** is defined as the chance of an event occurring.
- A scale from 0 to 1 inclusive is used to allocate the probability of an event as follows:

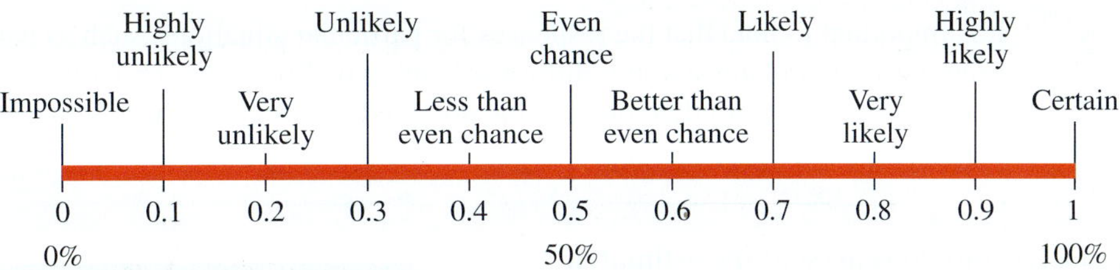

- A probability of 0 implies that the chance of an event happening is **impossible**.
- A probability of 1 implies that the chance of an event happening is **certain**.
- Probabilities may be written as fractions, decimals or percentages.

WORKED EXAMPLE 1

Describe the probability of each of the following events occurring, using a term from this list.

impossible	**highly unlikely**	**very unlikely**
less than even chance	**even chance**	
better than even chance	**very likely**	
highly likely	**certain**	

a **February follows January.**
b **You draw the queen of diamonds from a standard deck of playing cards.**
c **You will compete in gymnastics at the Olympics.**
d **You roll a standard die and obtain an even number.**
e **Every VCE student will obtain an ENTER score of 99.95%.**

THINK	WRITE
a 1 Read the statement and associate the likelihood of the event occurring with one of the given words from the list. *Note:* Provide reasoning.	**a** This is a true statement. February always follows January.
2 Answer the question.	It is *certain* this event will occur.
b Repeat steps 1 and 2 of part **a**.	**b** In a standard deck of 52 playing cards there is only one queen of diamonds. Thus, you have an extremely slim chance of drawing this particular card. It is *highly unlikely* this event will occur.
c Repeat steps 1 and 2 of part **a**.	**c** The chance of a person competing in the Olympics is very small. However, it could happen. It is *very unlikely* this event will occur.
d Repeat steps 1 and 2 of part **a**.	**d** There are six possible outcomes when rolling a die, each of which are equally likely. Three of the outcomes are even while three are odd. There is an *even chance* this event will occur.

e Repeat steps 1 and 2 of part **a**.	**e** Due to each student having different capabilities and the number of students involved, this situation could never occur. It is *impossible* that this event will occur.

It is important to note that the responses for particular situations, such as part **c** in Worked example 1, are not always straightforward and may differ for each individual. A careful analysis of each event is required before making any predictions about their future occurrences.

WORKED EXAMPLE 2

Assign a fraction to represent the estimated probability of each of the following events occurring:

a a high tide will be followed by a low tide
b everyone in the class will agree on every matter this year
c a tossed coin lands Heads
d a standard die is rolled and the number 5 appears uppermost
e one of your 15 tickets in a 20-ticket raffle will win.

THINK	WRITE
a 1 Determine the likelihood of an event occurring, with reasoning.	**a** The tide pattern occurs daily; this event seems *certain*.
2 Answer the question.	The probability of this event occurring is equal to 1.
b Repeat steps 1 and 2 of part **a**.	**b** Total agreement among many people on every subject over a long time is virtually *impossible*. The probability of this event occurring is equal to 0.
c Repeat steps 1 and 2 of part **a**.	**c** When tossing a coin there are two equally likely outcomes, a head or a tail. The probability of this event occurring is equal to $\frac{1}{2}$.
d Repeat steps 1 and 2 of part **a**.	**d** When rolling a die there are six equally likely outcomes: 1, 2, 3, 4, 5, 6. The probability of this event occurring is equal to $\frac{1}{6}$.
e Repeat steps 1 and 2 of part **a**.	**e** There are 15 chances out of 20 of winning. The probability of this event occurring is equal to $\frac{15}{20}$, which when simplified is equal to $\frac{3}{4}$.

REMEMBER

1. Probability is defined as the chance of an event occurring.
2. Probabilities range from 0 (impossible, no chance) to 1 (certain, every chance) inclusive.
3. Probabilities may be written as fractions, decimals or percentages.

EXERCISE 13A

Probability scale

INDIVIDUAL PATHWAYS

eBookplus

Activity 13-A-1 Probability scales doc-2388

Activity 13-A-2 More probability scales doc-2389

Activity 13-A-3 Advanced probability scales doc-7109

UNDERSTANDING

1 WE1 Describe the probability of each of the following events occurring using a term from the list below.

Impossible	Highly unlikely	Very unlikely
Less than even chance	Even chance	Better than even chance
Very likely	Highly likely	Certain

a The sun will set today.
b Every student in this class will score 100% in the next mathematics exam.
c It will rain tomorrow.
d Your shoelace will break next time you tie your shoes.
e Commercial TV stations will reduce time devoted to ads.
f A comet will collide with Earth this year.
g The year 2020 will be a leap year.
h You roll a standard die and an 8 appears uppermost.

i A tossed coin lands on its edge.
j World records will be broken at the next Olympics.
k You roll a standard die and an odd number appears uppermost.
l You draw the queen of hearts from a standard deck of playing cards.
m You draw a heart or diamond card from a standard deck of playing cards.
n One of your 11 tickets in a 20-ticket raffle will win.
o A red marble will be drawn from a bag containing 1 white marble and 9 red marbles.
p A red marble will be drawn from a bag containing 1 red and 9 white marbles.

2 Write two examples of events that are:
a impossible
b certain
c highly likely
d highly unlikely
e equally likely (even chance).

3 WE2 Assign a fraction or decimal to represent the estimated probability of each of the following events occurring.
a Heads appears uppermost when a coin is tossed.
b You draw a red marble from a bag containing 1 white and 9 red marbles.
c A standard die shows a 7 when rolled.
d You draw a yellow disk from a bag containing 8 yellow disks.
e The next baby in a family will be a boy.
f A standard die will show a 1 or a 2 when rolled.

g You draw the queen of hearts from a standard deck of playing cards.
h One of your 11 tickets in a 20-ticket raffle will win.
i A standard die will show a number less than or equal to 5 when rolled.
j You draw an ace from a standard deck of playing cards.
k A class captain will be elected from five candidates.
l You draw a king or queen card from a standard deck of playing cards.
m You spin a seven-sided spinner and obtain an odd number.
n Heads or Tails will show uppermost when a coin is tossed.

4 MC The word that best describes the probability for a standard die to show a prime number is:

A impossible
B very unlikely
C even chance
D very likely
E certain

5 MC The probability of Darwin experiencing a white Christmas this year is closest to:

A 1
B 0.75
C 0.5
D 0.25
E 0

REFLECTION

Can you think of some events that would have a probability of 0, 1 or $\frac{1}{2}$ of occurring?

13B Experimental probability

- **Experiments** are performed to provide data, which can then be used to forecast the outcome of future similar events.
- An experiment that is performed in the same way each time is called a **trial**.
- An **outcome** is a particular result of a trial.
- A **favourable outcome** is one that we are looking for.
- An **event** is the set of favourable outcomes in each trial.
- The **relative frequency** of an event occurring is the experimental probability of it occurring.
- Relative frequency of an event $= \dfrac{\text{frequency of an event}}{\text{total number of trials}}$.

WORKED EXAMPLE 3

The table at right shows the results of a fair coin that was tossed 20 times. What are the relative frequencies of:
a Heads?
b Tails?

Event	Frequency
Heads	8
Tails	12
Total	20

THINK / WRITE

a 1 Write the frequency of the number of Heads and the total number of trials; that is, tosses.
a Frequency of Heads = 8
Total number of tosses = 20

2 Write the rule for the relative frequency.
Relative frequency $= \dfrac{\text{frequency of a Head}}{\text{total number of tosses}}$

3 Substitute the known values into the rule.
Relative frequency of Heads $= \dfrac{8}{20}$

4 Evaluate and simplify if possible.
$= \dfrac{2}{5}$ (or 0.4)

5 Answer the question.
The relative frequency of obtaining Heads is $\dfrac{2}{5}$.

b 1 Write the frequency of the number of Tails and the total number of trials; that is, tosses.

b Frequency of Tails = 12
Total number of tosses = 20

2 Write the rule for the relative frequency.

$$\text{Relative frequency} = \frac{\text{frequency of Tails}}{\text{total number of tosses}}$$

3 Substitute the known values into the rule.

$$\text{Relative frequency of Tails} = \frac{12}{20}$$

4 Evaluate and simplify if possible.

$$= \frac{3}{5} \text{ (or 0.6)}$$

5 Answer the question.

The relative frequency of obtaining Tails is $\frac{3}{5}$.

WORKED EXAMPLE 4

Forty people picked at random were asked where they were born. The results were coded as follows:

Place of birth
1. **Melbourne**
2. **Elsewhere in Victoria**
3. **Interstate**
4. **Overseas.**

Responses
1, 3, 2, 1, 1, 4, 3, 1, 2, 1, 2, 1, 3, 4, 1, 2, 3, 1, 3, 4,
4, 3, 2, 1, 2, 3, 1, 4, 1, 2, 3, 4, 1, 2, 3, 1, 1, 4, 2, 3

a **Organise the data into a frequency table.**
b **Find the relative frequency of each category as a fraction and a decimal.**
c **What is the total of the relative frequencies?**
d **Where is a person selected at random most likely to have been born?**
e **How many people out of 100 would you expect to be born overseas?**

THINK

a 1 Draw a table with 3 columns. The column headings are in order, Score, Tally and Frequency.

2 Enter the codes 1, 2, 3 and 4 into the score column.

3 Place a stroke into the tally column each time a code is recorded.
Note: |||| represents a score of five.

4 Count the number of strokes corresponding to each code and record in the frequency column.

5 Add the total of the frequency column.

WRITE

a

Score	Tally	Frequency
Code 1	~~||||~~ ~~||||~~ ||||	14
Code 2	~~||||~~ ||||	9
Code 3	~~||||~~ ~~||||~~	10
Code 4	~~||||~~ ||	7
	Total	40

	THINK	WRITE
b	1 Write the rule for the relative frequency.	**b** Relative frequency $= \dfrac{\text{frequency of category}}{\text{total number of people}}$
	2 Substitute the known values into the rule for each category.	Category 1: People born in Melbourne
	3 Evaluate and simplify where possible.	Relative frequency $= \frac{14}{40}$ $= \frac{7}{20}$ or 0.35 Category 2: People born elsewhere in Victoria Relative frequency $= \frac{9}{40}$ or 0.255 Category 3: People born interstate Relative frequency $= \frac{10}{40}$ $= \frac{1}{4}$ or 0.25 Category 4: People born overseas Relative frequency $= \frac{7}{40}$ or 0.175
c	1 Add each of the relative frequency values.	**c** Total $= \frac{7}{20} + \frac{9}{40} + \frac{1}{4} + \frac{7}{40}$ $= 0.35 + 0.225 + 0.25 + 0.175$ $= 1$
	2 Answer the question.	The relative frequencies sum to a total of 1.
d	1 Using the results from part **b**, obtain the code that corresponds to the largest frequency. *Note:* A person selected at random is *most* likely to have been born in the place with the largest frequency.	**d** Melbourne (Code 1) corresponds to the largest frequency.
	2 Answer the question.	A person selected at random is most likely to have been born in Melbourne.
e	1 Write the relative frequency of people born overseas and the number of people in the sample.	**e** Relative frequency (overseas) $= \frac{7}{40}$ Number of people in the sample = 100
	2 Write the rule for the expected number of people. *Note:* Of the 100 people, $\frac{7}{40}$ or 0.175 would be expected to be born overseas.	Expected number = relative frequency × number of people
	3 Substitute the known values into the rule.	Expected number $= \frac{7}{40} \times 100$ $= \frac{700}{40}$
	4 Evaluate.	$= 17.5$
	5 Round the value to the nearest whole number. *Note:* We are dealing with people. Therefore, the answer must be represented by a whole number.	≈ 18
	6 Answer the question.	We would expect 18 of the 100 people to be born overseas.

REMEMBER

1. Relative frequency = $\dfrac{\text{frequency of an event}}{\text{total number of trails}}$
2. The total sum of the relative frequencies in an experiment is equal to 1.
3. Expected frequency = relative frequency × the number in the sample.

EXERCISE 13B

Experimental probability

INDIVIDUAL PATHWAYS

eBook*plus*

Activity 13-B-1 One in every two doc-2391

Activity 13-B-2 One in every six doc-2392

Activity 13-B-3 One in every five doc-2393

FLUENCY

1 WE3 The table at right shows the results of tossing a fair coin 150 times. What are the relative frequencies of:

a Heads?

b Tails?

Event	Frequency
Heads	84
Tails	66
Total	150

2 A fair coin was tossed 300 times. A Head came up 156 times.

a Find the relative frequency of the Head outcome as a fraction.

b Calculate the relative frequency of Tails as a decimal.

3 A die is thrown 50 times, with 6 as the favourable outcome. The 6 came up 7 times. Find the relative frequency of:

a a 6 occurring

b a number that is not a 6 (that is, any number other than a 6) occurring.

4 A spinner with 3 equal sectors, as shown at right, was spun 80 times, with results as shown in the table:

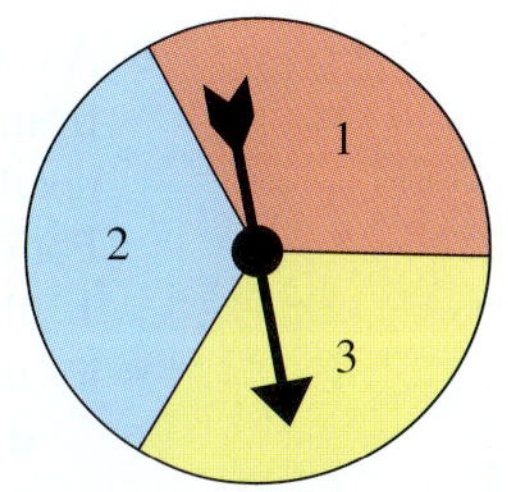

Score	1	2	3
Frequency	29	26	25

a What fraction of the spins resulted in a 3?

b What fraction of the spins resulted in a 2?

c Express the relative frequency of the spins that resulted in a 1 as a decimal.

eBook*plus*

Weblink Probability simulator

5 A die was rolled 200 times and the results recorded in the table below.

Score	1	2	3	4	5	6
Frequency	30	34	35	32	35	34

a Name the outcomes that make up each of the following events:

i an even number
ii a number less than 3
iii a number ≥ 3
iv a prime number
v a number > 6
vi the number 5 or more
vii a non-prime number
viii the number 4 or less
ix a multiple of three
x a number that is divisible by 5.

b Express the relative frequency of each of the face numbers as a percentage.

c What percentage of outcomes turned out to be even?

d What was the relative frequency of non-prime numbers, as a percentage?

e What was the relative frequency of numbers divisible by 5, as a percentage?

f What was the relative frequency of numbers greater than or equal to (≥) 3, as a percentage?

g What was the relative frequency of odd numbers, as a percentage?
h What was the relative frequency of numbers that are multiples of 3, as a percentage?
i What was the relative frequency of numbers that are 5 or greater, as a percentage?
j What was the relative frequency of numbers that are 2 or less, as a percentage?

6 WE4 100 people picked at random were asked which Olympic event they would most like to see. The results were coded as follows:
1. Swimming 2. Athletics 3. Gymnastics 4. Rowing.
The recorded scores were:
1, 1, 4, 3, 2, 2, 2, 4, 4, 3, 1, 1, 4, 2, 1, 1, 1, 4, 2, 2, 1, 3, 3, 3, 4, 1, 1, 3, 2, 2, 1, 2, 1, 1,
1, 1, 2, 3, 3, 3, 3, 2, 2, 4, 1, 1, 1, 3, 2, 2, 4, 1, 1, 1, 3, 3, 3, 3, 2, 1, 2, 2, 2, 2, 3, 4, 4, 1,
1, 1, 2, 3, 3, 2, 1, 4, 3, 2, 3, 1, 1, 2, 4, 1, 1, 3, 2, 2, 3, 3, 4, 4, 2, 1, 1, 3, 1, 2, 4, 1.
a Organise the data into a frequency table.
b Find the relative frequency of each category as a fraction and a decimal.
c What is the total of the relative frequencies?
d Which Olympic event selected at random is most likely to be seen?
e How many people out of 850 would you expect to see the gymnastics?

7 The following are results of 20 trials conducted for an experiment involving the 5-sector spinner at right.
1, 4, 2, 5, 3, 4, 5, 3, 2, 5, 1, 3, 2, 4, 2, 1, 4, 3, 3, 2
a Organise the data into a frequency table.
b Find the relative frequency of each outcome.
c How many times would you have expected each outcome to have appeared? How did you come to this conclusion?
d Which was the most common outcome?
e What is the total of all the relative frequencies?

8 A card is *randomly* (with no predictable pattern) drawn 60 times from a hand of 5 cards, it is recorded, then returned and the five cards are reshuffled. The results are shown in the frequency distribution table at right.
For each of the following, give:
i the favourable outcomes that make up the event
ii the relative frequency of these events.
a A heart b A diamond
c A red card d A 3
e A spade or a heart f A 3 or a queen
g The king of spades h A 3 or a diamond

Card	Frequency
3 ♥	13
Q ♦	15
3 ♦	12
3 ♣	9
3 ♠	11

eBook*plus*
Digital doc
WorkSHEET 13.1
doc-7107

UNDERSTANDING

9 The following table shows the progressive results of a coin-tossing experiment.

	Outcome		Relative frequency	
Number of coin tosses	Heads	Tails	Heads (%)	Tails (%)
10	6	4	60	40
100	54	46	54	46
1000	496	504	49.6	50.4

a What do you notice about the relative frequencies for each trial?
b If we were to repeat the same experiment in the same way, would the results necessarily be identical to those in the table? Explain your answer.

10 The square spinner at right was trialled 40 times and the results of how it landed were recorded as shown below.
2, 4, 3, 1, 3, 2, 1, 4, 4, 3, 3, 1, 4, 2, 1, 2, 3, 1, 4, 2,
4, 2, 1, 2, 1, 3, 1, 4, 3, 1, 3, 1, 4, 2, 3, 1, 3, 2, 4, 4

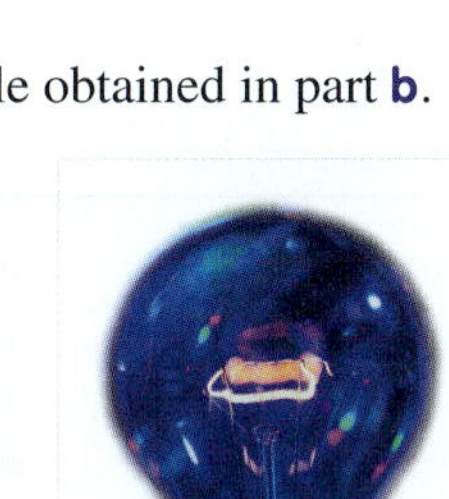

- **a** What would you expect the relative frequency of each outcome to be?
- **b** Organise the data into a frequency table and calculate the actual experimental relative frequency of each number.
- **c** Find the relative frequency of the event, *odd number*, from the table obtained in part **b**.
- **d** What outcomes make up the event, *prime number*?
  Hint: Remember a prime number has exactly 2 factors: itself and 1.
- **e** Calculate the relative frequency of the event, *prime number*, from the table obtained in part **b**.

11 When 60 light bulbs were tested, 3 were found to be faulty.
- **a** What was the relative frequency of faulty bulbs?
- **b** What fraction of the bulbs were not faulty?
- **c** In a carton of 600 such bulbs, how many would you expect to be faulty?

12 MC Olga observed that, in 100 games of roulette, red came up 45 times. Out of 20 games on the same wheel, how many would she expect to come up red?

A 4.5 **B** $\frac{4}{9}$ **C** $\frac{9}{4}$
D 9 **E** None of these

13 MC A fair coin was tossed 40 times and it came up Tails 18 times. The relative frequency of Heads was:

A $\frac{9}{11}$ **B** $\frac{11}{20}$ **C** $\frac{9}{20}$
D $\frac{20}{11}$ **E** unable to be calculated

REASONING

14 The game 'rock, paper, scissors' is played all over the world, not just for fun but also for settling disagreements.

The game uses the three different hand signs shown left.

Simultaneously, two players 'pound' the fist of one hand into the air three times. On the third time each player displays one of the hand signs. Possible results are shown below.

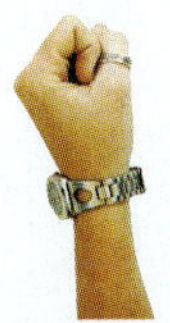

Rock

Paper

Scissors

Paper covers rock

Paper wins

Rock covers scissors

Rock wins

Scissors cut paper

Scissors wins

a Play 20 rounds of 'rock, paper, scissors' with a partner. After each round, record each player's choice and the result in a table like the one shown below.
(Use R for rock, P for paper and S for scissors.)

Round number	Player 1	Player 2	Result
1	P	R	Player 1 wins
2	S	R	Player 2 wins
3	S	S	Tie

b Based on the results of your 20 rounds, what is the experimental probability of
 i you winning?
 ii your partner winning?
 iii a tie?

c Do you think playing 'rock, paper, scissors' is a fair way to settle a disagreement? Explain.

REFLECTION
Explain why the experimental probability of an event can never be greater than one. What does it mean if the experimental probability is equal to one?

13C Sample spaces and theoretical probability

- The **theoretical probability** (or empirical probability) of a particular event occurring is denoted by the symbol P(event).
- The **sample space**, S, is the set of all the possible outcomes.
- $P(\text{event}) = \dfrac{\text{number of favourable outcomes}}{\text{number of possible outcomes}}$.
- If a very large number of trials is conducted, the relative frequency of an event will match the theoretical probability of the event.

WORKED EXAMPLE 5

A standard 6-sided die is rolled.
a List the sample space for this experiment.
b Determine the probability of obtaining the following appearing uppermost:
 i 4
 ii an odd number
 iii 5 or less.

THINK	WRITE
a Write all the possible outcomes for the given experiment.	a $S = \{1, 2, 3, 4, 5, 6\}$
b i 1 Write the number of possible outcomes.	b i Number of possible outcomes = 6
2 Write the number of favourable outcomes. *Note:* The favourable outcome is 4.	Number of favourable outcomes = 1
3 Write the rule for probability.	$P(\text{event}) = \dfrac{\text{number of favourable outcomes}}{\text{number of possible outcomes}}$

4 Substitute the known values into the rule and evaluate.	$P(4) = \frac{1}{6}$
5 Answer the question.	The probability of 4 appearing uppermost is $\frac{1}{6}$.
ii 1 Write the number of possible outcomes.	**ii** Number of possible outcomes = 6
2 Write the number of favourable outcomes. The favourable outcomes are 1, 3, 5.	Number of favourable outcomes = 3
3 Write the rule for probability.	$P(\text{event}) = \frac{\text{number of favourable outcomes}}{\text{number of possible outcomes}}$
4 Substitute the known values into the rule.	$P(\text{odd number}) = \frac{3}{6}$
5 Evaluate and simplify.	$= \frac{1}{2}$
6 Answer the question.	The probability of an odd number appearing uppermost is $\frac{1}{2}$.
iii Repeat steps 1 to 5 of part **b i**. *Note:* 5 or less means the favourable outcomes are 1, 2, 3, 4, 5. Therefore, the number of favourable outcomes is 5.	**iii** Number of possible outcomes = 6 Number of favourable outcomes = 5 $P(5 \text{ or less}) = \frac{5}{6}$ The probability of obtaining 5 or less is $\frac{5}{6}$.

WORKED EXAMPLE 6

A card is drawn at random from a standard well-shuffled pack.
Find the probability of drawing:
a a club
b a king or an ace
c not a spade.
Express each answer as a fraction and as a percentage.

THINK	WRITE
a 1 Write the number of outcomes in the sample space. There are 52 cards in a pack.	**a** Number of possible outcomes = 52
2 Write the number of favourable outcomes. There are 13 cards in each suit.	Number of favourable outcomes = 13
3 Write the rule for probability.	$P(\text{event}) = \frac{\text{number of favourable outcomes}}{\text{number of possible outcomes}}$
4 Substitute the known values into the rule and simplify.	$P(\text{a club}) = \frac{13}{52}$ $= \frac{1}{4}$

5 Convert the fraction to a percentage; that is, multiply by 100%.

$\text{Percentage} = \frac{1}{4} \times 100\%$
$= \frac{100}{4}\%$
$= 25\%$

6 Answer the question.

The probability of drawing a club is $\frac{1}{4}$ or 25%.

b 1 Write the number of outcomes in the sample space.

b Number of possible outcomes = 52

2 Write the number of favourable outcomes. There are 4 kings and 4 aces.

Number of favourable outcomes = 8

3 Write the rule for probability.

$$\text{P(event)} = \frac{\text{number of favourable outcomes}}{\text{number of possible outcomes}}$$

4 Substitute the known values into the rule and simplify.

$\text{P(a king or an ace)} = \frac{8}{52}$
$= \frac{2}{13}$

5 Convert the fraction to a percentage, rounded to one decimal place.

$\text{Percentage} = \frac{2}{13} \times 100\%$
$= \frac{200}{13}\%$
$\approx 15.4\%$

6 Answer the question.

The probability of drawing a king or an ace is $\frac{2}{13}$ or approximately 15.4%.

c Repeat steps 1 to 6 of part **a**.
Note: Not a spade means clubs, hearts or diamonds. Therefore, the number of favourable outcomes is 39.

c Number of possible outcomes = 52
Number of favourable outcomes = 39

$\text{P(not a spade)} = \frac{39}{52} = \frac{3}{4}$

$\text{Percentage} = \frac{3}{4} \times 100\% = \frac{300}{4} = 75\%$

The probability of drawing a card that is not a spade is $\frac{3}{4}$ or 75%.

WORKED EXAMPLE 7

A shopping centre car park has spaces for 10 buses, 300 cars and 20 motorbikes. If all vehicles have an equal chance of leaving at any time, find the probability that the next vehicle to leave will be:

a a motorbike

b a bus or a car

c not a car.

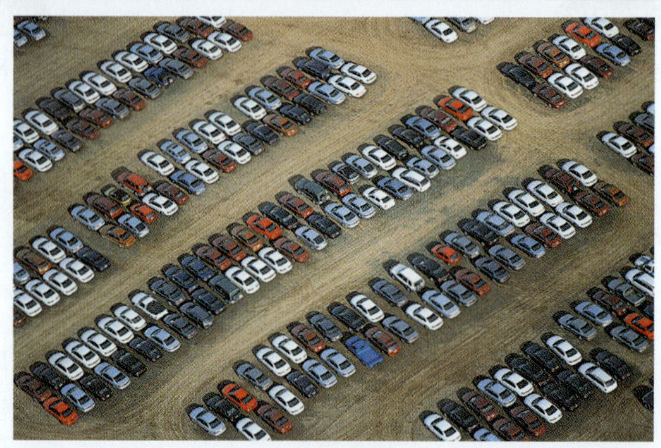

THINK | **WRITE**

a 1. Write the number of outcomes in the sample space. There are 330 vehicles.

a Number of possible outcomes = 330

2. Write the number of favourable outcomes. There are 20 motorbikes. Therefore, the number of favourable outcomes is 20.

Number of favourable outcomes = 20

3. Write the rule for probability.

$$\text{P(event)} = \frac{\text{number of favourable outcomes}}{\text{number of possible outcomes}}$$

4. Substitute the known values into the rule and simplify.

$$\text{P(a motorbike)} = \frac{20}{330} = \frac{2}{33}$$

5. Answer the question.

The probability of a motorbike next leaving the car park is $\frac{2}{33}$.

b 1. Write the number of outcomes in the sample space.

b Number of possible outcomes = 330

2. Write the number of favourable outcomes. There are 10 buses and 300 cars. Therefore, the number of favourable outcomes is 310.

Number of favourable outcomes = 310

3. Write the rule for probability.

$$\text{P(event)} = \frac{\text{number of favourable outcomes}}{\text{number of possible outcomes}}$$

4. Substitute the known values into the rule and simplify.

$$\text{P(a bus or a car)} = \frac{310}{330} = \frac{31}{33}$$

5. Answer the question.

The probability of a bus or car next leaving the car park is $\frac{31}{33}$.

c Repeat steps 1 to 5 of part **a**.
Note: There are 10 buses and 20 motorbikes. Therefore, the number of favourable outcomes is 30.

c Number of possible outcomes = 330
Number of favourable outcomes = 30

$$\text{P(not a car)} = \frac{30}{330} = \frac{1}{11}$$

The probability of a vehicle that is not a bus next leaving the car park is $\frac{1}{11}$.

REMEMBER

1. A sample space, S, is a list of all the possible outcomes (obtained from an experiment) and enclosed in a pair of curled brackets { }.
2. The theoretical probability of an event occurring is given by the rule:

$$\text{P(event)} = \frac{\text{number of favourable outcomes}}{\text{number of possible outcomes}}$$

EXERCISE 13C Sample spaces and theoretical probability

INDIVIDUAL PATHWAYS

eBook*plus*

Activity 13-C-1
Sample spaces and theoretical probability
doc-2394

Activity 13-C-2
More sample spaces and theoretical probability
doc-7110

Activity 13-C-3
Advanced sample spaces and theoretical probability
doc-7111

eBook*plus*

Weblink
Take the probability quiz

FLUENCY

1 WE5 A standard 6-sided die is rolled.

a List the sample space for this experiment.

b Determine the probability of obtaining the following appearing uppermost:

- **i** a 6
- **ii** an even number
- **iii** at most, 4
- **iv** a 1 or a 2
- **v** a prime number
- **vi** a number greater than 4
- **vii** a 7
- **viii** a number that is a factor of 60.

2 List the sample spaces for these experiments:

a tossing a coin

b selecting a vowel from the word 'ASTRONAUT'

c selecting a day of the week to go to the movies

d drawing a marble from a bag containing 3 reds, 2 whites and 1 black

e rolling a standard 6-sided die

f drawing a picture card from a standard pack of playing cards

g spinning an 8-sector circular spinner numbered from 1 to 8

h selecting even numbers from the first 20 counting numbers

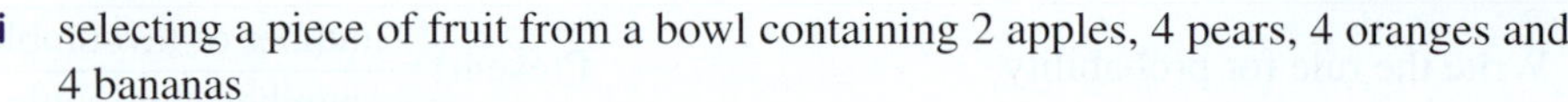

i selecting a piece of fruit from a bowl containing 2 apples, 4 pears, 4 oranges and 4 bananas

j selecting a magazine from a rack containing 3 *Dolly*, 2 *Girlfriend*, 1 *Smash Hits* and 2 *Mathsmag magazines*.

k selecting the correct answer from the options A, B, C, D, E on a multiple-choice test

l winning a medal at the Olympic games.

3 WE6 A card is drawn at random from a standard well-shuffled pack. Find the probability of drawing:

- **a** the king of spades
- **b** a 10
- **c** a jack or a queen
- **d** a club
- **e** a red card
- **f** an 8 or a diamond
- **g** an ace.

Express each answer as a fraction and as a percentage.

4 WE7 A shopping centre car park has spaces for 8 buses, 160 cars and 12 motorbikes. If all vehicles have an equal chance of leaving at any time, find the probability that the next vehicle to leave will be:

- **a** a bus
- **b** a car
- **c** a motorbike or a bus
- **d** not a car.

5 A bag contains 3 red, 2 black, 1 pink, 2 yellow, 3 green and 3 blue marbles. If a marble is drawn at random, calculate the chance that it is:

- **a** red
- **b** black
- **c** yellow
- **d** red or black
- **e** not blue
- **f** red or black or green
- **g** white
- **h** not pink.

6 A beetle drops onto *one* square of a chessboard. What are its chances of landing on a square that is:

a black?

b white?

c neither black nor white?

d either black or white?

7 What chance is there that the next person you meet has his/her birthday:

a next Monday?

b sometime next week?

c in September?

d one day next year?

8 For each of the following spinners:

a

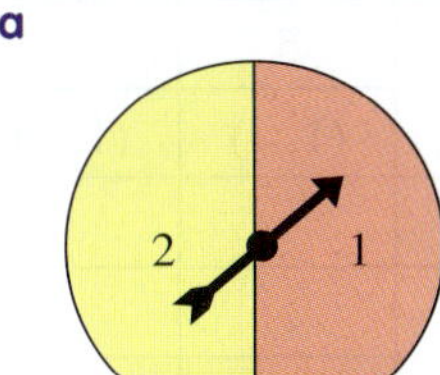

b

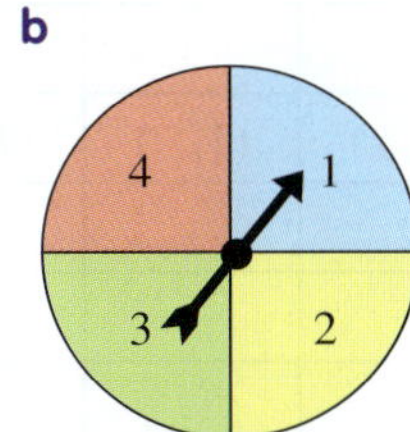

c

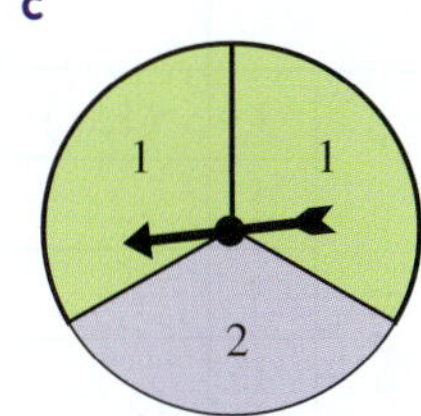

d

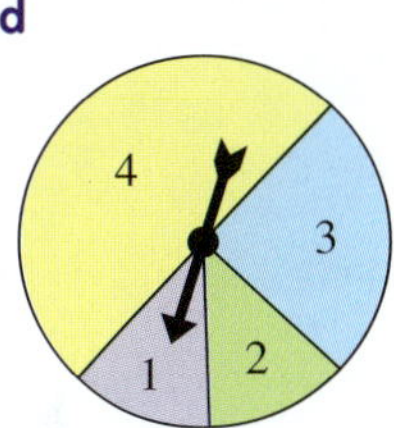

i state whether each of the outcomes are equally likely. Explain your answer.

ii find the probability of the pointer stopping on 1.

UNDERSTANDING

9 Hanna flipped a coin 5 times and each time a Tail showed. What are the chances of Tails showing on the *sixth* toss?

10 a Design a circular spinner coloured red, white, black, yellow and green so that each colour is equally likely to result from any trial.

b What will be the angle between each sector in the spinner?

11 a Design a circular spinner with the numerals 1, 2 and 3 so that 3 is twice as likely to occur as 2 or 1 in any trial.

b What will be the size of the angles in each sector at the centre of the spinner?

12 a Design a circular spinner labelled A, B, C and D so that $P(A) = \frac{1}{4}$, $P(B) = \frac{1}{3}$, $P(C) = \frac{1}{6}$, $P(D) = \frac{1}{4}$.

b What will be the size of the angles between each sector in the spinner?

13 a What is the total of all the probabilities in question **12**?

b What is the angle sum of the sectors in question **12**?

14 a List all the outcomes for tossing a coin once, together with their individual probabilities.

b Find the total.

15 a List all the outcomes for tossing a coin twice, together with their individual probabilities.

b Find the total.

16 a List the probabilities for the elements of the sample space for rolling a 6-faced die.

b Find the total of the probabilities.

c Do the totals for questions **14b**, **15b** and **16b** agree with that in **13a**?

d What conclusion can you draw?

17 MC If a circular spinner has 3 sectors, A, B and C, such that $P(A) = \frac{1}{2}$ and $P(B) = \frac{1}{3}$, then P(C) must be:

A $\frac{1}{4}$ **B** $\frac{2}{5}$ **C** $\frac{1}{6}$ **D** $\frac{5}{6}$ **E** none of these

18 MC For an octagonal spinner with equal sectors, numbered from 1 to 8, the chance of getting a number between (but not including) 5 and 8 is:

A $\frac{1}{4}$ **B** $\frac{1}{2}$ **C** $\frac{3}{8}$

D $\frac{5}{8}$ **E** none of these

19 a What is the sample space for rolling a standard 6-sided die?

b How many elements are in the sample space for rolling 2 standard 6-sided dice (think of the dice having different colours)?
Hint: The answer is not 12.

c Complete the following sample space for rolling two dice.
Note: Each colour in the table corresponds to the colour of the die.

		Die 2					
		1	2	3	4	5	6
Die 1	1	(1, 1)	(1, 2)	(1, 3)	(1, 4)	(1, 5)	(1, 6)
	2						
	3						
	4						
	5						
	6						

d Using the sample space, complete the following table.

Sum	2	3	4	5	6	7	8	9	10	11	12
Probability											

e Do you notice a pattern involving the probabilities in the table? Explain your answer.
The pattern observed in question **5** relates to symmetry. Investigate the symmetry property on tossing three coins.

f List the sample space for tossing three coins.

g Using the sample space obtained in question **6**, complete the following table.

Number of Heads	0	1	2	3
Probability				

h From the table above, which event is the probability of tossing three Tails the same as?

i By symmetry, which event has the same probability as tossing Heads twice and Tails once?

20 Toss a coin 60 times and record whether it shows Heads (H) or Tails (T) uppermost in a table like this.

Outcome	**Tally**	**Frequency**	**% Relative frequency** $\left(\frac{\textbf{frequency}}{\textbf{60}} \times 100\%\right)$
Heads (H)			
Tails (T)			

Once your results have been recorded, obtain the frequency results from each member of the class and add them together to obtain a total value for the class frequency. This is called *pooling* your results. Determine the percentage relative class frequency by using the rule given in the table below.

Outcome	Class frequency	% Relative class frequency $\left(\dfrac{\text{class frequency}}{\text{number of students} \times 60} \times 100\,\%\right)$
Heads (H)		
Tails (T)		

Now that both tables have been completed, answer the following questions.

a Does a larger sample group alter the percentage results?

b Are the class results closer to those predicted by theory?

c Compare your own result with the class result. Which do you think would be more reliable? Explain your answer.

d Complete the following sentence:

In the long run the *relative frequency* of an event will ____________________.

REASONING

21 The targets shown are an equilateral triangle, a square and a circle with coloured regions that are also formed from equilateral triangles, squares and circles. If a randomly thrown dart hits each target, find the probability that the dart hits each target's coloured region.

a
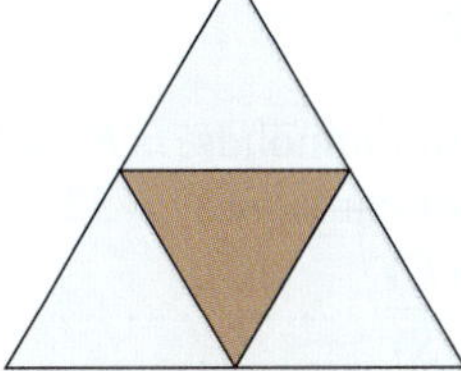

b

c
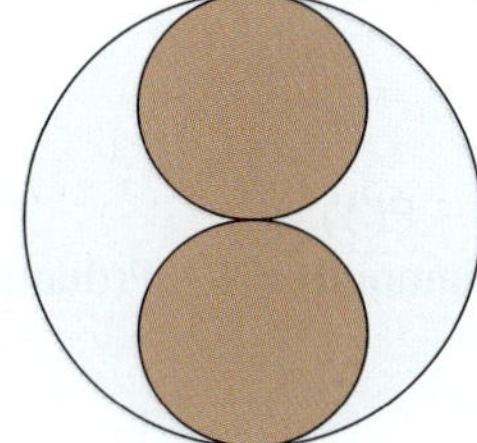

REFLECTION

How is theoretical probability similar to experimental probability?

13D Complementary events

- In some situations, there are only two possible outcomes.
- When there is nothing in common between these events and together they form the sample spaces, they are called **complementary events**.
- For example, when tossing a coin, there are only two possible outcomes, a Head or a Tail. They are complementary events.
- If an event is denoted by the letter A, its complement is denoted by the letter A', and the sum of their probabilities is equal to one.
- If we know the probability of one event, subtracting this probability from 1 will give us the probability of the complementary event.
- If events A and A' are complementary, then:
  $\text{P}(A) + \text{P}(A') = 1$
  and $\text{P}(A') = 1 - \text{P}(A)$ or $\text{P}(A) = 1 - \text{P}(A')$

WORKED EXAMPLE 8

Find the complement of each of the following events:
a selecting a red card from a standard deck
b rolling two dice and getting a total greater than 9
c selecting a red marble from a bag containing 50 marbles.

THINK	WRITE
a Selecting a black card will complete the sample space for this experiment.	a The complement of selecting a red card is selecting a black card.
b When rolling two dice, rolling a total less than 10 will complete the sample space.	b The complement of rolling a total greater than 9 is rolling a total less than 10.
c Selecting a marble that is not red is the only way to define the rest of the sample space for this experiment.	c The complement of selecting a red marble in this experiment is not selecting a red marble.

WORKED EXAMPLE 9

If a card is drawn from a pack of 52 cards, what is the probability that the card is not a diamond?

THINK	WRITE
1 Determine the probability of drawing a diamond.	Number of diamonds, $n(E) = 13$ Number of cards, $n(S) = 52$ $\text{P}(E) = \frac{n(E)}{n(S)}$ $\text{P(diamond)} = \frac{13}{52}$ $= \frac{1}{4}$
2 Write down the rule for obtaining the complement of drawing a diamond; that is, not drawing a diamond.	$\text{P}(A') = 1 - \text{P}(A)$ $\text{P(not a diamond)} = 1 - \text{P(diamond)}$
3 Substitute the known values into the given rule and simplify.	$= 1 - \frac{1}{4}$ $= \frac{3}{4}$
4 Answer the question.	The probability of drawing a card that is not a diamond is $\frac{3}{4}$.

REMEMBER

1. Complementary events have nothing in common but when added together form the sample space.
2. If events A and A' are complementary, then $\text{P}(A) + \text{P}(A') = 1$. This may be rearranged to $\text{P}(A') = 1 - \text{P}(A)$ or $\text{P}(A) = 1 - \text{P}(A')$.

EXERCISE

13D Complementary events

INDIVIDUAL PATHWAYS

eBook*plus*

Activity 13-D-1 Complementary events doc-2397

Activity 13-D-2 More complementary events doc-2398

Activity 13-D-3 Advanced complementary events doc-2399

UNDERSTANDING

1 WE8 For each of the following, state the complementary event.

a From a bag of numbered marbles selecting an even number
b From the letters of the alphabet selecting a vowel
c Tossing a coin and it landing Heads
d Rolling a die and getting a number less than 3
e Rolling two dice and getting a total less than 12
f Selecting a diamond from a deck of cards
g Selecting an E from the letters of the alphabet
h Selecting a blue marble from a bag of marbles

2 MC *Note:* There may be more than one correct answer.
A student is to be chosen from a class of 30 students. Each student in the class is either 14 or 15 years old. Which of the following represent complementary events?

A Selecting a 14-year-old boy and selecting a 14-year-old girl
B Selecting a boy and selecting a girl
C Selecting a 14-year-old and selecting a 15-year-old
D Selecting a 14-year-old boy and selecting a 15-year-old girl
E All of the above

3 For each of the following, state whether the pair of events are complementary or not. Explain your answer.

a Having Weet Bix or Corn Flakes for breakfast.
b Walking to your friend's house or riding your bike to your friend's house.
c Watching TV at night or listening to the radio.
d Passing your Mathematics test or failing your Mathematics test.
e Rolling a number less than 4 on a die or rolling a total greater than 4.

4 WE9 If a card is drawn from a pack of 52 cards, what is the probability that the card is not a queen?

5 MC The statement that does *not* involve complementary events is:

A travelling to school by bus and travelling to school by car
B drawing a red card from a pack of 52 playing cards and drawing a black card from 52 playing cards
C drawing a vowel from cards representing the 26 letters of the alphabet or drawing a consonant
D obtaining an even number on a six-sided die or obtaining an odd number on a die
E All of the above

6 When a six-sided die is rolled 3 times, the probability of getting 3 sixes is $\frac{1}{216}$. What is the probability of not getting 3 sixes?

7 Eight athletes compete in a 100 m race. The probability that the athlete in lane 1 will win is $\frac{1}{5}$. What is the probability that one of the other athletes wins? (Assume that there are no dead heats.)

8 A pencil case has 4 red pens, 3 blue pens and 5 black pens. If a pen is drawn randomly from the pencil case, find:

a P(drawing a blue pen)
b P(not drawing a blue pen)
c P(drawing a red or a black pen)
d P(drawing neither a red nor a black pen).

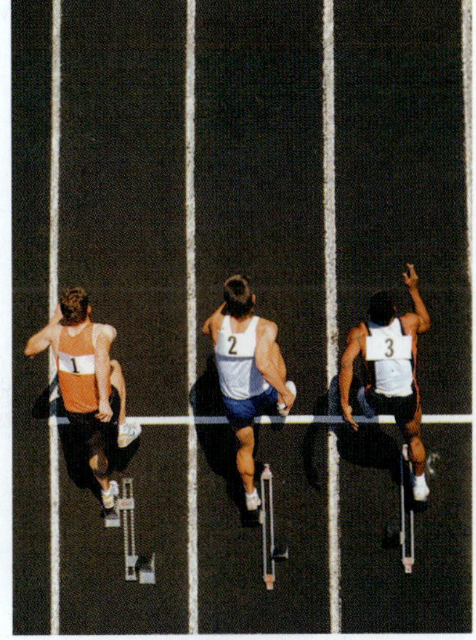

9 Holty is tossing two coins. He claims that getting two Heads and getting zero Heads are complementary events. Is he right? Explain your answer.

10 Seventy Year 9 students were surveyed.
Their ages ranged from 13 years to 15 years, as shown in the table below.

Age	13	14	15	Total
Boys	10	20	9	39
Girls	7	15	9	31
Total	17	35	18	70

A student from the group is selected at random. Find:
- **a** P(selecting a student of the age of 13 years)
- **b** P(not selecting a student of the age of 13 years)
- **c** P(selecting a 15-year-old boy)
- **d** P(not selecting a 15-year-old boy).

REFLECTION
Explain why the probability of an event and the complement of the event always sum to 1.

13E Venn diagrams

- A **set** is a collection of things or numbers that belong to a well defined category. For example, a bird is member of the set of two-legged animals; odd numbers belong to the set of integers.
- The elements of a set are enclosed in curly brackets, or braces. {}
- A Venn diagram is made up of a rectangle and one or more circles. It is used to show the relationships between different groups or sets of objects.
- The rectangle contains all the objects under consideration and is called the **universal set**.
- Each group or set of objects within the universal set is enclosed in its own circle inside the rectangle.
- The symbol for the universal set is ξ.

WORKED EXAMPLE 10

Draw a Venn diagram representing the relationship between the following sets below. Show the position of all the elements in the Venn diagram.
ξ = {counting numbers up to 10}
A = {first 3 prime numbers}
B = {odd numbers less than 9}

THINK	WRITE
1 List the elements in each of the sets.	ξ = {1, 2, 3, 4, 5, 6, 7, 8, 9, 10} A = {2, 3, 5} B = {1, 3, 5, 7}
2 Draw the universal set as a rectangle. *Note:* This contains the elements 1, 2, 3, 4, 5, 6, 7, 8, 9 and 10.	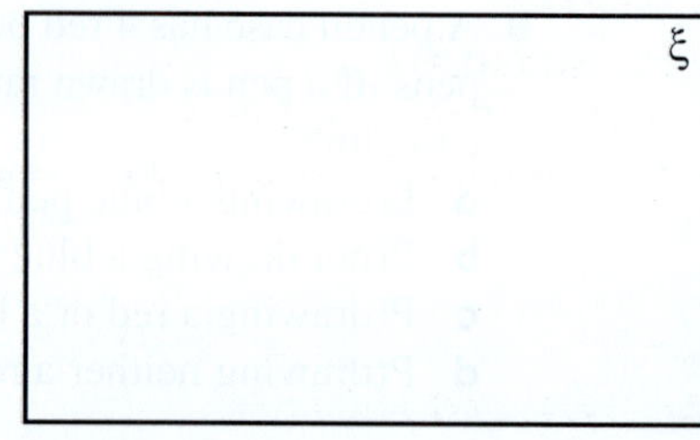

3 Draw and label a circle within the rectangle to represent set A. This circle contains the elements 2, 3 and 5.

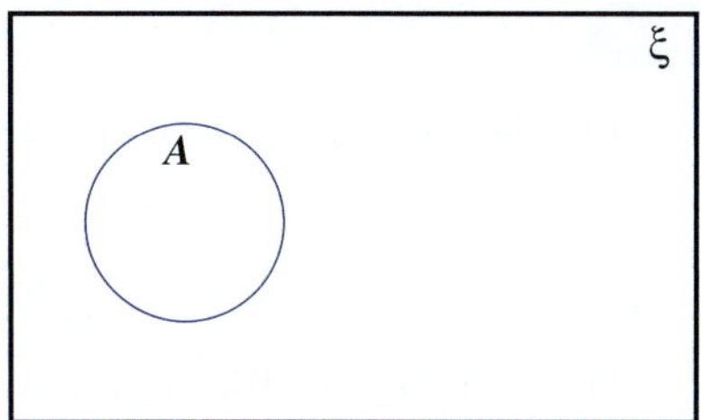

4 Draw and label a circle within the rectangle to represent set B. This circle contains the elements 1, 3, 5 and 7.
Note: Circles A and B will overlap as they have common elements, that is, 3 and 5.

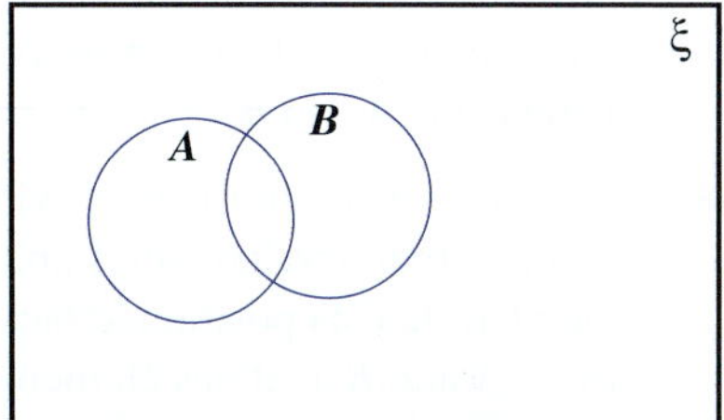

5 Enter the elements into the appropriate section of the Venn diagram.
a First label the overlapping section with the elements common to both A and B.
b Next label sets A and B with the elements not already included in the overlapping section.
c Lastly, label the rectangle with those elements in the universal set not already listed in sets A or B.

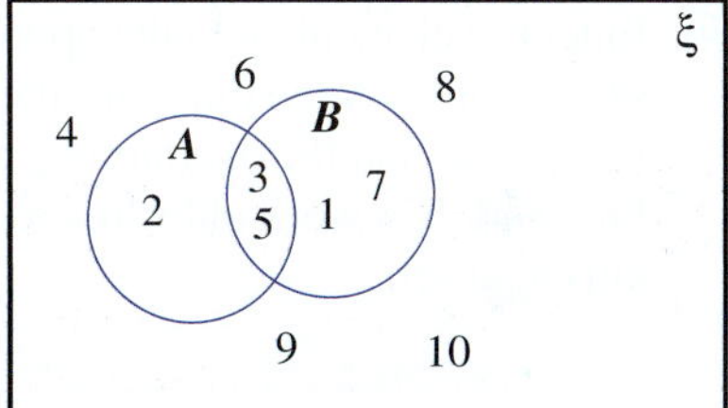

6 Check that circle A contains all the elements of set A. Similarly, check circle B and the universal set.

eBook*plus*

eLesson
Union and intersection of sets
eles-0049

Intersection of sets (∩) and union of sets (∪)

- When sets A and B overlap as in Worked example 10, this overlap is defined as the **intersection** of the two sets.
- This region is represented using notation $A \cap B$ (read as 'A intersection B').
  In Worked example 10, $A \cap B = \{3, 5\}$.
- The union of two sets, A and B, is the set of all elements in A or in B (or in both).
- This region is represented using the notation $A \cup B$ (read as 'A union B').
  In Worked example 10, $A \cup B = \{1, 2, 3, 5, 7\}$

WORKED EXAMPLE 11

a **Draw a Venn diagram representing the relationship between the following sets. Show the position of all the elements in the Venn diagram.**
ξ = {first 10 letters of the English alphabet}
A = {vowels}
B = {consonants}
C = {letters of the word *head*}

b **Use the Venn diagram to list the elements in the following sets.**
i B'
ii $B \cap C$
iii $A \cup C$
iv $(A \cap C) \cap (B \cap C)$

THINK	WRITE
a 1 List the elements in each of the sets.	**a** $\xi = \{a, b, c, d, e, f, g, h, i, j\}$ $A = \{a, e, i\}$ $B = \{b, c, d, f, g, h, j\}$ $C = \{a, e, d, h\}$
2 Draw the universal set as a rectangle. 3 Draw and label two separate circles within the rectangle to represent the disjoint sets *A* and *B*. 4 Draw and label a third circle within the rectangle that overlaps set *A* and set *B*. *Note:* Circle *C* is positioned between circles *A* and *B* as it has elements common to both sets.	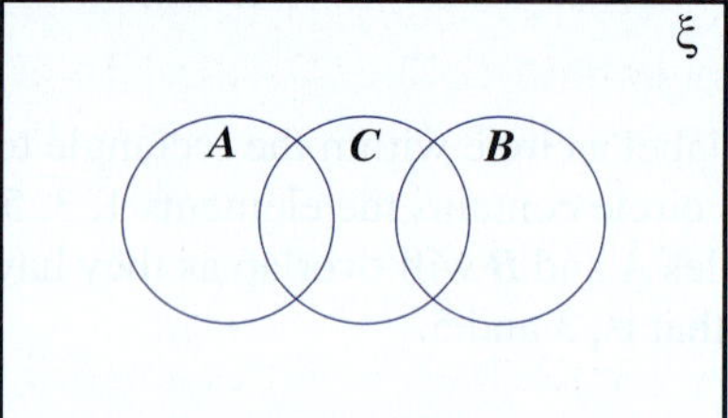
5 Enter the elements into the appropriate section of the Venn diagram; that is, fill in the letters in the overlapping areas first, and then work outwards to the universal set.	Sets *A* and *C* have *a* and *e* in common. Sets *B* and *C* have *h* and *d* in common. There are no remaining elements in *C*. The remaining element in *A* is *i*. The remaining elements in *B* are *b*, *c*, *f*, *g*, *j*. 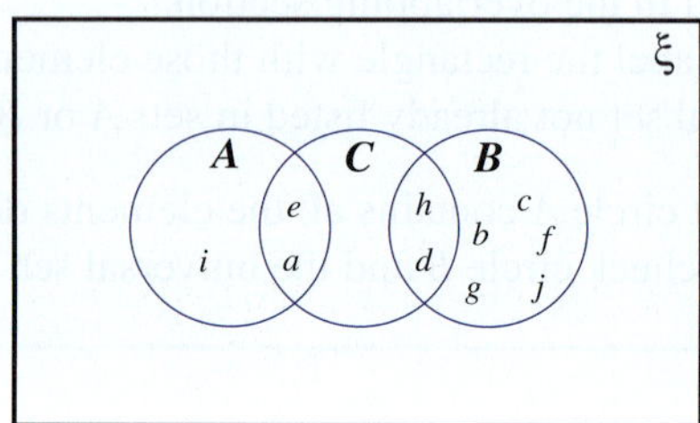
b i Carefully analyse the Venn diagram and identify the set required. *Note:* *B′* is the complement of set *B* and includes all the elements that are part of the universal set and not in set *B*.	**b** i $B' = \{a, e, i\}$
ii Carefully analyse the Venn diagram and identify the set required. *Note:* The intersection of *B* and *C* is the overlapping area of these two circles.	ii $B \cap C = \{d, h\}$
iii Carefully analyse the Venn diagram and identify the set required. *Note:* The union of *A* and *C* contain all the elements in circles *A* and *C*.	iii $A \cup C = \{a, d, e, h, i\}$
iv Carefully analyse the Venn diagram and consider the intersection of *A* with *C*. Next consider the intersection of *B* with *C*. Compare the sets obtained and answer the question.	iv $(A \cap C) \cap (B \cap C) = \{a, e\} \cap \{d, h\}$ $= \{\}$

WORKED EXAMPLE 12

An ice-creamery conducted a survey of 60 customers on a Monday and obtained the following results on two new ice-cream flavours. The results showed that 35 customers liked Product A, 40 liked Product B, and 24 liked both equally.

a Draw a Venn diagram to illustrate the above information.

b Use the Venn diagram to answer the following questions.

i How many customers liked Product A only?

ii How many customers liked Product B only?

iii How many customers liked neither product?

c If a customer was selected at random on this Monday morning what is the probability they would have liked neither new flavour?

d Calculate the probability that a customer liked Product A given that they liked Product B.

THINK	WRITE
a 1 Draw the universal set as a rectangle. 2 Draw and label two overlapping circles within the rectangle to represent Product A and Product B. *Note:* Circles for products A and B overlap because 24 customers liked both products equally.	a 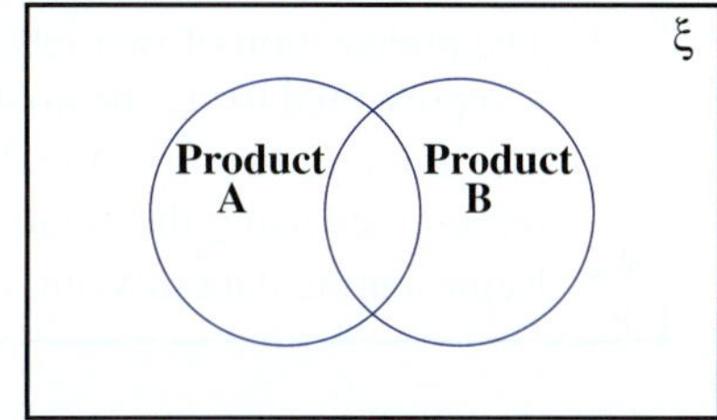
3 Working from the overlapping area outwards, determine the number of customers in each region. *Note:* The total must equal the number of customers surveyed, that is, 60.	There are 24 customers in both sets. Product A's set contains 11 customers (that is, 35 – 24) who like Product A but not Product B. Product B's set contains 16 customers (that is, 40 – 24) who like Product B but not Product A. The remaining 9 customers (that is, [60 – (11 + 24 + 16)]) like neither product. 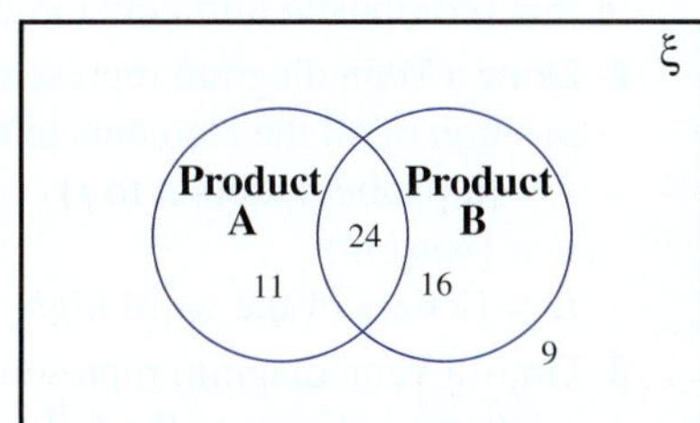
b i Refer to the Venn diagram and answer the question. *Note:* The non-overlapping part of Product A's circle refers to the customers that like Product A only.	b i 11 customers liked Product A only.
ii Refer to the Venn diagram and answer the question. *Note:* The non-overlapping part of Product B's circle refers to the customers that like Product B only.	ii 16 customers liked Product B only.
iii Refer to the Venn diagram and answer the question.	iii 9 customers liked neither product.

c There was a total of 60 customers and 9 customers liked neither new flavour.

c $P(\text{liking neither new flavour}) = \frac{9}{60}$

$= \frac{3}{20}$

d Forty customers liked Product B and 24 customers liked Products A and B.

d $P(\text{Liking Product A/Liked product B}) = \frac{24}{40} = \frac{3}{5}$

REMEMBER

1. Venn diagrams show the relationship between sets. The universal set ξ is drawn as a rectangle and other subsets of the universal set are drawn as circles within the rectangle.
2. If the circles within the universal set overlap, there are elements common to these subsets. If there is no overlap of the circles, the subsets are disjoint.
3. The intersection of two sets A and B is the set of elements common to both A and B. It is represented using the notation $A \cap B$.
4. The union of two sets A and B is the set of all elements in A or in B (or in both). It is represented using the notation $A \cup B$.
5. Representing data in Venn diagrams can assist in the calculation of probabilities.

EXERCISE 13E Venn diagrams

INDIVIDUAL PATHWAYS

eBook*plus*

Activity 13-E-1 Venn diagrams doc-2400

Activity 13-E-2 More Venn diagrams doc-2401

Activity 13-E-3 Advanced Venn diagrams doc-2402

FLUENCY

1 WE10 Draw a Venn diagram representing the relationship between the following sets. Show the position of all the elements in the Venn diagram.
ξ = {integers ranging from 10 to 20}
B = {odd numbers greater than 12 and less than 18}
A = {composite numbers ranging from 10 to 20}

2 Draw a Venn diagram representing the relationship between the following sets. Show the position of all the elements in the Venn diagram.
ξ = {alphabet letters a to j}
V = {vowels}
H = {letters of the word *high*}

eBook*plus*

Interactivity **Venn diagrams** int-2377

3 Draw a Venn diagram representing the relationship between the following sets. Show the position of all the elements in the Venn diagram.
ξ = {counting numbers up to 10}
P = {prime numbers}
E = {even numbers}

4 Draw a Venn diagram representing the relationship between the following sets. Show the position of all the elements in the Venn diagram.
ξ = {months of the year}
J = {months of the year beginning with j}
W = {winter months}
S = {summer months}

5 The Venn diagram at right shows the following sets.
ξ = {first 16 letters of the alphabet}
V = {vowels}
C = {consonants}
W = {letters of the word *padlock*}
Show the position of all the elements in the Venn diagram.

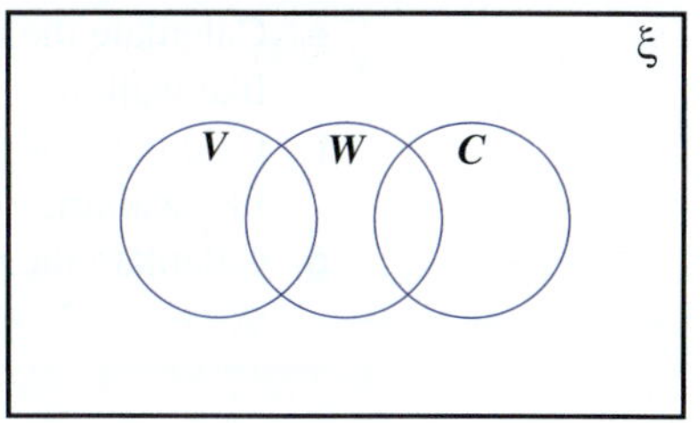

6 The Venn diagram at right shows the following sets.
ξ = {positive integers less than 15}
O = {odd numbers}
E = {even numbers}
M = {multiples of 3}
Show the position of all the elements in the Venn diagram.

7 **a** WE11 Draw a Venn diagram representing the relationship between the following sets. Show the position of all the elements in the Venn diagram.
$\xi = \{a, c, e, g, i, k, m, o, q, s, u, w, y\}$
A = {vowels}
B = {consonants}
C = {letters of the word *cages*}

b Use the Venn diagram to list the elements in the following sets.
i B' **ii** $B \cap C$ **iii** $A \cup C$ **iv** $(A \cap C) \cup (B \cap C)$

UNDERSTANDING

8 WE12 A tyre manufacturer conducting a survey of 2200 customers obtained the following results on two tyres: 1390 customers preferred Tyre A, 1084 preferred Tyre B, and 496 preferred both equally.

a Draw a Venn diagram to illustrate the above information.
b Use the Venn diagram to answer the following questions.
i How many customers preferred Tyre A only?
ii How many customers preferred Tyre B only?
iii How many customers preferred neither tyre?
c If a customer was selected at random, calculate the probability that they would have preferred neither type of tyre.
d Calculate the probability that a customer preferred Tyre A, given that they preferred Tyre B.

9 A sporting club has its members playing different sports, as shown in the Venn diagram.
a Copy the given Venn diagram and shade the areas that represent:
i members playing tennis only
ii members walking only
iii members both playing tennis and walking.

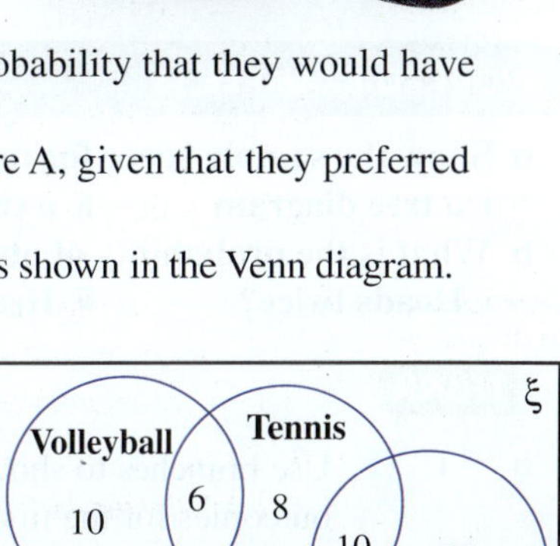

b How many members:
i play volleyball?
ii are involved in all three activities?
c How many members do not:
i play tennis? **ii** walk?
d How many members belong to the sporting club?

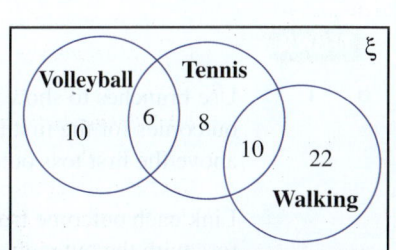

e Calculate the probability that a member likes playing volleyball or tennis but does not like walking.
f Calculate the probability that a member likes playing volleyball and tennis but does not like walking.
g Calculate the probability that a member likes playing tennis, given that they like walking.

REASONING

10 Margaret is in charge of distributing team uniforms for students representing the school in music, athletics and debating. Margaret knows that representing the school are 43 students, of whom some are involved in more than one activity. They must purchase a uniform for each activity in which they participate.

Margaret has the following information: 36 students are in the concert band, 31 students are in the athletics team, 12 students are in the debating team, 6 students are involved in all three. Nine students are involved in music and debating, 7 in athletics and debating and 26 students are in music and athletics.

a Show this information on a Venn diagram.
b Calculate the probability that a student will be required to purchase only the music uniform.
c Calculate the probability that a student will be required to purchase only the athletics uniform.
d Calculate the probability that a student will be required to purchase only the debating uniform.
e Calculate the probability that a student will be required to purchase music and debating uniforms but not an athletics uniform.
f Calculate the probability that a student will be required to purchase a music or athletics uniform but not a debating uniform.
g Calculate the probability that a student will be required to purchase a debating uniform given that they purchased a music uniform.

13F Tree diagrams and two-way tables

- A tree diagram is a branching diagram that lists all the possible outcomes.
- A two-way table can also be used to represent the sample space.

WORKED EXAMPLE 13

a Show the sample space for tossing a coin twice (or 2 coins together) by using:
i a tree diagram ii a two-way table.
b What is the probability of obtaining:
i Heads twice? ii Heads and Tails?

THINK

a i 1 Use branches to show the individual outcomes for the first toss. Place a **1** above the first toss outcomes.

2 Link each outcome from the first toss with the outcomes of the second toss. Place a **2** above the second toss outcomes.

WRITE

a i

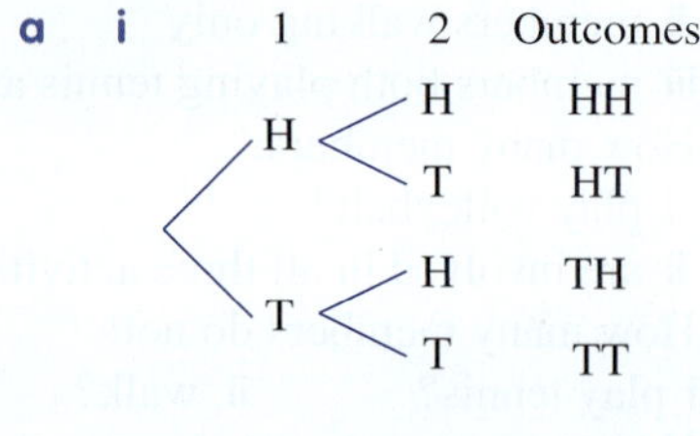

3 List each of the possible outcome pairs in the order they occur; that is, the first toss result followed by the second toss result.

ii 1 Draw a table consisting of three rows and columns. Leave the first cell blank.

ii 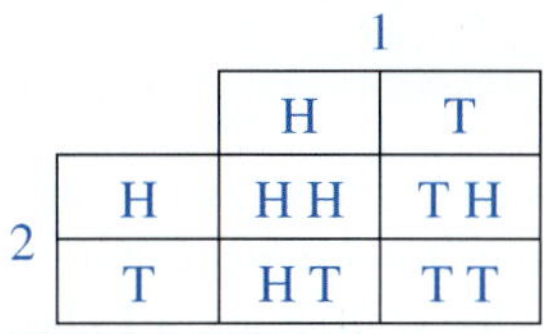

		1	
		H	T
2	H	H H	T H
	T	H T	T T

2 Label the second and third cells of the first row as H and T respectively. Place a **1** above the first row.

3 Label the second and third cells of the first column as H and T respectively. Place a **2** beside the first column.

4 Combine the outcome pairs in the order in which they occur in each of the remaining cells; that is, the first toss result followed by the second toss result.

b i 1 Using either the tree diagram or the two-way table, write the number of favourable outcomes and the total number of possible outcomes. *Note:* The outcome of two Heads occurs once.

b i Number of favourable outcomes = 1
Total number of possible outcomes = 4

2 Write the rule for probability.

$$\text{P(event)} = \frac{\text{number of favourable outcomes}}{\text{number of possible outcomes}}$$

3 Substitute the known values into the rule and evaluate.

$$\text{P(2 Heads)} = \frac{1}{4}$$

4 Answer the question.

The probability of obtaining 2 Heads when a coin is tossed twice is $\frac{1}{4}$.

ii 1 Using either the tree diagram or the two-way table, write the number of favourable outcomes and the total number of possible outcomes. *Note:* The outcome of 1 Heads and 1 Tails occurs twice.

ii Number of favourable outcomes = 2
Total number of possible outcomes = 4

2 Write the rule for probability.

$$\text{P(event)} = \frac{\text{number of favourable outcomes}}{\text{number of possible outcomes}}$$

3 Substitute the known values into the rule and simplify.

$$\text{P(1 Heads and 1 Tails)} = \frac{2}{4} = \frac{1}{2}$$

4 Answer the question.

The probability of obtaining 1 Heads and 1 Tails when a coin is tossed twice is $\frac{1}{2}$.

WORKED EXAMPLE 14

a A coin is tossed and then a die is rolled. Use i a tree diagram ii a two-way table to show all the possible outcomes.

b What is the probability of obtaining i Heads and an even number? ii an odd number?

THINK

a i 1 Use branches to show the individual outcomes for the first event; that is, the toss of the coin. Place a **1** above the first event outcome.

2 Link each outcome from the first event with each of the outcomes from the second event; that is, the roll of the die. Place a **2** above the second event outcomes.

3 List each of the possible outcome pairs in the order they occur; that is, the first event result followed by the second event result.

WRITE

a i

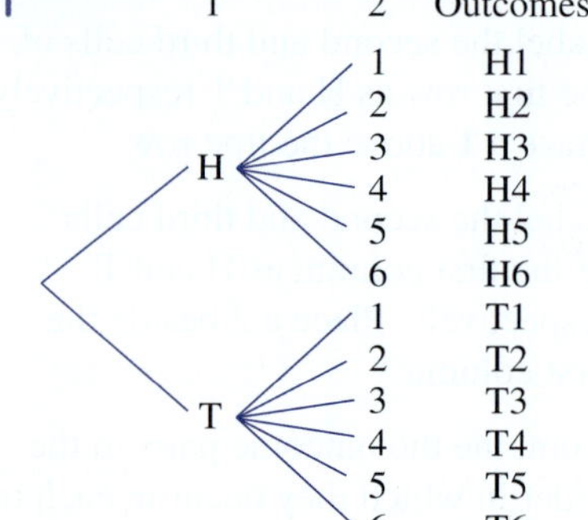

ii 1 Draw a table consisting of seven rows and three columns. Leave the first cell blank.

2 Label the second and third cells of the first row as H and T respectively. Place a **1** above the first row.

3 Label cells two to seven of the first column as 1, 2, 3, 4, 5, 6 respectively. Place a **2** beside the first column.

4 Combine the outcome pairs in the order they occur in each of the remaining cells; that is, the first event result followed by the second event result.

ii

1 (above table); **2** (beside first column)

	H	T
1	H 1	T 1
2	H 2	T 2
3	H 3	T 3
4	H 4	T 4
5	H 5	T 5
6	H 6	T 6

b i 1 Using either the tree diagram or the two-way table, write the number of favourable outcomes and the total number of possible outcomes.
Note: The outcome of Heads and an even number occurs 3 times.

b i Number of favourable outcomes = 3
Total number of possible outcomes = 12

2 Write the rule for probability.

$$\text{P(event)} = \frac{\text{number of favourable outcomes}}{\text{number of possible outcomes}}$$

3 Substitute the known values into the rule and simplify.

$$\text{P(Heads and an even number)} = \frac{3}{12} = \frac{1}{4}$$

4 Answer the question.

The probability of obtaining Heads and an even number when a coin is tossed and a die is rolled is $\frac{1}{4}$.

ii **1** Using either the tree diagram or the two-way table, write the number of favourable outcomes and the total number of possible outcomes. *Note:* The outcome of an odd number occurs 6 times.	**ii** Number of favourable outcomes = 6 Total number of possible outcomes = 12
2 Write the rule for probability.	$\text{P(event)} = \dfrac{\text{number of favourable outcomes}}{\text{number of possible outcomes}}$
3 Substitute the known values into the rule and simplify.	$\text{P(an odd number)} = \frac{6}{12}$ $= \frac{1}{2}$
4 Answer the question.	The probability of obtaining an odd number when a coin is tossed and a die is rolled is $\frac{1}{2}$.

WORKED EXAMPLE 15

a **Draw a tree diagram to show the combined experiment, tossing a coin and spinning a circular spinner with four equal sectors labelled 1, 2, 3, 4.**
b **Determine the probability of each possible result.**
c **What do you notice about the sum of the probabilities?**
d **Calculate the probability of obtaining:**
i **Heads and an even number** **ii** **a prime number** **iii** **Tails.**

THINK	WRITE
a **1** Use branches to show the individual outcomes for the first part of the experiment (that is, tossing a coin). Place a **1** above the coin toss outcomes. Label the ends of the branches H and T and place the probability of each along their respective branch.	**a** 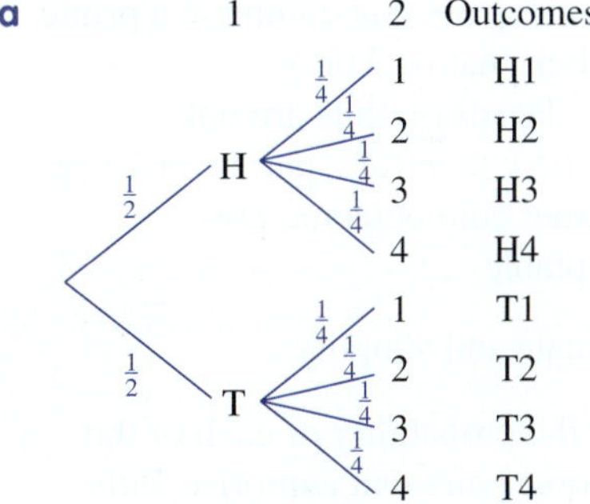
2 Link each outcome from the coin toss with the outcomes of the second part of the experiment (that is, spinning a circular spinner). Place a **2** above the spinning outcomes. Label the ends of the branches 1, 2, 3 and 4 and place the probability of each along its respective branch.	
3 List each of the possible outcome pairs in the order they occur; that is, the tossing of the coin result followed by the spinning result. *Note:* It doesn't matter which part of the experiment goes first, because the parts do not affect each other. They are called independent events. The coin toss will have two branches, and the spinning of the circular spinner will have four branches.	

b Determine the probability of each possible result by multiplying the first result probability by the second result probability of the ordered pair.

b $P(H, 1) = \frac{1}{2} \times \frac{1}{4} = \frac{1}{8}$ $\quad P(T, 1) = \frac{1}{2} \times \frac{1}{4} = \frac{1}{8}$

$P(H, 2) = \frac{1}{2} \times \frac{1}{4} = \frac{1}{8}$ $\quad P(T, 2) = \frac{1}{2} \times \frac{1}{4} = \frac{1}{8}$

$P(H, 3) = \frac{1}{2} \times \frac{1}{4} = \frac{1}{8}$ $\quad P(T, 3) = \frac{1}{2} \times \frac{1}{4} = \frac{1}{8}$

$P(H, 4) = \frac{1}{2} \times \frac{1}{4} = \frac{1}{8}$ $\quad P(T, 4) = \frac{1}{2} \times \frac{1}{4} = \frac{1}{8}$

c Add the probabilities together and answer the question.

c $\text{Total} = \frac{1}{8} + \frac{1}{8} + \frac{1}{8} + \frac{1}{8} + \frac{1}{8} + \frac{1}{8} + \frac{1}{8} + \frac{1}{8}$
$= 1$

The probabilities of each combined result in the tree diagram add up to 1.

d **i** **1** Add the probability of each of the outcome pairs that comprise Heads and an even number.

2 Evaluate and simplify.

d **i** $P(H, \text{even}) = P(H, 2) + P(H, 4))$

$P(H, \text{even}) = \frac{1}{8} + \frac{1}{8}$

$= \frac{2}{8}$

$= \frac{1}{4}$

ii **1** Add the probability of each of the outcome pairs that comprise a prime number; that is, 2 or 3.
Note: Heads or Tails are not specified; therefore, pairs consisting of either coin outcome are acceptable.

2 Evaluate and simplify.

ii $P(\text{prime}) = P(H, 2) + P(H, 3) + P(T, 2) + P(T, 3)$

$= \frac{1}{8} + \frac{1}{8} + \frac{1}{8} + \frac{1}{8}$

$= \frac{4}{8}$

$= \frac{1}{2}$

iii **1** Add the probability of each of the outcome pairs that comprise Tails.
Note: Numbers are not specified; therefore, pairs consisting of any spinner outcome are acceptable.

2 Evaluate and simplify.

iii $P(\text{tails}) = P(T, 1) + P(T, 2) + P(T, 3) + P(T, 4)$

$= \frac{1}{8} + \frac{1}{8} + \frac{1}{8} + \frac{1}{8}$

$= \frac{4}{8}$

$= \frac{1}{2}$

REMEMBER

When more than one event occurs within the same experiment, a representation of the sample space is useful in calculating the required probabilities. Sample spaces may be represented by:

1. a tree diagram, which is a branching diagram that lists all the possible outcomes
2. a two-way table.

EXERCISE
13F Tree diagrams and two-way tables

INDIVIDUAL PATHWAYS

eBook*plus*

Activity 13-F-1
What are my options?
doc-7112

Activity 13-F-2
So many choices
doc-7113

Activity 13-F-3
Options, options, options
doc-7114

FLUENCY

1 a WE13 Show the sample space for tossing a coin twice (or 2 coins together), by using
i a tree diagram **ii** a two-way table.
b What is the probability of obtaining:
i 2 Tails? **ii** Heads and then Tails?
iii Tails and then Heads? **iv** one of each?
v both the same?

2 a Use a tree diagram to show the sample space for two children that are born into a family.
b What are the chances that they are:
i 2 girls?
ii 2 boys?
iii both the same sex?
iv a boy, then a girl?
v a girl, then a boy?
vi one of each sex?

3 a Use a tree diagram to show the sample space for an electrical circuit that contains two switches, each of which can be on or off.
b What chance is there that the switches are:
i both on?
ii both off?
iii both in the same position?
iv one off, one on?

4 a Use a tree diagram to show the sample space for a true/false test that has 2 questions.
b What is the probability that the answers are:
i true, then false?
ii false, then true?
iii both false?
iv both true?
v one true, one false?

5 a Use a tree diagram and two-way table to show the sample space for the following. A light may be on or off and a door open or closed.
b What are the chances of the following situations?
i door open, light on **ii** door closed, light off
iii door closed, light on **iv** door open, light off

6 a WE14 A coin is tossed and then a die is rolled. Use **i** a tree diagram **ii** a two-way table to show all the possible outcomes.
b What is the probability of obtaining:
i Tails and the number 5? **ii** an even number?
iii Heads and a prime number? **iv** the number 3?

7 a Use a two-way table to show the sample space for the following. A coin is tossed and the spinner at right is twirled.
b What are the chances of obtaining:
i Heads and a 1?
ii Tails and a 2?
iii Tails and a 3?
iv Heads and a 2?
v Tails and an odd number?
vi Heads and an even number?
vii Tails and a prime number?

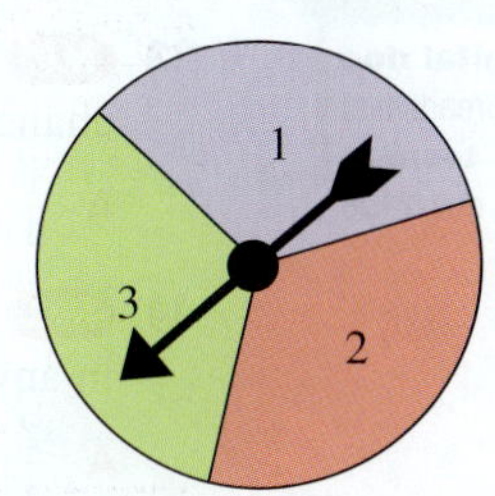

8 **a** Use a two-way table to show the sample space for the following. Zipper sports cars come in 3 colours (red, white and yellow) with manual or automatic transmissions available.

b What are the chances of a car selected at random being:

i red?
ii automatic?
iii yellow and automatic?
iv white and manual?
v red and automatic?

9 **a** Use a two-way table to show the sample space for the following. A die is rolled and a coin is tossed.

b What is the probability of obtaining the following?

i H, 6 **ii** T, 1 **iii** H, even **iv** T, odd **v** H, ≥ 4 **vi** T, < 3 **vii** H, not 6

10 A bag contains two red balls and one black. A ball is drawn, its colour noted, and then it is replaced. A second draw is then made. Use a tree diagram to list all possible outcomes. (*Hint:* Place each red ball on a separate branch.) Find the probability of drawing:

i black, black
ii red, red
iii red, then black
iv black, then red
v different colours
vi the same colour each time
vii no reds
viii no blacks
ix at least one red
x neither red nor black
xi at least one black.

11 **a** WE15 Draw a tree diagram to show the combined experiment, tossing a coin and spinning a circular spinner with six equal sectors labelled 1, 2, 3, 4, 5, 6.

b Determine the probability of each possible result.

c What do you notice about the sum of the probabilities?

d Calculate the probability of obtaining:

i a head and an even number
ii a prime number
iii a tail.

12 **a** Draw a tree diagram to show the combined experiment, rolling a die and spinning the circular spinner shown at right.

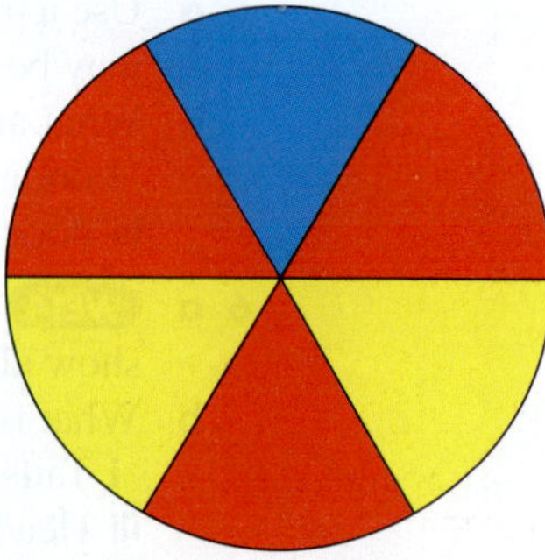

b Determine the probability of each possible result.

c What do you notice about the sum of the probabilities?

d Calculate the probability of obtaining:

i the number 2
ii the colour yellow
iii the colour red
iv an even number and the colour blue.

eBook*plus*

Digital doc
Spreadsheet
Coin tossing
doc-2408

UNDERSTANDING

13 MC Two sets of traffic lights each show red, amber or green for equal amounts of time. The chance of encountering 2 red lights in succession are:

A $\frac{1}{3}$ **B** $\frac{1}{6}$ **C** $\frac{2}{3}$ **D** $\frac{2}{9}$ **E** $\frac{1}{9}$

14 MC In the situation described in question **11**, the probability of experiencing amber and green in any order is:

A $\frac{2}{3}$ **B** $\frac{1}{9}$ **C** $\frac{1}{2}$ **D** $\frac{1}{3}$ **E** none of these

15 To get to school each morning, you are driven along Smith Street and pass through an intersection controlled by traffic lights. The traffic light for Smith Street drivers has a cycle of green and amber for a total of 40 seconds and then red for 20 seconds.

a What is the probability that the traffic light will be red as you approach the intersection?

b Over 3 school weeks, how many days would you expect the traffic light to be red as you approach the intersection?

c Design an experiment in which you simulate the operation of the traffic light to record whether the light is red as you approach the intersection. Explain what device you will use to represent the outcomes.

d Complete this experiment 10 times and calculate the experimental probability that the traffic light will be red as you approach the intersection.

e Repeat the experiment a further 40 times so that you have 50 results. Again calculate the probability that the traffic light will be red as you approach the intersection.

f Use the probabilities calculated in parts **d** and **e** to estimate the number of days that the traffic light would be red over 3 school weeks.

g Compare your results.

h Design an experiment to calculate the probability that the traffic light will be red every morning for a school week.

i What is the chance that the traffic light will be red every morning for a school week?

REASONING

16 People around the world have played games with dice for thousands of years. Dice were first mentioned in print in the *Mahabharata*, a sacred epic poem written in India more than 2000 years ago. The six-sided dice used today are almost identical to those used in China about 600 BC and in Egypt about 2000 BC.

Barbudey is a popular game in Greece and Mexico. Two players take turns rolling 2 dice until one of the following winning or losing rolls is obtained.

Winning rolls:        

Losing rolls:  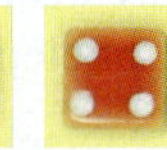      

a Calculate the probability of getting a winning roll.

b Calculate the probability of getting a losing roll.

c Calculate the probability of getting neither a winning nor a losing roll.

d Play the game a number of times with a partner. Set up an experiment to investigate the experimental probabilities of getting a winning roll and getting a losing roll. Compare your results.

eBook*plus*

Digital doc
WorkSHEET 13.2
doc-7108

REFLECTION

What are some things you need to be careful of when you are calculating the number of possible outcomes?

Summary

Probability scale

- Probability is defined as the chance of an event occurring.
- Probabilities range from 0 (impossible, no chance) to 1 (certain, every chance) inclusive.
- Probabilities may be written as fractions, decimals or percentages.

Experimental probability

- Relative frequency $= \dfrac{\text{frequency of an event}}{\text{total number of trails}}$
- The total sum of the relative frequencies in an experiment is equal to 1.
- Expected frequency = relative frequency × the number in the sample

Sample spaces and theoretical probability

- A sample space, S, is a list of all the possible outcomes (obtained from an experiment) and enclosed in a pair of curled brackets { }.
- The theoretical probability of an event occurring is given by the rule:

$$\text{P(event)} = \frac{\text{number of favourable outcomes}}{\text{number of possible outcomes}}$$

Complementary events

- Complementary events have nothing in common but when added together form the sample space.
- If events A and A' are complementary, then $P(A) + P(A') = 1$. This may be rearranged to $P(A') = 1 - P(A)$ or $P(A) = 1 - P(A')$.

Venn diagrams

- Venn diagrams show the relationship between sets. The universal set ξ is drawn as a rectangle and other subsets of the universal set are drawn as circles within the rectangle.
- If the circles within the universal set overlap, there are elements common to these subsets. If there is no overlap of the circles, the subsets are disjoint.
- The intersection of two sets A and B is the set of elements common to both A and B. It is represented using the notation $A \cap B$.
- The union of two sets A and B is the set of all elements in A or in B (or in both). It is represented using the notation $A \cup B$.
- Representing data in Venn diagrams can assist in the calculation of probabilities.

Tree diagrams and two-way tables

When more than one event occurs within the same experiment, a representation of the sample space is useful in calculating the required probabilities. Sample spaces may be represented by:

- a tree diagram, which is a branching diagram that lists all the possible outcomes
- a two-way table.

MAPPING YOUR UNDERSTANDING

Using terms from the summary, and other terms if you wish, construct a concept map that illustrates your understanding of the key concepts covered in this chapter. Compare this concept map with the one that you created in *What do you know?* on page 365.

Have you completed the two *Homework sheets*, the *Rich task* and the two *Code puzzles* in your *Maths Quest 8 Homework Book*?

Chapter review

FLUENCY

1 MC If a die is rolled 200 times and a 6 comes up 30 times, then its relative frequency is:

A $\frac{20}{3}$ B $\frac{3}{20}$ C $\frac{17}{20}$

D 30% E $\frac{1}{5}$

2 MC If a teacher found over the years that Year 8 students pass mathematics with a relative frequency of $\frac{2}{3}$, how many of her current class of 27 would she expect to pass?

A 2 B 3 C 18

D 15 E 24

3 An experiment involving rolling a die was conducted, with the results as shown in the following frequency table.

Score	1	2	3	4	5	6
Frequency	9	8	12	13	10	8

a How many trials were performed?
b How many outcomes were in the sample space?
c How many times would you have expected a 6 to come up?
d Find the relative frequency of:
i 5 ii 1 iii even numbers.

4 People from a random sample were asked how they would vote in an election. The results were coded as:

1. Liberal–National
2. Labor
3. One Nation
4. Democrats
5. other.

The recorded intentions were:

1, 2, 2, 1, 1, 2, 5, 3, 2, 1, 3, 1, 4, 2, 3, 1, 2, 1, 4, 2, 2, 4, 1, 2, 2, 3, 1, 2, 1, 1, 1, 2, 2, 1, 4, 1, 2, 1, 2, 3, 2, 2, 2, 1, 1, 1, 2, 3, 2, 5

a Organise the data into a frequency table.
b Find the relative frequency of each category, to the nearest whole per cent.
c A person selected at random from the general population would be highly likely to vote for one of which 2 parties?
d Out of 1000 people, how many could be expected to vote for One Nation?
e What should be the total of all the relative frequency percentages?

5 MC The chance of getting a 5 with the spinner at right is:

Weblink
Probability game

A $\frac{1}{3}$
B $\frac{1}{5}$
C $\frac{1}{6}$
D $\frac{2}{5}$
E none of these

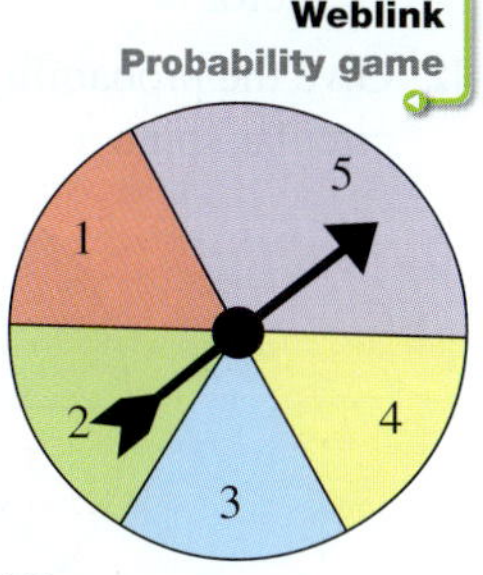

6 Study the spinner shown below.
a What is sample space?
b Are all outcomes equally likely? Explain your answer.
c In theory, what are the chances of spinning:
i a 2?
ii a 6?

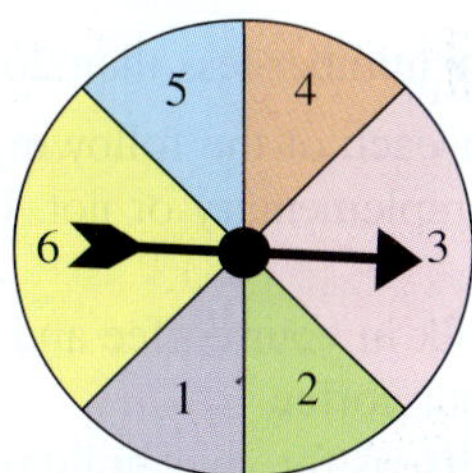

7 One thousand tickets were sold for a raffle. If you purchased five, what are your chances of winning the raffle?

8 A cube has 2 red faces, 2 white faces, 1 green and 1 yellow. If rolled, what is the probability of the top face showing:
a red?
b yellow?
c not red?
d green or white?

9 On each of the 5 days, Monday to Friday, garbage is collected. What are the chances that garbage is collected at an address chosen at random on:
a Wednesday?
b Thursday or Friday?
c Sunday?
d a day other than Monday?

10 A multiple-choice question has as alternatives A, B, C, D and E. Only one is correct.
a What is the probability of guessing:
i the right answer?
ii the wrong answer?
b What is the total of the probabilities?

11 a Design a circular spinner with the numbers 1 to 4 so that:

$P(1) = \frac{1}{2}, P(2) = \frac{1}{4}, P(3) = \frac{1}{8}, P(4) = \frac{1}{8}$.

b What will the size of the angle in each sector be?

12 Give the probability of each of the numbers in this circular spinner.

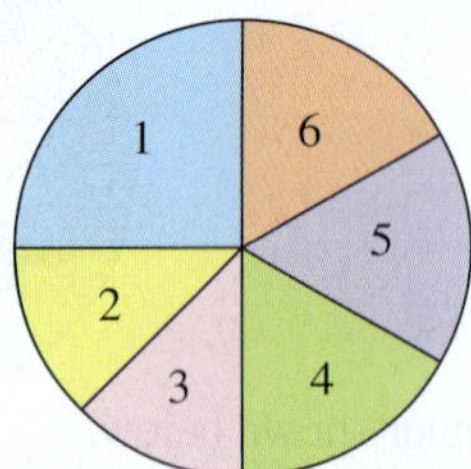

13 State the complement of each of the following events.

a Tossing a coin and it landing Tails
b Winning a race in which you run
c Answering a question correctly
d Selecting a black marble from a bag of marbles
e Selecting a number less than 20

14 State whether each of the following pairs of events are complementary or not. Explain your answer.

a Having milk in your coffee and not having milk in your coffee
b Going overseas for your holiday or holidaying in Australia
c Catching a train to work or catching a bus to work

15 The probability that a traffic light is green is $\frac{3}{7}$. Find the probability that the traffic light is not green.

16 Shoppers in a supermarket were given a taste test of two varieties of jellybeans — home brand (H) and brand X. Of the 168 shoppers to undertake the test, 111 liked the home brand, 84 liked brand X and 39 liked both.

a Represent these data as a Venn diagram.
b What is the probability that one of those shoppers did not like either of the two varieties?
c What is the probability that one of the shoppers liked brand H or brand X?
d What is the probability that one of the shoppers liked brand X given that they liked brand H?

17 Draw a two-way table to show the sample space for the situation in question **16**.

18 a Use a tree diagram and two-way table to show all the possible outcomes for the sex (B, G) and hair colour (blond, black, brown, red) of a baby.

b What are the chances (assuming all outcomes are equally likely) of a child being:

i a blond girl? **ii** a red-haired boy?
iii a redhead? **iv** not blond?
v a boy with black or brown hair?

19 Caryle is deciding what to order for lunch from her favourite restaurant. The table below provides her possible entree, main meal and dessert options.

Entree	Main	Desert
Pasta	Roast chicken	Creme caramel
Soup	Lamb cutlets	Ice-cream
	Seafood platter	Fruit salad

a Draw a tree diagram to show the possible combinations Caryle can order if she chooses to have an entree, main meal and dessert.
b How many different options can Caryle choose from?
c What is the probability that Caryle will order:

i lamb as her main meal?
ii ice-cream for dessert?
iii soup as her entree and fruit salad for dessert?
iv either pasta or soup for an entree, chicken or seafood as her main and crème caramel for dessert?

d Without drawing a tree diagram, how many different options would there be if Caryle could choose from:

i three entrees, three mains and three desserts?
ii four entrees, three mains and three desserts?
iii two entrees, four mains and three desserts?

e Explain how the total number of options were obtained in part **d**.

PROBLEM SOLVING

1 From a standard pack of cards, write down a set that would have:

a a probability of $\frac{1}{2}$ **b** a probability of $\frac{3}{13}$
c a probability of $\frac{1}{26}$ **d** a probability of $\frac{1}{13}$.

2 During her latest shopping trip, Karen's mother stocked up on a supply of icypoles for the summer. In one box there are 12 icypoles with four different flavours: orange, raspberry, lime and cola. Karen likes everything but lime.

- **a** What is the probability that when she reaches into the box randomly, she will select an icypole that she likes?
- **b** Two days later, 2 raspberry, 1 cola, and 1 lime have been eaten by various members of the family. Have Karen's chances of randomly choosing a lime popsicle gone up, down or stayed the same? Explain your answer.

3 One of the games suggested as a fund raiser at the local Auskick club was a coin tossing game. The children pay $1 and toss a coin three times. If they toss three Heads or three Tails they win a prize.

- **a** Draw a tree diagram to list all possible outcomes when a coin is tossed three times.
- **b** What is the probability of winning a prize at the fund raiser?
- **c** Gemma gets Heads with her first two tosses of the coin. What is the probability that she wins a prize?
- **d** Is the club likely to make money on this game? Explain.

4 In a certain school band there are 6 girls and some boys. A student is selected at random from this group. Find the number of boys in the group if the probability that a girl is selected is $\frac{1}{4}$.

5 Debbie and Ron, who are roughly of equal ability, play a squash tournament. The first person to win two games in a row, or who wins a total of three games, wins the tournament.

Draw a tree diagram to list all possible outcomes of the tournament.

6 Jar A contains 5 black, 3 white and 2 coloured marbles. Jar B contains 6 black, 4 white and 4 coloured marbles. From which jar are you more likely to draw a black marble?

7 How many 3-digit numbers are there?

8 A fair 4-sided die in the shape of a regular tetrahedron is tossed twice.

- **a** Draw the sample space.
- **b** What is the probability that the two numbers that are thrown are both even?

9 Ace Andrews and Dynamo Dawson, two famous tennis stars, are playing each other. The probability that Ace will win a game is 0.6.

- **a** Find the probability that in three games played, Ace wins the first but loses the next two.
- **b** Find the probability that Dynamo wins only one game.

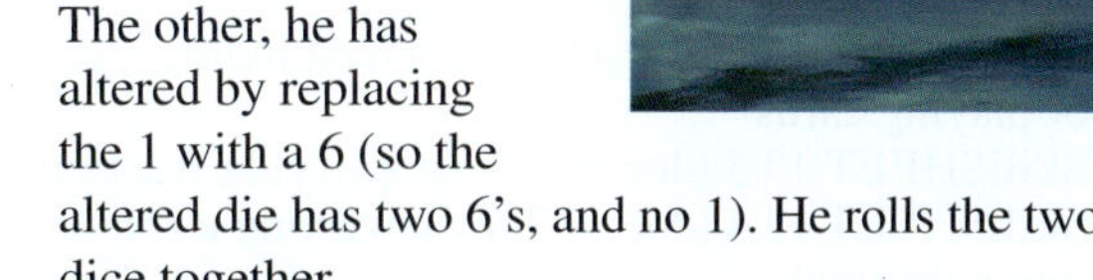

10 There are only three swimmers in the 100-m freestyle. Swimmer A is twice as likely to win as B and three times as likely to win as C. Find the probability that B or C wins.

11 James has two dice. One is a regular die. The other, he has altered by replacing the 1 with a 6 (so the altered die has two 6's, and no 1). He rolls the two dice together.

Determine the probability that a double is rolled when the two dice are thrown.

12 A coin is biased so that the probability of a Head appearing is $\frac{3}{5}$. Using a tree diagram (or otherwise) determine the probability that with three tosses of the coin, a tail appears at most once.

13 In a particular area, the probability of rain is 0.7 if it rained the day before. The probability that it does not rain is 0.8 if it did not rain the day before. It rains on Monday. Find the probability it will be fine on Wednesday.

14 In a club of 60 members, half support the sausage sizzles, one third support the raffles and some of these support both. One fifth of the members support neither of these fundraisers. Determine the probability that a club member, chosen at random, supports both.

15 There are four differently coloured marbles in a bag: red, blue, green and yellow. There are 8 blue marbles and 4 yellow marbles. The probability of drawing a blue or yellow marble is 0.6. If there are 3 green marbles in the bag, how many red marbles are there?

eBook*plus*

Interactivities
Test yourself
Chapter 13
int-2761
Word search
Chapter 13
int-2637
Crossword
Chapter 13
int-2638

eBookplus ACTIVITIES

Chapter opener

Digital doc *(page 365)*
- Hungry brain activity Chapter 13 (doc-6968)

Are you ready?

Digital docs *(page 366)*
- SkillSHEET 13.1 (doc-6969) Understanding chance words
- SkillSHEET 13.2 (doc-6970) Understanding a deck of playing cards
- SkillSHEET 13.3 (doc-6971) Simplifying fractions
- SkillSHEET 13.4 (doc-6972) Converting a fraction into a decimal
- SkillSHEET 13.5 (doc-6973) Converting a fraction into a percentage
- SkillSHEET 13.6 (doc-6974) Multiplying a fraction by a whole number
- SkillSHEET 13.7 (doc-6975) Listing the sample space
- SkillSHEET 13.8 (doc-6976) Multiplying proper fractions

13A Probability scale

Digital docs *(page 369)*
- Activity 13-A-1 (doc-2388) Probability scales
- Activity 13-A-2 (doc-2389) More probability scales
- Activity 13-A-3 (doc-7109) Advanced probability scales

13B Experimental probability

Digital docs *(page 373)*
- Activity 13-B-1 (doc-2391) One in every two
- Activity 13-B-2 (doc-2392) One in every six
- Activity 13-B-3 (doc-2393) One in every five
- WorkSHEET 13.1 (doc-7107) *(page 374)*

Weblink *(page 373)*
- Probability simulator

13C Sample spaces and theoretical probability

Digital docs *(page 380)*
- Activity 13-C-1 (doc-2394) Sample spaces and theoretical probability
- Activity 13-C-2 (doc-7110) More sample spaces and theoretical probability
- Activity 13-C-3 (doc-7111) Advanced sample spaces and theoretical probability

Weblink *(page 380)*
- Take the probability quiz

13D Complementary events

Digital docs *(page 385)*
- Activity 13-D-1 (doc-2397) Complementary events
- Activity 13-D-2 (doc-2398) More complementary events
- Activity 13-D-3 (doc-2399) Advanced complementary events

13E Venn diagrams

Digital docs *(page 390)*
- Activity 13-E-1 (doc-2400) Venn diagrams
- Activity 13-E-2 (doc-2401) More Venn diagrams
- Activity 13-E-3 (doc-2402) Advanced Venn diagrams

Interactivity *(page 390)*
- Venn diagrams (int-2377)

eLesson *(page 387)*
- Union and intersection of sets (eles-0049)

13F Tree diagrams and two-way tables

Digital docs *(page 397)*
- Activity 13-F-1 (doc-7112) What are my options?
- Activity 13-F-2 (doc-7113) So many choices
- Activity 13-F-3 (doc-7114) Options, options, options
- Spreadsheet (doc-2408) Coin tossing *(page 398)*
- WorkSHEET 13.2 (doc-7108) *(page 399)*

Chapter review

Interactivities *(page 403)*
- Test yourself Chapter 13 (int-2761) Take the end-of-chapter test to test your progress.
- Word search Chapter 13 (int-2637)
- Crossword Chapter 13 (int-2638)

Weblink *(page 401)*
- Probability game

To access eBookPLUS activities, log on to

www.jacplus.com.au

Coordinates and linear graphs

14A The Cartesian plane
14B Linear patterns
14C Plotting linear graphs
14D Extension: The y-intercept and gradient
14E Extension: Sketching linear graphs

WHAT DO YOU KNOW?

1 List what you know about graphing straight lines. Create a concept map to show your list.

2 Share what you know with a partner and then with a small group.

3 As a class, create a large concept map that shows your class's knowledge of graphing straight lines.

eBook*plus*

Digital doc
Hungry brain activity
Chapter 14
doc-6933

Radius (r)

OPENING QUESTION

The height of a male can be predicted from the length of his radius (the bone in the forearm) using the linear pattern $h = 3.6r + 81$. How tall would you expect a Year 8 boy to be, if his radius is 22 cm long?

Are you ready?

Try the questions below. If you have difficulty with any of them, extra help can be obtained by completing the matching SkillSHEET located on your eBookPLUS.

Use the table at right for questions 1 and 2.

	A	B	C	D	E
1	✂	☎	✆	❙	❖
2	●	❆	❄	❁	❑
3	▮	❘	◆	✶	❊
4	❍	✱	✥	✲	✳
5	✸	✦	✪	✷	■

eBook*plus*

Digital doc
SkillSHEET 14.1
doc-6934

Grid coordinates I

1 Give the coordinates for the following symbols.

a ◆ b ✪ c ✂
d ✱ e ●

eBook*plus*

Digital doc
SkillSHEET 14.2
doc-6935

Grid coordinates II

2 Draw the symbol that is found:

a 2 squares above B5
b 3 squares to the left of ❊.

eBook*plus*

Digital doc
SkillSHEET 14.3
doc-6936

Plotting coordinate points

3 a Plot the following points on a Cartesian plane (number plane).

i A(1, 4) ii B(−2, 3) iii C(3, −5)
iv D(−4, 0) v E(0, 0) vi F(0, −2)

b For each of the following, draw a number plane that extends from −5 to 5 on the horizontal axis and −5 to 5 on the vertical axis. Mark the points on the number plane and name the shape that is formed in each case.

i (0, 0) (1, 2) (4, 2) (3, 0)
ii (−2, 1) (3, 1) (3, −2) (−2, −2)
iii (−3, 0) $(\frac{1}{2}, 0)$ $(\frac{1}{2}, 3\frac{1}{2})$ $(-3, 3\frac{1}{2})$
iv (−5, −2) (−3, 3) (1, 3) (3, −2)

eBook*plus*

Digital doc
SkillSHEET 14.4
doc-6937

Substitution into rules

4 Substitute 5 for x in each of the following rules and then find the value of y.

a $y = x + 2$ b $y = x - 4$ c $y = 2x + 1$

eBook*plus*

Digital doc
SkillSHEET 14.5
doc-6938

Completing a table of values for a given rule

5 Complete the table of values for each of the following.

a $y = x + 4$

x	−2	−1	0	1	2
y	2	3			

b $y = 3x - 2$

x	−2	−1	0	1	2
y					

eBook*plus*

Digital doc
SkillSHEET 14.6
doc-6939

Plotting a line using a table of values

6 Draw up a table of values and plot the graph for each of the following rules.

a $y = x + 3$
b $y = x - 2$
c $y = 2x$

14A The Cartesian plane

The Cartesian plane

- A **Cartesian plane** (named after its inventor René Descartes) consists of two axes. The horizontal axis is called the x-axis; the vertical axis is called the y-axis.
- The centre of a Cartesian plane (where x- and y-axis intersect) is called the origin.
- Both axes are evenly scaled and numbered, with 0 (zero) placed at the origin. On the x-axis the numbers increase from left to right, while on the y-axis the numbers increase from bottom to top.
- Arrows are placed on the end of each axis to show that they continue infinitely.

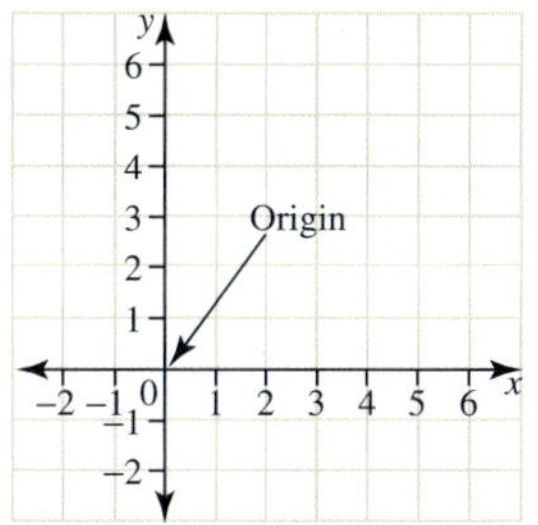

Coordinates

- To describe a position on a Cartesian plane, coordinates are used.
- A Cartesian coordinate is written as (x, y), where x and y are any numbers. The first number refers to the horizontal position of the point and is called 'the x-coordinate' of a point. The second number refers to the vertical position of the point and is called 'the y-coordinate' of a point. The coordinates of the origin are (0, 0).
- To locate a point on the Cartesian plane, move along the x-axis to the number indicated by the x-coordinate and then along the y-axis to the number indicated by the y-coordinate. For example, to locate the point with coordinates (1, 2), move 1 unit to the right of the origin and then 2 units up.

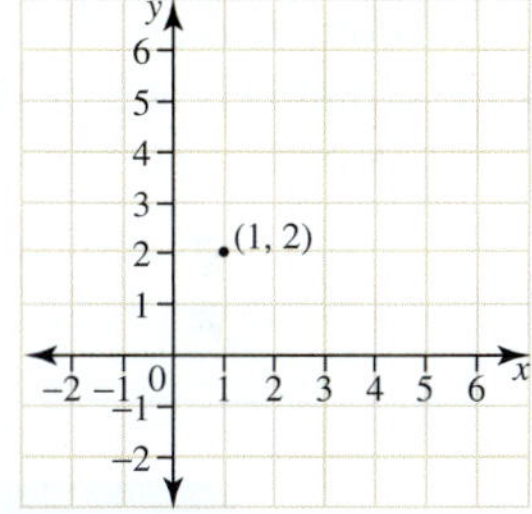

WORKED EXAMPLE 1

Draw a Cartesian plane that goes from –3 to 5 on the x-axis and –3 to 5 on the y-axis and plot the following points.

a **A(1, 2)** **b** **B(3, –2)** **c** **C$(-2, -2\frac{1}{2})$**
d **D(0, –1)** **e** **E(–2, 0)**

THINK

1. Draw a Cartesian plane that extends from –3 to 5 on both the x- and y-axes.
2. Find and plot the position of each point, and then label.
   - **a** Across to 1 on the x-axis and then up to 2 on the y-axis.
   - **b** Across to 3 on the x-axis and then down to –2 on the y-axis.
   - **c** Across to –2 on the x-axis and then down to $-2\frac{1}{2}$ on the y-axis.
   - **d** Stay at the origin (0 on the x-axis) and then down to –1 on the y-axis.
   - **e** Across to –2 on the x-axis and then stay at 0 on the y-axis.

DRAW

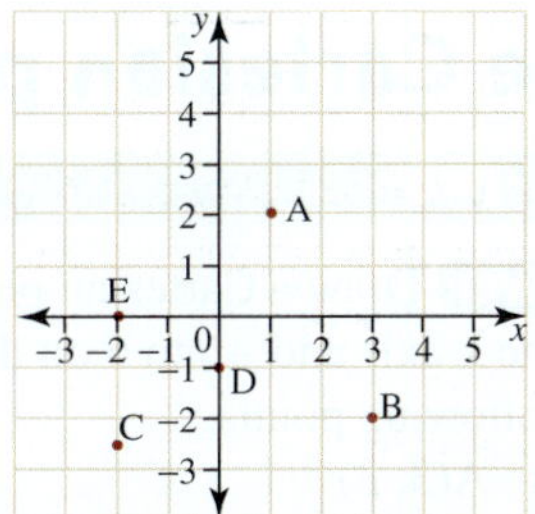

WORKED EXAMPLE 2

Write the Cartesian coordinates of the points A to E marked on the Cartesian plane at right.

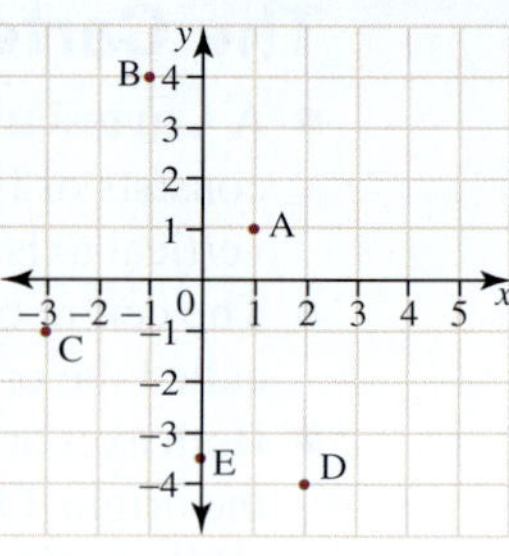

THINK	WRITE
1 Trace along the x-axis to find the first number, and then along the y-axis to find the second number. Point A is at 1 on the x-axis and 1 on the y-axis. Point B is at −1 on the x-axis and 4 on the y-axis. Point C is at −3 on the x-axis and −1 on the y-axis. Point D is at 2 on the x-axis and −4 on the y-axis. Point E is at 0 on the x-axis and $-3\frac{1}{2}$ on the y-axis.	
2 Write each point as a pair of coordinates.	A(1, 1) B(−1, 4) C(−3, −1) D(2, −4) E$(0, -3\frac{1}{2})$

REMEMBER

1. The Cartesian plane has a horizontal axis called the x-axis and a vertical axis called the y-axis.
2. The two axes cross at the origin, which has the coordinates (0, 0).
3. A Cartesian coordinate is written as (x, y).
4. The first number gives the position on the x-axis, and the second number gives the position on the y-axis.
5. To locate a point on the Cartesian plane, go across on the x-axis to the first number, and then up or down on the y-axis to the second number.

EXERCISE 14A The Cartesian plane

INDIVIDUAL PATHWAYS

eBook*plus*

Activity 14-A-1
The Cartesian plane
doc-6940

Activity 14-A-2
Using the Cartesian plane
doc-6941

Activity 14-A-3
Extending the Cartesian plane
doc-6942

FLUENCY

1 WE1 Draw a Cartesian plane that extends from −6 to 6 on the x-axis and −6 to 6 on the y-axis and plot and label the following points.

a A(3, 3) **b** B(2, 5)
c C(5, 1) **d** D(−1, 4)
e E(−4, 2) **f** F(−2, 0)
g G(−2, −3) **h** H(−4, −5)
i I(0, −3) **j** J(1, −2)
k K$(3, -1\frac{1}{2})$ **l** L$(4\frac{1}{2}, 0)$

2 WE2 Write the Cartesian coordinates of the points A to M marked on the Cartesian plane at right.

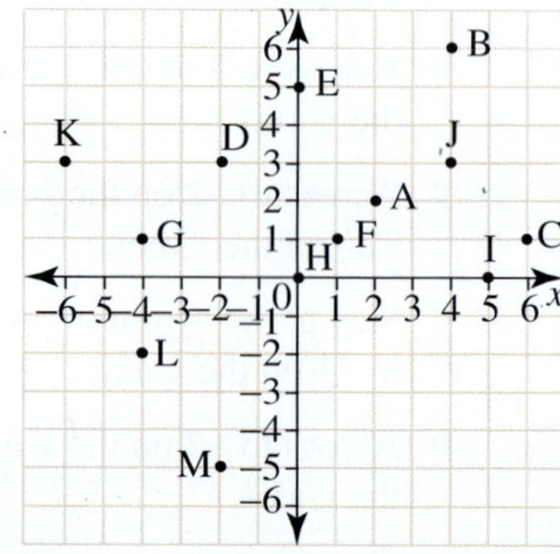

UNDERSTANDING

3 MC *Note:* There may be more than one correct answer.

a The point (3, 4) gives a position on the Cartesian plane of:

- **A** 3 on the y-axis, 4 on the x-axis
- **B** 3 left, 4 up
- **C** 4 right, 3 up
- **D** 3 on the x-axis, 4 on the y-axis
- **E** 3 right, 4 up

b The point (–2, 0) gives a position on the Cartesian plane of:

- **A** left 2, up 0
- **B** left 0, down 2
- **C** –2 on the x-axis, 0 on the y-axis
- **D** –2 on the y-axis, 0 on the x-axis.
- **E** 2 on the x-axis, 0 on the y-axis

4 On 1-cm graph paper, draw a Cartesian plane with an x-axis from –5 to 5 and a y-axis from –3 to 5. Connect these three groups of points.
START (0, 5) (–3, –3) (5, 2) (–5, 2) (3, –3) (0, 5) STOP
START (5, 2) (0, 0) (–5, 2) STOP
START (3, –3) (0, 0) (–3, –3) STOP

5 On 1-cm graph paper, draw a Cartesian plane with an x-axis from –6 to 6 and a y-axis from –6 to 6. Connect these groups of points.
START (4, 6) (–4, 6) (–6, 0) (–4, –6) (4, –6) (6, 0) (4, 6) (–6, 0) (4, –6) (4, 6) STOP
START (–4, 6) (–4, –6) (6, 0) (–4, 6) STOP
START (4, 0) (2, 2.5) (–2, 2.5) (–4, 0) (–2, –2.5) (2, –2.5) (4, 0) STOP
Colour the 6 triangles between the star and the hexagon. For example the triangle (6, 0) (4, 6) (4, 1) could be coloured red. Colour the 6 triangles inside the star. For example (4, 0) (4, 1) (2, 2.5) could be coloured green.

6 Draw a Cartesian plane using the following points. First check the coordinates to find the lowest and highest x- and y-values needed on each axis. Connect these groups of points.
START (4, 1) (3, 1) (4, 3) (5, 3) (5.5, 4) (5.5, 5) (6, 6) (6, 7) (5, 7.5) (4, 7.5) (3, 7.5) (2, 8) (1.5, 9) (1.5, 10) (2, 11) (3, 12) (4, 12.5) (5, 13) (6, 14) (7, 15) (8, 15) (10, 14) (11, 11) (11, 10) (10.5, 8.5) (10, 7.5) (9, 10.5) (8.5, 8) (7.5, 7) (8, 6.5) (8, 5) (9, 4) (10, 3) (10, 1) (4, 1) STOP
START (2, 8) (1.5, 7.5) (1, 8) (1.5, 9) STOP
START (4, 1) (4, 2) (5, 2.5) (6.5, 2.5) (5.5, 4) STOP
START (6, 6.5) (8, 6.5) (8, 6) (6, 6) STOP
EYE AT (5.5, 11)

7 Draw a Cartesian plane. Check the following coordinates to find the lowest and highest x- and y-value needed on the axes. Then draw a cartoon character.
START (6, 7) (7.5, 9) (5, 9) (4.5, 12) (2, 11) (0, 13) (–1.5, 10) (–5, 11) (–5, 8) (–8, 6) (–6, 4) (–8, 2) (–6, 1) (–7, –2) (–4, –1.5) (–4, –3.5) (–1.5, –3) (–2, –4) (–4, –7) (–5, –8) STOP
START (–2, –9) (–1, –7) (1, –8) (3, –8) (4, –7.5) (5, –10) STOP
START (4, –7.5) (3.5, –6) (3.5, –4) (4, –3) (5, –2.5) (5, –2) (4, –1.5) (4, –1) (5, 0.5) (7, 1) (8, 2) (8, 2.5) (6.5, 3) STOP
START (4, –2.5) (2, –3) (0.5, –3) (0, –2) (1, –1) (2, –0.5) (3, 0) (7, 1) STOP
START (6, 2.5) (6.5, 3) (6.5, 4) (6, 4) (4, 3) STOP
START (6, 7) (5, 7.5) (4, 7) (3, 6) (1, 6) (0, 5) (–1, 4) (0, 2) (1.5, 1.5) (3, 2) (4, 4) (6.5, 4) (7, 5) (7, 6) (6, 7) STOP
START (4, 4) (4, 5) (3, 6) STOP
START (1, –1) (5, 0) STOP
EYES AT (1, 3) AND (5, 5)
EYE LASHES (–1, 4) TO (–2, 4.5), (0, 5) TO (–0.5, 6), (1, 6) TO (0.5, 7), (2, 6) TO (2, 7), (4, 7) TO (3.5, 8), (5, 7.5) TO (5, 8.5), (6, 7) TO (6.5, 8), (6.5, 6.5) TO (7, 7)

8 On a piece of graph paper, draw a Cartesian plane that covers the entire page. Draw a simple picture on your graph paper. List the coordinates and instructions showing when to start and stop joining the points. The coordinates should be chosen carefully so that someone else can draw your picture, following your instructions.

REFLECTION

Think of an alternative way (that is, other than Cartesian coordinates) to specify the position of a point on a plane.

14B Linear patterns

- A set of points may be such that the x- and y-coordinates of each point are connected by the same rule. For example, each of the points (1, 2) (2, 3) (3, 4) (4, 5) have the same relationship (rule) between their x- and y-values; namely, the y-coordinate of every point is one more than its x-coordinate.
- If the set of points where x- and y-coordinates are connected by a certain rule is plotted on the Cartesian plane, the points will form a pattern.
- If the pattern formed by the set of points is a straight line, we refer to it as a linear pattern. For example, the points (1, 2) (2, 3) (3, 4) (4, 5), when plotted, will form a linear pattern as seen below.
- A diagram formed by plotting a set of points on the Cartesian plane is referred to as a graph. If the points form a straight line, then the graph is linear (a straight-line graph).
- A set of points with their coordinates can be presented in the form of a table. For example, the points (−2, 4) (−1, 2) (0, 0) (1, −2) (2, −4) can be presented as shown.

x	−2	−1	0	1	2
y	4	2	0	−2	−4

WORKED EXAMPLE 3

Plot the following points on a Cartesian plane and comment on any pattern formed. Check the lowest and highest values to help you decide the numbers to mark on the axes.
(−2, 1) (−1, 2) (0, 3) (1, 4) (2, 5)

THINK

1 Look at the x- and y-values of the points and draw a Cartesian plane.
The lowest value for the x-axis is −2, the highest is 2.
The lowest value for the y-axis is 1, the highest is 5.
Extend each axis slightly beyond these values.

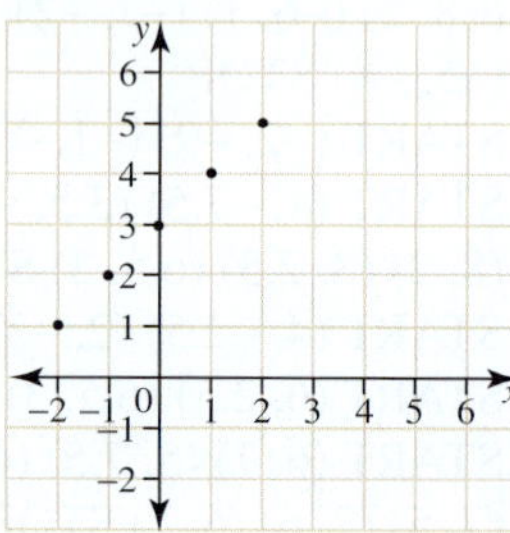

2 Plot each point.

3 Comment on any pattern formed.

A linear pattern is obtained as the points form a straight line.

WORKED EXAMPLE 4

a **Plot the points in the table at right on a Cartesian plane.**

x	−4	−3	−2	−1	0	1
y	−2	−1	0	1	2	3

b **Do the points form a linear graph? If so, what would the next point in the pattern be?**

THINK | WRITE/DRAW

a 1 Look at the x- and y-values of the points and draw a Cartesian plane.

2 Plot each point.

a

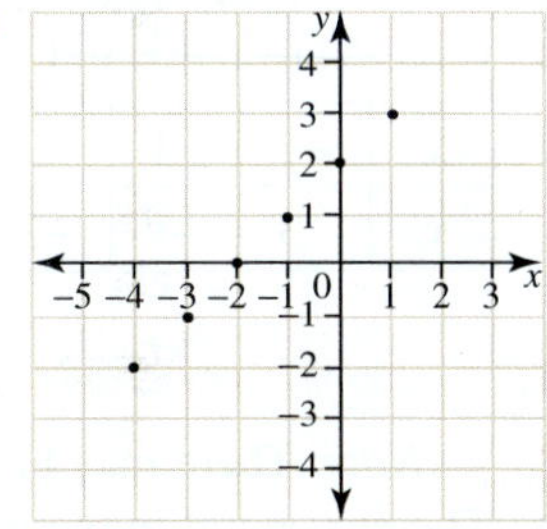

b 1 Look at the position of the points and answer the question.
Note: The points form a straight line, so we have a linear graph.

b Yes, the points do form a linear graph.

2 Study the pattern and answer the question.
Note: The pattern shows that the x-values increase by 1, and the y-values increase by 1. The next x-value will be 2 and the next y-value will be 4.

The next point in the pattern is (2, 4).

REMEMBER

1. Linear means 'in a straight line'.
2. When coordinates form a straight line on a Cartesian plane, we have a linear graph.

EXERCISE 14B Linear patterns

INDIVIDUAL PATHWAYS

eBook*plus*

Activity 14-B-1 Linear patterns doc-6943

Activity 14-B-2 More linear patterns doc-6944

Activity 14-B-3 Advanced linear patterns doc-6945

FLUENCY

1 WE3 Plot the points on a Cartesian plane and comment on any pattern formed. (Check the lowest and highest values to help you decide which numbers to mark on the axes.)

- **a** (−2, −3) (−1, −2) (0, −1) (1, 0) (2, 1)
- **b** (−2, 0) (−1, 1) (0, 2) (1, 3) (2, 4)
- **c** (−2, −4) (−1, −2) (0, 0) (1, 2) (2, 4)
- **d** (−2, −5) (−1, −2) (0, 1) (1, 4) (2, 7)
- **e** (−2, 2) (−1, 1) (0, 0) (1, −1) (2, −2)
- **f** (−2, 0) (−1, −1) (0, −2) (1, −3) (2, −4)

2 WE4a Plot the following points on a Cartesian plane.

a

x	−2	−1	0	1	2
y	1	2	3	4	5

b

x	−2	−1	0	1	2
y	−2	−1	0	1	2

c

x	−2	−1	0	1	2
y	−7	−4	−1	2	5

d

x	−2	−1	0	1	2
y	3	2	1	0	−1

e

x	−2	−1	0	1	2
y	−1	−0.5	0	0.5	1

f

x	−2	−1	0	1	2
y	4	2	0	−2	−4

3 WE4b Plot the following points on a Cartesian plane. Do the points form a linear graph? If so, state the next point in the pattern.

a (−3, −3) (−2, −1) (−1, 1) (0, 3) (1, 5) (2, 7) (3, 9)

b (−3, −5) (−2, −3) (−1, 0) (0, 1) (1, 4) (2, 5) (3, 7)

c

x	−2	−1	0	1	2
y	3	−1	−2	−3	−4

d

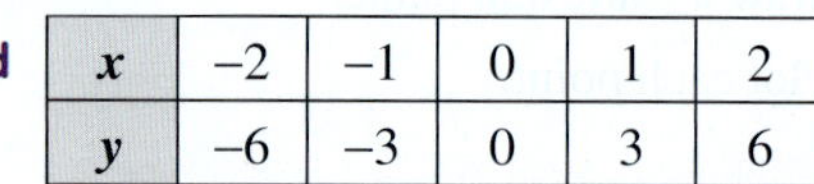

x	−2	−1	0	1	2
y	−6	−3	0	3	6

UNDERSTANDING

4 MC (*Note:* There may be more than one correct answer.)

a The next point in the linear pattern made by (−2, 0) (−1, 1) (0, 2) (1, 3) (2, 4) is:

A (5, 3) **B** (−3, −5) **C** (3, −5) **D** (3, 5) **E** (4, 6)

b The next point in the linear pattern made by (−2, 9) (−1, 8) (0, 7) (1, 6) (2, 5) is:

A (−3, 8) **B** (3, 4) **C** (3, 6) **D** (4, 3) **E** (6, 3)

c The next point in the linear pattern made by (−2, −18) (−1, −14) (0, −10) (1, −6) (2, −2) is:

A (−3, 3) **B** (−3, −20) **C** (3, 2) **D** (4, 6) **E** (6, 16)

eBook*plus*

Digital doc
Spreadsheet
Plotting points
doc-2439

d Which of the following set of points would make a linear pattern?

A (−2, −1) (−1, −2) (0, −3) (1, −4) (2, −5)

B (−2, 12) (−1, 10) (0, 8) (1, 6) (2, 4)

C (−2, −1) (−1, 0) (0, 1) (1, −1) (2, 0)

D (−2, −5) (−1, 0) (0, 4) (1, 5) (2, 8)

E (−2, 0) (−1, 3) (0, 6) (1, 9) (2, 12)

eBook*plus*

Digital doc
WorkSHEET 14.1
doc-2416

5 Plot the following points on a Cartesian plane and join the points with a straight line.

a (−3, −2) (0, 1) (1, 2) (4, 5)

b (−2, 4) (0, 2) (1, 1) (3, −1)

c (−1, −1) (0, −3) ($1\frac{1}{2}$, −6) (2, −7)

d ($-\frac{3}{2}$, −2) ($-\frac{1}{2}$, 0) (1, 3) (3, 7)

6 By extending each of the lines in question **5**, give three examples of points that also fit the same pattern and lie on the line.

REFLECTION

Is it possible to say whether or not a set of points will form a linear graph without actually plotting them?

14C Plotting linear graphs

- To plot the linear graphs whose equation is given, follow these steps.
  - (i) Create a table of values first.
    - Draw a table.
    - Select some x-values.
    - Substitute the selected x-values into the rule to find corresponding y-values.
  - (ii) Draw a Cartesian plane.
  - (iii) Plot the point from the table and join them with the straight line.
  - (iv) Label the graph.

WORKED EXAMPLE 5

Draw a table of values and plot the graph of $y = 2x + 1$ and label the line.

THINK

1. Write the rule.
2. Draw a table and choose simple x-values.
3. Use the rule to find each y-value and enter them in the table.
   When $x = -2$, $y = 2 \times -2 + 1 = -3$.
   When $x = -1$, $y = 2 \times -1 + 1 = -1$.
   When $x = 0$, $y = 2 \times 0 + 1 = 1$.
   When $x = 1$, $y = 2 \times 1 + 1 = 3$.
   When $x = 2$, $y = 2 \times 2 + 1 = 5$.
4. Draw a Cartesian plane and plot the points.
5. Join the points to form a straight line and label the graph.

WRITE/DRAW

$y = 2x + 1$

x	−2	−1	0	1	2
y	−3	−1	1	3	5

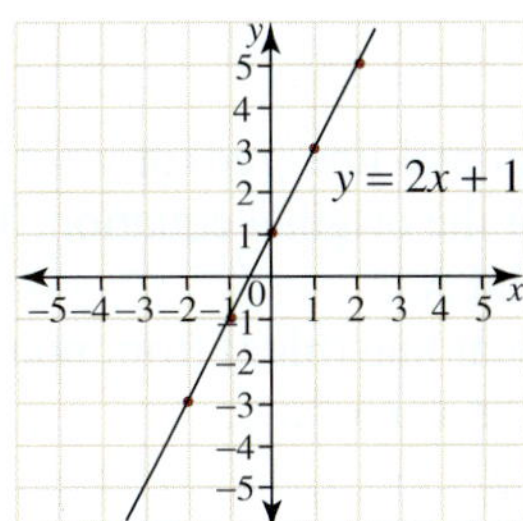

Function notation

- In mathematics, linear rules are also called **linear functions**.
- A linear function can be thought of as a machine with an 'input' of x and an 'output' of y.
- To write a rule in function notation, $f(x)$ is used in place of y.

WORKED EXAMPLE 6

Draw a table of values and plot the graph of $f(x) = -x + 2$.

THINK

1. Write the rule.
2. Draw a table and choose simple x-values.
3. Use the rule to find each function value and enter them in the table.
   Remember that $-x$ means $-1x$.
   When $x = -2$, $f(-2) = -1 \times -2 + 2 = 4$.
   When $x = -1$, $f(-1) = -1 \times -1 + 2 = 3$.
   When $x = 0$, $f(0) = -1 \times 0 + 2 = 2$.
   When $x = 1$, $f(1) = -1 \times 1 + 2 = 1$.
   When $x = 2$, $f(2) = -1 \times 2 + 2 = 0$.
4. Draw a Cartesian plane and plot the points.
5. Join the points to form a straight line and label the graph.

WRITE/DRAW

$f(x) = -x + 2$

x	−2	−1	0	1	2
$f(x)$	4	3	2	1	0

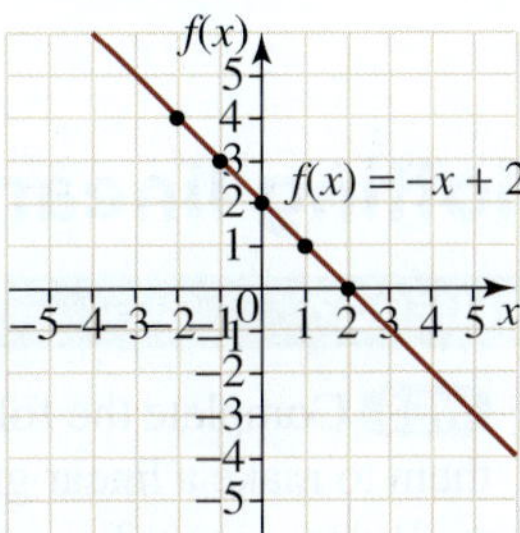

- Linear graphs can also be used to solve linear equations.

WORKED EXAMPLE 7

Use the graph at right to solve the linear equation $2x + 5 = 15$.

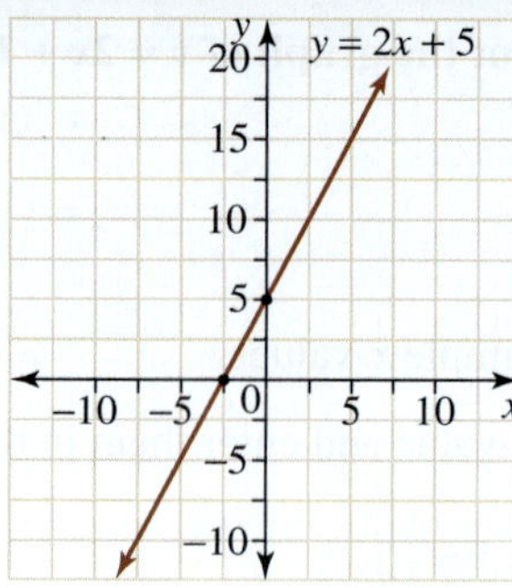

THINK

WRITE

1. Rule a horizontal line (red) at $y = 15$. This is the right-hand side of the original equation. This line meets the graph at point A.
   Rule a vertical line (blue) from point A to the x-axis. The line meets the x-axis at 5.

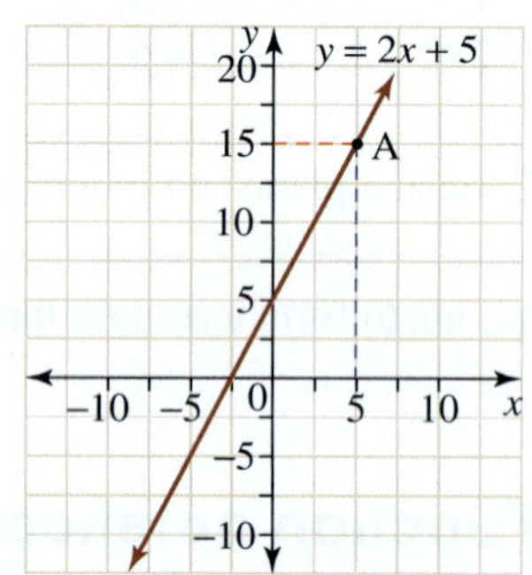

2. The solution to the linear equation $2x + 5 = 15$ is $x = 5$.

The solution to the linear equation $2x + 5 = 15$ is $x = 5$.

REMEMBER

To plot a linear graph, follow these steps.
1. Draw a table and choose some x-values.
2. Substitute each x-value into the rule to obtain the corresponding y-value.
3. Plot these coordinates as points on a Cartesian plane.
4. Rule a straight line through the plotted points.
5. Label the line with a rule.
6. To write a rule in function notation, $f(x)$ is used in place of y.

EXERCISE 14C Plotting linear graphs

FLUENCY

1 WE5 Complete the following tables of values, plot the points on a Cartesian plane, and join them to make a linear graph. Label the graphs with the rules.

a Rule: $y = x + 3$

x	−2	−1	0	1	2
y	1	2	3		

b Rule: $f(x) = x - 5$

x	−2	−1	0	1	2
$f(x)$		−6			−3

INDIVIDUAL PATHWAYS

eBook*plus*

Activity 14-C-1
Plotting linear graphs
doc-6946

Activity 14-C-2
More graphs of linear functions
doc-6947

Activity 14-C-3
Advanced linear functions
doc-6948

c Rule: $y = 5x$

x	−2	−1	0	1	2
y	−10		0		

d Rule: $f(x) = 2x + 4$

x	−2	−1	0	1	2
$f(x)$	0			6	

e Rule: $y = 3x + 2$

x	−2	−1	0	1	2
y					

f Rule: $f(x) = 2x - 2$

x	−2	−1	0	1	2
$f(x)$		−4			

g Rule: $y = 4x - 3$

x	−2	−1	0	1	2
y					

h Rule: $f(x) = -3x + 2$

x	−2	−1	0	1	2
$f(x)$		5			−4

2 a MC $y = 3x + 4$ means:

A The y-value equals the x-value, add 3 and then times 4.
B The y-value equals the x-value times 3 and then add 4.
C The x-value equals the y-value times 3 and then add 4.
D The y-value equals 4 times the x-value divided by 3.
E The x-value equals 4 times the y-value and then add 3.

b A table of values shows:

A a rule
B coordinates
C a linear graph
D an axis
E that a rule continues forever

3 WE6 Draw a table of values and plot the graph for each of the following rules. Label each graph.

a $y = x + 2$
b $f(x) = x - 4$
c $y = x - 1$
d $f(x) = x + 5$
e $y = 3x$
f $f(x) = 7x$
g $y = 4x + 1$
h $f(x) = 2x - 3$
i $y = 3x - 5$
j $f(x) = -2x$
k $y = -6x + 2$
l $f(x) = -5x + 4$

4 WE7 For each of the following, use the graph shown to solve the linear equation given.

a $3x + 5 = 8$

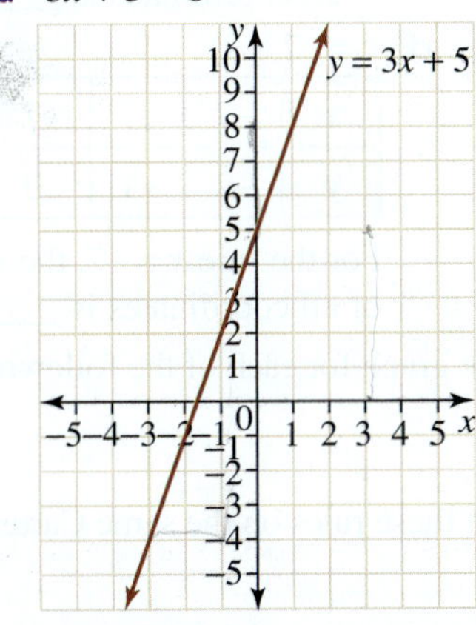

b $-5x + 6 = -9$

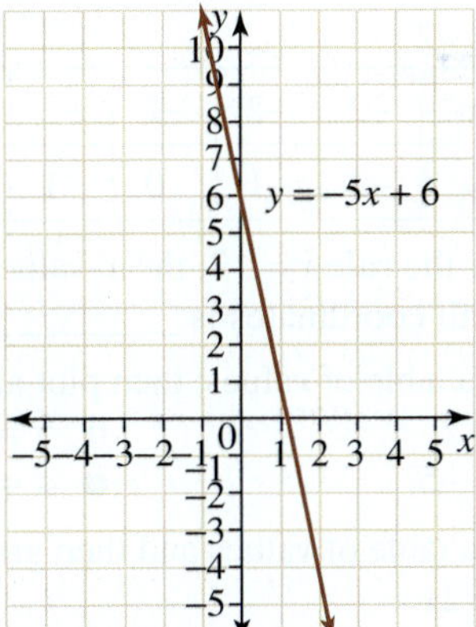

c $0.5x - 1 = -4$

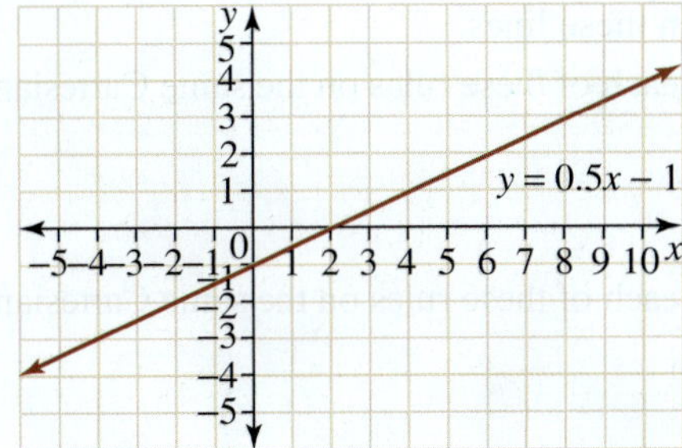

UNDERSTANDING

eBook*plus*

Digital doc
Spreadsheet
Plotting graphs with table
doc-2441

5 Plot a graph of the following rules from the tables of values provided. Label the graphs. Then copy and complete the sentences.

a $y = 4$

x	−2	−1	0	1	2
y	4	4	4	4	4

For the rule $y = 4$, the y-value of all coordinates is ____________.

b $y = 1$

x	−2	−1	0	1	2
y	1	1	1	1	1

For the rule $y = 1$, the y-value of all coordinates is ____________.

c $y = -2$

x	−2	−1	0	1	2
y	−2	−2	−2	−2	−2

For the rule $y = -2$, the y-value of all coordinates is ____________.

d $y = -5$

x	−2	−1	0	1	2
y	−5	−5	−5	−5	−5

For the rule $y = -5$, the y-value of all coordinates is ____________.

6 Make a table of values and plot the graph for each of the following rules.

a $y = 3$
b $y = 2$
c $y = -2$
d $y = -4$

7 Plot the graph of each of the following rules from the table of values provided. Label the graph. Then copy and complete the sentence.

a $x = 1$

x	1	1	1	1	1
y	−2	−1	0	1	2

For the rule $x = 1$, the x-value of all coordinates is ____________.

b $x = 3$

x	3	3	3	3	3
y	−2	−1	0	1	2

For the rule $x = 3$, the x-value of all coordinates is ____________.

c $x = -2$

x	−2	−2	−2	−2	−2
y	−2	−1	0	1	2

For the rule $x = -2$, the x-value of all coordinates is ____________.

d $x = -7$

x	−7	−7	−7	−7	−7
y	−2	−1	0	1	2

For the rule $x = -7$, the x-value of all coordinates is ____________.

8 Make a table of values; then plot and label the graph for each of the following.

a $x = 2$
b $x = 5$
c $x = -5$
d $x = 0$

9 Draw a table of values and then graph each of these rules on the same Cartesian plane.

a $y = 2x$
b $y = 2x - 1$
c $y = 2x + 1$

Describe the relationship between these lines.

10 Draw a table of values and graph each of these rules on the same Cartesian plane.

a $f(x) = 3x + 1$
b $f(x) = -2x + 1$

What do you notice?

11 Draw a table of values and graph each of these rules on the same Cartesian plane.

a $y = -x$
b $y = x + 2$

What do you notice?

12 The monthly cost in dollars, C, of renting a mobile phone is given by the equation $C = 15 + 0.5x$, where x is the call time in minutes.

a Plot the graph of the equation.

b Use the graph to determine the cost of the phone bill for each of the months February, March, April and May.

c If July's bill was \$100, what was your call time?

d If August's bill was only \$50, what was your call time?

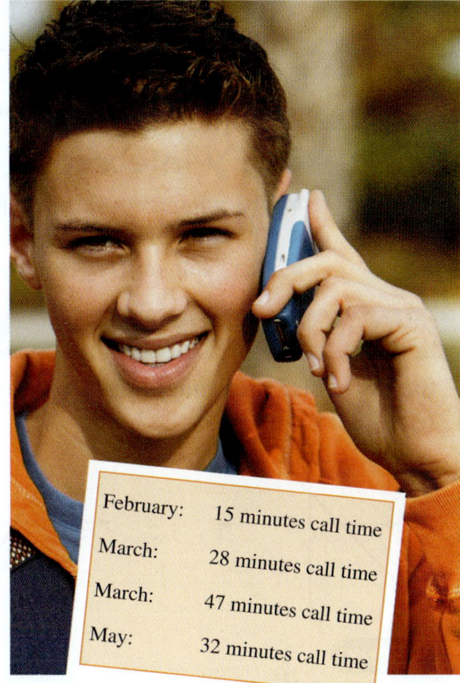

February: 15 minutes call time
March: 28 minutes call time
March: 47 minutes call time
May: 32 minutes call time

REFLECTION

How many points are needed to plot a linear graph?

14D Extension: The y-intercept and gradient

The gradient

- **Gradient** gives a measure of steepness. For example, the gradient of a road going up the hill would inform us of the steepness of the slope of the hill.
- The gradient of a straight line shows the change in vertical height as the horizontal distance increases by one unit.
- The gradient of a straight line is denoted by the letter m and is given by the formula: $m = \frac{\text{rise}}{\text{run}}$, where **rise** is the vertical distance between any two points on the line and **run** is the horizontal distance between the same two points.
- To find the gradient of a straight line on a Cartesian plane, draw a right-angled triangle anywhere along the line as shown below and use it to measure *rise* and *run*. The value of the gradient is given by the ratio $\frac{\text{rise}}{\text{run}}$. For example, in the diagram below, rise = 2 and run = 2, so the gradient $m = \frac{2}{2} = 1$.
- The gradient of a straight line is constant; that is, it will be the same when measured anywhere along the line.
- Since the gradient is the measure of steepness, the greater the value of the gradient, the steeper the line.
- If the line is horizontal, there is no slope; hence the value of the gradient is zero. If the line is vertical, we say that its gradient is **infinite** or **undefined**.

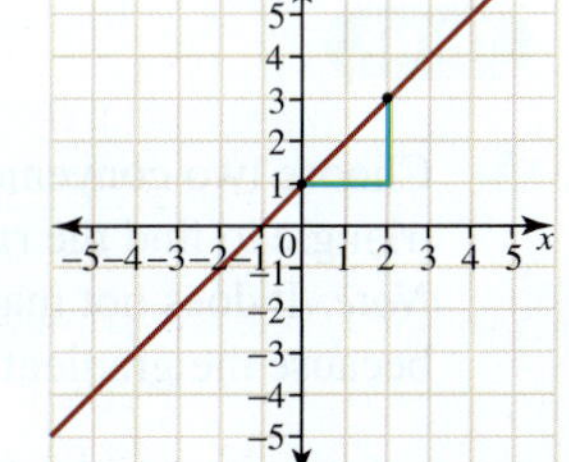

m is zero

m is undefined

- If the line slopes upwards from left to right (that is, it *rises*), the gradient is positive. If it slopes downwards from left to right (that is, it *falls*), the gradient is negative.

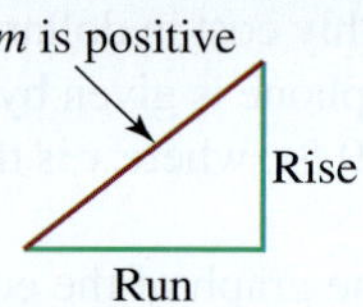

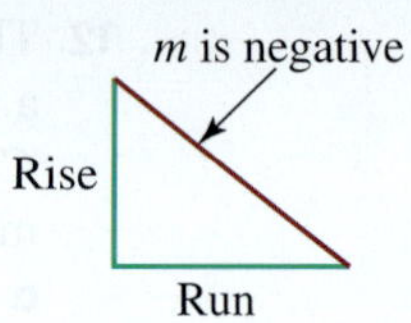

The *y*-intercept

- The *y*-intercept is the point where the graph crosses the *y*-axis.
- The symbol used to denote the *y*-intercept is *c*.
- The value of *c* is given by the *y*-coordinate of the *y*-intercept.

WORKED EXAMPLE 8

State whether these lines have a positive, negative, zero or undefined gradient.

a 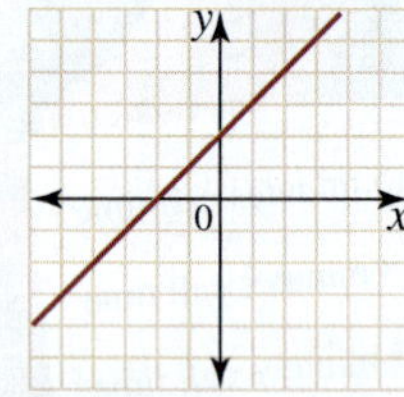

b 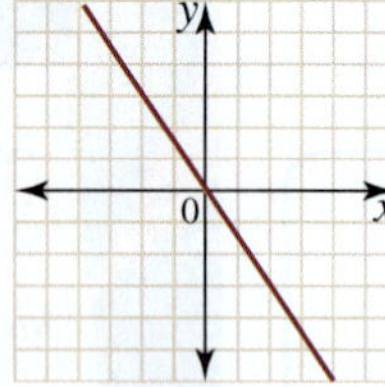

c 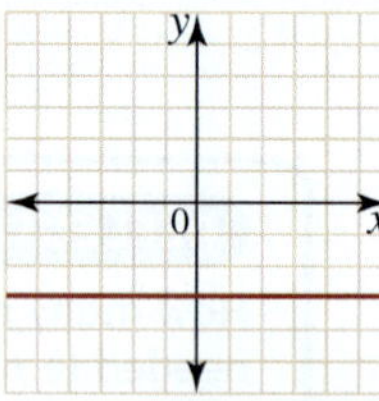

d 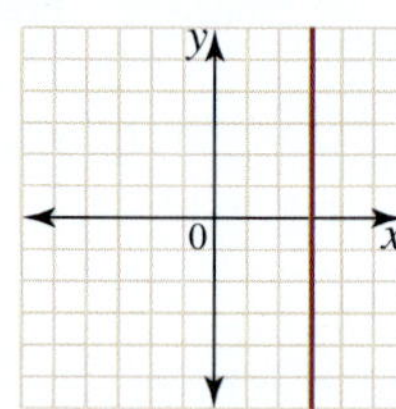

THINK	WRITE
a A line that rises from left to right, /, has a positive gradient.	**a** Positive gradient
b A line that drops from left to right, \, has a negative gradient.	**b** Negative gradient
c A line that is horizontal has a zero gradient.	**c** Zero gradient
d A line that is vertical has an undefined gradient.	**d** Undefined gradient

WORKED EXAMPLE 9

Find the gradient of the linear graph at right.

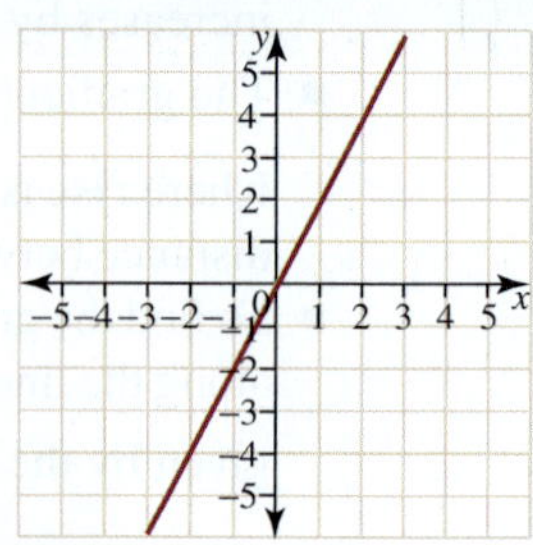

THINK	WRITE/DRAW
1 Choose two convenient points on the line and draw a triangle to find the rise and the run. *Note:* It does not matter which two points are chosen because the gradient of a straight line is constant.	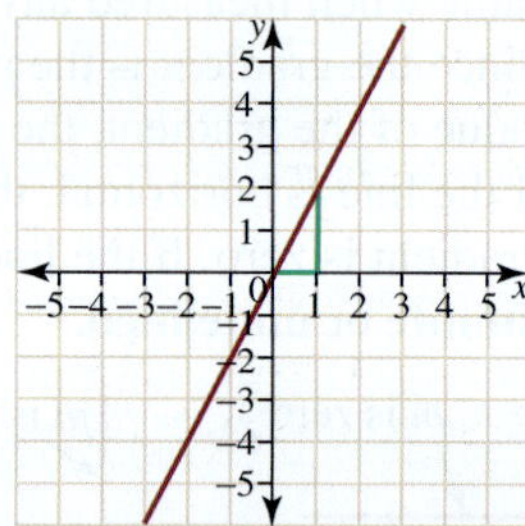

2 Read the rise and the run from the graph. — rise = 2, run = 1

3 Calculate the gradient. — Gradient: $m = \frac{\text{rise}}{\text{run}}$
$= \frac{2}{1}$
$= 2$

WORKED EXAMPLE 10

Find: a the gradient, *m*
b the *y*-intercept, *c*, of the linear graph at right.

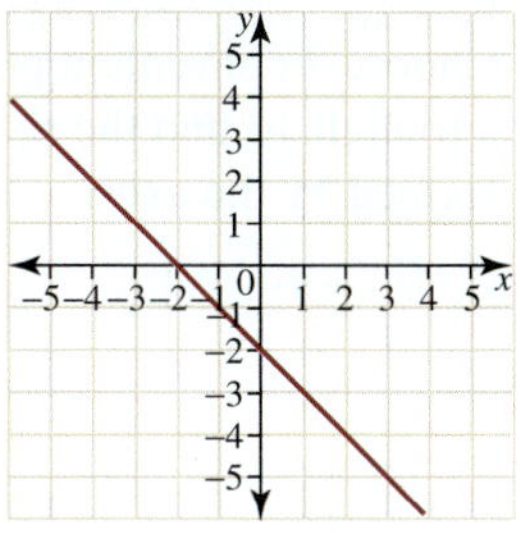

THINK / **WRITE/DRAW**

a 1 Choose two convenient points on the line and draw a triangle to find the rise and the run.

a

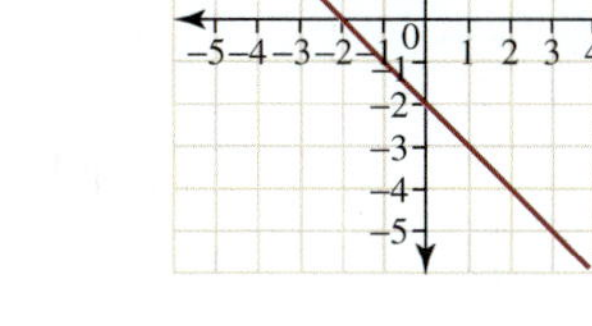

rise = −2, run = 2

2 Calculate the gradient. In this case the rise is negative since the line slopes down from left to right.

Gradient: $m = \frac{\text{rise}}{\text{run}} = \frac{-2}{2}$
$= -1$

b The *y*-intercept is where the graph crosses the *y*-axis, and *c* is the *y*-value at this point.

b $c = -2$

Finding the rule for the linear graph

- The **general rule** for all linear graphs is given by the equation $y = mx + c$, where x and y are variables, m is the gradient and c is the y-intercept.
- To find the equation of the line from its graph:
  - select any two points on the line, measure run and rise between these points and find the gradient; this gives the value of m;
  - locate the y-intercept (the point where the line crosses the y-axis) and read its y-coordinate; this gives the value of c;
  - substitute the values of m and c into $y = mx + c$ to obtain the equation of the given line.

WORKED EXAMPLE 11

For each of the linear graphs at right: Find the gradient, *m*, the *y*-intercept, *c*, and, using *m* and *c*, work out the rule.

a
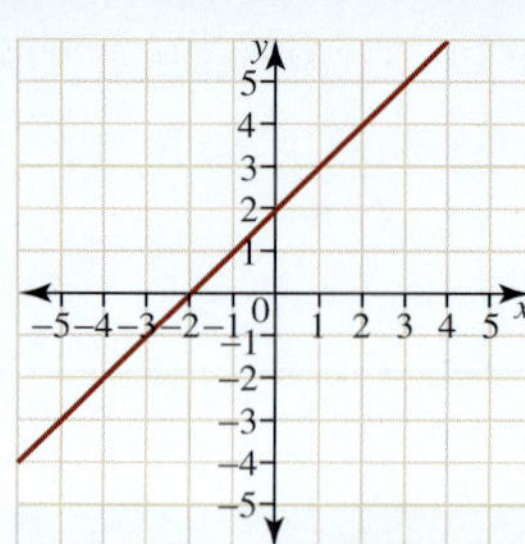

b
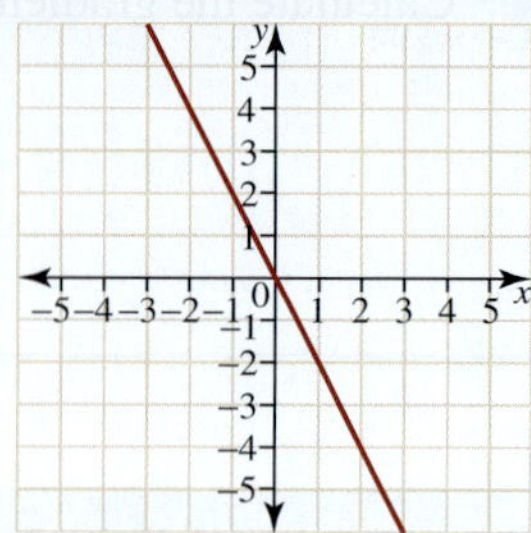

THINK / WRITE/DRAW

a 1 Choose 2 convenient points on the line and draw a triangle to find the rise and run. Use the triangle formed by the axes.

a
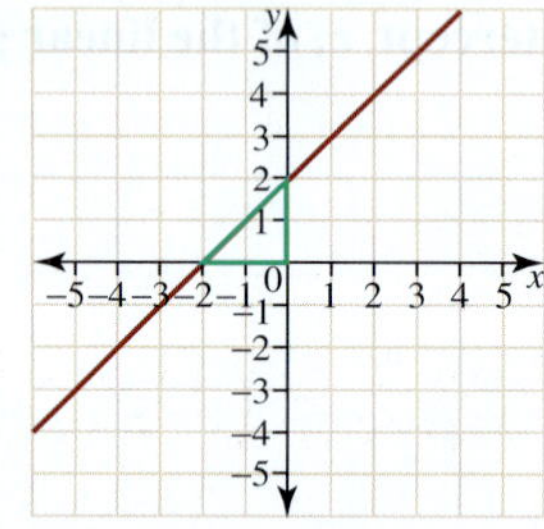

rise = 2, run = 2

2 Calculate the gradient.

Gradient: $m = \frac{\text{rise}}{\text{run}} = \frac{2}{2}$
$= 1$

3 State the value of c. The y-intercept is where the graph crosses the y-axis.

$c = 2$

4 Substitute the values of m and c into the general rule.

$y = mx + c$
$= 1 \times x + 2$
$= x + 2$

5 State the rule.

The rule is $y = x + 2$.

b 1 Choose 2 convenient points on the line and draw a triangle to find the rise and run. The rise is negative as the line slopes downwards from left to right.

b
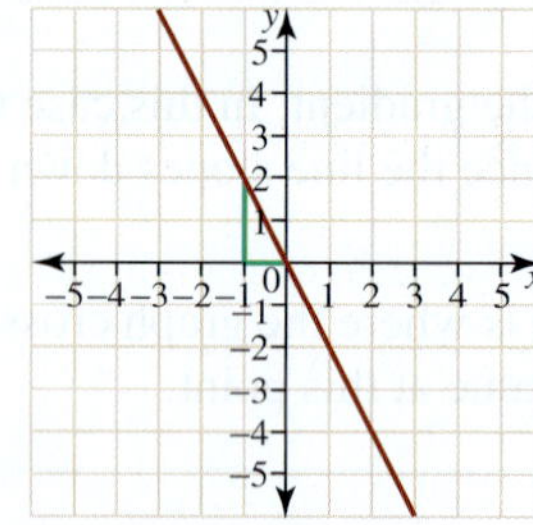

rise = −2, run = 1

2 Calculate the gradient.

Gradient: $m = \frac{\text{rise}}{\text{run}} = \frac{-2}{1}$
$= -2$

3 State the value of c. The y-intercept is where the graph crosses the y-axis.
Note: The graph passes through the origin.

$c = 0$

4 Substitute the values of m and c into the general rule.

$y = mx + c$
$= -2 \times x + 0$
$= -2x$

5 State the rule.

The rule is $y = -2x$.

WORKED EXAMPLE 12

State the gradient and *y*-intercept for each of the following linear rules.

a $y = 2x - 3$ **b** $y = -x + 1$

THINK		WRITE
a	1 Write the rule.	**a** $y = 2x - 3$
	2 Compare with the general rule.	$y = mx + c$
	3 The gradient is given by m.	Gradient: $m = 2$
	4 The y-intercept is given by c.	y-intercept: $c = -3$
b	1 Write the rule.	**b** $y = -x + 1$
	2 Compare with the general rule.	$y = mx + c$
	3 The gradient is given by m.	Gradient: $m = -1$
	4 The y-intercept is given by c.	y-intercept: $c = 1$

REMEMBER

1. Gradient is a measure of steepness and is denoted by the symbol m.
2. Gradient: $m = \frac{\text{rise}}{\text{run}}$.
3. The gradient of a straight line is constant.
4. A linear graph can have a positive gradient (/), a negative gradient (\ ), zero gradient (——) or an undefined gradient (|).
5. The y-intercept is where the graph crosses the y-axis. The symbol c stands for the y-value at this point.
6. The rule for any linear graph is given by:

$$y = mx + c$$

↑ Gradient ↑ y-intercept

EXERCISE 14D Extension: The *y*-intercept and gradient

INDIVIDUAL PATHWAYS

eBook*plus*

Activity 14-D-1 y-intercepts and gradients doc-6949

Activity 14-D-2 More y-intercepts and gradients doc-6950

Activity 14-D-3 Advanced y-intercepts and gradients doc-6951

FLUENCY

1 WE8 State whether each of the following lines has a positive, negative, zero or undefined gradient.

a
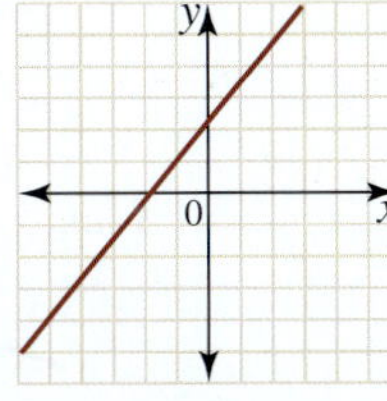

b
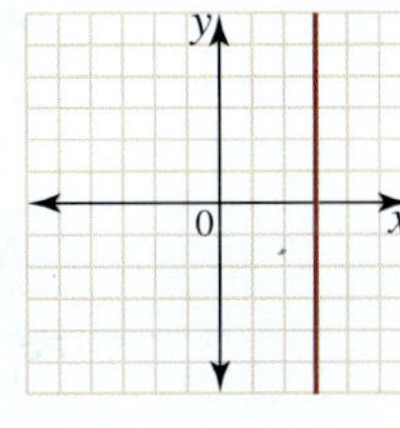

c
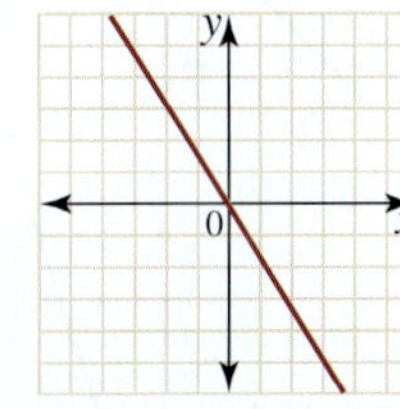

d
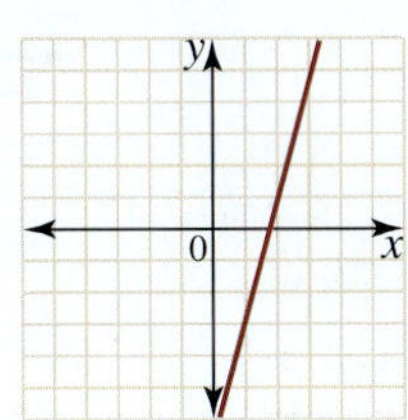

e
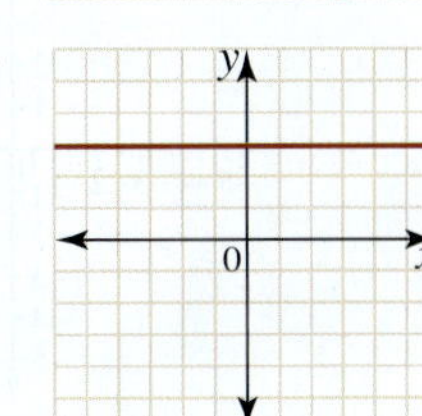

f
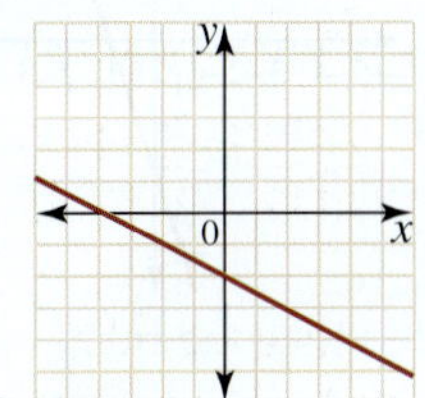

2 WE9 Find the gradient of the following linear graphs.

a
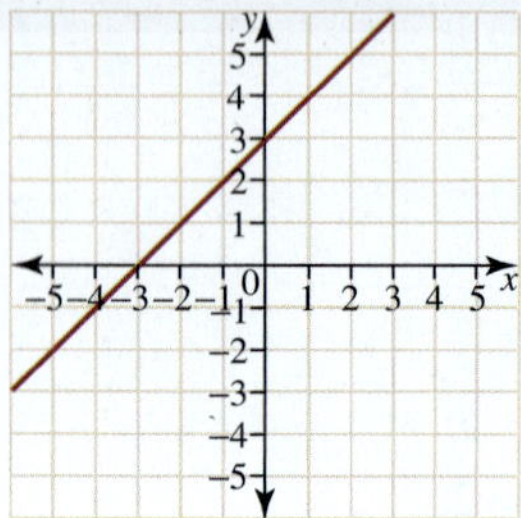

b
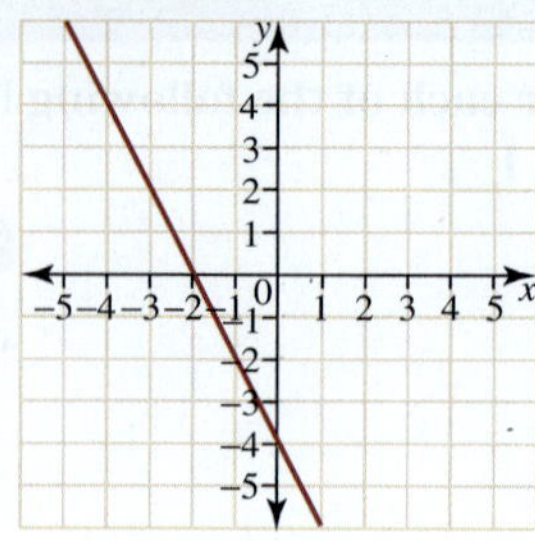

c
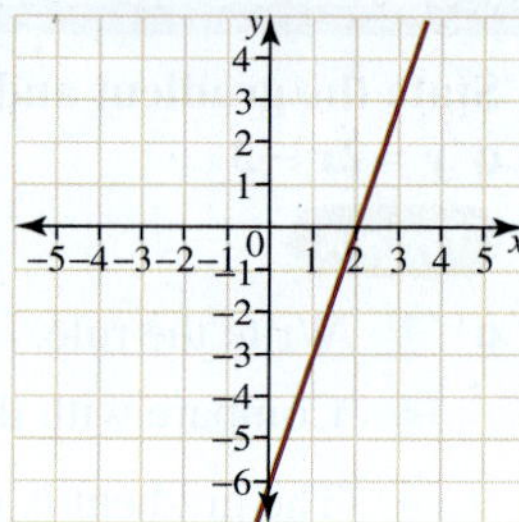

d
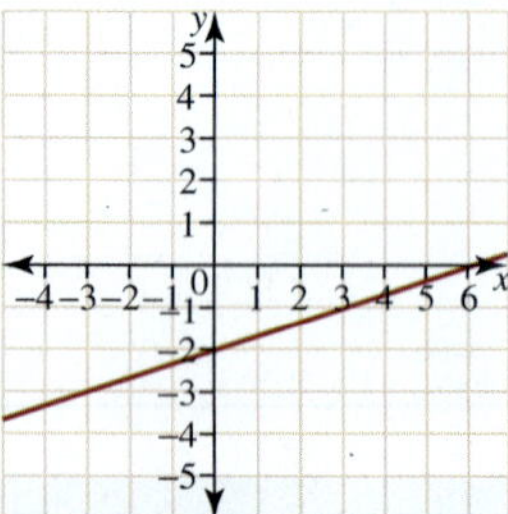

e
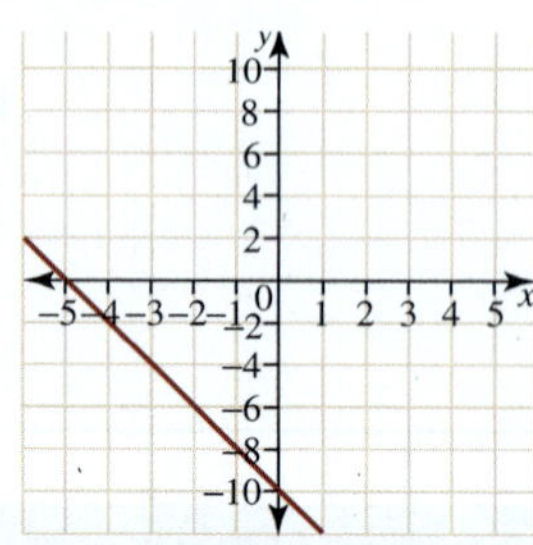

f
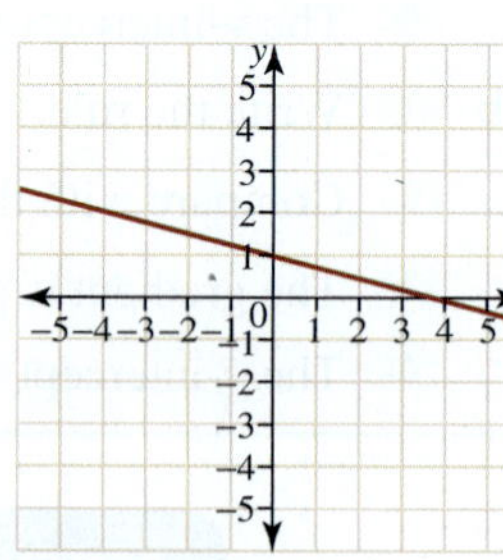

g
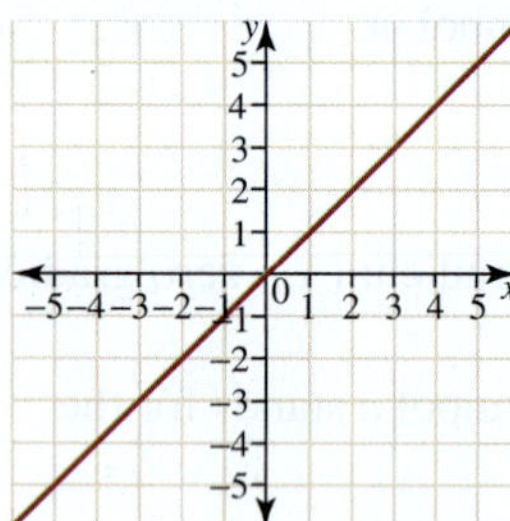

h
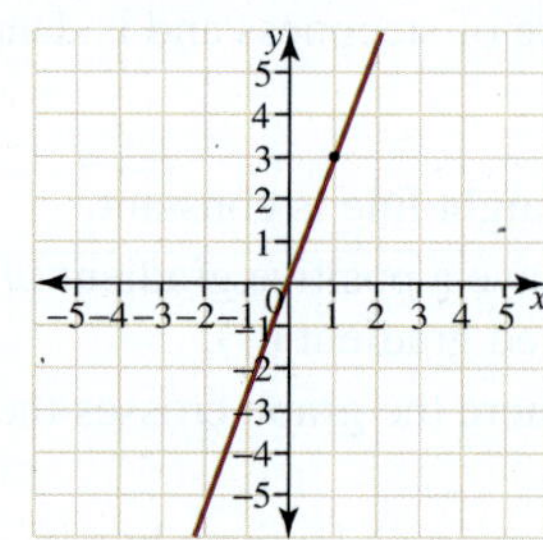

i
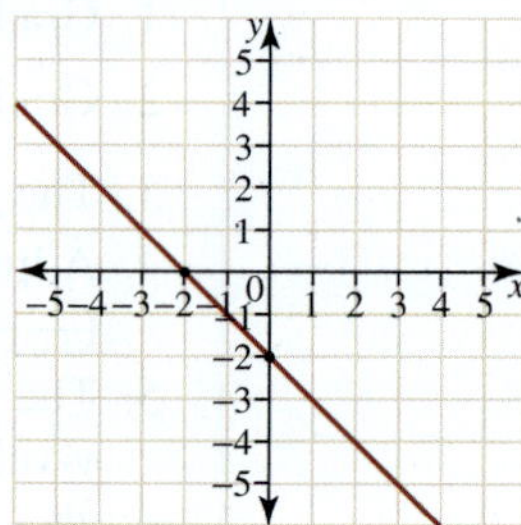

3 WE10 For each of the following linear graphs, find:

i the gradient, m

ii the y-intercept, c.

a
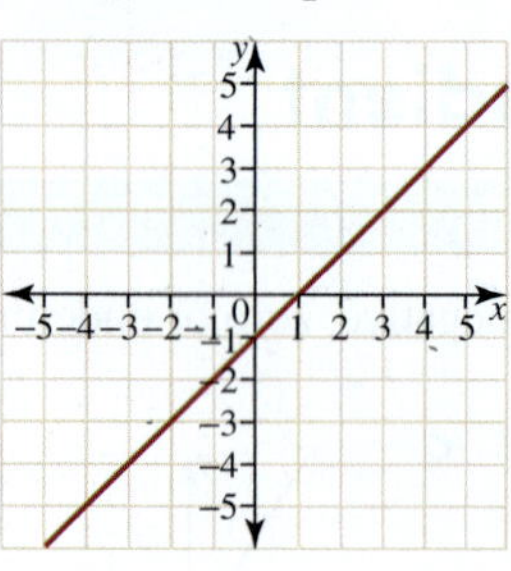

b
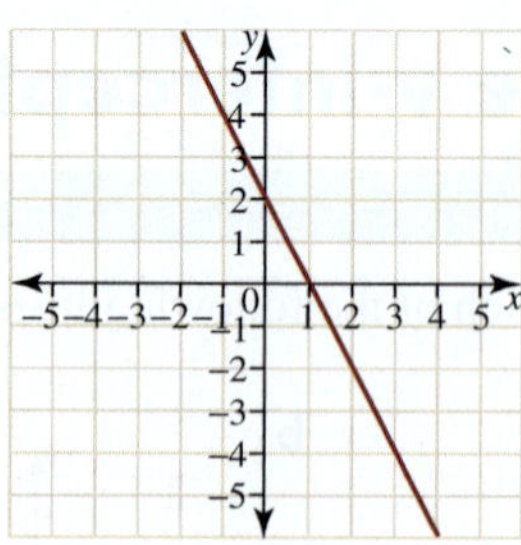

c
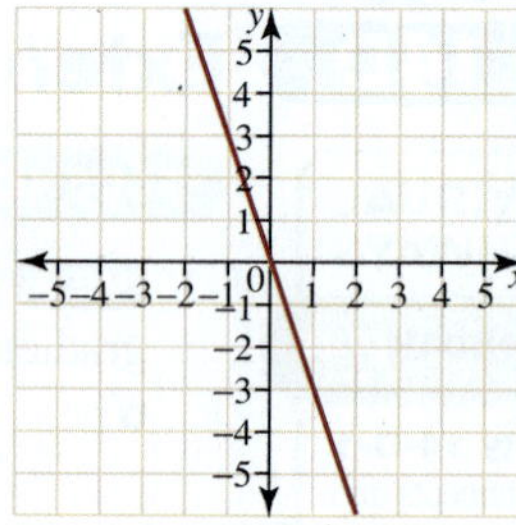

d
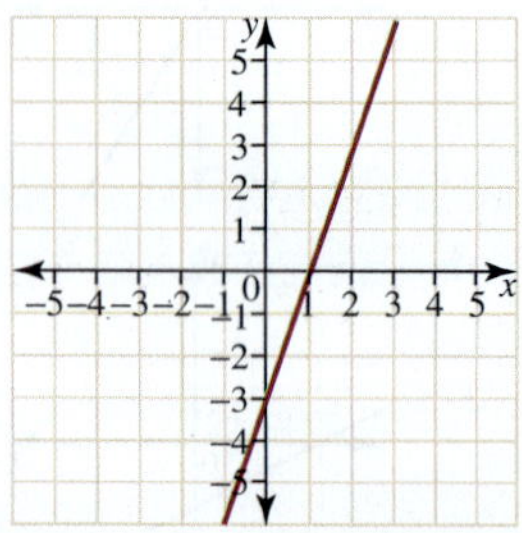

e
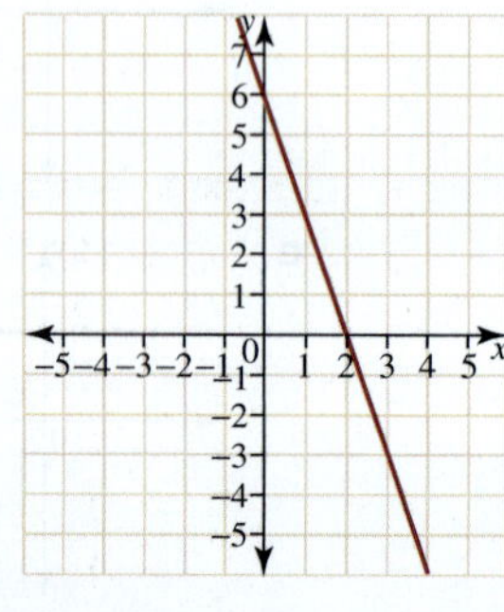

f
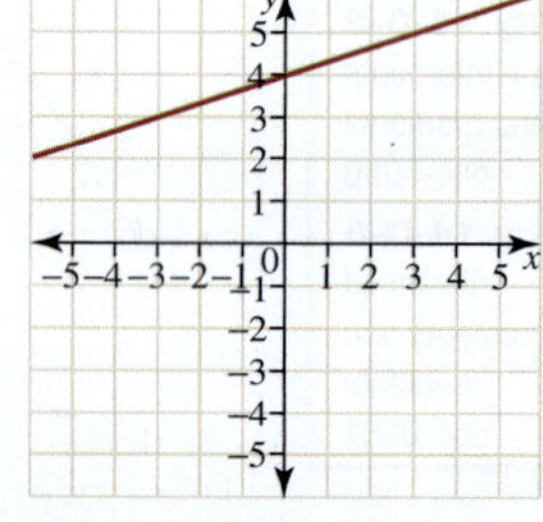

eBook*plus*

Digital doc
Spreadsheet
Plotting graphs with rule
doc-2443

4 MC For each of these graphs, choose the correct alternative.

a The gradient of this graph is:

A $\frac{1}{4}$ B -4 C 4 D $-\frac{1}{4}$ E 0

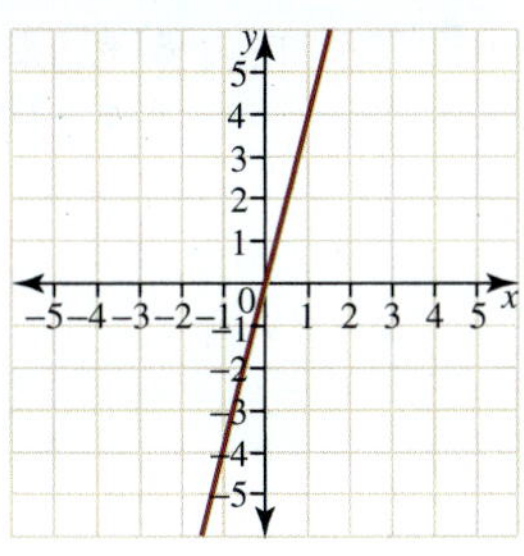

b The gradient and y-intercept of this graph are, respectively:

A 2, 4 B -2, 2 C -2, 4
D 2, 2 E -4, -2

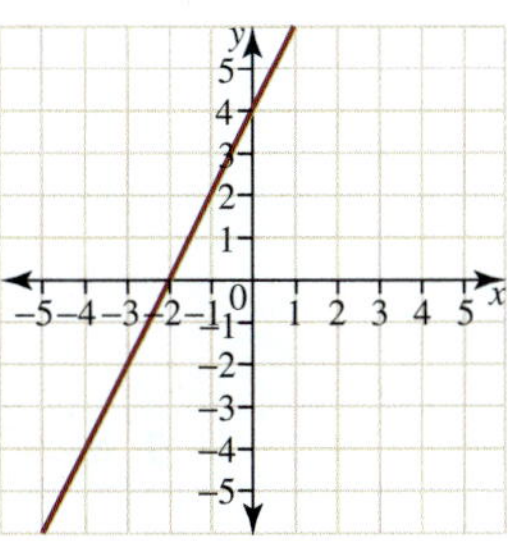

eBook*plus*

Digital doc
Spreadsheet
Gradient and intercepts
doc-2444

5 MC Hugo has developed greater skills with his skateboard. Earlier he mastered a ramp that has a run of 2 m and a rise of 1.5 m. The ramp has a gradient of:

A 0.75 B 3 C 1.5
D $-\frac{3}{2}$ E 2

6 WE11 For each of the following linear graphs, find **i** the gradient, m, **ii** the y-intercept, c, and, **iii** using m and c, work out the rule.

a
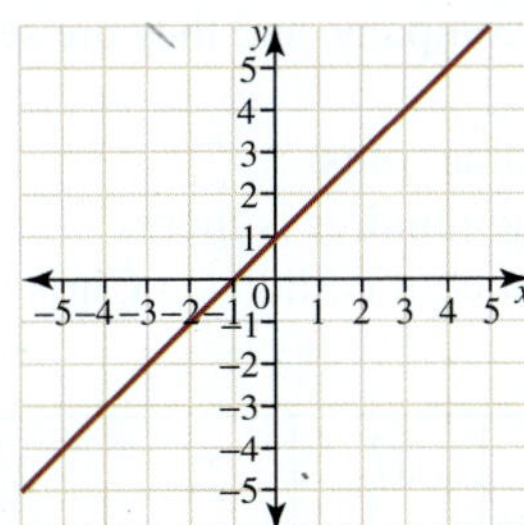

b
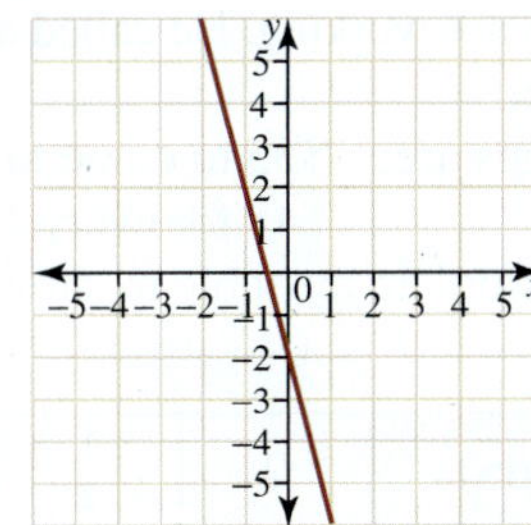

c
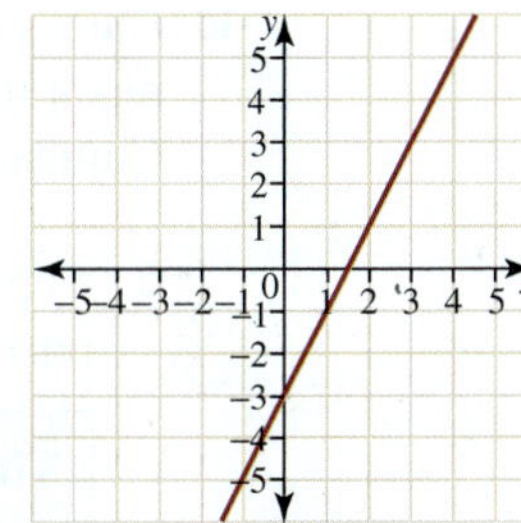

d
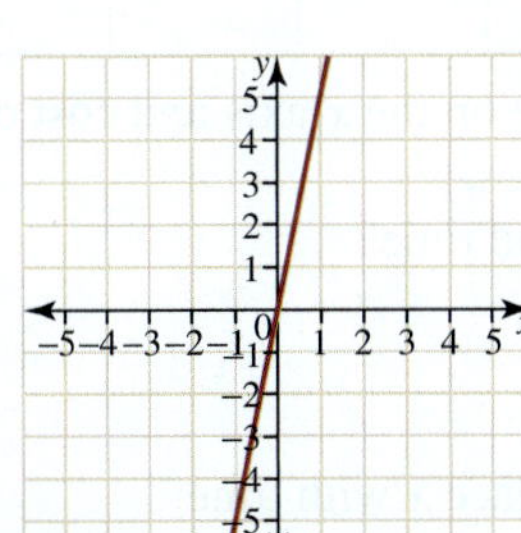

e
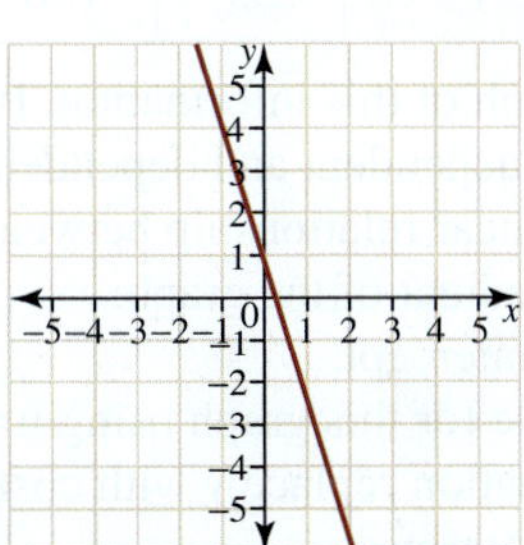

f
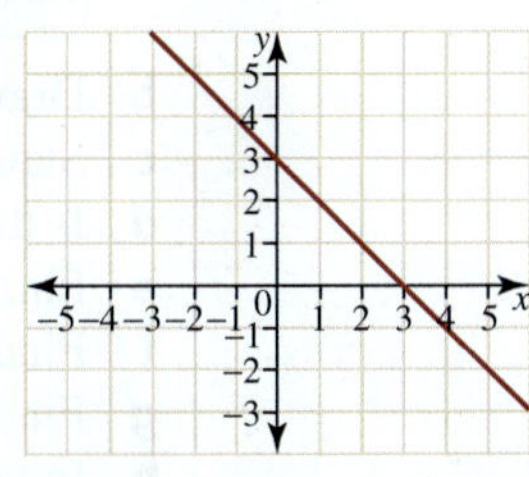

7 WE12 State the gradient and y-intercept for each of the following linear rules.

a $y = x + 3$
b $y = x - 4$
c $y = 3x + 1$
d $y = 5x - 2$
e $y = 6x + 10$
f $y = 8x - 7$
g $y = 5x + 3$
h $y = 9x - 4$
i $y = -3x + 4$
j $y = -6x + 2$
k $y = -4x$
l $y = x$

8 **MC** For each of the following graphs, choose the correct response.

a The rule for this linear graph is:

A $y = -3x$ **B** $y = x + 3$ **C** $y = 3x - 3$
D $y = x - 3$ **E** $y = x$

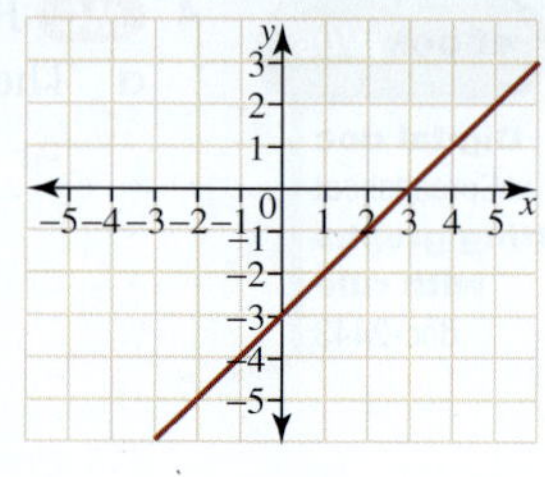

b The rule for this linear graph is:

A $y = -2x + 1$ **B** $y = -x + 1$ **C** $y = x + 1$
D $y = 2x + 1$ **E** $y = -\frac{1}{2}x + 1$

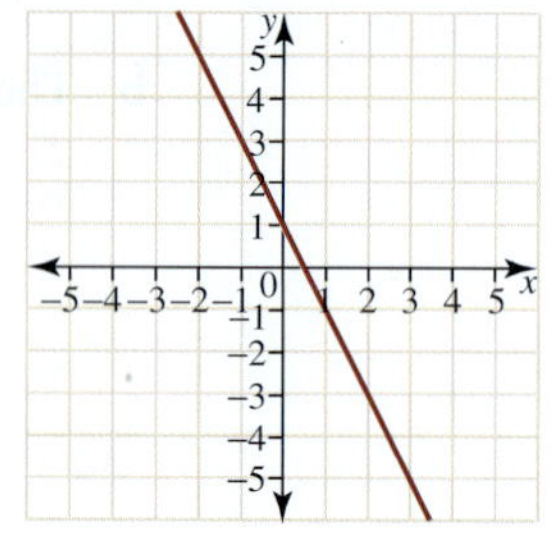

9 a **MC** A linear graph with the rule $y = 2x + 6$ would have:

A $m = 6, c = 2$ **B** $m = 2, c = 6$ **C** $m = -2, c = 6$
D $m = 1, c = 6$ **E** $m = 2, c = 2$

b A linear graph with the rule $y = 4x - 7$ would have:

A $m = -7, c = 4$ **B** $m = 7, c = 4$ **C** $m = 4, c = 4$
D $m = 4, c = 7$ **E** $m = 4, c = -7$

UNDERSTANDING

10 Chris's fridge is not working. He called a repair company, and they are sending someone to repair the fridge.

Company charges are: $55 to come to your home, plus
$45 for every $\frac{1}{2}$ hour the repairer is there.

a Copy and complete the table to show how much it could cost Chris to have his fridge repaired.

Time (hours)	0	$\frac{1}{2}$	1	$1\frac{1}{2}$	2	$2\frac{1}{2}$	3
Cost ($)	55	100	145				

b Draw a graph of this information. Place time on the x-axis and cost on the y-axis.
c State the independent and dependent variables.
d Is there a linear relationship between cost and time?
e Find the gradient of the graph.
f Find the y-intercept.
g Find the rule for this graph using $y = mx + c$.
h In your equation replace y with cost and replace x with time:
Cost = ___ × time + ___.
i Use your equation to find the cost if a repair person takes 4 hours to fix Chris's fridge.

11 Kyle was very bored on his holidays and decided to measure how much the grass grew every day for one week. His results are shown in the table.

Day number	0	1	2	3	4	5	6	7
Height of grass (mm)	10	12	14	16	18	20	22	24

- **a** Kyle knew his dad would want the grass cut as soon as it was 2.5 cm (25 mm) long. On which day would this occur?
- **b** Plot the points from the graph on a Cartesian plane putting day on the x-axis and height on the y-axis.
- **c** Do the points form a linear graph?
- **d** Find the gradient and y-intercept of the graph.
- **e** Find an equation for the height of the grass by filling in the blanks.
  Height = ___ × no. of days + ______
  or $h =$ ___ $d +$ ______
- **f** How long would the grass be after 14 days if it had not been cut?

12 Samantha has noticed that there are fewer students in her home group now than when she started school 3 years ago. The graph at right shows how the number of students has changed.

- **a** If the pattern continues, how many students will there be in Samantha's home group next year?
- **b** Find the gradient and y-intercept of the graph.
- **c** The equation for this graph would be:
  Number of students = _____ × time + _____.
  This could be shortened to
  $s =$ ____ $t +$ ____.
  Fill in the blanks in the equation above with the gradient and y-intercept.
- **d** Using the equation from part **c**, find the number of students in Samantha's home group after 6 years.

REFLECTION

In Question 12 above, will Samantha's home group have no students after a period of time? What does that tell you about the pattern?

14E Extension: Sketching linear graphs

- To sketch a straight-line graph only two points are needed.
- The two points can be obtained by substituting any two x-values into the rule to get the corresponding y-values. (The same process was used to obtain the table of values to plot the line.)
- There are two other convenient techniques of sketching straight lines: (a) gradient and y-intercept method and (b) intercept method. These are discussed below.

Sketching linear graphs using gradient and y-intercept method

- To sketch the line using the gradient-intercept method, follow these steps.
  - Identify the values of the gradient and the y-intercept from the equation; write the gradient in the form $m = \frac{\text{rise}}{\text{run}}$.
  - Plot the y-intercept; this is your first point.
  - To locate the second point, begin with the y-intercept and move up (or down) the number of units suggested by the rise, and then move forward the number of units suggested by the run.
  - Join the two points with the straight line; label your graph.

WORKED EXAMPLE 13

Sketch the graph of $y = 2x + 1$ using the gradient and y-intercept method.

THINK	WRITE/DRAW
1 Write the equation and compare with the general equation $y = mx + c$.	$y = 2x + 1 \quad m = 2, c = 1$
2 Plot a point at the y-intercept.	
3 Write the gradient as a fraction to identify the rise and the run.	$m = \frac{2}{1}$ So, rise = 2 and run = 1.
4 From the y-intercept at 1, move up 2 units and across 1 to plot the second point.	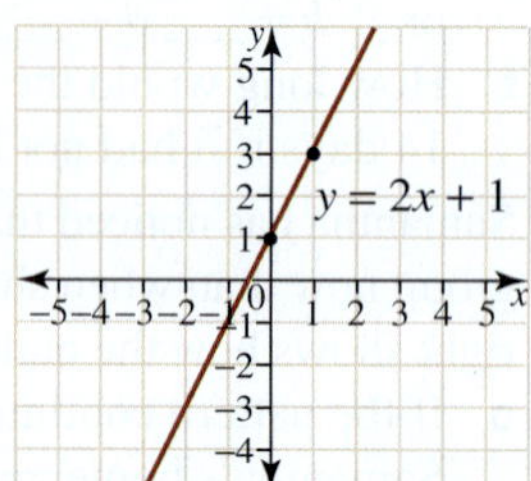
5 Join the 2 points to form a straight line. Extend and label the line.	

Intercept method

- The intercept method involves finding the coordinates of both the x- and the y-intercepts, and plotting them.
- At the x-intercept, $y = 0$. Therefore, to obtain the value of the x-intercept, substitute $y = 0$ into the equation and solve the equation for x.
- The y-intercept can be obtained directly from the equation (it is the value of c). Alternatively, at the y-intercept, $x = 0$. Therefore, to obtain the value of the y-intercept, substitute $x = 0$ into the equation and evaluate.
- To sketch the graph, plot both intercepts on the Cartesian axes and join them with the straight line. Label the line.

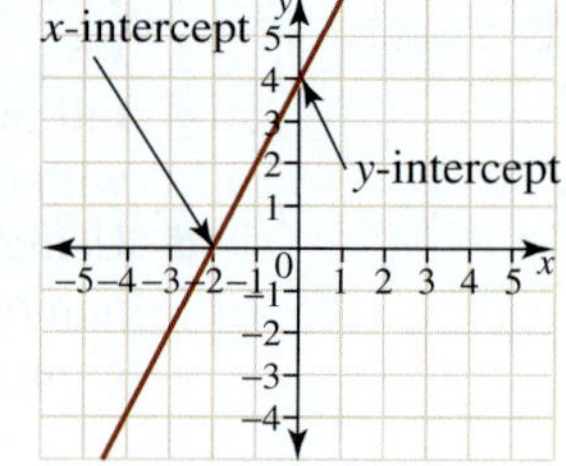

WORKED EXAMPLE 14

Sketch the graph of $y = x + 2$ using the intercept method.

THINK	WRITE/DRAW
1 Write the equation.	$y = x + 2$
2 At the y-intercept, $x = 0$. To find it, substitute $x = 0$ into the equation.	At y-intercept, $x = 0$ $y = 0 + 2$ $= 2$ y-intercept (0, 2)
3 At the x-intercept, $y = 0$. To find it, substitute $y = 0$ into the equation.	At x-intercept, $y = 0$ $0 = x + 2$
4 Rearrange the equation so that x is on the left-hand side.	$x + 2 = 0$
5 Subtract 2 from both sides of the equation.	$x + 2 - 2 = 0 - 2$ $x = -2$ x-intercept (−2, 0)

6 Plot the 2 intercepts and join them to form a straight line. Label the line.

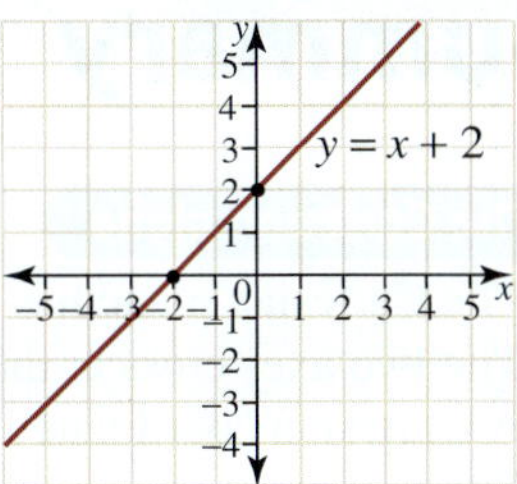

REMEMBER

1. To sketch a straight-line graph you need only two points.
2. To obtain two points you can use the gradient and y-intercept or the x- and y-intercepts.
3. Two methods can be used to sketch linear graphs.
   (a) Gradient and y-intercept method: plot a point at the y-intercept and then use the gradient to plot the second point.
   (b) Intercept method: find the x-intercept (substitute $y = 0$ into the equation), find the y-intercept (substitute $x = 0$ into the equation), or find c by comparing the equation with $y = mx + c$.

EXERCISE 14E

Extension: Sketching linear graphs

INDIVIDUAL PATHWAYS

eBook*plus*

Activity 14-E-1 Graph matching contest A doc-6952

Activity 14-E-2 Graph matching contest B doc-6953

Activity 14-E-3 Graph matching contest C doc-6954

FLUENCY

1 WE13 Sketch and label the following graphs using the gradient and y-intercept method.

a $y = x + 1$ b $y = x + 3$ c $y = x - 3$
d $y = x - 2$ e $y = 2x + 2$ f $y = 2x - 1$
g $y = 4x - 2$ h $y = 6x - 4$ i $y = -x + 4$
j $y = -x + 2$ k $y = -x - 5$ l $y = -2x + 3$

2 WE14 Sketch and label the following graphs using the intercept method.

a $y = x + 3$ b $y = x + 6$ c $y = x - 4$
d $y = x - 5$ e $y = x + 10$ f $y = x - 7$
g $y = x + 1$ h $y = x - 8$ i $y = x + 8$
j $y = x + 9$ k $y = -x + 1$ l $y = -x - 4$

3 a MC The gradient and y-intercept of the graph given by $y = 3x - 5$ is:
A $m = 3, c = 5$ B $m = 5, c = 3$ C $m = -3, c = 5$
D $m = 3, c = -5$ E $m = -5, c = 3$

b If $m = -6$ and $c = 4$, the rule for the linear graph would be:
A $y = 4x - 6$ B $y = -6x + 4$ C $y = 6x - 4$
D $y = -4x + 6$ E $y = -6x - 4$

eBook*plus*

Digital doc WorkSHEET 14.2 doc-2417

4 a MC The x- and y-intercepts for the linear graph whose rule is $y = x + 9$ are:
A 9 and 9 B 9 and –9 C –9 and 9
D 0 and 9 E 0 and –9

b The x- and y-intercepts for the linear graph whose rule is $y = x - 15$ are:
A 15 and –15
B –15 and –15
C 15 and 0
D 15 and 15
E 0 and 15

eBook*plus*

Interactivity Graphs of linear functions int-2379

REFLECTION

Why is it that only two points are necessary to sketch a straight line?

Summary

The Cartesian plane

- The Cartesian plane has a horizontal axis called the x-axis and a vertical axis called the y-axis.
- The two axes cross at the origin, which has the coordinates (0, 0).
- A Cartesian coordinate is written as (x, y).
- The first number gives the position on the x-axis, and the second number gives the position on the y-axis.
- To locate a point on the Cartesian plane, go across on the x-axis to the first number, and then up or down on the y-axis to the second number.

Linear patterns

- Linear means 'in a straight line'.
- When coordinates form a straight line on a Cartesian plane, we have a linear graph.

Plotting linear graphs

To plot a linear graph, follow these steps.
- Draw a table and choose some x-values.
- Substitute each x-value into the rule to obtain the corresponding y-value.
- Plot these coordinates as points on a Cartesian plane.
- Rule a straight line through the plotted points.
- Label the line with a rule.
- To write a rule in function notation, $f(x)$ is used in place of y.

Extension: The y-intercept and gradient

- Gradient is a measure of steepness and is denoted by the symbol m.
- Gradient: $m = \frac{\text{rise}}{\text{run}}$.
- The gradient of a straight line is constant.
- A linear graph can have a positive gradient (/), a negative gradient (\ ), zero gradient (——) or an undefined gradient (|).
- The y-intercept is where the graph crosses the y-axis. The symbol c stands for the y-value at this point.
- The rule for any linear graph is given by:

$$y = mx + c$$

↑ Gradient (m)   ↑ y-intercept (c)

Extension: Sketching linear graphs

- To sketch a straight-line graph you need only two points.
- To obtain two points you can use the gradient and y-intercept or the x- and y-intercepts.
- Two methods can be used to sketch linear graphs.
  - Gradient and y-intercept method: plot a point at the y-intercept and then use the gradient to plot the second point.
  - Intercept method: find the x-intercept (substitute $y = 0$ into the equation), find the y-intercept (substitute $x = 0$ into the equation), or find c by comparing the equation with $y = mx + c$.

MAPPING YOUR UNDERSTANDING

Using terms from the summary, and other terms if you wish, construct a concept map that illustrates your understanding of the key concepts covered in this chapter. Compare this concept map with the one that you created in *What do you know?* on page 405.

Have you completed the two *Homework sheets*, the *Rich task* and the two *Code puzzles* in your *Maths Quest 8 Homework Book*?

Chapter review

FLUENCY

1 Use the graph shown below to answer the following.

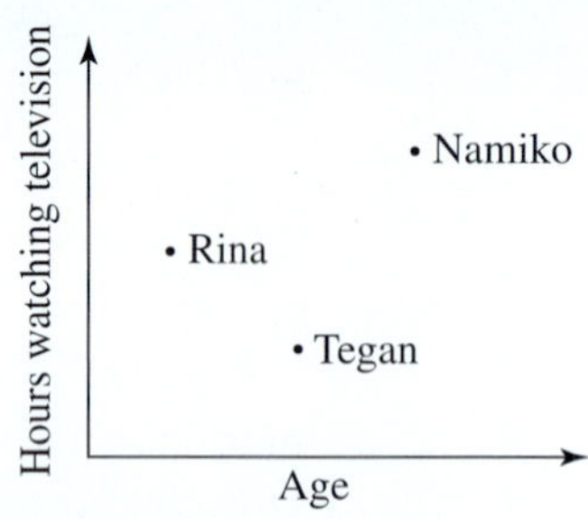

a Who watches the most television?
b Who is the youngest of the three?
c Does the youngest watch the least amount of television?

2 Place the following points on your Cartesian plane.

a A(1, 4) **b** B(5, 3)
c C(0, 2) **d** D(−2, 5)
e E(−4, 1) **f** F(−5, 0)
g G(−6, −6) **h** H(−5, −4)
i I(0, −5) **j** J(2, −1)
k K(2, −3) **l** L(2, 0)

3 Write down the coordinates of the points A to M, marked on the Cartesian plane below.

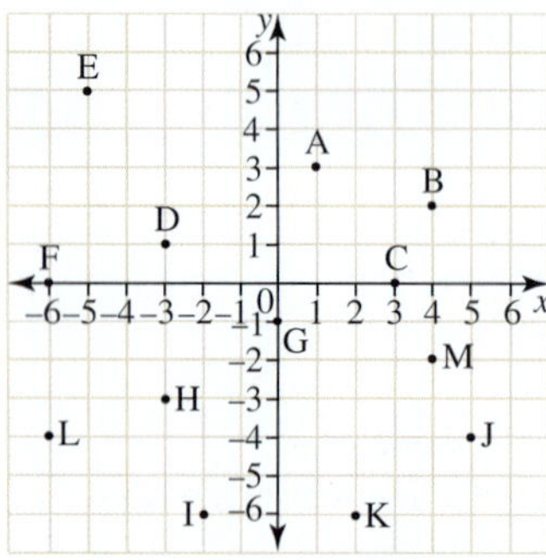

4 Plot the following points on a Cartesian plane.

a (−3, −1) (−2, 0) (−1, 1) (0, 2) (1, 3) (2, 4) (3, 5)
b (−3, −12) (−2, −9) (−1, −6) (0, −3) (1, 0) (2, 3) (3, 6)

5 Make a table of values and plot a graph for each of the following.

a $f(x) = x - 2$
b $f(x) = x + 5$
c $f(x) = 4x - 2$
d $f(x) = 3x + 2$

6 Find the gradient of the following linear graphs.

a

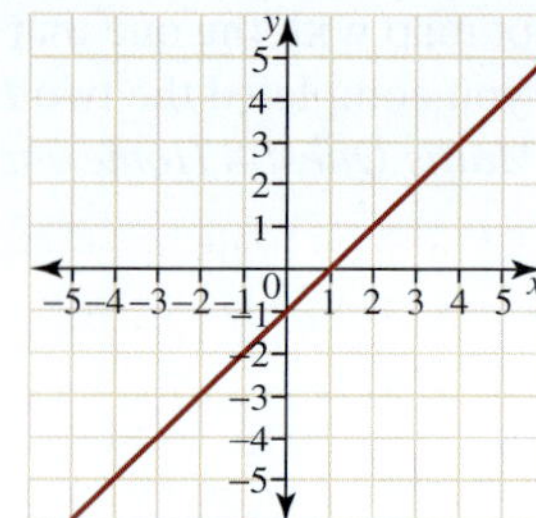

b

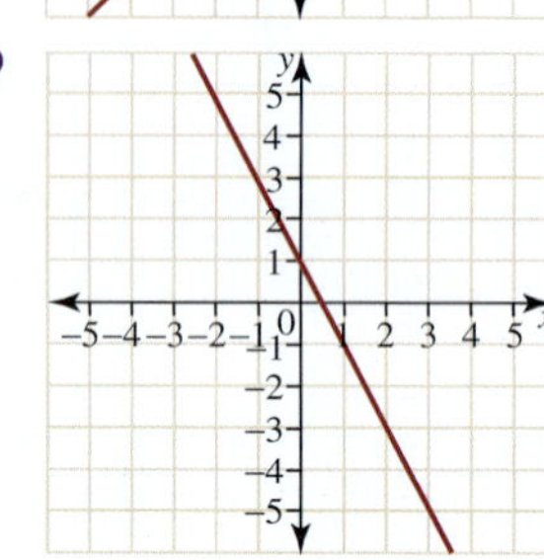

c

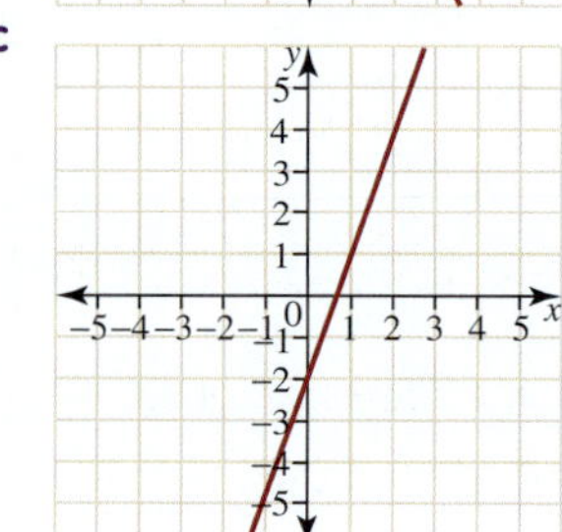

7 Sketch the following using the gradient and y-intercept method.

a $y = x + 7$ **b** $y = 2x - 2$
c $y = 3x - 5$ **d** $y = -2x + 4$

8 Sketch the following using the intercept method.

a $y = x + 7$ **b** $y = x - 3$
c $y = x - 5$ **d** $y = -x + 4$

PROBLEM SOLVING

1 Chris has the newspaper delivered 7 days a week. He saves his newspapers for recycling. Over a month the newspaper pile grows very high. The table below shows the height of the newspaper recycling pile at the end of each week.

Time (weeks)	0	1	2	3	4	5	6
Height (cm)		35	70	105	140		

a Copy and complete the table.
b Draw a set of axes showing height on the y-axis and time on the x-axis. Plot the information from your table on the axes and join the points to form a linear graph.

c Find the gradient, m, and the y-intercept, c.

d Find the rule for the graph using $y = mx + c$.

e Replace the y with height and x with time.
Height = __ × time + __.

f What would the height of the pile be after 20 weeks?

2 James and his sister are going for a bike ride. They know they can ride 25 km in an hour (average).

a Copy and complete the following table.

Distance (km)	0	25			100	
Time (hours)			2	3		5

b Plot these points on a Cartesian plane.

c Do the points form a linear graph?

d Find the gradient and y-intercept of the graph.

e Using the gradient and y-intercept from part **c**, copy and complete the equation below.
Distance = ______ × time + ______ or
d = _____ t + _____

f Use the equation found in part **e** to work out how far they would have ridden after 5 hours.

g If they leave home at 9.00 am and arrive home at 5.00 pm, how far would James and his sister have ridden?

3 Lara sells computers and is paid \$300 per week plus \$20 for every computer she sells.

a Draw a table to show how much money Lara would be paid if she sold between 0 and 10 computers per week.

b Plot the points in the table on a Cartesian plane.

c Do the points form a linear graph?

d Find the gradient and y-intercept of the graph.

e Find an equation for the graph in the form $y = mx + c$.

f If Lara sold 25 computers in a week, how much money would she be paid?

4 a Write an equation for the line shown below.

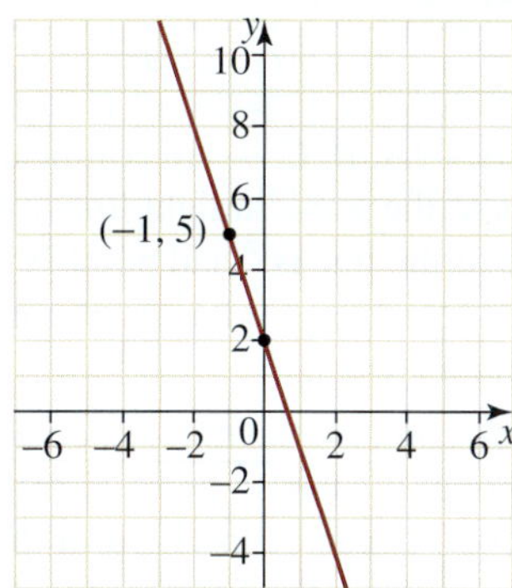

b Write an equation of another line that does not intersect the line in question **a**.

c Write an equation for a line that intersects the line in question **a** at one point.

d Explain generally how to write an equation of a line that intersects another line whose equation is given.

e Explain generally how to write an equation of a line that is parallel to another line whose equation is given.

f Explain how to determine where this graph cuts the x-axis.

5 The three lines shown below are parallel.

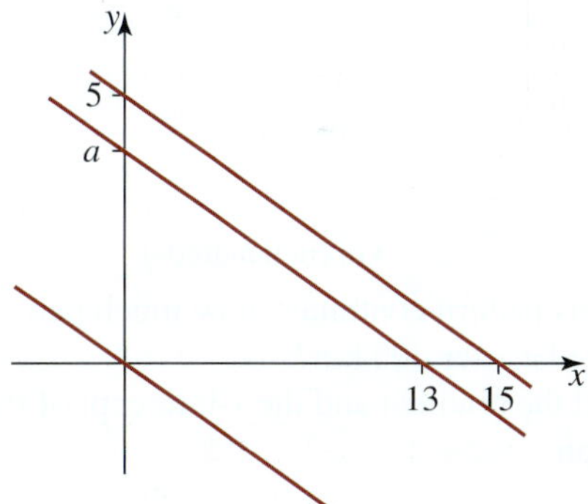

a Find the value of a.

b What are the equations of these lines?

c How do these equations and their graphs differ?

$$y = \frac{-1}{3}x + 5,\ y = \frac{-x}{3} + 5 \text{ and } y = \frac{-x + 15}{3}$$

6 Lena and Alex have set up savings accounts. Each month they write down their savings. If the trend continues, who will be the first to save \$300?

Lena's account:

t (months)	0	1	2
A (\$)	100	120	140

Alex's account:

t (months)	0	1	2
A ($)	150	160	170

7 Three points — A, B, C — are collinear (that is, they belong to the same straight line in that order). If the slope of the line is $\frac{3}{4}$ and point B is (2, 5), what are the possible coordinates of points A and C? Explain your answer.

8 A Fast Track company is fitting internet cable in the neighbourhood. It takes $1\frac{1}{2}$ hours to install 300 m. In 2 hours, 450 m can be installed. If this is a linear relationship, how much can be laid in 4 hours?

9 A trapezium ABCD is created by joining the points A(1, 1), B(1, 13) C(9, 13) and D(17, 1) with straight line segments. Find the gradients of the diagonals of this trapezium.

10 As Rachel has been driving her new car she has kept a watch on her petrol usage. The graph below shows how the amount of petrol has changed.

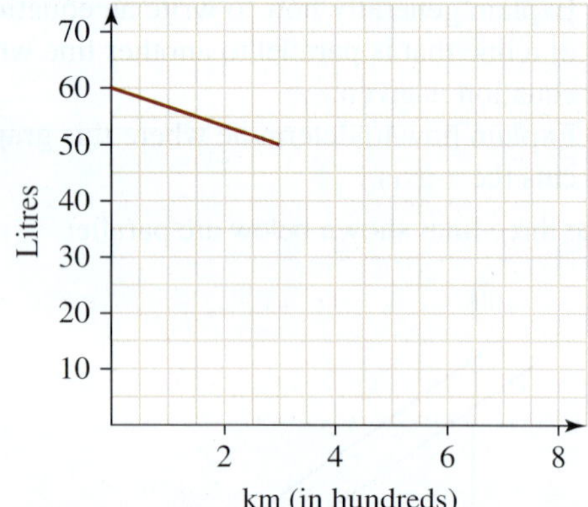

a If this pattern continues, how much petrol will there be after 400 km?

b Find the gradient and the y-intercept of the graph.

c The equation for this graph would be:
Number of litres used =_____ + _____ × number of km travelled.
This could be shortened to l = ____ + ____ k.
Fill in the blanks in the equation above with the gradient and y-intercept.

d Using the equation from part **c**, find the amount of petrol left when $k = 10$.

e How far will Rachel have travelled when she has used 120 litres of petrol?

11 Two yachts are sailing in Western Port Bay. At the end of a very windy day, rain begins to fall and visibility is markedly reduced. One yacht is travelling in the direction given by the equation $y = x + 6$ and the other in a direction given by $y = -2x + 3$.

a Could the yachts crash? (Assume both yachts are travelling towards the shore.) Use mathematical reasoning to justify your answer.

b If they could crash, state the coordinates of the point where they will meet.

c Explain how you found your answer.

eBook*plus*

Interactivities

Test yourself
Chapter 14
int-2380

Word search
Chapter 14
int-2639

Crossword
Chapter 14
int-2640

eBookplus ACTIVITIES

Chapter opener

Digital doc *(page 405)*
- Hungry brain activity Chapter 14 (doc-6933)

Are you ready?

Digital docs *(page 406)*
- SkillSHEET 14.1 (doc-6934) Grid coordinates I
- SkillSHEET 14.2 (doc-6935) Grid coordinates II
- SkillSHEET 14.3 (doc-6936) Plotting coordinate points
- SkillSHEET 14.4 (doc-6937) Substitution into rules
- SkillSHEET 14.5 (doc-6938) Completing a table of values for a given rule
- SkillSHEET 14.6 (doc-6939) Plotting a line using a table of values

14A The Cartesian plane

Digital docs *(page 408)*
- Activity 14-A-1 (doc-6940) The Cartesian plane
- Activity 14-A-2 (doc-6941) Using the Cartesian plane
- Activity 14-A-3 (doc-6942) Extending the Cartesian plane

14B Linear patterns

Digital docs *(page 411)*
- Activity 14-B-1 (doc-6943) Linear patterns
- Activity 14-B-2 (doc-6944) More linear patterns
- Activity 14-B-3 (doc-6945) Advanced linear patterns
- Spreadsheet (doc-2439) Plotting points *(page 412)*
- WorkSHEET 14.1 (doc-2416) *(page 412)*

14C Plotting linear graphs

Digital docs *(page 415)*
- Activity 14-C-1 (doc-6946) Plotting linear graphs
- Activity 14-C-2 (doc-6947) More graphs of linear functions
- Activity 14-C-3 (doc-6948) Advanced linear functions
- Spreadsheet (doc-2441) Plotting graphs with table *(page 416)*

14D Extension: The y-intercept and gradient

Digital docs *(page 421)*
- Activity 14-D-1 (doc-6949) y-intercepts and gradients
- Activity 14-D-2 (doc-6950) More y-intercepts and gradients
- Activity 14-D-3 (doc-6951) Advanced y-intercepts and gradients
- Spreadsheet (doc-2443) Plotting graphs with rule *(page 423)*
- Spreadsheet (doc-2444) Gradient and intercepts *(page 423)*

14E Extension: Sketching linear graphs

Digital docs *(page 427)*
- Activity 14-E-1 (doc-6952) Graph matching contest A
- Activity 14-E-2 (doc-6953) Graph matching contest B
- Activity 14-E-3 (doc-6954) Graph matching contest C
- WorkSHEET 14.2 (doc-2417)

Interactivity *(page 427)*
- Graphs of linear functions (int-2379)

Chapter review

Interactivities *(page 432)*
- Test yourself Chapter 14 (int-2380) Take the end-of-chapter test to test your progress.
- Word search Chapter 14 (int-2639)
- Crossword Chapter 14 (int-2640)

To access eBookPLUS activities, log on to
www.jacplus.com.au

15 Problem solving II

15A Problem set A
15B Problem set B
15C Problem set C
15D Problem set D
15E Problem set E
15F Problem set F
15G Problem set G
15H Problem set H
15I Problem set I
15J Problem set J

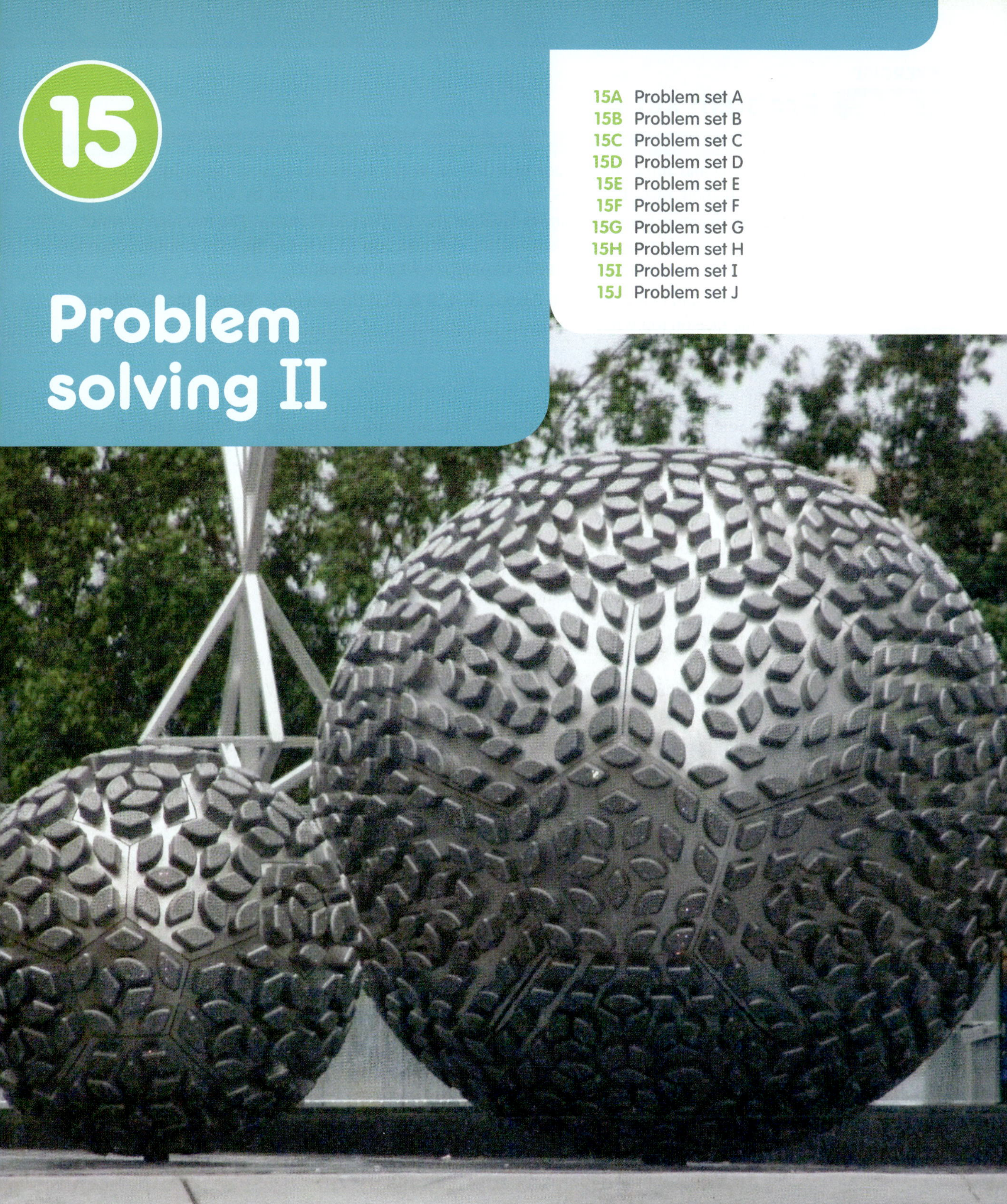

OPENING QUESTION

The height of the larger sphere is twice the smaller sphere. What is the ratio of the volumes?

EXERCISE

15A Problem set A

PROBLEM SOLVING

1. Josh, Ella and Jonte like to race over 100 m. When Josh races Ella, he wins by 10 m. When Ella and Jonte race, Ella wins by 10 m. How much will Josh win by when he races Jonte?
2. A drink machine has three buttons labelled *Tea*, *Coffee* and *Random*. The machine is wired incorrectly so that each label is incorrect. If drinks cost $1, what is the least amount of money you can spend to figure out which button gives which selection?
3. A wrongly numbered die (with faces 2, 3, 4, 5, 6, 6) is thrown once. What is the probability that the face on top will be:
   a. 2?
   b. 3, 4 or 5?
   c. 6?
4. On a Science test, Brendan scored twice as many marks as Damien but fifteen marks fewer than Maggie. The total of the three scores is 205 marks. How much did each student score on their Science test?
5. Tins of soup come in boxes of 12 when they are shipped to the large supermarkets. The diameter of each can of soup is 8 cm and the height is 12 cm.
   a. Find the dimensions of the base of the box.
   b. What is the volume of the box?
   c. What area of the base does not have a tin standing on it? (Give your answer to the nearest whole number.)
   d. What volume is empty space?

6. Teagan ordered some new stationery from a major distributor. Using the catalogue, she calculated that the total cost was $460. When she rang to place the order, however, she was told that the catalogue was old and there was a new one on-line. When she checked this, she found that the prices had risen by 8%.
   a. Find the new total cost.
   b. As Teagan was a good customer she was also given a discount of 15% off the new total cost. What did she pay for her stationery?
   c. If she had spent over $500 on stationery she would have received 20% discount. How much more would she have had to spend initially, and what is the new total cost after the extra discount. Would it be worth it?
7. You have 10 blue socks, 4 black socks and 2 white socks in your drawer. Getting dressed in the dark, you reach into the drawer. How many socks should you pull out to be certain that you have a pair of blue socks?
8. A painted cube is sliced into 64 smaller cubes as shown. How many smaller cubes have no paint on them?
9. Two cyclists are competing in a race of 8 km on a circular track of radius 25 metres. They begin at the same time. One biker's average speed is 40 km/h while the other biker's average speed is 48 km/h.
   How many laps will the slower cyclist have left to complete after the faster cyclist finishes?
10. In your science class you are asked to make up a 13.5-litre dye solution by using water and dye in the ratio of 5 : 4. How many litres of each should you use?

EXERCISE

15B Problem set B

PROBLEM SOLVING

1 In an old war movie, the army scout galloped up to his captain and said, 'Sir! We are outnumbered 3 to 2'. The captain had 500 soldiers. How many soldiers were going to do battle that day?

2 Adam bought 5 loaves of bread and Brian bought 3 loaves. A third man, Callum, joined them. The men shared the bread equally, and Callum offered them 8 coins to pay for his share.

Adam thought that he should share them with Brian 5 : 3, but Brian thought he should receive 4 coins. Callum suggested that Adam should receive 7 coins and Brian should receive 1. Which method is the fairest way to share the coins?

3 A cube has the letters C, H, A, N, C, and E printed on its faces. If it is rolled, what is the probability of getting:

a C? **b** a vowel? **c** N? **d** C, A or N?

4 Mrs Simpson has 4 children. How many gifts does she need to buy so that each child can give a gift to each of the other children?

5 On a standard die, opposite sides add to 7. Fill in the spaces on the net at right, so that when folded, it will form a standard die.

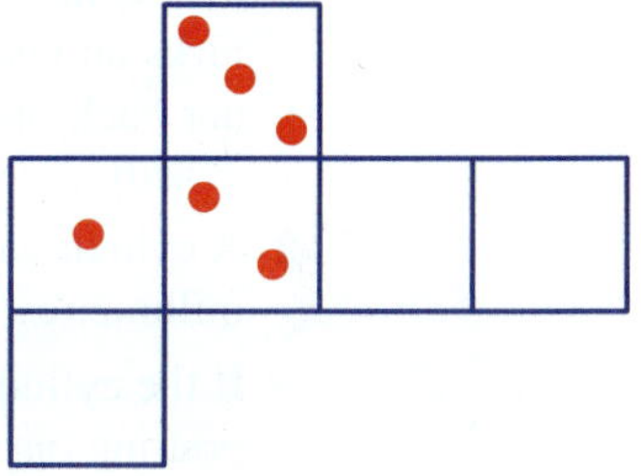

6 Triangle OPQ is isosceles, where OP = PQ, and has an area of 360 square units. What are the coordinates of P?

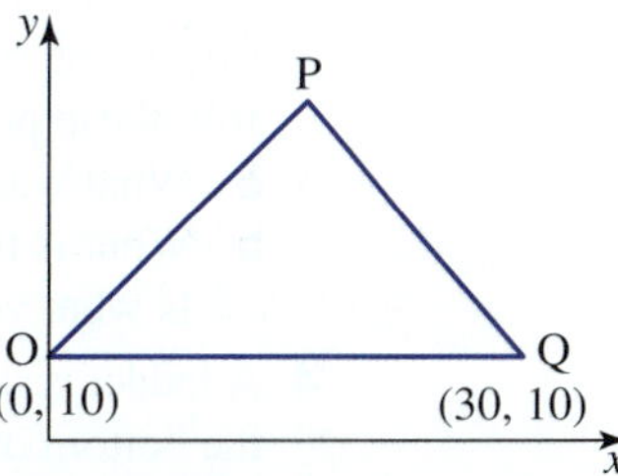

7 You worked on your mathematics assessment task for 4 days. Each day you worked half as long as you worked the day before. You spent a total of 4.2 hours on the task. How many hours did you work each day?

8 Calculate the shaded area of this circle:

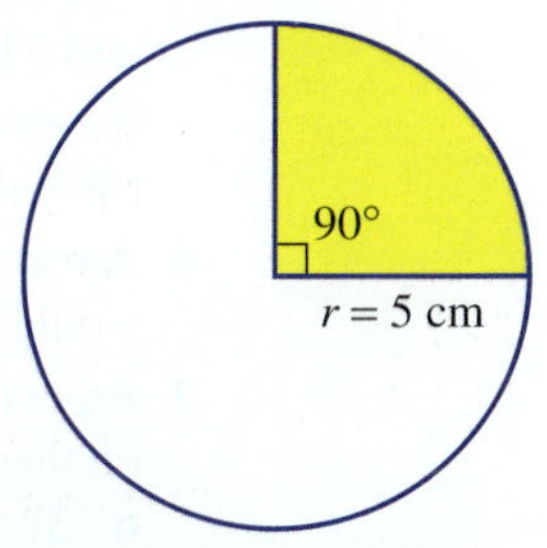

9 Tom wanted exactly 20% of his university classes for the year to be in mathematics, and he wanted to take a total of 6 classes.

a Is this possible? Why or why not?

b How many more total classes will Tom need to add to his schedule so that he can have 20% mathematics classes? Explain.

c How many of these will be mathematics classes? Explain.

d Tom does not want to take 10 total classes for the year, but decides to take 5. Can he achieve his goal of 20% mathematics classes? Explain.

10 Fine jewellery can be purchased in gold or silver. However, these metals would be too soft for jewellery if they were used on their own. They are mixed with other metals, the main ones being copper and zinc. Sterling silver, for example, contains 7.5 g of copper for every 92.5 g of pure silver. In 100 g of 18 carat yellow gold there are 12.5 g of copper. What mass of 18 carat yellow gold would contain the same amount of copper as 100 g of sterling silver?

EXERCISE

15C Problem set C

PROBLEM SOLVING

1 Little Red Riding Hood is going to visit her grandma. This time, there is no wolf to bother her on her walk. However, she does need to cross 7 bridges, and under each bridge there lurks an evil troll. Each troll insists that she hand over half of her cakes, but then gives her back one. How many cakes does she need to start with if she wants to arrive with exactly 2 cakes?

2 A cylindrical tube has a volume of 100 litres. If its cross-sectional area is 80 000 square millimetres, what is its height?

If the cylinder is half full of water, how long will the tank take to empty if the water is pouring out at a rate of 18 000 cubic millimetres per second?

3 Join the points A(−2, 4), B(2, 6), C(6, 0) and D(0, −2) to create a shape.

Locate the midpoints of AB, BC, CD and DA; and label them as P, Q, R and S respectively. Join these points to create a new shape.

- **a** What was the original shape?
- **b** What is the new shape? Justify your answer by using geometry or coordinate geometry. Is what you have found always true?

4 A ladder rests against a vertical wall with the top of the ladder being 7 m above the ground. If the bottom of the ladder was moved 1 m further away from the foot of the wall, the top of the ladder would rest against the foot of the wall.

What is the length of the ladder?

5 Music used to be recorded on vinyl records at speeds of 45 revolutions per minute (rpm) and $33\frac{1}{3}$ rpm. If it took $4\frac{1}{2}$ minutes to listen to a song recorded at 45 rpm, how long would it take to listen to the same song recorded at $33\frac{1}{3}$ rpm? Give your answer in minutes and seconds.

6 A rectangular board is 3 times as long as it is wide. If it was 3 m shorter and 3 m wider, it would be square. What are the dimensions of the board?

7 An octahedral die has eight faces with the digits (1 to 8) on them. What is the probability of rolling:

- **a** 3?
- **b** 1 to 4?
- **c** 7 or more?
- **d** 5 or less?

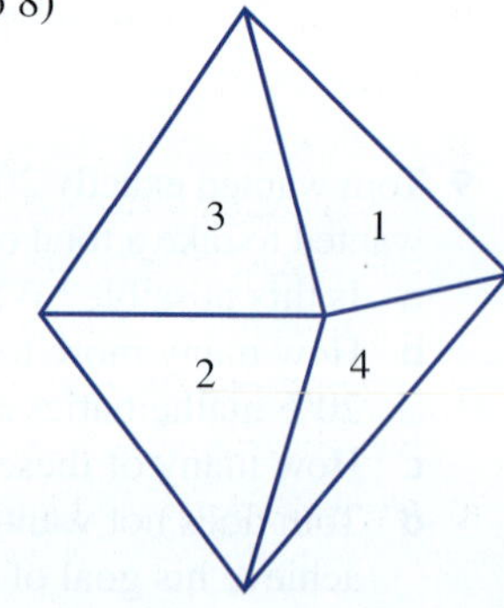

8 I am planning a 5000-km trip in my car. I have 4 tyres on my car at any time, and a spare tyre in the boot. I want to rotate my tyres during the trip so that they all do the same number of kilometres. How many kilometres would each tyre do?

9 This mobile balances perfectly when the unknown masses are properly assigned.

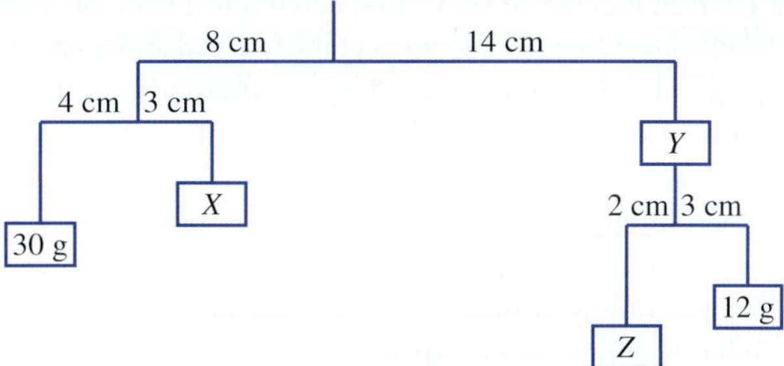

What are the masses of X, Y and Z to balance the mobile?

10 A circle and a square have the same area. The circle has the radius of 5 m. What is the width of the square?

EXERCISE

15D Problem set D

PROBLEM SOLVING

1 The angles of a triangle are in the ratio $2:3:5$. What is the difference in magnitude between the smallest and largest angles?

2 Pete has a new supply of birds for his pet store. If he puts one bird in each cage, he has one bird too many. If he puts two birds in each cage, he has one cage too many. How many birds and cages does Pete have?

3 You roll 2 tetrahedral dice, and you add the two numbers. Die 1 has the numbers $-1, -3, -5$ and -7; Die 2 has the numbers 1, 3, 5 and 6. What is the probability of the sum being less than 0.

4 A square is changed into a rectangle by increasing its length by 30% and decreasing its width by 30%. How does the area of the rectangle compare to that of the square?

5 Calculate the volume of the prism:

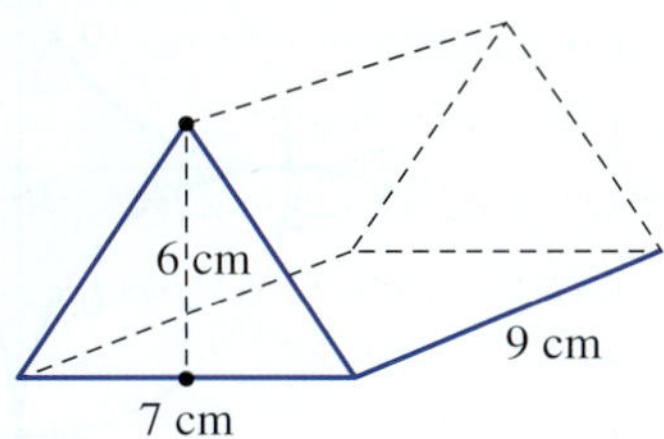

6 Two years ago, John was six times older than Betty. Now, he is four times older. How old was he two years ago?

7 Continuing from the previous question, how long from now will it be before John is twice Betty's age?

8 A shop assistant calculated 80% of an item on the shelf and changed the price tag to $160.00. He then threw out the old price tag. Later he realised that this item was not on special, so he calculated 20% of 160. This came to $32.00. He added this to $160, and wrote a new price tag showing $192. Was he right? Why? If not, what should he have done?

9 In the sport of indoor cricket, a team loses 5 runs every time a batsman gets out. When Dylan bats, he manages 13 runs and gets out 4 times. What is Dylan's score?

10 Given that $n(A) = 13$ and $n(B) = 15$ and $n(A \cap B) = 2$, find $n(A \cup B)$.

EXERCISE

15E Problem set E

PROBLEM SOLVING

1 Bob has 11 socks in his drawer: 5 identical school socks and 6 identical sports socks. What is the smallest number of socks Bob can remove from his drawer, without first looking at them, so he can be assured of having a pair of school socks and a pair of sports socks?

2 You can enter the school through three different gates. In order to reach your classroom on the first floor you have a choice of two doors followed by two sets of stairs. Draw a tree diagram to explain how many different ways can you reach your classroom. What is the probability that you enter through Gate 1, Door 1 and either of the two sets of stairs?

3 Rosemary drove her car at a constant speed for 40 seconds, travelling a distance of 560 metres.

a Represent this information on a distance time graph.

b What was Rosemary's speed?

c What is the gradient of your graph?

d Write down a rule for the distance travelled in terms of the time taken.

e Using this rule, work out how far Rosemary would have travelled after 1 minute if she had maintained the same speed.

f If Rosemary travelled 2 km at this speed, how long would it have taken her? (Give your answer in minutes.)

4 Show that $a = 90$ in this diagram. Assume X is the centre of the circle. (*Hint:* Use the dashed line to make two triangles.)

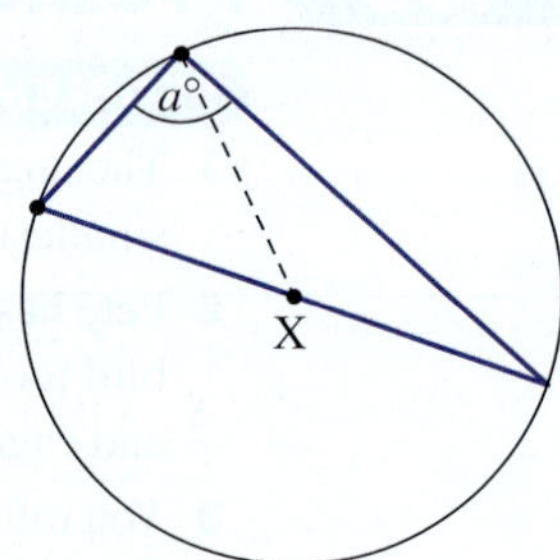

5 What is the area of the coloured region in the figure shown?

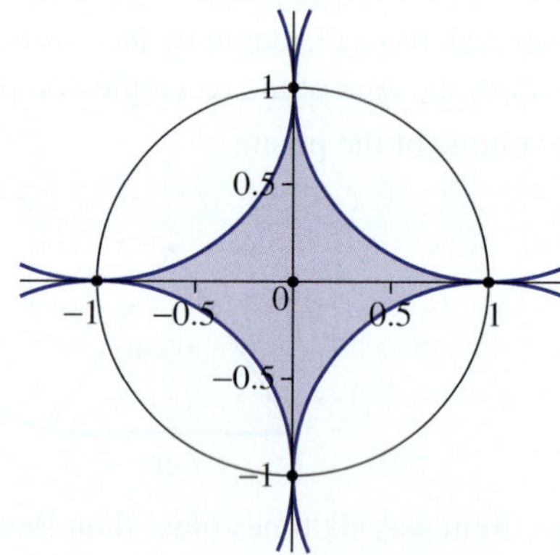

6 The mean of a set of 8 scores is 12. A score of 18 is added to the data set. Find the new mean.

7 Give an example of an equation that has:

- variables on both sides of the equation *and*
- a solution of $x = -4$.

8 The number ABCDEFGHI consists of the digits 1, 2, 3, 4, 5, 6, 7, 8 and 9. The pairs of numbers meet the following criteria.

- AB is divisible by 2.
- BC is divisible by 3.
- CD is divisible by 4.
- DE is divisible by 5.
- EF is divisible by 6.

- FG is divisible by 7.
- GH is divisible by 8.
- HI is divisible by 9.

9 Give an example of two numbers that fit each of the descriptions which follow. If no numbers fit the description, explain why.

a Both the sum and the product of two numbers are negative.

b The sum of two numbers is positive and the quotient is negative.

c The sum of two numbers is 0 and the product is positive.

10 On a test, each correct answer scores 5 points, each incorrect answer scores –2 points, and each question left unanswered scores 0 points.

a Suppose a student answers 16 questions on the test correctly, 3 incorrectly and does not answer 1 question. Write an expression for the student's score and find the score.

b Suppose you answer all 20 questions on the test. What is the greatest number of questions you can answer incorrectly and still get a positive score? Explain your reasoning.

EXERCISE **15F**

Problem set F

PROBLEM SOLVING

1 There are five more females than there are males in a squash club. A member of the club is chosen to play in a competition. Each member is equally likely to be chosen. If the probability that a male is chosen is $\frac{2}{5}$, how many males and females are there in the club?

2 A normal 6-sided die has the numbers 1 to 6 on its faces. When two of these dice are rolled and the numbers showing on the upper faces are added, there are 11 different outcomes (2, 3, 4, …, 12).

Explain the difference to the outcome if the two dice both contained the numbers 1, 2, 3, 5, 7 and 9.

3 There is a three-digit number that is divisible by 7. The sum of its digits is 10 and the product is 20. What is the number?

4 A drinking vessel in the shape of an inverted cone can hold 270 ml. When it is full to the brim the liquid level is 10 cm high? How wide is the vessel at the brim?

5 A menu has 4 entrees, 5 main courses and 3 desserts. How many different meals is it possible to choose from this menu?

6 The highest common factor of two integers is 12 and their lowest common multiple is a square number. What are the integers?

7 Arrange 5 different digits (from 0 to 9) into the cross below, keeping to the following conditions.
The sum of the four outside numbers is the inside number.
The product of the two top numbers is the middle number.
The sums of the numbers in the two diagonals are the same.

8 Giovanni bought enough square pavers to pave a square courtyard. When he'd finished, he decided that the area was too small, so he pulled up the tiles and bought another 100 tiles. If the new area was also square, how many tiles did he end up buying?

9 The diagram at right is a square section of square pavers. If the length of each side of the large square is 2 cm, what is the area of the smaller square?

10 Marion looks out of the window of her castle and spies Robin at 100 m down the road, riding at 2 m/s. She immediately starts to lower the drawbridge.

a If the drawbridge is 10 m high and takes 60 s to lower, what is the average change each second, in the height of the drawbridge?

b If Robin does not slow down as he approaches the castle, will he make it into the castle? Give reasons.

c If the point where the edge of the moat meets the road is taken as zero and Robin is +100 m from the moat when Marion first sees him, how far is he from the edge of the moat when the drawbridge hits the ground?

d Robin's horse is 2.8 m tall. If the distance from the horse's head to the surface of the water when the horse stands in the moat is 0.7 m, how far is the bottom of the moat from the surface of the water?

EXERCISE 15G Problem set G

PROBLEM SOLVING

1 A 'nude' number is a natural number whose digits are factors of the number. The number 1 is a factor of all numbers and so is not considered in this definition. An example of a nude number is 24 as both 2 and 4 are factors of 24.

A number is called 'cute' if it has exactly 4 factors including the number itself. For example, 10 is a cute number as it has the factors 1, 2, 5 and 10.

a What is the smallest 2-digit nude number?

b List all the 2-digit nude numbers.

c What is the smallest cute number?

d What is the smallest number which is both cute and nude?

e How many cute numbers are less than 100?

f Give an example of a square number that is nude.
g Are there any square numbers that are cute? Can you explain your answer?
h List 4 cubes that are cute. Cubes are numbers like 1 ($= 1^3 = 1 \times 1 \times 1$), 8 ($= 2^3 = 2 \times 2 \times 2$), 27 ($= 3^3 = 3 \times 3 \times 3$) and so on.

2 What is a four-digit number that satisfies the following?
The first digit is $\frac{1}{3}$ of the second.
The third digit is the sum of the first and second.
The last digit is three times the second.

3 In a party of 42 people, there are twice as many women as men and twice as many men as children. How many of each are there?

4 Kelty received one star (out of a possible 5) for her first homework assignment. How many 5-star assignments does she need to hand in if she wants a 4-star average?

5 If 30% of a is equal to 25% of b, what is the ratio of a to b?

6 The school tennis singles championship has attracted 23 players. How many matches must be played before a winner can be declared?

7 A gambler plays a game where he rolls a die after paying one dollar. If he lands a six, he is given back his dollar plus four more; otherwise, he loses his money. If he plays this 600 times, how much can he expect to lose?

8 Licia has bought her lunch from the school canteen for \$3.00. It consisted of a roll, a carton of milk and a piece of fruit. She paid 60 cents more for the milk than the fruit and 30 cents more for the roll than the milk. How much did the roll cost her?

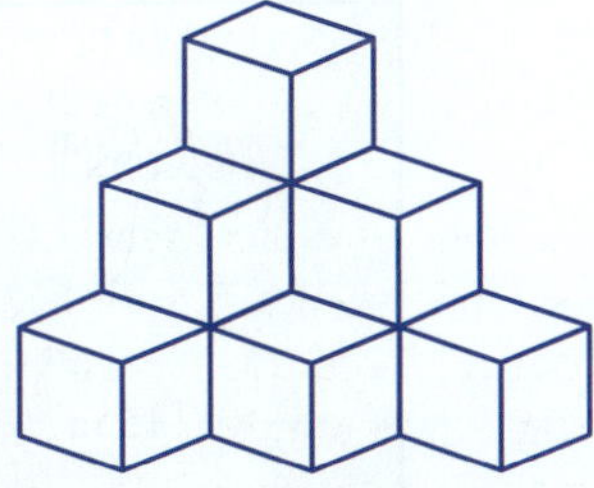

9 Find at least two 2-digit numbers that are equal to 7 times the sum of their digits.

10 Find 5 consecutive numbers that add to 120.

EXERCISE

15H Problem set H

PROBLEM SOLVING

1 If it takes 4 possums 4 minutes to eat 4 rose-buds, how long will it take 40 possums to eat 40 rose buds?

2 Three normal 6-sided dice are rolled. In how many ways can a total of 15 be obtained?

3 Here are the first three 'pyramid numbers'. 1, 5, 14, …

What are the next 3 numbers in the sequence?
Why are they called pyramid numbers?

4 A farmer has a field shaped like the trapezium shown. Where could he place a fence to divide the field in half? (There may be more than one possible answer.)

5 Arrange the digits 1, 1, 2, 2, 3, 3 so that there is one digit between the two 1s, two digits between the two 2s and three digits between the two 3s.

6 a Is it possible to draw a square with its diagonals without picking up your pencil or retracing your steps?

b Is it possible to draw a pentagon (5 sides) with its diagonals without picking up your pencil or retracing your steps?

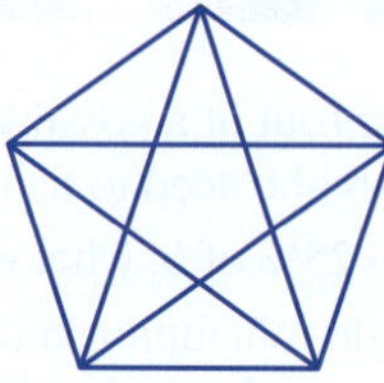

c Would it be possible with a hexagon (6 sides) and its diagonals or a heptagon (7 sides) and its diagonals?

d Find a rule for this problem that you can use with a polygon having 4 or more sides and its diagonals.

7 A goat is tied to the corner of a fence as shown. If the rope is 13 m long and the goat cannot eat through the rope or the fence, what area, to the nearest square metre, of grass can the goat graze on?

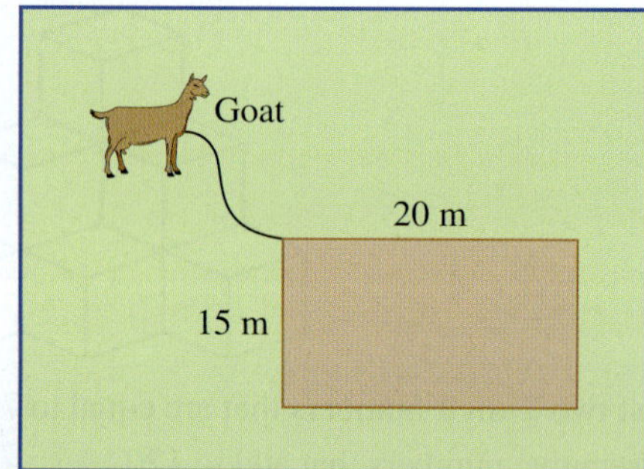

8 Sitting around this table are 3 girls (Anna, Cate and Ellen) and 3 boys (Brian, Dean and Francis).

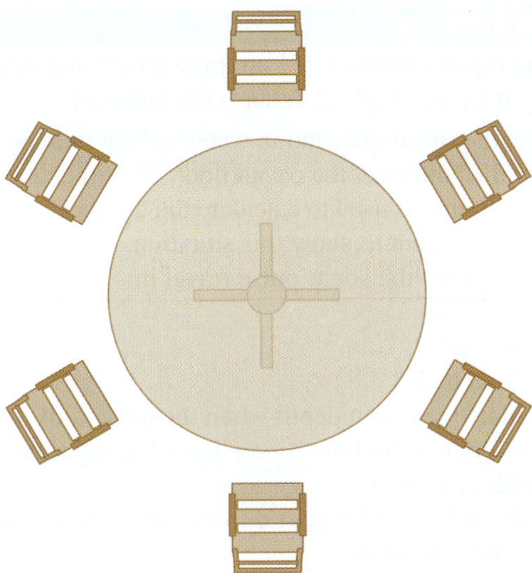

Arrange them so that Cate and Ellen sit together but do not sit with Anna; that Dean sits opposite from Ellen; and that Brian sits between 2 girls. (There are a number of possible answers.)

9 Place 6 crosses in the grid below so that there are exactly 2 crosses in each row and column. (There is more than one way to solve this problem.)

10 A group of mountain climbers were climbing one of the highest mountains in the world. From their base camp, the group travelled 506.3 m upwards. One climber started to suffer altitude sickness and was escorted down by another climber to a point 273.1 m below the base camp.

a Show the relative positions of the two groups on a vertical number line.

b How far apart were the two groups?

c How far would the smaller group need to travel to catch up with the main group if the main group has climbed a further 89.8 m?

d If the smaller group takes 5.5 hours to reach the base camp, how many hours of climbing time will be needed to reach the main group who are waiting for them? Assume they are climbing at a constant rate.

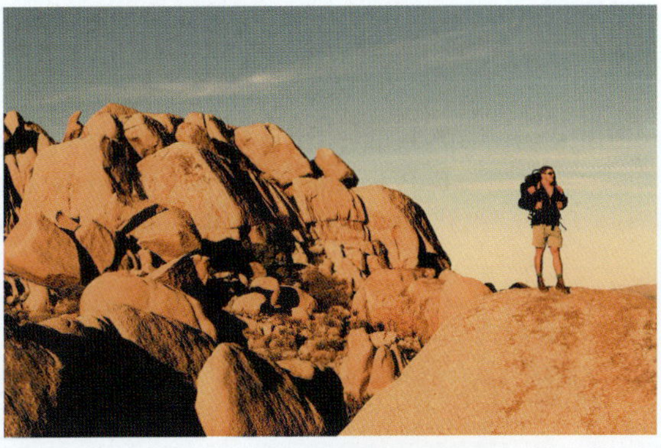

EXERCISE

15I Problem set I

PROBLEM SOLVING

1 I'm thinking of a number. If I multiply it by 5 and subtract 4, I get the same number as when I multiply it by 4 and add 2. What is the number?

2 Ships use the speed of sound in water to help find the water's depth. A sonar pulse from a ship is sent to the bottom of the ocean floor. The time takes for the pulse to hit the ocean floor and return to the ship is used to calculate the distance. The speed of sound in water is 1470 m/s.

a Draw a diagram to show this situation.

b How far does the sonar pulse travel in:

i 1 second?

ii 2 seconds?

iii 1.5 seconds?

c Calculate the ocean depth when the pulse took 1.5 seconds to return.

d Write a rule to find the ocean depth for any time measurement. Explain what each variable represents.

e Use the rule found in part **d** to calculate the ocean depth for the following pulse-return time measurements.

i 1.8 seconds

ii 4.22 seconds

iii 0.64 seconds

f The speed of sound in water is about 5 times the speed of sound in air. A person standing on the deck of the ship sends a sonar pulse through the air to a nearby cliff face. If the pulse takes 3 seconds to travel to the cliff face and return, calculate the distance to the cliff face. Write a rule to represent this situation.

3 A family has four children. Assuming that the chance of having a boy is the same as having a girl, what is the probability that this family had two children of one gender first and then two of the other?

4 If the length of a rectangle is increased by 10%, by what percentage is the width decreased if the area is unchanged?

5 Which is the better fit, a square peg in a round hole or a round peg in a square hole? Assume that the largest peg that will fit in each hole is used.

6 Two parallel roads, Ryrie St and Malop St, are crossed by a third street, Geringham St. Find the number of degrees of the smaller angle formed by the intersection of Ryrie and Geringhap Sts.

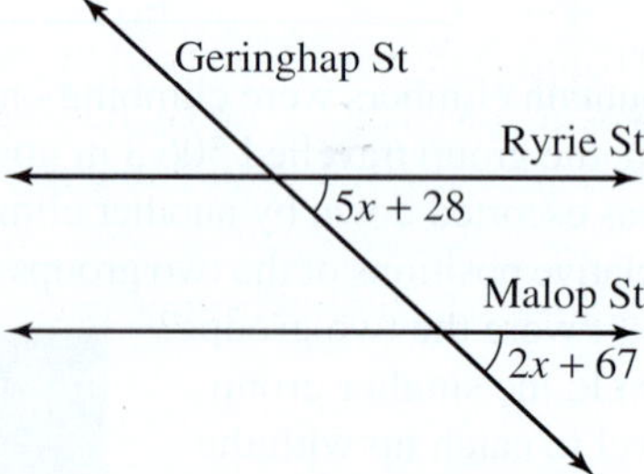

7 If $(x^2 - 5)^5 = 1$, what value/s could x be? Give your answer in exact form.

8 Place the numbers 1–10 in the triangle below. Each number is the difference between the two numbers below it. Some of the numbers have been placed for you.

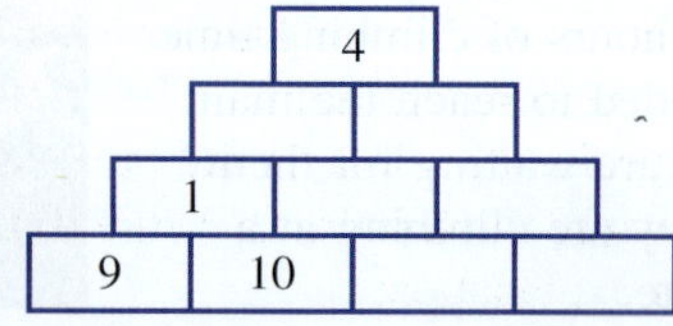

9 Six friends went to a theme park. They decided to go on the rides in pairs until each friend has ridden once with each of the others. How many rides did they go on?

10 If the small square has a side length of 2 cm and the line connecting the small square to the corner of the large square is also 2 cm, what is the area of the larger square?

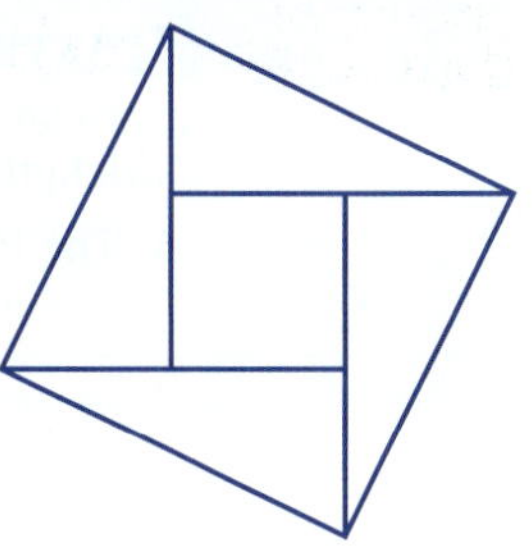

EXERCISE
15J Problem set J

PROBLEM SOLVING

1 In the final of a professional race there are three runners from the US, two from Cuba and one from Australia. The handicappers are satisfied that all the runners have an equal chance of winning. Use a two-way table to show that:
- a there is a 20% chance that first and second will both be American
- b the chance of first and second being Cuban is one in fifteen.

2 How could you number two cubes so that all of the days of the months from the 1st to the 31st can be shown?
Note: The order of the blocks can be changed and the blocks can be rotated if necessary.

3 Duke is a big dog and Candy is a small dog. Judy has 15 dog biscuits to feed the dogs. If she gives Duke 3 biscuits more than she gives to Candy, how many biscuits are given to each dog?

4 Can you draw a square so that the size of the area is equal to the size of the perimeter? (For example, 10 cm^2 and 10 cm.)

5 In Molly's kindergarten, the children were required to bring fruit to share. On Tuesday, $\frac{1}{4}$ of the children brought apples and $\frac{2}{5}$ bought bananas. Four children brought watermelon, two children brought plums and one child brought an orange. How many children were in the kindergarten?

6 a Calculate the values of the following pairs of expressions.
- i $\frac{1}{3}+\frac{1}{9}; \frac{1}{2}\times(1-\frac{1}{9})$
- ii $\frac{1}{3}+\frac{1}{9}+\frac{1}{27}; \frac{1}{2}\times(1-\frac{1}{27})$
- iii $\frac{1}{3}+\frac{1}{9}+\frac{1}{27}+\frac{1}{81}; \frac{1}{2}\times(1-\frac{1}{81})$

b What patterns can you see?

c Consider this sum: $\frac{1}{3}+\frac{1}{9}+\frac{1}{27}+\frac{1}{81}+\ldots$ It goes on forever. To express it we could include as many terms as we like, as long as we add the dashes to indicate a never ending series.
- i What are the next two terms?
- ii This sum cannot be done in the same fashion as ordinary fraction sums, but there are various ways to determine its value. Can you explain why it equals $\frac{1}{2}$? A diagram may help your explanation.

7 A cylindrical tank of radius r cm and height h cm has the same volume as another tank in the shape of a triangular prism. If the triangle is right-angled isosceles of hypotenuse l cm, find the length, g, of the prism in terms of r, h and l.

8 The following Venn diagram represents the information for two lines. Draw the two lines.

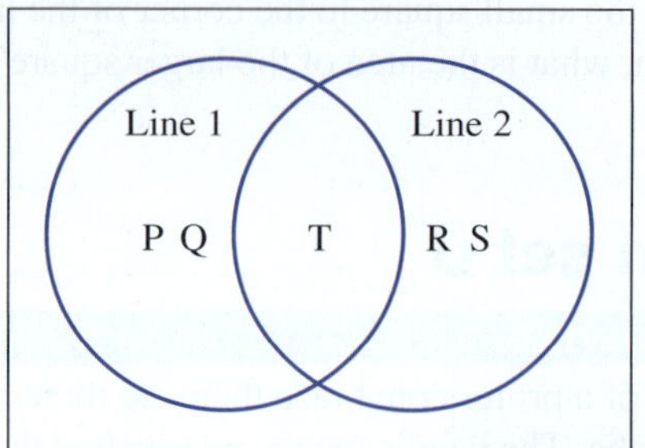

9 When two unbiased dice of the same kind are rolled, the probability of rolling a double depends on the number of sides on the dice. We can have 3-sided dice, 4-sided dice, 5-sided dice, …

Investigate, and determine how you are able to predict the probability of rolling a double with a pair of dice of the same kind that has any number of sides, without actually calculating the value. Write a general statement for your answer.

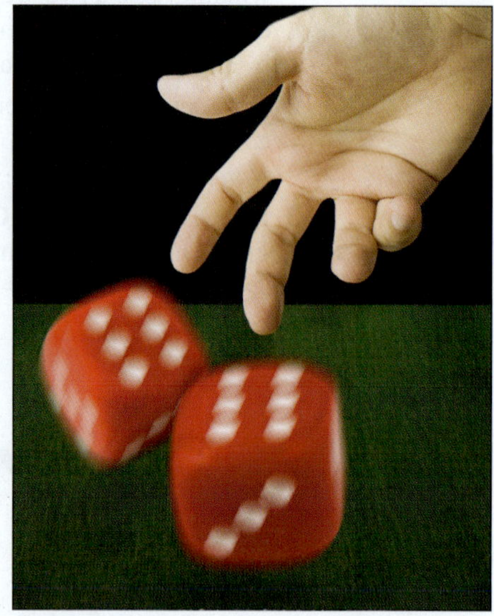

10 I have 2 bags containing red and green balls (as listed below). I draw out a green ball from one of the bags. What is the probability that I drew it from Bag B?
Bag A: 2 green, 2 red
Bag B: 2 green, 4 red.

Answers

CHAPTER 1

Numeracy

1A Set 1A

1 D **2** D **3** B
4 A **5** B **6** 31.25 cm^2
7 A **8** 120° **9** A
10 C **11** B **12** C
13 5582 cm^3 **14** D **15** B
16 2.1 m **17** $\frac{1}{4}$ **18** C
19 B **20** C **21** D
22 A **23** B **24** B
25 C **26** A **27** D
28 C **29** B **30** C

1B Set 1B

1 B **2** C **3** D
4 A **5** C **6** B
7 B **8** 47.56 s **9** C
10 C **11** B **12** D
13 B **14** D **15** C
16 B **17** C **18** C
19 C **20** D **21** D
22 205 **23** B **24** C
25 107° **26** 40%
27 7 pegs in each yellow bucket; 18 pegs in each blue bucket.
28 B **29** D **30** B

1C Set 1C

1 D **2** A **3** 11 pm
4 B **5** C **6** B
7 D **8** C **9** C
10 124 **11** 10 days **12** B
13 A **14** B **15** B
16 A **17** D **18** A
19 B **20** 58 cm **21** 4
22 B **23** B **24** C
25 D **26** A **27** C
28 B **29** B **30** D

1D Set 1D

1 B **2** C **3** D
4 D **5** C **6** A
7 D **8** A **9** B
10 D **11** C **12** B
13 A **14** B **15** $\frac{11}{15}$
16 A **17** D **18** A
19 D **20** D **21** C
22 C **23** 24 **24** C
25 C **26** B **27** B
28 A **29** C **30** B

1E Set 1E

1 A **2** B **3** B
4 D **5** C **6** 160 km
7 C **8** D **9** C
10 B **11** B **12** C
13 C **14** D **15** C
16 A **17** C **18** 4 km
19 C **20** C **21** 5
22 C **23** A **24** C
25 D **26** A **27** C
28 D **29** B **30** C

1F Set 1F

1 C **2** D **3** C
4 C **5** D **6** B
7 B **8** A **9** A
10 B **11** B **12** B
13 276 800 **14** C **15** 6
16 C **17** C **18** 32
19 9, 90 **20** D **21** True
22 C **23** A **24** A
25 35% **26** C **27** 220
28 B **29** B **30** C

CHAPTER 2

Integers

Are you ready?

1 0 1 2 3 4 5 6 7 8 9 10
2 a 2, 8 **b** 0, 4 **c** 2, 10
3 a 4869 **b** 635 **c** 2944
4 a 12, 17, 25, 29, 30, 39, 45, 56
b 56, 45, 39, 30, 29, 25, 17, 12
5 41 384
6 34 776
7 a 3 **b** 12 **c** 3
8 a 11 **b** 28 **c** 5
d 27 **e** 15 **f** 80

2A Adding and subtracting integers

1 3, –4, 201, –62
2 a 0, –2, –4
b –20, –25, –30
c 5, 3, 1
d –8, –6, –4
3 a –1 **b** –10 **c** –1 **d** –13
e 19 **f** 7 **g** –15 **h** 0
4 a 5 **b** –24 **c** –5 **d** 5
e 26 **f** –16 **g** 22 **h** 11
5 a –8 **b** 11 **c** –14 **d** –1
e 51 **f** –51 **g** –39 **h** 8
6 a –7 **b** –9 **c** 3 **d** 12
e –10 **f** 13 **g** –40 **h** 18
i 27 **j** –34 **k** –11 **l** 150
m –1 **n** 25 **o** –13 **p** 22
q 9 **r** –22
7 a

+	–8	25	–18	32
–6	–14	19	–24	26
–13	–21	12	–31	19
–16	–24	9	–34	16
–19	–27	6	–37	13

b

−	15	−17	−27	57
7	8	−24	−34	50
−6	21	−11	−21	63
−9	24	−8	−18	66
12	3	−29	−39	45

c

+	−11	19	13	−7
−5	−16	14	8	−12
17	6	36	30	10
−1	−12	18	12	−8
−28	−39	−9	−15	−35

d

−	9	21	−15	42
26	−17	−5	−41	16
−14	23	35	−1	56
−2	11	23	−13	44
23	−14	−2	−38	19

8 Check with your teacher.
9 a 22 °C **b** 176 °C **c** 198 °C
10 37 °C
11 a −301 **b** −5963
c 530 **d** 72
12 a 13 **b** −4 **c** 11
d −10 **e** 52 **f** 71
13 a Correct **b** Incorrect; 6
c Incorrect; −15 **d** Correct
e Correct **f** Incorrect; −21
14 a −3 **b** −2 **c** −5
15 The answers are the same.
16 a −7 **b** −11 **c** −13
17 The answers are the same.

2B Multiplying integers

1
$4 \times 4 = 16$
$4 \times 3 = 12$
$4 \times 2 = 8$
$4 \times 1 = 4$
$4 \times 0 = 0$
$4 \times -1 = -4$
$4 \times -2 = -8$
$4 \times -3 = -12$
$4 \times -4 = -16$

$-5 \times 4 = -20$
$-5 \times 3 = -15$
$-5 \times 2 = -10$
$-5 \times 1 = -5$
$-5 \times 0 = 0$
$-5 \times -1 = 5$
$-5 \times -2 = 10$
$-5 \times -3 = 15$
$-5 \times -4 = 20$

$-6 \times -4 = 24$
$-6 \times -3 = 18$
$-6 \times -2 = 12$
$-6 \times -1 = 6$
$-6 \times 0 = 0$
$-6 \times 1 = -6$
$-6 \times 2 = -12$
$-6 \times 3 = -18$
$-6 \times 4 = -24$

2 a −10 **b** −24 **c** 42 **d** −26
e 48 **f** −42 **g** −750 **h** 1150
i −63 **j** −72 **k** 55 **l** −300
3 a −800 **b** 112 **c** −192
d 42 **e** 160
4 a −9 **b** −7 **c** −2 **d** −12
e −6 **f** 8 **g** −20 **h** −6
i −11
5 a −8 **b** 9 **c** 16 **d** 81
e −32 **f** 16 **g** −125 **h** 256
i 625 **j** −216
6 a Positive **b** Negative
7 a ±5 **b** ±9 **c** ±7
d ±11 **e** ±10
8 a 48 **b** −36 **c** 72
d 16 **e** −12 **f** −576
9 Check with your teacher.
10 a Positive **b** Negative **c** Negative
11 If a positive number is multiplied by −1, the number becomes negative.
If a negative number is multiplied by −1, the number becomes positive.
12 a 2 **b** −3 **c** 5
d 5 **e** −7 **f** 4

2C Dividing integers

1 a −7 **b** −4 **c** −4 **d** 6
e −8 **f** 0 **g** −16 **h** −43
i 8 **j** −46 **k** 5 **l** −38
2 a 11 **b** −4 **c** 3
d −3 **e** 2 **f** 2
3 a −120 **b** −27 **c** 38
d 33 **e** −47 **f** −160
g −27 **h** −180 **i** 250
j 62 **k** 324 **l** 226
4 Check with your teacher.
5 a 3 **b** −2 **c** −9
d 3 **e** −35 **f** 24
g −12 **h** −10
6 a 1 **b** 6 **c** −20
7 a 3 **b** −4 **c** 2
d $\frac{-3}{4}$ **e** $\frac{-1}{2}$ **f** $\frac{2}{3}$
8 a 48 **b** −6 **c** −1
d −4 **e** $\frac{-1}{3}$ **f** −4

9 a

×	−2	4	−6	8
−3	6	−12	18	−24
−10	20	−40	60	−80
−5	10	−20	30	−40
−7	14	−28	42	−56

b

×	5	−3	−9	−7
6	30	−18	−54	−42
−12	−60	36	108	84
−11	−55	33	99	77
2	10	−6	−18	−14

10 a

÷	4	−10	12	−8
−2	−2	5	−6	4
7	$\frac{4}{7}$	$\frac{-10}{7}$	$\frac{12}{7}$	$\frac{-8}{7}$
−3	$\frac{-4}{3}$	$\frac{10}{3}$	−4	$\frac{8}{3}$
−10	$\frac{-2}{5}$	1	$\frac{-6}{5}$	$\frac{4}{5}$

b

÷	32	−24	−36	−4
12	$\frac{8}{3}$	−2	−3	$\frac{-1}{3}$
−8	−4	3	$\frac{9}{2}$	$\frac{1}{2}$
6	$\frac{16}{3}$	−4	−6	$\frac{-2}{3}$
−4	−8	6	9	1

2D Combined operations on integers

1 **a** −12 **b** −7 **c** −3 **d** 9
e 30 **f** −6 **g** −12 **h** −58
i −12 **j** 17 **k** 56 **l** −7

2 **a** −19 **b** −21 **c** −29 **d** −12
e −34 **f** −324

3 **a** −41 **b** −76 **c** −12 **d** 15
e −60 **f** 6 **g** −60 **h** 46

4 **a** −12
b 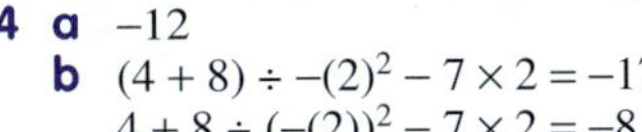
$(4+8) \div -(2)^2 - 7 \times 2 = -17$
$4 + 8 \div (-(2))^2 - 7 \times 2 = -8$

5

Round number	Points at the start of the round	Contacts during the round	Points at the end of the round
1	100	20 gnomes, 10 goblins and 3 healing potions	120
2	120	3 gnomes, 5 goblins, 6 orcs and 5 healing potions	177
3	177	3 orcs, 6 trolls and a cleric	152
4	152	5 trolls, 1 balrog and a cleric	52

Chapter review

Fluency

1 False
2 True
3 −10, −9, −8
4 −15, −3, 0, 7, 10
5 **a** −14 **b** 21 **c** −12 **d** 0
6 **a** 21 **b** 21 **c** 11 **d** −11
7 C
8 **a** 60 **b** −60 **c** 8 **d** −4
e 9 **f** −27 **g** 10 **h** −9

Problem solving

1 Check with your teacher.
2 **a** 74 **b** 14
3 **a** \$19.50 **b** 4431 m
4 **a**

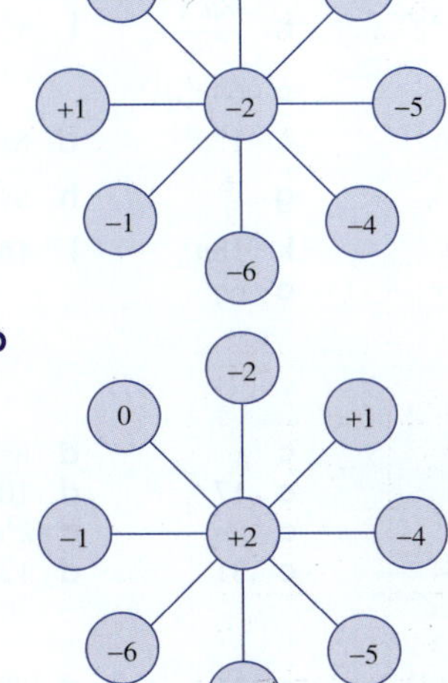

b

c 

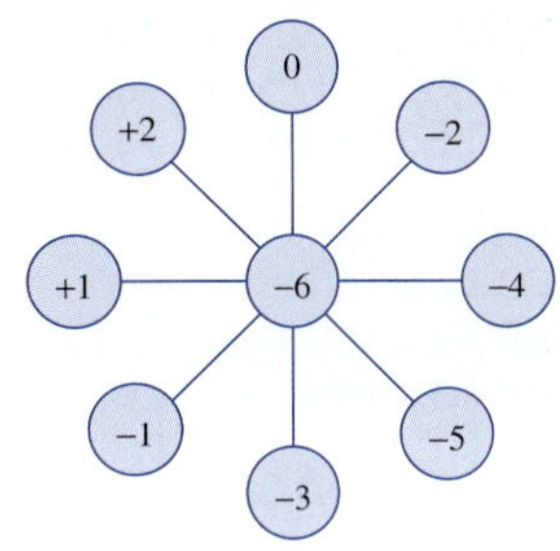

5 **a** **i** $2 \times 100 - 3 \times 75 + 20$ **ii** −\$5
b **i** 3×150 **ii** \$450
c **i** $3 \times 40 + 4 \times 10$ **ii** \$160
6 **a** −50 km **b** 750 km
7 **a** −200 km **b** 100 km

CHAPTER 3

Index laws

Are you ready?

1 **a** $32 = 2 \times 2 \times 2 \times 2 \times 2$ **b** $81 = 3 \times 3 \times 3 \times 3$
c $1000 = 2 \times 2 \times 2 \times 5 \times 5 \times 5$
2 **a** 36 **b** 121 **c** 2500
3 **a** $\frac{1}{3}$ **b** $\frac{2}{5}$ **c** $\frac{3}{4}$
4 **a** $6abc$ **b** $6zw$ **c** $20l^2$
5 **a** a **b** $\dfrac{m^2}{3}$ **c** $2k$

3A Review of index form

1 **a** Base = 8, power = 4
b Base = 7, power = 10
c Base = 20, power = 11
d Base = 19, power = 0
e Base = 78, power = 12
f Base = 3, power = 100
g Base = m, power = 5
h Base = c, power = 24
i Base = n, power = 36
j Base = d, power = 42
2 **a** 2^6 **b** 4^4 **c** x^5
d 9^3 **e** $11l^7$ **f** $44m^5$
3 **a** 4×4 **b** $5 \times 5 \times 5 \times 5$
c $7 \times 7 \times 7 \times 7 \times 7$ **d** $6 \times 6 \times 6$
e $3 \times 3 \times 3 \times 3 \times 3 \times 3$ **f** $n \times n \times n \times n \times n \times n \times n$
g $a \times a \times a \times a$
h $k \times k \times k \times k \times k \times k \times k \times k \times k \times k \times k \times k$
4 **a** 243 **b** 256 **c** 256
d 1331 **e** 2401 **f** 216
g 1 **h** 625
5 **a** B **b** D
6 **a** $2^2 \times 4^4 \times 6$ **b** $3^4 \times 7^4$ **c** $2^3 \times 19^5$
d $4^4 \times 13^2$ **e** $66p^2m^5s^2$ **f** $378n^2i^3r^3$
g $192ke^3p^2$ **h** $99j^5p^2l$
7 **a** $15 \times f \times f \times f \times j \times j \times j \times j$
b $7 \times k \times k \times k \times k \times k \times k \times s \times s$
c $4 \times b \times b \times b \times c \times c \times c \times c \times c$
d $19 \times a \times a \times a \times a \times n \times n \times n \times m$
e $8 \times r \times r \times l \times l \times l \times l \times t \times t$
8 **a** $64 = 2^6$ **b** $40 = 2^3 \times 5$ **c** $36 = 2^2 \times 3^2$
d $400 = 2^4 \times 5^2$ **e** $225 = 3^2 \times 5^2$ **f** $2000 = 2^4 \times 5^3$

9 **a** 120 **b** 100 **c** 216
d 308 **e** 1575 **f** 760 000
10 **a** **i** 10^1 **ii** 10^2 **iii** 10^3 **iv** 10^6
b **ii** 5×10^2
iii $4 \times 10^2 + 7 \times 10^1$
iv $2 \times 10^3 + 3 \times 10^2 + 6 \times 10^1$
v $1 \times 10^3 + 9 \times 10^2 + 8 \times 10^1$
vi $5 \times 10^3 + 4 \times 10^2 + 3 \times 10^1$
c **i** 75 000
ii 30 600
iii 5 200 480

3B First Index Law (multiplying numbers in index form with the same base)

1 **a** $2 \times 2 \times 2 \times 2 \times 2 \times 2 = 2^6$
b $5 \times 5 \times 5 \times 5 \times 5 \times 5 \times 5 \times 5 = 5^8$
c $f \times f \times f \times f \times f \times f \times f \times f \times f = f^9$
2 **a** 3^9 **b** 6^{17} **c** 10^{10} **d** 11^6
e 7^9 **f** 2^{14} **g** 5^4 **h** 8^{11}
i 13^{15} **j** q^{47} **k** x^{14} **l** e^4
3 **a** 3^{12} **b** 2^{18} **c** 5^{17} **d** 6^{11}
e 10^6 **f** 17^{12} **g** p^{22} **h** e^{23}
i g^{28} **j** e^{38} **k** $3b^{13}$ **l** $5d^{16}$
4 **a** A **b** B
5 **a** $20p^{11}$ **b** $6x^8$ **c** $56y^{10}$ **d** $21p^8$
e $84t^6$ **f** $30q^{15}$
6 **a** $6a^6e^7$ **b** $8p^6h^{12}$ **c** $80m^9$ **d** $6g^3h^6$
e $30p^6q^9$ **f** $48u^9w^7$ **g** $27d^{11}y^{17}$ **h** $42b^{14}c^9$
i $24r^{16}s^{18}$ **j** $60h^{38}v^{20}$
7 **a** 3^{x+4} **b** 3^{2y+2} **c** 3^{6y-5} **d** $3^{\frac{23}{12}}$
8 **a** $9 = 3^2$; $27 = 3^3$; $81 = 3^4$
b **i** 3^{10} **ii** 3^{2n+2}

3C Second Index Law (dividing numbers in index form with the same base)

1 **a** 2^3 **b** 7^4 **c** 10^3
2 **a** 3 **b** 11^7 **c** 5^4 **d** 12^5
e 3^3 **f** 13 **g** 6^4 **h** 10^4
i 15^{33} **j** h^{77} **k** b^{70} **l** f^{900}
3 **a** $3x^2$ **b** $6y^2$ **c** $8w^7$ **d** $3q^4$
e $8f^9$ **f** $10h^{90}$ **g** $4j^{10}$ **h** $5p^{10}$
i $8g^3$ **j** $\frac{3b^6}{2}$ **k** $\frac{9m^4}{2}$ **l** $\frac{5n^{90}}{2}$
4 **a** D **b** A
5 **a** $3p^4$ **b** $6r^4$ **c** $9a^3$ **d** $3b^6$
e $20r^4$ **f** $9q$
6 **a** $\frac{3p^5}{2}$ **b** $\frac{8b^5}{3}$ **c** $\frac{5m^{10}n^6}{6}$ **d** $\frac{9x^8y}{4}$
e $\frac{4hk^3}{3}$ **f** $3j^5f^3$ **g** $\frac{4p^2rs}{3}$ **h** $\frac{9a^5b^3c}{2}$
i $\frac{20f^6g^2h^4}{3}$
7 **a** 2^{10-p} **b** 2^{4e+4} **c** 5^{3x+y} **d** 3^{1-m}
8 **a** $\frac{2^3 \times 2^4 \times 2^2}{2^1 \times 2^5}$ **b** **i** 2^3 **ii** 8 **c** 8
9 **a** $\frac{2 \times 3 \times 3^3 \times 2^2 \times 3^2}{2^2 \times 3 \times 3^4}$
b **i** $2^1 \times 3^1$
ii 6

3D Third Index Law (the power of zero)

1 **a** 1 **b** 1 **c** 1 **d** 1
2 **a** 1 **b** 1 **c** 1 **d** 1
3 **a** 4 **b** 12 **c** 11 **d** 22
4 **a** $12m^3$ **b** 21 **c** 72 **d** $\frac{8}{7}$
e 2 **f** $10b^2$ **g** $3p^2$ **h** 1
5 **a** 1 **b** 1 **c** 1 **d** 7 **e** 3 **f** 3
6 **a** 1 **b** 4 **c** 2 **d** $2p^9$
e $\frac{3}{2}e^4$ **f** y **g** $\frac{m^3}{3}$ **h** $\frac{c^3}{4}$
7 **a** D **b** A **c** D
8 **a** 1 **b** 2 **c** 2 **d** 2
e 2 **f** $\frac{h^2}{2}$ **g** $\frac{q^4}{5}$ **h** $\frac{n^3}{5}$
i $4v^2$ **j** $2x^6$

3E Fourth Index Law (raising a power to another power)

1 **a** 3^6 **b** 6^{80} **c** 11^{100} **d** 5^{144}
e $3^8 \times 10^{12}$ **f** $13^5 \times 17^{15}$ **g** $\frac{3^{30}}{2^{20}}$ **h** $3^4w^{36}q^8$
i $\frac{7^2e^{10}}{r^4q^8}$
2 **a** p^8q^6 **b** $r^{15}w^9$ **c** $b^{10}n^{18}$ **d** $j^{18}g^{12}$
e q^4r^{20} **f** $h^{24}j^{16}$ **g** $f^{16}a^{21}$ **h** $t^{10}u^8$
i $i^{15}j^{12}$
3 **a** 2^{20} **b** t^{33} **c** a^{21} **d** b^{24}
e e^{66} **f** g^{39} **g** $324a^{20}$ **h** $216d^{27}$
i $40\,000r^{54}$
4 **a** B **b** B **c** D
5 **a** a^6 **b** m^4 **c** n^3 **d** b^8
e f^{17} **f** g^6 **g** p^9 **h** y^2
i c^{20} **j** f^7 **k** k^{14} **l** p^{16}
6 **a** $\frac{9b^8}{d^6}$ **b** $\frac{25h^{20}}{4j^4}$ **c** $\frac{8k^{15}}{27t^{24}}$ **d** $\frac{49p^{18}}{64q^{44}}$
e $\frac{125y^{21}}{27z^{39}}$ **f** $\frac{256a^{12}}{2401c^{20}}$
7 **a** $2g^8$ **b** $8p^8$ **c** w^{18} **d** $6x^5$
e $4d^6$ **f** $15a^{10}$ **g** $3s^6$ **h** $60b^4c^8$
i $2x^4$ **j** f^8g^6 **k** $\frac{8u^3v^4}{3}$ **l** x^3y^7
m $15a^9b^5$ **n** xy **o** $64p^6q^{15}$
8 **a** w^{10} **b** $6x^2$ **c** $12a^{11}$ **d** $8x^2$
e $7d^3 + d^2$ **f** k^2 **g** $\frac{2}{3}$ **h** $6s^7t^5$
i bc^4 **j** 0 **k** $18p$ **l** $16x^9y^7$
m $8a^6b^2$ **n** xy **o** $6q^2$

Chapter review

Fluency

1 **a** 5 **b** 9 **c** x **d** w
2 **a** 6 **b** 5 **c** 17 **d** 100
3 **a** 7^4 **b** 3^7 **c** m^5 **d** k^3n^5
4 **a** 36 **b** 64 **c** 81 **d** 128
e 125
5 **a** 33 **b** 83
6 **a** 3^{11} **b** 10^{15} **c** 7^9 **d** j^{19}
e t^{10} **f** $12z^7$ **g** $35w^{29}$ **h** $12e^5p^8$

7 a 6^3 **b** 12^9 **c** 5^{10} **d** 2^4
e 3^9 **f** m^{33} **g** p^{14} **h** h^{13}
i l^4 **j** y^6 **k** a^4 **l** $\frac{1}{c}$

8 a 1 **b** 1 **c** 1 **d** 1
e 1 **f** z **g** 7 **h** 6
i 64 **j** w^5 **k** 1 **l** kl
m d^2e^6 **n** r^4u^9

9 a 2^{12} **b** 6^{18} **c** 7^{40} **d** n^{126}
e $r^{32}i^{24}$ **f** $b^{40}d^{160}$ **g** $8p^3m^9$ **h** $81w^2z^8$

10 C

Problem solving

1 a i –1 **ii** 1 **iii** –1 **iv** 1
v –1 **vi** 1
b Positive one; negative one
c –2 if k and l are both odd; 0 if one of the powers is odd and one is even; 2 if both k and l are even.

2 a i 20 **ii** 40 **iii** 80 **iv** 10 240
b $N = 10 \times 2^t$
c 10×2^{60}

3 a i 25 **ii** 5^2
b i 125 **ii** 5^3
c i 780 **ii** $5 + 5^2 + 5^3 + 5^4$

4 a i 14 **ii** 28
b $P = 7 \times 2^{d-1}$
c 224
d Yes, the total for 6 days is 441, which is more than 400.

5 a \$20 000 **b** \$16 000
c 25 000 represents the purchase price of the car; 0.8 means 80% (expressed as a decimal) — this is the portion of the value that the car retains after each year.
d \$8192
e After 8 years

6 a 60
b i 69 **ii** 79
c 9 years

7 a \$2604.52 **b** \$12 250.40 **c** \$2250.40

8 a i 16 **ii** 256 **iii** 32 768
b i 29 491 **ii** 26 542 **iii** 11 426

9 a 880 **b** 10 880 **c** 2 170 880
d 2 161 947 723 463 393 280

10 a 3.0×10^9 **b** 4.0×10^4 **c** 5.0×10^6
d 3.0×10^5

11 a $2^2, 2^3, 2^4$
b i $2^{2x+3y-4}$ **ii** 1

12 a 50 **b** 686 **c** 833

13 a i 7.5 m **ii** 4.218 75 m **iii** 2.373 05
b After 8 bounces.

CHAPTER 4

Real numbers

Are you ready?

1 a 10 **b** 30
2 a 1, 2, 4, 5, 10, 20 **b** 1, 2, 3, 4, 6, 8, 12, 16, 24, 48
3 a 6, 12, 18, 24, 30 **b** 8, 16, 24, 32, 40
4 a $1\frac{2}{7}$ **b** $\frac{1}{8}$
5 a $\frac{7}{27}$ **b** $\frac{5}{6}$
6 a 22.7 **b** 42.86
7 a 4.44 **b** 36.544
8 a 90 **b** 500
9 a $\frac{5}{6}$ **b** $\frac{11}{35}$ **c** $4\frac{5}{12}$
d $\frac{5}{14}$ **e** $1\frac{1}{2}$ **f** $1\frac{9}{25}$
10 a 0.76 **b** 1.24 **c** 0.06
d 0.16 **e** 9.6 **f** 0.8

4A Addition and subtraction of fractions

1 a $\frac{13}{20}$ **b** $1\frac{3}{8}$ **c** $\frac{1}{5}$ **d** $\frac{18}{25}$
e $1\frac{7}{12}$ **f** $\frac{43}{70}$ **g** $\frac{37}{42}$ **h** $2\frac{13}{30}$

2 a $\frac{9}{17}$ **b** $\frac{5}{27}$ **c** $\frac{12}{17}$ **d** $\frac{4}{5}$

3 a $1\frac{2}{5}$ **b** $1\frac{1}{4}$ **c** 2 **d** $\frac{23}{50}$

4 a $-1\frac{3}{5}$ **b** $3\frac{2}{9}$ **c** $4\frac{3}{5}$ **d** $4\frac{2}{3}$
e $2\frac{1}{2}$ **f** 7 **g** $9\frac{1}{2}$ **h** $21\frac{8}{45}$
i $2\frac{3}{4}$ **j** $2\frac{7}{15}$

5 a $3\frac{3}{10}$ **b** $2\frac{2}{3}$ **c** $4\frac{17}{20}$ **d** $1\frac{21}{40}$

6 a –4 –3 **b** –3 –2
c –5 –4 **d** 6 7
e –2 –1 0 1 **f** –2 –1 0 1
g –7 –6 –5 –4 **h** 2 3
i –2 –1 **j** 2 3 4

7 a $x > -1\frac{1}{2}$ **b** $x \le 6\frac{3}{4}$
c $-7\frac{1}{2} < x \le -6\frac{1}{3}$ **d** $x < \frac{2}{3}$
e $x \ge -4\frac{2}{5}$ **f** $10\frac{3}{4} \le x < 11\frac{3}{4}$
g $x > -8.7$ **h** $-2\frac{1}{2} < x < \frac{2}{3}$

8 a $-4\frac{1}{2}, -3, 0, 5.8, 6$ **b** $-4.2, -1, -\frac{3}{4}, 1\frac{1}{2}, 3\frac{2}{3}$
c $-8.6, -6.8, -\frac{2}{3}, 0, \frac{1}{4}$

9 a $-\frac{2}{5}$ **b** $-\frac{8}{8}$ or –1 **c** $-\frac{1}{4}$ **d** $-\frac{5}{6}$
e $\frac{1}{8}$ **f** $-\frac{5}{6}$ **g** $-\frac{1}{10}$ **h** $\frac{5}{12}$
i $-4\frac{1}{4}$ **j** $-\frac{14}{15}$ **k** $-5\frac{5}{6}$ **l** $4\frac{17}{20}$

10 a $-\frac{1}{4}$ **b** $-\frac{5}{6}$ **c** $-\frac{11}{15}$ **d** $-\frac{7}{20}$
e $-\frac{3}{4}$ **f** $-2\frac{4}{15}$

11 1 — whole or all of it **12** $1\frac{7}{9}$ bottles were left over.

13 He has $\frac{4}{15}$ of his pay left.

14 $\frac{5}{12}$ of the class get a lift.

15 $\frac{11}{8}$ or $1\frac{3}{8}$ of the cake was left.

4B Multiplication and division of fractions

1 a $\frac{3}{8}$ **b** $\frac{1}{56}$ **c** $\frac{6}{25}$ **d** $\frac{5}{21}$
e $\frac{5}{12}$ **f** $\frac{1}{3}$ **g** $\frac{11}{30}$ **h** $\frac{1}{5}$
i $\frac{11}{32}$ **j** $\frac{3}{5}$ **k** $\frac{4}{5}$ **l** $\frac{1}{4}$

2 a $5\frac{3}{5}$ **b** $1\frac{11}{25}$ **c** 4 **d** $8\frac{3}{4}$
e $6\frac{23}{100}$ **f** $13\frac{4}{5}$ **g** 13 **h** 1
i $11\frac{7}{8}$

3 a $\frac{2}{3}$ **b** $\frac{7}{12}$ **c** $\frac{6}{7}$ **d** $1\frac{3}{5}$
e $\frac{6}{7}$ **f** $\frac{15}{16}$ **g** $\frac{3}{5}$ **h** $\frac{6}{25}$
i 2

4 a 1 **b** $1\frac{5}{7}$ **c** $\frac{7}{12}$ **d** $5\frac{1}{7}$
e $1\frac{3}{5}$ **f** $\frac{14}{25}$ **g** $2\frac{3}{16}$ **h** $4\frac{8}{25}$
i $1\frac{7}{135}$

5 a $-\frac{1}{6}$ **b** $\frac{3}{20}$ **c** $-4\frac{2}{3}$ **d** $-\frac{1}{4}$
e $-\frac{5}{8}$ **f** $-\frac{1}{4}$ **g** $-1\frac{5}{9}$ **h** $2\frac{3}{4}$
i −2

6 a $-\frac{2}{5}$ **b** $-\frac{8}{9}$ **c** $\frac{7}{8}$ **d** $-\frac{3}{8}$
e $-\frac{1}{6}$ **f** $-\frac{3}{10}$ **g** $4\frac{1}{2}$ **h** $-2\frac{2}{5}$
i $-\frac{8}{35}$

7 12

8 a $\frac{1}{5}$ **b** 15 lollies each

9 a $-\frac{11}{15}$ **b** $-2\frac{3}{16}$ **c** 0 **d** $1\frac{11}{21}$
e $-8\frac{5}{6}$ **f** $1\frac{4}{17}$

10 128 non-American caps **11** $\frac{1}{16}$ of the cake each

12 \$30 to the children's charity, \$80 to the cruelty to animals charity, \$10 left over

4C Terminating and recurring decimals

1 a 0.8 **b** 0.25 **c** 0.75
d $0.41\dot{6}$ **e** $0.\overline{81}$ **f** 0.84
g 1.75 **h** $2.\dot{1}6$ **i** $0.4\dot{6}$
j $0.\dot{6}$

2 a $1.8\dot{3}$ **b** 1.75 **c** 3.4
d 8.8 **e** 12.9 **f** 6.75
g $5.\dot{6}$ **h** $11.7\dot{3}$ **i** 6.5
j $4.\dot{3}$

3 a −0.8 **b** −0.78 **c** −1.6
d −0.27 **e** −0.375 **f** −2.25
g −6.6 **h** −3.14 **i** −1.83
j −5.89

4 a $\frac{2}{5}$ **b** $\frac{4}{5}$ **c** $1\frac{1}{5}$
d $3\frac{1}{5}$ **e** $5\frac{3}{5}$ **f** $\frac{3}{4}$
g $1\frac{3}{10}$ **h** $7\frac{7}{50}$ **i** $4\frac{21}{100}$
j $10\frac{1}{25}$ **k** $1\frac{333}{1000}$ **l** $8\frac{1}{20}$
m $7\frac{39}{125}$ **n** $9\frac{47}{50}$ **o** $12\frac{9}{200}$
p $84\frac{63}{500}$ **q** $73\frac{9}{10}$ **r** $\frac{21}{5000}$

5 0.75 **6** 1.1

7 0.56 **8** $\frac{2}{5}$

4D Addition and subtraction of decimals

1 a 12.9 **b** 13 **c** 19.68
d 20.3 **e** 17.26 **f** 8.14
g 132.44 **h** 42.719 **i** 6.239
j 20.672 **k** 59.434 **l** 394.132
m 126.157 **n** 7113.556

2 a 2.24 **b** 7.32 **c** 121.66
d 54.821 **e** 42.33 **f** 1674.93
g 53.16 **h** 124.966 **i** 22.897
j 26.03 **k** 33.028 **l** 474.104

3 a E **b** B

4 a 115.09 **b** 31.953 **c** 821.48
d 1954.291 **e** 1493.875 **f** 433.98
g 1553.589 **h** 8.884 **i** 598.018
j 4224.296

5 a −0.9 **b** −0.7 **c** −0.57
d −0.991 **e** 7.606 **f** 0.6343

6 a −0.7 **b** −1.32 **c** 3.4
d −4.3 **e** −2.55 **f** −0.818

7 a 27 **b** 46 **c** 21
d 129

8 a Salmah spent \$157.22.
b She would have \$42.78 left.

9 41.37 seconds

10 9.88 km

11 763.4 km

12 15.8 km

13 Spending decreased by \$10.5 billion.

4E Multiplication and division of decimals

1 a 4.96 **b** 9.48 **c** 210.24
d 613.2 **e** 2.036 **f** 78.624
g 582.659 **h** 1153.96 **i** 2183.14
j 40.74 **k** 156.78 **l** 0.2616
m 624.036 **n** 0.344 55 **o** 0.147 62

2 a 6.17 **b** 130.98 **c** 790.14
d 95.54 **e** 6.41 **f** 2.53

3 a 88.83 **b** 1920.86 **c** 5355
d 536 515 **e** 29 933.75 **f** 954 087.50
g 6466.25 **h** 89 920 **i** 134.60
j 1714.36 **k** 7012.80 **l** 6.56

4 a −0.06 **b** −0.72 **c** 0.024
d 0.36 **e** 0.09 **f** −0.16
g −2000 **h** 0.008 **i** 0.0025
j −0.294 **k** −1.6 **l** 0.1296

5 a −42 **b** −0.3 **c** 0.135
d −30 **e** −0.7 **f** 400
g −0.06 **h** −9000 **i** 0.000 05
j −5 **k** 36 **l** 45

6 a 13.9 **b** 1.5 **c** 7.6
d 2.0

7 a D **b** B

8 a 133 **b** 90 **c** 501
d 46

9 \$5.30

10 10

11 43.98

12 2.015

4F Percentages, fractions and decimals

1 a 87.5%
b 60%
c 83.33% (correct to 2 decimal places)
d 233.33% (correct to 2 decimal places)

2 **a** 15% **b** 85% **c** 310% **d** 2.4%
3 **a** $\frac{1}{5}$ **b** $\frac{7}{20}$ **c** $\frac{61}{100}$ **d** $\frac{21}{20}$
4 **a** 0.24 **b** 0.13 **c** 0.015 **d** 2.50
5 **a** 10%, 25%, 75%, $\frac{7}{8}$, 1.6, 2.4, $3\frac{1}{2}$
b 150%, $2\frac{1}{3}$, 2.8, 3, 330%, $3\frac{4}{5}$, 4.5
6 30%
7 56.67%
8 30%
9 35.29%
10 $55.99
11 64
12 Yes, 5%
13 26.67%

4G Estimation

1 Estimate: 72. Kim is correct.
2 **a** **i** 200 **ii** 300 **iii** 200
b **i** 5000 **ii** 5000 **iii** 4000
c **i** 20 **ii** 30 **iii** 20
d **i** 50 000 **ii** 60 000 **iii** 50 000
e **i** 600 **ii** 600 **iii** 500
f **i** 1000 **ii** 2000 **iii** 1000
3 **a** 230 **b** 4520 **c** 20 **d** 53 620
e 590 **f** 1040
4 **a** 300 **b** 4600 **c** 100 **d** 53 700
e 600 **f** 1100
5 **a** 4 **b** 340 **c** 520 **d** 1170
e 300 **f** 24 000 **g** 54 000 **h** 20
i 9680 **j** 10 **k** 108 000 **l** 20
m 28 000 **n** 600 **o** 4000 **p** 810 000
6 **a** 4000 **b** 500 **c** 70 000 **d** 12 000
e 8000 **f** 400
7 **a** 20.5 **b** 150.175 **c** 20.25 **d** 5.13
e 54.4 **f** 64.8
8 $500
9 **a** 4 and 5 **b** 10 and 11
c 13 and 14 **d** 15 and 16

10

	Question	Simplified question	Estimated answer	Exact answer
a	789 × 56	800 × 60	48 000	44 184
b	124 ÷ 5	100 ÷ 5	20	24.8
c	678 + 98 + 46	700 + 100 + 50	850	822
d	235 × 209	200 × 200	40 000	49 115
e	7863 − 908	8000 − 900	7100	6955
f	63 × 726	60 × 700	42 000	45 738
g	39 654 ÷ 227	40 000 ÷ 200	200	174.69
h	1809 − 786 + 467	2000 − 800 + 500	1700	1490
i	21 × 78 × 234	20 × 80 × 200	320 000	383 292
j	942 ÷ 89	900 ÷ 90	10	10.58
k	$\frac{492 \times 94}{38 \times 49}$	$\frac{500 \times 100}{40 \times 50}$	25	24.84
l	$\frac{54\,296}{97 \times 184}$	$\frac{50\,000}{100 \times 200}$	2.5	3.04

11 **a** $300 000 **b** 640 mL
c $200 **d** 5000 seconds
e $1 080 000 **f** $16 000
g 4 000 000 pieces of litter

Chapter review

Fluency

1 **a** 8 **b** −13 **c** −86 **d** 0
2 **a** 48 **b** −4 **c** 8 **d** −300
e −200
3 **a** $1\frac{11}{21}$ **b** $5\frac{1}{10}$ **c** $1\frac{5}{8}$ **d** $1\frac{7}{20}$
e $4\frac{7}{64}$ **f** $4\frac{2}{5}$
4 0, 1.2, 2.4
5 **a** $x \le 10\frac{4}{5}$ (or 10.8) **b** $-3.9 \le x \le -3.2$
6

7 **a** $-1\frac{1}{15}$ **b** $-1\frac{3}{10}$
8 **a** $\frac{7}{20}$ **b** $\frac{6}{7}$ **c** $2\frac{2}{3}$ **d** $41\frac{1}{6}$
e 18 **f** $\frac{9}{34}$ **g** $-\frac{5}{16}$ **h** $7\frac{1}{3}$
9 **a** 0.75 **b** 1.40 **c** 6.25 **d** 1.80
e $4.\dot{6}$ **f** 12.375
10 **a** $\frac{7}{10}$ **b** $\frac{9}{20}$ **c** $1\frac{23}{100}$ **d** $3\frac{2}{25}$
e $24\frac{73}{200}$ **f** $17\frac{1}{25}$
11 **a** 6.1 **b** 6.73 **c** 14.94 **d** 5.56
e 30.192 **f** 3514.5903 **g** −0.577 **h** −4.17
12 **a** 865.8 **b** 265.27 **c** 4530.83 **d** 8.77
e 0.42 **f** 106 042.86 **g** 0.2 **h** 2.04
13 **a** 26% **b** 75% **c** 212.5% **d** 435%
14 **a** **i** 40 000 **ii** 40 000 **iii** 30 000
b **i** 200 **ii** 300 **iii** 200
c **i** 3000 **ii** 4000 **iii** 3000
15 **a** 70 **b** 800 **c** 1000
16 3.75
17 **a** 3600 **b** 103 330 **c** 200 **d** 15 000

Problem solving

1 **a** $2\frac{1}{8}$
b No. 3 pieces short
c Red Cross $30, World Vision $100, $20 left over
2 **a** Check with your teacher.
b 2.145
c No because the number could have any number of decimal places, but must be less than 2.155.
3 **a** $\frac{21}{28}$ **b** $\frac{15}{20}$
4 7 grey horses
5 NPQR is $\frac{1}{8}$ the area of ABCD.
6 218.04
7 $\frac{13}{20}$
8 **a** Mix A
b 90 cups
c 36 cups of cordial, 54 cups of water
9 $3.20/kg
10 $1892

11 The magic sum is 1.3.

0.34	0.48	0.02	0.16	0.3
0.46	0.1	0.14	0.28	0.32
0.08	0.12	0.26	0.4	0.44
0.2	0.24	0.38	0.42	0.06
0.22	0.36	0.5	0.04	0.18

12 $\frac{5}{6}$ is an answer. There are others. Check with your teacher.

13 $\frac{7}{16}=\cfrac{1}{2+\cfrac{1}{8+\cfrac{1}{2}}}$

14 63%

15 Yes, rounded to two decimal places, Jack's percentage mark is 73%, which is higher than the other students' marks.

16 28%

17 $68.20

CHAPTER 5

Ratios and rates

Are you ready?

1 **a** 300 **b** 5200 **c** 4250 **d** 2000 **e** 500 **f** 6400 **g** 8200 **h** 240 **i** 150 **j** 28 **k** 24 **l** 104

2 **a** 3 **b** 4 **c** 3 **d** 5

3 **a** $\frac{3}{4}$ **b** $\frac{4}{5}$ **c** $\frac{3}{5}$ **d** $\frac{18}{25}$

4 **a** $\frac{4}{12}, \frac{9}{12}$ **b** $\frac{9}{24}, \frac{14}{24}$ **c** $\frac{8}{12}, \frac{5}{12}$ **d** $\frac{14}{20}, \frac{15}{20}$

5 **a** $\frac{7}{4}$ **b** $\frac{13}{5}$ **c** $\frac{37}{10}$ **d** $\frac{83}{8}$

6 **a** 12.37 **b** 0.84 **c** 28.4 **d** 0.784

7 **a** 20 **b** 48 **c** 150 **d** 60

8 **a** $\frac{1}{4}$ **b** $\frac{2}{3}$ **c** $\frac{3}{5}$ **d** $\frac{9}{10}$

5A Introduction to ratios

1 **a** 4 : 5 **b** 5 : 4 **c** 5 : 9 **d** 9 : 4 **e** 1 : 2

2 **a** 5 : 3 **b** 3 : 5 **c** 1 : 5 **d** 5 : 1 **e** 1 : 3 **f** 5 : 4 **g** 1 : 8 **h** 5 : 9 **i** 1 : 9 **j** 1 : 3

3 **a** 5 : 7 **b** 7 : 5 **c** 5 : 12

4 **a** 4 : 3 **b** 3 : 4 **c** 6 : 1 **d** 4 : 1 **e** 2 : 5

5 **a** 3 : 5 **b** 6 : 19 **c** 4 : 11 **d** 7 : 9 **e** 1 : 5 **f** 9 : 4 **g** 3 : 4 **h** 3 : 10 **i** 17 : 60 **j** 53 : 100 **k** 11 : 100 **l** 1 : 1000 **m** 1 : 2000 **n** 7 : 24 **o** 5 : 12 **p** 1000 : 27 **q** 7 : 12 **r** 13 : 24 **s** 3 : 5 **t** 1 : 22

6 **a** 3 : 59 **b** 59 : 38 **c** 38 : 3 **d** 3 : 97 **e** 59 : 41

7 **a** 24 : 17 **b** 21 : 17 **c** 2 : 1 **d** 4 : 39 **e** 4 : 1 **f** 1 : 1 **g** 1 : 2 **h** 3 : 1 **i** 9 : 1 **j** 1 : 3 **k** 1 : 6 **l** 1 : 4

8 **a** 215 : 179 **b** 215 : 36

9 **a** 97 : 3 **b** 3 : 100

10 **a** Yes (same units) **b** Yes (same units) **c** No (different units) **d** No (different units) **e** Yes (same units) **f** Yes (same units) **g** No (different units) **h** Yes (same units)

11 **a** 17 : 83 **b** 97 : 3

5B Simplifying ratios

1 **a** 1 : 2 **b** 1 : 3 **c** 1 : 2 **d** 1 : 3 **e** 3 : 4 **f** 5 : 6 **g** 3 : 2 **h** 3 : 2 **i** 5 : 3 **j** 1 : 2 **k** 3 : 7 **l** 3 : 4 **m** 4 : 5 **n** 3 : 2 **o** 5 : 6 **p** 10 : 3 **q** 7 : 8 **r** 3 : 4 **s** 7 : 12 **t** 2 : 3

2 **a** 1 : 3, 2 : 6, 3 : 9, 4 : 12, 5 : 15 **b** 2 : 1, 4 : 2, 8 : 4, 16 : 8, 20 : 10 **c** 2 : 3, 4 : 6, 6 : 9, 8 : 12, 16 : 24 **d** 64 : 32, 32 : 16, 16 : 8, 8 : 4, 2 : 1 **e** 48 : 64, 24 : 32, 12 : 16, 6 : 8, 3 : 4

3 **a** 2 : 3 **b** 1 : 3 **c** 5 : 3 **d** 2 : 5 **e** 1 : 4 **f** 8 : 3 **g** 3 : 40 **h** 1 : 5 **i** 9 : 4 **j** 8 : 13 **k** 5 : 4 **l** 5 : 4 **m** 1 : 5 **n** 11 : 2 **o** 2 : 5 **p** 16 : 9 **q** 3 : 10 **r** 3 : 2 **s** 7 : 3 **t** 1 : 6

4 **a** 4 : 5 **b** 2 : 3 **c** 3 : 2 **d** 4 : 1 **e** 4 : 3 **f** 5 : 4 **g** 1 : 8 **h** 10 : 3 **i** 8 : 1 **j** 9 : 2

5 **a** 1 : 20 **b** 1 : 9 **c** 12 : 11 **d** 7 : 300

6 **a** 1 : 2 **b** 5 : 6 **c** 1 : 2 **d** 4 : 5 **e** 16 : 9 **f** 10 : 9 **g** 3 : 10 **h** 5 : 1 **i** 5 : 6 **j** 4 : 3 **k** 5 : 8 **l** 65 : 56

7 **a** 7 : 9 **b** 1 : 7 **c** 1 : 3 **d** 4 : 5 **e** 1 : 6 **f** 15 : 32 **g** 10 : 1 **h** 4 : 5 **i** 1 : 10 **j** 48 : 35 **k** 1 : 20 **l** 25 : 46

8 **a** $a : 5b$ **b** 2 : 1 **c** $2x : 3$ **d** $y : 2$ **e** $3m : 4$ **f** $1 : 4b$ **g** $10^2 : x^2$ **h** $2cd^2 : 1$

9 **a** 5 : 8 **b** 2 : 3 **c** 3 : 5 **d** 4 : 3 **e** 4 : 13

10 **a** 929 : 321 **b** 217 : 22 **c** 9 : 16 **d** 11 : 9 **e** 6 : 29

11 **a** 85 : 103 **b** 50 : 71 **c** 2 : 3 **d** **i** $425 000 **ii** 1 : 2 **e** In a period of just over 6 years, the price of the house has increased by half its purchase price (in 2003).

12 **a** A **b** D **c** E **d** A **e** B

5C Proportion

1 **a** Yes **b** Yes **c** Yes **d** Yes **e** No **f** Yes **g** No **h** No **i** No **j** Yes **k** No **l** Yes

2 **a** $a = 1$ **b** $a = 4$ **c** $a = 6$ **d** $a = 4$ **e** $a = 24$ **f** $a = 50$ **g** $a = 12$ **h** $a = 6$ **i** $a = 6$ **j** $a = 1$ **k** $a = 4$ **l** $a = 3$

3 **a** 9 boys **b** 10 m **c** 21 wins **d** 24 chickens

e 5 litres
f 7 tables
g 4 cups
h 33 g
i 75 cartons
j 3280 women

4 a 11.2 b 4.8 c 2.1 d 8.1
e 7.1 f 9.3 g 7.7 h 10.8
i 11.7 j 10.3

5 a $\frac{1}{3}=\frac{n}{5}$, $n = 1.7$ b $\frac{2}{6}=\frac{n}{11}$, $n = 3.7$ c $\frac{15}{4}=\frac{50}{n}$, $n = 13.3$
d $\frac{2}{17}=\frac{5}{n}$, $n = 42.5$ e $\frac{2}{3}=\frac{15}{n}$, $n = 22.5$

6 a No b No c No d Yes e Yes
f No g Yes h Yes i Yes j No

7 a C b E c A d D

8 The 16-year-old receives \$32, the 14-year-old receives \$28, the 10-year-old receives \$20.

9 a White gold $\frac{3}{4}$, pink gold $\frac{3}{4}$.
b Because $\frac{18}{24}=\frac{3}{4}$.
c 6 g
d \$210

10 4 : 5

5D Comparing ratios

1 a 3 : 4 b 7 : 9 c 6 : 5 d 7 : 10
e 7 : 9 f 2 : 5 g 3 : 4 h 7 : 8
i 7 : 12 j 6 : 5

2 a Colac b Bright 50
c Seymour d Bairnsdale

3 Jenny

4 a i 1 ii $\frac{2}{3}$ iii $\frac{2}{5}$ iv $\frac{3}{14}$
b AB c GH d iv, iii, ii, i

5 a b 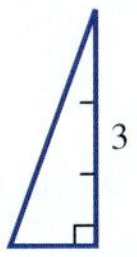 c 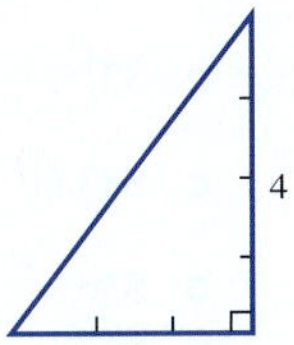 d 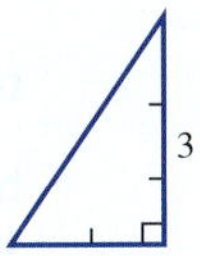 e

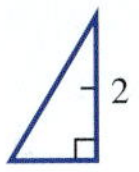

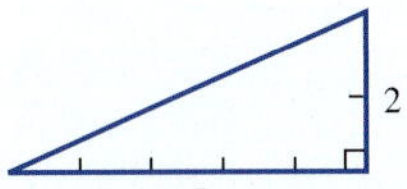

6 a C b A c C

7 a 3 : 4 : 5
b The ratio of the 3 sides stays the same.
c 0.75 m, 1 m, 1.25 m

5E Dividing in a given ratio

1 a 3 b 5 c 4 d 8 e 13
f 13 g 13 h 19 i 6 j 12

2 a \$400, \$600 b \$750, \$250
c \$200, \$800 d \$500, \$500
e \$375, \$625 f \$625, \$375
g \$300, \$700 h \$900, \$100
i \$350, \$650 j \$450, \$550

3 a \$5000, \$5000 b \$4000, \$6000
c \$6000, \$4000 d \$3000, \$7000
e \$7000, \$3000 f \$2000, \$8000
g \$9000, \$1000 h \$3750, \$6250
i \$4800, \$5200 j \$4600, \$5400

4 a \$10 000, \$40 000 b \$15 000, \$35 000
c \$20 000, \$30 000 d \$25 000, \$25 000
e \$12 500, \$37 500

5 a 2 m^3 b 0.5 m^3 c 1.6 m^3
d 1.6 m^3 e 1.2 m^3

6 a \$90 000, \$210 000, \$300 000
b \$180 000, \$180 000, \$240 000
c \$30 000, \$240 000, \$330 000
d \$150 000, \$180 000, \$270 000
e \$150 000, \$225 000, \$225 000

7 \$25, \$20, \$15

8 a 90
b 75

9 a 120 b 45 c \$6 d \$19.50

10 a D b D c A d D

11 30°, 60°, 90°

12 96°

5F Rates

1 a 10 m^2/min b 5 kL/min
c 300 cm^3/s d \$1.38/L
e 8 L/100 km or 12.5 km/L f \$2.50/m
g 40 cows/hectare or (250 m^2/cow)
h \$12.50/person i \$3.20/m^2
j 25 c/min k 16 points/game
l \$5.40/kg m $8\frac{1}{3}$ m/s
n 5.2 runs/over o \$26.50/h
p \$3.50/kg q 52 words/min
r 2 °C/h s 6.5 cm/year
t 16 km/h

2 \$108.50

3 396 points

4 60.5 L **5** 21

6 70 min **7** 12 days

8 49 **9** 1500 m^2

10 42

11 a $\frac{\text{distance}}{\text{time}}$ b $\frac{\text{volume}}{\text{time}}$ c $\frac{\text{capacity}}{\text{distance}}$
d $\frac{\text{money}}{\text{time}}$ e $\frac{\text{money}}{\text{length}}$ f $\frac{\text{capacity}}{\text{time}}$
g $\frac{\text{money}}{\text{capacity}}$ h $\frac{\text{money}}{\text{number}}$ i $\frac{\text{mass}}{\text{time}}$
j $\frac{\text{number}}{\text{area}}$

12 a mL/min b m/s c cm/year
d cm/h e mm^2/sec f L/km
g Runs/over h Words/min

13 360 L **14** Packs of 10

15 Car A **16** 250 g jar; 75c

17 a C b C c D d B

18 a 4 patients per hour
b 15 min
c \$62.50 per patient

19 4 min

20 $1\frac{7}{8}$ hours or 1 hour 52 minutes 30 seconds

Chapter review

Fluency

1 a 3 : 5 b 1 : 17 c 17 : 3
d 5 : 1 e 5 : 21
2 a 1 : 2 b 2 : 3 c 7 : 20
d 10 : 3 e 2 : 9 f 1 : 4
g 2 : 5 h 7 : 10 i 3 : 1
j 15 : 4
3 a $n = 4$ b $n = 20$ c $n = 12$
d $n = 15$ e $n = 9.6$ f $n = 1.2$
4 a 1 : 6 b 1.5 L
5 a $\frac{4}{5}$ b $\frac{5}{8}$
6 10 or 11
7 a Slide A: $\frac{2}{3}$, slide B: $\frac{2}{5}$ b Slide A
8 a $10, $15 b $420, $300
9 $880
10 8.57 L/100 km
11 a David's b 432 km c 42 L
12 1 kg packet

Problem solving

1 96 cm 2 32.9 cm
3 10 cm 4 16
5 32 km/h 6 28 064.5 km/h
7 a 13.5 km/min b 808.3 km/h
8 a 45 km b 15 km/h
9 4.5 kg 10 20 cm
11 68.61 km/h 12 $700
13 1 h 6 min 40 s

CHAPTER 6

Application of percentages

Are you ready?

1 a $23.50 b $207.90
2 a 0.34 b 0.79 c 0.04
d 0.672 e 0.0825 f 0.175
3 a 85% b 87.5%
c 10% d 94.5%
4 a $35 b $356
c $1620 d $571.25
5 a 14% b 65% c 20%
6 a 125% b 105%
c 200% d 112.5%

6A Common percentages and shortcuts

1 a $1.00 b $1.80 c $4.50
d $8.10 e $15.00 f $11.20
g $9.30 h $7.90 i $4.70
j $2.20 k $1.65 l $1.70
m $1.25 n $0.15 o $3.30
p $4.80 q $8.15 r $19.25
s $50.70 t $462.00 u $192.60
v $304.15 w $721.95 x $200.00
2 a $1.50 b $5.10 c $1.70
d $0.90 e $13.70 f $17.20
g $0.45 h $0.65 i $0.80
j $3.90 k $7.50 l $1.40
m $10.30 n $6.80 o $4.30
p $51.80 q $30.50 r $62.85
s $10.05 t $20.70
3 a $0.40 b $0.30 c $0.10
d $0.10 e $7.00 f $4.05
g $2.10 h $0.55 i $12.15
j $15.25 k $50 l $32.15
m $5.15 n $1.60 o $0.30
4 a $4.30 b $8.45 c $1.65
d $0.65 e $14.80 f $0.20
g $0.15 h $3.30 i $27.15
j $52.35 k $247.40 l $1013.80
5 a $1.80 b $1.20 c $3.00
d $9.00 e $7.50 f $11.25
g $22.50 h $55.00 i $4.50
j $7.50 k $14.25 l $30.65
6 a $2.70 b $7.15 c $5.75
d $6.05 e $0.05 f $0.10
g $0.15 h $0.15 i $0.20
j $0.80 k $0.20 l $4.30
m $0.05 n $0.05 o $0.10
p $0.00 q $0.00 r $12.65
7 a $1.30 b $10.50 c $3.30
d $0.65 e $2.40 f $2.20
g $1.80 h $73.50 i $18.00
j $1.55 k $1.05 l $2.05
m $32.20 n $4.80 o $1.60
p $0.45 q $14.40 r $492
8 a D b B c A
d C
9 $855 10 54 000 residents
11 $322.50 12 110 students
13 27.9 seconds
14 a 2 people b 38 people
15 a 13 608 people b 17 820 people
16 $10\% + 5\% + 2\frac{1}{2}\% = \$7.60 + \$3.80 + \$1.90 = \$13.30$
17 $26.40
18 $7.90
19 $2800
20 20 years old
21 $0.80
22 8.2 kg
23 50 years old
24 9 years old, 90 years old

6B Discount

1 a $42 b $46.25 c $49.50
d $76
2 a 10% b 50% c $33\frac{1}{3}\%$
d 25%
3 a $850 b $200 c $83.60
d $104 e $64.70
4 a $45 b $45 c $36
5 a 40% b 28% c 28%
d 22%
6 Estimate 20%
7 a Mobile phone $95
b Surfboard and bike
c $8.35
d No
8 a $70 b $280
9 $62.96
10 a $41.65 b Yes
11 $75.76
12 20% 13 25%
14 17.3%
15 30%
16 60%
17 $243.70
18 a $121.60 $140.80 b Gain

19 A
20 \$1.00/\$12.00 × 100% = 8.33%, so this is a 8.33% discount.
21 B
22 No, the statement is not correct. For example, if you have a cost of \$100, a 50% discount = \$50 and a 40% discount = \$20.
Total discount = \$70; this represents a 70% discount, not 90%.
23 Yes (difference in the meanings) 75% off \$200 = \$150 off the price so would pay only \$50.
75% of \$200 = \$150 does not represent a discount.
24 Henry pays \$954; Sancha pays \$991.20. Henry has the best buy.

6C Profit and loss

1 **a** \$25.20 **b** \$87 **c** \$1690 **d** \$53.25 **e** \$932
2 **a** $33\frac{1}{3}$% profit **b** 25% profit **c** 25% loss **d** $13\frac{1}{3}$% profit **e** 22.2% loss
3 60%
4 **a** \$545 **b** 156%
5 **a** 1 : 4 **b** 25% **c** 1 : 5 **d** 20%
e The ratio of the profit to the cost price as a fraction is the same as the percentage profit on the cost price.
6 **a** \$325 **b** 27% **c** 21%
d The percentage profit is greater on the cost price.
7 **a** \$79.95 **b** 57%
8 18.75%
9 166.5%
10 \$1643.40
11 **a** \$39 **b** \$27 **c** \$274.45 **d** \$66
12 **a** \$1.00 profit per kg
b 55.6%
c 35.7%
d The percentage profit is greater on the cost price.
13 **a** \$77 **b** 49% **c** 33%
14 C
15 172%
16 60%, 40%
17 50%
18 GST = \$9.60. The restaurant overcharged the group by \$2.40

Chapter review

Fluency

1 **a** \$21.70 **b** \$178.35 **c** \$67.55
2 \$5.95
3 **a** \$6.30 **b** \$4.20 **c** \$10.50 **d** \$21.60 **e** \$0.35 **f** \$4.25 **g** \$11.85 **h** \$212.60
4 **a** \$0.40 **b** \$1.05 **c** \$3.20 **d** \$5.20 **e** \$1.75 **f** \$2.60 **g** \$10.30 **h** \$3.85
5 **a** \$0.15 **b** \$0.30 **c** \$5.05 **d** \$27.00 **e** \$48.40 **f** \$11.60 **g** \$2.95 **h** \$2.95
6 \$1.80
7 \$0.30
8 \$2.75
9 \$1.80
10 **a** 32%
b 24.24%
c The percentage profit is greater on the cost price.

Problem solving

1 \$164.35
2 \$175
3 \$3792.67
4 \$85
5 Estimates are total, \$140; change, \$10; exact amounts are \$138.35, \$11.65.
6 13%
7 \$1.99
8 **a** \$140.40
b 44.4%
9 \$77.03
10 \$83.68
11 34%
12 9.375%
13 \$32.20
14 \$144.65
15 \$1125
16 **a** 488%
b \$415
17 Options are 50c per CD, 49.9c per CD, 54.17c per CD. Therefore the \$4.99 pack is best buy.
18 First pack costs 76c per 100 g; second pack costs 66c per 100 g; so the second pack is the best buy.
19 **a** Saved \$40.81 **b** 40.5% saved
20 **a** \$121 **b** \$120. No

CHAPTER 7

Congruence and transformations

Are you ready?

1 ∠PQR or ∠RQP
2 ΔFGH, ΔFHG, ΔGHF, ΔGFH, ΔHFG, ΔHGF
3 **a** $x = 72$ **b** $y = 26$ **c** $z = 59$
4 **a** **i** Co-interior
ii Corresponding
iii Alternate
b $a = 52°$ (alternate), $b = 128°$ (co-interior), $c = 52°$ (corresponding), $d = 128°$ (vertically opposite)
c AB is not parallel to CD as the alternate angles are not equal.
5

X | X Y | Y P | ꟼ N | И

6

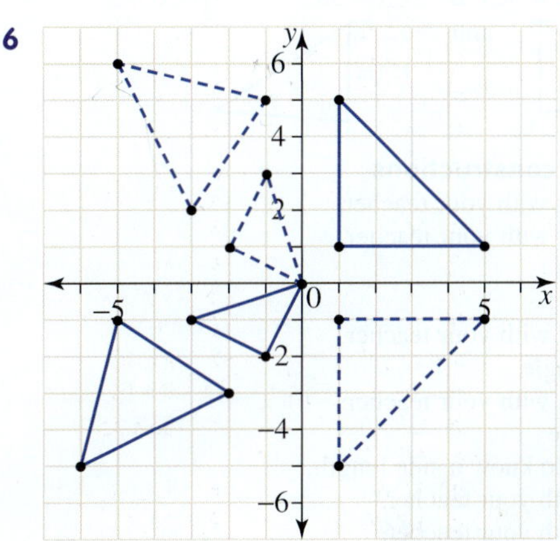

7

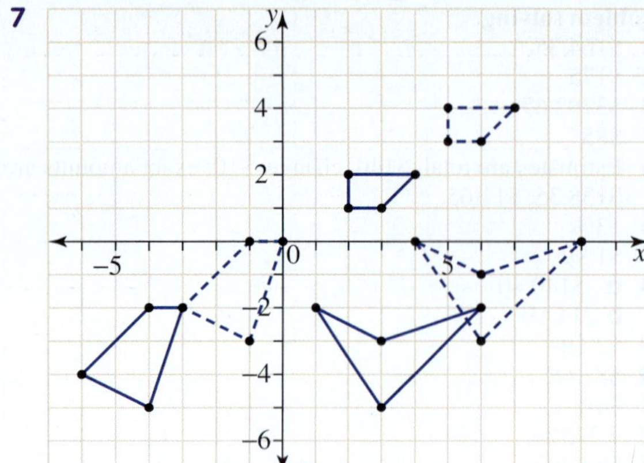

7A Congruent figures

1 a–c

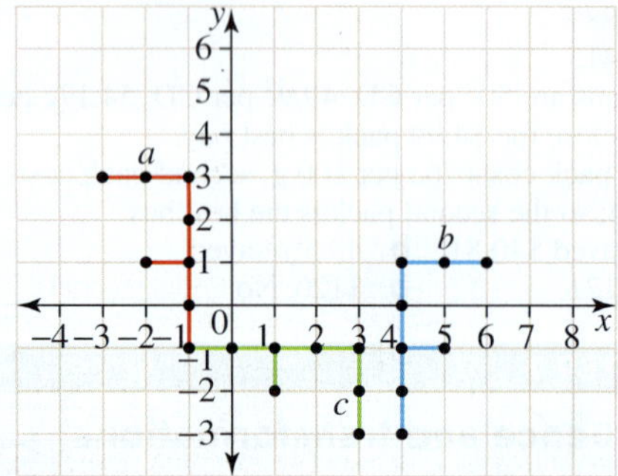

d Yes

2 a **i** and **iii**
b **i** and **iv**
c **ii** and **iv**

3 a $\Delta ABC \equiv \Delta PQR$, $x = 25°$
b $\Delta ABC \equiv \Delta PQR$, $x = 70°$, $y = 40°$
c $\Delta ABC \equiv \Delta CDA$, $x = 40°$, $y = 55°$
d $\Delta ABC \equiv \Delta ADC$, $x = 30°$, $y = 30°$, $z = 120°$
e $\Delta ABC \equiv \Delta ADC$, $x = 40°$, $y = 40°$, $z = 100°$
f $\Delta ABC \equiv \Delta PRQ$, $x = 35°$, $y = 55°$

4 C

5 a $\Delta ABC \equiv \Delta ADC$ $x = 30°$ $y = 60°$
b $\Delta KLN \equiv \Delta MNL$ $x = 75°$ $y = 60°$ $z = 45°$
c $\Delta PSR \equiv \Delta QRS$ $x = 8$ cm
d $\Delta SWT \equiv \Delta UVT$ $w = y = 70°$ $x = z = 55°$
e $\Delta EFG \equiv \Delta EHG$ $x = 8$ cm
f $\Delta WXZ \equiv \Delta WYZ$ $x = 45°$ $y = 3$ cm
g $\Delta ABE \equiv \Delta CDB$ $x = 58°$ $y = 65°$

6 15 cm, 20°, 89° and

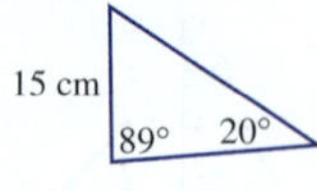

7B Triangle constructions

1 to **3** Check with your teacher.

4 a Check with your teacher.
b 89°
c **i**

5 a Check with your teacher.
b 1 triangle

6 a Check with your teacher.
b Infinite
c Need to know a side length.

7 Check with your teacher.

8 Check with your teacher.

7C Congruent triangles

1 a $\Delta ABC \equiv \Delta PQR$ (SSS)
b $\Delta ABC \equiv \Delta PQR$ (SSS)
c $\Delta LMN \equiv \Delta PQR$ (SAS)
d $\Delta ABC \equiv \Delta PQR$ (ASA)
e $\Delta ABE \equiv \Delta ADE$ (SSS)
f $\Delta FKJ \equiv \Delta GKH$ (SSS)

2 a $x = 3$ cm
b $x = 83°$
c $x = 75°$ $y = 25°$ $z = 80°$
d $x = 25°$ $y = 8$ cm
e $x = 35°$ $y = z = 55°$ $n = m = 90°$

3 Check with your teacher.

4 Check with your teacher.

5 Check with your teacher.

6 a Congruent (SSS)
b Congruent (ASA)

7 Check with your teacher.

8 Check with your teacher.

7D Quadrilaterals

1 a $\Delta WXA \equiv \Delta YZA$ (ASA)
b **i** $WA \equiv YA$
ii $XA \equiv ZA$
c Diagonals bisect each other.

2 a $\Delta ABE \equiv \Delta CBE$ (SSS)
b **i** $\angle AEB \equiv \angle CEB$
ii $\angle ABE \equiv \angle CBE$
c 90°
d ΔCBE, ΔADE, ΔCDE
e Diagonals bisect the angles.

3 a $\Delta PQR \equiv \Delta SRP$ (SAS)
b Diagonals of a rectangle are congruent.

4 a $\Delta ABD \equiv \Delta CBD$ (SSS)
b **i** $\angle ABD \equiv \angle CBD$
ii $\angle BAD \equiv \angle BCD$
iii $\angle BDA \equiv \angle BDC$
c $\Delta ABD \equiv \Delta CBD$ (SAS)
d **i** $AE \equiv CE$
ii $\angle AEB \equiv \angle CEB$
e No
f **i** No
ii No
iii No
iv Yes
v No

5 a $\Delta QPR \equiv \Delta SRP$ (SSS)
b **i** $\angle SRP$ **ii** $\angle SPR$
c **i** RS **ii** SP
d Quadrilateral

6 a $\angle BAC \equiv \angle DCA$
b $\Delta ABC \equiv \Delta CDA$ (SAS)
c $\angle BCA \equiv \angle DAC$ (alternate angles)
d Parallelogram

7 Trapezium

Chapter review

Fluency

1 **a, c**

2 Check with your teacher.

3 a $\Delta ABC \equiv \Delta PQR$ (ASA) $x = 5$ cm
b $\Delta PQR \equiv \Delta QPS$ (ASA) $x = 5$ cm
c $\Delta PQR \equiv \Delta PST$ (SAS) $x = 10$ mm
$y = 11$ mm $z = 12$ mm
d $\Delta ABC \equiv \Delta ADC$ (SAS) $x = 23$ mm

4

Properties of quadrilaterals	Parallelogram	Rhombus	Rectangle	Square	Kite
Opposite sides parallel	✓	✓	✓	✓	✗
Opposite sides congruent	✓	✓	✓	✓	✗
All sides congruent	✗	✓	✗	✓	✗
All angles congruent (90°)	✗	✗	✓	✓	✗
Diagonals congruent	✗	✗	✓	✓	✗
Diagonals bisect each other	✓	✓	✓	✓	✗
Diagonals intersect at 90°	✗	✓	✗	✓	✓
Diagonals bisect angles	✗	✓	✗	✓	✗

Problem solving

1 Check with your teacher.
2 Check with your teacher.
3 Check with your teacher.
4 Claim is not correct.

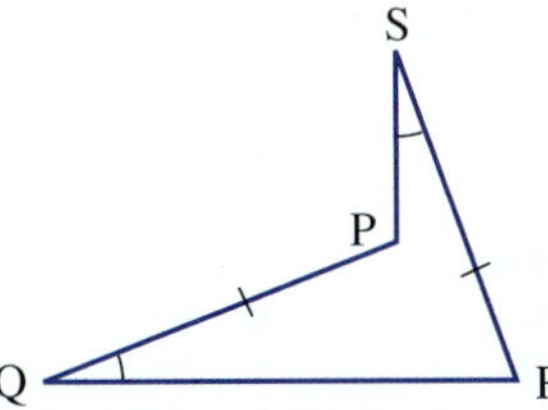

5 Check with your teacher.
6 Square
7 Check with your teacher.

CHAPTER 8

Algebra

Are you ready?

1 a $M - C$ b $\$2B$ c XY
d $H + 12$ e $10D$ cents
2 a 15 b 6 c −39
3 a 12 b 18
4 a −18 b 25 c −52
d 8
5 a $7g$ b $6y$ c $3gy$
d $x + 11$ e $15g + 17$ f $4h + 4t$
6 a $\frac{1}{3}$ b $\frac{2}{5}$ c $\frac{3}{4}$
7 a 4 b 7 c 9

8A Using variables

1 a $x + 420$
b $3x$
c $x - 130$
d The nearby nest has 60 more ants.
e The nearby nest has 90 fewer ants.
f The nest is one quarter of the size of the original nest.
2 a $x + y$ b $x + y + 260$
c $x + y + 90$ d $x + y - 260$
3 Between 9.00 am and 9.15 am one Danish pastry was sold. In the next hour-and-a-half, a further 11 Danish pastries were sold. No more Danish pastries had been sold at 12.30 pm, but in the next half-hour 18 more were sold. No Danish pastries were sold after 1.00 pm.
4 a $a + b$ b $a + b + c$
c $b + 4$ d $a - 6$
5 a $y + 7$ b $y - 8$
c $5y$ d $14 - y$
e $\frac{y}{3}$ f $8y + 3$
6 a $a + b$ b $a - b$
c $2b - 3a$ d ab
e $2ab$ f $3a + 7b$
g a^2 h $\frac{a^2}{5}$
7 a $\$27y$ b $\$14d$
c $\$(27r + 14h)$
8 a $t + 2$ b $t + g$
c $t - 5$ d $2t$
9 a The number of passengers doubled at the next stop and continued to increase, more than quadrupling in the first nine minutes. At 7.22 pm, 5 people alighted the train, and by 7.25 pm the same number of passengers were on the train as there were at the beginning. By 7.34 pm there were 12 fewer passengers than there were at the beginning.
b 7.22 pm c 7.19 pm d 7.34 pm
10 a The number of bacteria in each of these intervals is double the number of bacteria in the previous interval.
b The bacteria could be dividing in two.
c It is lower than expected, based on the previous pattern of growth.
d Some of the bacteria may have died, or failed to divide and reproduce.
11 a Odd b Even
c i $n + 2$, $n + 4$ and $n + 6$ ii $n - 2$

8B Substitution

1 a 6 b 14 c 30
d 1 e 9 f 1
g 7 h 3 i 6
j 15 k 19 l 4
m 5 n 10 o 20
p 5 q 22 r 2
s $\frac{89}{10}(8\frac{9}{10})$ t $\frac{39}{10}(3\frac{9}{10})$
2 a 42 b 3 c 54 d 1
e 9 f 15 g 15 h 21
i 24.3 j 21 k 1 l 4.8
m 18.3 n 8.1 o 16.2 p $\frac{7}{4}(1\frac{3}{4})$
3 a 7 b 7 c −3 d 3
e 4 f 10 g 50 h 1
i −15 j −4 k 37 l 15
m 40 n $2\frac{1}{3}$ o 19 p 1

4 150 m
5 10 cm
6 $C = \$64$
7 **a** 48 cm^2
b 8400 m^2
c 4.472 m^2 or 44 720 cm^2
8 **a** $F = 212$ °F **b** 28 °C = 82.4 °F
c 32 °F
9 **a** 100 km ≈ 60 miles
b 248 km ≈ 148.8 miles
c 12.5 km ≈ 7.5 miles
10 If $x = 0$, then the expression becomes $\frac{0}{0}$, which is indeterminate.

8C Working with brackets

1 **a** 36 **b** 4 **c** 84 **d** 18
e 56 **f** 35 **g** 90 **h** 350
i 55 **j** 20 **k** 133 **l** 147
m 784 **n** 250 **o** 9800 **p** 200
2 **a** 90 **b** 16 **c** 6 **d** 32
e 72 **f** 90 **g** 7 **h** 36
i 60 **j** 58 **k** 21 **l** 180
m 576 **n** 32 **o** –26 **p** 33
3 **a** 62 cm **b** 97.8 cm
4 B
5 **a** 720° **b** 540° **c** 180°
d 360° **e** 3240°
6 **a** CD = $m + 4n$
b BC = $3m + n$
c Perimeter = $8m + 18n$

8D Substituting positive and negative numbers

1 **a** 3 **b** 9 **c** –9 **d** 3
e –9 **f** –12 **g** –12 **h** 2
i 5 **j** –13 **k** 9 **l** 3
m –2 **n** –3 **o** –8 **p** –2
q 0 **r** –109 **s** 6 **t** 16
2 **a** 18 **b** 32 **c** –15 **d** 12
e 16 **f** 24 **g** 22 **h** 155
i 32 **j** 3 **k** 6 **l** 21
3 **a** –9 **b** 1 **c** 3 **d** 40
e –8 **f** 2 **g** –3 **h** 12
i $-\frac{4}{5}$ **j** –2 **k** –1 **l** –6
m 125 **n** 175 **o** –5 **p** –12.5
q –74 **r** –117 **s** –104 **t** –15.5
4 $\frac{30}{7}$ or $4\frac{2}{7}$
5 If x is negative then $5x$ will also be a negative integer (less than or equal to –5). Subtracting this number is equivalent to adding a positive integer. The result will be positive.

8E Number laws and variables

1 **a** **i** 11 **ii** 11 Same
b **i** 25 **ii** 25 Same
c **i** 31 **ii** 31 Same
d **i** 32 **ii** 32 Same
e **i** –5 **ii** 5 Different
f **i** –18 **ii** 18 Different
g **i** –28 **ii** 28 Different
h **i** 1 **ii** –1 Different
2 **a** **i** –10 **ii** –10 Same
b **i** –180 **ii** –180 Same
c **i** –40 **ii** –40 Same
d **i** –350 **ii** –350 Same
e **i** $-\frac{2}{5}$ **ii** $-\frac{5}{2}$ Different
f **i** –1 **ii** –1 Same
g **i** $-\frac{4}{5}$ **ii** $-\frac{5}{4}$ Different
h **i** $-\frac{14}{45}$ **ii** $-\frac{45}{14}$ Different
3 **a** True **b** False **c** False
d True **e** True **f** True
g False **h** False **i** False
j True **k** False **l** True
4 **a** **i** 13 **ii** 13 Same
b **i** 24 **ii** 24 Same
c **i** 40 **ii** 40 Same
d **i** –3 **ii** –7 Different
e **i** –35 **ii** –71 Different
f **i** –43 **ii** –67 Different
5 **a** **i** –64 **ii** –64 Same
b **i** 768 **ii** 768 Same
c **i** –1536 **ii** –1536 Same
d **i** –4 **ii** –1 Different
e **i** –6 **ii** $-\frac{1}{6}$ Different
f **i** $\frac{8}{5}$ **ii** $\frac{1}{10}$ Different
6 **a** False **b** False **c** False
d True **e** True **f** False
7 C **8** D

8F Simplifying expressions

1 **a** $6c$ **b** $-3c$ **c** $4a$
d q **e** $-3h$ **f** $2x$
g $-6a$ **h** $4f$ **i** $-3p$
j h **k** $18b$ **l** $3t$
m $13m$ **n** $-x$ **o** $20z$
p $10p$ **q** $17g$ **r** $3b$
s $14t$ **t** $-7j$ **u** $-15l$
v $8m$ **w** 0 **x** $10t$
2 **a** $10x - 2y$ **b** $7x - 12$ **c** $11 - 2f$
d $6 - u$ **e** $7m + 3p$ **f** $4r - 5h$
g $17a - 5b$ **h** $9t - 2$ **i** $17 - 3g$
j $10m - 2n$ **k** $7k - 12$ **l** $4n - 9$
m $12 - 2b$ **n** $20 - 12h$ **o** $9y - 2g - 6$
p $11h - 8$ **q** $4s - 2t$ **r** $14l - 5m$
s $3k - 13h + 7$ **t** $5 - 4t$ **u** $7g - 2$
v $19f - 10k$
3 **a** $3x^2$ **b** $5y^2$ **c** $4a^3$
d $7d^2$ **e** $-g^2$ **f** $10y^3$
g $7b^2$ **h** a^2 **i** $-g^2$
j $4a^2 + 9$ **k** $23x^2$ **l** $11s^2 + 4$
m $8a^2 + 5a$ **n** $b^2 + 23b$ **o** $t^2 - 4g - 7$
p $8g^3 - g^2 + 22$
q $18ab + 3$ **r** $11xy$ **s** $3fg + 3s$
t $12ab - 5$ **u** $20ab^2 - 14ac$
4 Check with your teacher.
5 Check with your teacher.

8G Multiplying and dividing expressions with variables

1 **a** $12g$ **b** $21h$ **c** $24d$
d $15z$ **e** $30r$ **f** $35t$
g $12u$ **h** $42p$ **i** $21gy$
j $22ht$ **k** $24gx$ **l** $70ah$
m $36dm$ **n** $15ch$ **o** $18gx$
p $12.5bt$ **q** $156mn$ **r** $72ad$
s $6abc$ **t** $12fgh$ **u** $48wx$
v $231abd$ **w** $24xy$ **x** $10.5xy$
y $132qs$ **z** $24abc$
2 **a** $4f$ **b** $2h$ **c** $5x$ **d** $3g$
e $2r$ **f** 2 **g** 2 **h** 2

i $\frac{2}{3}$ **j** $\frac{1}{2}$ **k** $\frac{6}{7}$ **l** $\frac{2}{3}$
m $\frac{1}{3}$ **n** $\frac{1}{2}$ **o** $\frac{2}{3}$ **p** $\frac{1}{34}$
q 9 **r** $\frac{5}{12}$ **s** $\frac{16}{11}(1\frac{5}{11})$ **t** 3

3 a $5fg$ **b** $3cd$ **c** $\frac{2xy}{3}$ **d** cg
e y **f** $\frac{p}{2}$ **g** $\frac{3a}{4}$ **h** $\frac{3d}{4}$
i 5 **j** $\frac{5r}{7}$ **k** $\frac{2y}{7}$ **l** $\frac{4b}{3}$
m $13y$ **n** $\frac{2}{5}$ **o** $2a$ **p** $\frac{g}{2}$
q $\frac{11m}{5}$ **r** $\frac{1}{6}$ **s** $\frac{2d}{5}$ **t** $\frac{b}{7}$

4 a $-15f$ **b** $12d$ **c** $-33ag$
d $27gt$ **e** $20dht$ **f** $-18st$
g $42dw$ **h** $24abce$ **i** $-33abf$
j $18absx$ **k** $-75hqt$ **l** $144pw$
m $-21abg$ **n** $-51abgh$ **o** $-49gh$
p $-40hjk$ **q** $112.5xy$ **r** $-144prtz$
s $30abc$ **t** $-408wx$ **u** $-90a^2bcde$

5 a $-\frac{a}{2}$ **b** $-\frac{a}{3}$ **c** $-12j$ **d** $\frac{1}{2d}$
e $-\frac{4}{5l}$ **f** $-\frac{x}{4}$ **g** $-\frac{6}{7}$ **h** $\frac{f}{5j}$
i $-\frac{2x}{3}$ **j** $-\frac{1}{6}$ **k** $-\frac{m}{4}$ **l** $\frac{st}{2}$
m -2 **n** $\frac{b}{3}$ **o** $-\frac{d}{5h}$ **p** $-\frac{12}{11p}$
q $\frac{14ef}{9}$ **r** $-\frac{18x}{7}$ **s** $\frac{3}{2r}$ **t** $-\frac{11}{12t}$

6 a $2a^2$ **b** $25p^2$ **c** $-30x^2$
d $7a^2b$ **e** $6b^2cd$ **f** $-160x^2y$
g $42p^2q^2$ **h** $-30mn^2t^2$ **i** $-18xy^2z^2$
j $-42abc^2$ **k** 0 **l** $-18w^2x^2y^2z^2$
m $6a^{11}$ **n** $2x^5y^3$ **o** $10m^9$
p $\frac{5p^{10}q^5}{6}$ **q** $\frac{4x^2yz^2}{3}$ **r** $\frac{3b}{5}$

7 a $\frac{6}{a^2}$ **b** $\frac{10b^2}{3}$ **c** $\frac{5}{w}$ **d** $\frac{9k}{5}$
e $-\frac{3g}{5a}$ **f** $\frac{16h^2}{9d^2}$ **g** $\frac{5t}{n}$ **h** $-\frac{27h^2}{2g^2}$
i $\frac{8y}{w}$ **j** $6fz$

8H Expanding brackets

1 a $3d + 12$ **b** $2a + 10$
c $4x + 8$ **d** $5r + 35$
e $6g + 36$ **f** $2t + 6$
g $7d + 56$ **h** $18x + 54$
i $48 + 12c$ **j** $42 + 21x$
k $90g + 135$ **l** $1.5t + 9$
m $11t - 22$ **n** $6t - 18$
o $t^2 + 3t$ **p** $x^2 + 4x$
q $g^2 + 7g$ **r** $2g^2 + 10g$
s $3fg + 9f$ **t** $6mn - 12m^2$

2 a $9x - 6$ **b** $3x^2 - 18xy$
c $15xy - 45y^2$ **d** $100y - 250$
e $-3c - 9$ **f** $-15x - 20$
g $-5x^2 - 30x$ **h** $-12y - 2y^2$
i $-6t + 18$ **j** $-20f + 8f^2$
k $27xy - 18x$ **l** $-6bh + 18h^2$
m $20ab + 12ac$ **n** $-6ag + 21a^2$
o $15ab + 30ac$ **p** $-18w^2 + 10wz$
q $48m^2 + 120m$ **r** $6k^2 - 15k$

3 a $35x + 49$ **b** $3c - 4$
c $22c - 2c^2$ **d** $6v + 30$
e $5d^2 - 12d$ **f** $11y + 12$
g $26r + r^2$ **h** $9g - 37$
i $11f - 12g - 7$ **j** $9x$
k $-5k - 10$ **l** $18x + 6rx$
m $8r - 13$ **n** $18gh - 24g$
o $11t + 1$ **p** $24 + 11r - 11r^2$

4 a $5x + 8$ **b** $9x + 23$
c $6y + 26$ **d** $d + 22$
e $14h$ **f** $21m - 4$
g $28f - 1$ **h** $4a - 3a^2 - 35$
i $6 - t^2 + 2t$ **j** $7m$

5 a $10hk + 21h + 20k$ **b** $15n - 6ny$
c $8gm + 24g - 18$ **d** $18ab + 67b$
e $5a^2 - 35a - 35$ **f** $11cf + 3c$
g $28x - 5xy - 29$ **h** $37vw + 55v - 24$
i $6xy - 45x$ **j** $77mn - 16m + 12n$

6 a

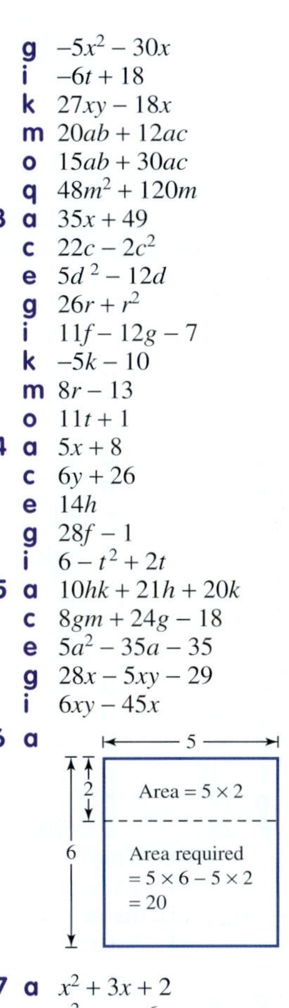
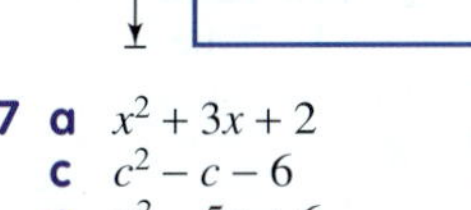

b

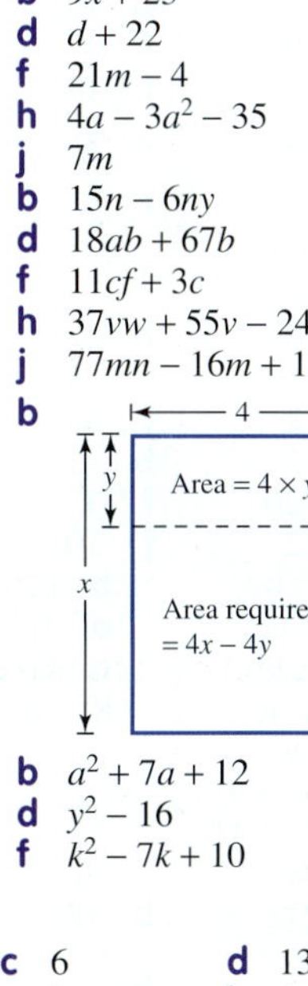

7 a $x^2 + 3x + 2$ **b** $a^2 + 7a + 12$
c $c^2 - c - 6$ **d** $y^2 - 16$
e $u^2 - 5u + 6$ **f** $k^2 - 7k + 10$

8I Factorising

1 a 2 **b** 3 **c** 6 **d** 13
e 7 **f** 2 **g** 3 **h** 4

2 a $2g$ **b** $3m$ **c** 11 **d** $2m$
e $2a$ **f** $12g$ **g** $2g$ **h** $11l$
i $4mn$ **j** $4c$ **k** $4c$ **l** x

3 a $3(x + 2)$ **b** $2(y + 2)$
c $5(g + 2)$ **d** $4(2x + 3)$
e $3(2f + 3)$ **f** $4(3c + 5)$
g $2(d + 4)$ **h** $2(x - 2)$
i $6(2g - 3)$ **j** $11(h + 11)$
k $4(s - 4)$ **l** $4(2x - 5)$
m $12(g - 2)$ **n** $2(7 - 2b)$
o $16(a + 4)$ **p** $12(4 - q)$
q $8(2 + f)$ **r** $12(1 - d)$

4 a $3(gh + 4)$ **b** $2y(x + 3)$
c $4p(3q + 1)$ **d** $7g(2 - h)$
e $2k(8j - 1)$ **f** $2g(6e + 1)$
g $4(3k + 4)$ **h** $m(7n + 6)$
i $7b(2a + 1)$ **j** $5a(1 - 3bc)$
k $2r(4 + 7t)$ **l** $12ab(2m + 1)$
m $2b(2 - 3a)$ **n** $4g(3f - 4h)$
o $b(a - 2c)$ **p** $7x(2 - 3y)$
q $k(11j + 3)$ **r** $3p(1 + 9q)$
s $c(12a - 4 + 3d)$ **t** $4(g + 2h - 4)$
u $14s(2 + t)$ **v** $3v(5u + 9w)$

5 $2ab$ **6** $12a^3b^2c$

7 $\frac{3}{5}$

8 $\frac{3(x+1)}{2(x-1)}$

9 $\frac{28}{3}$ or $9\frac{1}{3}$

10 $7y$

Chapter review

Fluency

1 a $x+y$ b $y-x$ c $3x-5y$ d $5x$ e $2xy$ f $6x+7y$ g y^2 h $2x-7$ i $3(p+q)$

2 a $15x$ b $9y$ c $15k+9m$

3 a $m+5$ b $m-p$ c $5m$

4 a 4 b 12 c 30 d 1 e 10 f 4 g 8 h 4 i 8 j 13 k 22 l 10 m 14 n 3 o $\frac{1}{3}$ p −36 q $\frac{5}{3}$ r $\frac{2}{3}$

5 $13.90

6 5 cm

7 a 16 b 4 c 40 d 16 e 35 f 15 g 24 h 180 i 18 j 500 k 96 l −72

8 a −3 b −3 c −10 d −2 e −20 f 3 g 22 h 2 i 12 j 10 k 28 l −20

9 a False b False c True d True e True f False g False h True i False j True k False l True

10 a $7d$ b $-2c$ c $3d+a$ d $2g$ e $2x+11$ f $g-1$ g $9xy$ h $15t^2+2t$

11 a $21g$ b $18y$ c $42d$ d $-24z$

12 a $\frac{a}{4}$ b $\frac{1}{4}$ c $-3r$ d $\frac{h}{2}$ e $\frac{4}{5sv}$ f $3x$ g $-\frac{6}{7}$ h $\frac{e}{6j}$

13 a $2x+6$ b $10x-5$ c $-2f-14$ d $3bm-3m^2$ e $3y^2-21y$ f $9bc-18b$

14 a $12v$ b $16t-35$ c $17p+3$ d $7x+15$ e $5g^2-33g$ f $42-3t$

15 a $3(g+4)$
b $y(x+5)$
c $5(n-4)$
d $4n(3m+p)$
e $6g(2-h)$
f $12y(x-3z)$

16 Check with your teacher.

Problem solving

1 a $3(2+1)=3\times2+3\times1$ or $3(2-1)=3\times2-3\times1$
b $-10\times8+-10\times-6=-10(8+-6)$ or $-10\times8--10\times-6=-10(8--6)$
c $8(6+5)=8\times5+8\times5$ or $8(6-5)=8\times5-8\times5$
d $-4\times7+1\times7=-4(1+7)$ or $-4\times7-1\times7=-4(1-7)$
e $2(x+y)=2\times x+2\times y$ or $2(x-y)=2\times x-2\times y$
f $3\times a(a+b)=3\times a\times a+3\times a\times b$

2 a $120-a$ cm
b $b-12a-96$ cm
c $b-13a+24$ cm

3 a 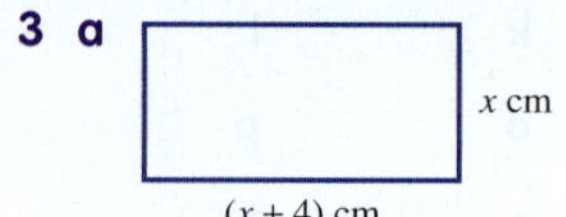

b $x(x+4)$ cm^2
c x^2+4x
d 21 cm^2
e Volume $=x^3+4x^2$ cm^3
f 63 cm^3

4 a P (points), G (goals) and B (behinds)
b $6G+B$
c 76 points
d 72 points
e (G, B): (7, 45), (8, 39), (9, 33), (10, 17), (11, 21), (12, 12), (13, 9), (14, 3)

5 $34

6 a 36 barrels b 120 barrels

7 a–c 2.5 L in Tin B and 5.5 L in Tin A

8 $\frac{7}{12}$

9 $\frac{125}{27}$ or $4\frac{17}{27}$

10 The sum is twice the middle number.

11 Yes

12 The final digit of 2^{81} is 2.

CHAPTER 9

Problem solving I

9A Introduction to problem solving — create a table

1 174 feet 2 inches

2 Peta has 7 kg 400 g remaining in her 20 kg bag of flour.

3 Better to double your dollar for 21 days.

4 6

5 a $1400
b 11

6

	Blue	Purple	Red	Green
Bed	Papa	Mama	Goldi	Baby
Chair	Goldi	Papa	Mama	Baby
Spoon	Papa	Mama	Baby	Goldi
Bowl	Papa	Goldi	Mama	Baby

7 36 s

8 Polly 66, Neda 58

9 19 bottles

10 When the interest is paid in month 7.

9B Draw a diagram

1 32 rabbits

2 Nigel would have 54 rabbits after the third litter.

3 75 000 000 km

4 a Brisbane is 8 hours ahead of Paris.
b Tokyo is 4 hours behind Auckland.

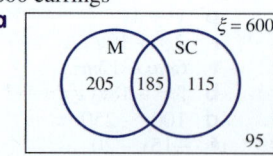

5 600 earrings

6 a

ξ = 600
M SC
205 185 115
95

b

	SC	SC'	Total
M	185	205	390
M'	115	95	210
Total	300	300	600

c 41 : 23

7 16 : 81

8 30°

9 52.5 km/h

10 21

9C Look for a pattern

1 $33 693.51

2 $2\frac{5}{19}$ or $\frac{43}{19}$

3 48

4 $\frac{1}{256}$

5 56.637

6 220

7 Tuesday

8 364

9 **a** **i** $\frac{7}{8}$ **ii** $\frac{15}{16}$ **iii** $\frac{31}{32}$

b **i** $\frac{1}{256}, \frac{1}{512}$

ii

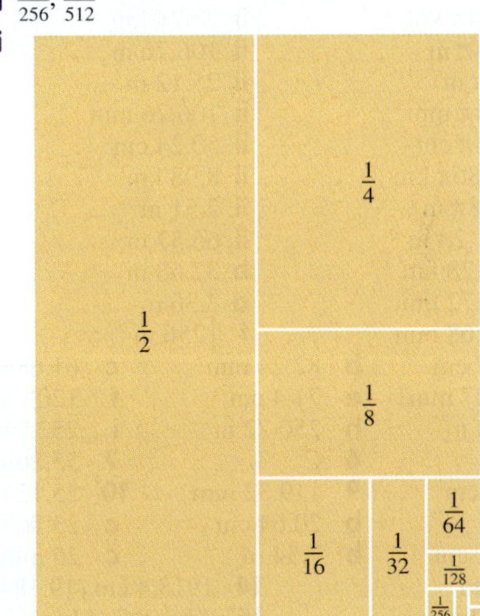

10 34

9D Work backwards from the answer

1 245 **2** $789.91

3 207

4 The initial purchase was 48 roses.

5 Dan had 112 emails in his inbox on Monday morning.

6 $37.02

7 Answers will vary. Check with your teacher. One possible answer is 4, 5, 8, 9, 9.

8 30. Therefore, pass 10 of the remaining tasks.

9 16

10 Bucket 1: 12 L, Bucket 2: 3 L, Bucket 3: 3 L

9E Elimination

1 $550 **2** 0.579

3 64 is a perfect square (8^2) and a perfect cube (4^3)

4 −12 and +1 multiply to give −12 and add to give −11

5 36 is both triangular and square

6 The sequences begin with 4 and 7.

7 76 **8** Rhombus

9

	Prime	Triangular	Square	Multiple of 3	Multiple of 5
Odd	7	1	9	45	55
Even	2	6	36	12	30
Less than 20	11	10	16	18	15
Greater than 20	23	21	25	24	35
Factor of 60	5	3	4	60	20

10 From top to bottom: Pistachio, Bubblegum, Chocolate, Strawberry, Vanilla

9F Simplify the problem

1 42.5 days

2 At this rate it would take approximately 7 years.

3 The digit 1 appears 10 times.

4 **a** 204

b 650

5 54 m

6 10 lockers are open

7 **a** Each child receives $5.

b Each child receives $4. Mrs Smith won $16.

c $64 and $\frac{1}{9}$

8 Yes

9 1.8 s

10 10 000

9G Guess and check

1 1st group: 17, 2nd group: 21, 3rd group: 63.

2 White; 87

3 $11

4 6, 24, 20

5 2 735

6 2 bracelets and 4 necklaces

7 There are many possible answers. Some could be:

$-1 = (1 \times -2) - 3 + 4$

$-2 = 1 - 2 + 3 - 4$

$-3 = (1 \times -2) + 3 - 4$

$-4 = (1 - 2 + 3) \times -\sqrt{4}$

$-5 = (1 - 2) \times (3 + \sqrt{4})$

$-6 = (1 - 2) \times (3 \times \sqrt{4})$

$-7 = 1 - (2 \times 3) - \sqrt{4}$

$-8 = 1 - 2 - 3 - 4$

$-9 = 1 - (2 \times 3) - 4$

$-10 = -(1 \times 2 \times 3) - 4$

8 625 and 5 776 **9** 18

10 There is more than one solution. Here is one:

$$\begin{array}{r} 583 \\ +\ 146 \\ \hline 729 \end{array}$$

9H Mixed problems I

1 208 stone 3 pounds

2 36 different combinations

3 Approximately 2 cars

4 82 L 700 mL
5 36 different types of sandwiches
6 65 536
7 16 pairs of shoes in Sue's cupboard at the beginning of the year
8 87 or 96
9 65 m every 100 paces
10 2, 8 and 25

9I Mixed problems II

1 777 visits
2 20 people
3 129 km 900 m
4 Increase of 11.55%; multiply the selling price by 1.155.
5 Decrease of 1%; multiply the selling price by 0.99.
6 Use the formula $1.05x - 1$
7 Multiply the sum of money by 1.2597.
8 $m = 2d$ or $d = \frac{m}{2}$
9 $p = \frac{1000d}{40}$ (with d in megabytes)
10 $m = 4p$

9J Mixed problems III

1 839 years 1 month
2 Gordon walked approximately 1.7 km every 15 minutes.
3 There will be 1024 bacteria after 5 minutes.
4 $V = 0.05A + 0.1B + 0.2C + 0.5D$
5 128 cm
6 Length of wire: $4\sqrt{2}$ m; area: 2 m^2. Length of arms: $\sqrt{3}$ m
7 a 913 L per day b 182.6 L per person per day
c 71.3 kL per quarter d $109.20
8 a $2\frac{1}{2}$ m b 10 m
9 $26\frac{2}{3}$ L
10 12.9 km

CHAPTER 10

Measurement

Are you ready?

1 a 0.32 b 40
2 a 3.4 cm b 1600 mm c 0.045 km
3 a 5.85 cm^2 b 7.82 cm^2
4 112.5 cm^3
5 a 4 o'clock
b A quarter past 10
6 a 2100 b 1000 c 1400

10A Perimeter

1 a 20 mm = 2 cm b 13 mm = 1.3 cm
c 130 mm = 13 cm d 1.5 cm = 15 mm
e 0.03 cm = 0.3 mm f 2.8 km = 2800 m
g 0.034 m = 3.4 cm
h 2400 mm = 240 cm = 2.4 m
i 1375 mm = 137.5 cm = 1.375 m
j 2.7 m = 270 cm = 2700 mm
k 0.08 m = 80 mm
l 6.071 km = 6071 m
m 670 cm = 6.7 m
n 0.0051 km = 5.1 m
2 a 14 cm b 12 cm
c 106 mm d 18 cm
e 240 mm f 32 mm
g 23 cm h 72 mm
i 73 mm j 1260 cm (12.6 m)
k 192 cm (1.92 m) l 826 cm
3 a 1800 mm × 900 mm = 180 cm × 90 cm
= 1.8 m × 0.9 m
b 2400 mm × 900 mm = 240 cm × 90 cm
= 2.4 m × 0.9 m
c 2700 mm × 1200 mm = 270 cm × 120 cm
= 2.7 m × 1.2 m
4 $5.40 5 $38.16
6 41 400 m or 41.4 km
7 a 7 m b $26.60
8 86 m
9 980 cm
10 86 cm
11 a 510 m b $749.70
12 $15.88
13 a 11 cm b 22 cm c 6.9 m
14 5.5 m
15 a 5 cm b 20 cm c 2 bottles
16 9 cm

10B Circumference

1 a i 2π cm ii 6.28 cm
b i 10π cm ii 31.40 cm
c i 7π mm ii 21.98 mm
d i 0.82π m ii 2.57 m
e i 7.4π km ii 23.24 km
f i 34π m ii 106.76 m
2 a i 8π m ii 25.12 m
b i 34π mm ii 106.76 mm
c i 16π cm ii 50.24 cm
d i 2.86π km ii 8.98 km
e i 0.8π m ii 2.51 m
f i 21.2π m ii 66.57 m
3 a 241.78 km b 37.68 m
c 150.72 mm d 3.36 m
e 194.68 mm f 1256 m
4 a 25.7 cm b 82.24 mm c 61.68 m
d 39.27 mm e 71.4 cm f 120.78 cm
g 5.88 m h 250.72 m i 252.75 cm
5 B 6 C 7 55.26 m
8 100.48 cm 9 119.32 mm 10 25.12 m
11 a 6 m b 20.64 cm c 23.76 mm
12 a 2.01 cm b 7.54 m c 25 mm
13 21.56 cm 14 1918.4 cm (19.184 m)
15 15.7 m further 16 About 41.8 km/h
17 About 9.6 cm

10C Area of rectangles, triangles, parallelograms, rhombuses and kites

1 a 530 000 m^2 b 2.35 cm^2
c 254 000 mm^2 d 54.2 m^2
e 0.074 m^2 f 3 km^2
g 9.8563 ha h 17 800 m^2
i 987 000 mm^2 j 1 275 000 cm^2
2 a 36 cm^2 b 1125 mm^2 c 4.5 m^2
d 1215 km^2 e 2.5 m^2 f 336 mm^2
3 a 25 mm^2 b 256 cm^2 c 5.29 m^2
4 C 5 B
6 a 1258 mm^2 b 1771.54 m^2 c 9932.63 mm^2
d 17 537 cm^2 e 11 566.8 mm^2 f 257.645 m^2
7 a 275 mm^2 b 24 000 m^2 c 656 cm^2
d 11.04 mm^2 e 2.7 m^2 f 2400 mm^2
g 17.36 m^2 h 4760 m^2 i 8.48 m^2
8 a 42.65 m^2, 60.81 m^2, 42.65 m^2 b 146.11 m^2

9 351.98 cm^2

10 a 15 000 m^2 **b** 60 000 m^2

11 a 15.64 m^2 **b** 3

12 42 cm

13 a 400 m **b** 375 min or $6\frac{1}{4}$ h

14 50.4 cm^2 **15** 2052 m^2 **16** D

17 17.28 cm^2 **18** 1584 cm^2

19 a 3.6 cm **b** 9.2 cm

20 $b = h = 9.5$ cm

21

Area of $\Delta ABC = \frac{1}{2} \times \text{base} \times \text{height}$

$= \frac{1}{2} \times a \times \frac{1}{2} b$

$= \frac{1}{4} \times a \times b$

Area of rhombus $ABCD = 2 \times$ area of ΔABC

$= 2 \times \frac{1}{4} \times a \times b$

$= \frac{1}{2} \times a \times b$

22 $A_K = \frac{1}{2} \times a \times b$

10D Area of a circle

1 a 452.16 cm^2 **b** 4.9 km^2
c 2.27 m^2 **d** 0.38 cm^2
e 10 563 cm^2 **f** 206 mm^2

2 a 78.5 cm^2 **b** 482.81 mm^2
c 615.44 m^2 **d** 254.34 cm^2

3 a 37.68 cm^2 **b** 1281.12 cm^2
c 3187.9 m^2

4 a 157 cm^2 **b** 0.39 cm^2 **c** 201 mm^2
d 13.85 m^2 **e** 39.25 cm^2 **f** 1038.56 cm^2
g 77.89 cm^2 **h** 132.5 cm^2 **i** 9.73 cm^2

5 1133.54 cm^2 **6** 4.52

7 25 packets **8** 173.4 g

10E Area of trapeziums

1 a 9 cm^2 **b** 33.75 m^2
c 12.75 m^2 **d** 351 mm^2 (3.51 cm^2)
e 4.68 cm^2 **f** 3120 m^2

2 E

3 3062 cm^2

4 $88.30

5 a $2730.60
b i $333.30
ii $3063.90

6 2 m **7** B

10F Volume of prisms and other solids

1 **b** and **e**

2 a 84 cm^3 **b** 81 m^3 **c** 14 130 cm^3
d 31 400 cm^3 **e** 667.6 m^3 **f** 4776 cm^3
g 84 cm^3 **h** 120 cm^3 **i** 320 m^3
j 126 cm^3 **k** 7.5 cm^3 **l** 1.875 m^3

3 1200 m^3

4 60.3 m^3

5 a 60 cm^3
b 84 cm^3

6 7376 cm^3 (or 7375.86 litres)

7 18 563 cm^3 (1.86 litres)

8 Length 18 cm, width 15 cm and height 10 cm. Volume is 2700 cm^3.

9 16.5 cm

10G Time

1 a–f A cricket test match — 5 days, writing your name — 10 seconds, eating breakfast — 15 minutes, building a house — 6 months, flying time from Melbourne to Hong Kong — 7 hours, being in Year 7 — 1 year.

2 a 5:00 **b** 5:04 **c** 7:23
d 1:05 **e** 9:14 **f** 6:47

3

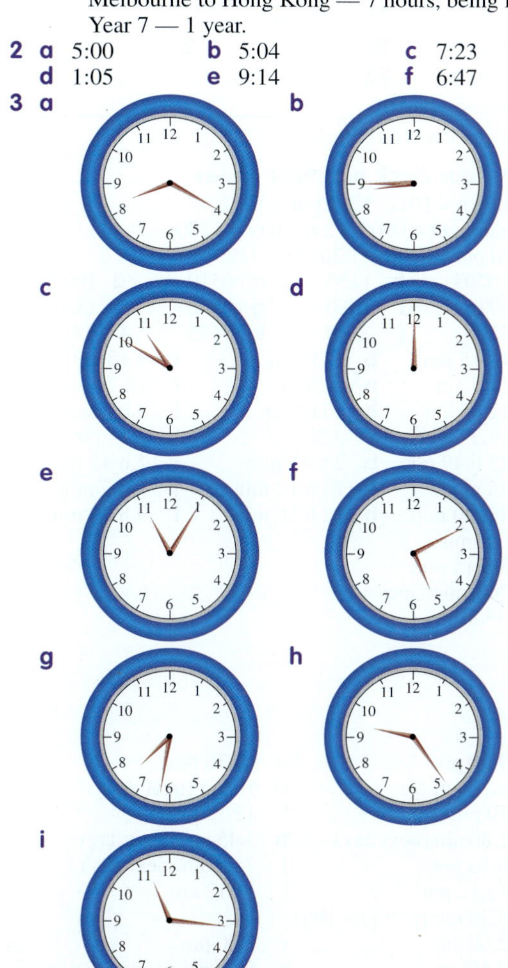

4 Sundial and hourglass

5 2.25 hours = $2\frac{1}{4}$ hours, which is 2 hours and 15 minutes

6 a 120 **b** 150 **c** 195
d 30 **e** 45 **f** 465
g 1440 **h** 12 960

7 a 3 h 20 min **b** 3 h 5 min **c** 2 h 40 min
d 3 h 50 min **e** 6 h 45 min **f** 1 h 35 min
g 10 h 10 min **h** 1 h 12 min **i** 5 h 5 min

8 a 75 min **b** 130 min **c** 110 min
d 265 min **e** 455 min **f** 192 min
g 1005 min **h** 330 min **i** 375 min

9 a 7 **b** 52 **c** 60
d 3600 **e** 86 400 **f** 24
g 8760 **h** 1440 **i** 525 600

10 a 5 pm **b** 3 pm **c** 6.30 am
d 11.50 am **e** 8.40 am **f** 5.18 pm
g 2.00 am **h** 2.20 am **i** 5.30 pm
j 6.35 am **k** 7.41 pm **l** 10.20 am

11 a 15 min **b** 1 h 5 min **c** 1 h 13 min
d 1 h 15 min **e** 53 min **f** 1 h 53 min
g 32 min **h** 3 h 45 min **i** 5 h 15 min
j 12 h **k** 8 h 45 min
12 a 35 h 10 min **b** 32 h 47 min
c 13 h 31 min **d** 43 h 49 min
13 C **14** D **15** A
16 48 min
17 $7\frac{1}{2}$ h **18** 7.25 am
19 6.30 am **20** 11.45 pm **21** 10.35 pm
22 52 min **23** 4 h 2 min
24 25 minutes past 10
25 12 o'clock and 6 o'clock

10H 24-hour clock and time zones

1 10.12 am = 1012, 1212 pm = 1212, 12 midnight = 0000, 12 midday = 1200, 11.20 pm = 2320, 11.20 am = 1120
2 a 1020 **b** 1130 **c** 0510 **d** 0415
e 1715 **f** 1830 **g** 0830 **h** 2040
i 1200 **j** 2330 **k** 0435 **l** 1430
3 a 11.15 pm **b** 1.10 pm **c** 8.15 am
d 1.15 am **e** 6.18 pm **f** 12.20 pm
g 12.05 am **h** 10.05 am **i** 8.05 pm
j 11.35 am **k** 3.20 pm **l** 2.14 pm
4 a 12 h 49 min **b** 2 h 15 min **c** 1 h 45 min
d 45 min **e** 13 h 10 min **f** 3 h 5 min
g 7 h 30 min **h** 12 h 56 min **i** 9 h 20 min
5 6 h 31 min
6 a 3 h 15 min
b 240-min tape
7 3 h 45 min
8 B
9 E
10 A
11 E
12 a 9.00 pm **b** 10.30 pm
c 8.20 pm **d** 10 am (next day)
e 10 pm **f** 12.15 pm
g 1.30 am (next day) **h** 3.45 am (next day)
i 6.10 pm **j** 7.35 am (next day)
k 11.12 pm **l** 11.12 am
13 a 5.30 pm (previous day)
b 2.00 am **c** 2.00 pm
d 7.50 am **e** 8.40 pm (previous day)
f 9.20 am **g** 1.10 am
h 0325 **i** 0550
j 2015 **k** 0855
l 0935
14 5.30 pm
15 3 hours
16 a Basic light: 2 h 50 min, basic medium: 3 h, basic dark: 3 h 10 min
b 1.40 pm, timer set to start process at 1340.
17 B
18 a 1 pm **b** 3 pm **c** 12 pm
19 a 12 midday **b** 10 pm **c** 7 pm
20 a 8.30 am **b** 4.30 pm **c** 6.30 pm
21 Brother 8.59 pm, parents 10.29 pm
22 Answers could include:
Perth — Singapore, Kuala Lumpur, Cebu City in the Phillipines, Denpasar in Bali
Brisbane — Port Moresby in Papua New Guinea.
23 Connor misses the train by 20 minutes.

Chapter review

Fluency

1 a 0.53 cm **b** 76 mm
c 0.15 m **d** 460 cm
e 0.25 km **f** 6500 m
g 1500 mm **h** 0.125 km
2 a 11.6 m **b** 96 cm **c** 111 mm
3 a 69.08 cm **b** 138.16 mm **c** 56.52 m
4 a 241.6 m **b** 257.88 **c** 28.56 cm
5 a 627 cm^2 **b** 96 m^2 **c** 1344 cm^2
6 1000 m^2
7 a 1228.5 cm^2 **b** 978.5 m^2
8 a 37.5 cm^2 **b** 42.6 cm^2 **c** 433.5 cm^2
9 a 112 538 cm^3
b 8008 cm^3
c 8.4 cm^3
10 a 180 min **b** 315 min **c** 450 min
d 105 min **e** 1440 min **f** 4320 min
11 a 2 h 45 min **b** 2 h 20 min **c** 3 h 30 min
d 3 h 40 min **e** 13 h 20 min **f** 1 h 15 min
12 a 80 min **b** 160 min **c** 190 min
d 258 min **e** 635 min **f** 222 min
13 8 h 15 min
14 a 2235 **b** 0715 **c** 0320
d 1642 **e** 2150 **f** 0105
15 a 12.40 pm **b** 7.25 am **c** 3.50 pm
d 9.09 am **e** 9.21 pm **f** 11.20 am
16 a 9 h 20 min **b** 9 h 57 min
c 15 h 38 min **d** 6 h 35 min
17 a 9.20 pm **b** 1.30 am (next day)
c 7.15 am (next day) **d** 4.23 pm
18 a 1.30 pm **b** 1.30 am
c 0450 **d** 2235 (previous day)

Problem solving

1 2.9 m^2
2 a 16 000 cm^2 **b** 10 000 cm^2 **c** 2.6 m^2
3 7040 cm^2
4 a 380 cm^2 **b** 1519.76 mm^2 **c** 254.34 m^2
5 452.39 mm^2
6 6 cm
7 a 945.3 mm^2 **b** 120.25 mm
8 72 000 cm^2 (or 7.2 m^2)
9 5 cm
10 a 12.6 m further **b** 389.6 m^2
c 2647.4 m^2 **d** 106 packets
11 a 77.4 m **b** 204 m^2 **c** 61.2 m^3
12 52.15 cm
13 a If B is 25 square units, then each side is 5 units long. If F is 16 square units then each side is 4 units long. Then E is $1 \times 1 = 1$ square unit, C is $6 \times 6 = 36$ square units and D is $7 \times 7 = 49$ square units. A is made up of B and F, which means it is $9 \times 9 = 81$ square units, and then G is $8 \times 8 = 64$ square units.
b Total area: A = 81, B = 25, C = 36, D = 49, E = 1, F = 16, G = 64, H = 25.
Sum of all areas = 297 square units.
c 75 units
14 a 27 cubes. **b** 9 cm
15 10.2 m
16 42 cm^2
17 14 cm
18 900 days
19 $\frac{2}{\pi}$

20 $\frac{1}{8}$ **21** 3600 m^2

22 The best buy is the party size (at \$0.031 per cm^2).

23 24 m^2

24 The shaded plot has dimensions 5 m × 4 m and an area of 20 m^2.

25 1.50 m and 0.75 m

CHAPTER 11

Linear equations

Are you ready?

1 a Add 2 to obtain the next number in the sequence. The next three numbers are 15, 17, 19.

b Subtract 4 to obtain the next number in the sequence. The next three numbers are 12, 8, 4.

c Multiply by 2 to obtain the next number in the sequence.The next three numbers are 48, 96, 192.

d Divide by 10 to obtain the next number in the sequence. The next three numbers are 100, 10, 1.

2 a

Number of squares	1	2	3	4	5	6
Number of sides	4	8	12	16	20	24

b 40

3 a Each first number is one more than the previous first number and each second number is one more than the previous second number. Each second number is always 6 more than the matching first number.

b Each first number is two more than the previous first number and each second number is six more than the previous second number. Each second number is three times the matching first number.

4 a 11 **b** 2

5 a ÷ 2 **b** − 8 **c** + 17 **d** × −5

6 a

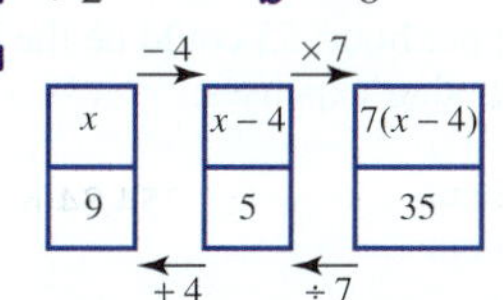

Solution is $x = 9$.

b

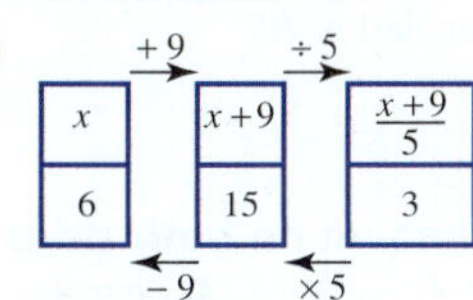

Solution is $x = 6$.

7 a $10v + 7$ **b** $c + 7$

8 a $6x + 10$ **b** $-7m + 7$

9 a Yes **b** No

10 a $x + 2 = 9$ **b** $8x = 40$

c $x - 11 = 3$ **d** $\frac{x}{6} = 2$

11A Identifying patterns

1 a Add 2; 10, 12, 14

b Add 5; 23, 28, 33

c Subtract 3; 15, 12, 9

d Multiply by 3; 81, 243, 729

e Divide by 2; 8, 4, 2

f Squares of numbers 1; 25, 36, 49

2 a 6, 15, 18 **b** 10, 12, 16

c 16, 64 **d** 9, 11, 17

e 88, 110 **f** 95, 90, 75

3 a 1, 5, 9, 13, 17 **b** 5, 15, 45, 135, 405

c 50, 42, 34, 26, 18 **d** 64, 32, 16, 8, 4

e 1, 4, 10, 22, 46 **f** 1, 6, 16, 36, 76

4 a Even numbers/multiples of 2

b Cubes **c** Prime numbers

d Fibonacci sequence **e** Factors of 12

f Multiples/powers of 3

5 a 2, 4, 6, 8 **b** 3, 9, 7, 1

c 4, 6 **d** 5

e 8, 4, 2, 6

6 a i

ii

Number of squares	1	2	3	4	5
Number of matches	4	7	10	13	16

iii Number of matches = Number of squares × 3 + 1

iv 61

b i

ii

Number of triangles	1	2	3	4	5
Number of matches	3	5	7	9	11

iii Number of matches = Number of triangles × 2 + 1

iv 41

c i

ii

Number of houses	1	2	3	4	5
Number of matches	6	11	16	21	26

iii Number of matches = Number of houses × 5 + 1

iv 101

d i

ii

Number of fence units	1	2	3	4	5
Number of matches	4	7	10	13	16

iii Number of matches = Number of fence units × 3 + 1

iv 61

7 a, b

2
4 6
8 10 12
14 16 18 20
22 24 26 28 30
32 34 36 38 40 42
44 46 48 50 52 54 56
58 60

c–e Check with your teacher.

11B Backtracking and inverse opearations

1 a 8 **b** 20 **c** −4

d −19 **e** −1 **f** −1

g −2 **h** −44 **i** 8

j 4 **k** 1.075 **l** 4.4

2 a $2x - 7$ **b** $2(w - 7)$ **c** $-5s + 3$

d $-5(n + 3)$ **e** $\frac{m}{2} + 7$ **f** $\frac{y + 7}{2}$

g $\frac{6z - 3}{2}$ **h** $\frac{-3(d + 5)}{4}$ **i** $\frac{2e}{5} + 1$

j $4(3 - x)$ **k** $\frac{-2(w - 5)}{7}$ **l** $-3(z + 6) - 11$

m $\frac{v-3}{6}-8$ **n** $-7(8m-4)$

o $\frac{-5k}{6}+2$ **p** $\frac{-5p-7}{3}$

3 a $\boxed{x} \xrightarrow{+7} \boxed{x+7} \xrightarrow{\times 2} \boxed{2(x+7)}$

b $\boxed{x} \xrightarrow{-8} \boxed{x-8} \xrightarrow{\times -2} \boxed{-2(x-8)}$

c $\boxed{m} \xrightarrow{\times 3} \boxed{3m} \xrightarrow{-6} \boxed{3m-6}$

d $\boxed{m} \xrightarrow{\times -3} \boxed{-3m} \xrightarrow{-6} \boxed{-3m-6}$

e $\boxed{x} \xrightarrow{-5} \boxed{x-5} \xrightarrow{\div 8} \boxed{\frac{x-5}{8}}$

f $\boxed{x} \xrightarrow{\div 8} \boxed{\frac{x}{8}} \xrightarrow{-5} \boxed{\frac{x}{8}-5}$

g $\boxed{x} \xrightarrow{\times -5} \boxed{-5x} \xrightarrow{+11} \boxed{-5x+11}$

h $\boxed{x} \xrightarrow{\times -1} \boxed{-x} \xrightarrow{+11} \boxed{-x+11}$

i $\boxed{x} \xrightarrow{\times -1} \boxed{-x} \xrightarrow{-13} \boxed{-x-13}$

j $\boxed{x} \xrightarrow{\times -2} \boxed{-2x} \xrightarrow{+5} \boxed{-2x+5}$

k $\boxed{x} \xrightarrow{\times 3} \boxed{3x} \xrightarrow{-7} \boxed{3x-7} \xrightarrow{\div 4} \boxed{\frac{3x-7}{4}}$

l $\boxed{x} \xrightarrow{-2} \boxed{x-2} \xrightarrow{\times -3} \boxed{-3(x-2)} \xrightarrow{\div 4} \boxed{\frac{-3(x-2)}{4}}$

m $\boxed{x} \xrightarrow{+5} \boxed{x+5} \xrightarrow{\div 8} \boxed{\frac{x+5}{8}} \xrightarrow{-3} \boxed{\frac{x+5}{8}-3}$

n $\boxed{x} \xrightarrow{\div 5} \boxed{\frac{x}{5}} \xrightarrow{-2} \boxed{\frac{x}{5}-2} \xrightarrow{\times -7} \boxed{-7(\frac{x}{5}-2)}$

o $\boxed{x} \xrightarrow{\times 2} \boxed{2x} \xrightarrow{\div 7} \boxed{\frac{2x}{7}} \xrightarrow{+4} \boxed{\frac{2x}{7}+4} \xrightarrow{\times 3} \boxed{3(\frac{2x}{7}+4)}$

p $\boxed{x} \xrightarrow{\times 6} \boxed{6x} \xrightarrow{\div 11} \boxed{\frac{6x}{11}} \xrightarrow{-3} \boxed{\frac{6x}{11}-3} \xrightarrow{\times \frac{1}{4}} \boxed{\frac{1}{4}(\frac{6x}{11}-3)}$

11C Keeping equations balanced

1 a $x+5=11$ **b** $7x=42$

c $x-4=2$ **d** $\frac{x}{3}=2$

e $-4x=-24$ **f** $-x=-6$

g $-x=-6$ **h** $x-9=-3$

i $\frac{2x}{3}=4$ **j** $\frac{3x}{2}=9$

k $x-\frac{2}{3}=5\frac{1}{3}$

2 a $2x=4$ **b** $x=2$

3 a $x+3=5$ **b** $x=2$

4 a $3x+1=7$ **b** $3x+4=10$

5 a $2x+1=5$ **b** $4x+2=10$

6 B **7** E

8 C **9** C

11D Using algebra to solve problems

1 a $x=-1$ **b** $r=-5$

c $t=24$ **d** $w=2.7$

e $m=\frac{1}{2}$ **f** $j=-\frac{19}{7}$ or $-2\frac{5}{7}$

g $q=19$ **h** $r=9$

i $t=32$ **j** $y=14.5$

k $z=-\frac{19}{21}$ **l** $f=\frac{4}{13}$

2 a $d=8$ **b** $p=-14$

c $u=\frac{4}{5}$ or 0.8 **d** $g=5$

e $m=\frac{1}{32}$ **f** $j=-\frac{1}{15}$

g $t=24$ **h** $k=-60$

i $l=-21.2$ **j** $v=4$

k $c=-\frac{5}{3}$ or $-1\frac{2}{3}$ **l** $h=-\frac{35}{12}$ or $-2\frac{11}{12}$

3 a $m=3$ **b** $w=-5$

c $k=-4$ **d** $t=-3$

e $m=1$ **f** $n=-18$

g $k=-9$ **h** $s=-7$

i $m=3.5$ **j** $p=-14$

k $g=-3$ **l** $f=5$

m $q=9.05$ **n** $r=-3.2$

o $t=3.6$ **p** $k=-0.2$

q $g=-\frac{1}{4}$ or -0.25 **r** $f=\frac{15}{16}$

4 a $x=21$ **b** $x=9$

c $m=-17$ **d** $h=-12$

e $m=-20$ **f** $w=-10$

g $m=2\frac{1}{3}$ **h** $c=1$

i $m=-8$ **j** $t=-37$

k $c=-19.5$ **l** $x=-20.8$

5 a $m=-5$ **b** $x=-20$

c $m=1\frac{1}{5}$ **d** $x=3$

e $x=-7$ **f** $x=11$

g $x=7$ **h** $b=10$

i $f=-9$ **j** $z=6$

k $m=5$ **l** $u=-11$

m $m=-3$ **n** $w=-1\frac{3}{5}$

o $x=8$ **p** $d=3$

q $n=9$ **r** $t=-2$

6 a The solution is not correct.

b Alex should have also divided 3 by 2 in the second line or subtracted 3 from both sides first before dividing both sides by 2. The solution should be $x=5\frac{1}{2}$.

7 a $x=2$ **b** $v=-2$

c $m=-1$ **d** $y=4$

e $y=-6$ **f** $t=-5$

g $w=2\frac{2}{9}$ **h** $w=\frac{2}{3}$

i $u=-4$ **j** $c=6$

8 a $2\frac{1}{2}$ hours

b 40 could be the charge per hour; 55 could be the flat fee covering travel and other expenses.

9 $l+286=517$, $l=\$231$

10 a $10x+54=184$, $x=13$ cm

b $11x+12=287$, $x=25$ cm

11 9 and 4

12 2

13 Yes, when Tom is 45 and his dad is 90.

14 $80 per month

15 $y=2x+\frac{1}{3}$

11E Equations with the unknown on both sides

1 a $x=3$ **b** $y=4$ **c** $n=4$

d $t=4$ **e** $w=5$ **f** $y=3\frac{2}{3}$

g $z=4$ **h** $a=-4$ **i** $s=2$

j $k=4$ **k** $w=-3$ **l** $v=-4$

2 a $w=2$ **b** $b=2$ **c** $n=2$

d $s=3$ **e** $a=-3$ **f** $m=2$

g $p=4$ **h** $d=3$ **i** $m=0$

j $s=1$ **k** $t=-2$ **l** $x=4$

3 a $x=3$ **b** $m=10$ **c** $n=12$

d 5 **e** $d=2\frac{5}{6}$ **f** $w=1\frac{2}{9}$

g $k=10$ **h** $s=-3$ **i** $z=-17$

j $v=1\frac{1}{2}$ **k** $m=11\frac{2}{3}$ **l** $d=3\frac{7}{10}$

m $d=-19$ **n** $k=-10$ **o** $v=2$

p $l=18$

4 $x=-\frac{13}{33}$ **5** $x=\frac{13}{5}$ or $2\frac{3}{5}$

6 6.25 cm

7 a $6(x+3)=\frac{1}{2}\times 6\times(x+5+2)$
b $x=1$
c Parallelogram: base 4 cm, height 6 cm, Trapezium: base 6 cm, top 2 cm, height 6 cm.
8 24 **9** 3
10 Mick is 14, his father is 42.
11 16
12 12

Chapter review

Fluency

1 a $5(x-1)$ **b** $\frac{3x}{8}$
c $\frac{x+8}{5}+3$ **d** $\frac{3x-7}{2}$

2 a $m \xrightarrow{+4} m+4 \xrightarrow{\times -3} -3(m+4)$
b $n \xrightarrow{\div 3} \frac{n}{3} \xrightarrow{+5} \frac{n}{3}+5$
c $m \xrightarrow{-7} m-7 \xrightarrow{\div 5} \frac{m-7}{5} \xrightarrow{-4} \frac{m-7}{5}-4$
d $w \xrightarrow{\times -15} -15w \xrightarrow{+7} 7-15w$

3 a $2x+2=8$ **b** $2x=6$

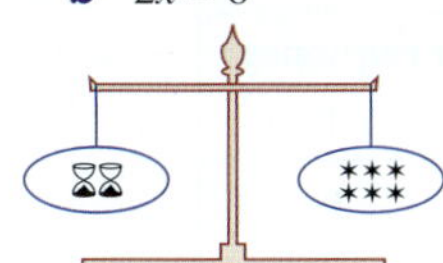

4 B **5** E
6 a 11 **b** 7 **c** $\frac{4}{9}$
d $\frac{1}{27}$ **e** -43.5 **f** $-\frac{48}{13}$ or $-3\frac{9}{13}$
7 a $v=3$ **b** $s=-4$ **c** $d=47$
d $r=-9$ **e** $y=33$ **f** $x=25$
8 a $k=3$ **b** $s=-2$
c $t=4$ **d** $x=2$
9 a $v=2$ **b** $m=5$

Problem solving

1 a $C=65t+80$ **b** $1\frac{1}{2}$ hours
c 1 hour 45 minutes
d \$54: charge per half hour, \$86: flat call-out fee.
2 Katie scored 58% for her Algebra test.
3 Eldest is 23 years old.
4 Truck weighs 5.11 tonnes.
5 You are 16 and your sister is 4.
6 5
7 \$5, \$10, \$30
8 832 mm
9 a 1. $y=0.15+0.3x$
2. $y=0.4x$
3. $y=0.4+0.19x$ where x in the time of the call and y is the cost of the call.
b 1 minute choose Plan 2; 2 minutes choose Plan 1; 3 minutes choose Plan 3.
c Switch to Plan 3 for calls over 2.27 minutes.
10 22 m × 7 m
11 a $n=2r+1$
b 32 rows
12 1 L in the black bucket, 3 L in the white bucket, 4 L in the red bucket.

13 2 hours 20 minutes

Time	Amy	Ben
0	\$3	\$10
20	\$6	\$12
40	\$9	\$14
60	\$12	\$16
80	\$15	\$18
100	\$18	\$20
120	\$21	\$22
140	\$24	\$24

14 \$134.57 **15** \$356.25

CHAPTER 12

Representing and interpreting data

Are you ready?

1

Score	Tally	Frequency
1	|||	3
2	~~||||~~	5
3	~~||||~~ ||	7
4	||||	4
5	||	2
6	|||	3

2 a 1 cm **b** 0.2 m **c** 20 mm **d** 5%
3 a 3 **b** 13 **c** 4.6 **d** 468
4 a 20, 21, 22, 25, 25, 29, 34
b 215, 276, 277, 298, 304, 325, 345, 381, 400
c 0.3, 1.8, 2.8, 2.9, 3.1, 3.5, 3.6, 3.6, 4.6, 5.8, 5.8
5 a 4 **b** 11 **c** 5 **d** 8
6 a 7 **b** 0.5
7 a 2 **b** 25 **c** 8

12A Samples and populations

1 Census, sample
2 Census — every member of the population participates.
3 Survey
4 a Survey **b** Survey
c Census **d** Survey
5 a Survey **b** Census
c Census **d** Survey
6 Open questions have no boundaries for response. Closed questions require answers to fall within a category. A variety of examples is possible.
7 A variety of categorical responses is suitable; check with your teacher.
8 A variety of categorical responses is suitable; check with your teacher.
9 a This is a personal question.
b This question is vague. Define what is meant by 'exercise' and 'regularly'.
c What do the abbreviations stand for?
d What is the Premier's policy on wildlife preservation?
e Is this question capable of being answered? What is a 'foot'?
f This is a double-barrelled question.
Check with your teacher for alternative wording of questions.

10 22, 30, 49, 3, 14 is one possible solution.

11 a 94, 1, 54 **b** 60, 47, 33, 43 **c** 25, 49, 10

12 D

13 A variety of answers is available here.
- **a** Typically, the choir members would not be the ones using the pool. The sample is biased.
- **b** These people may or may not know about the PM's health-care package. In any case, the sample is biased as it is not truly representative of the population.
- **c** If the visitors had just arrived at the airport, they would not have had time to experience the transport system into the city. The sample is biased.
- **d** This sample size is far too small.

14 Generally only those people with strong points of view participate in telephone surveys. This type of sample is often not representative of the whole population. The high telephone cost for the response is also a deterrent to responding.

15 Check with your teacher.

16 A variety of answers is possible.

17 Discuss this question as a class.

12B Organising and displaying data

1 a The sample is random and is of sufficient size, so calculations from the data could be considered reliable.

b

x	Frequency
0	5
1	8
2	13
3	7
4	5
5	2
Total	40

c

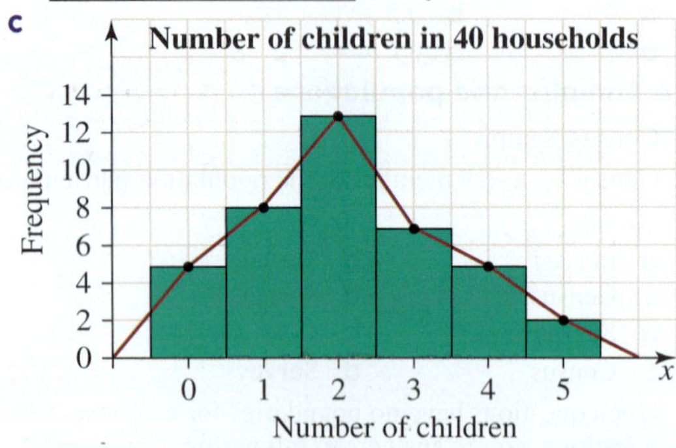

d The data is distributed fairly evenly around 2 children per household, and there appear to be no outliers. The graph clearly shows a maximum at 2 children per household.

e The sample is a random one, and of sufficient size; we can be confident that the suburb also exhibits these same properties.

2 a i

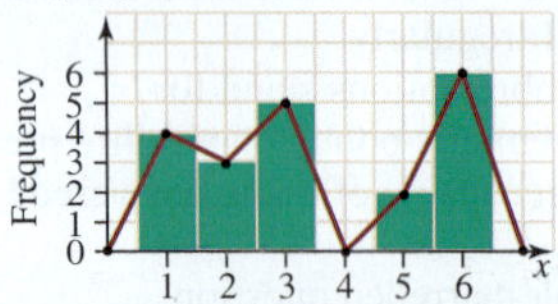

ii This graph is quite inconsistent, showing no particular trend.

b i

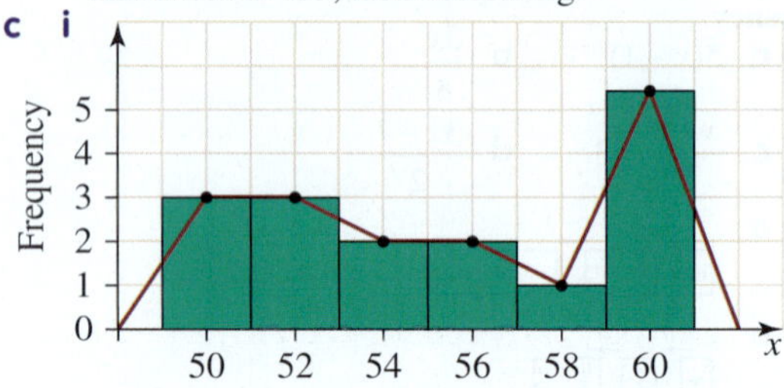

ii This graph is almost symmetrical, rising to a maximum at 153, then decreasing.

c i

ii This graph is quite unusual. It shows a group of smaller values, then a maximum at the upper limit of the data.

3 a The sample is a random one, so it seems to be a reliable reflection of the population of the portable CD players.

b

x	Frequency
0	1
1	6
2	8
3	5
4	2
5	3
Total	25

c There was only 1 box with no defective CD players. Most boxes had only 1, 2 or 3 defective CD players, while 3 boxes were found to have 5 defective CD players.

d Since the sample was randomly selected, it seems to be a reliable reflection of the characteristics of the population. It would be reasonably safe to say that most boxes would have only 1, 2 or 3 defective CD players.

4 a

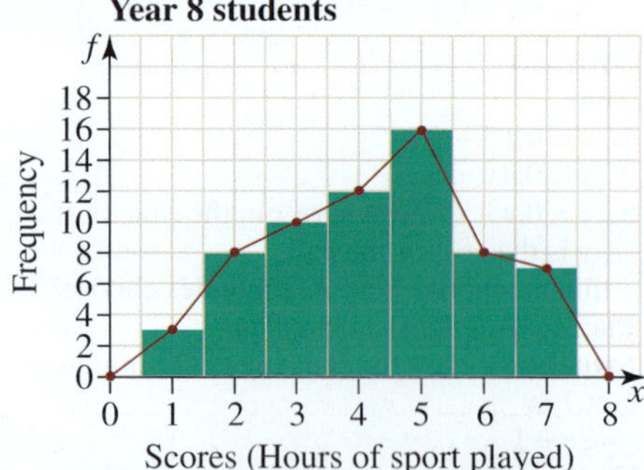

b The graph rises steadily to a maximum, then falls away sharply at the upper end of the data.

c This is likely to be a true reflection of the sporting habits of Year 8 students. Some do a minimum of only 1 hour per week, quite a few do 2, 3 or 4 hours per week, with the maximum number doing 5 hours per week. The committed sports players would put in 6 or 7 hours per week.

5 a

f

Size of house (m^2)

b The graph is roughly symmetrical, rising to a maximum at the 200-m2 to 250-m2 size, then decreasing slowly.

c Since this is one block of houses in the suburb, it is not a random sample. We often find all the houses in a block of a suburb are of similar style. For this reason, we could not say it reflects the size of houses in the whole suburb.

6 a

Mass of people joining a weight loss program

Frequency

Mass (kg)

b The graph is quite symmetrical, rising to a maximum at the 90-kg to 100-kg mass, then decreasing more rapidly to the 130-kg mass.

c This would most likely not reflect the masses of people in the community because these are people who have enrolled in a program to lose weight.

7 a

Class interval	Midpoint (class centre)	Tally	Frequency
5–<10	7.5	𝍸 𝍸 |	11
10–<15	12.5	𝍸 𝍸 𝍸 ||||	19
15–<20	17.5	𝍸	5
20–<25	22.5	||	2
25–<30	27.5	|||	3
		Total	40

b

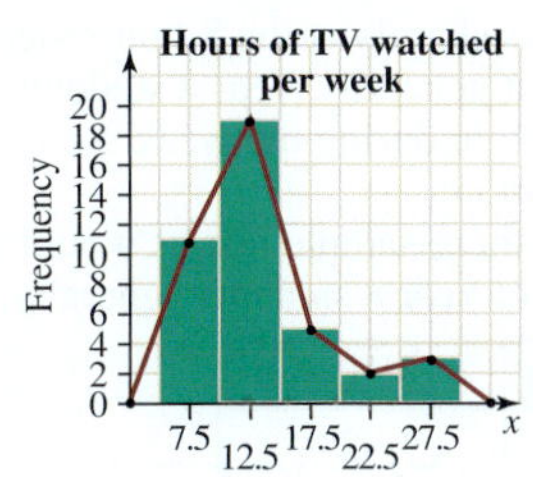

c The graph is heavily weighted towards the lower end of the scale, with most people watching fewer than 15 hours of TV per week. There were 3 people who watched almost 30 hours of TV per week.

d Since these people were interviewed in a shopping centre, the sample is not a random one. It could not therefore be taken to reflect the viewing habits of the community.

8 a

Test results	Frequency
2	2
3	2
4	2
5	3
6	6
7	5
8	7
9	3
Total	30

b

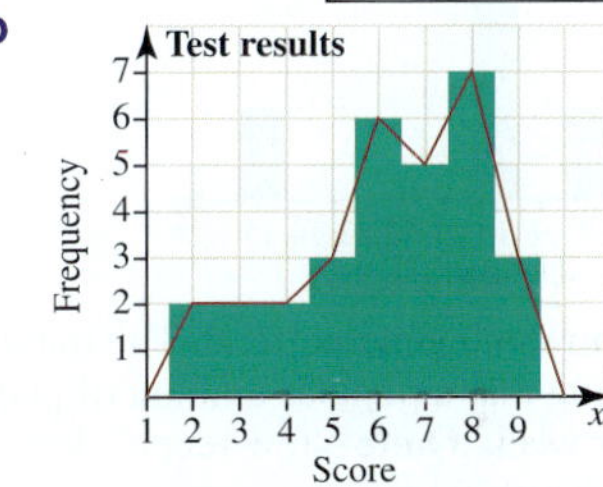

c Most Year 8 students achieved a score of about 5 to 9. There were 6 students who received less than 5. This is probably a typical spread of marks for a multiple-choice test.

9 a

Hours of sleep	Frequency
6	1
$6\frac{1}{2}$	2
7	3
$7\frac{1}{2}$	3
8	7
$8\frac{1}{2}$	2
9	2
Total	20

b

Number of hours sleep on school nights

Frequency

Number of hours' sleep

c The histogram peaks sharply at the 8-hours sleep mark, indicating that generally, Year 8 students get 8 hours of sleep per night during the week. Some get less, and a few get more.

d It seems likely that these sample results would reflect the sleeping habits of Year 8 students generally.

10 a

Pocket money ($)	Frequency
4	2
5	4
6	3
7	0
8	2
9	0
10	7
11	0
12	0
13	0
14	0
15	2
Total	20

b

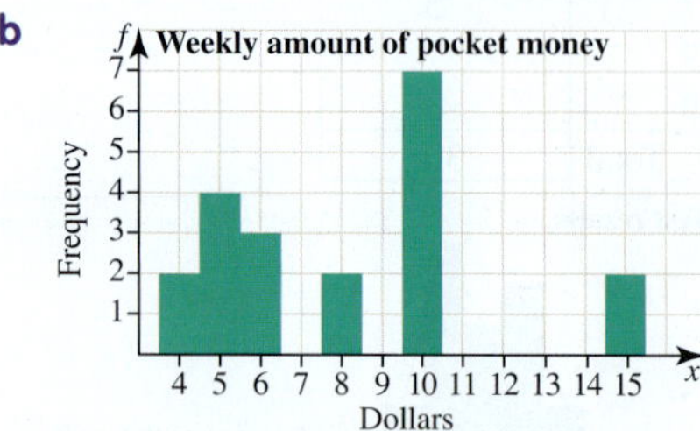

c The histogram shows no general trend. The maximum is at $10, indicating that a popular amount of pocket money is $10 per week. Quite a few receive less than this, with only 2 receiving more.

d Since this is a random sample, it is quite likely that this is the trend amongst 13-year-olds when it comes to pocket money.

11 a

Life time (hours)	Frequency
20–<25	16
25–<30	16
30–<35	18
35–<40	25
40–<45	15
45–<50	10
Total	100

b

Lifetime of torch batteries

Frequency

Lifetime (hours)

c The histogram shows that the majority of torch batteries last for about 40 hours. A few last longer than this.

d It seems reasonable that the torch battery population would display a similar trend.

12 a

Class interval	Midpoint (class centre)	Tally	Frequency
145–<150	147.5	||	2
150–<155	152.5	||||	4
155–<160	157.5	卌 |||	8
160–<165	162.5	卌 ||	7
165–<170	167.5	卌	5
170–<175	172.5	|||	3
175–<180	177.5	|	1
		Total	30

b

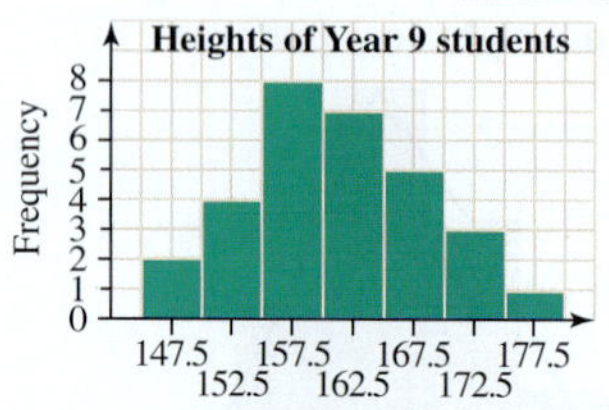

c

Class interval	Midpoint (class centre)	Tally	Frequency
145–<148	146.5	|	1
148–<151	149.5	||	2
151–<154	152.5	||	2
154–<157	155.5	||||	4
157–<160	158.5	卌	5
160–<163	161.5	||||	4
163–<166	164.5	|||	3
166–<169	167.5	卌	5
169–<172	170.5	||	2
172–<175	173.5	|	1
175–<178	176.5	—	0
178–<181	179.5	|	1
		Total	30

d

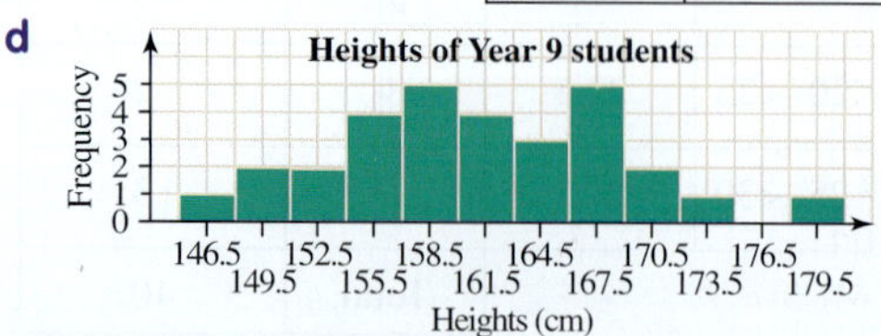

e The two histograms represent the same data set, but appear to be quite different. The first histogram appears to be roughly symmetrical, with a maximum number of students having a height about 155 cm to 160 cm. The second histogram is bimodal, with the most common height for students being about 157 cm to 160 cm, or 166 cm to 169 cm. It illustrates the fact that the interpretation of a histogram displaying grouped data is dependent on the class interval used.

12C Measures of centre

1 26.8

2 **a** 4.33 **b** 7.33 **c** 36.3 **d** 6.91

3 **a** 18 **b** 10 **c** 1.8 goals

4 C

5 4.6

6 **a** Group A: 6.1; Group B: 6.8. Group B has a larger mean.
b Group A has a larger spread of values; that is, from 2 to 9. Group B's spread is from 5 to 9.

7 2

8 7.8

9

x	*f*	*xf*
1	4	4
2	5	10
3	4	12
4	2	8
5	1	5
Total	16	39

Mean = 2.4

10 80

11 **a** 7 **b** 17

12 **a** 48 **b** 1.8

13 Question **11:** **a** 5 **b** 17
Question **12:** **a** 52 **b** 1.5, 1.7, 1.8

14 C

15 E

16 **a** 6.7 **b** 10

17

x	*f*	*xf*
0	1	0
1	2	2
2	7	14
3	3	9
4	4	16
5	2	10
6	1	6
Total	20	57

Mean = 2.85

18 **a** 36 **b** 7

19 **a** 3 **b** 3 **c** Both

20 **a** 4 **b** 3
c Three strokes. Factors include wind, difficulty of hole, performance on the day, and so on.

21 **a** 49 **b** 55 **c** 56
d Median

22 **a** \$18 000 **b** \$26 000 **c** \$30 000
d Mean **e** Mode

23 One possible answer is 5, 6, 12, 13, 14. If the five numbers are in ascending order, the third number must be 12 and the other 4 numbers must total 38.

24 Highest score is 49 and lowest score is 0.
The scores would be 0, 1, 12, 13, 49.

25 Largest value for median is 15. Scores would be 0, 2, 15, 16, 17. Smallest value for median is 2. Scores would be 0, 1, 2, a, b, where $a + b = 47$.

26 43; highest score: 100; lowest score: 57. The scores would be 57, 77, 78, 79, 80, 97, 98, 99, 100.

12D Measures of spread

1 **a** 8 **b** 15
c 50 **d** 2.5

2 **a** 4 **b** 5
c 15 **d** 4

3 **a** Yes **b** 8 **c** Both equal 8.

4 **a** No **b** 31–40 **c** No

5 **a** 4–5 **b** Negatively skewed

6 **a**

Frequency
Number of goals
1–10, 11–20, 21–30, 31–40, 41–50

b Negatively skewed

7 B

8 **a** **i** 35
ii The data are irregular, with no obvious skewness.
b **i** 46
ii The data are negatively skewed.
c **i** 35
ii The data are negatively skewed.

9 This distribution seems to have two outliers — one at 8 and the other at 18. If these two scores are disregarded, the remaining part of the distribution is almost symmetrical.

10 **a**

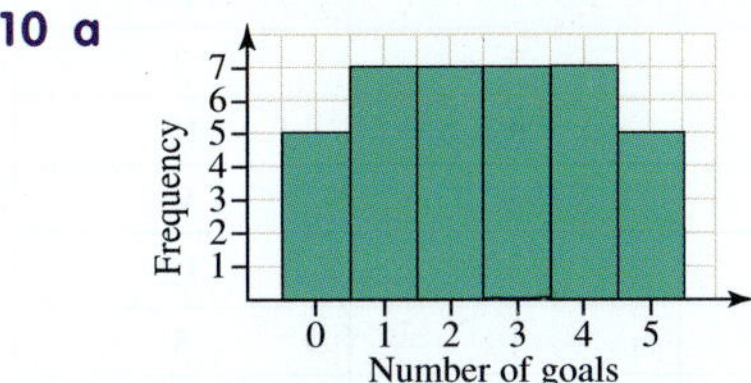

b Yes
c 1, 2, 3 and 4 **d** Yes, both equal 2.5.

11 **a**

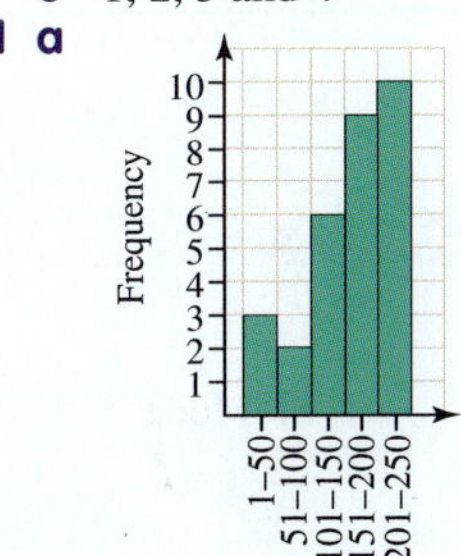

b No
c 201 – 250
d The distribution is negatively skewed. Reasons could include the size of cinemas or the target audience of the movie.

12 a No
b Science: positively skewed, Maths: negatively skewed
c The science test may have been more difficult.
d Science: 61–70, Maths: 71–80
e Maths has a greater standard deviation (2.6) than Science (11.9).

13 Answers will vary. Check with your teacher.

12E Analysing data

1 a Range b Mean c Mode
d Mean e Median

2 a 6.4 b 6 c 6
d They are all quite close, so any would do.
e The distribution is negatively skewed, with more scores towards the upper end.
f Since these were the results of half the class, and the sample was random, it seems likely that the population results would be similar.

3 a i 2 ii 2 iii 1
iv Mean or median
v Positively skewed
b i 7.8 ii 7 iii 7
iv Any of the three
v Slightly positively skewed

4 a i 22.6 ii 23 iii 23
iv Any of the three
v Possibly positively skewed with an outlier at 44
b i 117.5 ii 116 iii 112 iv Mean
v Symmetrical

5 a i 4.5 ii 5 iii 5 iv Any of the three
v The distribution is very scattered, with an outlier at 10.
b i 82.4 ii 82.5 iii 81 iv Mean or median
v Slightly positively skewed

6 a

Score (x)	Frequency (f)	Freq. × score ($f \times x$)
0	1	0
1	3	3
2	6	12
3	3	9
4	3	12
5	1	5
6	1	6
	$n = 18$	$\Sigma fx = 47$

b $\bar{x} = 2 - 6$

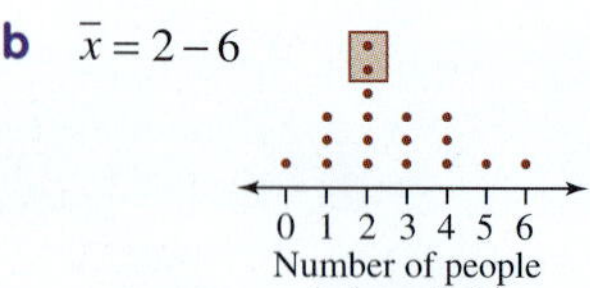

c 2
d i Median ii Mean iii Mode

7 a \$18 000 b \$29 444
c \$26 000
d i Mode ii Mean

8 a

Score (x)	Frequency (f)	Freq. × score ($f \times x$)
137	2	274
138	3	414
139	5	695
140	3	420
141	6	846
142	1	142
	$n = 20$	$\Sigma fx = 2791$

b 141, 139.5, 139.6
c Mean
d

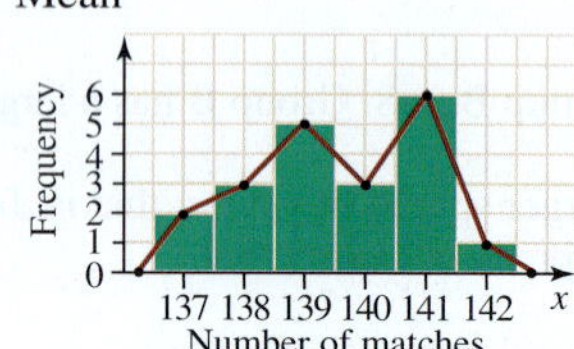

9 a The median was calculated by taking the average of the 2 middle scores.
b 13

10 2

11 a 55 250 km, 52 000 km, 52 000 km
b Discuss in class.
c 51 810 km; it is reduced by 3440 km.
d 52 000 km
e 3333
f 50 000 km; 92% last that distance or more.

Chapter review

Fluency

1 a Survey b Census
c Census d Survey

2 D
3 B
4 Discuss as a class.
5 The appropriate sample size is $\sqrt{\text{population size}}$.

6 a

Video rating	Frequency
0	8
1	6
2	3
3	2
4	0
5	1
Total	20

b

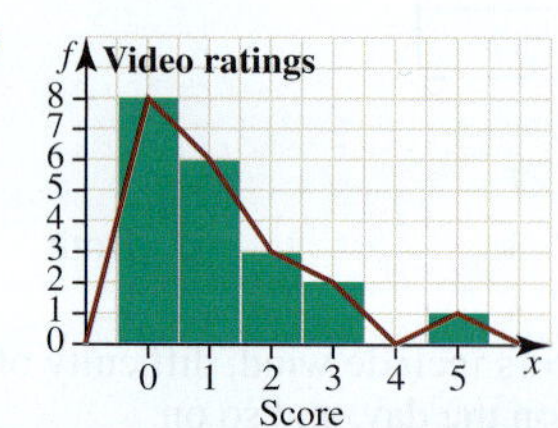

c The graph is positively skewed with an outlier at 5.
d 0 e 1 f 5

7 a

Class interval	Frequency (f)
0–9	2
10–19	3
20–29	6
30–39	5
40–49	9
50–59	14
60–69	9
70–79	2
	$n = 50$

b

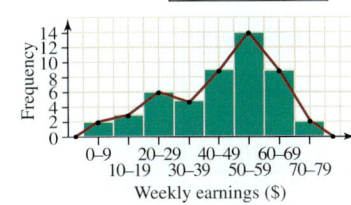

c The graph is negatively skewed.

8 3.1 **9** 8 **10** 4.3

11 a 5 **b** 5 **c** 4

12 a There is no mode since none of the values occurs more than once.

b 7 **c** 40

13 a Yes **b** Yes. Both are 3.

c 3

14 a

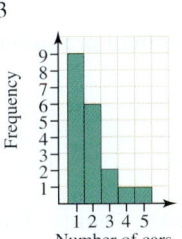

b Positively skewed

15 a 2.3 **b** 2.0 **c** 2.0

d Mode **e** Positively skewed

16 a 6.27 **b** 6.28 **c** 6.34

d Mean or median **e** Negatively skewed

17 a 2.6 **b** 2.55 **c** 2.4

d Mean **e** The distribution shows no pattern.

Problem solving

1 a

x	f	xf
11	6	66
12	10	120
13	11	143
14	8	112
15	8	120
16	5	80
17	2	34
Total	50	675

b

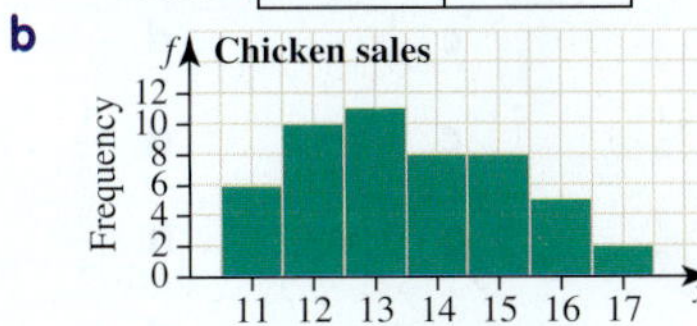

c 13 **d** 13.5, 13

e 13; as this is the most frequently sold size.

f 6 **g** 58% **h** Discuss

2 a 2 **b** 2.6 **c** 9

d Most homes get up to about 3 pieces of mail. Some do get more.

CHAPTER 13

Probability

Are you ready?

1 a Impossible **b** Fifty–fifty

c Certain **d** Impossible

e Fifty–fifty

2 a 26 **b** 4 **c** 2 **d** 1

e 4 **f** 12

3 a $\frac{1}{2}$ **b** $\frac{4}{5}$ **c** $\frac{9}{25}$ **d** $\frac{1}{4}$

4 a 0.2 **b** 0.75 **c** 0.3 **d** 0.85

5 a 25% **b** 60% **c** 70% **d** 35%

6 a 16 **b** 72 **c** $10\frac{1}{2}$ **d** 16

7 a {1, 2, 3, 4, 5, 6} **b** {Heads, Tails}

c {1, 2, 3, 4, 5}

8 a $\frac{3}{14}$ **b** $\frac{8}{27}$ **c** $\frac{7}{24}$ **d** $\frac{8}{39}$

13A Probability scale

1 a Certain **b** Highly unlikely

c Discuss **d** Discuss

e Highly unlikely **f** Highly unlikely

g Certain **h** Impossible

i Highly unlikely **j** Highly likely

k Even chance **l** Highly unlikely

m Even chance **n** Better than even chance

o Highly likely **p** Highly unlikely

2 a–e Should be discussed in class

3 a $\frac{1}{2}$ **b** $\frac{9}{10}$

c 0 **d** 1

e $\frac{1}{2}$ **f** $\frac{1}{3}$

g $\frac{1}{52}$ **h** $\frac{11}{20}$

i $\frac{5}{6}$ **j** $\frac{1}{13}$

k $\frac{1}{5}$ **l** $\frac{2}{13}$

m $\frac{4}{7}$ **n** 1

4 C **5** E

13B Experimental probability

1 a $\frac{14}{25}$ (0.56) **b** $\frac{11}{25}$ (0.44)

2 a $\frac{13}{25}$ **b** 0.48

3 a $\frac{7}{50}$ (0.14) **b** $\frac{43}{50}$ (0.86)

4 a $\frac{5}{16}$ **b** $\frac{13}{40}$ **c** 0.3625

5 a **i** 2, 4, 6 **ii** 1, 2

iii 3, 4, 5, 6 **iv** 2, 3, 5

v Impossible **vi** 5, 6

vii 1, 4, 6 **viii** 1, 2, 3, 4

ix 3, 6 **x** 5

b 1 → 15%
2 → 17%
3 → 17.5%
4 → 16%
5 → 17.5%
6 → 17%

c 50% **d** 48%
e 17.5% **f** 68%
g 50% **h** 34.5%
i 34.5% **j** 32%

6 a

Score	Frequency
1	34
2	27
3	24
4	15
Total	100

b Swimming = $\frac{34}{100}$ (0.34)

Athletics = $\frac{27}{100}$ (0.27)

Gymnastics = $\frac{24}{100}$ (0.24)

Rowing = $\frac{15}{100}$ (0.15)

c 1 **d** Swimming **e** 204

7 a

Score	Frequency
1	3
2	5
3	5
4	4
5	3
Total	20

b 1 → $\frac{3}{20}$ (0.15)

2 → $\frac{1}{4}$ (0.25)

3 → $\frac{1}{4}$ (0.25)

4 → $\frac{1}{5}$ (0.2)

5 → $\frac{3}{20}$ (0.15)

c 4
Since there are five possible outcomes, each has an equal chance of occurring. Therefore, in 20 trials each outcome would be expected to occur 4 times.

d 2 and 3 **e** 1

8 a i 3 of hearts
ii $\frac{13}{60}$

b i Queen of diamonds and 3 of diamonds
ii $\frac{9}{20}$

c i 3 of hearts, queen of diamonds and 3 of diamonds
ii $\frac{2}{3}$

d i 3 of each suit
ii $\frac{3}{4}$

e i 3 of both spades and hearts
ii $\frac{2}{5}$

f i All cards drawn
ii 1

g i None of the cards drawn **ii** 0
h i All cards drawn **ii** 1

9 a The greater the number of trials, the closer the results come to what we would expect; that is, a relative frequency of 50% for each event.
b No, the results would not be identical because this is an experiment and values will differ for each trial.

10 a $\frac{1}{4}$

b

Score	Frequency
1	11
2	9
3	10
4	10
Total	40

c $\frac{21}{40}$ **d** 2, 3 **e** $\frac{19}{40}$

11 a $\frac{1}{20}$ (0.05) **b** $\frac{19}{20}$ (0.95) **c** 30

12 D **13** B

14 Check with your teacher.

13C Sample spaces and theoretical probability

1 a {1, 2, 3, 4, 5, 6}
b i $\frac{1}{6}$ **ii** $\frac{1}{2}$ **iii** $\frac{2}{3}$ **iv** $\frac{1}{3}$
v $\frac{1}{2}$ **vi** $\frac{1}{3}$ **vii** 0 **viii** 1

2 a {Heads, Tails} **b** {a, a, o, u}
c {Monday, Tuesday, Wednesday, Thursday, Friday, Saturday, Sunday}
d {R, R, R, W, W, B} **e** {1, 2, 3, 4, 5, 6}
f {king of: hearts, diamonds, clubs, spades queen of: hearts, diamonds, clubs, spades jack of: hearts, diamonds, clubs, spades}
g {1, 2, 3, 4, 5, 6, 7, 8}
h {2, 4, 6, 8, 10, 12, 14, 16, 18, 20}
i {apple, apple, pear, pear, pear, pear, orange, orange, orange, orange, banana, banana, banana, banana}
j {*Dolly, Dolly, Dolly, Girlfriend, Girlfriend, Smash Hits, Mathsmag, Mathsmag*}
k {A, B, C, D, E} **l** {gold, silver, bronze}

3 a $\frac{1}{52}$, 1.9% **b** $\frac{1}{13}$, 7.7%
c $\frac{2}{13}$, 15.4% **d** $\frac{1}{4}$, 25%
e $\frac{1}{2}$, 50% **f** $\frac{4}{13}$, 30.8%
g $\frac{1}{13}$, 7.7%

4 a $\frac{2}{45}$ **b** $\frac{8}{9}$ **c** $\frac{1}{9}$ **d** $\frac{1}{9}$

5 a $\frac{3}{14}$ **b** $\frac{1}{7}$ **c** $\frac{1}{7}$ **d** $\frac{5}{14}$
e $\frac{11}{14}$ **f** $\frac{4}{7}$ **g** 0 **h** $\frac{13}{14}$

6 a $\frac{1}{2}$ **b** $\frac{1}{2}$ **c** 0 **d** 1

7 a $\frac{1}{365}$ (or $\frac{1}{366}$) **b** $\frac{7}{365}$ (or $\frac{7}{366}$)
c $\frac{30}{365} = \frac{6}{73}$ (or $\frac{30}{366} = \frac{5}{61}$) **d** $\frac{1}{365}$ (or $\frac{1}{366}$)
Note: In a leap year there are 366 days.

8 a i Yes, equal sectors **ii** $\frac{1}{2}$
b i Yes, equal sectors **ii** $\frac{1}{4}$
c i No, sector 1 occupies a larger area. **ii** $\frac{2}{3}$
d i No, sector 1 occupies the smallest area. **ii** $\frac{1}{8}$

9 $\frac{1}{2}$

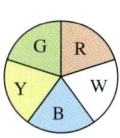

10 a
b Each sector has an angle of 72° at the centre of the spinner.

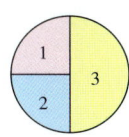

11 a
b Sectors 1 and 2 have angles of 90° and sector 3 has an angle of 180° at the centre of the spinner.

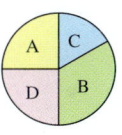

12 a
b Sectors A and D: 90°, sector B: 120° and sector C: 60°.

13 a 1 **b** 360°

14 a Heads, $\frac{1}{2}$; Tails, $\frac{1}{2}$ **b** 1

15 a H H, $\frac{1}{4}$ H T, $\frac{1}{4}$ T H, $\frac{1}{4}$ T T, $\frac{1}{4}$
b 1

16 a $\frac{1}{6}$ **b** 1 **c** Yes
d The total of probabilities for all elements in a sample space is always 1.

17 C **18** A

19 a {1, 2, 3, 4, 5, 6}
b 36
c

		Die 2					
		1	2	3	4	5	6
Die 1	1	(1, 1)	(1, 2)	(1, 3)	(1, 4)	(1, 5)	(1, 6)
	2	(2, 1)	(2, 2)	(2, 3)	(2, 4)	(2, 5)	(2, 6)
	3	(3, 1)	(3, 2)	(3, 3)	(3, 4)	(3, 5)	(3, 6)
	4	(4, 1)	(4, 2)	(4, 3)	(4, 4)	(4, 5)	(4, 6)
	5	(5, 1)	(5, 2)	(5, 3)	(5, 4)	(5, 5)	(5, 6)
	6	(6, 1)	(6, 2)	(6, 3)	(6, 4)	(6, 5)	(6, 6)

d

Sum	2	3	4	5	6	7	8	9	10	11	12
Probability	$\frac{1}{36}$	$\frac{2}{36} = \frac{1}{18}$	$\frac{3}{36} = \frac{1}{12}$	$\frac{4}{36} = \frac{1}{9}$	$\frac{5}{36}$	$\frac{6}{36} = \frac{1}{6}$	$\frac{5}{36}$	$\frac{4}{36} = \frac{1}{9}$	$\frac{3}{36} = \frac{1}{12}$	$\frac{2}{36} = \frac{1}{18}$	$\frac{1}{36}$

e The probabilities are symmetric.
f {HHH, HHT, HTH, HTT, THH, THT, TTH, TTT}
g

Number of Heads	0	1	2	3
Probability	$\frac{1}{8}$	$\frac{3}{8}$	$\frac{3}{8}$	$\frac{1}{8}$

h 3 Heads **i** Heads once and Tails twice

20 Ask your teacher.

21 a $\frac{1}{4}$ **b** $\frac{5}{9}$ **c** $\frac{1}{2}$

13D Complementary events

1 a Selecting an odd number
b Selecting a consonant
c The coin landing Tails
d Getting a number greater than 2
e Getting a total of 12
f Not selecting a diamond
g Not selecting an E
h Not selecting a blue marble

2 B and C

3 a Not complementary, as there are other things that you could have for breakfast.
b Not complementary, as there are other ways of travelling to your friend's house.
c Not complementary, as there are other things that you could be doing.
d Complementary, as this covers all possible outcomes.
e Not complementary, as neither case covers the possibility of rolling a 4.

4 $\frac{12}{13}$ **5** A

6 $\frac{215}{216}$ **7** $\frac{4}{5}$

8 a $\frac{1}{4}$ **b** $\frac{3}{4}$ **c** $\frac{3}{4}$ **d** $\frac{1}{4}$

9 No, the two events are not complementary, as the sum of their probabilities does not equal one. Getting one Head is also an outcome.

10 a $\frac{17}{70}$ **b** $\frac{53}{70}$ **c** $\frac{9}{70}$ **d** $\frac{61}{70}$

13E Venn diagrams

1

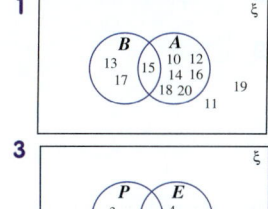

2

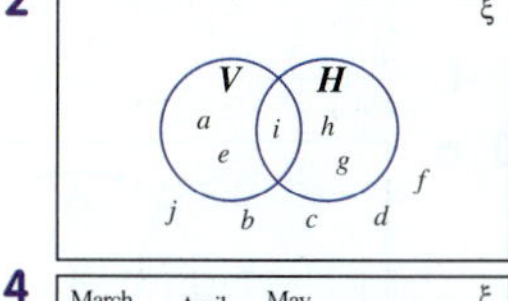

3

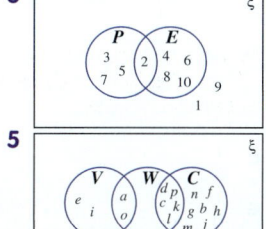

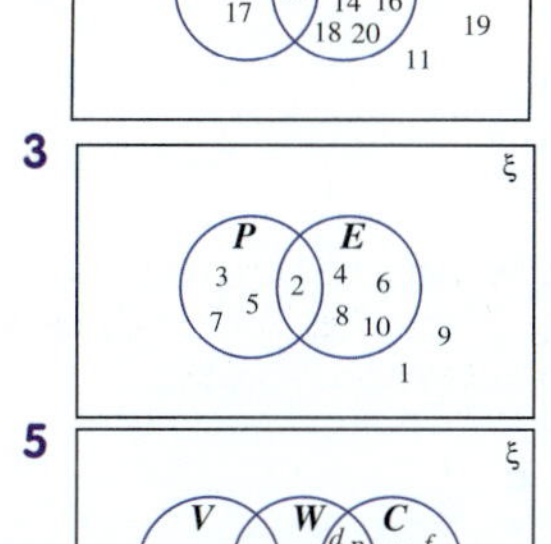

4

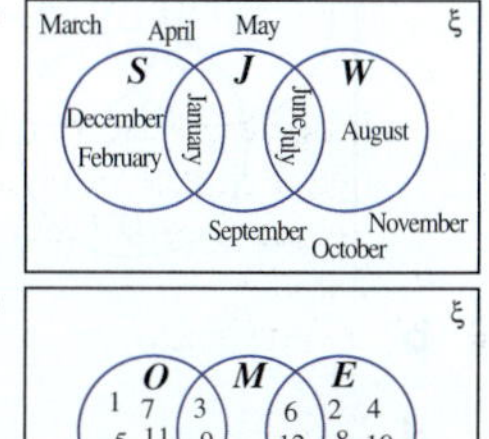

5

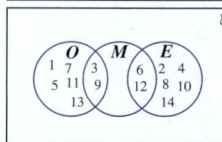

6

7 a

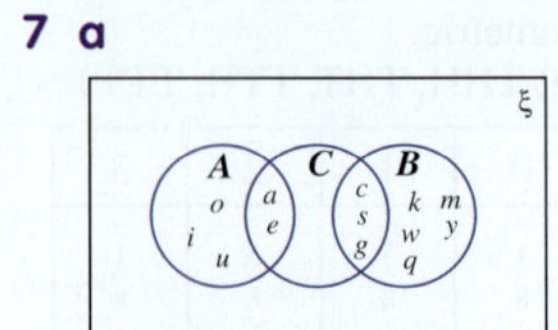

b **i** $\{a, e, i, o, u\}$ **ii** $\{c, g, s\}$
iii $\{a, c, e, g, i, o, s, u\}$ **iv** $\{c, a, g, e, s\}$

8 a

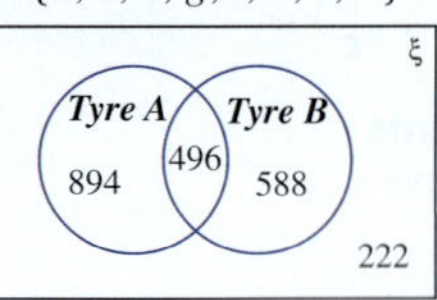

b **i** 894 **ii** 588
iii 222

c $\frac{222}{2200} = \frac{111}{1100}$ **d** $\frac{124}{271}$

9 a **i**

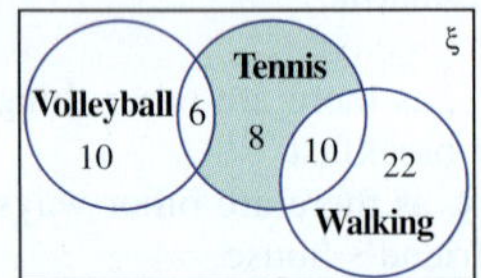

ii

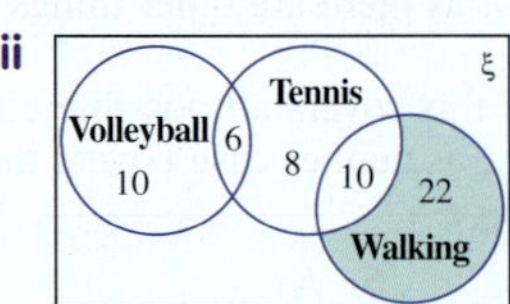

iii

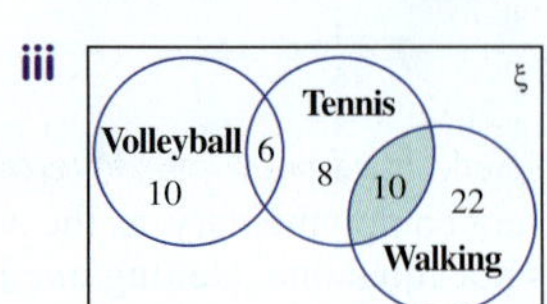

b **i** 16 **ii** 0
c **i** 32 **ii** 24

d 56 **e** $\frac{24}{56} = \frac{3}{7}$

f $\frac{6}{56} = \frac{3}{28}$ **g** $\frac{10}{32} = \frac{5}{16}$

10 a

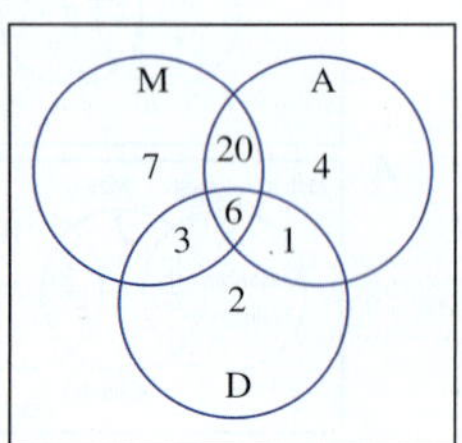

b $\frac{7}{43}$ **c** $\frac{4}{43}$

d $\frac{2}{43}$ **e** $\frac{3}{43}$

f $\frac{31}{43}$ **g** $\frac{1}{12}$

13F Tree diagrams and two-way tables

1 a i

1	2	Outcomes
H	H	HH
	T	HT
T	H	TH
	T	TT

ii

		1	
		H	T
2	H	H H	T H
	T	H T	T T

b **i** $\frac{1}{4}$ **ii** $\frac{1}{4}$ **iii** $\frac{1}{4}$ **iv** $\frac{1}{2}$ **v** $\frac{1}{2}$

2 a

1	2	Outcomes
B	B	BB
	G	BG
G	B	GB
	G	GG

b **i** $\frac{1}{4}$ **ii** $\frac{1}{4}$ **iii** $\frac{1}{2}$ **iv** $\frac{1}{4}$ **v** $\frac{1}{4}$ **vi** $\frac{1}{2}$

3 a

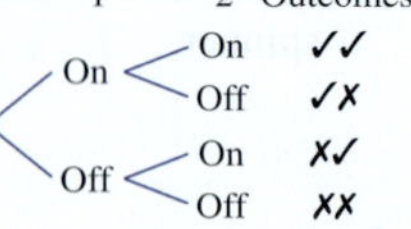

b **i** $\frac{1}{4}$ **ii** $\frac{1}{4}$ **iii** $\frac{1}{2}$ **iv** $\frac{1}{2}$

4 a

1	2	Outcomes
T	T	TT
	F	TF
F	T	FT
	F	FF

b **i** $\frac{1}{4}$ **ii** $\frac{1}{4}$ **iii** $\frac{1}{4}$ **iv** $\frac{1}{4}$ **v** $\frac{1}{2}$

5 a

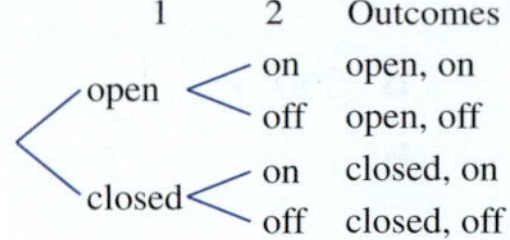

		Light	
		On	Off
Door	Open	open, on	open, off
	Closed	closed, on	closed, off

b **i** $\frac{1}{4}$ **ii** $\frac{1}{4}$ **iii** $\frac{1}{4}$ **iv** $\frac{1}{4}$

6 a i

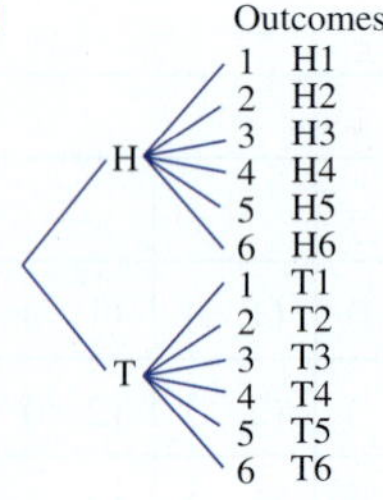

ii

		1	
		H	T
2	1	H 1	T 1
	2	H 2	T 2
	3	H 3	T 3
	4	H 4	T 4
	5	H 5	T 5
	6	H 6	T 6

b **i** $\frac{1}{12}$ **ii** $\frac{1}{2}$ **iii** $\frac{1}{4}$ **iv** $\frac{1}{6}$

7 a

		Spinner		
		1	2	3
Coin	H	H 1	H 2	H 3
	T	T 1	T 2	T 3

b **i** $\frac{1}{6}$ **ii** $\frac{1}{6}$ **iii** $\frac{1}{6}$ **iv** $\frac{1}{6}$ **v** $\frac{1}{3}$ **vi** $\frac{1}{6}$ **vii** $\frac{1}{3}$

8 a

		Colour		
		Red	White	Yellow
Transmission	Manual	MR	MW	MY
	Auto	AR	AW	AY

b **i** $\frac{1}{3}$ **ii** $\frac{1}{2}$ **iii** $\frac{1}{6}$ **iv** $\frac{1}{6}$ **v** $\frac{1}{6}$

9 a

		Die					
		1	2	3	4	5	6
Coin	H	H 1	H 2	H 3	H 4	H 5	H 6
	T	T 1	T 2	T 3	T 4	T 5	T 6

b **i** $\frac{1}{12}$ **ii** $\frac{1}{12}$ **iii** $\frac{1}{4}$ **iv** $\frac{1}{4}$ **v** $\frac{1}{4}$

vi $\frac{1}{6}$ **vii** $\frac{5}{12}$

10

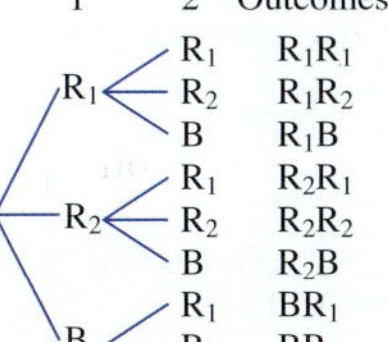

i $\frac{1}{9}$ **ii** $\frac{4}{9}$ **iii** $\frac{2}{9}$ **iv** $\frac{2}{9}$

v $\frac{4}{9}$ **vi** $\frac{5}{9}$ **vii** $\frac{1}{9}$ **viii** $\frac{4}{9}$

ix $\frac{8}{9}$ **x** 0 **xi** $\frac{5}{9}$

11 a

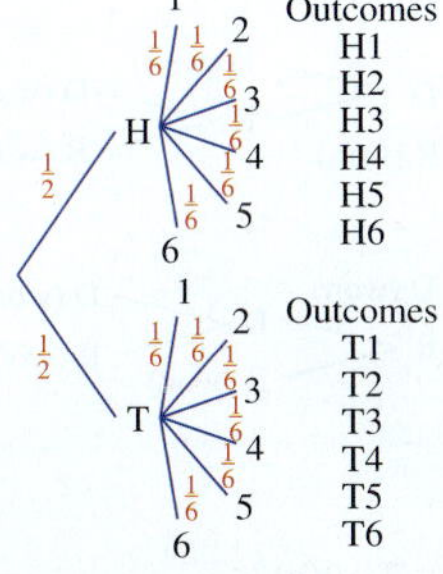

b $P(H, 1) \rightarrow P(T, 6) = \frac{1}{12}$

c 1

d **i** $\frac{1}{4}$ **ii** $\frac{1}{2}$ **iii** $\frac{1}{2}$

12 a

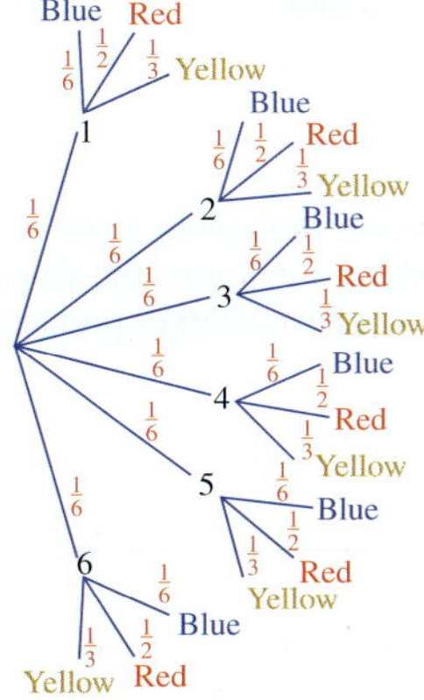

b $P(1, \text{Blue}) \rightarrow P(6, \text{Blue}) = \frac{1}{36}$

$P(1, \text{Red}) \rightarrow P(6, \text{Red}) = \frac{1}{12}$

$P(1, \text{Yellow}) \rightarrow P(6, \text{Yellow}) = \frac{1}{18}$

c 1

d **i** $\frac{1}{6}$ **ii** $\frac{1}{3}$ **iii** $\frac{1}{2}$ **iv** $\frac{1}{12}$

13 E **14** E

15 a $\frac{1}{3}$ **b** 5

c Check with your teacher.
d Check with your teacher.
e Check with your teacher.
f Check with your teacher.
g Check with your teacher.
h Check with your teacher.
i For the lights described, P(red every morning of a school week) = $\frac{1}{243}$.

16 a $P(\text{winning roll}) = \frac{5}{36}$ **b** $P(\text{losing roll}) = \frac{5}{36}$

c $P(\text{neither win or lose}) = \frac{26}{36}$

d Check with your teacher.

Chapter review

Fluency

1 B **2** C

3 a 60 **b** 6 **c** 10

d **i** $\frac{1}{6}$ **ii** $\frac{3}{20}$ **iii** $\frac{29}{60}$

4 a

Score	Frequency
1	18
2	20
3	6
4	4
5	2
Total	50

b $1 \rightarrow 36\%$
$2 \rightarrow 40\%$
$3 \rightarrow 12\%$
$4 \rightarrow 8\%$
$5 \rightarrow 4\%$

c 1 Liberal–National or 2 Labor
d 120
e 100%

5 A

6 a {1, 2, 3, 4, 5, 6}
b No, because the sectors are of varying angle size. 3 and 6 have sectors which are double the size of others, therefore they will have a larger probability.
c i $\frac{1}{8}$ **ii** $\frac{1}{4}$

7 $\frac{1}{200}$

8 a $\frac{1}{3}$ **b** $\frac{1}{6}$ **c** $\frac{2}{3}$ **d** $\frac{1}{2}$

9 a $\frac{1}{5}$ **b** $\frac{2}{5}$ **c** 0 **d** $\frac{4}{5}$

10 a i $\frac{1}{5}$ **ii** $\frac{4}{5}$ **b** 1

11 a

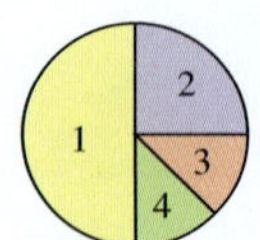

b Sector 1: 180° Sector 2: 90°
Sector 3: 45° Sector 4: 45°

12 Sector 1: $\frac{1}{4}$ Sector 2: $\frac{1}{8}$ Sector 3: $\frac{1}{8}$
Sector 4: $\frac{1}{6}$ Sector 5: $\frac{1}{6}$ Sector 6: $\frac{1}{6}$

13 a The coin lands Heads.
b Losing the race
c Answering the question incorrectly
d Not selecting a black marble
e Selecting a number greater than 19

14 a Complementary, as all possible outcomes are covered.
b Complementary, as all possible outcomes are covered.
c Not complementary, as there are other means to travel to work.

15 $\frac{4}{7}$

16 a

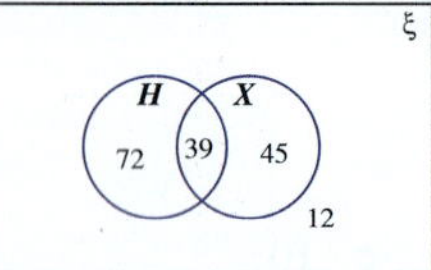

b $\frac{12}{168} = \frac{1}{14}$ **c** $\frac{156}{168} = \frac{13}{14}$
d $\frac{13}{37}$

17

		Answer 1	
		Y	N
Answer 2	Y	YY	NY
	N	YN	NN

18 a

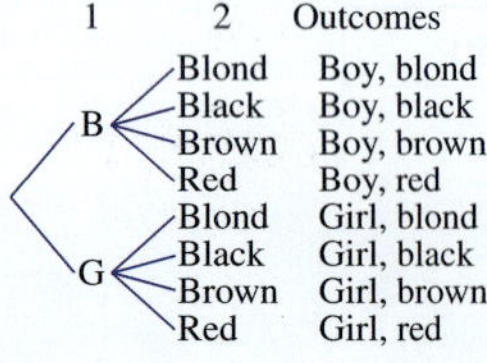

		Hair colour			
		Blond	Black	Brown	Red
Sex	B	B Blond	B Black	B Brown	B Red
	G	G Blond	G Black	G Brown	G Red

b i $\frac{1}{8}$ **ii** $\frac{1}{8}$ **iii** $\frac{1}{4}$ **iv** $\frac{3}{4}$ **v** $\frac{1}{4}$

19 a

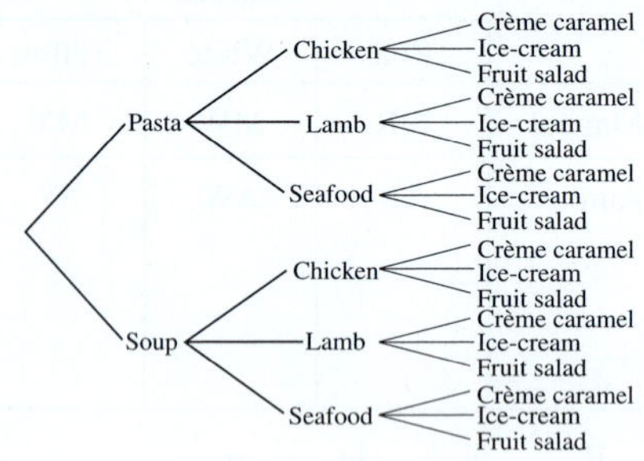

b 18
c i $\frac{1}{3}$ **ii** $\frac{1}{3}$ **iii** $\frac{1}{6}$ **iv** $\frac{2}{9}$
d i 27 **ii** 36 **iii** 24
e Multiply the total number of options from each category.
For example, 4 entrees, 3 mains and 2 desserts give $(4 \times 3 \times 2)$ 24 different meal combinations.

Problem solving

1 Check with your teacher.

2 a $\frac{3}{4}$ **b** Stayed the same

3 a

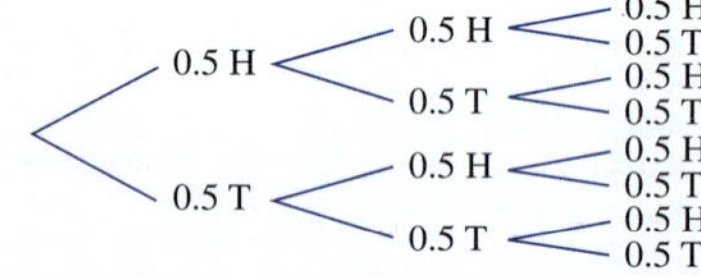

b $\frac{1}{4}$ **c** $\frac{1}{2}$
d Yes. The probability of a child winning is $\frac{1}{4}$ and the probability of the club winning is $\frac{3}{4}$.

4 18 boys

5

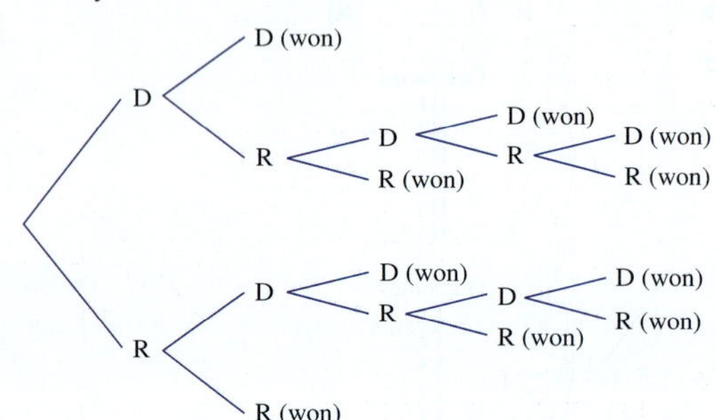

6 Jar A **7** 900

8 a {(1, 1), (1, 2), (1, 3), (1, 4), (2, 1), (2, 2), (2, 3), (2, 4), (3, 1), (3, 2), (3, 3), (3, 4), (4, 1), (4, 2), (4, 3), (4, 4)}
b $\frac{1}{4}$

9 **a** 0.096 **b** 0.432

10 $\frac{5}{11}$ **11** $\frac{1}{6}$ **12** $\frac{81}{125}$

13 0.45 **14** $\frac{1}{30}$ **15** 5

CHAPTER 14

Coordinates and linear graphs

Are you ready?

1 **a** C3 **b** C5 **c** A1
d B4 **e** A2

2 **a** I **b** I

3 **a** i–vi

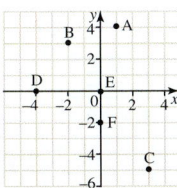

b i

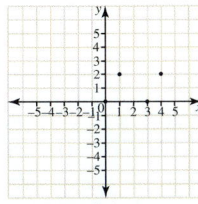

Parallelogram

ii

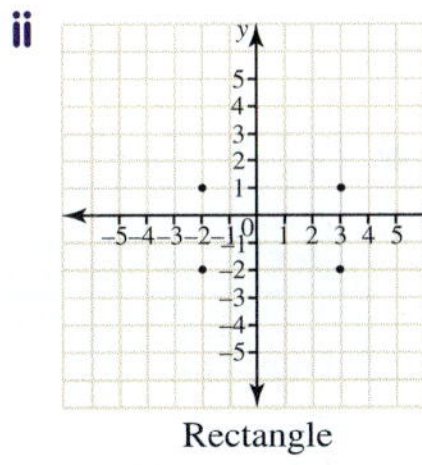

Rectangle

iii

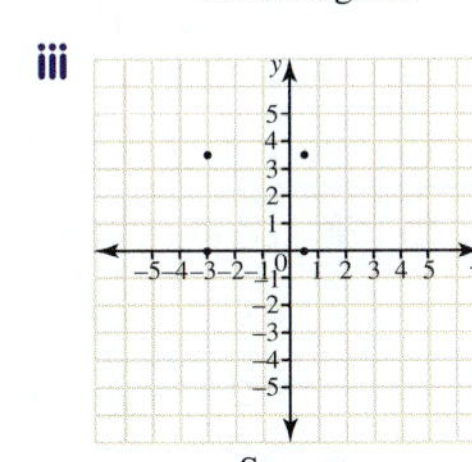

Square

iv

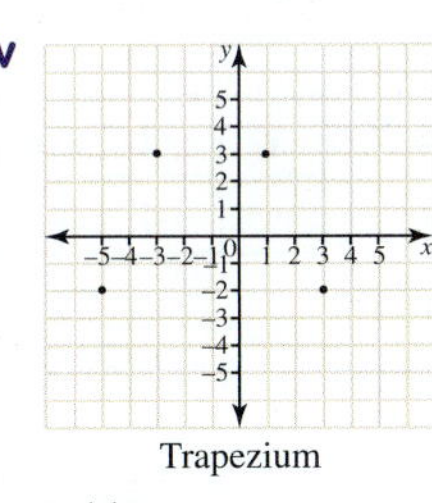

Trapezium

4 **a** $y = 7$ **b** $y = 1$ **c** $y = 11$

5 **a** $y = x + 4$

x	−2	−1	0	1	2
y	2	3	4	5	6

b $y = 3x - 2$

x	−2	−1	0	1	2
y	−8	−5	−2	1	4

6 **a** $y = x + 3$

x	−2	−1	0	1	2
y	1	2	3	4	5

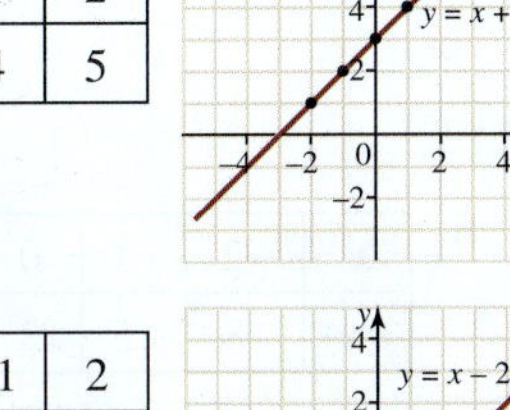

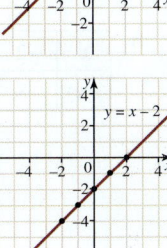

b $y = x - 2$

x	−2	−1	0	1	2
y	−4	−3	−2	−1	0

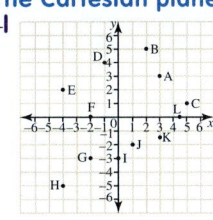

c $y = 2x$

x	−2	−1	0	1	2
y	−4	−2	0	2	4

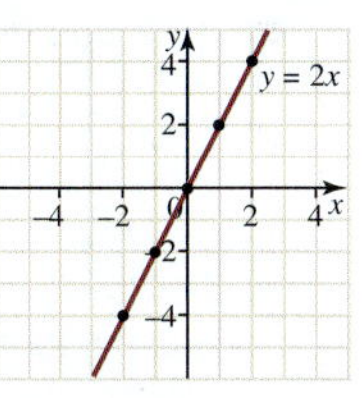

14A The Cartesian plane

1 **a–l**

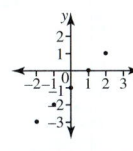

2 A(2, 2) B(4, 6) C(6, 1) D(−2, 3) E(0, 5) F(1, 1) G(−4, 1) H(0, 0) I(5, 0) J(4, 3) K(−5, 3) L(−4, −2) M(−2, −5)

3 **a** E
b A, C

4–8 Check with your teacher.

14B Linear patterns

1 **a**

Linear

b

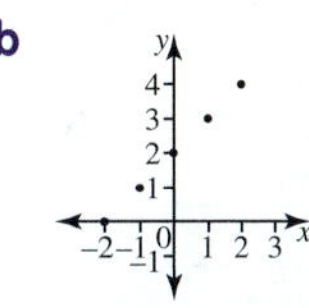

Linear

c

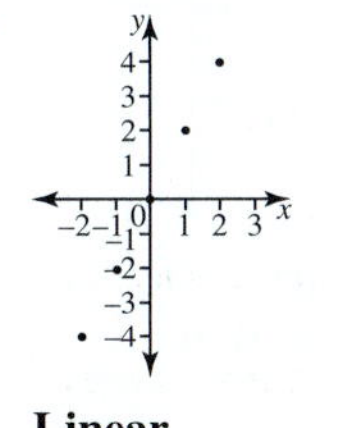

Linear

d

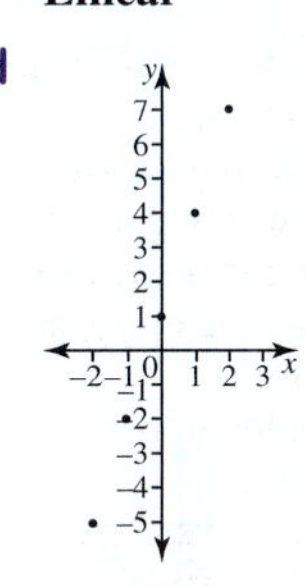

Linear

e

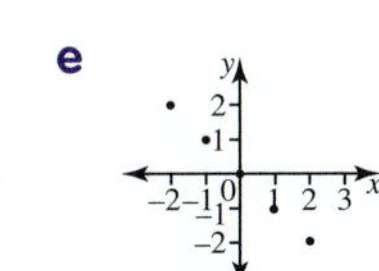

Linear

f

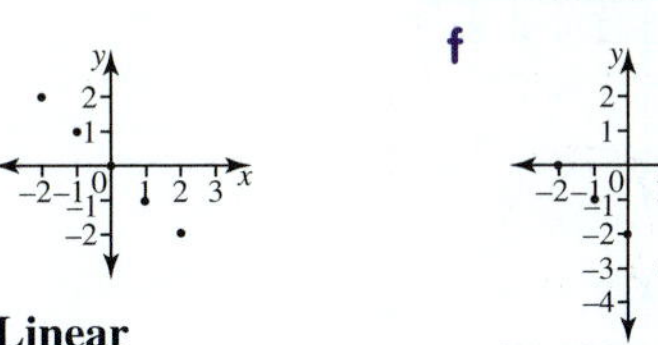

Linear

2 **a**

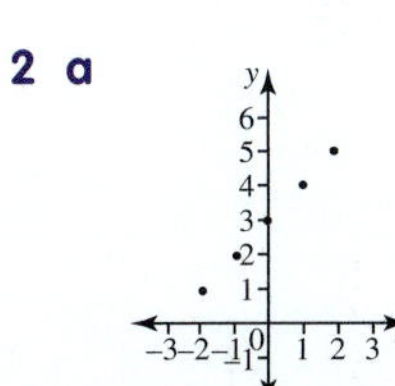

b

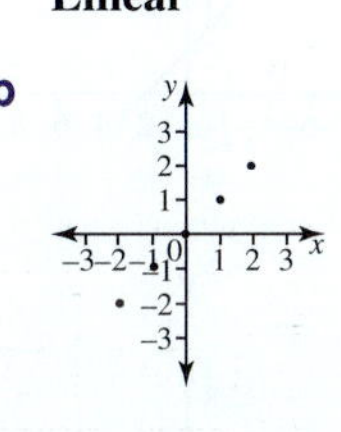

c

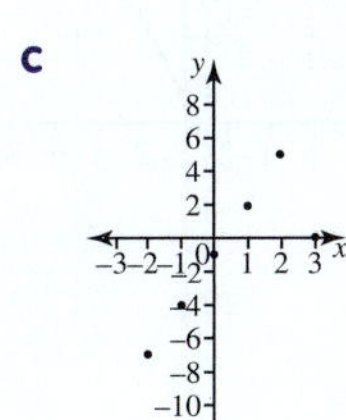

d

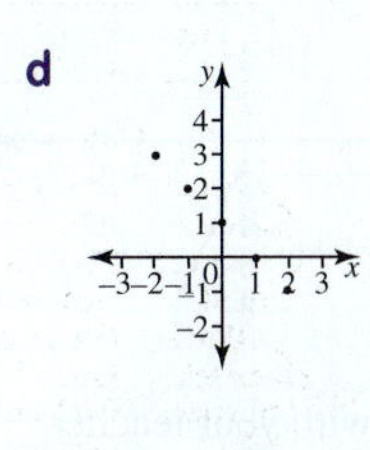

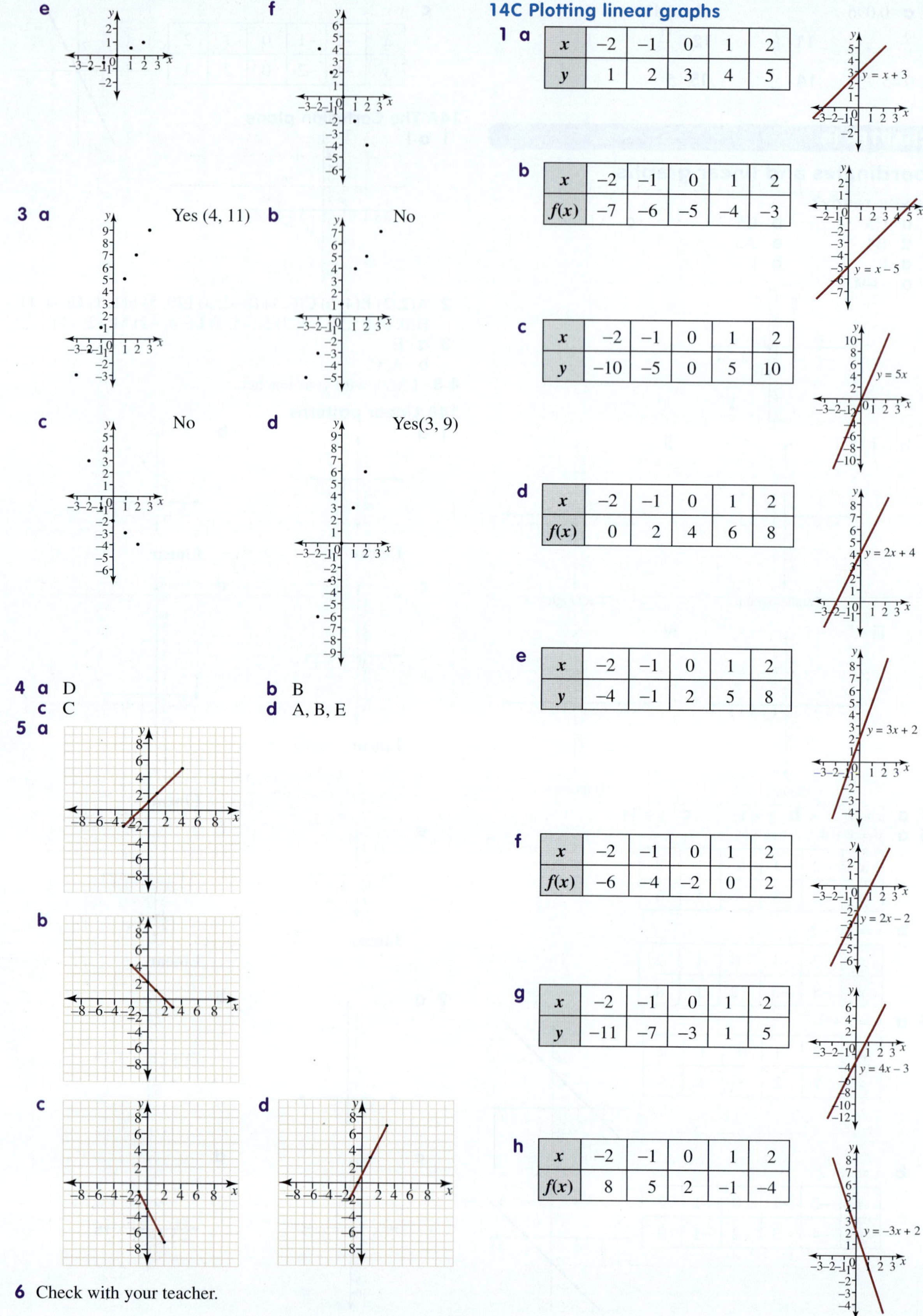

e

f

3 a Yes (4, 11) b No

c No d Yes(3, 9)

4 a D b B
c C d A, B, E

5 a

b

c d

6 Check with your teacher.

14C Plotting linear graphs

1 a

x	−2	−1	0	1	2
y	1	2	3	4	5

b

x	−2	−1	0	1	2
$f(x)$	−7	−6	−5	−4	−3

c

x	−2	−1	0	1	2
y	−10	−5	0	5	10

d

x	−2	−1	0	1	2
$f(x)$	0	2	4	6	8

e

x	−2	−1	0	1	2
y	−4	−1	2	5	8

f

x	−2	−1	0	1	2
$f(x)$	−6	−4	−2	0	2

g

x	−2	−1	0	1	2
y	−11	−7	−3	1	5

h

x	−2	−1	0	1	2
$f(x)$	8	5	2	−1	−4

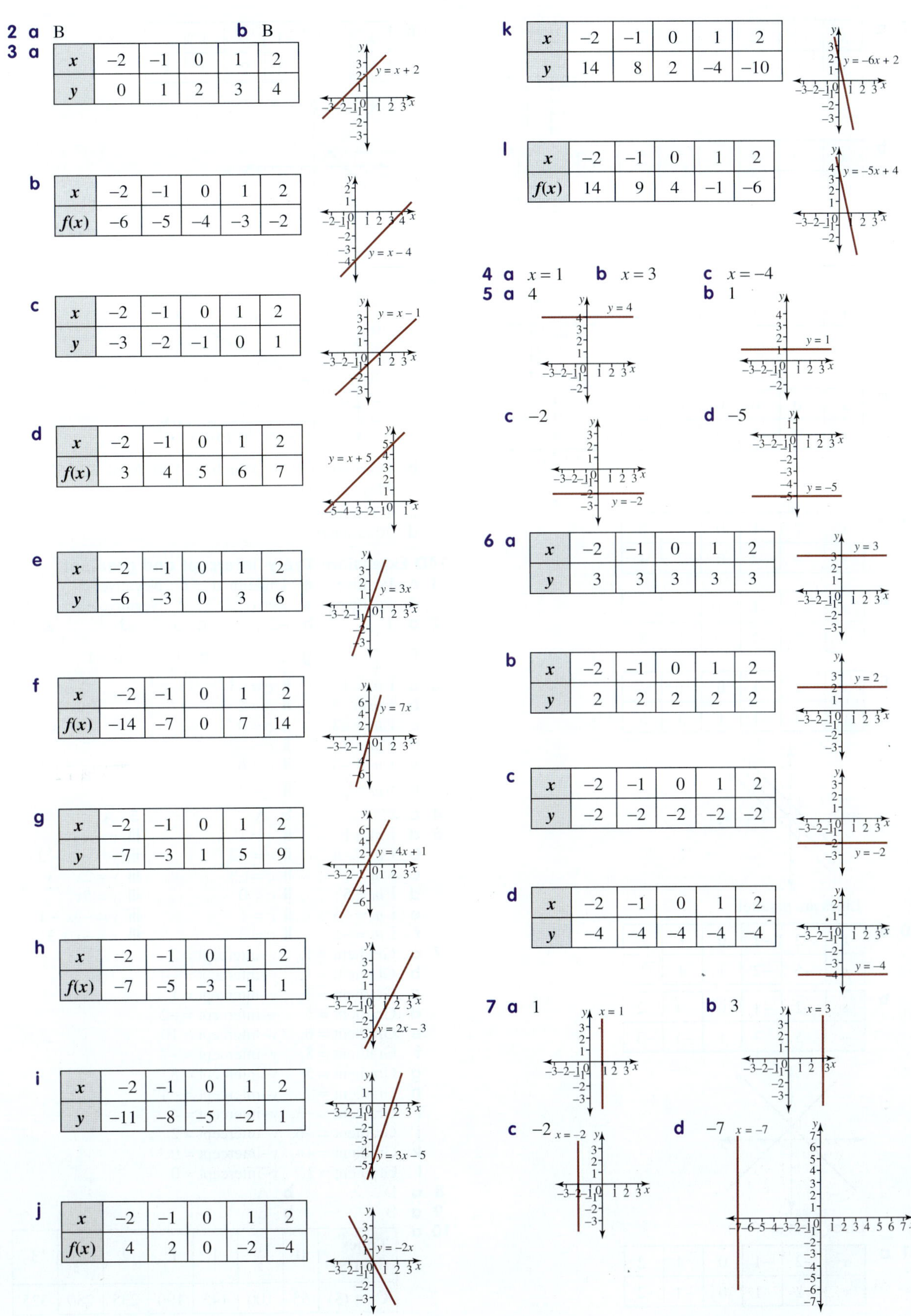

2 a B **b** B

3 a

x	–2	–1	0	1	2
y	0	1	2	3	4

b

x	–2	–1	0	1	2
$f(x)$	–6	–5	–4	–3	–2

c

x	–2	–1	0	1	2
y	–3	–2	–1	0	1

d

x	–2	–1	0	1	2
$f(x)$	3	4	5	6	7

e

x	–2	–1	0	1	2
y	–6	–3	0	3	6

f

x	–2	–1	0	1	2
$f(x)$	–14	–7	0	7	14

g

x	–2	–1	0	1	2
y	–7	–3	1	5	9

h

x	–2	–1	0	1	2
$f(x)$	–7	–5	–3	–1	1

i

x	–2	–1	0	1	2
y	–11	–8	–5	–2	1

j

x	–2	–1	0	1	2
$f(x)$	4	2	0	–2	–4

k

x	–2	–1	0	1	2
y	14	8	2	–4	–10

l

x	–2	–1	0	1	2
$f(x)$	14	9	4	–1	–6

4 a $x = 1$ **b** $x = 3$ **c** $x = -4$

5 a 4

b 1

c –2

d –5

6 a

x	–2	–1	0	1	2
y	3	3	3	3	3

b

x	–2	–1	0	1	2
y	2	2	2	2	2

c

x	–2	–1	0	1	2
y	–2	–2	–2	–2	–2

d

x	–2	–1	0	1	2
y	–4	–4	–4	–4	–4

7 a 1

b 3

c –2

d –7

8 a

x	2	2	2	2	2
y	−2	−1	0	1	2

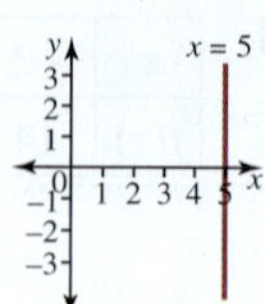

b

x	5	5	5	5	5
y	−2	−1	0	1	2

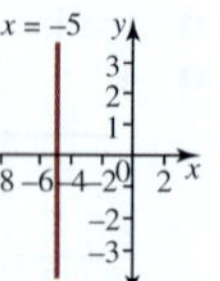

c

x	−5	−5	−5	−5	−5
y	−2	−1	0	1	2

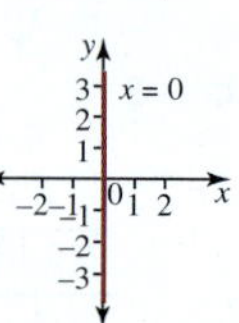

d

x	0	0	0	0	0
y	−2	−1	0	1	2

$x = 0$

9 a

x	−2	−1	0	1	2
y	−4	−2	0	2	4

b

x	−2	−1	0	1	2
y	−5	−3	−1	1	3

c

x	−2	−1	0	1	2
y	−3	−1	1	3	5

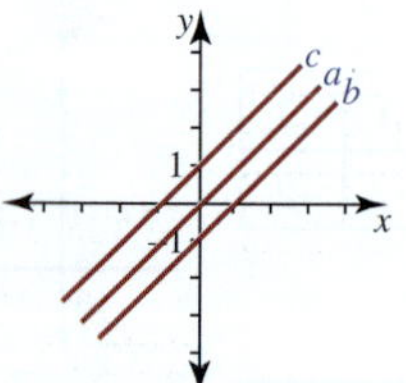

Lines are parallel.

10 a

x	−2	−1	0	1	2
y	−5	−2	1	4	7

b

x	−2	−1	0	1	2
y	5	3	1	−1	−3

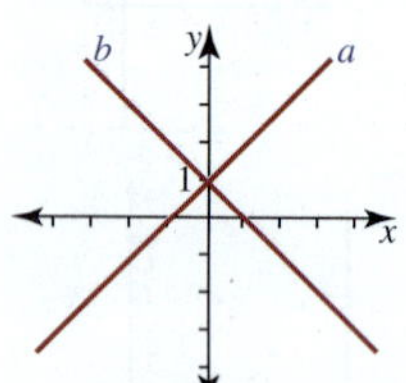

Lines meet at (0, 1).

11 a

x	−2	−1	0	1	2
y	2	1	0	−1	−2

b

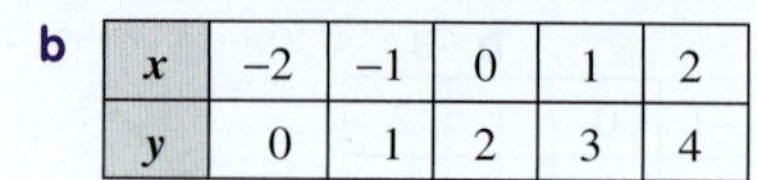

x	−2	−1	0	1	2
y	0	1	2	3	4

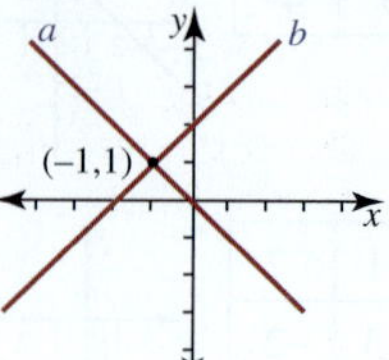

Lines meet at (−1, 1).

12 a

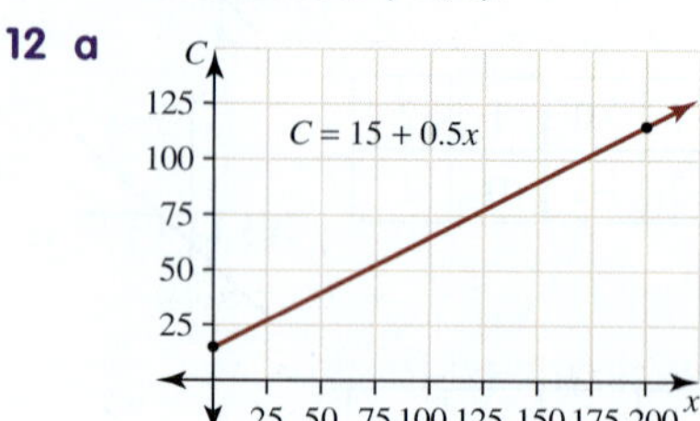

b February: $22.50; March: $29.00; April: $38.50; May: $31.00

c 170 minutes

d 70 minutes

14D Extension: The y–intercept and gradient

1 a Positive **b** Undefined **c** Negative
d Positive **e** Zero **f** Negative

2 a 1 **b** −2 **c** 3 **d** $\frac{1}{3}$ **e** −2
f $-\frac{1}{4}$ **g** 1 **h** 3 **i** −1

3 a i $m = 1$ **ii** $c = -1$
b i $m = -2$ **ii** $c = 2$
c i $m = -3$ **ii** $c = 0$
d i $m = 3$ **ii** $c = -3$
e i $m = -3$ **ii** $c = 6$
f i $m = \frac{1}{3}$ **ii** $c = 4$

4 a C **b** A

5 A

6 a i $m = 1$ **ii** $c = 1$ **iii** $y = x + 1$
b i $m = -4$ **ii** $c = -2$ **iii** $y = -4x - 2$
c i $m = 2$ **ii** $c = -3$ **iii** $y = 2x - 3$
d i $m = 5$ **ii** $c = 0$ **iii** $y = 5x$
e i $m = -3$ **ii** $c = 1$ **iii** $y = -3x + 1$
f i $m = -1$ **ii** $c = 3$ **iii** $y = -x + 3$

7 a Gradient = 1, y–intercept = 3
b Gradient = 1, y–intercept = −4
c Gradient = 3, y–intercept = 1
d Gradient = 5, y–intercept = −2
e Gradient = 6, y–intercept = 10
f Gradient = 8, y–intercept = −7
g Gradient = 5, y–intercept = 3
h Gradient = 9, y–intercept = −4
i Gradient = −3, y–intercept = 4
j Gradient = −6, y–intercept = 2
k Gradient = −4, y–intercept = 0
l Gradient = 1, y–intercept = 0

8 a D **b** A

9 a B **b** E

10 a

Times (hours)	0	$\frac{1}{2}$	1	$1\frac{1}{2}$	2	$2\frac{1}{2}$	3
Cost ($)	55	100	145	190	235	280	325

b

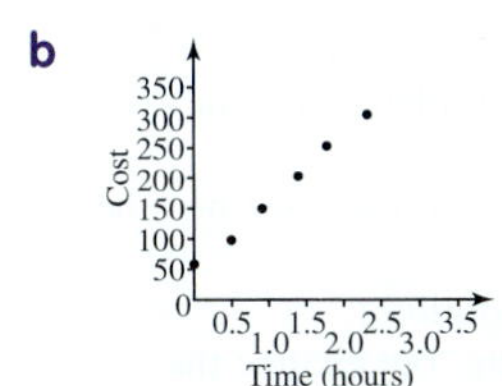

c Independent: time
Dependent: cost
d Yes
e $m = 90$
f $c = 55$
g $y = 90x + 55$
h Cost = 90 × time + 55
i $C = \$415$

11 a Day 8

b

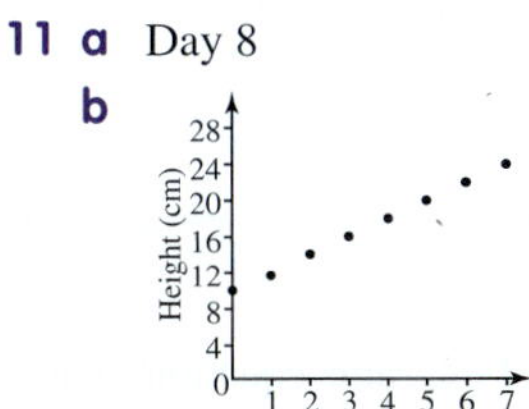

c Yes
d $m = 2, c = 10$
e $h = 2d + 10$
f $h = 38$ mm

12 a 18 **b** $m = -2, c = 26$
c $s = -2t + 26$ **d** $s = 14$

14E Extension: Sketching linear graphs

1 a

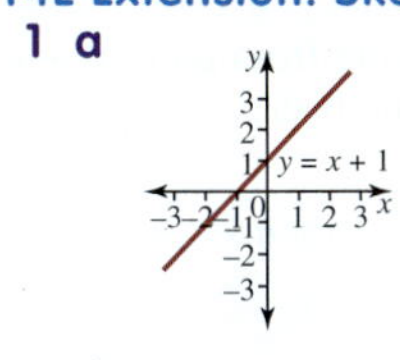

b

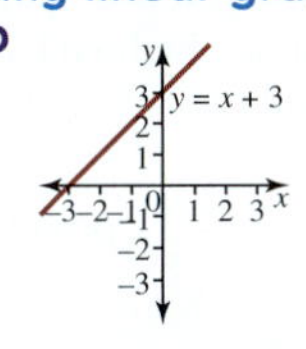

c

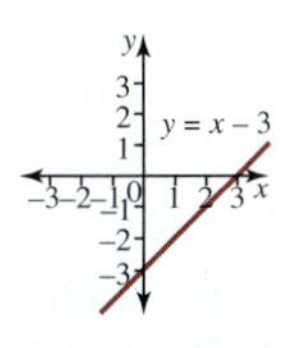

d

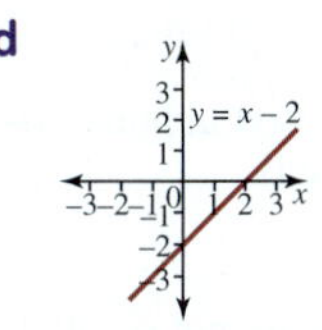

e

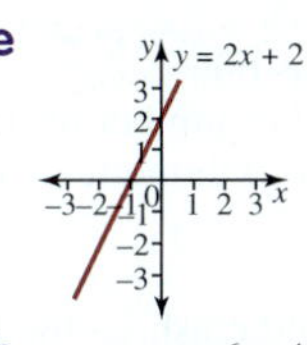

f

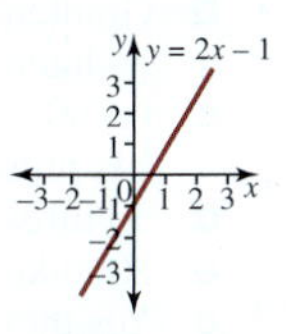

g

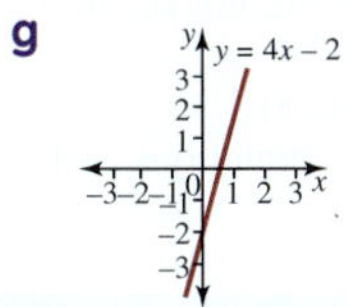

h

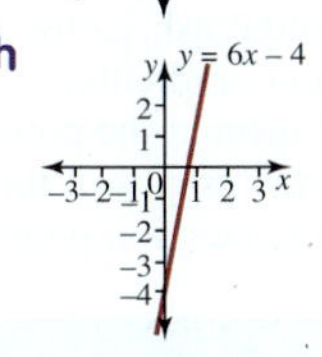

i

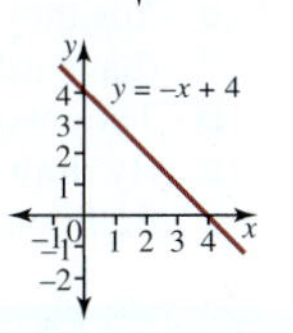

j

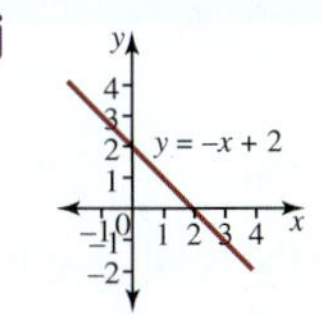

k

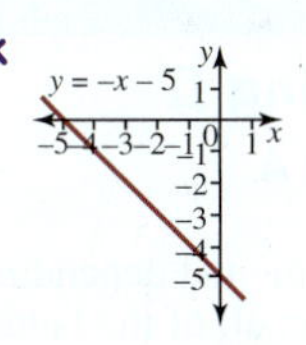

l

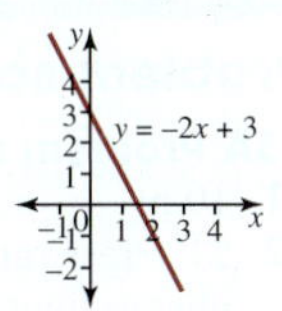

2 a

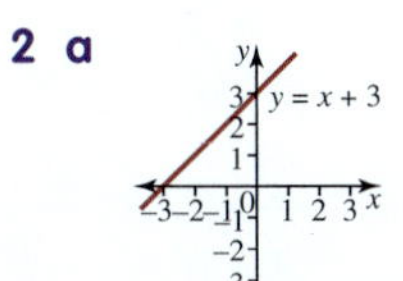

b

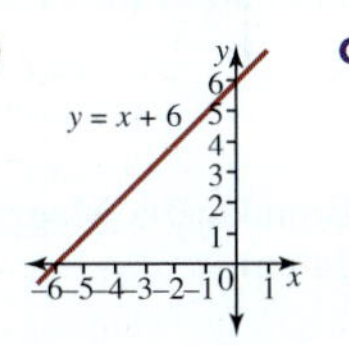

c

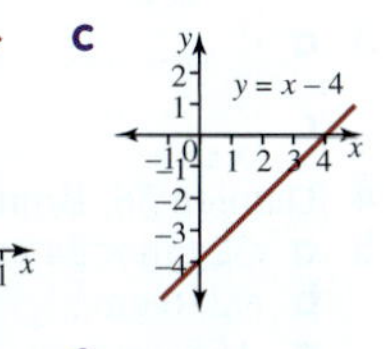

d

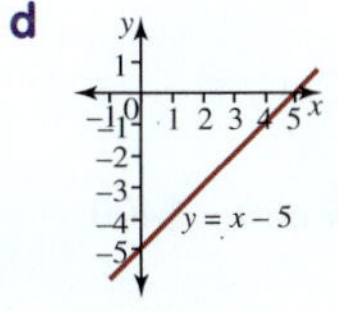

e

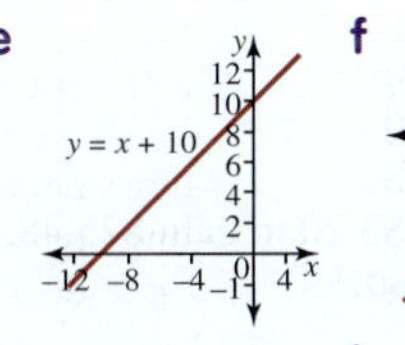

f

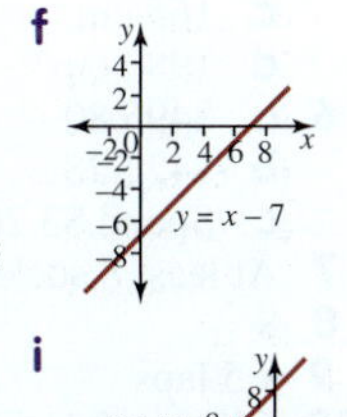

g

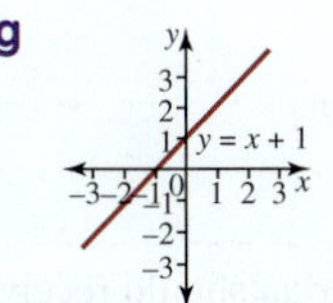

h

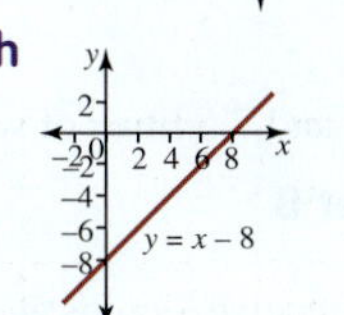

i

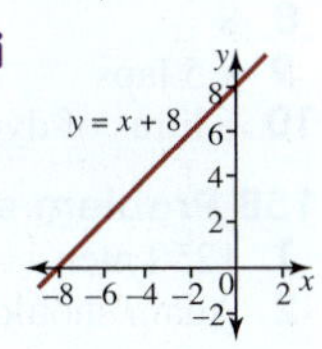

j $y = x + 9$

k $y = -x + 1$

l $y = -x - 4$

3 a D **b** B
4 a C **b** A

Chapter review

Fluency

1 a Namiko **b** Rina **c** No

2 a–l

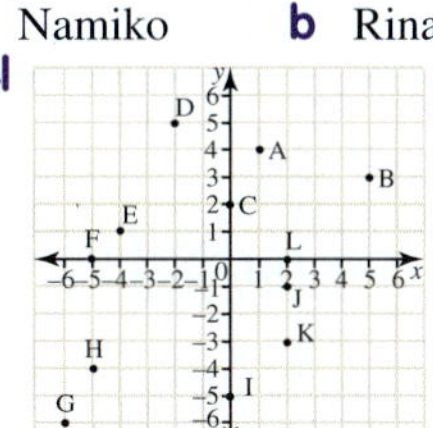

3 A(1, 3) B(4, 2) C(3, 0) D(−3, 1) E(−5, 5) F(−6, 0)
G(0, −1) H(−3, −3) I(−2, −6) J(5, −4) K(2, −6)
L(−6, −4) M(4, −2)

4 a

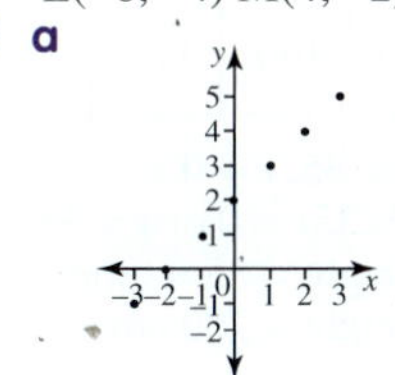

b

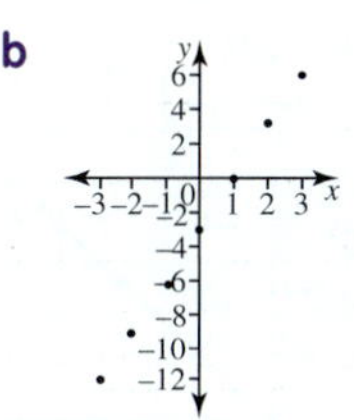

5 a

x	−2	−1	0	1	2
$f(x)$	−4	−3	−2	−1	0

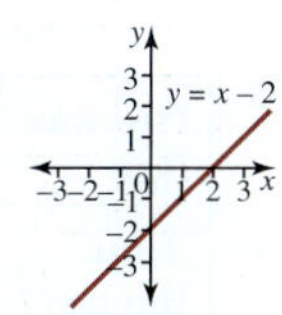

b

x	−2	−1	0	1	2
$f(x)$	3	4	5	6	7

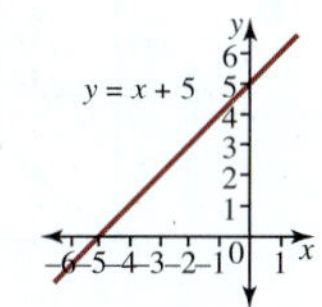

c

x	−2	−1	0	1	2
$f(x)$	−10	−6	−2	2	6

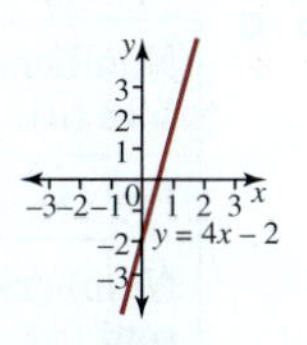

d

x	−2	−1	0	1	2
$f(x)$	−4	−1	2	5	8

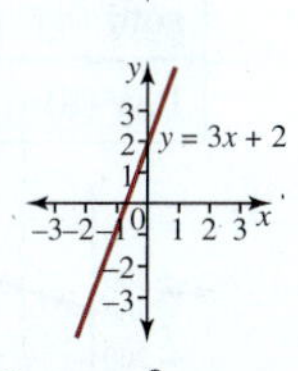

6 a $m = 1$ **b** $m = -2$ **c** $m = 3$

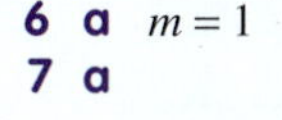

7 a

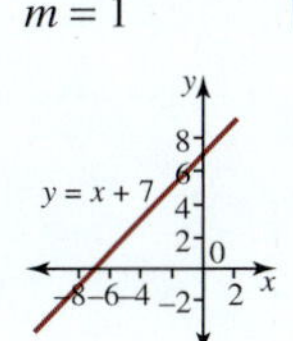

b

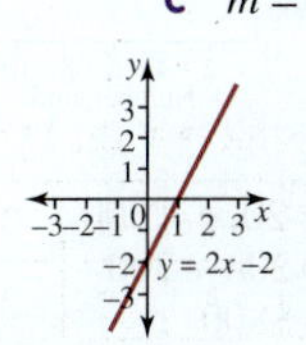

c

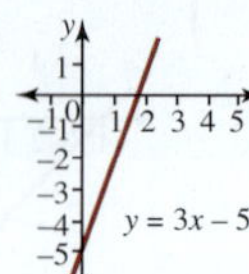

d

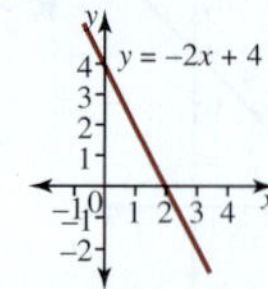

8 a

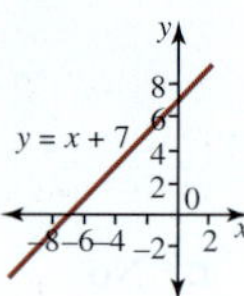

b

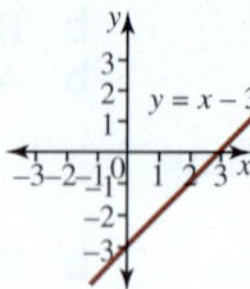

c

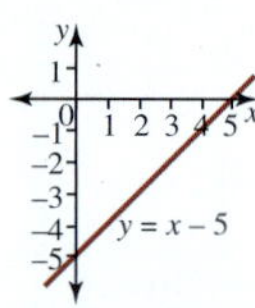

d

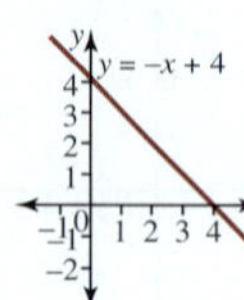

Problem solving

1 a

Time (weeks)	0	1	2	3	4	5	6
Height (cm)	0	35	70	105	140	175	210

b

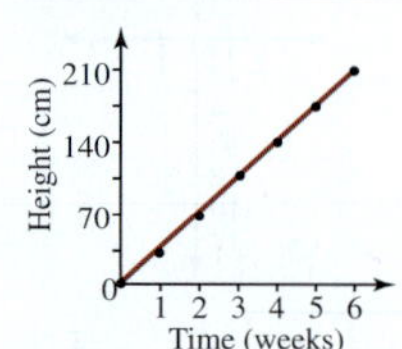

c $m = 35$, $c = 0$
d $y = 35x + 0$ or $y = 35x$
e Height = 35 × time
f Height = 700 cm

2 a

Distance (km)	0	25	50	75	100	125
Time (hours)	0	1	2	3	4	5

b

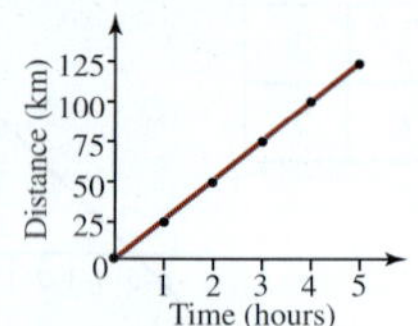

c Yes
d $m = 25$, $c = 0$
e $d = 25t + 0$ or $d = 25t$
f $d = 125$ km
g $d = 200$ km

3 a

Numbers sold (n)	0	1	2	3	4	5
Pay ($)	300	320	340	360	380	400
Numbers sold (n)	6	7	8	9	10	
Pay ($)	420	440	460	480	500	

b

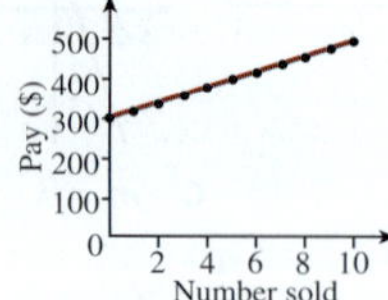

c Yes
d $m = 20$, $c = 300$
e $P = 20n + 300$
f $P = \$800$

4 a $y = -3x + 2$
b Various answers, but the gradient must be −3, e.g. $y = -3x + 5$
c Various answers, but the gradient must be other than −3, e.g. $y = 2x + 1$
d Change the value of the gradient.
e Do not change the gradient, but change the y–intercept.
f Substitute $x = 0$ into the equation and solve the equation for y.

5 a $a = 4\frac{1}{3}$
b The equations are: $y = -\frac{1}{3}x + 5$ and $y = -\frac{1}{3}x + 4\frac{1}{3}$ and $y = -\frac{1}{3}x$.
c These are different forms of the same equation (which is the equation of the top line).

6 Lena (it will take her 10 months, while Alex will need 15 months)

7 Various answers. One possible solution: C(6, 8) and A(−2, 2)
Coordinates can be obtained by starting from point B and using rise = 3 and run = 4 forward and back.

8 1050 m

9 $m_{AC} = \frac{3}{2}$ $m_{BD} = -\frac{3}{4}$ product of gradients = −1

10 a 48 litres
b Gradient is −3
y–intercept is 60
c $l = 60 - 3k$ (l is number of litres used in hundreds; k is number of kilometres travelled)
d 30 litres
e 2000 km

11 a Yes they could crash, as the lines are not parallel (have different gradients).
b They would meet at the point (−1, 5).
c By drawing the graphs of the two equations and finding the intersection point.

CHAPTER 15

Problem solving II

15A Problem set A

1 19 m
2 $1. Press random, and depending on the result you'll be able to figure out all of the buttons.
3 a $\frac{1}{6}$ **b** $\frac{1}{2}$
c $\frac{1}{3}$
4 Damian 38, Brendan 76, Maggie 91
5 a 32 cm × 24 cm
b 9216 cm^3
c 165 cm
d 1980 cm^3
6 a $496.80
b $422.28
c Spend $3.20 to gain $25.48. New cost = $400
7 At least 8 socks
8 8
9 8.5 laps
10 6 litres of dye and 7.5 litres of water

15B Problem set B

1 1250 men
2 Adam should receive 7 coins and Brian should receive 1.

3 **a** $\frac{1}{3}$ **b** $\frac{1}{3}$ **c** $\frac{1}{6}$ **d** $\frac{2}{3}$

4 12 presents

5

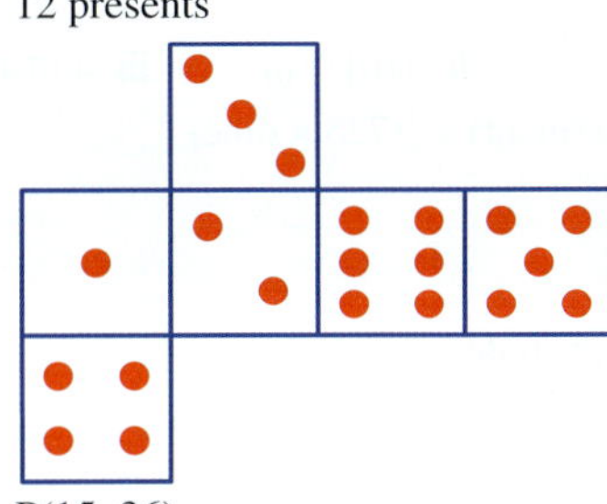

6 P(15, 36)

7 Day 1, 2.24; Day 2, 1.12; Day 3, 0.56; Day 4, 0.28

8 6.25π

9 **a** No. One-fifth of 6 is not a whole number.
b 4 classes; total of 10 **c** 2 Maths classes
d Yes, if he studies 1 maths class.

10 60 g of 18 carat gold

15C Problem set C

1 2

2 46 minutes 18 seconds; height is 1250 mm

3 **a** Quadrilateral **b** Parallelogram

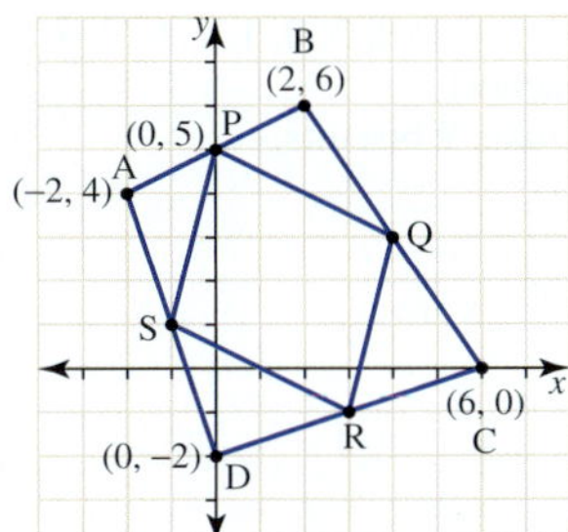

4 25 m **5** 6 min 4.5 s **6** 3 m × 9 m

7 **a** $\frac{1}{8}$ **b** $\frac{1}{2}$ **c** $\frac{1}{4}$ **d** $\frac{5}{8}$

8 4000 km **9** $X = 40$ g, $Y = 10$ g and $Z = 18$ g

10 8.86 m

15D Problem set D

1 54° **2** 4 birds and 3 cages

3 $P(\text{sum} < 0) = \frac{7}{16}$

4 The area of the rectangle is 9% less than the area of the square.

5 189 cm^3 **6** John was 18 years old 2 years ago.

7 John will be twice Betty's age 10 years from now.

8 He wasn't correct. The original price was $200.

9 −7 **10** 26

15E Problem set E

1 8 socks **2** $\frac{1}{6}$

3 **a**

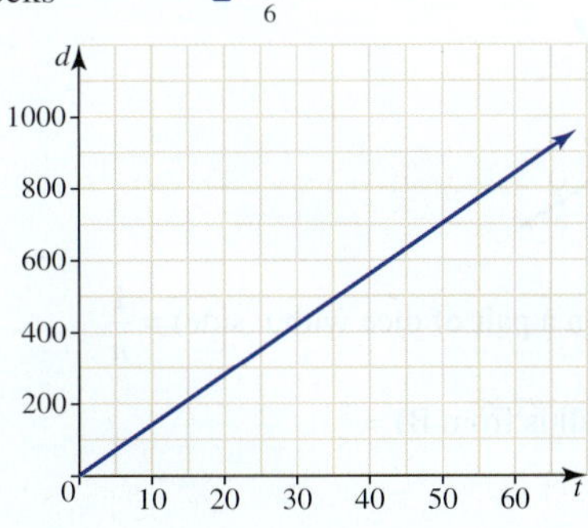

b 50.4 km/h **c** 14
d $d = 14t$ **e** 840 m
f 2.38 minutes

4 Ask your teacher. **5** $4 - \pi$

6 $12\frac{2}{3}$

7 Answers will vary. An example is $x - 3 = 2x + 15$.

8 187 254 963 or 781 254 963

9 **a** 3 and −7, the sum is −4 and the product is −21.
b −2 and 6, the sum is 4 and the quotient is −3.
c Not possible. For the sum to be 0, one is −ve and the other is +ve. The product is −ve.

10 **a** $16 \times 5 + 3 \times -2 + 1 \times 0$; 74 **b** 14

15F Problem set F

1 15 females

2 The new outcomes are 2, 3, 4, 5, 6, 7, 8, 9, 10, 11, 12, 14, 16, 18.

3 154 **4** 10.16 cm

5 60 **6** 24 and 36

7

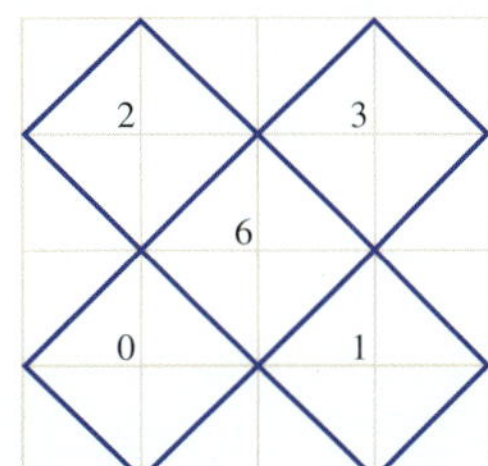

8 676 **9** 0.8 cm^2

10 **a** $\frac{1}{6}$ m/s
b No. He will travel 120 m in the time.
c −20 m **d** 2.1 m

15G Problem set G

1 **a** 12
b 12, 15, 22, 24, 33, 36, 44, 48, 55, 66, 77, 88, 99
c 6 **d** 15 **e** 32
f 36 **g** No
h 8, 27, 125, 343 (cubes of primes)

2 1349

3 6 children, 12 men and 24 women

4 3

5 5 : 6

6 22

7 $100

8 $1.40

9 21, 42, 63 or 84

10 22, 23, 24, 25, 26

15H Problem set H

1 4 minutes

2 10 different ways

3 30, 55, 91. They can be arranged in square-based pyramids.

4 One method is to place the fence between the midpoints of the parallel sides.

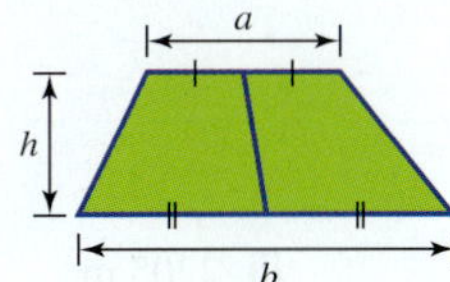

5 231 213 or 312 132

6 **a** No **b** Yes **c** No; Yes

d The polygon needs to have an odd number of sides.

7 398 m^2

8

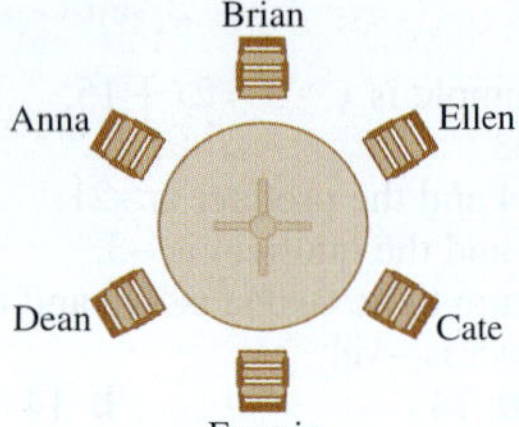

9 Solution 1 (cross in centre)

X		X
X	X	
	X	X

Solution 2 (centre empty)

X	X	
X		X
	X	X

10 **a**

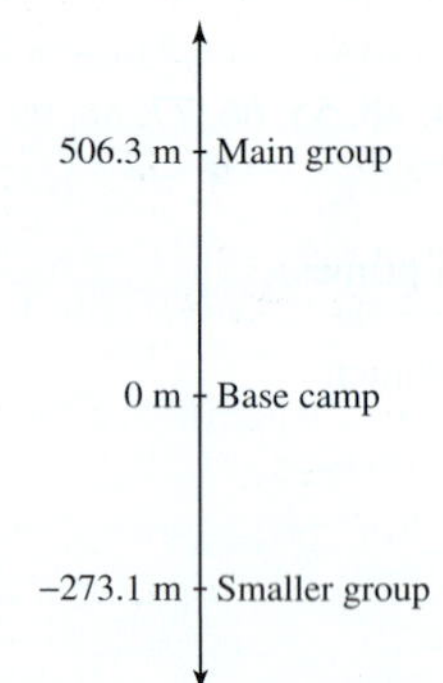

b 779.4 m **c** 869.2 m

d 12 hours from base camp or 17.5 hours from where they started

15I Problem set I

1 6

2 **a**

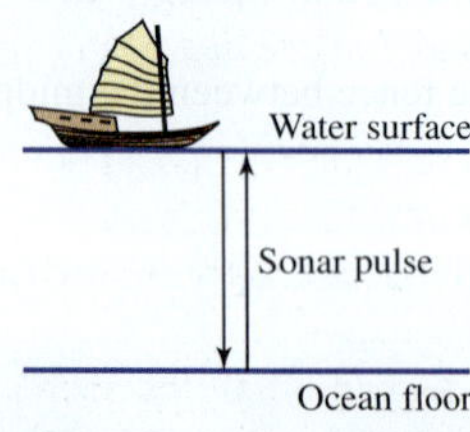

b **i** 1470 m **ii** 2940 m **iii** 2205 m

c 1102.5 m

d Let the ocean depth be d m and the time to return be t s.
$d = 735t$

e **i** 1323 m **ii** 3101.7 m **iii** 470.4 m

f 441 m. Distance (in air) = $\frac{1}{5}(735 \times \text{time})$

3 $\frac{1}{8}$

4 $9\frac{1}{11}\%$

5 Round peg in a square hole

6 93°

7 $x = \pm\sqrt{6}$

8

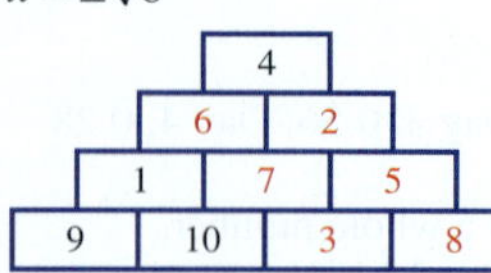

9 15 rides

10 20 cm^2

15J Problem set J

1 **a** $\frac{1}{5}$

b $\frac{1}{15}$

2 Block 1: 0, 1, 2, 3, 4, 5; Block 2: 0, 1, 2, 6, 7, 8 (check with your teacher)

3 Candy, 6 biscuits; Duke, 9 biscuits.

4 Square side 4 cm

5 20 children

6 **a** **i** $\frac{4}{9}$

ii $\frac{13}{27}$

iii $\frac{40}{81}$

b They are getting closer to $\frac{1}{2}$.

c **i** $\frac{1}{243}$ and $\frac{1}{729}$

ii

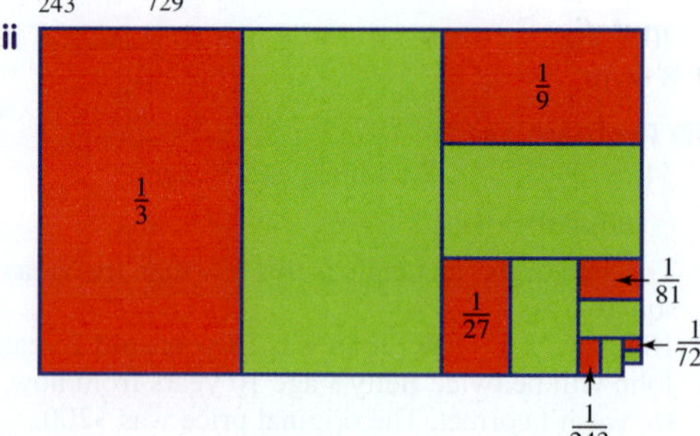

7 $g = \frac{4\pi r^2 h}{l^2}$

8

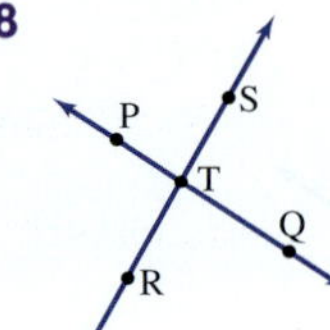

9 P(double on a pair of dice with n side) = $\frac{1}{n}$

10 P(Green ball is from B) = $\frac{2}{5}$

Glossary

2-dimensional representation: a plan or net that can be folded to form a polyhedron

3-dimensional: a view of a shape that has depth, as well as length and width

3-dimensional object: a shape that has depth, as well as length and width; also called a polyhedron

Allied angles: *see* Co-interior angles

Alternate angles: angles on opposite sides of the transversal positioned between the parallel lines. These angles are equal in size.

Annulus: the shape formed between two circles with a common centre (called concentric circles)

Associative Law: a number law that refers to the order in which three numbers may be added, subtracted, multiplied or divided, taking two at a time

Biased sample: a non-randomly selected sample obtained from a population

Census: the collection of data in which every member of a target population is surveyed

Certain: used in probability to describe an event that will definitely occur

Circumference: the distance around the outside of a circle. It is equal to $2\pi r$ or πD, where r = radius and D = diameter of the circle.

Class interval: an equal-sized group of scores

Closed question: a question with one possible solution

Congruent: refers to figures that have exactly the same shape and size

Co-interior angles (allied angles): angles on the same side of the transversal positioned between the parallel lines. These angles are supplementary.

Commutative Law: a number law that refers to the order in which two numbers may be added, subtracted, multiplied or divided

Compass: an instrument for determining direction

Complementary angles: angles that sum to 90°

Complementary events: events that together form a sample space

Composite shape: figure made up of more than one basic shape

Corresponding angles: angles on the same side of the transversal that are both either above or below the parallel lines. These angles are equal in size.

Data: various forms of information

Denominator: the bottom term of a fraction. It shows the total number of parts the whole has been divided into.

Diagonal: a line that runs from one corner of a closed figure to an opposite corner

Diameter: the straight-line distance across a circle through its centre

Directed number: a number that has both size and direction; for example, +3 and −7

Distributive Law: a rule that states that each term inside a pair of brackets is to be multiplied by the term outside the brackets

Equivalent ratios: ratios that describe the same relationship; for example, 2 : 8 and 1 : 4 are equivalent

Equivalent fractions: fractions that are equal in value; for example, $\frac{1}{2} = \frac{3}{6}$

Estimate: an approximate answer when an accurate answer is not required

Evaluate: to obtain an answer

Event: a set of favourable outcomes in each trial of a probability experiment

Experiment: the process of performing repeated trials of an activity in probability for the purpose of obtaining data in order to be able to predict the chances of certain things happening

Factorise: to break down a number or expression into smaller factors

Favourable outcome: the desired result in a probability experiment

Frequency polygon: the line graph created when the midpoints of the tops of the columns of a histogram are joined by straight lines. The polygon is closed by drawing lines at each end down to the x-axis (score).

Gradient: a measure of how steep something is; that is, its slope. The gradient of a straight line is given by:

$$m = \frac{\text{vertical distance}}{\text{horizontal distance}}.$$

Histogram: a type of column graph in which no gaps are left between columns and each column 'straddles' an x-axis score, such that the column starts and finishes halfway between scores. The x-axis scale is continuous and usually a half-interval is left before the first column and after the last column.

Hypotenuse: the longest edge of a right-angled triangle

Impossible: used in probability to describe an event that will not occur

Improper fraction: a fraction whose numerator is larger than its denominator; for example, $\frac{5}{4}$

Included angle: the angle formed between two lines that meet at a point

Index form: the short way of writing a number or variable when it is multiplied by itself repeatedly

Infinite: not finite; never ending; unlimited

Integer: positive whole numbers, negative whole numbers and zero

Irrational numbers: numbers that can not be written as fractions

Kite: a quadrilateral in which two pairs of adjacent sides are equal in length and one pair of opposite angles (those between the sides of unequal length) are equal

Like terms: terms that contain exactly the same variables (letters); for example, $3ab$ and $7ab$ are like terms, but $5a$ and $6ab$ are not

Linear equation: an equation in which the dependent variable has an index (power) of 1

Linear function: a function that is a straight line when drawn

Mean: in summary statistics, the sum of all the scores divided by the number of scores. It is also called the average.

Median: in summary statistics, the middle value if the number of data is odd, or the average of the two middle values if the number of data is even. Data must first be arranged in numerical order.

Mixed number: a number made up of a whole number and a fraction; for example, $2\frac{3}{4}$

Mode: in summary statistics, the most common value (score) or values in a set of data

Normal distribution: a set of data that forms a bell-shaped curve when graphed

Numerator: the top term of a fraction. It shows how many parts there are.

Open question: a question with more than one possible answer

Opposite angles: angles in a polygon that are opposite

Opposite sides: sides in a polygon that are opposite

Outcome: the particular result of a trial in a probability experiment

Outlier: a piece of data that is much larger or smaller than the rest of the data

Paralellogram: a quadrilateral with both pairs of opposite sides parallel to each other. Rectangles, squares and rhombuses are parallelograms.

Per cent: out of 100

Perimeter: the distance around the outside (border) of a shape

Prisms: solid shapes with identical opposite ends joined by straight edges. They are 3-dimensional objects, which can be cut into identical 'slices', called cross-sections.

Probability: the likelihood or chance of a particular event (result) occurring.

$$\text{P(event)} = \frac{\text{number of favourable outcomes}}{\text{number of possible outcomes}}$$

The probability of an event occurring ranges from 0 (impossible — will not occur) to 1 (certain — will definitely occur).

Pronumeral: a letter used in place of a number; another name for a variable

Proper fraction: a fraction whose numerator is smaller than its denominator; for example, $\frac{3}{4}$

Proportion: equality of two or more ratios

Quadrilateral: a 2-dimensional, closed shape formed by four straight sides

Questionnaire: a set of questions used in a survey

Radius: a straight line from a circle's centre to any point on its circumference

Random: following no particular order or pattern. To ensure that they are free from bias, surveys should be as random as possible.

Range: in summary statistics, the difference between the highest and lowest values (scores)

Ratio: comparison of two or more quantities of the same kind

Rational numbers: numbers that can be expressed as fractions

Real numbers: the set of all rational and irrational numbers

Rectangle: a parallelogram in which the opposite sides are equal in length and all angles are equal to 90°

Recurring decimal: a number with an infinitely repeating pattern of decimal places

Relative frequency: chance of an event happening expressed as a fraction or decimal

$$\text{relative frequency} = \frac{\text{frequency of an event}}{\text{total number of trials}}$$

Rhombus: a parallelogram in which all sides are equal and opposite angles are equal

Right-angled triangle: a triangle that has one of its angles equal to 90° (a right angle)

Rise: the vertical distance from one point to another on a Cartesian plane

Rounding: expressing a number with a certain number of decimal places

Rounding down: A number ending in 0, 1, 2, 3 or 4 is rounded down.

Rounding up: A number ending in 5, 6, 7, 8 or 9 is rounded up.

Run: the horizontal distance from one point to another on a Cartesian plane

Sample: part of a whole population

Sample space: in probability, the complete set of outcomes or results obtained from an experiment. It is shown as a list enclosed in a pair of braces, {}.

Sequence: a set of numbers that follow a pattern

Set: a collection of things or numbers that belong to a well-defined category

Skewed: describes data that is not symmetrical about the mean

Square: a parallelogram in which all sides are equal and all angles are equal to 90°

Statistics: the branch of mathematics that deals with the collection, organisation, display, analysis and interpretation of data, which are usually presented in numerical form

Substitution: the process by which a number replaces a variable in a formula

Supplementary angles: angles that sum to 180°

Surd: any *n*th root of a number that results in an infinite, non-recurring decimal pattern

Terms: a group of numbers and variables connected by the operations of multiplication or division

Terminating decimal: a number with a set number of decimal places

Theoretical probability: the probability of an event based on the number of possible favourable outcomes and the total number of possible outcomes

Transformations: reflections, rotations, translations and dilations of shapes in the plane

Transversal: a line that intersects a pair (a set) of parallel lines

Trapezium: quadrilateral in which one pair of opposite sides is parallel

Trial: a single experiment

Undefined: a numeric value that cannot be calculated

Universal set: the universal set contains all the elements specific to a particular problem. It is denoted by the symbol ξ.

Unknown: a variable in an algebraic equation or expression

Variables: letters or symbols in an equation or expression that may take many different values

Vertically opposite angles: special angles formed when two straight lines intersect. The two non-adjacent angles are called vertically opposite angles. These angles are equal in size.

Index

addition
  decimals 88–9
  fractions 76, 77
  integers 33
algebra 183–212
  to solve problems 303–7
  see also equations; expressions
allied angles 172
alternate angles 172
analysing data 349–53
angles
  alternate 172
  co-interior 172
  corresponding 172
  and parallel lines 172–3
  in quadrilaterals 171
  vertically opposite 172
area 251
  circle 258–9
  kite 254
  parallelogram 253–4
  rectangle 252
  rhombus 254
  trapezium 262–3
  triangle 252–3
  units of 251–2
ASA congruency test 167
Associative Law 195–6

backtracking 298–9
biased samples 325
BIDMAS 42
brackets
  expanding 205–7
  working with 189–90

Cartesian coordinates 407–8
Cartesian plane 407–8, 410–11
census 321
certain event 367
circle
  area 258–9
  circumference 246–8
circumference 246–8
closed questions 322
clustering around a common value (estimation) 98
co-interior angles 172
collecting data 321–5
column graphs 329–33
communicating, reasoning and reflecting (problem solving) 233–5
Commutative Law 193–5
comparing ratios 124–5
complementary events 383–4
cone 265
congruency tests for triangles 167
congruent figures 160–1
congruent parallelograms 172–3
congruent triangles 166–9
  congruency tests 167
constructing triangles 163–5
  given three side lengths 163–4
  given two angles and the side between them 164
  given two sides and the angle between them 164–5
conversions
  decimals to fractions 86–7
  fractions to decimals 85–6, 87
  percentages to decimals 95–6
  percentages to fractions 95–6
  units of area 251–2
  units of length 241
  units of volume 265
coordinates 407–8
corresponding angles 172
cube, volume 265

data 321
  analysing 349–53
  collecting 321–5
  displaying 329–33
  examining 328
  measures of centre 337–41
  measures of spread 343–6
  organising 328–9
daylight-saving time 277–8
decimals
  addition 88–9
  converting to fractions 86–7
  division 92–3
  fractions converted to decimals 85–6, 87
  multiplication 91, 92–3
  negative 89, 92–3
  percentages converted to decimals 95–6
  positive 88–9, 91–3
  recurring 75, 85–6
  subtraction 88–9
  terminating 75, 85–6
denominator 76
diagrams, for problem solving 222–3
diameter 246
directed numbers 77–8
  dividing 40–1
  multiplying 38–9
  powers 38
  square roots 38
discount 143–5
displaying data 329–33
Distributive Law 205–7
dividing in a given ratio 126–8
division
  decimals 92–3
  expressions with variables 201–3
  fractions 82–3
  integers 40–1
  numbers in index form 56–8

elements of a set 386
elimination (problem solving) 227–8

equations
backtracking 298–9
inverse operations 298–9
keeping balanced 301–2
linear 303–7
one-step 304
two-step 304–5
with unknown on both sides 309–12
using flowcharts 298–9, 304–6
equivalent fractions 76
equivalent ratios 116
estimation 98
clustering around a common value 98
rounding 99–101
event 370
examining data 328
expanding brackets 205–7
experimental probability 370–3
experiments 370
expressions
Distributive Law 205–7
dividing 201–3
expanding brackets 205–7
factorising 208–9
multiplying 201
pronumerals 183, 303
simplifying 199–200
substitution in 187, 191–2
variables 183–4, 193–7, 201–3, 205–7, 303
working with brackets 189–90

factor form 51, 52
factorising 208–9
favourable outcome 370
First Index Law 53–5
flowcharts 298–9, 305
Fourth Index Law 62–3
fractions 75
addition 76, 77, 78
converted to decimals 85–6, 87
decimals converted to fractions 86–7
denominator 76
division 82–3
equivalent 76
improper 76
mixed numbers 76–7
multiplication 81–3
negative 77–8, 79, 82–3
numerator 76
percentages converted to fractions 95–6
positive 78, 82–3
proper 76
subtraction 76, 77, 79
frequency polygon 331–3
frequency tables 328–9, 330–1
function notation 413–14

geometric patterns 295–6
gradient 417
gradient–intercept method (sketching linear graphs) 425–6
gradient of a straight line 417–19
positive or negative gradient 418

graphs
column 329–33
linear 410–11, 412–14, 417–21
guess and check (problem solving) 232–3
hexagonal prism 265

highest common factor (HCF) 208–9
histograms 329–33

Identity Law 196
impossible event 367
improper fractions 76
included angle 164
index form 51–2
dividing with coefficients 57–8
dividing numbers in 56–7
multiplying numbers in 53–5
index laws
First Index Law 53–5
Second Index Law 56–8
Third Index Law 59–60
Fourth Index Law 62–3
infinite gradient 417
integers 33, 75
addition 33
combined operations 42–3
dividing 40–1
multiplying 37–8
subtraction 33–4
intercept method (sketching linear graphs) 426–7
intersection of sets 387–9
Inverse Law 196
inverse operations 298–9
irrational numbers 75, 76

kite 172
area 254

length, units of 241
linear equations 303–7
graphical solutions 413–14
linear functions 413
linear graphs 410–11
general rule 419–21
gradient 417–19
plotting 412–14
sketching 425–7
y-intercept 418
linear patterns 410–11

mean 337–8, 350
measurement
area 251–4, 258–9, 262–3
circumference 246–8
perimeter 240–4
time 270–4
units of area 251–2
units of length 241
units of volume 265
volume 265–7
measures of centre 337–40
outlier effects 340
which is the most useful? 340
see also mean; median; mode

measures of spread 343–6
see also range; skewness
median 338–9, 350
mixed numbers 76–7
mode 339–40, 350
money
discount 143–5
profit and loss 148–9
selling price 144–5, 148–9
multiplication
decimals 91, 92–3
expressions with variables 201
fractions 81–3
integers 37–8
numbers in index form 53–5

negative decimals 89, 92–3
negative fractions 77–8, 79, 82–3
negative numbers, substitution 191–2
normal distribution 344
number laws 193–7
Associative Law 195–6
Commutative Law 193–5
Identity Law 196
Inverse Law 196
number line 78
number patterns 294–5
numeracy sets 2–30
numerator 76

one-step equations 304
open questions 322
order of operations 42
organising data 328–9
origin 407
outcome 370
outliers 328
effect on measures of centre 340

parallel lines, and angles 172–3
parallelograms 171
area 253–4
congruency 172–3
patterns
geometric 295–6
linear 410–11
looking for in problem solving 224–5
number 294–5
per cent 95
percentages 95
common 139
converting to decimals 95–6
converting to fractions 95–6
and discount 143–5
increase and decrease 96–7
and profit and loss 148–9
shortcut methods 139–41
perimeter 241–3
circle 246–8
rectangle 242, 243
square 243
π (pi) 76, 246
plotting linear graphs 412–14
population 321, 324
using sample properties to predict characteristics of 351–2
positive decimals 88–9, 91–3
positive fractions 78, 82–3
positive numbers, substitution 191–2
powers
negative numbers 38
raising to another power 62–3
zero 59–60
prisms 265–6
volume 265–6
probability 367
complementary events 383–4
experimental 370–3
theoretical 376–9
tree diagrams 392–6
two-way tables 392–6
probability scale 367–9
problem solving methods 218, 220
communicating, reasoning and reflecting 233–5
create a table 218–19
drawing a diagram 222–3
elimination 227–8
guess and check 232–3
look for a pattern 224–5
simplify the problem 229–30
work backwards from the answer 226
problem solving sets 436–48
profit and loss 148–9
pronumerals 183, 303
proper fractions 76
proportion 120–1

quadrilaterals 171
angles 171
properties 171, 172
special types of 171–2
terms and rules 171–2
questionnaires 322–3
planning 323–4

radius 246
random sample 321
range 343–4, 350
rates 129–30
rational numbers 75
ratios 113
comparing 124–5
dividing in a given ratio 126–8
equivalent 116
simplifying 116–18
see also proportion
real numbers 75–6
rectangle 171
area 252
perimeter 242, 243
rectangular prism, volume 265
recurring decimals 75, 85–6
relative frequency (of an event) 370
rhombus 171
area 254
RHS congruency test 167

rise 417
rounding 99
  the dividend to a multiple of the divisor 100–1
  to the first digit 99–100
rounding down 99
rounding up 99
run 417

sample space 376, 383, 392
sample(s) 321
  biased 325
  selecting 324
  using to predict population characteristics 351–2
SAS congruency test 167
Second Index Law 56–8
selling price 148–9
  of discounted item 144–5
sets 386
  intersection of 387–9
  union of 387–9
  universal 386
simplifying
  expressions 199–200
  problems 229–30
  ratios 116–18
sketching linear graphs 425–7
  gradient–intercept method 425–6
  intercept method 426–7
skewed distribution 344, 345–6
skewness 344–6
sphere 265
square 172
  perimeter 243
square pyramid 265
square root 38
SSS congruency test 167
statistics 321
straight line, gradient of 417–18
substitution
  in expressions 187
  positive and negative numbers 191–2
subtraction
  decimals 88–9
  fractions 76, 77
  integers 33–4
surveys 321, 322

tables
  frequency 328–9, 330–1
  for problem solving 218–29
  two-way 392–6
terminating decimals 75, 85–6
theoretical probability 376–9
Third Index Law 59–60
time 270
  24-hour system 275–6
  calculations 271–4
  units of 270
time zones 276–7, 281
  and daylight-saving time 277–8
transversal 172
trapezium 172
  area 262–3
tree diagrams 392–6
trial 370
triangles
  area 252–3
  congruent 166–9
  constructing 163–5
triangular prism 265
24-hour time 275–6
two-step equations 304–5
two-way tables 392–6

undefined gradient 417
union of sets 387–9
units of area 251–2
units of length 241
units of time 270
units of volume 265
universal set 386
unknowns 183

variables 183–4, 303
  Associative Law 195–6
  Commutative Law 193–5
  Distributive Law 205–7
  dividing expressions with 201–3
  Identity Law 196
  Inverse Law 196
  multiplying expressions with 201
Venn diagrams 386–90
  see also sets
vertically opposite angles 172
volume 265
  cube 265
  prisms 265–6
  rectangular prism 265
  solids with uniform cross-section that
    are not prisms 266–7
  units of 265

working backwards from the answer (problem solving) 226

x-axis 407

$y = mx + c$ 419–21
y-axis 407
y-intercept 418

zero, power of 59–60
zero gradient 417